International Handbook of Historical Studies

International
Handbook
of Historical Studies
CONTEMPORARY RESEARCH
AND THEORY

Edited by
Georg G. Iggers
and Harold T. Parker

 GREENWOOD PRESS
WESTPORT, CONNECTICUT

Library of Congress Cataloging in Publication Data
Main entry under title:

International handbook of historical studies.

   Bibliography: p.
   Includes index.
   1. Historiography—Addresses, essays, lectures.
2. History—Methodology—Addresses, essays, lectures.
I. Iggers, Georg G. II. Parker, Harold Talbot,
1907-
D13.I62   907'.2   79-7061
ISBN 0-313-21367-4

Library of Congress Catalog Card Number: 79-7061
ISBN: 0-313-21367-4

First published in 1979 in the United States of America by

Greenwood Press, Inc.
51 Riverside Avenue, Westport, Connecticut 06880

First published in 1980 in Great Britain by

Methuen & Co Ltd
London EC4P 4EE

Printed in the United States of America

10 9 8 7 6 5 4 3 2 1

Contents

Preface

The period since World War II, particularly the last two decades, has witnessed a remarkable reorientation in historical studies throughout the world. Whole new areas of human existence have become the subject of historical inquiry, and new methodological approaches have been tested. This volume seeks to assess the present state of the discipline, to examine innovations in historical method and perspective as well as continuities with older patterns of scholarship. The editors have asked themselves to what extent new approaches have succeeded or failed in bridging ideological differences and national traditions which divided scholarship in the past.

One important attempt at an assessment of contemporary historical studies has been made in the excellent volume edited by Felix Gilbert and Stephen Graubard, *Historical Studies Today* (New York, 1971), the result of a conference of Western scholars in 1970. The present collection to some degree overlaps this preceding work, but it moves beyond in several respects. It seeks to analyze the rapid changes which have marked historical studies in the 1970s. A major section of the volume (Part I) deals systematically with new approaches and new areas of inquiry. The collection, moreover, is more comprehensive in scope than the volume by Gilbert and Graubard. Another major section (Part II) deals extensively with national and regional developments not only in Western Europe and the United States but in the socialist countries and in Japan, India, sub-Saharan Africa, and Latin America as well. The volume offers a truly international perspective.

At the same time the book is not intended to be an encyclopedic survey of present scholarship. Contributors were asked to present and to examine major tendencies in historical studies with an emphasis on methodological and conceptual approaches. Beyond this, each author was free to develop the subject as he or she thought best. The result is a rich diversity of approaches and interpretations, the latter at times reflecting very divergent ideological and methodological positions. This pluralism of viewpoints, the editors believe, enhances the value of the volume.

By necessity, the articles are selective, reflecting the areas of competence of the authors. The price to be paid for this is that at times important aspects of the topic under discussion are omitted. Thus Louis Mink, in the article on contemporary theories of history, restricts himself to analytical philosophy in the English-speaking world; the chapters dealing with regional or national developments in France, West Germany, Poland, and Latin America partially make up for this selectivity. Philip VanderMeer's article focuses on the new political history in the United States; again other chapters deal with new approaches to political history elsewhere. There is no separate essay on quantitative history—a topic on which much has been written in recent years—but various essays deal, even if marginally, with quantitative approaches in recent studies. After we were unable to obtain a contribution from a Soviet historian, Samuel Baron was kind enough to offer on short notice an essay which concentrates on the political and ideological aspects of Soviet scholarship. His article is complemented by that of Jerzy Topolski on the work done in the Soviet Union on social history.

Diversity among the essays has extended even to the choice of subject matter. Two or three authors stressed coverage of the literature with minimum attention to analysis, while in one instance the author singled out for analysis a cluster of works which he considered valuably paradigmatic for historical studies in the region. However, the editors believe that on the whole the essays reflect a balance between information and analysis.

The editors regret that they were unable to obtain an article on historiography in the contemporary Islamic world. Space did not permit inclusion of essays on Spain, Scandinavia, the Low Countries, or Hungary, all of which have made important contributions to contemporary historiography. Yet despite these omissions the editors are convinced that the volume offers a sense of the intellectual and scholarly climate of historical endeavor throughout the contemporary world.

November 1978

Georg G. Iggers and Harold T. Parker

Notes on the Contributors

J. F. ADE. AJAVI, Vice-Chancellor of the University of Lagos, was formerly Professor of History at the University of Ibadan.

E. J. ALAGOA is Dean of the School of Humanities, University of Port Harcourt. His specialty is African oral traditional history and historiography. His publications include *The Small Brave City-State* (1964), *A Chronicle of Grand Bonny* (1972), and *A History of the Niger Delta: An Historical Interpretation of Ijo Oral Tradition* (1972).

SAMUEL H. BARON, Alumni Distinguished Professor of History at the University of North Carolina, Chapel Hill, is the author of *Plekhanov: The Father of Russian Marxism* and numerous articles on the merchants of Muscovite Russia; translator and editor of *The Travels of Olearius in Seventeenth Century Russia;* and coeditor of *Windows on the Russian Past: Essays on Soviet Historiography Since Stalin.*

NORMAN GERALD BARRIER, Professor of South Asian History, University of Missouri-Columbia, specializes on the religious and political history of Northwest India during the nineteenth and twentieth centuries. His publications include *The Punjab Alienation of Land Bill* (1966), *The Sikhs and Their Literature* (1969), *Banned* (1975), and *The Roots of Communal Politics* (1976).

CHARLES BERGQUIST, Department of History at Duke University, has written *Coffee and Conflict in Colombia, 1886–1910* (1978) and is presently at work on a study of organized labor in the export sector in twentieth-century Latin American societies.

LUCIAN BOIA is Lecturer in Historiography at the University of Bucharest. His main research interests are modern history and the history of historiography. Along those lines his published works include *Eugen Brote (1850–1912)* (1974), *Evolutia istoriografiei române* (The Evolution of Rumanian Historiography) (1976), *The Relationships Between Romanians, Czechs, and Slovaks, 1848–1914* (1977), and *Mari istorici ai lumii* (Great World Historians) (1978).

ARIF DIRLIK, Department of History of Duke University, is a specialist on modern Chinese historical and political thought. His book *Revolution and History: Origins of Marxist Historiography in China 1919–1937* came out in 1978.

GEOFF ELEY, after a tenure as Fellow and Director of Studies in History at Emmanuel College, University of Cambridge, became a member of the faculty of the University of Michigan in September 1979. His general field of research is German society and politics in the nineteenth and twentieth centuries. His book on the political formation of the German right between the 1890s and the 1920s is to be published by the Yale University Press in 1979. His other publications include "Defining Social Imperialism: Use and Abuse of an Idea," *Social History*, vol. 1, no. 3 (1976) and "The German Right: How It Changed," in R. J. Evans, ed., *Society and Politics in Wilhelmine Germany* (1978).

JEAN GLENISSON, Director of the *Institut de Recherche et d'Histoire des Textes* of the *Centre National de la Recherche Scientifique,* is primarily interested in economic and social history, notably that of France during the fourteenth century, and in the history of the papal state during the same century. His books include: (with Guillaume Mollat) *L'administration des Etats de l'Eglise au XIVe siècle. Correspondance des légats et vicaires-généraux* (1964); (with C. Higounet) *Remarques sur les comptes et sur l'administration financière des villes françaises entre Loire et Pyrénées (XIVe-XVIe siècles)* (1964); (with John Day and Odile Grandmottet) *Textes et documents d'histoire du Moyen Age, XIVe-XVe siècles* (1970–).

ANDRZEJ F. GRABSKI, Extraordinary Professor at the Institute of History of the Polish Academy of Sciences, medievalist and historiographer, is author in Polish of the following principal books: *Polish Military Art in the Early Medieval Period* (1959); *Poland as Viewed by Foreigners During the Tenth to Thirteenth Centuries* (1964); *Boleslas the Great* (1964; 2nd edition, 1966); *Poland in the Opinions of Western Europe During the Fourteenth and Fifteenth Centuries* (1968); *Orientations of Polish Historiography* (1972); *The Historical Thought of the Polish Enlightenment* (1976); and *Historiography and Politics* (in press).

GEORG G. IGGERS, Distinguished Professor of History at the State University of New York at Buffalo, specializes on nineteenth- and twentieth-century German and French intellectual history, on historiography, and on the philosophy of history. His books include *The Cult of Authority* (1958), *The German Conception of History* (1968), *New Directions in European Historiography* (1975), and (with Konrad von Moltke as coeditor) *Leopold von Ranke: The Theory and Practice of History* (1973).

LEONARD KRIEGER is University Professor of History at the University of Chicago. His main research interests are modern intellectual history, historiography, and philosophy of history. On those subjects his publications include *The German Idea of Freedom* (1957, 1973), *The Politics of Discretion* (1965), *Kings and Philosophers 1689–1789* (1970), *An Essay on the Theory of Enlightened Despotism* (1975), *Ranke: The Meaning of History* (1977), "The Horizons of History," in *The American Historical Review* (1958), and "Culture, Cataclysm, and Contingency," in the *Journal of Modern History* (1968).

LOUIS O. MINK is Professor of Philosophy and Senior Tutor in the College of Social Studies at Wesleyan University. He is an editor of *History and Theory* and the author of *Mind, History and Dialectic: The Philosophy of R. G. Collingwood* (1969), *A Finnegans Wake Gazetteer* (1978), and numerous articles on philosophy of history in books and journals.

HAROLD T. PARKER, Professor Emeritus of History, Duke University, researches the administrative history of the French Revolution and Napoleon and teaches European intellectual history since Rousseau, historiography, and historical methodology. His publications include *The Cult of Antiquity and the French Revolutionaries* (1937), *Three Napoleonic Battles* (1944), "Herbert Butterfield" in S. William Halperin, ed., *Some 20th-Century Historians* (1960), (with Marvin Brown) *Major Themes in Modern Euro-*

pean History (1974), *Liberty and Democracy in English-speaking Countries (1767–1885)* (1974), *The Industrial Policies of the Bureau of Commerce in 1781* (1979), and (with Richard Herr as coeditor) *Ideas in History* (1965).

A. WILLIAM SALOMONE is Wilson Professor of European History at the University of Rochester. His major publications are *Italian Democracy in the Making,* with an Introduction by Gaetano Salvemini (1945); *L' età giolittiana* (1949); *Italy in the Giolittian Era* (1960); and *Italy from the Risorgimento to Fascism* (1970). His numerous essays and monographs, ranging from the Renaissance to the Risorgimento and the anti-Fascist Resistance, include bio-critical studies on Machiavelli and Croce, Salvemini and Chabod, and Mazzini. They reflect his increasing interest in modern European and Italian cultural and intellectual history.

HANS SCHLEIER, member of the Zentralinstitut für Geschichte der Akademie der Wissenschaften of the German Democratic Republic, specializes in historiography and historical methodology. His interest in the history and theory of German bourgeois historiography is manifested in his books, which include: *Sybel und Treitschke: Antidemokratismus und Militarismus in historisch-politischen Denken grossbourgeoiser Geschichtsideologen* (1965); *Die bürgerliche deutsche Geschichtsschreibung der Weimarer Republik* (1975); *Theorie der Geschichte, Theorie der Geschichtswissenschaft: Zu neueren theoretisch-methodologischen Arbeiten der Geschichtsschreibung in der BRD* (1975).

LAURENCE A. SCHNEIDER, Department of History, State University of New York at Buffalo, is concerned with the intellectual history of modern China. Chinese historiography and the development of modern science in twentieth-century China are among his special research fields. He is author of *Ku Chieh-Kang and China's New History* (1971) and *A Madman of Ch'u: The Chinese Myth of Loyalty and Dissent* (in press).

RICHARD L. SCHOENWALD is Professor of History at Carnegie-Mellon University; his main research interest is the psychological study of modern Western intellectual history. He is now writing a biography of Herbert Spencer; his major publications include: *Freud: The Man and His Mind* (1956) and the articles listed at the end of his essay in this volume.

NANCY S. STRUEVER is Professor at Johns Hopkins University, with a joint appointment with the Department of History and the Humanities Center. Her field is Renaissance intellectual history, with a focus on the history of the theory of language. She has published *The Language of History in the Renaissance* (1970), and is currently working on a book on the language of morality in the Renaissance.

JERZY TOPOLSKI is Professor of History at the University of Poznań, Vice-Director of the Institute of History of that University, and coeditor of the journal *Studia Historiae Oeconomicae*. His other appointments include visiting professorships at California State University at Hayward (1972/1973) and at the Ecole des Hautes Etudes en Sciences Sociales in Paris (1977). His more important books reflect his research interests in early modern history, especially economic history, and in historical methodology. They include *Methodology of History* (several editions and translations, 1968–1976); *Birth of Capitalism in Europe from the XVIth to the XVIIIth Centuries* (1965; Italian translation, 1978), *The Polish and European Economy from the XVIth to the XVIIIth Centuries* (in Polish, 1977), and *Understanding of History* (in Polish, 1978).

PHILIP R. VANDERMEER, Department of History at Purdue University, focuses his research on political recruitment, political career patterns, and the religious bases of politics in the Midwest of the United States, 1870–1930. He has previously published in *Computers and the Humanities* the "Annual Bibliography—History" for 1975 and 1976. Since 1978 he has served as the Associate Book Review Editor for *Computers and the Humanities*.

RICHARD T. VANN is Professor of History and Letters at Wesleyan University in Connecticut and is Executive Editor of *History and Theory*. He is the author of *The Social Development of English Quakerism, 1655–1755* (1969) and is currently working on a history of the family in the early modern period.

LAURENCE VEYSEY, Professor of History at the University of California, Santa Cruz, specializes in the social and intellectual history of the United States in the late nineteenth and twentieth centuries. He is author of *The Emergence of the American University* and *The Communal Experience*.

YASUSHI YAMANOUCHI is Professor of Foreign Studies at Tokyo University. His major fields of research are the economic history of modern Europe and the methodology of the social sciences. He is author of *Historical Analysis of the English Industrial Revolution* (1966), *Marx's and Engels's Ideas on World History* (1969), and *Methodology of Social Science and Anthropology* (1973).

GEORG G. IGGERS

INTRODUCTION: The Transformation of Historical Studies in Historical Perspective

In the past several decades, although the link with older traditions of historical writing has not been broken, patterns of inquiry which had directed historical writing since the days of classical antiquity have lost their predominance. There had been a high degree of continuity in the way historians had investigated and written history from the ancient Greeks until the most recent years. Although it is erroneous to perceive only one pattern in historical writing, nevertheless Thucydides' *Peloponnesian War* presented a model which historians not only followed in the classical period but revived at the beginning of the Renaissance, a tradition by no means destroyed but to an extent even enhanced by the professionalization of historical studies in the nineteenth century. It is not without significance that Ranke wrote his doctoral dissertation on Thucydides.

This model sharply distinguished the main tradition of historiography in the West from that of other cultures, for example, China, and from both the chronicles and the sacred histories of the Middle Ages. The orientation of this historiography was secular. Its form of presentation was the narrative. History was conceived of as a form of literature, governed by standards of rhetoric and at the same time concerned about the truthful reconstruction of the past on the basis of the critical examination of evidence. A number of presuppositions underlay this history. Perhaps the most important was that men make their own history. Historical explanation rested upon an understanding of the conscious motivations of man. Linked with this essentially humanistic conception of history was the essentially aristocratic perspective which pervaded historical writing into the twentieth century. History dealt with the actions and aspirations of the eminent, particularly with the ruling elites. The key institution which gave unity to society and provided the thread of historical narrative was the state, a state whose conduct could be understood in terms of the deliberate actions of its statesmen guided by the requirements of power in a world marked by interstate conflict. The primary focus of historians from Thucydides to Ranke was thus on the narration of political and military events, with a concentration not on internal conflicts, inspired by social or economic interests, but on external affairs, governed by a logic of their own.

Such a history necessarily narrowed the perspective of the historian. It established a sharp line of distinction between areas which deserved historical interest and those which essentially were unhistorical in character. The history of Thucydides and its concentration on the politics of the Greek world stood in sharp contrast to the broadly social and cultural cosmopolitan history of Herodotus. This distinction between the barbaric and the civilized world, between the spheres of life worthy of historical attention and those not, permeated historical writing from the fifth century B.C. to the twentieth century A.D. and contributed to the parochialism of a history which concentrated on the Greek or Roman world or later the European state system.

The interest in universal history was never fully extinguished; it was kept alive, however, largely by a tradition of sacred and ecclesiastical history. The eighteenth century saw not only the reassertion of a tradition of secular history but also the conscious attempt to break the narrow confines of the classical paradigm. Voltaire provided a model for a new approach which aimed at a history of civilization in the broadest sense. Politics for Voltaire in his *Age of Louis XIV,* as for the famous Göttingen school of historians indebted to him, continued to occupy the central place in the historical account. But the attempt was made to combine the narration of political events with an analysis of institutions, customs, and opinions which would recreate the "spirit of an age." In some ways, the work of the Göttingen circle foreshadowed certain aspects of modern social history with its interest in statistics, demography, and economics and its concern not only with the European but also with the non-Western world. But both Voltaire and the Göttingen historians lacked any comprehensive theory of social organization or of social change which would have permitted them to integrate the great masses of data they accumulated. The result, particularly in the case of the Göttingen historians, was an additive history which lacked any clearly definable principles of organization.

The mainstream of historical scholarship went in other directions which were both more innovative and more traditional. The nineteenth century saw the acceleration on a worldwide scale of the process of professionalization which had begun in the eighteenth-century German universities. Very consciously now historians conceived of their discipline as a science—albeit a science in the broader, continental sense of the term, distinct from the natural sciences and never totally separable from literary considerations, but capable of reliable knowledge. Neither the professionalization of history nor the search for scientific rigor was going to be reversed in the twentieth century despite the philosophic skepticism regarding the possibilities of a historical science. History was now pursued less by people in public life, statesmen, military men, or men of letters, than by a group of technically trained scholars who increasingly wrote for a scholarly audience rather than an educated public.

The scientific character of the new historiography consisted in its heightened emphasis on the critical examination of evidence. But the "scientific" history of the Ranke school did not stop here. It was closely interwoven with basic notions about human beings, society, and the historical process which were "metahistorical" in character and represented an implicit philosophy of history. It was this conception of history which enabled the scholarly historians of the nineteenth century to write the cohesive historical accounts which the historians of the Enlightenment had been incapable of sustaining. They overcame the gulf which had existed in the seventeenth and early eighteenth centuries between a tradition of historical erudition, critical of sources but essentially antiquarian in outlook, and the classical heritage of narrative history. Their new conception of history has been labeled "historicism." In several aspects, it represented a profound rupture with the notions of man and history which had informed the classical tradition of historical writing. The new outlook stressed the radical "historicity" of all cultural phenomena. If the tradition from Thucydides to Gibbon had assumed the constancy of human nature and from this had deduced the possibility of seeing in the past exemplars for the present, the new historicist outlook stressed the incomparability of historical epochs. In the place of a unity of human history, the new outlook saw a diversity of societies and cultures, each possessing certain inherent principles of structure and development similar to those of a single organism. This organicist view of human society prevented the new historical school from lapsing into historical relativism or skepticism. While history could no longer be the *magister vitae* which provided lessons applicable to the present, history alone provided the key to the understanding of things human in their diversity. All sciences relating to man—linguistics, economics, jurisprudence, art, literature, and theology—were historical disciplines. Mankind was thus seen as being in continuous development. This stress on development contained an optimistic note, the belief, based on a residual religious faith, that the history of man itself constituted a progressive revelation of human values in concrete historical, cultural contexts.

One might have expected the historicist outlook to bring about an extension of the scope of the historian. In theory everything human was of historical interest—all ages, all cultures, all aspects of life. In practice, however, the new historical scholarship retreated from the broad cosmopolitan, social perspective of the Enlightenment historians. In part this was a result of the exigencies of specialization introduced by professionalization, which laid emphasis on a history that proceeded on the basis of certain evidence, particularly written documentary sources found in archives. Although Ranke still wrote comprehensive histories in which he sought to reveal the political and intellectual tendencies operating in modern history, a later generation, stressing the technical aspects of scholarship, turned increasingly to monographic studies. This was the case not only in Germany but generally in the Western world and elsewhere, as in Japan, wherever German patterns of professionalized historical research were imitated. The new nationalism provided an impetus for historical study, but its increasing emphasis on political integration restricted the areas of history of concern to the historian. In Germany at least, historical scholarship strove in the face of industrialization to legitimize a state in which broad segments of the middle classes, whose status rested on property or education, sought support in a conservative political establishment against the fear of rising working-class influence.

The new "scientific" school of history proceeded with a theory of knowledge which was essentially idealistic in character. History, it assumed, could be understood only in terms of human behavior which was guided by conscious ideas. A society always constituted an integrated complex of values and purposes. In this sense, men made their own history, whether they made it collectively or individually. The historians of the new "scientific" orientation fought a running battle, first in Germany and later in France and Italy, with the positivism represented by Auguste Comte, Hippolyte Taine, and Thomas Buckle. Where positivists sought historical explanation in terms of generalizations and laws of development, historians with historicist views insisted that history dealt with human purposes and meanings which could never be reduced to abstract formulae but had to be "understood" in their unique historical setting. History was the scene of free, purposive human actions. A clear distinction was drawn between areas which were peculiarly historical and others which were not. "The repetitive, the irrational, the quasi-instinctual, [might] be the substratum of history—but it [could] not be the subject matter of history itself."[1] Whole areas of human existence thus fell outside the purview of the historian. The focus rested on the decision makers, on the elites who formulated and executed policies. An aristocratic bias guided historical studies. The history of the masses, of everyday life, and of popular culture were not of historical interest. Only the realm of consciousness was of legitimate concern to the historian. Connected with this was an explicit rejection of theory. History dealt with the concrete motivations and actions of individuals. These in the last instance were ineffable. They had to be empathetically understood or reexperienced. History, therefore, was the science of the unique and the narrative form of presentation was most suitable to it.

There were indeed alternative forms of historical writing in the nineteenth century—we need only think of Alexis de Tocqueville and Jakob Burckhardt—but these stood outside the main current of professionalized scholarship. By the turn of the century, however, a conscious challenge to the dominance of the German school of "scientific" history arose almost simultaneously in various countries in the world, in the United States with the New Historians (F. J. Turner, Charles Beard, J. H. Robinson), in France with Paul Lacombe, Emile Durkheim, and Henri Berr, and in Germany with Karl Lamprecht. Their criticism proceeded not from the basis of the contention made by Nietzsche and others that history could not be a science, but rather from the position that traditional historiography was insufficiently scientific. Berr, Lamprecht, and others challenged the objectivistic notion that historians could reconstruct the past purely by immersing themselves in the evidence free from presuppositions. They instead insisted that history, like any form of scientific or scholarly inquiry, must approach its subject matter with explicit questions and hypotheses: no history is possible without theory. At the same time the critics accepted the traditional school's insistence on critical scholarship. They thus rejected macrohistorical speculations in the manner of Hegel or Spengler and sought to formulate theories of limited range which could be applied to and tested against concrete historical situations. From a different perspective, closer to the philosophic tradition of German historicism with its emphasis on human consciousness, Wilhelm Dilthey and Max Weber came to similar conclusions. They agreed that a closer relationship had to be established between the phenomena of consciousness and their sources in the subconscious. Events had to be understood in the structural context in which they occurred. Pure narration was therefore insufficient and had to be supplemented by analysis. Politics, moreover, was no longer viewed as the keystone to history; not only was it necessary to approach politics in interaction with social and economic factors, but a history could legitimately be written which devoted itself to nonpolitical spheres of society.

These new patterns of historical writing were to be explored in the period after World War I by a small minority of historians, such as Lucien Febvre and Marc Bloch in France and Henri Pirenne in Belgium. By the late 1920s several important journals were founded which represented the new approaches: The *Annales d'histoire économique et sociale* (1929) in France; a journal by the same name, *Dziejow Społecznych i Gospodarczych* (1926) in Poland; and the *Economic History Review* (1929) in England, which originally addressed itself broadly to problems of social as well as economic history. Max Weber's influence made itself felt in the conceptualized approaches to social history of Otto Hintze in Germany. But as a whole, as reflected in the journals that represented the major national organizations of historians, the *American Historical Review,* the *Historische Zeitschrift,* the *English Historical Review,* and the *Revue Historique,* the profession remained resistant to the new orientations.

Only after 1945, and then slowly, did the new approaches gain a dominant voice. The earliest and most remarkable breakthrough was in France: in 1946 the Sixth Section of the Ecole Pratique des Hautes Etudes (since 1975 the Ecole des Hautes Etudes en Sciences Sociales) was established as a research and teaching center for the integration of history and the social sciences; it also assumed the publication of the *Annales.* In England, *Past and Present* began to appear in 1952. In the United States a large number of interdisciplinary journals was founded reflecting the new historical interests, beginning with *Comparative Studies in Society and History* (1958) and including the *Journal of Social History* (1967) and the *Journal of Interdisciplinary History* (1970). The *International Review of Social History,* founded but suspended in Amsterdam in the late 1930s, reappeared in 1956. *Geschichte und Gesellschaft* began publication in West Germany in 1975, *Social History* and the *History Workshop* in England in 1976. The *Jahrbuch für Wirtschaftsgeschichte,* founded in the early 1960s in the German Democratic Republic as an international forum, also deserves mention here. Nowhere else in the West, however, did the new interdisciplinary history possess the firm institutional basis and the influence over the profession that it did in France. In the socialist countries, Marxist ideology and the coordinating role of the Academies of Science provided for the integration of historical research and social theory.

The rapidly changing historiographical situation in the 1950s, and more particularly in the 1960s and 1970s, reflected the delayed impact of fundamental changes in both the political, social, and economic structures and the intellectual attitudes in the twentieth century. Traditional historiography proved increasingly unable to understand the complex processes at work in a highly technological society and its social concomitants. The traditional political order had been replaced by democratization in the West and by the establishment of socialist governments in the East, both of which effected the destruction of the social and political monopoly of the traditional elites. European domination of the world had come to an end as areas of the world previously regarded by Western historians as ahistorical achieved national consciousness. At the same time the national state, while still firmly established, lost relative importance in Western Europe. Disillusionment regarding the course of history replaced the once deeply felt optimism regarding the quality of modern civilization. While the idea of progress had never been generally accepted by nineteenth-century historians and was explicitly rejected by Ranke, there had existed a broad consensus, questioned by relatively few cultural pessimists like Burckhardt, that the course of history, particularly that of the modern Western world, represented a qualitatively positive process. The idea of progress gave way among thinkers as different as Spengler and Max Horkheimer to pessimistic visions of the self-destructive forces inherent in modern technological societies. A broad group of thinkers, including theorists as diverse as Max Weber, Theodor Lessing, Karl Popper, Claude Lévi-Strauss, and Michel Foucault but excluding the Marxists, now held that history had no meaning or structure. Much greater emphasis was now placed on a history which took into consideration the discontinuities and ruptures in history. The conception of the "historical process as a continuous development" was termed by Lévi-Strauss to be "fallacious" and "contradictory"[2] as was the nineteenth-century faith that "men make their own history." If, as we cited before, "the repetitive, the quasi-instinctual" had once been rejected as the subject matter of history, historians, including Marxists, now assigned a much greater significance to this "substratum of history." Forces outside human consciousness and control, whether economic and social processes possessing a high degree of autonomy, depth psychological determinants, or concealed anthropological or linguistic structures, were now assigned a decisive significance for historical understanding.

There is broad diversity in history writing. To be sure among all professional historians there are certain communalities. For all of them history is a reality-seeking enterprise. They seek to discover what happened in human affairs in the past and to understand why it occurred. Ideally, they proceed by canons of scientific research: through critical rational investigation, publication of results, and review by one's peers. Indeed, with respect to procedure, their work has become scientifically ever more rigorous with self-conscious testing of assumptions, concepts, and hypotheses.

Nevertheless, there are divisions among professional historians. Roughly speaking, they seem to fall into three categories, or perhaps four: the narrators of eventful history, usually concerned with establishing from written evidence the detailed record of the activities of elites; the French *Annales* school, with its adventurous, wide-ranging, insatiable curiosity about almost all aspects of the past, consciously neglecting only the eventful political story but approaching economies, societies, and civilizations with an inventive problem-as-you-go attitude, not bound by system, creating (and at times borrowing) ideas, theories, concepts, and methods in a virtuosity fireworks display of human ingenuity; the social scientific group, usually analytical in their approach, who in the solution of their problems invent (or borrow from neighbor disciplines) concepts, techniques, and hypotheses, frequently about structures, movements, and processes that lie beneath or within the story of population, economy, and society; and the Marxists, stimulated, guided, and restrained by the comprehensive theory and method of understanding founded by Karl Marx and Friedrich Engels. Viewed abstractly, each category of historians forms a self-contained unity or bloc, but in actuality there are divisions within each category and intermarriages among the blocs. Thus, despite the repeated insistence in France, the United States, West Germany, and elsewhere that history must become a social science (major proponents are Pierre Chaunu and Charles Tilly) or a historical social science (H.-U. Wehler), there is little agreement on what constitutes a science or a social science. Ideological differences, such as those between empirical functionalists, structural anthropologists, Weberians, and Marxists, are reflected in conflicting conceptions of what is meant by social science. Even in the realm of political history, an area relatively resistant to contemporary social-scientific concepts, there is division between those who tell an often fascinating story of unique events and those who seek consciously to relate the political story to broader social or even cultural factors. Two very different examples come to mind, one being Lewis Namier's attempts in the 1920s and 1930s to move from political history oriented toward great ideological issues to a minute analysis of the personal and social setting of the individual members of Parliament, the other being the attempts by West German (E. Kehr, Fritz Fischer, H.-U. Wehler and others) and East German (Fritz Klein, W. Gutsche) but also of American New Left historians (William A. Williams, Walter Lefever, Gabriel Kolko) to examine foreign-policy decisions in terms of domestic social and economic factors. Although modern historiography has not often attempted to write the broad "history of society" of which Eric Hobsbawm speaks,[3] the perspective of historical studies has grown immensely. It is dealing relatively less with traditional elites and increasingly with aspects of the life of broad segments of the population, no longer almost exclusively with high culture but with popular life-styles, sexuality, the family, leisure time, and popular attitudes. New categories of sources have been utilized. The written document found in the public archives has been supplemented by oral history, parish records and censuses, and archeological findings. The new kinds of evidence opened the way not only to the history of the many and to an exploration of deeper layers of consciousness but also provided the methods for studies of non-Western societies, like those of sub-Saharan Africa, which lacked the written sources and often the highly structured political institutions to which the historian of the Western, the Islamic, or the Far Eastern world had been accustomed.

Despite the warnings of such historians as J. H. Hexter, G. R. Elton, Paul Veyne, and Hayden White against the adoption of any scientific, even social-scientific model, for historical inquiry, and White's insistence that history is an intellectual enterprise akin to rhetoric or poetry,[4] historians have become more committed than ever to the scientific ideal of history as a methodologically and conceptually rigorous discipline. At one extreme is the notion, reminiscent of nineteenth-century positivism and embodied in Carl Hempel's "covering law," that scientific explanation in history is similar to that of other disciplines. The idea has fascinated small groups of historians who have sought to introduce highly mathematical models explaining historical behavior. This has been the case of the New Economic Historians in the United States (notably Robert Fogel, Stanley Engerman, and Douglas North).[5]

Yet the impact of theory building and quantification has made itself felt in other orientations of historical writing as well, although historians have generally been highly eclectic in their use of social-science theories and have remained aware of the qualitative aspects of human meaning which require historical understanding. The chapters which follow throw light on this rich diversity of theoretical and technical approaches. There is a danger in modern social history, as there was in the older professionalized history, to succumb to narrow specialization. At the same time there have been conscious attempts to arrive at a broader conception of history, at a "history of society," which overcomes compartmentalization. In the following pages, I want to examine two modern traditions of historical study, which while they represent only a small segment of contemporary historical writing internationally, have offered two important models for a social history which seeks to overcome disciplinary compartmentalization—the historiography of the French *Annales* school and modern Marxist historiography. Both represent rich, diversified traditions which cannot be reduced to a simple common denominator. Yet despite fundamental divergences in their conceptions of science and history, they point in important ways to directions in which modern social history might move.

Both the *Annales* and the Marxist traditions proceed from the assumption that the realm of conscious human actions, including political behavior, must never be taken at face value, but must rather be understood in terms of underlying forces, material conditions of life, which determine or at least in part explain these. In their conception of the role which conscious human action plays in the course of historical events and hence the relevance of politics for history, the two differ, *Annales* historians being generally more concerned with exploring the silent, impersonal processes which underlie human behavior in time, while Marxist scholars continue to view man as an active agent who transforms the society in which he lives. Marxism in its concern with human consciousness and political action, seen within the context of economic and social structure, preserves essential elements of the historicist belief in the primacy of man in the historical process. Marxism continues to ascribe a special role to understanding in a historical perspective the forces operating in the modern world, while *Annales* historians, hostile to the idea of unilinear developments, reject as a specifically Western prejudice the notion that the "history of the world can be measured from the particular experience" of a modern industrialized society.[6]

Not that *Annales* historians have neglected the history of consciousness. From the beginnings of the movement in the 1920s, Marc Bloch and Lucien Febvre were centrally concerned with "mentalities," especially with those of collective groups. In seeking to reconstruct "feudal society" as a structure of interpersonal relationships, Bloch took into account not only geographic, technological, and economic factors but the "mental climate" as well. He sought evidence not solely in written sources but also in the hard material artifacts of tools and field patterns as well as in the less material remnants of superstitions, folklore, and legal practices. In his study of the problem of unbelief in the age of Rabelais, which appeared in 1943, Febvre sought through an analysis of language to examine the "mental tools" which shaped the thinking of the period.[7] The historian was no longer interested in development *per se* but in the uniqueness of a historical epoch. In Fernand Braudel's magisterial *The Mediterranean and the Mediterranean World in the Age of Philip II* (1949) the concept of historical time was redefined and the unity of a linear historical time denied. Side by side with the time of fast-moving but ephemeral political events there was the much slower time of long-enduring cultural, social, and economic patterns and the even slower time of almost immobile geological, geographical, and climatic factors. It was the sphere of the impersonal, material, and collective factors which deserved primary historical consideration. It was this sphere which, moreover, set effective limits to human freedom. Here the political structures, which are still focal in Bloch's *Feudal Society,* recede into the background. In this new history, people appear as the object rather than as the subject of historical processes. Under the direction of Febvre and Braudel, who in 1956 succeeded Febvre as director of the Sixth Section, studies in the 1950s and 1960s concentrated on the economic and demographic patterns of the Old Regime. Extensive quantified studies were undertaken, utilizing land registers, parish records, and tax books and even taking into consideration climatic conditions. A model was set up of a preindustrial society in which Malthusian laws regulated the interrelation of birth, morbidity, nutrition, wages, and land prices. There was a fascination with numbers and the conviction, repeated by various of the historians of the movement, that "from a scientific point of view, the only social history is quantitative history."[8] Even the history of consciousness was to be approached, where possible, not on the basis of literary evidence but of hard data. Thus *Annales* historians in the 1970s turned increasingly to the exploration of popular consciousness, approaching attitudes towards such existential concerns as death and sexual experience by computerizing information gained from wills and by investigating sexuality on the basis of demographic data. There was indeed a singular attempt by Emmanuel Le Roy Ladurie in his analysis of the Protestant Reformation in the Languedoc[9] to relate religious and political conflict to demographic-economic cycles. Increasingly, however, *Annales* historians turned their interest away from the analysis of change to an analysis of relatively stable or slow-moving structures, to what Le Roy Ladurie has called an "immobile history,"[10] which in many *Annales* works has taken the form of a retrospective anthropology.[11]

The ambition of the *Annales* historian was to overcome the narrow confines of specialized studies and lay the foundation of a "global" or "total" history of a unit of historical study, a unit which was seldom a political entity, such as a nation, but more likely a region like the Languedoc or the Beauvaisis[12] or a larger geographic whole such as the Mediterranean. Not politics or ideology but the underlying material forces of the interaction of population and economic factors provided a unifying element for the subject under study. *Annales* methods thus proved to be particularly applicable to relatively stable societies in which political intervention and technological controls had relatively little impact on the processes of production and reproduction. Yet despite the positivistic implications of their concern with figures and hard data, the *Annales* approach challenged the empiricism of a positivistic orientation. The figures did not speak for themselves. They were instruments for establishing underlying structures which permitted the historian to "decode" the multiplicity of signifiers which constitute a culture or society.

The *Annales* historians indeed originated neither the methods of demographic or economic study nor the exploration of popular cultures. They sought, however, to provide a view which would contribute to a synthesis. They intensified the concern for areas of study which until then had been neglected, the everyday life of the many as well as the realm of the subconscious. Yet at the same time they increasingly gave up or at least neglected the analysis of change, particularly of change in a modern technological world in which the state played a crucial role. History written in the *Annales* tradition, with few exceptions, was the history of society with politics left out. It reflected the conviction that history was not a continuous process, but instead was marked by discontinuity and by a plurality of societies and cultures, among which the modern West deserved no special place.

A broad segment of modern social history, Marxist and non-Marxist, has gone in different directions. The main concern of these new orientations has been an understanding of the forces which determine the modern world. Like the *Annales* historians, the historians of these new orientations are aware of fundamental ruptures in the course of history that were ushered in by industrialization. Non-Marxists, such as the new critical school of political historians in West Germany, have sought to integrate theories of modernization, Weberian concepts of power and status, and Marxist conceptions of economic conflict in order to analyze the catastrophic course of modern German history. Marxist ideas, however, in one form or another have had a considerable impact on contemporary historical writing, perhaps less so in the United States or West Germany than in France, Italy, Japan, and Latin America, not to mention the socialist countries.

There is, however, not one Marxist approach to historiography. In his writings Marx himself offered a rich and ambiguous legacy of thought. The interpretation of Marxism as a form of economic determinism, fashionable in the Social Democratic movements of the 1890s and 1900s, which demanded a relatively rigid relation between an economic basis and a political and cultural superstructure, and a theory of stages through which all societies passed in the course of the development of productive forces, has yielded in recent decades to a more flexible conception which has given its due place, as Marx had done, to the role of political consciousness as itself an active factor of change. In the period after World War I, Marxism as a theory of understanding society and history moved diversely. An older direction continued to deal with the "lawful" processes by which society moved from one social formation to the next, determined by the conflicts inherent in productive relations and relatively unaffected by conscious human intervention. The interminable discussions about the transformation from "feudalism" to "capitalism" at times reflect the relatively mechanical conception of what is offered as a dialectical movement.[13] A second direction, written from a Leninist perpective, while it recognized the crucial role of consciousness, often tended in almost idealistic manner to stress the role of the party, its leaders, and its ideology. A history of the working class could thus become highly elitist and ignore the actual conditions under which workers lived and struggled.[14]

Recent Marxist historiography, as these essays will show, has gone a good way in overcoming these limitations by giving a greater role to popular consciousness and yet not abandoning the firm material basis which a Marxist approach provides. The frequent schematism of an older generation of Marxist theorists has given way to a more complex understanding of historical change. Georg Lukács, Karl Korsch, and Antonio Gramsci's reexaminations of Marx's thought in the 1920s contributed to this new openness by stressing Marx's view of society as a totality in movement and by seeking out the dialectical relationship between social being, rooted in productive processes and class struggle, and social consciousness as a central theme in Marx's thought. This opened the way to an approach to history, increasingly current since the 1950s, which in the works of Eugene Genovese, Christopher Hill, Eric Hobsbawm, Walter Markov, Albert Soboul, E. P. Thompson, and others turned to the analysis of popular consciousness and everyday life, subjects which also concerned the *Annales,* but which the Marxists examined in the context of economic and social conflict. At the same time a critical openness developed towards social science techniques and concepts as is apparent, for example, in Witold Kula and Jerzy Topolski's use of quantifiable models in the analysis of feudal economies in specific national and historical contexts. Marxist historiography thus moved closer to a broad current of modern social history, in both its increasing attention to broader segments of the population and its greater openness to the empirical social sciences. But this new Marxist history specifically rejected the conception of societies as systems marked by equilibrium as they were portrayed by the *Annales* school and the sociological functionalists. Rather, they viewed popular life and all other social and economic phenomena in terms of their relationships to productive and reproductive processes in societies that are marked and moved by conflict.

Marxian historiography has obviously affected non-Marxist historians. It attracted their attention to economic factors in history. It drew them to study the exploited and oppressed. But perhaps Marx's most important contributions to modern historiography were his emphasis on the concept that society moves as a totality of interrelated elements and his attempts to find the structural content in which historical phenomena occurred, to relate these to the processes of production and reproduction, and to formulate conceptual models which would permit an analysis of the factors making for change. The primacy which Marx assigned to the dialectical movement of history, to the changing forces of production, and to the class conflicts resulting therefrom remained open to debate with non-Marxists. Yet debate between non-Marxists and Marxists was itself fructifying. A great deal of non-Marxist social and economic theory—the classical examples are works by Max Weber and Joseph Schumpeter—and a broad segment of modern social history arose from the critical dialogue with Marxist theory.

The debate between the Marxists and the New Economic Historians illustrates some of the resemblances and differences between two schools of thought. They share a concern with economic factors. They also share a willingness to quantify and to apply conceptual models. What distinguishes the Marxists from the New Economic Historians is the former's insistence that economic factors—or similarly, political events or sociological data—can never be separated from the broader context of social relations and historical development. This concern with the broader context enables Marxists to apply several correctives to contemporary historiography and social sciences. Willing (as we see in Topolski's essay) to apply strict conceptual models and mathematics to the analysis of economic processes, Marxists are nevertheless unwilling to reduce economic or social phenomena to mathematical functions. In the final analysis, the Marxist conception of history is highly political. Marxist science rejects a conception of objectivity which makes it possible to reconstruct reality dispassionately and to dissect it; rather it sees science—and historical study—as a revolutionary praxis seeking not only to "interpret" but to "change" the world.

We have perhaps oversimplified the diversity of modern historiography by dwelling at such extent on the *Annales* school and the Marxists. Yet these two orientations reflect two important types of modern social history, both concerned with seeing historical phenomena in a social context, one reflecting the disillusionment with the belief in the continuity of historical development and seeking to create a retrospective anthropology, the other focusing on the transformations of the present.

No unified historical science or paradigm has emerged to dominate the field as did the "paradigm" which emerged from Ranke's seminars. Historians in recent years have indeed spoken frequently of history as a historical social science and have adapted methodologies and theories derived from the systematic social sciences. But they have done so very eclectically because they have been unable to draw on an integrated body of social-science theory. Ideological divergences, although fruitful in providing a diversity of perspectives and cognitive interests and thus contributing to an ongoing dialogue among historians, have thus far prevented consensus on what constitutes historical science. Yet a certain new style has made itself felt in historical writing. Historians today write history differently than they did thirty years ago. They have doubtless become more aware of the assumptions underlying their investigations and of the need to define clearly the questions and hypotheses with which they approach their subject matter. Greater demand has been placed on the historian not merely to narrate but to conceptualize. In this sense there has undoubtedly been a gain in scholarly rigor.

At the same time the field of history has been enormously enriched. The scope of historical study, as the following chapters will show, has been extended dramatically in these past thirty years. The Europocentric bias has been broken, as has the limitation of historical studies to the public life of small groups of elites. The non-European world has increasingly become an area for study. Within the areas of the non-Western world which were once regarded as not having a history, indigenous traditions of history have become known. New classes of the population have become the subject of historical studies. Not only the history of the articulate but that of the less articulate has been explored as historians have begun to delve into new sources, not only literary ones, which give insights into popular life and popular culture and into the realm of the nonconscious.

It is difficult, of course, to assess the gains and losses which have accompanied the transformation of historical studies. The great narrative tradition has declined although by no means disappeared, and the best historians of our age, such as Marc Bloch, Emmanuel Le Roy Ladurie, and E. P. Thompson, give us reason to believe that analytical history and literary quality are not incompatible. The dangers of new methodological dogmatisms and of a fascination with the new technological tools at the disposal of the historian, which may lead to a dehumanization of historical studies under the guise of a new social-scientific positivism, are present, but few historians have succumbed to them. We may perhaps conclude on a note of moderate optimism that in its attempt to explore a broad diversity of human experiences by means of new methods, contemporary historical scholarship has come a step closer to the Enlightenment ideal that all aspects of human life are worthy of rational historical inquiry.

Notes

1. H. Stuart Hughes, *Consciousness and Society: The Reorientation of European Social Thought 1890–1930* (New York, 1958), p. 6.

2. Claude Lévi-Strauss, *The Savage Mind* (Chicago, 1966), p. 260.

3. E. J. Hobsbawm, "From Social History to the History of Society," in Felix Gilbert and Stephen R. Graubard, *Historical Studies Today* (New York, 1971), pp. 1–26.

4. See Hayden White, *Metahistory: The Historical Imagination in Nineteenth-Century Europe* (Baltimore, 1973).

5. The attempt to analyze a complex social phenomenon like slavery in the United States quantitatively, as Robert Fogel and Stanley Engerman did in *Time on the Cross: The Economics of American Negro Slavery*, 2 vols. (Boston, 1974), has aroused considerable controversy. See the review essay by Thomas L. Haskell, "The True and Tragic History of 'Time on the Cross,' " *New York Review of Books*, 2 October 1975, pp. 33–39.

6. See André Burguière, "Préface" to the special issue "Histoire et structure," *Annales, économies, sociétés, civilisations* 26 (1971): iv.

7. Lucien Febvre, *Le Problème de l'incroyance au XVIe siècle, la religion de Rabelais* (Paris, 1942).

8. François Furet and Adeline Daumard, "Méthode de l'histoire sociale: les archives notariales et la mécanographie," *Annales, économies, sociétés, civilisations* 14 (1959): 676; see also Emmanuel Le Roy Ladurie, *Le Territoire de l'historien* (Paris, 1973), p. 22.

9. *Les Paysans du Languedoc*, 2 vols. (Paris, 1966); English translation: *The Peasants of Languedoc* (Urbana, Ill., 1974).

10. See Emmanuel Le Roy Ladurie, "L'Histoire immobile," *Annales, économies, sociétés, civilisations* 29 (1974): 673–692.

11. See Emmanuel Le Roy Ladurie, *Montaillou village occitan, 1294–1324* (Paris, 1975); English translation: *Montaillou: Cathars and Catholics in a French Village 1294–1324* (London, 1978).

12. Pierre Goubert, *Beauvais et le Beauvaisis de 1600 à 1730, contribution à l'histoire sociale de la France du XVIIe siècle* (Paris, 1960).

13. See Jon S. Cohen, "The Achievements of Economic History: The Marxist School," *Journal of Economic History* 38 (1978): 29–57.

14. See, for example, the Introduction to Institut für Marxismus-Leninismus beim Zentralkommitee der SED, *Geschichte der deutschen Arbeiterbewegung* (Berlin/GDR, 1966), I, 7.

Some Methodological Reorientations

PART: I

1 LOUIS O. MINK

Philosophy and Theory of History

Modern philosophy of history can be dated, arbitrarily but conveniently, from the year 1938. In that year appeared both Raymond Aron's *Introduction à la philosophie de l'histoire* and Maurice Mandelbaum's *The Problem of Historical Knowledge*. While neither volume was of significant direct influence on Anglophone philosophy—and Aron's book did not appear in English translation until 1961—they were the first full-dress philosophical studies of the problems of historical knowledge to appear in their own countries for an audience not directly acquainted with the controversy over historicism in Germany in the late nineteenth and early twentieth centuries. In retrospect they can be seen to have anticipated many of the themes and problems which have occupied recent discussions of the relation of causal explanation and historical understanding. In 1938 it was still necessary for Aron and Mandelbaum to dis-associate themselves from the then-current meaning of "philosophy of history" as the claim to discern the pattern, meaning, or direction of the historical process as a whole, in the various forms of that claim by Hegel (and post-Hegelian systems including Marxism), by Comte, and by Spengler or Toynbee. The ambiguity of the term "history" in English and other languages has been repeatedly noted. On the one hand it refers to *res gestae,* the course of human events, on the other to *historia rerum gestarum,* the inquiries undertaken and accounts rendered by historians. In 1951, W. H. Walsh's *The Philosophy of History: An Introduction* introduced the terms "critical (or analytic) philosophy of history" and "speculative philosophy of history," corresponding to the two meanings of "history," and in succeeding years "critical philosophy of history" has constituted the discipline of philosophy of history, while "speculative philosophy of history" has virtually ceased to be a center of original thought and has itself passed over to become part of the subject matter of intellectual history—along with, say, monarchical theories of politics. The one fully contemporary, speculative theory of history in the tradition of Spengler, Toynbee, and Sorokin is Eric Voegelin's *Order in History,* with four published volumes and a fifth and concluding volume still projected. But the fourth volume of that work (1974), published seventeen years after the third, acknowledges the abandonment of the original project of demonstrating a single line of "meaning" in Western history from the ancient Near East to the present.

Not all critical philosophers of history, however, have accepted the categorical distinction between straightforward historiography and "speculative" philosophy of history. In rather similar but independent ways, it has been argued by both Haskell Fain, in *Between Philosophy and History* (1970; the subtitle is "The Resurrection of Speculative Philosophy of History Within the Analytic Tradition"), and the historian Peter Munz, in *The Shapes of Time* (1977), that narrative historiography of any scope inescapably presupposes some conception of historical significance and direction—the plot line of the narrative, as it were—and that such conceptions if explicitly articulated amount to speculative philosophies of history. Nevertheless, both philosophers and historians have come with near unanimity to accept R. G. Collingwood's dictum that philosophy is "thought about thought," and that the philosophy of history is therefore the second-order activity of reflection upon the nature and structure of historical thinking. As with logic and conceptual analysis, of course, such reflection is at once descriptive and critical.

History as a discipline shares one characteristic with philosophy: neither is defined by a prescriptive method of inquiry or by the dominance of a single methodology or set of theoretical assumptions. Thus in the nineteenth and early twentieth centuries parts of both history and philosophy split off to become separate disciplines as they became amenable to inquiry according to a discipline-specific methodology such as laboratory experimentation. In this way psychology broke away from its earlier identity with philosophy, as sociology broke away from history by "operationalizing" the theoretical vocabulary for the comparison of social systems. Nevertheless, history remains a discipline not defined by any theory but open to the concepts and theories of other disciplines, especially the social sciences, while reserving the right to determine their utility in historical research; and correspondingly the modern critical philosophy of history has reflected developments in general philosophy. Even though the philosophy of history has, in the decades since 1938, achieved the status of an acknowledged discipline, it continues to reflect the differing interests of historians and philosophers. Historians, for example, are naturally interested in any analysis of *historical* explanation which throws light on the difference between good and bad, adequate and inadequate explanations in history; but they are not necessarily interested in the special problems of explanation in, say, psychoanalysis or astrophysics. Philosophers, on the other hand, may have regard for the discipline-specific problems of explanation in history, as in other fields, but their natural interest is in a *general* theory of explanation, even though such a general theory may be complicated by qualifications when applied to different disciplines or types of inquiry. So philosophy of history is subject to a double demand. On the side of history it cannot ignore the special characteristics of history (or the problem of what those characteristics may be); on the side of philosophy it cannot assume that historical knowledge is incommensurable with other forms of inquiry and understanding. There may or may not be specifically historical laws, or uniquely historical causes. But the concept of law and the concept of cause, as these appear in historical thinking, must be related to, even though not identical with, similar concepts in any other form of inquiry.

Philosophy of history, in the decades since 1938, has therefore gone through a series of developments in which it has drawn upon other areas of philosophy in the formulation and reformulation of problems. In the 1940s and 1950s the philosophy of science (specifically, natural science) provided the main challenge; in the 1960s the focus shifted to a newly developing philosophy of social science, and in the 1970s new directions in the philosophy of history have come mainly from studies of the linguistic and literary form of the historical writing which embodies the claims of historical knowledge.

Until the 1960s, the central controversy in philosophy of history was the continuing debate over the so-called covering-law model of historical explanation. This was first formulated by Karl Popper in his comprehensive philosophy of science *Logik der Forschung* (1935) but given application to history and made current among English-speaking philosophers and historians by C. G. Hempel in "The Function of General Laws in History" (1942). According to the covering-law analysis of explanation, the satisfactory explanation of any event (whether natural or social) requires that the description of the event—the *explanandum*—be logically deducible from a set of empirical laws, together with statements asserting the initial and boundary conditions referred to in the laws; the laws and statements of initial conditions together constitute the *explanans*. Such a model, of course, gives only the formal conditions of explanation, but that is its explicit intent, since it purports to be a perfectly general model; it is in fact intended to show the formal or methodological unity of all science, independent of the differences of subject matter, concepts, or theories of particular sciences.

The covering-law model has a number of implications of particular interest for historiography, since it calls into question many *prima facie* satisfactory explanations. For one thing, it implies that explanations and predictions have the same logical structure; a prediction differs from an explanation only with respect to the time of occurrence of the *explanandum:* the prediction of an eclipse, for example, involves exactly the same calculations from the laws of motion and the state of the solar system at a given moment before the beginning of the eclipse as does the explanation of that eclipse at any subsequent time. The implication for history is that an explanation falls short of being satisfactory unless the historical event *could* have been predicted on the basis of no more knowledge than the explanation explicitly adduces. A second feature of the covering-law model is that it displays the *explanandum* as *necessary* relative to the covering laws and initial conditions because it is logically implied by the *explanans*. Such an explanation therefore shows not only why an event occurred but also why it did *not* occur. Third, the covering-law model proscribes the claim to explain unique events exactly insofar as they are unique, because an event falls under a covering law, or set of covering laws, only to the extent that it shares the relevant properties with the entire class of instances which fall under the same laws. The unique, in whatever respect it truly is unique, cannot be explained at all. Finally, the covering-law model incorporates an essentially Humean theory of causality as the regularity of succession of classes of events. The *explanandum*-event is linked to the initial conditions as its cause only by the empirical laws adduced in the *explanans*; and these laws do not express an intelligible link between cause and effect but only the contingent fact that events of the type of the "cause" are observed regularly to be followed by events of the type of the "effect"—that is, the *explanandum*.

The covering-law model is descriptive insofar as it purports to make explicit the logical features of adequate explanation particularly as such explanations have been achieved in the physical sciences. At the same time, it is prescriptive insofar as it formulates a schema of explanation which is satisfied by very few, if any, explanations of individual action and social change. Few historians have been inspired to redirect historical research toward the discovery of laws of historical change. But a generation of social scientists, especially but not exclusively in the United States, did in fact accept the covering-law model and the positivist—or "logical empiricist"—philosophy of science of which the covering-law model was a major tenet. To historians who objected that the covering-law model was remote from the actual practice of historical explanation, positivist philosophers and social scientists could reply, following Hempel, that so-called explanations in history are as a rule "explanation sketches," that is, truncated explanations which cannot achieve canonical form until (*a*) the required laws of individual and social behavior are discovered and confirmed by the social sciences themselves; and (*b*) historians redescribe historical events in the scientific vocabulary of the search for appropriate laws.

Three decades of criticism of the covering-law model of explanation, however, have led to a progressive weakening of its claims and of its scope of application. First of all, the requirement that an *explanans* contain at least one universal law was abandoned when Hempel himself proposed an alternative model in which the covering laws are statistical rather than universal. This modification was made in order to adapt the model to quantum-theoretical explanations in physics, but its effect was to eliminate the requirement that *explananda* be deducible, since in an explanation in which the covering laws are statistical or probability laws, the *explanans* does not imply the *explanandum* but only a certain probability of the latter; and moreover, the same *explanans* "explains" the nonoccurrence of an event as well as its occurrence. A second weakening of the model was initiated by Morton White in his *Foundations of Historical Knowledge* (1965). Recognizing that at least some historical explanations are adequate without the invocation of general laws, he admitted the possibility of singular causal explanations, in history and elsewhere, while continuing to maintain that an adequate causal explanation entails the existence of *some* law or laws, even though the latter are not now known and may even never be known. Finally, Murray Murphey in *Our Knowledge of the Historical Past* (1973), while continuing to defend the covering-law theory of historical explanation, proposed to accept as typical laws generalizations of all sorts about the customs and practices of particular societies at specific times. Thus the explanation of a particular piece of human behavior may be simply that the agent was doing the accepted or expected thing in those circumstances. And it is the historian, not the "social scientist," who discovers and describes the practices local to particular societies at particular times. By this point of modification, the covering-law model had been brought into close agreement with the actual practice of historical inquiry; but at the same time it had been emptied of most of the normative criteria of adequacy—particularly the deducibility criterion and the logical requirements for the formulation of universal empirical laws—that had initially made it a challenge to the practice of historiography.

A different line of criticism of the covering-law theory of explanation, beginning with W. H. Dray's *Laws and Explanation in History* (1957), called into question the claim of the covering-law model, however modified, to represent the form of *all* explanations; manifestly, that model is relevant only to the explanation of *events*, and historians appear to give many different kinds of explanations, as well as explanations for different purposes. Dray, for example, identified "how-possibly" explanations (making an unexpected course of events intelligible by rebutting the presumption that it was unlikely), and "explaining-what" explanations (relating a number of events to a whole, e.g., seeing otherwise unrelated events as parts of the same social revolution). Genetic or process explanations afford yet another disputed category. No one has yet succeeded in producing an inventory of types of noncausal explanation or in formulating criteria of adequacy for the assessment of such explanations, no doubt because they are variable with subject matter, and do not lend themselves to formal modeling as does the covering-law model.

The most discussed type of explanation also reflects a shift in philosophy of history away from the positivist emphasis on a general theory of knowledge based on natural science to a newly developing philosophy of social science (including psychology) of antipositivist persuasion. This type is the explanation, or understanding, of rational action, that is, human action in the fulfillment of a purpose or the carrying out of a policy through changing circumstances. Against the covering-law theory, the argument is that actions are intelligible in virtue of an intrinsic connection between purpose (the "reason" for action) and action. For the covering-law theorist, the connection must be interpreted as contingent and empirical; that is, it can be invoked as an explanatory causal generalization only on the basis of repeated observations of the regular association of intentions of a certain type with actions of a certain type. The attack on the positivist interpretation of rational action is therefore an attack on behavioristic psychology and behavioristic social science and turns on the claim that actions are not just instances of "behavior" (as objectively describable by a scientific observer) and that reasons (motives, intentions, purposes) are not just instances of "causes," of the same order as causality in nature.

One consequence of the debate over reasons for actions versus causes of behavior has therefore been to call into question the Humean account of causality as observed regularity or frequency of succession—an account which in one way or another has been part of every attempt to model historical knowledge on knowledge in the natural sciences. It is clear at least that on Humean presuppositions putative causes and putative effects must be separately identifiable and describable, otherwise the connection between cause and effect would not be contingent and empirical—"loose and separate," in Hume's terms. Morever, both historians and philosophers have tended unconsciously to accept the Humean notion that a completely satisfactory causal explanation of an event must state the necessary and sufficient conditions for the occurrence of the event; this principle is in fact built into the covering-law model. Since few, if any, historical explanations can satisfy the principle, it has been customary to distinguish between causes and conditions, the "conditions" being those parts of the total cause which are necessary but not jointly sufficient, the "cause" being that part of the total cause which is sufficient, given the conditions; thus the lighted match is the "cause" of the fire, the combustibility of the material and the presence of oxygen among the "conditions." Historians have tended to say that historical explanations are justifiably incomplete because it is neither necessary nor usually possible to discern *all* the conditions of an event in order to understand its proximate cause.

Philosophers of history, however, have in various ways called into question the Humean account of causality. In their *Causation in the Law* (1959), which has been widely influential because of its thesis that historical reasoning is more closely allied with legal reasoning than with scientific thinking, H. L. A. Hart and A. M. Honoré argue that the identification of causes cannot be separated from the imputation of *responsibility,* and that in this way we draw the line between "cause" and "condition" variously from case to case. Voluntary action, however, ordinarily is an ultimate cause beyond which the chain of causality is not pursued. In a more fundamental attack on the Humean theory of causality, Maurice Mandelbaum has argued, in both *The Problem of Historical Knowledge* (1938) and *The Anatomy of Historical Knowledge* (1977), that the analysis of processes of change into sequences of "events" is artificial, and that there is direct perception of causal efficacy, not in the connection between events, but in the unity of a continuous process. Thus, in his view, there can be causal ascription independent of any empirical generalizations, and historical knowledge can be both idiographic and causally explanatory.

Causality in history has been even more radically called into question, however, by "idealist" philosophers of history. In *Experience and Its Modes* (1933), Michael Oakeshott forcefully denies that historical consciousness requires the concept of causality at all: the historian tells an intelligible story of the course of events (supported at every point by evidence, of course) and responds to the question "why" of any event by telling *more* of the details of the story. R. G. Collingwood's well-known thesis that "history is the reenactment of thought" (which includes human actions, since to understand them is to reenact the purposive thought which they express) has also the implication that causality is an irrelevant concept. In fact, Collingwood's thesis can in retrospect be seen to have anticipated by more than twenty years the replacement of covering-law explanations of human actions by rationale-explanations.

Rationale-explanations are of course not peculiar to history, and have been extensively discussed with particular reference to psychology, anthropology, sociology, and political science. They therefore illustrate the area of problems common to philosophy of history and philosophy of social science, an area typified by Peter Winch's influential *The Idea of a Social Science* (1958), a book which does not mention philosophy of history but is relevant to it throughout. With sociology and anthropology particularly in mind, Winch's thesis, adapted from Wittgenstein, is that meaningful behavior within a society consists of actions governed by rules which determine whether different actions are equivalent or different in meaning (for example, quite different actions may all count as "worshiping" or as "paying a debt"). Understanding social behavior is therefore not a matter of discovering and confirming empirical laws of behavior according to the *investigator's* rules for scientific inquiry, but rather of understanding the *agent's* own rules of meaning as the agent understands them. Clearly this thesis is as prescriptive for history as for anthropology.

Among other discussions of problems arising in the relation of history to the social sciences, one important contribution has not yet been followed up by philosophers of history. In *Our Knowledge of the Historical Past* (1973), Murray Murphey (although holding a modified positivist view of historical knowledge) concluded that historians cannot successfully adapt much of contemporary social science to their own purposes. His argument is a close examination of the statistical theories and techniques used in social science, which shows that statistical social science depends on the ability to *produce* data (for example, by questionnaires) adaptable to the statistical methods available for their analysis. Statistics, so to speak, has developed in symbiosis with the ability of social science to elicit new responses as data, but these statistical techniques are not technically appropriate for drawing inferences in situations in which historians cannot add to or change the evidence which the past has bequeathed to the present. This provides a further strong reason for discerning in history a type of understanding, however limited, which resists assimilation to scientific studies of social processes, at least in the present state of that art.

Recent developments in philosophy of history have looked less and less to an analysis of historical inquiry as "scientific" or even as a branch of "social science" and more to the structure of historical *writing*, an emphasis which restores the traditional but often neglected link between history and literature. Yet the relevant emphasis has been on the epistemological significance of narrative structure, not on the graces of literary style. The premise of this turn in attention is that in narrative history the *form* of the narrative is both essential and cognitive; it cannot be summarized, abstracted, divided into self-contained parts, or formulated in alternative ways. The contributions to philosophy of history by practicing historians have been almost entirely in this area. Geoffrey Elton's *The Practice of History* (1967) and J. H. Hexter's *The History Primer* (1971), neither of which touches on other issues in the critical philosophy of history, both stress the indispensability of narrative form; and the latter book goes beyond this to argue that there is a uniquely historical or "processive" type of explanation which can be exhibited in no other way than by narrative form.

The earliest attempt by a philosopher to deal with the epistemological significance of narrative was W. B. Gallie's *Philosophy and the Historical Understanding* (1964). Gallie's strategy was to analyze "understanding something historically" in terms of what is required to follow a story and to recognize it as displaying continuity and coherence. Causal explanations, Gallie asserted in unconscious agreement with Oakeshott's earlier claim, are resorted to by historians only at points where evidence fails to support narrative continuity. Gallie's analysis of following a narrative served to call attention to the experience of intelligibility, despite the obvious difficulty that it throws no light on historical *inquiry*, since the historian does not "follow" a narrative but constructs it. Other early attempts to characterize the significance of narrative sought to make narrative form compatible with covering-law explanation, a vehicle for the latter, as it were. In Arthur Danto's *Analytical Philosophy of History* (1965), this compatibility was achieved by the argument that events are knowable only under some description or other, and the same event may be (correctly) described in different ways—very concretely, for example, or very abstractly. A death may be described physiologically and impersonally, as in a clinical report, or politically or personally, as, say, in the death of a king, in circumstances of great import. So for Danto, the *same* event may be subject to a covering-law explanation under one description but belong to a narrative account under a different description; and even though both descriptions are correct, it may not be possible to infer one from the other and therefore a description appropriate to narrative cannot be *replaced* by a covering-law explanation of the same event.

It is evident that while Danto did not reject the possibility in principle of covering-law explanation of any event, his account does bring about a *conceptual* separation between covering-law explanation and historical understanding expressed in narrative form. The conceptual independence of narrative intelligibility was sharpened in Haskell Fain's *Between Philosophy and History* (1970). Since we are capable with a high degree of agreement of recognizing whether a given incident belongs to or is required by a certain narrative account, it would seem that we possess shared criteria of narrative relevance (as we have implicit criteria for the correct use of words), and it is the philosophical task to bring implicit criteria to explicit formulation. Fain therefore investigated a number of possible criteria for the coherence of narratives (for example, "a narrative is unified if every statement refers to or is equivalent to a statement referring to a single central subject''), only to conclude that every suggested criterion is inadequate. The problem of stating positive criteria for narrative coherence—and coherence is at least one of the conditions of cognitively significant narrative—therefore remains open and programmatic.

These developments converge toward an increasing tendency to regard narrative structure as incorporating and communicating a primary and irreducible type of cognitive understanding, and one typically if not uniquely appropriate to historical knowledge. There is also a conceptual connection between the understanding of rational action and narrative as the formulation and expression of such understanding; this was pointed out by Frederick Olafson in ''Narrative History and the Concept of Action'' (*History and Theory* 9 [1970], 265–289). Nevertheless, as the center of emphasis in philosophy of history has shifted from logical and conceptual problems associated with the *explanation* of *events* to logical and conceptual problems associated with the *understanding* of *narrative syntheses*, the question of historical relativism has been reopened in a new form. It is evident that the historian is in a different relationship to his evidence with regard to the construction of narrative than he is with regard to the assertion of particular statements. Each statement of a narrative account may be grounded in evidence (granting that the *assessment* of evidence is a problem, but this is a problem of historical practice, not of the critical philosophy of history). But the form of any narrative which goes beyond bare chronicle is not perceived in or abstracted from any body of evidence; it is constructed by the historian himself. Moreover, if the cognitive content of written history is in part exhibited in its form (over and above that part of its cognitive content which consists of the referential meaning of its factual statements), then it is difficult to see in what sense two different histories can be said to agree or be incompatible with each other, since complex forms cannot be restated as propositional assertions, which alone can be compatible or incompatible.

The response of what might be called the New Rhetorical Relativism in historiography to these considerations is that indeed narrative syntheses are cognitively incommensurable with each other. This view is implicitly present in J. H. Hexter's *The History Primer* as a consequence of its insistence on narrative structure as the historian's invention—but only implicitly and unconsciously, since Hexter also wishes to insist on the historian's Rankean responsibility to the past *wie es eigentlich gewesen*. The most considered rejection of the ideal of historical objectivity is that of Hayden White's *Metahistory: The Historical Imagination in Nineteenth-Century Europe* (1973). According to White's ''theory of the historical work,'' significant narrative consists of the emplotment of an established chronicle of events which is common to alternative emplotments. White identifies four categorical types of emplotment: Romance, Comedy, Tragedy, and Satire, represented in the nineteenth century by Michelet, Ranke, Tocqueville, and Burckhardt, respectively. These types of emplotment are in turn associated with different strategies of explanation and different possibilities of ideological implication. It is not merely derivative that the four types of emplotment correspond to established literary genres; in White's view they are not imitations of literary genres but rather derive directly from the linguistic tropes of metaphor, metonymy, synecdoche, and irony (respectively), which generate alternative structures of historical imagination. Although White's examples, discussed in much detail, are from nineteenth-century historiography, his theory of the sources of historical imagination is perfectly general. And it is uncompromisingly relativistic, since although the varieties of narrative emplotment make cognitive claims, the choice of a particular mode of emplotment cannot be justified on cognitive grounds but only as an aesthetic or political preference.

Critical philosophy of history has yet to come to grips with the New Rhetorical Relativism, although it is evident that the arguments traditionally marshaled against historicism cannot be simply transposed or reformulated to meet this new challenge. Nor, on a broader scale, have critical philosophers of history yet examined the theory and practice of hermeneutics, despite such suggestions as Paul Ricoeur's that human actions can be regarded as analogous to texts, thus extending the scope of "interpretation" and its supporting theory from literary texts to the domain of history itself. It may well be that the direction of development in philosophy of history will reveal as yet unsuspected affinities with the development of literary theory and analysis. This does not prejudge the perennial question whether history is an art or a science; but the meanings of "art" and "science" are themselves, like all concepts, subject to historical change.

Bibliography

Aron, Raymond. *Introduction à la philosophie de l'histoire* (Paris, 1938; rev. ed., 1948; English trans., London and Boston, 1961).

Berlin, Isaiah. *Historical Inevitability* (Oxford, 1953; reprinted in Isaiah Berlin, *Four Essays on Liberty*, Oxford, 1969).

Borger, Robert, and Frank Cioffi, eds. *Explanation in the Behavioral Sciences* (Cambridge, 1970).

Carr, David. *Phenomenology and the Problem of History* (Evanston, Ill., 1974).

Collingwood, R. G. *Autobiography* (Oxford, 1939).

———. *The Idea of History* (Oxford, 1946).

Danto, Arthur D. *Analytical Philosophy of History* (Cambridge, 1965).

Dray, William H. *Laws and Explanation in History* (Oxford, 1957).

———. *Philosophy of History* (Englewood Cliffs, N.J., 1964).

Elton, Geoffrey. *Political History* (New York and London, 1970).

———. *The Practice of History* (Sydney and New York, 1967).

Fain, Haskell. *Between Philosophy and History* (Princeton, N.J., 1970).

Funke, Gerhard. "Phenomenology and History," in Maurice Natanson, ed., *Phenomenology and the Social Sciences* (Evanston, Ill., 1973), II, 3–101.

Gallie, W. B. *Philosophy and the Historical Understanding* (London, 1964).

Goldstein, Leon J. *Historical Knowing* (Austin, Texas, and London, 1976).

Hart, H. L. A., and Honoré, A. M. *Causation in the Law* (Oxford, 1959).

Hempel, C. G. "Explanation in Science and History," in R. G. Colodny, ed., *Frontiers of Science and Philosophy* (Pittsburgh, Pa., 1962).

————. "The Function of General Laws in History," *Journal of Philosophy* 39 (1942): 35–48; reprinted in C. G. Hempel, *Aspects of Scientific Explanation* (New York, 1965).

Hexter, J. H. *Doing History* (Bloomington, Ind., and London, 1971).

————. *The History Primer* (New York, 1971).

Leff, Gordon. *History and Social Theory* (London, 1969).

Louch, A. R. *Explanation and Human Action* (Berkeley and Los Angeles, 1966).

Mandelbaum, Maurice. *The Anatomy of Historical Knowledge* (Baltimore and London, 1977).

————. *The Problem of Historical Knowledge* (New York, 1938).

Manninen, Juha, and Raimo Tuomela, eds. *Essays on Explanation and Understanding* (Dordrecht, Netherlands, and Boston, 1976).

Martin, Rex. *Historical Explanation* (Ithaca, N.Y., and London, 1977).

Meiland, Jack W. *Scepticism and Historical Knowledge* (New York, 1965).

Munz, Peter. *The Shapes of Time* (Middletown, Conn., 1977).

Murphey, Murray. *Our Knowledge of the Historical Past* (Indianapolis and New York, 1973).

Nagel, Ernest. *The Structure of Science* (New York, 1961).

Oakeshott, Michael. *Experience and Its Modes* (Cambridge, 1933).

Popper, Karl. *Logik der Forschung* (Vienna, 1935; English trans., *The Logic of Scientific Discovery*, New York, 1959).

————. *The Poverty of Historicism* (London, 1957).

Reiner, G. J. *History, Its Purpose and Method* (London, 1950).

Skagestad, Peter. *Making Sense of History: The Philosophies of Popper and Collingwood* (Oslo, 1975).

Stover, Robert. *The Nature of Historical Thinking* (Chapel Hill, N.C., 1967).

Voegelin, Eric. *Order and History* (Baton Rouge, La., 1956–1974): *Israel and the Revelation* (Vol. I, 1956), *The World of the Polis* (Vol. II, 1957), *Plato and Aristotle* (Vol. III, 1957), and *The Ecumenic Age* (Vol. IV, 1974).

Walsh, W. H. *An Introduction to the Philosophy of History* (London, 1951; rev. ed., 1967).

White, Hayden V. *Metahistory: The Historical Imagination in Nineteenth-Century Europe* (Baltimore and London, 1973).

White, Morton G. *The Foundations of Historical Knowledge* (New York, 1965).

Wright, G. H. von. *Explanation and Understanding* (London, 1971).

2 RICHARD T. VANN

The New Demographic History

Demography is a protean subject, standing where many disciplines converge. From its origins among the "political arithmeticians" of late seventeenth-century England, it has tended to be associated with economics, as in the pioneering work of Malthus (1798), but in North America it is more often categorized as a subfield of sociology. Some important demographers, particularly in France, have been trained as geographers. The mathematical theory of demography is highly developed, going well beyond the repertoire of statistics which is adequate for most social sciences. Human reproduction and mortality certainly fall within the scope of biology, and human reflection upon these profound topics is the staple of psychology, not to mention literature and philosophy.

Given its interdisciplinary nature, it is not surprising that demography should have many points of contact with history, which also lays tribute on so many other disciplines. It is perhaps more surprising that these potential relationships have taken so long to be developed. A start, at least, has been made in the past twenty-five years. It would be premature to salute any record of immense accomplishment, though a few studies have shown what remarkable results can be achieved with immense labor and patience, and it has become almost impossible to write social history, at least, without some attention to the distinctive concerns and concepts of demography. How this has come to be and what salient problems remain to be solved will be the subject of this essay.

Historical Demography

Hollingsworth[1] usefully distinguishes historical demography from demographic history. The former is simply the extension of the established techniques of demography to past populations, with the aim of discovering their size. Sometimes this can only be estimated for a single year or for widely scattered points in time, but it is always better to have estimates at regular intervals (like the decennial census totals) over a long span of time. If the data permit, the historical demographer can proceed to questions which come closer to explanations of population change: how many people married, at what ages, how large their families were, and how long they lived.

Historical demography is a subfield of analytic demography, whose aim has always been largely descriptive.[2] Development of better explanations of demographic change would be the first step towards what Hollingsworth calls "demographic history"—history reconceived with variations in the size and composition of the population made salient. Not only would changes in social structure be investigated to see how far they are causes or results of observed changes in population, but the deep rhythms of demographic change might also be shown to underlie the military struggles and political decisions which are the traditional staples of historiography.

Individual scholars made contributions to historical demography long before 1945, but the end of World War II saw the beginning of an organized attack on the subject from the Institut National d'Etudes Démographiques in Paris and its journal, *Population*. In 1947 *Population Studies* began publication in London. (*Annales, économies, sociétés, civilisations* also began its current series in 1945, but it is a mistake to treat it, or the Sixth Section, as pioneers in this subject, in which the editors of *Annales* at that time were not much interested.)[3] By 1955 *Population Index* had introduced a separate rubric for historical demography in its annual bibliography of demographic studies, and the subject could be said to be established.[4]

The attempt to apply demographic analysis to past populations grows logically out of any attempt to understand the demography of a present population. That this logic was so slow to unfold has been explained by the fact that so many of the earliest demographers concentrated upon mortality, where it is possible to study events concentrated in a very narrow span of time, by so-called transversal analysis. Once the attention of demographers fell primarily on births and marriages, the best technique was seen to be "longitudinal analysis": studying the experience over their lifetimes, or just over their fertile years, of a group of people ("cohort," in demographic terminology) who were born about the same time.[5] The most familiar example of longitudinal or cohort analysis is the figure for expectation of life at various ages, on which life insurance premiums are calculated. Although it is generally calculated from a census, expectation of life at birth in a given year is the median age at which all the people born in that year die. It thus (in advanced countries) directs our attention back to births that occurred in the first decade of the twentieth century, or even earlier. A complete life table, as a full set of such figures is called, could only be constructed on the basis of events a century apart.

An even longer time span is desirable for the full understanding of demographic change, since it takes a long time for the full consequences of a change in fertility or marriage patterns to work themselves out. Suppose that married women adopt the habit of completing their child-bearing by the age of thirty-five. This reduces the birthrate, and it also shortens the time between generations. The age structure of the population is changed by the reduced birthrate, and thus twenty years later the birthrate falls again. It has been estimated that even if there were no intervening demographic changes, about a century would pass before a new stabilization of demographic rates, and that ideally a series 150 years long should be available in order to isolate and study demographic changes.[6] This would mean, for most Western countries, pushing an analysis back from today to the beginning of the reliable census data.

Even if not lured well back into the past in the quest for such long series, the demographer has other good reasons to exploit past materials, even though his interest might be in present-day populations. For example, he might want some point of contrast to the voluntary control of births which has become widespread throughout the developed countries and is being vigorously promoted in most of the rest of the world. Since so few modern populations for which satisfactory records are available are free of family limitation, it is mainly in populations living before 1800—and not even all of them—in which "natural fertility" (where there was no conscious effort to limit family size) can be found. It was this reason (rather than any interest in history) which led Louis Henry to his path-breaking studies of the Genevan *haute bourgeoisie* and of the parish of Crulai in Normandy.[7]

Historical demography shares the body of demographic theory, though quite often its data are too sparse for some of the theory to be applicable. The critique of sources—the quintessential historian's task—is more difficult and more important, and historical demographers are forced to use evidence of a lower order of reliability than a modern demographer would bother with. The sources most often used in historical demography, in approximate order of usefulness, are as follows: (1) censuses, especially if names and not simply totals are given, (2) vital registration of births, marriages, and deaths (before the mid-nineteenth century this usually takes the more problematic form of registration of baptisms and burials), (3) bills of mortality, (4) fiscal records, such as poll or hearth taxes, (5) military records, (6) genealogies, (7) probate records (wills and inventories of property), (8) marriage settlements, (9) eyewitness estimates, (10) long-term price series, (11) physical remains of towns, houses, and so on, (12) evidence of new agricultural techniques and clearance of new lands, and (13) evidence from burial places, both from skeletons and from tombstone inscriptions.[8]

Only skeletons, the least reliable of these sources, are available as a basis for estimating the size of prehistoric populations (or, indeed, that of Greece until classical times). Skeletons do at least tell us approximately at what age prehistoric people died (which was almost always under forty), because the sutures in the skull close as one grows older, at a rate which can be approximately dated. Beyond this we cannot go, because we have little idea what the burial customs of prehistoric people were and thus cannot tell how representative the distribution of available prehistoric skeletons is. (It seems highly skewed; men predominate, and children of either sex are surprisingly unrepresented.) Nevertheless, even this most exiguous evidence has been used to construct population models for

Greek and even for prehistoric populations.[9] It is noteworthy that an evaluation of the reliability of the demographic evidence requires a purely historical investigation into the burial customs, which in turn rest on religious beliefs.

Naturally the evidence improves the closer one comes to modern times, but the three best sources are still almost entirely lacking for the Middle Ages. Just to estimate population at a single time during this period may demand the most curious knowledge from the historian. For example, Marco Polo says that a customs official told him that 43 cartloads of pepper, each weighing 223 pounds, were consumed daily in Hangchow in the thirteenth century. This amounts to 153,424 ounces of pepper—a figure which can be used to estimate the population, if we can guess how much pepper each person would use each day. Not much, surely: but if we reckon one fiftieth of an ounce rather than one twenty-fifth, we double the size of the estimate (which, even if pepper addiction were widespread, points to a population of several millions). For medieval Baghdad, one important source is the number of bathhouses, reported to be 120,000. If 800 persons used each bathhouse, the population becomes an incredible 96,000,000—but perhaps two of the zeroes (written as dots in Arabic) were really specks on the paper.[10]

It is not surprising that the interest of historical demography has centered on the period just before the national censuses—that is, the eighteenth century and the last half of the seventeenth. Here are preindustrial populations which might help us understand the demography of currently developing countries. Furthermore, there is evidence that seems to allow a highly accurate appraisal of their population patterns, though it is unlike the evidence that is available for developing countries today, where there have usually been censuses for some decades, but no effective system of vital registration; whereas in preindustrial Europe there are parish registers of baptisms, marriages, and burials which in some countries go back to the sixteenth century and even earlier, but no national censuses of the modern kind. The lack of a comprehensive national census is, however, partly offset by a large number of local community listings, which survive in considerable numbers in many parts of Europe and also in Japan. (There were also, in England, a number of national enumerations of communicants in the Church of England, with estimates of the numbers of Catholic recusants and Nonconformists.) These local censuses, if they supply the ages of those enumerated and the enumeration looks thorough, can be used for the estimate of demographic rates.

Since most of the historical demography of the early modern period rests on the inferences that can be made from parish-register material, a discussion of the way it has been exploited can touch on most of the issues in the field. One approach to the registers is simply to count the entries, treating any persistent surplus of baptisms over burials as a sign of rising population, and trying to note any apparent correlations between peaks in the various events. For example, in many parts of Western Europe marriage was quite late, because marriage required an independent economic base for the new couple; this might mean that a large number of deaths would lead to a peak in marriages, as the tempo of inheritance would be speeded up. This "aggregative" approach was much out of fashion a decade ago but has since made a comeback. One intrinsic difficulty with it is that it can produce only totals of the various demographic events, but what the demographer really wants is rates, for which he must know the size of the population at risk. There is no way the parish register can tell him this. Further problems arise in determining how complete the coverage of the parish register was. It was a register of sacramental acts by the parish priest, rather than a true vital registration. Persons who had withdrawn from the ministrations of the national church, like the English Nonconformists, might not figure at all. Baptisms, also, were sometimes delayed days or even weeks after birth. This would mean that many babies died before they could be baptized by the priest. The first day of life carries a higher risk of death than any other, and mortality in preindustrial Europe was especially high throughout the first week of life; so if baptism were customarily delayed even for a week, substantial differences between totals of baptisms registered and the true number of births can be expected.[11]

Totals of vital events in a single parish are likely to be misleading. Most rural parishes usually had a surplus of baptisms over burials, but this did not mean they were necessarily becoming more populous, because some young adults migrated permanently from the parish, and thus their burials were recorded elsewhere. In Crulai in Normandy about one in five young adults emigrated, so that the size of the population remained relatively unchanged.[12] It has been established that much migration was over very short distances—under ten miles—so it makes sense to count up the totals in several contiguous parishes embracing a settlement area of perhaps fifty square miles.[13] An early and still instructive use of this method may be seen in David Eversley's survey of parish records in Worcestershire.[14] Another approach is to make a random sample of several hundred parishes from a country. Such a national sample was projected in France but never carried through. An aggregative study based on an English sample has been completed.[15]

Although simple counting is all that is needed to compile the data, refined mathematics may be required for the analysis. An example is spectral analysis, designed to reveal periodic fluctuations in a series. The method, which was originally developed to detect radio signals amidst high background noise, requires a vast amount of computation. It can hardly be said to have proved itself, but preliminary studies seem to offer a way of assessing (and apparently disproving) such claimed connections as that between peaks of deaths and subsequent marriages.[16]

The various difficulties in aggregative analysis have led demographers to another approach to the parish registers which has been worked out in the past twenty-five years—"family reconstitution."[17] The procedure is that employed by genealogists in tracing the ancestors of descendants of a single person. In the latter part of the nineteenth century, Cyprien Tanguey compiled mass genealo-

gies attempting to trace the descendants of entire communities in seventeenth-
and eighteenth-century Quebec; in the first full-scale study to employ "family
reconstitution" techniques, Jacques Henripin drew upon Tanguey's work to
make his demographic survey of Canadian population at the dawn of the eighteenth century.[18]

With the multiple genealogies that a family-reconstitution study gives him,
a demographer can in effect set the limits and know the exact size of the population he is studying. This is done by excluding any family from the calculation
if insufficient information about it is available. To study fertility, for example,
we need to know the age of the mother at the time the children were born, how
long she had been married, and how many children she had borne previously.
Pure fertility, unaffected by the death of parents, can only be studied in the so-
called completed family (one where the wife remained married until her forty-
fifth or fiftieth birthday). No family can be considered "completed" unless the
date of the wife's birth or baptism, marriage, and burial are all known, together
with evidence that her husband, too, was still alive when the wife reached the
end of her fertile years. In an English parish, where many people did not live
their entire lives in a single place, fewer than one quarter of the births in the
parish register might figure in age-specific fertility calculations for completed
families.* Unfortunately, it seems unlikely that people who moved around had
the same demographic behavior as those who stayed put—particularly with respect to age at marriage.[19] So the precise control of the population under observation has been bought at the cost of limiting it to what is to some degree an
unrepresentative fraction of the whole population.

Since "family reconstitution" is appropriate to a minority of families in any
case, it lends itself to elite studies, such as that of the Genevan bourgeoisie or
the British peerage.[20] These were both based on genealogies rather than parish
registers. The problems presented by mobility can also be circumvented to some
extent by studying a group like the British Quakers, whose registration unit was
much wider than the parish.

Seasonal migration, where a family might be in a parish for part of a year and
out of it the rest, would still disturb the results of family reconstitution. So would
the deaths of unbaptized children. Nevertheless, it seems clear that careful family-reconstitution studies can not only yield rates which reflect the full analytical
repertoire of modern demography, but also approach the accuracy and completeness of information available for contemporary populations (where errors
and under-enumerations of up to 5 percent are by no means unknown, even in
advanced countries). In fact we have more information about some past populations than we are likely to get for present ones.

The shared analytical framework of demography also allows for comparisons
to test for underregistration or bias in the sources. This is particularly valuable

---

*This is the most severe shrinkage. For infant mortality calculations the family need only stay
in observation for a few years, so that the data are more abundant.

when invoking a biological regularity, as in the analysis of mortality. Mortality rates at different ages are bound to bear some relationship to one another which can be expressed in a series of model life tables. The ones prepared under United Nations auspices have not proved especially useful in historical demography, but the construction of model life tables for past populations by Ansley Coale and Paul Demeny was a great advance. Since then others have been prepared by Lederman and Demonet, Dupâquier, and LeBras.[21] If the observed mortality between birth and age four seems to correspond on a model life table with a life expectancy at birth of forty-five, but the mortality between ten and fifteen with an expectancy of only thirty-five, underregistration of infant mortality must be suspected, though there is always the possibility that the population in question has unique mortality patterns. Another way of detecting unrecorded infant deaths rests on the ratio between deaths in the first month of life and in the remainder of the first year, which are normally about even. If few deaths in the first weeks of life are recorded, underregistration must again be suspected.[22]

The historical demographer has done his job when he produces an array of measures which give an adequate account of a past population. He need not tell us very much, if anything, about the institutions of the people he studies, their social milieu, or even their responses to the political crises of their times. Hollingsworth's study of the British peerage is almost devoid of such details, and Henry's of the Genevan bourgeoisie even more so. Even his study of Crulai, despite its subtitle, does not succeed in bringing history and demography into a significant relationship; the bits of history in the first chapter are of the sort that antiquarians introduce into parochial histories, and the last chapter is based on a documentary series which begins seventy-five years after the end of the period to which the demographic study relates.

Henry has never professed to be a historian, and many demographers (even those who study past populations) have scant interest in history. Is there any reason why they should? If not, is there any reason why historians should interest themselves in the niceties of demographic analysis? The answer to this question depends on the way a transition from historical demography to demographic history is made.

Toward a Demographic Social History

Just after World War II, when historical demography was getting organized, a few historians, such as Jean Meuvret, were looking to population change— particularly the short-term "subsistence crisis"—to help explain the political uprisings of the seventeenth and eighteenth centuries. The early classics of demographic history are Chambers' *Vale of Trent* and Goubert's *Beauvais et le Beauvaisis,* studies of the population of a region in a broad social context.[23] These works are quite unlike those produced by mathematical demographers, who are interested only in ever more refined operations on single bodies of data.

Yet important historical questions are raised by the very act of checking the accuracy of demographic data. Just as the attitudes of primitive people toward death determine their burial practices, so changes in attitude towards baptism, with all they may imply of differing beliefs about childhood innocence or original sin, may produce those delays in baptism which bedevil our efforts to calculate infant mortality. The demographer may not be able to explain why attitudes towards baptism changed, but he must be interested in any explanation the historian can offer.

Also, the closer demographers can come to explanations as opposed to descriptions of demographic change, the more they will be drawn into the mainstream of history. Such explanations may not come quickly; even so recent a phenomenon as the unexpected rise and then fall of fertility after World War II remains rather mysterious. Indeed, even the main outlines of the history of the world's population are not entirely clear. The paradigm explanation is that of the "demographic transition," which holds that in most peasant societies there was very high ("natural") fertility offset by an equally high mortality (at least in the long run). This stable population with very high fertility and mortality then underwent growth because for some reason the death rate declined sharply. After a period of rapid population growth, the birth rate also declined, and the stable pattern of a modern population with low fertility and low mortality was reached.

Although this explanation has not been overthrown, it does not fit some of the evidence which has come to light. In particular, "natural" fertility turns out to be surprisingly variable and not always high. The variance can be as high as 1.7 to 1, even though family limitation is not in effect.[24] This means, among other things, that it is possible that a rise in fertility was as important as a fall in mortality in the great increase in European population which began around 1750. Also, the causes of the decline in mortality have not yet been elucidated; nor are we sure whether family limitation was really practiced in the seventeenth century or how it spread in the nineteenth.

With so much remaining unexplained in the classic problem, it might seem premature for demographic historians to make excursions into other aspects of social history, but in fact, it is the massive central puzzle which has led us to think that the pieces are very widely scattered. Marriage, the demographic event which falls most clearly within the sphere of human volition and culture, has been the natural bridge into social history. A good example of what mathematically sophisticated scholars who are also alert to broader historical problems can achieve is the recent study of the effects of the Napoleonic Civil Code on marriage patterns in nineteenth-century France. It subjects one of the oldest and most influential theories in demographic history, that of Frédéric le Play (1871), to a searching statistical analysis.[25]

Other obvious links to a broader social history arise from the study of sources used for the computation of demographic rates, or from the study of phenomena which can be ordered in the same way as vital events. Local censuses are a good example of the former; mobility, literacy, and illegitimacy of the latter. Local censuses do provide demographic information, but much else besides, and most of the use made of them thus far has been directed toward the light which they cast on the social structure. Much effort has been devoted to devising a standard notation in which the information from a community listing from any part of the world can be expressed—an obvious prerequisite for computer analysis. The most comprehensive system thus far has been worked out by the Cambridge Group for the History of Population and Social Structure[26] but various other notations remain in use.

Very few series of local censuses survive. They are almost always snapshots of the community at a single moment. An advance in understanding them came with the application of the same longitudinal perspective that we have already noted in demography. Thus, even though relatively few households might have been extended (as by widowed or retired parents living in the same household as married children) at the time a census was made, it could still have been true that in the life cycle of most persons, living with widowed parents and later with married children was the norm for anyone who lived long enough to do so.[27] The frequency of this pattern can be estimated by simulations of population change based on the relationship between rules for household formation on the one hand and known demographic rates on the other. Devotees of this approach, pointing out the hazards of accepting single observations as typical, have even claimed that "in the sense of experimental reliability, the results of [a large series of] simulation runs are more dependable than the direct historical evidence."[28] Though this sounds outrageous, it is in fact a truism, since "experimental reliability" is not a concept which can be applied to history.

However this may be, evidence relating household structure to demographic behavior and to broader social institutions is beginning to be presented.[29] Theories about the relationships among larger kinship groups are hard to test just through community listings, but Michael Anderson has shown that contrary to the view of Parsons and Bales, the isolated nuclear-family household is not always the form most appropriate to an industrializing society, since the households of workers in the Lancashire cotton mills in the early nineteenth century had more coresident kin than households in the country parishes from which the workers had migrated.[30]

The very discovery of how much mobility hinders our attempts to compute demographic rates has important consequences for social history. The picture of an immobile peasantry has been challenged[31] and the study of mobility, both social and geographic, seems to have become the principal theme in urban history. Literacy, at first sight, might seem far removed from demography, except for the fact that some sources—wills, hearth-tax records, marriage licenses—can be used to study both. In fact the connection is considerably closer; literacy is one of the best indicators of the general modernization of a society, and rising literacy is often a good predictor of falling fertility within marriage.

Thus far we have discussed questions for which economic and sociological concepts are perfectly adequate, but the discussion of family limitation, illegitimacy, and sexuality in general brings us to a more controversial frontier, that between demography and psychology. There has been one ambitious attempt to suggest a relationship between character structure and stages in the demographic transition. David Riesman distinguished three character types: the traditional, appropriate to the high-fertility, high-mortality stage; the "inner-directed," which flourished during the period of rapid population growth (familiar to us through its manifestations in evangelical religion and aggressive entrepreneurship); and the "other-directed," valuing above all conformity with the peer group, which to Riesman typifies the modern pattern of low fertility and low mortality.[32] Unfortunately the suggested connection between demography and personality development specified by Riesman has not been followed up.

Recourse to psychology has been stimulated by the problem of the great rise in prenuptial pregnancies noticed throughout most of Western Europe and North America in the late eighteenth century. It has been argued that this represents widespread rebellion against paternal authority on the part of working-class women, in particular, together with an upsurge of romantic love;[33] but it also has been asserted that the young domestic servants who were particularly vulnerable to pregnancy outside marriage were thoroughly imbued with familistic values.[34]

A common mistake has been to take a single demographic index—these are seldom significant in isolation—and try to explain it by some psychological consideration for which it is the only evidence.[35] Confusion of causes with effects is also easy. In his well-known *Centuries of Childhood* Philippe Ariès argues that high infant-mortality rates led parents (his evidence really pertains only to fathers) to make very low emotional investments in their children until they were sure they would survive, but J. L. Flandrin has stood this argument on its head by claiming that it was precisely the low emotional investment and lack of nurturance—extending all too often to outright cruelty and "accidental" infanticide—which accounts for the high infant mortality.[36]

At present it is difficult to resolve such differences, not only because there is not even enough descriptive demography available, but also because we lack any convincing psychosocial theory. For example, apart from our difficulties in getting evidence about early childhood, we find that Freudianism suffers from the absence of any convincing demonstration of the consequences of childrearing practices for the adult character structure. Also, a variety of Freudian interpretations can be proffered about the same general subject, and as there is no obvious way to exclude any of them, theorizing becomes rank. The work of the English psychologist John Bowlby on maternal attachment avoids some of these difficulties, but is only narrowly applicable.[37] Still, these theories, or indeed any psychological theory, are improvements over the lay psychology inherent in most sociological or economic models. A model that proceeds on the assumption that everyone wants to get married as early as society makes available the necessary resources (as if, for example, there were no homosexuals) or a view which reduces family interaction to a calculus of the exchange of benefits is far too crude for historical reality, whatever the advantages in analysis. The creation of a demographically grounded *histoire des sentiments* is perhaps the most difficult task on our current agenda, but also one of the most urgent.

The fact that so much remains to be done probably explains why demographic history thus far has made comparatively little impression on the popular historical consciousness. In 1968 Landes showed that many general history textbooks ignored population questions altogether, and even those which did not often got them muddled. His survey has not been brought up to date, but the situation does not seem much better. Yet if this essay has had any success, it should have made clear that demographic history is not just another subspecialty within a specialized (i.e., disintegrated) historical enterprise. Its jargon may be forbidding and its mathematics esoteric; when the ordinary historian reads that the data, which are seen through a Parzen window, have first been detrended and prewhitened before being recolored,[38] he may well wonder whether he has not blundered into a laundromat instead of the historian's workshop. But a college freshman's mathematics will go a long way, and the trip is worthwhile because there is hardly any historical problem—even in political history—which is not also a demographic problem. The struggles of dynastic states, and certainly of modern nations, were usually decided by the mobilization of superior populations, and the differential rates of fertility and mobility in early modern English as opposed to French populations account for the fact that the United States is an English-speaking nation. Demographic history directs us to the people behind the statesmen. In the words of Brecht, "The Pharoahs built the pyramids—all by themselves?"

Notes

1. T. H. Hollingsworth, *Historical Demography* (London, 1969), p. 37.

2. Ronald D. Lee, ed., *Population Patterns in the Past* (New York, 1977), p. 1.

3. Pierre Goubert, "Historical Demography and the Reinterpretation of Early Modern French History," *Journal of Interdisciplinary History* 1 (1970): 37–48.

4. A. M. van der Woude, "De historische demografie in de ontwikkeling van de geschiedwetenschap," *Tijdschrift voor Geschiednis* 82 (1969): 186.

5. Louis Henry, "Historical Demography," *Daedalus* 97 (Spring 1968): 388.

6. T. H. Hollingsworth, *Historical Demography*, p. 38.

7. Louis Henry, *Anciennes Familles genevoises: étude démographique* (Paris, 1956); Etienne Gautier and Louis Henry, *La Population de Crulai, paroisse normande: étude historique* (Paris, 1958).

8. Based on Hollingsworth, *Historical Demography*, pp. 43–44.

9. Molly Miller, *The Sicilian Colony Dates* (Albany, N.Y., 1970), p. 126; J. M. Datta, "Demography of Prehistoric Man," *Man in India* 39 (1959): 257–70.

10. Hollingsworth, *Historical Demography*, pp. 245, 285.

11. E. A. Wrigley, "Births and Baptisms: The Use of Anglican Baptism Registers as a Source of Information about the Numbers of Births in England before the Beginning of Civil Registration," *Population Studies* 31 (1977): 281–83.

12. Gautier and Henry, *La Population de Crulai*, p. 231.

13. J. D. Chambers, *Population, Economy, and Society in Pre-Industrial England*, ed. W. A. Armstrong (London, 1972), p. 46.

14. David Eversley, "A Survey of Population in an Area of Worcestershire from 1660–1850 on the Basis of Parish Records," *Population Studies* 10 (1957): 253–79.

15. Roger Schofield and E. A. Wrigley, *English Population Change, 1540–1840* (London, 1978).

16. Lee, *Population Patterns*, pp. 337–70.

17. Described in E. A. Wrigley, ed., *An Introduction to English Historical Demography* (London, 1966).

18. Cyprien Tanguey, *Dictionnaire généalogique des familles canadiennes*, 9 vols. (Montreal, 1871–1890); Jacques Henripin, *La Population canadienne au début du XVIIIe siècle* (Paris, 1954).

19. Daniel Scott Smith, "A Homeostatic Demographic Regime: Patterns in Western European Family Reconstitution Studies," in Lee, *Population Patterns*, p. 25.

20. Henry, *Anciennes Familles genevoises;* T. H. Hollingsworth, "The Demography of the British Peerage," supplement to *Population Studies* 18, no. 2 (1964).

21. Ansley J. Coale and Paul Demeny, *Regional Model Life Tables and Stable Populations* (Princeton, N.J., 1966); M. Demonet, J. Dupâquier, and N. LeBras, "A Repertory of Stable Populations," in Lee, *Population Patterns*, pp. 297–309; Sully Lederman, *Nouvelles Tables-types de mortalité* (Paris, 1969).

22. Wrigley, "Births and Baptisms," p. 290.

23. J. D. Chambers, *The Vale of Trent 1670–1800: A Regional Study of Economic Change*, supplement to *Economic History Review* 3 (1957); Pierre Goubert, *Beauvais et le Beauvaisis de 1600 à 1730* (Paris, 1960).

24. Louis Henry, *Population: Analysis and Models*, trans. Etienne Van de Walle and Ellise F. Jones (London, 1976), p. 90.

25. Albert I. Hermalin and Etienne Van de Walle, "The Civil Code and Nuptiality: Empirical Investigation of an Hypothesis," in Lee, *Population Patterns*, pp. 71–111; Frédéric LePlay, *L'Organisation de la famille selon le vrai modèle signalé par l'histoire de toutes les races* (Paris, 1871).

26. Peter Laslett, *The World We Have Lost: England Before the Industrial Age* (London, 1971), pp. 31–44.

27. Lutz K. Berkner, "The Stem Family and the Development Cycle of the Peasant Household: An Eighteenth-Century Austrian Example," *American Historical Review* 77 (1972): 398–418.

28. E. A. Hammel and Kenneth Wachter, "Primonuptiality and Ultimonuptiality: Their Effect on Stem-Family-Household Frequency," in Lee, *Population Patterns*, pp. 116–17.

29. See, for example, Lutz K. Berkner, "Peasant Household Organization and Demographic Change," in Lee, *Population Patterns*, pp. 53–69.

30. Michael Anderson, *Family Structure in Nineteenth-Century Lancashire* (Cambridge, 1971); Talcott Parsons, Robert Bales, et al., *Family, Socialization, and Interaction Processes* (Glencoe, Ill., 1955).

31. Laslett, *The World We Have Lost*.

32. David Riesman, with Reuel Denny and Nathan Glazer, *The Lonely Crowd: A Study of the Changing American Character* (New Haven, Conn., 1950).

33. Edward Shorter, *The Making of the Modern Family* (New York, 1975).

34. Joan Scott and Louise Tilly, "Women's Work and the Family in Nineteenth Century Europe," in *The Family in History*, ed. Charles E. Rosenberg (Philadelphia, 1975).

35. See, for example, Shorter, *The Making of the Modern Family*, p. 156.

36. Philippe Ariès, *Centuries of Childhood*, tr. Robert Baldick (London, 1962); Jean Louis Flandrin, "La Cellule familiale et l'oeuvre de procréation dans l'ancienne société," *XVIIe Siècle*, no. 79 (1974): 3–14.

37. Bowlby's work is described in Randolph Trumbach, *The Rise of the Egalitarian Family* (New York, 1978).

38. Lee, *Population Patterns*, p. 370.

Bibliography

Anderson, Michael. *Family Structure in Nineteenth Century Lancashire* (Cambridge, 1971).

Ariès, Philippe. *Centuries of Childhood,* trans. Robert Baldick (London, 1962).

Berkner, Lutz K. "Peasant Household Organization and Demographic Change," in Ronald D. Lee, *Population Patterns in the Past* (New York, 1977), pp. 53–69.

————. "The Stem Family and the Development Cycle of the Peasant Household: An Eighteenth-Century Austrian Example," *American Historical Review* 77 (1972): 398–418.

Chambers, J. D. *Population, Economy, and Society in Pre-Industrial England,* ed. W. A. Armstrong (London, 1972).

————. *The Vale of Trent 1670–1800: A Regional Study of Economic Change (Economic History Review,* Supplement, no. 3, 1957).

Coale, Ansley J., and Paul Demeny. *Regional Model Life Tables and Stable Populations* (Princeton, N.J., 1966).

Datta, J. M. "Demography of Prehistoric Man," *Man in India* 39 (1959): 257–70.

Demonet, M., J. Dupâquier, and N. LeBras. "A Repertory of Stable Populations," in Lee, *Population Patterns,* pp. 297–309.

Eversley, David. "A Survey of Population in an Area of Worcestershire from 1660–1850 on the Basis of Parish Records," *Population Studies* 10 (1957): 253–79.

Flandrin, Jean Louis. "La Cellule familiale et l'oeuvre de procréation dans l'ancienne société," *XVIIe Siècle,* no. 79 (1974): 3–14.

Gautier, Etienne, and Louis Henry. *La Population de Crulai, paroisse normande: étude historique* (Paris, 1958).

Glass, D. V., and D. E. C. Eversley, eds. *Population in History: Essays in Historical Demography* (London, 1965).

Goubert, Pierre. *Beauvais et le Beauvaisis de 1600 à 1730* (Paris, 1960).

————. "Historical Demography and the Reinterpretation of Early Modern French History," *Journal of Interdisciplinary History* 1 (1970): 37–48.

Hammel, E. A., and Kenneth Wachter. "Primonuptiality and Ultimonuptiality: Their Effect on Stem-Family-Household Frequency," in Lee, *Population Patterns,* pp. 113–34.

Henripin, Jacques. *La Population canadienne au début du XVIIIe siècle* (Paris, 1954).

Henry, Louis. *Anciennes Familles genevoises: étude démographique* (Paris, 1956).

————. "Historical Demography," *Daedalus* 97 (Spring 1968): 385–96.

————. *Manuel de démographie historique* (Geneva and Paris, 1967).

————. *Population: Analysis and Models,* trans. Etienne Van de Walle and Elise F. Jones (London, 1976).

Hermanlin, Albert I., and Etienne Van de Walle. "The Civil Code and Nuptiality: Empirical Investigation of an Hypothesis," in Lee, *Population Patterns,* pp. 71–111.

Hollingsworth, T. H. *The Demography of the British Peerage,* supplement to *Population Studies* 18, no. 2 (1964).

————. *Historical Demography* (London, 1969).

Landes, David. "The Treatment of Population in History Textbooks," *Daedalus* 97 (Spring 1968): 363–84.

Laslett, Peter. *Household and Family in Past Time* (Cambridge, 1972).

————. *The World We Have Lost: England Before the Industrial Age,* 2nd ed. (London, 1971).

Lederman, Sully. *Nouvelles Tables-types de mortalité* (Paris, 1969).

Lee, Ronald D., ed. *Population Patterns in the Past* (New York, 1977).

LePlay, Frédéric. *L'Organisation de la famille selon le vrai modèle signalé par l'histoire de toutes les races* (Paris, 1871).

Lockridge, Kenneth A. "Historical Demography," in Charles F. Delzell, ed., *The Future of History* (Nashville, Tenn., 1977), pp. 53–64.

Malthus, Thomas R. *An Essay on the Principle of Population as it Affects the Future Improvement of Society* (London, 1798).

Miller, Molly. *The Sicilian Colony Dates* (Albany, N.Y., 1970).

Parsons, Talcott, Robert Bales, et al. *Family, Socialization, and Interaction Processes* (Glencoe, Ill., 1955).

Riesman, David, with Reuel Denny and Nathan Glazer. *The Lonely Crowd: A Study of the Changing American Character* (New Haven, Conn., 1950).

Schofield, Roger. "Historical Demography: Some Possibilities and Some Limitations," *Transactions of the Royal Historical Society*, 5th ser., 21 (1971): 119–32.

Scott, Joan, and Louise Tilly. "Women's Work and the Family in Nineteenth Century Europe," in Charles E. Rosenberg, ed., *The Family in History* (Philadelphia, 1975).

Shorter, Edward. *The Making of the Modern Family* (New York, 1975).

Smith, Daniel Scott. "A Homeostatic Demographic Regime: Patterns in West European Family Reconstitution Studies," in Lee, *Population Patterns*, pp. 19–51.

Tanguey, Cyprien. *Dictionnaire généalogique des familles canadiennes*, 9 vols. (Montreal, 1871–1890).

Tilly, Charles, ed. *Historical Studies of Changing Fertility* (Princeton, N.J., 1978).

Trumbach, Randolph. *The Rise of the Egalitarian Family* (New York, 1978).

Van der Woude, A. M. "De historische demografie in de ontwikkeling van de geschiedwetenschap," *Tijdschrift voor Geschiednis* 82 (1969): 184–205.

Vann, Richard T. "History and Demography," *History and Theory* 9 (1969): 64–78.

Wrigley, E. A. "Births and Baptisms: The Use of Anglican Baptism Registers as a Source of Information about the Numbers of Births in England before the Beginning of Civil Registration," *Population Studies* 31 (1977): 281–312,

———. *Population and History* (London, 1969).

———, ed. *An Introduction to English Historical Demography* (London, 1966).

3 JERZY TOPOLSKI

The Role of Theory and Measurement in Economic History

From the very beginning of its autonomous existence, economic history has belonged to the most dynamic branches of historical inquiry. Generally speaking, the attacks against traditional historiography launched over the past years by writers who wished to replace a narrative of atomic facts with the explanation of the "totality," processes, tendencies, or structures, that is, of the "deeper" layers of historical process, were executed to a large extent by economic historians, who played the part of shock troops. The attacks grew more intensive with the growth of theoretical and methodological awareness among historians and with transformations within the social sciences. The changes were especially important within political economy, which, pressed hard by practical requirements, began to express interest in processes and structures. It developed a new branch—econometrics—and left behind the previous preference for investigations of producer and consumer behavior in an ideal market and for abstract striving towards the maximization of profits. At the same time the strong development of sociology, psychology, social psychology, cultural anthropology, and other sciences linked to the explosive growth of social history in which economic historians also played important roles contributed (as much as did political economy and econometrics) to the changes within economic history. The changes consisted basically of a transition from traditional economic history, which displayed no interest in theory, to modern economic history saturated with theory and models and generally prone to quantifications. From this point of view three kinds of inquiry can be distingushed, although the division is not very sharp:

(1) inquiry inspired by general theories of historical process;
(2) inquiry inspired by economic theory;
(3) inquiry inspired by theories of society.

In each case the role of a theory in investigation consists of furnishing general knowledge about classes of facts and relations between these classes, which is employed by a historian to select the object of inquiry, select and group data,

provide a conceptual framework which facilitates presentation of empirical data
and their interpretation, and construct (sometimes also test) models. Sometimes
theoretical knowledge is produced by historians themselves, as in research on
feudalism, which still lacks complex theory.

Inquiry Inspired by General Theories of Historical Process

Studies involving the intervention of some general theory of historical process
are usually of two types: either the application of some set of theoretical concepts
(with various philosophical roots) to a problem or the employment of some complete theory which often furnishes the foundation for adding an explanatory interpretation of the entire process under consideration. From this point of view
historical writing conceived under the influence of the global Marxist theory of
social reality is saturated with general theory. Early attempts toward the construction of general models in economic theory and discussion of the decline of
feudalism and the growth of capitalism owe much to the Marxist inspiration,
too.

When speaking about the construction of general models by economic historians, it is apparent that they belong either to the subjective aspect of the historical process, that is, human actions, their motivations, and decisions (variant
S) or to the objective aspect of history, that is, processes and facts expressed not
in categories of human actions (variant *O*). In the first case models tend to be
more general and indicate human economic behavior within some class of conditions (for example, in the feudal period or in investing). In the second case
they indicate either the global effects of human actions in a given area and at
a given period (variant *Op*—for example, economic decline of some country)
or they describe some type of productive workshop or enterprise (for example,
peasant holding), which makes the model more general, for it goes beyond a
definite spatial and temporal framework (variant *Ot*). For instance, a model of
economic regression in Poland of the seventeenth and eighteenth centuries is
linked more strongly to time and space than a type of peasant holding for the
same period constructed on Polish data.

J. Rutkowski's model[1] belongs to the earliest attempts to construct a general
model of the *Ot* type for some type of economy. It looks for the basic features
of the manorial-serf economy in Poland and finds them in the distribution of
income between a peasant and a nobleman. In W. Kula's model,[2] built with
respect to the same economy, the analysis was divided into the research on objective (*longue durée*) and subjective (*courte durée*) aspects. However, as international discussions clearly indicate, the author failed to link two types of
analysis (i.e., the models *Ot* and *Op*). Jerzy Topolski did try to link them through
the analysis of different classes' incomes, but only to explain the birth of capitalism and only with respect to Europe.[3] Thus Topolski, following Kula, took
part in the former discussion on reasons of the decline of feudalism and the

growth of capitalism which was started in the 1950s by M. Dobb,[4] P. Sweezy, H. K. Takahashi, R. Hilton, and C. Hill, but drew from previous debates—namely from M. Weber, R. H. Tawney, A. Fanfani, et al. This discussion offered a first approach toward the theory of feudalism. The meaning of the then-fashionable attempts to get rid of the term "capitalism" introduced by Marx and associated so strongly with "exploitation"[5] also diminished when no better definition was found. The same holds true with respect to feudalism, understood increasingly as an economic-social system. The model of D. C. North and R. P. Thomas,[6] which suggests a nonexploitive interpretation of feudalism, is interesting as an attempt toward theory, but does not grasp the essence of this system. E. J. Nell[7] is right in suggesting a network of explanations instead of explanation by factor but does not account for the social factor and thus fails to provide a satisfactory explanation. I. Wallerstein[8] thinks that European commercial expansion by creating economic regional disparities was responsible for the growth of capitalism—this, however, is only a fragmentary explanation. The book by G. Bois[9] proved to be a considerable step forward in theoretical progress: the author defended a thesis attributing the fall of the nobility's income to the fundamental contradiction of feudalism—the contradiction between large property and the small (family-type) peasant economic unit obliged to discharge feudal rent with noneconomic means. At the same time he criticized the model of a peasant economy introduced by A. Chayanov-Thorner (the same model for different modes of production did not observe the principle of historicism which tells us about qualitative differentiation of the modes of production). In this context one should also mention the studies of P. Anderson, P. A. Khromov, or J. Varga.[10]

All these attempts enriched the theory of feudalism and capitalism to some extent, thus facilitating conceptualization in further studies in economic history. If they do not always refer directly to an explicit model (which was the case with E. J. Nell), they do illustrate the application of a theory by a particular mode of thought, that is, with reasoning that uses a conscious model in the *Op* sense. These studies find important complementation in studies where the models of *S* type linked to *Ot* are constructed in order to explain peasant economy,[11] manor,[12] or enterprise[13] and to facilitate an analysis of feudal, capitalist, or socialist economy.

An interest in a given theory is best demonstrated by numerous studies (and discussions which focus on them) that point to significant problems of historical growth of interest to an economic historian: the crisis of feudalism (K. Barg, G. Duby, L. Genicot, F. Graus, E. A. Kosminskij, M. M. Postan), the crisis of the seventeenth century (E. J. Hobsbawm, R. Romano, E. Le Roy Ladurie et al.), English enclosures (J. D. Chambers, D. Landes, W. M. Lawiuswkij, W. F. Semionov), the reasons for the Industrial Revolution (P. Bairoch, M. W. Flinn, C. Flohen, D. Landes, R. M. Hartwell, M. Lévy-Leboyer, P. Mathias, G. E. Mingay, J. Nadal, J. Purš, F. J. Wright et al.), and other problems (for instance—the role of the state in the economy or models of the economy during

World War II). The problem of the influence exerted by science and technology upon economic life also belongs here (R. Cameron, F. Furet, P. Mathias et al.). The waves of interest arising out of theoretical reasoning give rise to many studies and discussions which, in turn, saturate inquiry with theory even more. It proved fruitful, for instance, to focus attention on the phenomenon of domestic industry and rural handicraft in the period of the making of capitalism and to introduce a theoretical concept of protoindustrialization (F. F. Mendels, H. Medick et al.). Likewise, a growth of interest in production during the feudal epoch and early capitalism, characteristic of the Marxist theoretical inspiration but also very popular outside Marxist circles, brought about a huge number of works on agricultural production, among which we can find the studies of P. Goubert, E. Le Roy Ladurie, J. Goy, H. Kellenbenz, J. de Vries, G. G. Kotovski, C. Poni, B. H. Slicher van Bath, Ch. Pfister, M. Morineau. Theoretical reflection of the Marxist historical writers in the 1960s also contributed to the growth of studies in the history of commerce and the market, heretofore neglected (M. Bogucka, A. L. Khoroshkevitch, A. Mączak, Z. Pach, I. Rychlikova et al.). Out of a number of such studies I. D. Kovalchenko's and L. W. Milov's work on the agrarian market in Russia in the nineteenth and twentieth centuries merits attention from the standpoint of theoretical inspiration (an analysis of commodity market and capitalist market).[14] A considerable increase of studies in material culture and technique has also been backed by general theories of historical process, and within Marxist historiography by the theory of socioeconomic formations. "Life" pressed historians to study the processes of inflation in the past, the natural environment, and raw materials, and these pressures also enriched theoretical reflection. The investigations of the processes of urbanization have also been saturated with theory.

Finally, one should point out the influence of such general theoretical constructs as the "*longue durée*" of F. Braudel, which guided many French historians towards investigations of more stable processes, such as modernization (partly in opposition to the theory of socioeconomic formations which pointed to the mechanisms of change), productivity (labor and capital), investment strategy, and economic growth. The latter influenced historians who expressed increasing interest in those problems of the unequal economic development of various regions and of the decline or growth of economy that force the investigator to look for reasons beyond the economic sphere. Many studies have been devoted to the economic regression of Spain or Italy in the early modern period (for example, those by C. Cippola, J. Gentil de Silva).

The statement that theory influences investigations to a growing degree does not mean that in every investigation there is a model which is made explicit, nor that models determine precisely the variables under investigation.[15] However, the number of such models increases. Apart from this, there is an increasing awareness of the existence of hidden models which furnish a significant instrument of interpretation. It has been pointed out (for instance, by E. J. Nell, R. Brenner) that three models (or theories) can be distinguished with respect to the interpretation of long-term economic change in medieval and early modern Europe: demographic[16] (according to which the economic growth of the twelfth to eighteenth centuries is a sequence of the following cycles: population growth, climatological crisis, food crisis, a decline in population, better weather, better food situation, growth of population, and so on), commercial (commerce and market propel the development), and class struggle (class conflict propels growth). The Marxist model also has to be mentioned, for it points out various planes of internal contradictions which set a given system in motion; among the latter there is a space for class struggle, but it is conceived of in less abstract manner.

The increase of influences of a general theoretical inspiration upon the inquiry made us examine the procedures of measurement—of quantification—in a different light. Statistical data are increasingly often quoted not just to present some phenomenon (its structure or dynamics) but to concretize quantitatively[17] or to test a model. We are dealing here with quantification of a new type arising out of theoretical requirements, not from descriptive needs. In cases where a reference is made to general (more or less complex) concepts of historical process the quantitative concretization is linked to a qualitative one (that is, the one which does not operate with numbers). The requirements of a model in which relations are pointed out often make us go beyond the elementary techniques of descriptive statistics and employ, for instance, multiple correlation or regression method or an analysis of variance and force us to a repeated employment of computers (which was the case with the above-mentioned study by Kovalchenko and Milov).

Inquiry Inspired by Economic Theories

The most considerable progress has been made with respect to quantification by inquiries inspired by economic theories. This inspiration has often shown a double face: apart from progress in saturating investigations with theory it has often brought about an ahistorical point of view which consisted of analyzing the feudal epoch as a dominant natural economy and early capitalism from the vantage point of advanced market relations. The latter resulted in exaggerating the importance of data on prices as economic indicators and in seeking to decipher the real rhythm of economic life from fluctuations of prices and wages.

We may safely argue that the following economic theories exerted the strongest influence upon economic history: (1) theories proposed by J. M. Keynes, (2) theory of crises and booms, (3) dynamic theories of J. Schumpeter which pointed out the role of the entrepreneur and of his striving towards profit and innovation, (4) theories of economic growth, (5) investigations of national accounts of income and wealth developed under the influence of S. Kuznets, and (6) neoclassical political economy based on the concepts of the perfect market, economic equilibrium, and simple models of supply and demand. Except for the last theory they all point to the processes of dynamic change and growth and thus suit economic history much better than the static neoclassical approach, which at best could only suggest the *S*-type models. At the same time we should point out that Marxist political economy began to play an increasingly inspiring role. Here attention focused on the following social messages and categories: primitive accumulation, surplus value, imperialism, and unequal economic growth.

Even before World War II, Keynes's theory (along with the study of E. Hamilton on the inflow of precious metals to Europe in the sixteenth century), which opted for a rewriting of economic history in which the growth and decline of civilization was linked to the inflow or outflow of precious metals, the theories of crises and booms stemming from the so-called Swedish school (voiced, for instance, by F. Simiand), and the concepts of Schumpeter all influenced the investigation of prices and wages and resulted in long sequences of data on prices and wages in various countries. These data in turn became a starting point for a demonstration of economic cycles in the past (for instance, the decennial cycles of Kondratieff).[18] There have also been numerous increasingly modern, quantitative studies. Some of them were rather similar to systematic publications of historical sources containing directly observable quantitative and economic data, while others suggested different interpretations of economic phenomena (for example, they referred to various concepts of crises) and constructed series of data which were not directly observable, by economic theory. The works of such authors as J. Ruwet, C. Verlinden, H. Van der Wee (Belgium); A. Friis, K. Glamann (Denmark); M. Baulant, E. Labrousse, J. Meuvret, R. Romano, F. Spooner (France); A. Eiras Real, R. Usero Gonzales (Spain); I. G. van Dillen (Holland); G. L. Basini, C. M. Cippola, A. De Maddalena (Italy); E. Ashtor (Near East); S. Hoszowski, H. Madurowicz-Urbanska (Poland); V. Magelhaes Godhino (Portugal); V. Zsimanyi, T. Molnar (Hungary); A. Chapman, W. G. Hoskins, R. C. D. Matthew (Great Britain); and A. G. Mankov (Soviet Union) enriched our knowledge of the economic past and at the same time inspired the development of statistical-quantitative and graphic methods and techniques.

The comparison of long series which referred to prices, wages, foreign trade, or money, and of series of demographic data filled historical writings with quantified data reflecting dynamic states and crises. These data clearly coincided and enriched our knowledge of a qualitative difference between the relatively static feudal economy and a dynamic capitalist one. In the Marxist historical writings, which did not respond too favorably to the investigations of fluctuations as market phenomena, scholars focused on studies of agricultural and industrial production, completing them only after some time with works on the problems of market, prices, and crisis (for example, the Great Depression of 1929–1933).

A distinct thematic coincidence of the Marxist and non-Marxist studies occurred (and the same held true, in part, with respect to the interpretative coincidence) when the influence of theory and of models of economic growth and the investigations of national accounts became prominent in historical writings in many countries. The historians now paid attention to the problems of the growth of production and of national income, accumulation, investment, and consumption. Statistical investigations of agricultural and industrial production have also flourished. Differences remained in methods of calculating national income and in the attitude toward the theory of socioeconomic formations, which furnished the general framework of conceptualization in the Marxist research. Thus the investigations of the problem of modernization or of industrial society that have been undertaken over the past few years are viewed by the Marxists as falling under the categories of the Marxist theory of formations and not as phenomena that render this theory obsolete.

The concepts of economic growth, of national income, and of investments became regular concepts of economic historians. In 1952 S. Kuznets published his study *Long-Term Changes in the National Income of the United States of America Since 1870*. In 1957 Rostow's *The Stages of Economic Growth* was first issued, and because of its range it gave rise to immediate discussion—it was supposed to furnish an alternative to the Marxist theory of social growth. It made some concepts popular (traditional society, takeoff, mass consumption) but failed to exert a visible influence in the field of general theory. There have also been studies by the economists who pointed out the role of economic growth in the past—B. F. Hoselitz, J. Marczewski, and F. Perroux. There has been a flood of case studies in economic growth of particular regions, countries, branches of industry, and sectors of economy. By way of example we may cite the following general studies: Ph. Deane and W. A. Cole, *British Economic Growth 1688–1959* (1962), W. G. Hoffmann, *Das Wachstum der Deutschen Wirtschaft seit der Mitte des 19. Jahrhunderts* (1965), R. Baehrel, *Une croissance: la Basse-Provence rurale: fin du XVIe siècle à 1789* (2 vols., 1961); L. H. Feinstein, *Capital Formation in the United Kingdom 1920–1938* (1965), and an analysis of the interactions between wages and productivity by E. H. Phelps Brown and M. H. Browne, *A Century of Pay: The Course of Pay and Product in France, Germany, Sweden, the United Kingdom, and the United States of America* (1968). Numerous structural studies on the quantitative reconstruction of the major categories of national economy were closely linked to them—they were chiefly concerned with the income and wealth of the nation. Among the studies prepared by economic historians (we bypass those which were written by economists and served other cognitive aims) one should point out those by M. Lévy-Leboyer, F. Crouzet (problems of France), O. Johansson (Sweden), A. Caracciolo (Italy), J. Borke (Denmark), and many others on various European and non-European countries. At the same time the Marxist synthetic and qualitative studies of economic growth (especially with respect to the countries of central and eastern Europe, industry, manufactures, and agriculture) have also increased in number. The most important ones (from the standpoint of quantitative methods) are the investigations on the Soviet Union (S. G. Strumilin, I. N. Pawlenko, K. Jatsunski, A. L. Weinstein, et al.), Poland (S. Borowski, A. Jezierski, J. Łukasiewicz, Z. Landau, et al.), Hungary (I. Berend, P. Gunst,

L. Makkay, G. Ránki, et al.), Yugoslavia (u.a. I. Erceg), and also the German Federal Republic, Czechoslovakia, Bulgaria, and Rumania. Before the period in question we used to write monographic studies which did not cover the whole national economy (this is true with respect to all works in economic history, not just in the above-mentioned countries), but now we do.

The influence of J. Schumpeter's views has been felt primarily in the United States, where a special line of research has been established—the so-called business and entrepreneurial history (also influenced by other sociological theories and based on the A. H. Cole Center for Entrepreneurial History and a periodical, *Explorations in Entrepreneurial History*). These investigations are conducted in the history of enterprise and institutions and stress the role of an entrepreneur (and of the state) in economic life and his behavior. The major works of this line of research are A. D. Chandler's *Strategy and Structure* (1962) and Th. Cochran's *Railroad Leaders 1845–1890* (1953), which provide a collective portrait of a railroad entrepreneur based on quantitative study of the correspondence of railway officials. L. E. Davis and D. C. North, the authors of *Institutional Change and American Economic Growth* (1971), have also been reared in the school of entrepreneurial history.

As the study of Davis and North is based on a simple neoclassical concept (i.e., also on a concept of *homo economicus*) they have been often linked to the so-called New Economic History represented by such authors as R. W. Fogel, J. R. T. Hughes, S. L. Engerman, A. Fishlow, R. P. Thomas, et al. This is at present the most theoretical and most mathematical school in economic history. Quantification is considered by New Economic historians to be a quantitative concretization of models derived from a theory of the economy (such as models of input-output, of supply and demand, and of economic growth—all assuming perfect competition and the Cobb-Douglas Production Function). The starting point was purely economic: verification by means of model analysis and quantification (sometimes counterfactual models) of certain current views on the American economy in the past (for instance, the profitability of black slavery or the role of women in economic growth). An example of advanced method employed in New Economic History is R. W. Fogel's *Railroads and American Growth* (1964). In order to investigate the role of railroads, Fogel built a counterfactual model with no railroads present and quantified numerous variables by means of linear programming (among these variables there were some which no one had calculated before, such as national saving).

European sophisticated models inspired by theoretical economy have been constructed either under the spell of the New Economic History or as a result of the evolution of native historiography. The former are rare (for examples, see the studies by S. Fenoaltea, R. Floud, G. R. Hawke, W. Vamplev), but the trend has not died yet. Native model attempts with a strong theoretical charge are more frequent. For instance, H. J. Habakkuk (1962) writes on differences in the technical level of English and American industry in the nineteenth century; J. P. Lewis (1965) discovers construction cycles in Britain; F. Mauro explores the commercial expansion of Europe in modern times with a theory of commercial capitalism in mind; and H. van der Wee presents the growth of world trade in the twelfth to the eighteenth centuries (1970). Many instances of modern quantification can be found in European studies in business history (for example, those by J. Kocka, R. Tilly).

Inquiry Inspired by Theories of Society (Social Theory)

The search for inspiration in the areas of social theory and social history on the part of economic historians—conducted for reasons sometimes as slight as selection of problems and explanatory factors—turned economic history into something less strictly resembling economic history and more akin to a part of global or total history. Economic historians began to fulfill a double role—they were economic historians, but also social ones. The French *Annales* school has its share of responsibility for this situation,[19] for it went—as a matter of principle—beyond the borders of traditional historical inquiry toward an explanation of social life, toward grasping the totality of society. The *Annales* school looks for theoretical support from sociology, social psychology, and geography—less so from economics. The title of its major publication is *Annales, économies, sociétés, civilisations*. In the course of its development, the school tried to shed an early and excessive stress on the geographic element, the processes of *longue durée*, and scorn for events. Its representatives criticized the New Economic History for its purely economic point of view. Along with the older works by M. Bloch or L. Febvre, the book by F. Braudel, *La Méditerranée et le monde méditerranéen à l'époque de Philippe II* (1949) became a sort of manifesto of the new school in the making. After a period of certain methodological dogmatism, various propositions have been put forward within the school that have led toward the postulate of total history. A focus on people resulted in stimulating demographic research, which in the *Annales* version has social undertones. The traditional demographic model (described in the previous section) was reconstructed by J. Dupâquier in order to rid it of its Malthusian aspect.[20] Some historians from the *Annales* school refer to Marxist theory (for example, P. Vilar) or look for new paths—always united with the idea of a holistic investigation of the past. Structuralist and psychoanalytical theories, on the whole, have failed to gain support among the Annalistes. An interest in problems of mentality, displayed in the studies of G. Duby, J. Le Goff, F. Furet, R. Mandrou, and J. Gentil de Silva, broadened the set of explanatory factors and allowed them to penetrate deeper strata of the historical process. Increasingly complex explanations provided by the historians from the *Annales* school do not fit any elegant models but have nothing whatsoever to do with traditional event-oriented historiography. Explanations abound in their warnings that the context of the whole situation influencing a given factor should be accounted for.

The influence of the *Annales* school upon modern economic history has already been significant. A look through successive publications of *Annales* is sufficient to see this. Studies like P. Deyon's *Etude sur la société urbaine au 17e siècle: Amiens, capitale provenciale* (1967); P. Goubert's *Beauvais et Beauvaisis de 1600 à 1730: contribution à l'histoire sociale de la France du XVIIe Siècle* (2 vols., 1960); H. and P. Chaunu's *Seville et l'Atlantique 1504–1650* (8 vols., 1955–1959); E. Le Roy Ladurie's *Les Paysans de Languedoc* (2 vols., 1965); H. Neveux's *Les grains du Cambrésis (fin du XIVe, début du XVIIe Siècle) vie et déclin d'une structure économique* (1974); J. Bouvier's *Crédit Lyonnais de 1863 à 1892* (1961); and the works of J. Meuvret and J. F. Bergier have already been granted a place among the classic basic works of modern economic history.

Investigations of various social classes and groups have also been undertaken: of peasants and nobility (for example, by J. Meyer), and of bourgeoisie (for example, by A. Daumard). Quantitative research on a large scale is characteristic of the *Annales* school. For instance, they investigate such sources as data from military lists of the nineteenth century with seventy-eight variables (E. Le Roy Ladurie, P. Dumont, M. Demonet) and data on 50,000 Florentine households (D. Herlihy, Ch. Klapisch), derived from a register of Florence from the end of the fifteenth century. The computer is very helpful as are factor analysis and other special quantitative methods.

It is worth noting that the *Annales* school has influenced historians not only in Western Europe but in socialist Europe as well. Its focus on social matters and processes is close to Marxism, while the major importance attached by the *Annales* circle to the demographic factor and their attitude toward the Marxist theory of formation are the principal domains of differences.

The influence exerted by the interests of society at large upon the structure of research in economic history is clearly noticeable in European and non-European historical writings. Even within the New Economic History social and demographic matters became more frequently discussed: for instance R. W. Fogel and S. L. Engerman's *Time on the Cross: The Economics of American Negro Slavery* (1975) caused lively discussion and stimulated counterstudies (undertaken for instance by Gutman). It turned out that subtle mathematical methods based on neoclassic models of reasoning failed to provide an image as persuasive or as subtle as the Marxist analysis of the same topics undertaken earlier by E. Genovese.[21] Other orientations of the American economic history linked their investigations to social problems (for example, studies by A. Gerschenkron, B. Moore). The influence of the *Annales* was also noticeable—the so-called new rural history is an example (M. Curtis, M. P. Conzen). There has been a distinct school—the so-called new urban history—which linked demographic, social, and economic points of view (S. Thernstrom). One encounters an increasing number of historians who write studies from the borderland between economic and social history (for example, J. H. Hexter, R. Lichtfeld, T. Rabb, L. Stone, Ch. Tilly) and who account for various social classes and groups by probing their economic backgrounds. British studies by E. J. Hobsbawm and E. P. Thompson on the aristocracy, the working class, and the problem of social mobility are a case in point. One may also mention numerous studies in urban history and historical demography (E. A. Wrigley, D. E. C. Eversley, P. Laslett, Michael Anderson, et al.). In West Germany there are many interesting studies in the so-called Sozialgeschichte (for example, those by R. Koselleck). Developments have been similar in other countries. The social factor has played a role in studies of the Industrial Revolution and of feudal and capitalist economies. There have also been studies of various social classes (E. van Cauwebberge's and P. Janssen's investigations of Dutch nobility in the fourteenth through the eighteenth centuries; J. Jedlicki's of Polish nobility in the eighteenth to nineteenth centuries).

Within Marxist historiography there have been investigations of the working class (J. Kuczynski, S. Kalabinski), peasants (J. Kahk, I. Kovalchenko, E. Tarvel [USSR]; A. Wyczański, K. Groniowski, H. Słabek [Poland]; J. Nichtweiss [GDR]; J. Petráň [Czechoslovakia]; Zs. Pach [Hungary]; V. Vukosavlevic [Yugoslavia]), and various groups of bourgeoisie (for instance, the studies by E. Fugedi [Hungary] and B. Geremek [Poland]). A broad perspective and thorough elaboration of these studies, traditionally classified as economic history, often termed also as social and economic history at that, demonstrate their inspiration by both Marxist theory and the increasingly dynamic social history.

Economic history is presently in a period of stormy growth, full of internal contradictions which have become the source of its constant methodological and theoretical progress. It is a branch of knowledge fully aware of the role played by theory and measurement, but already past the period of excessive enthusiasm for quantification.

Notes

1. J. Rutkowski, *Badania nad podziatem dochodów w Polsce w czasach nowazytnych* (Studies Concerning the Repartition of Incomes in Poland in Early Modern Times) (Krakow, 1938).

2. W. Kula, *Théorie économique du système féodal: pour un modèle de l'économie polonaise 16e–18e siècles* (Paris-The Hague, 1970; Polish edition, 1962).

3. J. Topolski, *Narodziny kapitalizmu w Europie XIV–XVII wieku* (Birth of Capitalism in Europe, 14th–17th Centuries) (Warsaw, 1965; Italian translation, Turin, 1978).

4. M. Dobb, *Studies in the Development of Capitalism* (London, 1946).

5. F. A. Hayek, ed., *Capitalism and the Historians* (Chicago, 1954). See also the comment by R. Romano in *Annales, économies, sociétés, civilisations* 10 (1956): 175.

6. D. C. North and R. P. Thomas, *The Rise of the Western World: A New Economic History* (Cambridge, 1973), pp. 19–45; D. C. North and R. P. Thomas, "The Rise and Fall of the Manorial System: A Theoretical Model," *Journal of Economic History* 31 (1971): 777–803. For comments see A. Jones, S. Fenoaltea, and others.

7. E. J. Nell, "Economic Relationship in the Decline of Feudalism: An Examination of Economic Interdependence and Social Change," *History and Theory* 6 (1967): 313–350.

8. I. Wallerstein, *The Modern World-System: Capitalist Agriculture and the Origins of the European World-Economy in the Sixteenth Century* (New York, 1974).

9. G. Bois, *Crise du féodalisme* (Paris, 1976).

10. P. Anderson, *Passages from Antiquity to Feudalism* (London, 1974); P. A. Khromov, *Ocherki ekonomiki feodalizma w Rossii* (Studies in the Feudal Economy in Russia) (Moscow, 1957); J. Varga, *Jobbágyrendeszer a maguaroszagi feudalizmus kései századaban 1556–1767* (Serfdom in Late Feudal Hungary) (Budapest, 1969).

11. See the many works, covering the period from the sixteenth to the twentieth centuries, written by such authors as J. Kahk, H. Ligi, I. D. Kovalchenko, N. Selunskaya, E. Schremmer, E. Tarvel, and A. Wyczański.

12. For example, A. Wyczański, *Studia nad folwarkiem szlacheckim w Polsce w latach 1500–1580* (Studies Concerning the Manors in Poland in the Years 1500–1580) (Warsaw, 1966).

13. For example, the studies of H. van der Wee or W. Fischer.

14. I. D. Kovalchenko and L. V. Milov, *Vserosiĭskiĭ agrarnyĭ rynok XVIII-nachalo XX veka* (All-Russian Agrarian Market XVIII-XXth Centuries) (Moscow, 1974).

15. Cf. W. N. Parker, "Through Growth and Beyond: Three Decades in Economic and Business History," in Louis P. Cain and Paul J. Uselding, eds., *Business Enterprise and Economic Change* (Kent, Ohio, 1973), pp. 15–47.

16. R. Brenner, "Agrarian Class Structure and Economic Development in Pre-industrial Europe," *Past and Present* 70 (1976): 31–75.

17. See J. Topolski, "Quantitative Concretization in the Model Method in Economic History," *Studia Historiae Oeconomicae* 8 (1974): 21–26.

18. See G. Imbert, *Des mouvements de longue durée Kondratieff* (Aix-en-Provence, 1959).

19. See G. G. Iggers, *New Directions in European Historiography* (Middletown, Conn., 1975); J. H. Hexter, "Fernand Braudel and the Monde Braudellien," *Journal of Modern History* 44 (1972): 480–539; T. Stoianovich, *French Historical Method: The Annales Paradigm* (Ithaca, N.Y., and London, 1976).

20. J. Dupâquier, "De l'animal à l'homme: le mécanisme autorégulateur des populations traditionelles," in G. Kurgan and Ph. Moureaux, eds., *La Quantification en histoire* (Brussels, 1973), pp. 39–73.

21. See R. M. Bell, "Slavery as an Investment: Dollars and Humans," *Historical Methods Newsletter* 10 (1976): 1–9.

Bibliography

Heffer, J. "Le Dossier de la question," in Ralph Andreano, ed., *La Nouvelle Histoire économique: exposé de méthodologie sous la direction de Ralph Andreano* (Paris, 1977).

Hexter, J. H. "Fernand Braudel and the Monde Braudellien," *Journal of Modern History* 44 (1972): 480–539.

Iggers, G. G. *New Directions in European Historiography* (Middletown, Conn., 1975).

Kellenbenz, H. *Die Methoden der Wirtschaftshistoriker* (Cologne, 1972).

Le Goff, J., and P. Nora. *Faire de l'histoire,* 3 vols. (Paris, 1975).

Leskiewicz, J., and S. Kowalska-Glikman, eds. *Historia i nowoczesność* (History and Modernization) (Warsaw, 1974).

Matematicheskie metody w issledovaniĩakh po soĩsialnó-ekonomicheskoĩ istorii (Moscow, 1975).

McClelland, P. *Causal Explanation and Model Building in History: Economics and the New Economic History* (Ithaca, N.Y., and London, 1975).

Parker, W. N. "Through Growth and Beyond: Three Decades in Economic and Business History," in Louis P. Cain and Paul J. Uselding, eds., *Business Enterprise and Economic Change* (Kent, Ohio, 1973), pp. 15–47.

Shorter, J. H. *The Historian and the Computer* (Englewood Cliffs, N.J., 1971).

Stoianovich, T. *French Historical Method: The Annales Paradigm* (Ithaca, N.Y., and London, 1976).

Supple, B. H., ed. *Research in Economic and Social History* (London, 1971).

van der Wee, H., and P. M. M. Klep. "Quantitative Economic History in Europe since the Second World War: Survey, Evaluations, and Prospects," *Recherches économiques de Louvain* 41 (1975): 195–218.

4 GEOFF ELEY

Some Recent Tendencies in Social History

In 1971 Eric Hobsbawm concluded his survey of social history by "noting, and welcoming, the remarkably flourishing state of the field." Seven years later it is still, as he put it, "a good moment to be a social historian,"[1] partly because of the very scale of the activity (for example, the proliferation of new journals, standing conferences, subdisciplinary societies, courses, chairs, theses-in-progress, and as with all waves of "enthusiasm," dramatic individual conversions). But with this expanding activity has also come an enlargement of ambition. In Britain, for instance, to call oneself a social historian is no longer to signify automatically an interest in the trade unions or the poor law (valid interests in themselves naturally), to be shunted off into obscure sidings of economic history departments, or to be excluded from the main thoroughfares of the profession. Each of these things naturally persists, as do the sillier excesses of middle-brow, coffee-table journalism, in which social history is identified mainly with colorful and nostalgic evocations of "manners and morals."[2] But, on the whole, social history is fast outgrowing this subaltern status, and there are few areas of the discipline to which it now lays no claim.

This is a recent development—as late as 1970 one perfectly competent survey of historical studies could still avoid giving social history a separate treatment of its own[3]—and much could be written about why it has happened. Much could also be said about the longer origins and the differential progress of social history in different countries. But given the limited space available, it makes sense to concentrate on the most interesting feature of social history as it has become today, namely its new *totalizing potential*. In the past the term "social history" could easily imply indifference to the political institutions of a society and even to the problem of generalizing in the abstract about society as a whole. Of course, the best *historians* have always maintained a sense of social totality in their work, but until recently the category of the social historian tended to suggest something more specialized and narrow, even antiquarian. It has consequently been something of a novel departure for some social historians to begin claiming a totalizing potential as a specific virtue of their field. In Germany, where the innovators have cast themselves as the advocates of a "historical social science," this has been especially marked, with predictable cries of outrage from the patriarchs of traditional political and diplomatic history.[4] It would be fair to say that the recent social historians are interested not only in specific social practices like trade union activity, poor relief, and education, but also in their relation to the social formation as a whole. There are the beginnings of a move toward the investigation of structures and social relations proper rather than mere organizations. Beyond this there is quite a new commitment in certain quarters to attempting to understand *all* facets of human existence in terms of their social determinations—to "be as much concerned with questions of culture and consciousness as with those of social structure and the material conditions of life," as the first editorial of the new journal *Social History* put it.[5] To think of social history as the "history of society" in general, as opposed to a series of discrete specialisms (labor, the "social problem," education, demography, and so on), is becoming relatively conventional. The extent to which this general rethinking of social history has become embodied in the actual practice of social history writing is the main object of the following brief remarks.[6]

***

It is necessary to begin with a paradox. At a time when any subject seems fair game and the boundaries of social history's possible scope have expanded to become virtually coterminous with those of the discipline as a whole, the practice of *individual* social historians can often be even more specialized than before. Subdisciplinary organizations have followed one another with alarming rapidity. In Britain labor history is perhaps the oldest of these sectional interests, with an increasingly formal and institutionalized existence, embracing its own society, bulletin, regular conferences and regional affiliates. Demography and local history are other older examples, with strong organizational bases in Cambridge and Leicester. More recently they have been joined by many others, including urban history, family history, social history of education, oral history, women's history, peasant studies, history of childhood, social history of medicine, and so on. Cutting across these divisions are others which separate the historians of different national areas. In Britain it is hard enough to establish extensive intellectual contacts between historians of Europe and those of Britain, let alone with those of North America, Latin America, Africa, or Asia. This academic division of labor—which is almost universal—has often been accompanied by a distinct methodology and technical jargon: though a necessary procedure in fields like demography, this also serves to legitimate the specialism's exclusiveness and renders it inaccessible to outsiders. Though the individual practitioners of these respective fields often see themselves as contributing to the "history of society" and define their projects accordingly, they seldom emerge from a self-made methodological ghetto in order to pool analytical resources with colleagues elsewhere.

In other words, though a new holistic pattern is undeniable at the level of theory, in practice older habits of fragmentation tend to persist. The resultant tension between theorizing potential and the infrastructure of empirical practice is best exemplified perhaps in the burgeoning field of family history. Over a decade ago, for instance, Peter Laslett demanded a new "social structural history" which embraced entire societies and examined the basic "structural function of the family in the pre-industrial world."[7] Yet after massive expenditures of labor Laslett's own achievement has been remarkably prosaic, substituting a problematic of extreme narrowness (that of mean household size) for his ambitious statements of intent. Of course, his celebrated "null hypothesis" concerning the continuity of the nuclear family across the great divide of the Industrial Revolution was a pioneering achievement, which cleared the ground for important departures. Likewise the emphasis on quantification and the allied procedures of family reconstitution has been exemplary, and in a time of promiscuous numeracy within the profession it is only too easy to forget just how hard a battle Laslett had to fight.

But the criticisms of Laslett are now very familiar. Any exclusion of literary or "attitudinal" sources is indefensible, and in any case the original attempt to distinguish the superior reliability of parish registers is probably spurious.[8] In the end the exclusion of non-numerate evidence imposes analytical categories of an empirical rather than a properly theoretical kind. Though Laslett successfully exposes the inadequacy of the sociological notion of progressive nucleation of the family in relation to industrialization, his failure to propose alternative ways of linking family and household to the sphere of production and class relations effectively vacates the field for the intrusion of other sociological models which are equally arbitrary and unhistorical. By adhering obsessively to his original research brief (nailing the myth of the extended family, pioneering quantitative techniques), Laslett has merely trapped his historical imagination within a microsociological approach and has singularly failed to deliver the goods he was supposedly producing (a "social structural history"). Disappointingly, he has confined the social historian's enterprise to the mere collection of evidence, thus maintaining the conventional division of academic labor and abandoning the field of theory to the sociologists. In this stance he appears to be unrepentant. Despite the title of his new book, we learn actually very little about the social *texture* of "family *life* and illicit *love* in earlier generations," still less about their relationship to the social relations of production.[9]

Fortunately—not least thanks to Laslett's tireless efforts in originally opening up the field—other social historians have started to make good this deficit. The attempt to theorize the problem of the family in general terms, both as change across time and as a particular relationship to production and society as a whole, is one of the most encouraging developments of recent years. The two most ambitious claims to have delivered a general history of the "modern family" are, it is true, somewhat misguided,[10] and their wild generalizations from inadequate sources are enough to send one scurrying back to the security of Laslett's methodological caution. But despite the idealist excesses of Shorter and Stone in their desire to impute an immanent purpose to the historical process ("the making of the modern family," the "rise of affective individualism"), there is much of value in their general approach. They at least raise *as problems* two badly neglected questions: the inner life of the family in a cultural and psychological sense, and the role of the family in the larger ideological arena of social reproduction. By their own formulation of these questions they have placed both the understanding of "modern" sexuality and the sociological concept of "socialization" more firmly on the agenda of future discussion.

However, neither author tackles these questions with conspicuous success, and they provide only the crudest notions of cultural diffusion to explain how their new family "values" spread through society. Moreover, the idea of "socialization" is used uncritically, without explaining how the family has interacted with other institutions and forms of social relations. There is also an implicit assumption (shared with most other work on the subject) that the family was and is an effective "socializing" agency, whereas in reality family life is constituted by a series of *contradictory* relationships with the "outside world."[11] In most usage "socialization" contains an essential functionalist bias which gives the family a key role in integrating and maintaining the existing social structure and its value system—conservative belief in the family as the ultimate guardian of moral order is only the most obvious ideological form of this syndrome. It is, therefore, a pity that neither Stone nor Shorter tries to discuss the wider ideological significance of the value changes they are so keen to diagnose. As it is they confine the process of socialization implicitly to the interior of the family itself in general isolation from society at large. This indifference to matters of theory also mars a superior work, that of Herbert Gutman on the black family, which is notably silent on how the outside world (for example, the state, politics, work) might affect the content of family relations.[12]

Recent work has been far more successful in relating the family to the sphere of production. Since Smelser's original work, there have been major contributions from Michael Anderson and John Foster from within a sociological and a Marxist tradition respectively, and Anderson has recently returned for a systematic reexamination of Smelser's model.[13] The work of Hans Medick is especially important in this respect, for he sets out directly to define "the structural function of household and family during the transition from peasant society to industrial capitalism."[14] Significantly, he actually puts Laslett's "null hypothesis" to work by arguing that it was precisely the continuity of household organization which facilitated the development of cottage industries in the process of "protoindustrialization." Whether or not Medick's analysis proves to be right, he has at least begun the process of resituating the discussion in the larger context of the economy and society. As Edward Thompson argued some years ago, "How is it possible to get very far with the discussion of household or family if we don't know whether the households were of serfs or freemen, of fishermen or bakers, nomadic shepherds or miners, were cultivating rice or silk or chestnuts, what kind of inheritance customs determined the transmission of land, what kind of dowries or marriage settlements, what customs of apprenticeship or of migrant labour?''[15] When measured against these necessary social-historical concerns, the nuclear family debate appears increasingly as an issue of staggering unimportance. Thus Karin Hausen has insisted on the need to set the discussion in the determinate context of the rural economy and its social relations. In a majestic survey of the field as a whole she has also mapped out a detailed agenda for the future. Proceeding from the general principle that ''history can only begin to be written as the history of human beings when the basis of human reproduction is given a central rather than a marginal role,'' she proposes four main constituents for a general history of the family: that family and household always be situated in the context of the productive system; that their character varies by social class; that they perform historically specific functions for their members and society; and that they are sustained by a range of normative ideologies.[16]

It is worth dwelling at some length on work in this field, because it reveals both the strengths and weaknesses of the recent social history. On the one hand, the general thrust of the best work carries it in the direction of the totalizing ambition identified at the outset of this essay. One of the great virtues of Medick's essay is that it brings family history out of its self-made ghetto, makes it available to historians in other fields, and redeploys its findings to shed light on questions of larger importance. Moreover, Medick, Hausen, and Thompson, like Genovese in another field,[17] employ a Marxist framework of social reproduction (the reproduction of labor power and the reproduction of relations of production), which is far more fruitful than those of structural functionalism and exchange theory used by Smelser and Anderson—in the simple sense that it engages more directly with the larger social and economic context (that is, the goal of ''social history''). But on the other hand, the narrower work in the field reveals an uncritical dependence on the existing fund of sociological concepts and an unwillingness to subject them to the proper kind of historical scrutiny.

In fact, if there is a salient weakness of the new work in social history, it has been a tendency to slake the thirst for more theory by scooping up mouthfuls of unpurified concepts from the waters of conventional sociology. Though presented as a new openness to theory and as such extremely welcome, the ambition of recent work frequently appears as an uncontrolled theoretical eclecticism, which easily reproduces the old division between the thoeretical and the empirical which has bedeviled historical studies in the past: the conventional labors of the researcher continue willy-nilly much as before, whereas the adoption of ''concepts'' or ''models'' is left to shorter think-pieces or specially convened conferences. The two enterprises are rarely brought into proper critical tension: more commonly the relationship is an arbitrary one, comprising the schematic ''testing'' of preconceived ''models'' against the ''evidence.'' Still more frequently, the well-meaning social historian, understandably embarrassed by the empiricist habits of his or her profession, simply goes to the general storehouse of sociological concepts, and after rummaging around amongst the available wares, emerges contentedly with an appropriate selection. The theoretical status of such concepts is taken on trust, and recent social history has been shot through with a reluctance to confront working assumptions of this kind on a theoretical level. Concepts are borrowed from all manner of sources as the need of the moment dictates but are seldom integrated into an open, internally consistent conceptual framework of the historian's own. More often than not, the vital preconceptions, which may determine in advance the selection of problems and evidence, are never explicated and are present only as a fine network of concealed preferences.[18] To illustrate this failing further, it may be worth considering a number of its particular sources.

***

The first of these is the most obvious, and is normally regarded as a traditional Anglo-Saxon empiricism, though it is certainly not confined to Britain and North America. Very often the historian simply proceeds on an archival odyssey, returning laden with important facts, which are then slotted with a minimum of further reflection into the interpretative framework established by the chosen school of interpretation. It makes little real difference whether the latter derives from contemporary sociological discourse or from the older frame of high politics and statecraft. Naturally it would be unfair to suggest that such work is unanalytical, for it often contains sensitive explorations of a given locality or social milieu and some tightly argued analyses of political events. But on the whole it tends to rely on common sense or an intuitive imagination for its insights rather than any use of systematizing social theory. At most one finds the almost indispensable conceptual vocabulary of *any* attempt to talk about social relations—for example, the language of social structure and stratification, elite theory, social control, socialization, and so on.

The best illustrations are the revisionist historiographies of the English and French Revolutions. An immensity of fine empirical scholarship has appeared in these areas, which adds immeasurably to our understanding of the events in question. But in each case an existing general interpretation has been gradually disintegrated by an accumulation of local, regional, and sectoral studies, without any notable attempt to construct an alternative in its place. Thus in Britain there have been a succession of "county studies" which militate intentionally against any general interpretation of the Civil War in the name of some notional "county community" and its superior social and political solidarities: yet such work resolutely abstains from commenting on its significance for larger problems like the character of the state or the evolving class structure, let alone the meaning of the English Revolution or the forms of the transition from feudalism to capitalism. Of course, such work often denies (not always explicitly) the legitimacy of the historical problematic which these terms connote, and not the least of the determinants of this particular form of empiricism is an overt self-definition against a *particular* general interpretation, namely the Marxist. It is a pity that the *theoretical* objections to the latter are never given a proper airing in this work, instead of being smuggled through in the name of empirical scruples and some higher scholarly morality of fact-grubbing. In the case of the English Revolution this has been especially debilitating, whereas in France it has been partially compensated by the influence of Richard Cobb and his extraordinary historical imagination. More generally, it is striking that the three major Anglo-American voices in French history (Richard Cobb, Theodor Zeldin, Eugen Weber) are all notable "refusers of systems."[19] At its best their work produces stunning explorations of the significant instance; at its worst it fetishizes the detail. Necessarily all three use global assumptions to rationalize their imagination (those about "modernization" are the commonest), and it is unfortunate that they remain insufficiently reflected in the texts themselves.[20]

A second source of residual empiricism comes from the various traditions of national labor history and their more recent academic offspring. The oldest form of weakness was the classic organizational history of the trade unions, sects, and parties, invariably with a whiggish coloration. This could confer a disproportionate degree of attention to often quite transitory phenomena, largely because the organizations in question were to be appropriated for the historical legitimation of a specific political tradition. In some ways the publication of Edward Thompson's magnificent work of 1963 did little to change this tendency, but had the effect rather of simply relocating it from the organizations of the labor movement onto the larger social milieu of which they were a part, while merely replacing the older organizational partisanships with a newer and vaguer commitment to the history of ordinary people. This could lead to a higher antiquarianism, in which the study of particular groups of workers and their life-styles was justified simply because they were of the working class—a self-enclosed project, removed from the broader setting of national history, without theoretical ambition and animated by a populist belief in the superior morality of the working class. The worst excesses have been prompted by a sentimental desire to demonstrate the vitality of popular culture and its resistance to the attempts of the ruling class to control it, legitimated by the late 1960s slogan of "history from the bottom up." This type of work has generally isolated its subject from the relations of subordination and exploitation in which it was held and from the larger context of the class structure and the state, a point tellingly made by Genovese.[21] But again, this line of populist labor history has produced some work of enormous sensitivity—witness the best achievements of the Ruskin History Workshop, with their meticulous reconstruction of working-class styles of life.[22] But in this latter case the divorce from both theory and larger context has often been at its most extreme, so much so that it has seemed more like the German discipline of *Volkskunde* than social history proper.

Other sources of theoretical weakness have, paradoxically, developed from some of social history's more important technical advances. The misuse of quantitative techniques by exaggerating the value of data to which they can be applied and neglecting the evidence to which they cannot has already been mentioned. Moreover, the extension of quantification to phenomena which are not statistically comparable or even susceptible to statistical measurement in the first place is potentially one of the most disturbing developments of the new social history. The curious belief that food riots in the 1830s may be compared with Social Democratic street demonstrations in 1911 and reduced to a single category of "collective violence" is only the most striking example of this technocratic malaise.[23] One does not have to relapse into blanket rejection of quantification[24] to recognize muddled historical thinking. Another important area of recent innovation, likewise the product of cheap technology (the tape recorder), has also allowed its methodological procedures and type of evidence to dictate the terms of the analysis in this way: though an indispensable tool for the twentieth-century historian, oral history can easily substitute a disguised sociology of meaning (social history as the product of "social perception" and the "experiences and consciousness of individuals") for a more measured evaluation of its findings.[25] Even the reception of the *Annales* outside France, not to speak of some of the recent work of the school itself, has taken forms which are a far cry from Marc Bloch's vision of complex social totality and its change across time. The discrete emphasis on climate, ecology, social ritual, or *mentalités* can easily obscure their very interrelatedness with the levels of production and the state, with which Bloch was above all concerned. Braudel's great works[26] may be "total history," but they lack all totalizing coherence in this sense.

A final form of indifference to theory—or to the theoretically confusing consequences of certain methodological and analytical habits—concerns the attempts to use sociological concepts without thinking through carefully enough the possible drawbacks and disadvantages. The commonest instance of this has been the adoption of apparently serviceable concepts without first exploring their relation to the larger sociological problematic on which they subsist. The notion of "social control" has been a particularly striking example of this defect. The concept has delivered an organizing interpretative perspective for large numbers of British and American social historians, in work covering everything from the operation of the criminal law to the attack on violent sports in the early nineteenth century, philanthropy, religion, and the commercialization of leisure. The concept has proved particularly attractive to social historians of the left, often Marxist, implying as it seems to do a manipulation and imposition of a system of bourgeois class power onto a popular mass. Yet as has recently been pointed out, this idea has its origins in a specific body of functionalist sociology which postulates a three-stage model of order, breakdown, and restabilization and has little to do with Marxist notions of class struggle. As Stedman Jones says: "Contradiction is not episodic, but continually present; the antagonism between the producers of the surplus and the owners and controllers of the means of production extracting the surplus, is a structural and a permanent feature. Thus class conflict is a permanent feature and not a sign of breakdown, and the conditions in which class conflict may assume explosive or revolutionary form bear only the emptiest of resemblances to a crude notion conveyed by the phrase 'breakdown of social control.' ''[27] Whether this Marxist critique proves acceptable or not, it at least points to the paramount need for greater theoretical self-awareness among those social historians who make use of the idea under attack.

In principle the idea of social control has a short-circuiting analytical function very similar to the ideas of "incorporation," "accommodation," "bourgeoisification," and so on, in that it affords a generalized descriptive category for "explaining" the perplexing absence of a revolutionary politics in a given working class. It also normally goes with a Lukácsian understanding of "class consciousness," in which an idealized model of "revolutionary consciousness" is devised as a measure for the real situations of particular working classes, and whose absence is explained by the simple opposite of "false consciousness," or ideological subordination to the bourgeoisie. This pattern of thinking bears some affinities to the notion of "socialization" employed by German historians of the period before World War I to explain the persistence of an authoritarian political system.[28] Here the maintenance of a "traditional value system" occurs as an unproblematic one-way transmission of authoritarian values downward into the populace, orchestrated through the manipulation of key institutions, from the army, police, and courts, to the school, the church, and the media. Yet like its sister concept of social control, this notion of socialization contains a remarkably crude idea of ideology. It betrays a simplistic understanding of how ideas get formed in people's minds, and of how one particular view of the world *becomes* dominant so that other competing views are subsumed or eliminated. But the moral authority of a ruling class cannot be reduced to a series of stabilizing functions, performed in accordance with the "natural" requirements of a particular social order. On the contrary, that authority needs to be constructed and continually reconstructed by material processes of struggle which may always be contested by the subordinate classes and are therefore unpredictable. It is, therefore, the *specific* range of those determinations which decide the outcome of the processes in *particular* historical conjunctures that requires our attention as historians, and not some universal sociological model of "social control" or "socialization." To this extent there can be no theory of ideology in general, but only the history of particular ideological processes.

In other words, the general tendency to appropriate sociological concepts uncritically for use on the past invariably conceals a specific deficit of concrete theoretical work—in this particular case a failure to theorize the problem of ideology. The latter bears directly on most of the growth areas of social history mentioned above and simultaneously restates the primary need for a grasp of social totality. This is clearest perhaps in the area of family history, where the overwhelming volume of new work is constituted mainly by a *retreat* from social history of the more ambitious sort. Here the *ideological* role of the family "as mediator between the public and private spheres" has been barely tackled by the growing armies of social historians: it encompasses "not only relations between men and women; the induction of the young into the ranks of the rulers, citizenry, or work force; the disposition of property; and the virtues and violence of intimate domestic life; but also the much thornier ones of the causal relationship between private preferences and public structures."[29] Much the same may be said of the newer labor history, where the celebration of past popular struggles (that is, invariably dramatic or violent defeats, or individualized "human" achievements) has been a poor substitute for analyzing the changing forms and limits of popular subordination.[30] In both cases—family and labor history— the object of study tends to become isolated from a larger set of determinations: the class structure, the public sphere of civil society, and finally the level of politics and the state.

Given the general characteristics of recent social history discussed above—its application to new areas, its commitment to theory, and its actual dependence on conventional sociology—it is a pity that social historians have shown so little interest in recent developments of Marxist theory, for in at least three areas— the sexual division of labor and domestic production, the problem of ideology, and the theory of the state—the latter is directly relevant to the weaknesses under discussion. Despite a massive expansion of social-historical interest in women in the family, for instance, recent Marxist discussions of domestic labor and housework have had surprisingly little impact, as have those of women's role in production more generally.[31] Likewise, most social historians remain unaware of recent Marxist thinking about ideology and continue to reduce the history of ideas to the social origins of those who espouse them.[32] But it is the third area, that of the state as the organizing instance of social life, in which Marxist theory could perhaps be most helpful. Though social historians have justifiably resented their past subordination to political history in the formal structures of the profession, their own practice has tended to perpetuate this old division. In practice social history has evolved as a subdiscipline of history in general, making its claims to legitimacy by a kind of self-denying ordinance to avoid generalizing about "high politics"; the latter has been left to the "political historian" while the "social historian" stays in his or her ghetto, only rarely venturing more ambitious judgments concerning the political importance of his or her findings. But unless the importance of the latter is theoretically instated at the center of social-historical discussion, social history will remain what Trevelyan, in a much derided epigram, called it—"history with the politics left out."

***

Thus although the possible scope of social history has expanded out of all recognition and its *potential* ability to recast the discipline as a whole has grown accordingly, the actual realization of any new totalizing ambition has remained comparatively rare. Despite the popularity of the *slogan*, social historians seldom discuss the "history of society" as such. It is striking, for instance, that the most stimulating discussion of British historical development in this larger social-historical sense has taken place outside the ranks of the profession altogether in journals of sociology and Marxist theory, even though partly conducted by professional historians.[33] Similarly, it is no accident that the discussion of the transition from feudalism to capitalism—which has recently been revitalized by a remarkable series of major interventions—should also have been conducted either by Marxists or by nonhistorians.[34] It is arguably within the context of these and other general debates that the most productive detailed social-historical work will be done, constituted by a fertile theoretical relation between the general and particular. Moreover, the recent revival of interest in the problem of transition from feudalism to capitalism may also help dislodge the unhistorical assumptions of ''modernization theory'' from their undoubted supremacy among most historians of the sixteenth through the twentieth centuries: that is, the series of sociological couplets which lie at the foundation of most non-Marxist social theory, including ''preindustrial/industrial,'' ''rural/urban,'' ''traditional/rational,'' ''undifferentiated/differentiated,'' ''community/association,'' ''mechanical/organic,'' and so on.[35] These terms are used almost universally by non-Marxist historians (and by many Marxists, too) as part of a general conceptual vocabulary, but without on the whole much awareness of their precise theoretical provenance or implications.

Of necessity there are many important areas which this essay has been unable to cover. Thus it has made no attempt to discuss the strengths or weaknesses of the *Annales* school, largely because this would require a major essay in itself to do the problem full justice. Similarly, though the opening comments focused on the specific field of family history, a similar analysis might apply to other fields equally well—sexuality, women's history, peasant studies, history of education, social history of ideas, and so on. Much could also have been said concerning the relationship of social history to disciplines other than sociology, where the interaction has been considerably more productive: social anthropology and historical geography are both examples which spring to mind.[36] In many ways the last decade has introduced an exciting period of redefinition of history as a discipline, and for this social historians must take most of the credit, if only by the cumulative consequences of their practice. Ultimately, the main effect of redefining social history as the ''history of society'' in general may be to make the older label redundant altogether, except as an indication of a general emphasis and commitment to seeing work in all fields in its appropriate social and economic context. But for the reasons set out above these are still mainly *possibilities*. If there is a single priority facing social historians—that is, historians in general—at the present time, in fact, it is to reach a better and more reflected understanding of the meaning, associations, and limitations of the conceptual vocabulary they habitually use. Currently the latter connotes a long-standing dependence of social history on the theoretical corpus of conventional sociology, and it is only when this fine web of assumptions has been subjected to some careful critical thought that the pursuit of a theoretically informed history of society can properly begin.

Notes

1. E. J. Hobsbawm, "From Social History to the History of Society," *Daedalus* 100 (1971): 43.

2. The recent policy of the *Times Literary Supplement*, where "social history" signifies amusing society memoirs, historic sexual scandals, or gossipy surveys of popular taste, is a particularly sad example of the latter syndrome. This is naturally not to say that "manners and morals," when treated correctly, are not the proper concern of the social historian. See for instance, M. Elias, *The Civilizing Process: The History of Manners* (New York, 1978; originally published 1936).

3. A. Marwick, *The Nature of History* (London, 1971).

4. The main vehicle for this "historical social science" in the Federal Republic of Germany is the new journal *Geschichte und Gesellschaft*. For a masterly reply to its critics, see H.-U. Wehler, "Kritik und kritische Antikritik," *Historische Zeitschrift* 225 (1977): 347–84.

5. *Social History* 1 (1976): 3.

6. My observations make no claims to completeness, and many areas of recent advance, not to speak of whole national historiographies, have necessarily been left out of the account. In such small space I cannot hope to cover all aspects of social history, and in any case when the volume of work has expanded so rapidly, when the theoretical orientations are so diverse (and often so vague and ill-defined), when the national particularities are so important, and the future direction of the field so open, any general survey would be premature. My observations are deliberately general and confined to literature of the past decade. They claim no great originality. My main intellectual debts are clear enough from the cited literature, but whatever virtues my comments might possess derive in no small part from discussions with Gareth Stedman Jones and David Crew. The vices are entirely my own.

7. Peter Laslett, *The World We Have Lost*, 2nd ed. (London, 1971), pp. 241–53, 20.

8. E. P. Thompson, "Under the Same Roof-Tree," *Times Literary Supplement*, 4 May 1973, p. 486; K. Thomas, "The Changing Family," *Times Literary Supplement*, 21 October 1977, p. 1226; H. Rosenbaum, "Zur neueren Entwicklung der Historischen Familienforschung," *Geschichte und Gesellschaft* 1, nos. 2/3 (1975): 210–25.

9. P. Laslett, *Family Life and Illicit Love in Earlier Generations* (Cambridge, 1977).

10. E. Shorter, *The Making of the Modern Family* (London, 1976); L. Stone, *The Family, Sex and Marriage in England 1500–1800* (London, 1977).

11. See C. Lasch, *Haven in a Heartless World: The Family Besieged* (New York, 1977); E. Fox-Genovese and E. D. Genovese, "The Political Crisis of Social History: A Marxian Perspective," *Journal of Social History* 10 (1976): 213 ff.

12. Herbert Gutman, *The Black Family in Slavery and Freedom, 1750–1925* (New York, 1976). A similar tendency to assume the essential privacy of the domestic sphere in the generation of ideology has not been absent from recent feminist historiography as well. See the helpful comments in M. B. Macintyre, "Recent Australian Feminist Historiography," *History Workshop* 5 (1978): 98–110.

13. N. J. Smelser, *Social Change in the Industrial Revolution* (London, 1959); Michael Anderson, *The Family in Nineteenth-Century Lancashire* (Cambridge, 1971); John Foster, *Class Struggle and the Industrial Revolution* (London, 1974); and Michael Anderson, "Sociological History and the Working-Class Family: Smelser Revisited," *Social History* 1, no. 3 (1976): 317–34.

14. Hans Medick, "The Proto-Industrial Family Economy: The Structural Function of Household and Family During the Transition from Peasant Society to Industrial Capitalism," *Social History* 1, no. 3 (1976): 291–316.

15. Thompson, "Under the Same Roof-Tree," p. 486.

16. Karin Hausen, "Familie als Gegenstand historischer Sozialwissenschaft: Bermerkungen zu einer Forschungsstrategie," *Geschichte und Gesellschaft* 1, nos. 2/3 (1975): 171–209.

17. E. D. Genovese, *Roll, Jordan, Roll: The World the Slaves Made* (New York, 1974).

18. These points have recently been made to great effect by G. Stedman Jones, "From Historical Sociology to Theoretical History," *British Journal of Sociology* 27 (1976): 295–305; E. P. Thomp-

son, "On History, Sociology and Historical Relevance," *British Journal of Sociology* 28 (1976): 387–402; and S. Macintyre, "The Making of the Australian Working Class: An Historiographical Survey," *Historical Studies* (Melbourne) 72 (1978). See also R. Ashcraft, "Marx and Weber on Liberalism as Bourgeois Ideology," *Comparative Studies in Society and History* 14 (1972): 130–68; and for a related critique in another discipline, see D. Slater, "The Poverty of Modern Geographical Enquiry," *Pacific Viewpoint* 16 (1975): 159–76.

19. See T. Judt, review of E. Weber, *Peasants into Frenchmen: The Modernization of Rural France 1870–1914* (London, 1977) in *Social History* 3, no. 1 (1978): 110–14.

20. Emphasis on the "infinite variety of human experience" (R. Cobb, *Reactions to the French Revolution* [London, 1972], p. 14) can in less imaginative or sensitive hands easily lead to a philistine denial of larger historical analysis and a retreat from large-scale historical change. Thus an understanding of revolutionary change at the level of the state is sacrificed to the postulated primacy of "personal and family loyalties and regional or municipal traditions" (C. Wilson, "Velvet Revolution?" *New York Review of Books,* 9 June 1977).

21. E. D. Genovese, "Solidarity and Servitude," *Times Literary Supplement,* 25 February 1977.

22. For example, see R. Samuel, ed., *Village Life and Labour* (London, 1975).

23. C. Tilly, L. Tilly, and R. Tilly, *The Rebellious Century 1830–1930* (London, 1975).

24. For example, see R. Cobb, "History by Numbers," in *Tour de France* (London, 1976).

25. R. Gray, review of P. Thompson, *The Edwardians: The Remaking of British Society* (London, 1975) in *Social History* 2 (1977): 695–7. Again, as with quantification, these remarks are not meant to deny the validity of oral history when properly applied. For an example of the problems which an excess of enthusiasm for oral history can create, see Thompson's *The Edwardians.* For an eloquent defense of the method see D. Smith, "What Does History Know of Nailbiting?" *Llafur* 1, no. 2 (1973): 34–41.

26. Fernand Braudel, *Capitalism and Material Life 1400–1600* (London, 1973), and *The Mediterranean and the Mediterranean World at the Time of Philip II,* 2 vols. (London, 1973).

27. G. Stedman Jones, "Class Expression *versus* Social Control?" *History Workshop* 4 (1977): 165.

28. See H.-U. Wehler, *Das Deutsche Kaiserreich 1871–1918* (Göttingen, 1973), pp. 122ff.

29. Fox-Genovese and Genovese, "The Political Crisis of Social History," pp. 213ff.

30. See A. S. Kraditor, "American Radical Historians on Their Heritage," *Past and Present* 56 (1972): 136–53.

31. There are notable exceptions: see the fine essay by S. Alexander ("Women's Work in Nineteenth-Century London: A Study in the Years 1820–50," in J. Mitchell and A. Oakley, eds., *The Rights and Wrongs of Women* [London, 1976], pp. 59–111), and T. Mason ("Women in Germany, 1925–1940: Family, Welfare and Work," Parts I and II, *History Workshop* 1 and 2 [1976]: 74–113 and 5–32).

32. Again there are important exceptions: for example, see G. Stedman Jones, *Outcast London* (London, 1971); E. P. Thompson, *Whigs and Hunters: The Origin of the Black Act* (London, 1975); and D. Hay, "Property, Authority and the Criminal Law," in D. Hay, P. Linebaugh, and E. P. Thompson, eds., *Albion's Fatal Tree* (London, 1975), pp. 17–64.

33. See, for example, P. Anderson, "Origins of the Present Crisis," in P. Anderson and R. Blackburn, eds., *Towards Socialism* (London, 1965); E. P. Thompson, "The Peculiarities of the English," *Socialist Register 1965,* pp. 311–62; N. Young, "Prometheans or Troglodytes?" *Berkeley Journal of Sociology* 12 (1967): 1–27; and H. Johnson, "Barrington Moore, Perry Anderson and English Social Development," *Working Papers in Cultural Studies* 9 (1976): 7–28.

34. See the following. M. Dobb, *Studies in the Development of Capitalism* (London, 1946); E. J. Hobsbawm, Introduction to K. Marx, *Pre-Capitalist Economic Formations* (London, 1964), J. Saville, "Primitive Accumulation and Early Industrialization in Britain," *Socialist Register 1969,* pp. 247–71; I. Wallerstein, *The Modern World-System* (New York, 1974); P. Anderson, *Lineages of the Absolutist State* (London, 1974); P. Anderson, *Passages from Antiquity to Feudalism* (London, 1974); B. Hindess and P. Q. Hirst, *Pre-Capitalist Modes of Production* (London, 1975); R. Hilton, ed., *The Transition from Feudalism to Capitalism* (London, 1976); R. Brenner, "Agrarian Class

Structure and Economic Development in Pre-Industrial Europe," *Past and Present* 70 (1976): 30–75; R. Brenner, "The Origins of Capitalist Development: A Critique of Neo-Smithian Marxism," *New Left Review* 104 (1977): 25–93; and W. Kula, *An Economic Theory of the Feudal System* (London, 1976). The major non-Marxist contribution, C. Tilly, ed., *The Formation of the National States in Western Europe* (Princeton, N.J., 1975), is markedly inferior. Though non-Marxist historians have been largely indifferent to the general problems of transition, the debate conducted in *Past and Present* around the idea of the "general crisis of the seventeenth century" has been a partial exception to this generalization; see T. Aston, ed., *Crisis in Europe, 1550–1660* (London, 1970).

35. See C. Lasch, "The Family and History," "The Emotions of Family Life," and "What the Doctor Ordered," *New York Review of Books*, 13 November 1975, 27 November 1975, and 11 December 1975.

36. History and anthropology have met most productively perhaps on the terrain of African history, where some challenging social history is starting to appear. For a useful conspectus, see T. O. Ranger, "Towards a Usable African Past," in C. Fyte, ed., *African Studies Since 1945* (London, 1976); for an agenda, see G. Prins, "The End of the Beginning of African History," *Social History* (forthcoming, 1979). For work in historical geography, see the issues of the *Journal of Historical Geography* (1975–).

Select Bibliography

Select Journals

Annales, économies, sociétés, civilisations
Archiv für Sozialgeschichte
Bulletin of the Society for the Study of Labour History
Comparative Studies in Society and History
Geschichte und Gesellschaft
History Workshop
Journal of Historical Geography
Journal of Interdisciplinary History
Journal of Peasant Studies
Journal of Social History
Le Mouvement social
Past and Present
Social History

General Discussions of Social History

Ashcraft, R. "Marx and Weber on Liberalism as Bourgeois Ideology," *Comparative Studies in Society and History* 14 (1972): 130–68.

Braudel, F. "History and Social Science," in P. Burke, ed., *Economy and Society in Early Modern Europe* (London, 1972), pp. 11–42.

Crossick, G. "L'Histoire sociale de Grand-Bretagne moderne: un aperçu critique des recherches récentes," *Mouvement social* 100 (1977): 101–20.

Fox-Genovese, E., and E. D. Genovese, "The Political Crisis of Social History: A Marxian Perspective," *Journal of Social History* 10 (1976): 205–20.

Gray, R. Review of P. Thompson, *The Edwardians: The Remaking of British Society* (London, 1975) in *Social History* 2 (1977): 695–7.

Hausen, K. "Familie als Gegenstand historischer Sozialwissenschaft: Bemerkungen zu einer Forschungsstrategie," *Geschichte und Gesellschaft* 7, nos. 2/3 (1975): 171–209.

Hay, D. "Property, Authority and the Criminal Law," in D. Hay, P. Linebaugh, and E. P. Thompson, eds., *Albion's Fatal Tree* (London, 1975), pp. 17–64.

Hilton, R., ed. *The Transition from Feudalism to Capitalism* (London, 1976).

Hindess, B., and P. Q. Hirst. *Pre-Capitalist Modes of Production* (London, 1975).

Hobsbawm, E. J. Introduction to K. Marx, *Pre-Capitalist Economic Formations* (London, 1964).

Johnson, H. "Barrington Moore, Perry Anderson and English Social Development," *Working Papers in Cultural Studies* 9 (1976): 7–28.

Judt, T. Review of E. Weber, *Peasants into Frenchmen: The Modernization of Rural France 1870–1914* (London, 1977) in *Social History* 3, no. 1 (1978): 110–14.

Kula, W. *An Economic Theory of the Feudal System* (London, 1976).

Lasch, C. "The Family and History," "The Emotions of Family Life," and "What the Doctor Ordered," *New York Review of Books*, 13 November 1975, 27 November 1975, and 11 December 1975.

———. *Haven in a Heartless World: The Family Besieged* (New York, 1977).

Laslett, P. *Family Life and Illicit Love in Earlier Generations* (Cambridge, 1977).

Macintyre, M. B. "Recent Australian Feminist Historiography," *History Workshop* 5 (1978): 98–110.

Marwick, A. *The Nature of History* (London, 1971).

Mason, T. "Women in Germany, 1925–1940: Family, Welfare and Work," Parts I and II, *History Workshop* 1 and 2 (1976): 74–113 and 5–32.

Medick, H. "The Proto-Industrial Family Economy: The Structural Function of Household and Family during the Transition from Peasant Society to Industrial Capitalism," *Social History* 1, no. 3 (1976): 291–316.

Ranger, T. O. "Towards a Usable African Past," in C. Fyte, ed., *African Studies Since 1945* (London, 1976).

Richardson, R. C. *The Debate on the English Revolution* (London, 1977).

Rosenbaum, H. "Zur neueren Entwicklung der Historischen Familienforschung," *Geschichte und Gesellschaft* 1, nos. 2/3 (1975): 210–225.

Samuel, R., ed. *Village Life and Labour* (London, 1975).

Saville, J. "Primitive Accumulation and Early Industrialization in Britain," *Socialist Register 1969*, pp. 247–71.

Shorter, E. *The Making of the Modern Family* (London, 1976).

Smelser, N. J. *Social Change in the Industrial Revolution* (London, 1959).

Thompson, E. P. "Anthropology and the Discipline of Historical Context," *Midland History* 1 (1972): 41–55.

———. "On History, Sociology and Historical Relevance," *British Journal of Sociology* 28 (1976): 387–402.

Vilar, P. "Marxist History, a History in the Making: Dialogue with Althusser," *New Left Review* 80 (1973): 65–106.

Wehler, H.-U. "Kritik und kritische Antikritik," *Historische Zeitschrift* 225 (1977): 347–84.

Other References

Alexander, S. "Women's Work in Nineteenth-Century London: A Study in the Years 1820–50," in J. Mitchell and A. Oakley, eds., *The Rights and Wrongs of Women* (London, 1976), pp. 59–111.

Anderson, M. *The Family in Nineteenth-Century Lancashire* (Cambridge, 1971).

———. "Sociological History and the Working-Class Family: Smelser Revisited," *Social History* 1, no. 3 (1976): 317–34.

Anderson, P. "Origins of the Present Crisis," in P. Anderson and R. Blackburn, eds., *Towards Socialism* (London, 1965).

———. *Lineages of the Absolutist State* (London, 1974).

———. *Passages from Antiquity to Feudalism* (London, 1974).

Aston, T., ed. *Crisis in Europe, 1550–1660* (London, 1970).

Braudel, F. *Capitalism and Material Life 1400–1600* (London, 1973).

————. *The Mediterranean and the Mediterranean World at the Time of Philip II*, 2 vols. (London, 1973).

Brenner, R. "Agrarian Class Structure and Economic Development in Pre-Industrial Europe," *Past and Present* 70 (1976): 30–75.

————. "The Origins of Capitalist Development: A Critique of Neo-Smithian Marxism," *New Left Review* 104 (1977): 25–93.

Cobb, R. "History by Numbers," in *Tour de France* (London, 1976).

————. *Reactions to the French Revolution* (London, 1972).

Dobb, M. *Studies in the Development of Capitalism* (London, 1946).

Elias, M. *The Civilizing Process: The History of Manners* (New York, 1978; original edition 1936).

Foster, J. *Class Struggle and the Industrial Revolution* (London, 1974).

Genovese, E. D. *Roll, Jordan, Roll: The World the Slaves Made* (New York, 1974).

————. "Solidarity and Servitude," *Times Literary Supplement*, 25 February 1977.

Gutman, H. G. *The Black Family in Slavery and Freedom, 1750–1925* (New York, 1976).

Hobsbawm, E. J. "From Social History to the History of Society," *Daedalus* 100 (1971): 20–45.

————. "Labour History and Ideology," *Journal of Social History* 7 (1974): 371–81.

Jones, G. Stedman. "Class Expression *versus* Social Control?" *History Workshop* 4 (1977): 162–70.

————. "From Historical Sociology to Theoretical History," *British Journal of Sociology* 27 (1976): 295–305.

————. *Outcast London* (London, 1971).

Kocka, J. "Recent Historiography of Germany and Austria," *Journal of Modern History* 47 (1975): 101–19.

Kraditor, A. S. "American Radical Historians on Their Heritage," *Past and Present* 56 (1972): 136–53.

Laslett, P. *The World We Have Lost*, 2nd ed. (London, 1971).

Lorwin, V. R., and J. M. Price, eds. *The Dimensions of the Past* (New Haven, Conn., and London, 1972).

Macintyre, S. "The Making of the Australian Working Class: An Historiographical Survey," *Historical Studies* (Melbourne) 72 (1978).

Prins, G. "The End of the Beginning of African History," *Social History* (forthcoming, 1979).

Slater, D. "The Poverty of Modern Geographical Enquiry," *Pacific Viewpoint* 16 (1975): 159–76.

Smith, D. "What Does History Know of Nailbiting?" *Llafur* 1, no. 2 (1973): 34–41.

Stoianovich, T. *French Historical Method: The Annales Paradigm* (Ithaca, N.Y., and London, 1976).

Stone, L. *The Family, Sex and Marriage in England 1500–1800* (London, 1977).

Thomas, K. "The Changing Family," *Times Literary Supplement*, 21 October 1977.

Thompson, E. P. "Happy Families," *New Society*, 8 September 1977.

————. *The Making of the English Working Class* (London, 1963).

————. "The Peculiarities of the English," *Socialist Register 1965*, pp. 311–62.

————. "Under the Same Roof-Tree," *Times Literary Supplement*, 4 May 1973.

————. *Whigs and Hunters: The Origin of the Black Act* (London, 1975).

Thompson, P. *The Edwardians: The Remaking of British Society* (London, 1975).

Tilly, C., ed. *The Formation of the National States in Western Europe* (Princeton, N.J., 1975).

Tilly, C., L. Tilly, and R. Tilly. *The Rebellious Century 1830–1930* (London, 1975).

Wallerstein, I. *The Modern World-System* (New York, 1974).

Weber, E. *Peasants into Frenchmen: The Modernization of Rural France 1870–1914* (London, 1977).

Wehler, H.-U. *Das Deutsche Kaiserreich 1871–1918* (Göttingen, 1973).

Wilson, C. "Velvet Revolution?" *New York Review of Books*, 9 June 1977.

Young, N. "Prometheans or Troglodytes?" *Berkeley Journal of Sociology* 12 (1967): 1–27.

Zeldin, T. *France 1848–1945*, vol. I, *Ambition, Love and Politics* (Oxford, 1973); vol. II, *Intellect, Taste and Anxiety* (Oxford, 1977).

5 RICHARD L. SCHOENWALD

The Psychological Study of History

Psychohistory, essentially, is the study
of individual and collective life
with the combined methods of psychoanalysis
and history.[1]

Psychohistorians believe now that a new day has broken: years of savage attacks have given way at least to benign indifference within the profession and often enough to real sympathy and support from many colleagues. Psychohistory must be proving its true worth, a value that can only increase as time goes on (Wehler 1971; Friedländer 1975; Strout 1976). In this essay I am going to speak out of my own considerable experience over several decades both in practicing psychohistory and in studying its development, and that experience leads me to a quite different conclusion.

Fifty or sixty years ago the enterprise of psychohistory looked so promising and plausible. History meant studying human behavior; the rise of scientific psychology foretold an end to the philosophical mustiness and uncritical common sense that had long masqueraded as reliable knowledge of human behavior; therefore, the application of psychology to history appeared well worth undertaking. The growth of history in the last hundred years has often been distinguished by the acceptance and transformation of concepts and techniques drawn from fields outside history and then molded to history's narrative and analytic concerns. Thus the use of psychology would stand in good company with resorting to insights from economics and sociology (Barnes 1919; Ratner 1941; Garraty 1954; Ross 1974).

From those earliest days into the 1970s psychohistorians have contended that the youth and fragility of their venture deserve special consideration, and they have urged patience upon skeptics and critics. Yet we can now survey half a century of work, and one profoundly disturbing conclusion stands out: the best psychohistorical work has been done not by historians, but by psychoanalysts or by workers in fields other than history. When at last a masterpiece of psychohistorical biography appeared, its author was a psychoanalyst, John E. Mack

(1976*, 1977). Professors and Ph.D.'s in history have generally restricted psychological consideration to articles or to a limited part of a larger study, or, as in the work of Rudolph Binion, the outstanding American psychohistorian, they have focused relentless attention on a single kind of psychic outcome studied in a variety of individuals and, recently, in a group.

Why have historians not done more and better work? Almost all existing psychohistorical writing derives, not from psychology as a field comparable to fields such as economics or sociology, but from one particular form of psychology: psychoanalysis. In retrospect, the choice of psychoanalysis was inevitable. Except for psychoanalysis, psychology either dealt with human behavior at a level meaningless to historians, by mapping pain-sensitive skin areas, for example, or it required the genius of a William James for its use. Not so in the case of Freud and his followers: their literary talents made psychoanalysis accessible and convinced some historians that here indeed was a psychology about human beings that was waiting to be tapped by the historian. In addition, Freud and his followers actually applied psychoanalysis nonmedically, to literature, art, and the study of figures from the past (Lindauer 1974). They unmasked these figures; they uncovered the hidden, unconscious conflicts at the very core of the lives of the great and the significant. Psychoanalysis promised thrilling discoveries for historians.

The main orientations of psychoanalysis, however, operated to hamstring historians. The fundamental mode of classical psychoanalytic explanation depends upon the discovery of a kernel or nucleus from which all of an individual's conduct radiates. It would be an exaggeration to call this procedure reductionistic, yet its basic import does run counter to the historian's leading imperative. Far from discovering one key, all-embracing conflict or all-explaining trauma, the historian must unfold a tale rich in change and reversals, a maze rather than a neat trajectory.

Furthermore, for a long time psychoanalysis stressed the unconscious or irrational nature of the core it was seeking. Not the daytime world of thinking and planning and trying, but the dark, underground swamps of wishes and fantasies provided the preferred territory for discovering that core. Here again, the historian trained to discuss treaties and contracts would find himself bewildered. In addition, the highly individualistic bent of psychoanalysis handicapped the historian who thought of himself as charged with writing about the past of large numbers of people. In its pioneering decades, and even later, psychoanalysis focused on single individuals and regarded multipersonal or group situations as problems to be treated by translating crowd psychology of the late nineteenth century into psychoanalytic terms or to be left for a future time when it could be hoped that better developed social sciences would draw somehow on what psychoanalysis had found out about individual functioning.

---

*Details for asterisked references will be found at the end of this paper in the section entitled "Notable Works of Psychohistory."

Until the 1940s, then, some historians urged the use of psychology and even spun out programs for its use, but they could not carry out this aim very impressively or extensively because they could not cope with the prevailing direction of what they understood psychology to be: psychoanalysis. The work of the psychoanalyst Erik H. Erikson disclosed a new path to them. Erikson stressed the meaning of certain views developed by psychoanalysts in the 1930s and later: man did not live by passion alone. A part of man's personality, his "ego," thought, planned, and remembered so that satisfying man's passions did not entail his destruction. These psychoanalysts saw life as a series of strategies powered in part by obscure prompting deep within, but also unmistakably meant as adaptive responses to a real and changing world outside.

In his studies of gifted and outstanding individuals—Freud, Luther, George Bernard Shaw, William James, Gandhi—Erikson fulfilled the first psychoanalytic intent, to set forth the array of a person's inner drives and their interplay as, in time, they came to constitute his character. He also carried out a second task imposed by more recent advances in understanding the workings of the ego. He showed how an individual fused creatively in thought and action the demands of his inner life and his grasp of realities in the world around him (Erikson 1950*, 1958*, 1959, 1968, 1969*, 1970; Schoenwald 1977).

In dealing with the problem of the group, Erikson offered two solutions later taken over by many psychohistorians. First, he saw the family and its pattern of childrearing as the major mechanism for imparting society's values and directives to the oncoming generation. Second, he provided an interpretation of the nature of leadership. For Erikson, leader and led must resemble each other closely. Then a leader's innovative use of the external world, of its institutions, language, and culture, to solve his own inner problems would find a deeply sympathetic response within thousands and millions of followers floundering as they sought to accommodate their own needs to the world around them. A leader would function as a model or teacher because he resembled so closely the throngs who became his followers.

Erikson carried out much of the best psychohistorical work published thus far. Many psychohistorians have sought to follow his example, especially in his attention to critical periods such as adolescence and his conception of the tie binding leader and masses. Erikson wrote books and long, virtually monograph-size articles, but historians under his spell have succeeded only in making pieces of books, and some articles, sound Eriksonian. A number of factors account for this striking difference in magnitude of accomplishment.

Erikson wrote with the verve and self-possession of a master because in fact he had created a synthesis between psychoanalysis as he had learned and practiced it, starting from his own training in analysis by Freud's daughter, and the social sciences as he found them burgeoning in America of the 1930s and 1940s. Erikson very largely discovered and made his own tools, working with an added zest and freshness of spirit, perhaps, because he had escaped formal higher education.

Erikson was born in 1902. Until the 1950s one person could reasonably expect to read and absorb most of the important psychoanalytic literature. The first great compendium of psychoanalytic theory, in one volume, appeared in 1945, and it has proved to be the last. Articles and books have poured forth torrentially since then. Today the would-be psychohistorian eager to grasp psychoanalytic theory scarcely knows where to begin, and once he plunges in, often finds himself overcome by faintness of spirit.

Psychohistorians have tried to follow Erikson on the question of the nature of groups, but they have been restrained by a realization that he did not really crack that problem. In fact, the historian Fred Weinstein and the sociologist Gerald Platt have shown that Erikson's interpretation of leadership can scarcely serve as a general model.[2] Deep interior likenesses of leaders and their multitudes of followers are simply too improbable. Thus the historian cannot make very much use of Erikson in actually working out his central concern, the activities of large numbers of people in the past. Actually, no psychoanalytically oriented writer has yet offered a successful interpretation of a period or an episode in which many people took part. The two best psychohistorically oriented books about groups that I know both deal with very small numbers of people who resembled each other rather closely and led fairly uncomplicated psychic existences: Weston La Barre's *They Shall Take Up Serpents* (1962*), and Kai T. Erikson's *Everything in Its Path* (1976*).

Playing the epigone to Erikson, then, does not help the psychohistorian very much because Erikson belongs to another world, a universe that he could indeed bestride. Following Erikson serves only to depress the morale of psychohistorians and their productivity as well, rather than to end in lifting the first and, as a consequence, the second. Morale must suffer because psychohistorians are, after all, historians, and they realize that the writing of history never advances by mere imitation of the example of a significant pioneer.

Tying psychohistory exclusively to psychoanalysis has not proven fruitful, nor will it in the future. In a series of publications, Weinstein and Platt (jointly 1973, 1975; Platt 1976) labored mightily amid a multiplicity of abstruse and scattered publications to disclose the fundamental concern of contemporary psychoanalysis most useful to psychohistorians—that psychoanalysts are on the way to accepting the primacy of the real world in psychic development! My own survey of the frontiers of psychological knowledge makes clear that not very much new knowledge that seems promising for psychohistorians is actually coming from psychoanalysis (for flickers see Searles 1960, 1965; Bowlby 1969–1973; Schoenwald 1973; Schafer 1974; Stoller 1975, 1976; *Journal of the American Psychoanalytic Association* 1976; Wolf 1976). So far as psychohistorians ought to be concerned, psychoanalysis has done its work. It has disclosed an unforgettable truth, that human lives center around conflicting urges and intentions that lie outside conscious awareness to varying degrees (Klein 1973). Psychoanalytic contributions of value to psychohistorians will continue to appear, without any question, but the fullest light on the mind now streams from other sources.

A new conception of psychohistory would hold that

The psychological study of history
means investigating the past
with some ideas, techniques, and findings
from psychology and the social sciences.

This statement's terms compress several propositions.

''THE PAST''

Psychohistorians have not had much success in dealing with everyday life; in fact, they have scarcely attempted such studies, so that one of the charges most often and most justly leveled against them remains their virtually exclusive concentration on great and famous individuals. Much of the history written throughout the world since 1945 has portrayed the fate of ordinary men and women, and psychohistory as a part of the total historical venture can no longer avoid this challenge.

For psychohistorians ''the past'' means uncovering how the interior lives of human beings have changed with the passing of time. Exterior lives remain the province of other historical specialties, and on these specialties the psychohistorian must draw heavily for his grasp of the real world surrounding his subjects.

''SOME''

Until now, psychohistorians have not ceased weeping and castigating themselves for not being able to metamorphose into psychoanalysts. Then, of course, they would have ceased thinking as historians for the most part, because the demands of the highly individualistic world view of psychoanalysis rule out the accumulation of knowledge and insight about the historic past that marks a historian. Some psychoanalysts, it is true, sometimes can manage to think as historians do, and with success that is notable—for instance, in the cases of Erik Erikson and John Mack. Yet in the main, psychoanalysis and psychohistory consist of efforts to attain two different goals.

Psychohistory will stand as the only systematic attempt to study the history of man's inner world as it has developed within the frame of the history of his outer world. The historian's unceasing need to grasp both worlds will forever prevent his mastering both, except in delicious fantasizing that magically grants his cherished wish to know everything. The historian will have to admit that ''some'' is better than ''all,'' because ''all,'' like turning into a psychoanalyst, is just not possible.

''PSYCHOLOGY''

The hope dear to Freud and many of his followers that psychoanalysis would emerge as a general psychology, indeed as the only true general psychology, has escaped fulfillment. It may never be fulfilled. Many psychologists, such as George Mandler (1975), seem very content for the present to work on particular problems with partial theories and allow a big scheme, a really general theory, to take shape in the future, if it is going to.

Psychological knowledge grows so rapidly nowadays that it cannot be squeezed within psychoanalytic confines. Translating new findings and conceptions from studies in perception or cognition seems a pointless endeavor, especially because so much of the work in areas such as these already rests upon acceptance of a central psychoanalytic premise, a person's dominant unawareness of exactly what he is doing when he is engaged in perceiving or thinking or learning. In fact, a more probable outcome may prove to be the translation and absorption of psychoanalytic findings into other psychological domains (Guterman 1970; Lindauer 1974; Segall 1976; Flavell 1977). Such a result will be even more likely if the recruitment of bright and gifted thinkers and investigators for psychoanalysis declines, a result toward which some signs presently point (Stone 1976).

"THE SOCIAL SCIENCES"

Despite their jargon and their often forbiddingly mathematical guise, the social sciences constitute the best arsenal from which the psychohistorian will draw the most effective weapons in his attack on the problem of collective human life in the past. Somehow, in time and with patience, he will find ways of connecting psychological knowledge about individual conduct with suggestions and conclusions from the social sciences about the performance of many individuals (Wellman 1975). He will come upon these ways if he can resist being detoured, befuddled, and depressed by talk about behavioral "levels" at which it is right and proper for him to work (Kuhn 1962; Calhoun 1973*; Stokes 1974*, forthcoming*; Gablik 1976; Perkins and Leondar 1977). Let him take from cognition some ideas that may throw new light on episodes in the history of education; let him gather from work in perception some hunches that might explain part of the reception of romantic painting.

Psychohistorians need to remind themselves constantly that they are historians, not scientists. They have suffered too long under the sway of the "covering-law" principle advanced some decades back as a way of applying propositions from the social sciences to history, a principle sanctified by certain philosophers. According to the "covering law," a historian intent on discovering "truth" would show that a general finding from another field, preferably a social or behavioral science, covers every particular item of historical data that he was treating. The philosopher Leon Goldstein has shown (1976) that Sisyphean difficulties must ensue: a historian would exhaust both himself and the patience of any reader, if he ever found a reader, by relentlessly fitting even the slightest bit of evidence to a general theorem in order to attain truthfulness in his work by following the "covering-law" procedure.

The psychohistorian urgently needs to recognize that he must leave much to

art, to the consciously planned and unconsciously stumbled-on skill of his presentation. A psychohistorian demonstrates, he does not prove. For the most part,
he shows his readers "connections between otherwise isolated pieces of experience." Pressed to estimate the truthfulness of his work, he replies with Daniel
Calhoun, "There come times when an interpreter asks not What can we prove?
but What if it should be true that all these threads do hang together?"[3]

Trapped between feeling driven to prove and sensing that they must demonstrate, psychohistorians have settled for a dogged and wooden style that they
probably feel makes them more acceptable because they end up sounding more
like their disciplinary brethren. Yet the point of working free from the old en-
slavements—to psychoanalysis and to Erikson, for instance—is to be able to
choose freely how to present findings. Erik Erikson here has pointed the way
because the artistic power manifest in his organization of his material and in his
style contributes so greatly to his impact. Psychohistorians have scarcely paid
any attention to his example, just as historians generally have failed to pick up
Oscar Handlin's injunction (1971) to seek innovative ways of communicating.
Style, of course, is not meant to replace substance. Every historian must unfold
a sequence of argued steps underpinned by evidence (Weinstein 1977a). Precisely, however, because the psychohistorian shuttles back and forth between
everyday outer realities and more hidden inner realities, he must make his work
operate on more levels than a historian is accustomed to hit. The psychohistorian
who wants to send messages on several tracks because his material and analysis
actually follow several tracks will gain by heeding the example of those well
experienced in many-leveled signaling—artists (Kai T. Erikson 1970).

"IDEAS, TECHNIQUES, AND FINDINGS"

Only a few promising possibilities can receive mention here.

1. Suppose that a psychohistorian wanted to experiment . . .

Growing contact with nonpsychoanalytic psychology and with the social sciences might lead to experimental efforts involving historians. These ventures
need not reek immoderately of the laboratory. They would, most likely, be distinguished principally by the temporary abandonment of the principle that a historian ought to toil alone, and by an equally temporary effort to devise some
way of calling on several people to monitor a single historian's tendency to
nudge and squeeze his data unconsciously or semiconsciously into certain favored patterns.

The psychologist David McClelland, for instance, has long urged historians
to follow his practice in using numbers to indicate the degree to which artifacts
from the past showed evidence of psychological functions such as a particular
motive: the data studied might include plays, proclamations, vases, and similar
objects for everyday use (1961, 1972). McClelland has used panels of judges
to rate data and thus tried to correct for the vagaries of individual bias, taste,
and ignorance. Panels do not lead magically to a grail wherein truth reposes;

they do offer one way of checking observations that deserves consideration ([National Association of Social Workers] 1959).

A collaborative effort by the historians Peter Hoffer and Steven Allen and the psychologist N. E. H. Hull, soon to be published (*; Hoffer*), uses judges to see whether people uninvolved in devising a historical hypothesis can attain confirming results when applying it. This work, which deals with divisions among the colonists on the eve of the American Revolution, carries greater conviction because of its successful testing than an outstanding recent psychohistorical study, somewhat psychoanalytically oriented, by Edwin Burrows and Michael Wallace dealing in part with the same subject (1972*). The latter proceeded as historians always have, by multiplying quotations from the sources in support of a complex argument, but without trying to determine if others could arrive at similar results using their hypothesis. (Kenneth Lynn's effort [1977] is much slighter and also as yet untested by anyone but him.) Another group, which seems to have been composed mainly of psychologists, found that it could produce descriptions of the personalities of historical figures "within the same range of inter-observer agreement and reliability as those obtained in extensive face-to-face personality assessment programs" (Historical Figures Assessment Collaborative, 1977).

The primary maxim here for psychohistorians, as everywhere else, ought to be: move around, take up, consider, adapt, reject! A number of experimental and quasi-experimental possibilities are open. The fearful rigidity of psychohistorians has even kept them from the sizable body of literature reporting tests of psychoanalytic propositions through experimental psychological studies, longitudinal studies of human development, and the scrutiny of cross-cultural anthropological data (Stephens 1962; Block 1971; Kline 1972; Elder 1974; Shapiro and Alexander 1975; Fisher and Greenberg 1977; Vaillant 1977). Furthermore, historians, whose profession teaches them how to understand man in so many times and places, have frozen stock-still and failed to see how they could contribute by testing psychological findings across time. Who stands better situated than historians to attack difficulties perennially raised, such as the alleged exclusively bourgeois nature of psychoanalytic psychology, or what is sometimes supposed to be its ineradicably Western orientation (Croizier 1977; Schoenwald 1977)? The psychologist Michael Cole, through his own experimental work and his discussion of the efforts of others, has raised most intriguingly the whole question of how Western-type schooling leads to Western-type intellectual accomplishment (Luria 1971; Cole and Scribner 1974). Cole's work lacks what resourceful psychohistorians could supply: sampling in past time to begin formulating the impact of various educational systems in other ages (Kuhn 1962; Kedrov 1966–1967; Calhoun 1973*; Ross 1976).

2. The use of information-processing models

Recent psychological theorizing and investigation draw upon the conception and the capabilities of the computer to portray the human being as someone who lives by taking information from the world outside and the world within and acting on the basis of that information (Dember and Jenkins 1970: 502–511; Posner 1973). Structures and systems within human beings route and utilize information. Human behavior depends upon what is done with information, the signals that report events in both the external and internal universes.

George Mandler (1975) has suggested that emotion may be better understood than it ever has been by conceiving of a "flow chart" in which certain structures determine the disposition of information. Human beings learn from their social groups how and when to allow the autonomic nervous system—hormones and "guts"—to affect their systems for thinking and action. Emotion results from the impact of the autonomic nervous system on the other systems that produce thinking and action. Human beings feel disorganized and helpless when they cannot master and subject inner and outer information to the processes summed up as "thinking": they are then experiencing anxiety. Much of the significance of emotion for Mandler derives from its representing structured, systematic ways to maintain courses of action important to the individual. Interruptions of ongoing behavior, for instance, may result in signals from the autonomic nervous system that lead the organism to take a closer look at the cause and meaning of the interruption. For Mandler a psychoanalytic concept such as repression entails keeping "out of consciousness those meaning analyses that would, if present, produce the interruption of either action or plans."[4]

The unconscious aspects of behavior remain: no individual ever recalls how he learned to think about what he could do, what he should do, and what he must never think about doing; but learn all those proprieties and improprieties he most certainly did, or tried to. Information-processing models show more economically what recent psychoanalytic theorizing has sought to portray but has achieved more cumbersomely because of the amorphousness of its central concept, the ego.

According to some psychologists, what people think about aggression tends to determine how aggressive they are: information flows, or does not flow, from the cognitive system to other systems, telling them when to be aggressive and when not (Aronson 1976). The psychohistorian's problem then becomes how to grasp the ways in which societies, social classes, families and other groups develop and instill patterns prescribing the nature of suitable occasions for being aggressive. The psychohistorian must—and here the psychoanalytic insight is never lost—make conscious what scarcely ever becomes fully conscious to anyone.

In a particularly striking recent piece of work the psychologists J. W. Getzels and M. Csikzentmihalyi (1976) have studied the interaction of personality and culture in the production of art by using a cognitive approach. They tested the notion that those art students who excelled at finding significant problems became successful young artists. Such students turned out to be able to process information about elements and materials available for the construction of works of art so that they chose parts later combinable into richly complex creations. Other students appeared to settle for materials that could be fused in far less manifold and compelling ways. Customarily art history fixes on how artists solved problems, rather than how they sensed where important problems lay. The findings of Getzels and Csikzentmihalyi would appear to lead a psychohistorian to a new point of view from which to study creativity not only in art, but in other fields marked by the impress of "genius" (White 1949; Kubler 1962). That concept would lose much of its woolliness if it were attacked on three fronts: the culture from which a creator learns and for which he creates, the individual personality that leads him to pick out certain items to learn while forgetting or bypassing others, and the cognitive or information-processing capacities that he learns as do others around him but which he exercises with some greater skill and concentration than they muster.

3. A place for riders of hobbyhorses

Far too few psychohistorians have allowed themselves to gain from some important students of human behavior who notoriously flout orthodoxies. Norman O. Brown (1959*, 1966*) has long been well known for his daring inventiveness; yet he has virtually no followers (except for Thorpe 1972*), though he sought, in his own Dionysian way, precisely what Weinstein and Platt are seeking so earnestly, a psychology for historians. Julian Jaynes (1977) has opened a dazzling vista backward into the past of the human brain by building daringly on his historical, neurological, and psychological knowledge. Manfred Clynes (1977) contends that composers leave fundamental patterns all over their music. These very small curves rise and fall; they are distinctive and unmistakable, like fingerprints, and the great performer is someone who has become expert at detecting them. Amid all this crankish grinding of axes the psychohistorian needs to move with discretion but mainly with freedom, and it is precisely that—freedom—which has proved to be so disastrously lacking until now.

> The psychological study of history means
> investigating the past with some
> ideas, techniques, and findings
> from psychology and the social sciences.

Psychohistory looks almost too difficult. The past unfolded in its own good time, and perversely destroyed most of the evidence for its own reality. Every historian nevertheless manages to dare to reconstruct, to recreate and assert, "I have made a past." The psychohistorian intent on adding "and I show you its mind" seems to top all conceivable folly. Yet if he perseveres he may one day feel, "I am coming to see man as he was, in the life that his mind made for him."

Notes

1. Erik H. Erikson, *Dimensions of a New Identity* (New York, 1974), p. 13.
2. Fred Weinstein and Gerald M. Platt, *Psychoanalytic Sociology: An Essay on the Interpretation of Historical Data and the Phenomena of Collective Behavior* (Baltimore and London, 1973), pp.

65–69; Fred Weinstein, "The Transference Model in Psychohistory: A Critique," *Psychohistory Review* 5, no. 4 (1977): 12–17.

3. Daniel Calhoun, *The Intelligence of a People* (Princeton, N.J., 1973), p. xii; see also John Chynoweth Burnham, review of several books in *Literature and Psychology* 10 (1960): 28–31.

4. George Mandler, *Mind and Emotion* (New York, 1975), p. 82.

Bibliography

References

American Psychiatric Association. *The Psychiatrist as Psychohistorian*. Task Force Report No. 11 (Washington, 1976).

Aronson, Elliot. *The Social Animal*. 2nd edition. (San Francisco, 1976).

Barnes, Harry Elmer. "Psychology and History," *American Journal of Psychology* 30 (1919): 337–76.

Block, Jack, and Haan, Norma. *Lives Through Time* (Berkeley, Calif., 1971).

Bowlby, John. *Attachment and Loss* (New York, 1969–1973).

Burnham, John Chynoweth. "Review of several books," *Literature and Psychology* 10 (1960): 28–31.

Clynes, Dr. Manfred. *Sentics. The Touch of Emotions* (Garden City, N.Y., 1977).

Cole, Michael, and Scribner, Sylvia. *Culture and Thought. A Psychological Introduction* (New York, 1974).

Croizier, Ralph C. *Koxinga and Chinese Nationalism. History, Myth, and the Hero* ([Cambridge, Mass.], 1977).

Dember, William N., and Jenkins, James J. *General Psychology* (Englewood Cliffs, N.J., 1970).

Elder, Glen H., Jr. *Children of the Great Depression* (Chicago and London, 1974).

Erikson, Erik H. *Identity and the Life Cycle* (New York, 1959).

———. "Identity, Psychosocial," and "Life Cycle," *International Encyclopedia of the Social Sciences*, 7:61–65 and 9:286–92 (N.p., 1968).

———. "Autobiographic Notes on the Identity Crisis," *Daedalus* 99 (1970): 730–59.

———. *Dimensions of a New Identity* (New York, 1974).

Erikson, Kai T. "Sociology and the Historical Perspective," *American Sociologist* 5 (1970): 331–38.

Fisher, Seymour, and Greenberg, Roger P. *The Scientific Credibility of Freud's Theories and Therapy* (New York, 1977).

Flavell, John H. *Cognitive Development* (Englewood Cliffs, N.J., 1977).

Friedländer, Saul. *Histoire et psychoanalyse* (Paris, 1975).

Gablik, Suzi. *Progress in Art* (London, 1976).

Garraty, John A. "Preserved Smith, Ralph Volney Harlow, and Psychology," *Journal of the History of Ideas* 15 (1954): 456–65.

Getzels, Jacob W., and Csikzentmihalyi, M. *The Creative Vision* (New York, 1976).

Gilmore, William J., Critical bibliographies on psychohistory, *Newsletter of the Group for the Use of Psychology in History*, 1972–1976; *The Psychohistory Review*, 1976–.

Goldstein, Leon J. *Historical Knowing* (Austin, Texas, and London, 1976).

Guterman, Stanley S. *The Machiavellians, A Social Psychological Study of Moral Character and Organizational Milieu* (Lincoln, Neb., 1970).

Handlin, Oscar, "History: A Discipline in Crisis?" *American Scholar* 40 (1971): 447–65.

Historical Figures Assessment Collaborative. "Assessing Historical Figures: The Use of Observer-based Personality Descriptions," *Historical Methods Newsletter* (forthcoming).

Hofling, Charles. "Current Aspects of Psychohistory," *Comprehensive Psychiatry* 17 (1976): 227–39.

Jaynes, Julian. *The Origin of Consciousness in the Breakdown of the Bicameral Mind* (Boston, 1977).

Journal of the American Psychoanalytic Association, 24, no. 5 (1976), special issue on feminine psychology.

Kedrov, B. M., trans., and introduction by Herbert A. Simon. "On the Question of the Psychology of Scientific Creativity," *Soviet Psychology* 5, no. 2 (1966–1967): 16–37; reprinted, *The Soviet Review* 8, no. 2 (1967): 24–45.

Klein, George S. "Is Psychoanalysis Relevant?" in Benjamin B. Rubenstein, ed., *Psychoanalysis and Contemporary Science,* II, 3–21 (New York and London, 1973).

Kline, Paul. *Fact and Fantasy in Freudian Theory* (London, 1972).

Kubler, George. *The Shape of Time* (New Haven, Conn., and London, 1962).

Kuhn, Thomas S. *The Structure of Scientific Revolutions* (Chicago, 1962; 2nd edition, 1970).

Lindauer, Martin S. *The Psychological Study of Literature* (Chicago, 1974).

Luria, Alexander K., trans. M. Cole, "Towards the Problem of the Historical Nature of Psychological Processes," *International Journal of Psychology* 6 (1971): 259–72.

Lynn, Kenneth S. *A Divided People* (Westport, Conn., 1977).

McClelland, David C. *The Achieving Society* (Princeton, N.J., 1961).

———. "How and Why to Code Historical Documents, or, The Psychological Interpretation of History." Paper presented at the meeting of the Organization of American Historians, 1972.

Mack, John E. "T. E. Lawrence and the Uses of Psychology in the Biography of Historical Figures," in L. Carl Brown and N. Itzkowitz, eds., *Psychological Dimensions of Near Eastern Studies* (Princeton, N.J., 1977), pp. 27–59.

Mandler, George. *Mind and Emotion* (New York, 1975).

[National Association of Social Workers]. *Use of Judgments as Data in Social Work Research* (New York, 1959). I owe this reference to Judah Rubinstein.

Perkins, David, and Barbara Leondar, eds. *The Arts and Cognition* (Baltimore, 1977).

Platt, Gerald M. "The Sociological Endeavor and Psychoanalytic Thought," *American Quarterly* 28 (1976): 343–59.

Posner, Michael I. *Cognition: An Introduction* (Glenview, Ill., and Brighton, England, 1973). I owe this reference to J. R. Hayes.

Ratner, Sidney. "The Historian's Approach to Psychology," *Journal of the History of Ideas* 2 (1941): 95–109.

Ross, Dorothy. "The 'New History' and the 'New Psychology': An Early Attempt at Psychohistory," in Stanley Elkins and Eric McKitrick, eds., *The Hofstadter Aegis* (New York, 1974), pp. 207–34.

———. Review of Daniel Calhoun, *The Intelligence of a People, The Journal of Interdisciplinary History* 6 (1976): 741–44.

Schafer, Roy. "Problems in Freud's Psychology of Women," *Journal of the American Psychoanalytic Association* 22 (1974): 459–85.

Schoenwald, Richard L. "Using Psychology in History: A Review Essay," *Historical Methods Newsletter* 7 (1973): 9–24.

———. "The Problem of Erikson," *The Psychohistory Review* 6, no. 1 (1977): 76–87.

Searles, Harold F. *The Nonhuman Environment in Normal Development and in Schizophrenia* (New York, 1960).

———. *Collected Papers on Schizophrenia and Related Subjects* (New York, 1965).

Segall, Marshall H. *Human Behavior and Public Policy: A Political Psychology* (New York, 1976).

Shapiro, Kenneth Joel, and Alexander, Irving. *The Experience of Introversion: An Integration of Phenomenological, Empirical and Jungian Approaches* (Durham, N.C., 1975).

Stephens, William N. *The Oedipus Complex, Cross-cultural Evidence* (New York, 1962).

Stoller, Robert J. *Perversion: The Erotic Form of Hatred* (New York, 1975).

———. "Sexual Excitement," *Archives of General Psychiatry* 33 (1976): 899–909.

Stone, Alan A. "Psychiatry: Dead or Alive?" *Harvard Magazine* 79, no. 4 (1976): 17–23.

Strout, Cushing. "The Uses and Abuses of Psychology in American History," *American Quarterly* 28 (1976): 324–42.

Vaillant, George E. *Adaptation to Life* (Boston and Toronto, 1977).

Wehler, Hans-Ulrich, ed. *Geschichte und Psychoanalyse* ([Cologne], 1971).

Weinstein, Fred. "The Transference Model in Psychohistory: A Critique," *The Psychohistory Review* 5, no. 4 (1977): 12–17.

———. Contribution to Discussion Forum on Rudolph Binion's *Hitler Among the Germans, The Psychohistory Review* 6, no. 1 (1977): 50–61. (Referred to in text as 1977*a*).

Weinstein, Fred, and Platt, Gerald M. *Psychoanalytic Sociology: An Essay on the Interpretation of Historical Data and the Phenomena of Collective Behavior* (Baltimore and London, 1973).

———. "The Coming Crisis in Psychohistory," *Journal of Modern History* 47 (1975): 202–28.

Wellman, Judith. "Culture and Character: Some Perspectives from Psychological Anthropology for Psychohistorians," *Newsletter of the Group for the Use of Psychology in History* 4, no. 3 (1975): 12–30.

White, Leslie A. *The Science of Culture* (New York, 1949).

Wolf, Ernest S. "Recent Advances in the Psychology of the Self: An Outline of Basic Concepts," *Comprehensive Psychiatry* 17 (1976): 37–46.

Notable Works of Psychohistory

Abell, Walter. *The Collective Dream in Art* (Cambridge, Mass., 1957).

Bakan, David. *Sigmund Freud and the Jewish Mystical Tradition* (Princeton, N.J., 1958).

Barbu, Z. *Problems of Historical Psychology* (New York, 1960).

Beckman, Alan C. "Hidden Themes in the Frontier Thesis: An Application of Psycho-Analysis to Historiography," *Comparative Studies in History and Society* 8 (1966): 361–82.

Benton, John F. "The Personality of Guibert of Nogent," *Psychoanalytic Review* 57 (1970–1971): 563–86.

Berg, J. H. van den. *The Changing Nature of Man*. Translated by H. F. Croes (New York, 1961).

Binion, Rudolph. *Frau Lou: Nietzsche's Wayward Disciple* (Princeton, N.J., 1968).

———. "Repeat Performance: A Psychohistorical Study of Leopold III and Belgian Neutrality," *History and Theory* 8 (1969): 213–59.

———. "From Mayerling to Sarajevo," *Journal of Modern History* 47 (1975): 280–316.

———. *Hitler Among the Germans* (New York, Oxford, and Amsterdam, 1976).

Blanchard, William H. *Rousseau and the Spirit of Revolt* (Ann Arbor, Mich., 1967).

Brown, Norman C. *Life Against Death* (Middletown, Conn., 1959).

———. *Love's Body* (New York, 1966).

Burrows, Edwin G., and Wallace, Michael. "The American Revolution: The Ideology and Psychology of National Liberation," *Perspective in American History* 6 (1972): 167–306.

Bushman, Richard L. "On the Uses of Psychology: Conflict and Conciliation in Benjamin Franklin," *History and Theory* 5 (1966): 225–40.

Calhoun, Daniel. *The Intelligence of a People* (Princeton, N.J., 1973).

Cody, John. *After Great Pain: The Inner Life of Emily Dickinson* (Cambridge, Mass., 1971).

———. "Richard Wagner and the Ur Maternal Sea," *Bulletin of the Menninger Clinic* 39 (1975): 556–77.

Demos, John. "Underlying Themes in the Witchcraft of Seventeenth-Century New England," *American Historical Review* 75 (1970): 1311–26.

Eaton, Leonard K. *Two Chicago Architects and Their Clients: Frank Lloyd Wright and Howard Van Doren Shaw* (Cambridge, Mass., 1969).

Erikson, Erik H. *Childhood and Society* (New York, 1950; 2nd edition, 1963).

———. *Young Man Luther* (New York, 1958).

———. *Gandhi's Truth. On the Origins of Militant Nonviolence* (New York, 1969).

Erikson, Kai T. *Everything in Its Path. Destruction of Community in the Buffalo Creek Flood* (New York, 1976).

Fromm, Erich, and Maccoby, Michael. *Social Character in a Mexican Village* (Englewood Cliffs, N.J., 1970).

George, Alexander L., and George, Juliette L. *Woodrow Wilson and Colonel House, A Personality Study* (New York, 1956).

Greene, Jack P. "Search for Identity: An Interpretation of the Meaning of Selected Patterns of Social Response in Eighteenth-Century America," *Journal of Social History* 3 (1970): 189–219.

Hoffer, Peter C. "Psychohistory and Empirical Group Affiliation, Extraction of Personality Traits from Historical Manuscripts," *Journal of Interdisciplinary History* 9 (1978): 131–45.

————. "Choosing Sides: A Quantitative Study of Personality Determinants of Loyalist and Revolutionary Political Affiliation in New York," *Journal of American History* (forthcoming).

Holfing, Charles K. "Percival Lowell and the Canals of Mars," *British Journal of Medical Psychology* 37 (1964): 33–42.

Hunter, Doris M., and Babcock, Charlotte. "Some Aspects of the Intrapsychic Structure of Certain American Negroes as Viewed in the Intercultural Dynamic," in W. Muensterberger, ed., *The Psychoanalytic Study of Society* (New York, 1967), IV, 124–69.

Kakar, Sudhir. *Frederick Taylor: A Study in Personality and Innovation* (Cambridge, Mass., and London, 1970).

Kovel, Joel. *White Racism: A Psychohistory* (New York, 1970).

Künzli, Arnold. *Karl Marx. Eine Psychographie* (Vienna, Frankfurt, and Zürich, 1966).

La Barre, Weston. *They Shall Take Up Serpents. Psychology of the Southern Snake-Handling Cult* (Minneapolis, 1962).

Levi, A. W. "The 'mental crisis' of John Stuart Mill," *Psychoanalytic Review* 32 (1945): 86–101.

Little, Lester K. "The Personal Development of Peter Damian," in William C. Jordan and others, eds., *Order and Innovation in the Middle Ages: Essays in Honor of Joseph R. Strayer* (Princeton, N.J., 1976), pp. 317–41.

Lockspeiser, Edward. *Debussy: His Life and Mind* (New York, 1962).

Loewenberg, Peter. "The Psychohistorical Origins of the Nazi Youth Cohort," *American Historical Review* 76 (1971): 1456–1502.

Mack, John E. *A Prince of Our Disorder. The Life of T. E. Lawrence* (Boston and Toronto, 1976).

McLaughlin, Mary M. "Abelard as Autobiographer: The Motives and Meanings of His 'Story of Calamities'," *Speculum* 42 (1967): 463–88.

McRandle, James H. *The Track of the Wolf. Essays on National Socialism and Its Leader, Adolf Hitler* (Evanston, Ill., 1965).

Manuel, Frank E. *A Portrait of Isaac Newton* (Cambridge, Mass., 1968).

Moller, Herbert. "The Meaning of Courtly Love," *Journal of American Folklore* 73 (1960): 39–52.

Monaco, Paul. *Cinema and Society. France and Germany During the Twenties* (New York, Oxford, and Amsterdam, 1976).

Parker, Harold T. "The Formation of Napoleon's Personality: An Exploratory Essay," *French Historical Studies* 7 (1971): 6–26.

Patterson, James T. *Mr. Republican: A Biography of Robert A. Taft* (Boston, 1972).

Pflanze, Otto. "Toward a Psychoanalytic Interpretation of Bismarck," *American Historical Review* 77 (1972): 419–44.

Raack, R. C. "When Plans Fail: Small Group Behavior and Decision-Making in the Conspiracy of 1808 in Germany," *Journal of Conflict Resolution* 14 (1970): 3–19.

Roelker, Nancy L. "The Appeal of Calvinism to French Noblewomen in the Sixteenth Century," *Journal of Interdisciplinary History* 2 (1972): 391–418.

Rogin, Michael Paul. *Fathers and Children. Andrew Jackson and the Subjugation of the American Indian* (New York, 1975).

Rosenzweig, Linda W. "The Abdication of Edward VIII: A Psycho-Historical Explanation," *Journal of British Studies* 14 (1975): 102–19.

Sagan, Eli. *Cannibalism: Human Aggression and Cultural Form* (New York, 1974).

Schoenwald, Richard L. "Town Guano and 'Social Statics'," *Victorian Studies* 11, Supplement (1968), 691–710.

———. "Training Urban Man: A Hypothesis About the Sanitary Movement," in H. J. Dyos and M. Wolff, eds., *The Victorian City* (London, 1973), II, 669–92.

Seigel, J. E. "Marx's Early Development: Vocation, Rebellion,and Realism," *Journal of Interdisciplinary History* 3 (1973): 475–508.

Shore, Miles F. "Henry VIII and the Crisis of Generativity," *Journal of Interdisciplinary History* 2 (1972): 359–90.

Shorter, Edward. "Illegitimacy, Sexual Revolution, and Social Change in Modern Europe," *Journal of Interdisciplinary History* 2 (1972): 237–72.

———. "Female Emancipation, Birth Control, and Fertility in European History," *American Historical Review* 78 (1973): 605–40.

Slater, Philip E. *The Glory of Hera: Greek Mythology and the Greek Family* (Boston, 1968).

Stites, Raymond S. *The Sublimations of Leonardo de Vinci* (Washington, 1970).

Stokes, Gale. "Cognition and the Functions of Nationalism," *Journal of Interdisciplinary History* 4 (1974): 525–42.

———. "The Undeveloped Theory of Nationalism," *World Politics* (forthcoming).

Strout, Cushing. "William James and the Twice-Born Sick Soul," *Daedalus* 97 (1968): 1062–82.

Thorpe, Earl E. *The Old South: A Psychohistory* (Durham, N.C., 1972).

Weinstein, Fred, and Platt, Gerald M. *The Wish to Be Free. Society, Psyche, and Value Change* (Berkeley and Los Angeles, 1969).

Weisskopf, Walter A. *The Psychology of Economics* (Chicago, 1955).

Willcox, William B. *Portrait of a General: Sir Henry Clinton in the War of Independence* (New York, 1964).

Woods, Joseph M. "Towards a Psychoanalytic Interpretation of Charles Stewart Parnell," *Bulletin of the Menninger Clinic* (forthcoming).

6 PHILIP R. VANDERMEER

The New Political History: Progress and Prospects*

The "new" history is no longer a minor deviation from the norm of historical studies. In the past decade the volume of such works has grown enormously, as evidenced in frequent bibliographic reviews[1] and the annual bibliographies appearing in journals. More noteworthy are the new questions and topics which these works consider. Demographic and mobility studies have emerged as staples of social history, and the mere mention of *Time on the Cross* brings to mind a virtual industry of writing about the economics of slavery.[2] The rather sudden growth of interest in these fields has somewhat overshadowed developments in the new political history. This is unfortunate, for it tends to deny attention to the increasing sophistication, both methodological and conceptual, and the significant findings of the new political history.

Political history has traditionally focused on the episodic and the unique, emphasizing biographies of major politicians, studies of particular election campaigns, and the like. While this approach has by no means disappeared, substantial progress has been made in the reorientation toward the systematic analysis of structure and of process and the utilization of theory. Many examples of new political history fit into one of three categories: studies of mass voting behavior, legislative roll-call analyses, and collective biographies. In their findings, their systematic approach, and their analysis of the social context of politics, these works demonstrate the strengths, but also the weaknesses, of the reorientation of American political history. Because it invokes a broader conception of politics, a full evaluation of this new political history must also consider the extent to which it succeeds in integrating many different elements and in providing a comprehensive portrait of political life. Implicit in this task is the obligation to provide guidelines for future research.

Voting Behavior

The analysis of elections and mass voting behavior owes much to work of V. O. Key.[3] A prolific writer, Key used historical data and developed theories

*Reprinted with permission from *Computers and the Humanities* II, No. 5 (1977): 265–78, Pergamon Press, Ltd.

of electoral behavior that students of politics continue to examine.[4] Most important was his analysis of the nature of electoral change, distinguishing slow, "secular" change from "critical" elections in which there was a sharp and durable realignment within the electorate.[5] This theory has inspired substantial commentary and, as will be discussed later, has become a framework for linking the various elements of a political system. Focusing here on its implications for voting behavior, one can distinguish three major issues: election typologies and classification, the shape and nature of the electorate, and the determinants and patterns of party voting behavior.

The literature on election typologies is of several types. The first is theoretical and involves the construction of election typologies, with some trend towards increasing complexity.[6] Unfortunately, the proliferating number of categories threatens to equal the number of presidential elections being classified. While the aim is to identify the full range of variable combinations, the result is to make analysis and comparison unnecessarily difficult. Consequently, there is fairly common acceptance of a three-part classification: maintaining elections (in which basic patterns remained stable), deviating elections (in which there was a temporary shift), and realigning or critical elections (where there was a sharp and durable change).

More significant and controversial are efforts to classify particular elections and examine Key's definition of "critical" elections.[7] Since he wrote, most authors have come to agree that realignment has occurred not in one election but in a short series—a critical period.[8] Debate continues, however, over the precise boundaries of those periods, which elections were most critical, and the best methods for classifying certain borderline elections such as 1912 and 1964. While there is some dispute concerning the relative importance of the elections in the period 1852 to 1864, even less consensus exists about the contests between 1928 and 1936, largely because of the complex interaction of such factors as prohibition, religion, ethnicity, and the depression.[9] A second problem is the perspective for comparing electoral change in different areas. Analysis on the national level often shows a definite pattern, but, as Walter Burnham notes, further investigation reveals "how complex electoral movement over time becomes when we move to the state level—a complexity which becomes even more humbling when smaller geographical areas of analysis are employed."[10] Thus, studies which focus on particular states or cities do not in themselves establish or disprove the critical nature of a given election. Rather, they provide essential data for constructing a complex model of electoral change in a specific period.

A second aspect of recent election analysis concerns the shape and nature of the electorate. Voter turnout has become an important topic, in part because it is linked with a traditional concern of political historians: evaluating the extent of democracy. In general, the extent of turnout during various periods has been fairly well established.[11] The directions of change are also clear: a decline in the mid-eighteenth century, a rise in the early 1800s, a downward trend after 1896 which was not reversed until 1928, and a gradual reduction since 1960. The reasons for this variation, however, are vigorously debated. Some historians have probed the influence of competition, the frontier, and rural residence.[12] More important is debate over the effects and purpose of legal changes. J. Morgan Kousser demonstrates that Southern voter turnout in the late nineteenth century was reduced primarily by various suffrage restriction laws and for partisan purposes.[13] Walter Burnham, Jerold Rusk, and others disagree about the impact of laws initiating voter registration and the secret ballot. Rusk views these measures as the cause of lower turnout and a growing proportion of split tickets, while Burnham argues that declining party loyalty was more important.

The question is by no means settled. Clearly, legal change was important, and declining party attachment has been characteristic of twentieth-century American politics.[14] A more definite conclusion requires additional specific studies of voting change. One matter that especially needs systematic analysis is corruption, which Rusk and others assert was a cause of high turnout. Similarly in need of investigation is Burnham's contention that socioeconomic changes weakened party loyalty. Historians should also consider the attempts in non-Southern states to duplicate the other restrictive laws passed in the South.[15] Finally, the subject needs to be placed in the social and intellectual context, particularly with regard to attitudes towards political parties.

Most election studies have focused primarily on the patterns and determinants of party voting behavior. Since 1970 systematic studies of voting behavior have mushroomed, covering cities, states and occasionally groups of states, and using data from county, ward, township, and precinct levels. Although historians are beginning to examine other areas and time periods, they have thus far concentrated on the late nineteenth century (especially the 1890s) and the years 1830 to 1860, and the locus has most often been the Midwest or the Mid-Atlantic region. This distribution is explained by many factors, including both the nature of the debate over those time periods and the relative availability of data, and also raises the danger of generalizing about national patterns on the basis of geographically or temporally limited evidence.

An equally significant trend is the rising use of sophisticated statistical techniques.[16] Historians have been shifting from percentages and correlation coefficients to multivariate regression and factor analysis, a gain in distinguishing the relative influence of different factors. One notable use is calculating the effect of changing voter turnout rates on electoral outcomes.[17] Intertwined with this development has been the movement from description to analysis and theory construction.

For many years historians have been trying to develop theories of party identification and voting.[18] Some have taken models based on contemporary evidence and tested them on historical data. This procedure has been less than satisfactory, for such ahistorical efforts tend to ignore important differences between present and past. Basing a model on historical evidence is more difficult, but in recent years considerable progress has been made. In the early 1960s, Lee Benson and

Samuel Hays directed historians to consider the importance of ethnicity and religion in shaping voter preferences, and since then, this ethnocultural model has
been more thoroughly explicated and tested by Richard Jensen, Paul Kleppner,
and Ronald Formisano.[19] The essential elements include an emphasis on religion
as the major voting determinant, a division of religious groups into "liturgicals"
and "pietists" (or other terms suggesting a type of division between doctrine
and emotion), the description of religious-based world views, and the analysis
of other group-related influences such as ethnicity and negative referents. In
addition, there are other studies which emphasize the central importance of religion, ethnicity, or both, but which do not explicitly use the model.[20]

Opposition to the ethnocultural model has taken two forms. First, a series of
monographs, concentrating on Populism and on Southern or Western states, has
emphasized socioeconomic factors.[21] Even so, the studies by Stanley Parsons
and James E. Wright did find ethnicity and religion important during certain
periods. Secondly, several students of political history have offered explicit critiques of the methodology, theological analyses, and causal assumptions which
underlie the ethnocultural model.[22] Because of the important implications of this
criticism, it deserves detailed examination. These critics cite as methodological
errors the use of correlation coefficients, the reliance on ethnically or religiously
homogeneous districts, and the failure to consider turnout or to define clearly
the ethnic or religious proportions in the geographical units being discussed. In
general, while these points reflect the healthy trend toward greater methodological sophistication, and they identify areas of imprecision, they do not by themselves invalidate the ethnocultural approach.[23] Moreover, the charge that this
approach relies on the analysis of homogeneous districts is inaccurate; although
many studies do consider areas containing a relatively high proportion of some
group, yet few of the districts could actually be called homogeneous, and virtually no study ignores the more heterogeneous areas. To evaluate this issue
fully requires some estimates of the degree of heterogeneity in most districts and
communities of a given state or region. To test how appreciably voting behavior
has differed within diverse contexts also requires multivariate studies of areas
with various levels of heterogeneity.

The typology is faulted on several grounds. The critics' argument that liturgical religion was political only when it was on the defensive misinterprets an
important aspect of liturgical theology: the perspective was inherently defensive
and, hence, always politically salient. A more valid objection involves the category of "pietism," for some pietist churches, like the Church of Christ, opposed government coercion on moral issues.[24]

A related issue is church membership: the critics observe that many persons
did not belong to a church. This is perhaps a less serious problem than it might
seem, for many people attended services, often frequently, while others joined
or participated in Bible study groups or Sunday school. Different levels of religious commitment, however, may well have been reflected in political attitudes. It has also been noted that many members were women. In fact, not only
were women a majority of church members (averaging 56.9 percent in 1906),

but their proportion varied considerably by denomination.[25] Consequently, statistical analyses should use figures for male membership only. While a wife's piety might conceivably have influenced her spouse or even reflected his own beliefs to some degree, testing such hypotheses is difficult.

Finally, the critics suggest that religion simply could not have been so important. Instead, they argue, other factors or a combination of them (class, status, local context, tradition, and individual variability) account for the apparent influence of religion and ethnicity. This argument, resting on little more than assertion, simply ignores both the nature of religious belief and the variety of evidence for its importance at many different times in the American past. That voting decisions were influenced by many factors is certainly true, but the question is not whether a unicausal model should be accepted or rejected. Rather, explanations of voting behavior must take into account political socialization, psychological orientation, and social position. Such models, while allowing for multiple causes and exceptions, should outline a general pattern and dominant influences.[26] Most important, they must help the historian recognize and evaluate basic perspectives and world views. These requirements do not at all suggest that voting was always a direct product of basic beliefs. Even if religion was the variable most strongly related to voting behavior, the influence of religion as a system of beliefs must still be distinguished from its role as an organization involved in an individual's socialization. This does argue, however, for sensitivity to the possible influence of beliefs.

In sum, while the ethnocultural model represents an advance over previous descriptions of voting behavior, it is neither universally accepted nor without serious problems.[27] The socioeconomic approach used in the Populist studies certainly has much to commend it. In focusing on the social context and the group-based character of political identification, it helps to illuminate conflicts over economic development and political power. Yet in most of its varieties this approach is flawed by insufficient regard for the possible influence of religion and ethnicity. Moreover, it may be that either Populism or the 1890s were unique. Thus, theories of voting behavior have emerged from infancy into troubled adolescence.

Legislative Roll-Call Voting

The analysis of roll-call voting in legislatures,[28] a traditional concern, was transformed in the mid-1960s when the new political historians began systematically analyzing many roll-calls from the mid-nineteenth century Congresses. They were attempting to discover the strength of party loyalty over sectional issues, and to identify and analyze who among Republican Congressmen could properly be termed "Radicals."[29] There have been subsequent studies of this era, and the technique has also been used for other Congresses, notably those of the Federalist decade, the early nineteenth century, and the Gilded Age.[30] Since Congressional roll-calls are now available in machine-readable form, this trend will no doubt continue. Historians have also recently begun to examine voting in state legislatures, such as colonial Massachusetts, states during the Confederation era, various Northern states in the Jacksonian era, and several Southern and Western states in the late nineteenth century.[31]

Historians have used roll-call analysis to look at several types of questions. First, they have both isolated particular voting blocs, such as Radical Republicans in the 1860s, and clarified factional voting in the late eighteenth century.[32] Second, they have considered whether parties were clearly divided over issues or simply competing electoral machines.[33] Finally, they have uncovered the general pattern of legislative voting within particular periods, especially the level and trends of party voting.[34]

Like historians of mass voting behavior, students of roll-call analysis have turned to computers for both management and analysis of data. Many have used increasingly sophisticated statistical techniques, such as indices of likeness and of cohesion, cluster bloc matrices, Guttman scaling, rank-order polarity scaling, and factor analysis. These methods can greatly improve the identification of patterns. There is also a shift towards using a greater number of roll-calls. Rather than isolating a few key votes, many historians are now looking at virtually all the votes in a given period. This trend does not, however, include even a majority of investigators; most continue to select key votes and analyze them by cross-tabulation or relatively simple indices. This is partly because the complicated work requires considerably more time, a major factor when roll-call analysis is only a secondary concern. Yet reliance on a simpler approach seems also to reflect a skepticism that newer methods can cut through the web of unknown circumstances, accidents, personal connections and the like, to portray legislators' attitudes with accuracy.[35]

A standard criticism of quantitative history is that assumptions shape the results. This is no less true, of course, for traditional studies. Moreover, quantitative history has clearly strengthened the practice of making assumptions explicit. Examining several roll-call analyses, however, serves to reinforce the importance not only of stating, but also of refining the assumptions.

The debate over partisanship in late nineteenth-century Congresses provides an example. Two studies, one of the House and one of the Senate, contended that party voting rose abruptly in the 1890s, especially after 1896.[36] A subsequent review of the Senate concluded that a high level of party voting began in the 1870s and actually declined in the 1890s.[37] An examination of House roll-calls since 1861 presented data showing a similar pattern.[38] The cause of disagreement lies in the definition of "party voting." The first two studies used that term to mean roll-calls in which 90 percent of one party voted against 90 percent of the other party. The second two studies, arguing for continuity of party voting, used a level of 50 percent. Thus, different definitions lead to different conclusions because, in this case, different phenomena are being measured.

A second example of the importance of assumptions is the debate over Congressional voting blocs in the 1860s. Michael Benedict's findings are shaped by a crucial decision: to analyze the performance of only those Congressmen who voted in at least two Congresses.[39] As a result, many individuals were excluded from analysis. In addition, his search for consistent voting and Allan Bogue's interest in fluidity led them in different directions.[40] It is no accident, therefore, that lists of various blocs differ substantially. Such problems are probably not insoluble, nor do the categories reflect merely the caprice of the author. Many different approaches not only can be justified, but are quite valuable. It is, however, worth reemphasizing the vital connection between theory, hypotheses, and conclusions.[41]

Collective Biographies

A major reason for the popularity of a third category of new political history, collective biographies of political groups, is the simplicity of the basic technique—collecting and analyzing information about the activities and characteristics of some group.[42] With a multitude of diverse groups having been covered, studies of legislators are the single most common type,[43] but there are also works on state and county party leaders, local party activists, and ward committeemen;[44] various collections of political appointees, governors, and state and federal judges;[45] as well as studies of local elites and pressure groups.[46]

Collective biography of these communities is very useful, for it submits to systematic investigation questions about the nature of leadership and officeholding, as well as the distribution of privilege and power. Yet despite its beguiling simplicity and promise of important findings, this type of analysis has many hidden problems, the most serious being a general need for context and perspective. The basic profile of virtually *any* political group is somewhat predictable: middle-aged men who, compared with the general population, ranked higher in such categories as education, occupation, wealth, and social standing. The problem is evaluating the information. A notable example is the suggestion some years ago by Alfred Chandler, George Mowry, and Richard Hofstadter that the progressive movement was uniquely middle-class. That notion has been buried by a series of subsequent studies which compared progressive and old guard leaders and discovered that both were middle-class and largely similar.[47]

A second problem for those and other studies is the composition of the group being analyzed. Politicians differed substantially by position (party officer, party activist, elected officer, or appointed officer) and by level (national, state, county, city, township, or ward).[48] Consequently, any analysis (for example, of "party leaders") which combines politicians from several levels and position types runs a serious risk of misinterpreting the aggregate characteristics.[49] Not only will that analysis depend on the proportion of leaders from each group, but comparisons over time and between places will also be affected. Similarly, one must be aware of the possible effects of geographical bias in sources of information. For example, William Barney's useful study of secessionist leaders in 1860 includes a comparison of four groups in five noncontiguous Alabama counties which were anti-Breckenridge and had a high proportion of slaveholders.

Unfortunately, the number of leaders in each group ranged from 47 to 135, and the number of counties in which they were found ranged from one to four. Since the author did not check, it is impossible to know how much the intergroup differences actually stemmed from source bias rather than political or social factors.[50]

The distinction between political recruitment and political career patterns is an important and often neglected one. The former refers to conditions of political mobility, focusing on social structure and characteristics, the latter relates more to political structure.[51] As many authors have argued, we need to know what types of people became politicians, for while their general characteristics may be somewhat predictable, important variations did exist. For instance, Parsons and Clanton discovered that in Nebraska and Kansas an unusually high proportion of Populist legislators were farmers.[52] Also significant is the type and extent of politicians' political experience. First, it is a crucial variable in comparing groups of politicians from different parties or different factions.[53] Second, it is essential for analyzing political career patterns, political mobility, and fundamentally, the nature of the political system. Whether politicians were amateurs or professionals, whether political mobility was rapid or slow, tells much about the distribution and perception of power.

The best collective biographies done thus far have generally been of legislators, for these groups are well defined and relatively large, and substantial information on them is readily available. Since Congress is so important, and since biographical information on all Congressmen serving before 1961 is now machine-readable, we will in the near future undoubtedly learn more about them.[54] State legislatures are especially significant, a study of recent Oregon legislators claims, because that is more commonly the starting point for electoral careers and the stepping stone to higher office.[55] How true this was for most times and states is unknown, for there are still too few studies to permit many generalizations.

Collective biographies have demonstrated the nature of recruitment for various political positions, but still too little is known in a comparative sense about differences between positions, times, and places. As for political career patterns, it is clear that since the late eighteenth century there have been enormous changes in the pattern and tenure of officeholding, suggesting a general shift from amateur to professional politicians.[56] This point is significant, but it requires both additional evidence and some attention to the broader ramification of this transformation.

Political Institutions and Organizations

A fourth and much less developed field involves political institutions and organizations. The most frequently studied institutions are legislative bodies. Here too the interest is an old one, and studies (for example, of the U.S. Congress) have been done for many years. What is different about this recent work is the systematic and quantitative examination of structure and operation.[57] A major boost to the study of legislatures came from the insights in two key essays by Nelson Polsby on the institutionalization of the U.S. House and the growth of its seniority system.[58] Specifically, Polsby discussed the rise and fall of the Speaker's power, the growth of the committee system and seniority, the complexity of Congressional business, the increasing party organization, and the effect of changing tenure levels. Also, he argued that an evaluation of each of these topics showed a marked increase in organizational complexity during the 1890s.

The examination of these ideas has merely begun. Several capable works cover the nature of Congressional leadership since 1900, but leadership in the preceding years needs further systematic study.[59] Similarly, Polsby's probing of seniority and committee chairmen after 1880 needs duplication for earlier Congresses. The committee system as a whole deserves greater attention, as does the membership of individual committees. Their composition in terms of prior committee experience, party affiliation, region, and type of constituency can explain much about political structure and policy decisions.[60] On the state level the paucity of systematic studies is more evident, and still fewer questions have been asked, let alone answered.[61] An additional consideration for state legislatures is the amount of time required and the compensation given. These are essential factors in understanding the desirability or unattractiveness of being a state legislator and, thus, in explaining political career patterns.

While we know little about legislatures, we know even less about other institutions. There are several studies of early nineteenth-century patronage and bureaucracy, but little else. The multitudinous state offices, agencies, and bureaus have largely escaped systematic evaluation. As for courts, our information is skimpy about judges, not to mention procedures, prosecutors, and clerks. Clearly, these areas need substantial investigation.[62]

The study of political organizations has fared little better. In the past, most authors who dealt with parties looked at major public figures, platforms, and elections and thus gave little attention to organization. This neglect is unfortunate, for an understanding of that topic may provide significant insights into the nature of politics.[63] For example, knowing the structure of party positions from the local to the national level, the extent to which they were filled, and the persons who filled them, would yield a better sense of interparty competition and of political participation. Nor should one ignore the variety of political clubs, which might have served either as an aid to the party or as a means of disassociating oneself from it. Attitudes about party organizations have been scrutinized by several authors, producing very useful results, but here too there is more to be done.[64] Thus, while the study of political institutions and organizations offers significant possibilities, they are far from being realized.

Comprehensive Political History

An important characteristic of the new political history, especially in recent years, is the emphasis on a complex analysis of politics, one which integrates the various dimensions of political life. This has not been the aim in every instance, of course, for the investigation of new subjects and the time-consuming problems of data collection have obliged some historians to limit their scope. Yet, the increasing number of studies and the growth of data archives have made a comprehensive approach more feasible.

The concepts of party systems and critical periods provide a framework for relating different political elements, and the analysis of popular voting behavior serves as their primary foundation.[65] Several state studies have linked popular voting behavior with legislative roll-call analysis or collective biography. On the national level Walter Burnham tied a thorough analysis of voting behavior to a study of institutional changes, but he touched only slightly on issues and not at all on voting in Congress.[66]

Legislative voting is a second element of the political system which is often used as the basis for integration, or linkage. Given the availability of data it is not surprising that many studies have considered how a member's voting is influenced by his personal characteristics, such as ethnicity, religion, wealth, and occupation.[67] Another approach, sometimes by the same authors, has focused on the relationship between a legislator's voting and the nature of his constituency.[68] A still more inclusive framework, devised by David Brady, tries to link voting, personal characteristics, constituencies, and the level of organization in the legislature.[69] While these studies of linkage are clearly important, they are not without difficulties. The most serious of these involve the attempt to link constituencies and legislative voting. Too often constituencies are classified on only a few variables and along too simple a scale. Moreover, the assumption that most legislative voting represents a general constituency preference is inaccurate, for the relationship is much more complex. As Ballard Campbell put it: "To establish linkages between the behavior of the elected and their electorate one must clearly delineate the mechanisms connecting the expectations and demands of the constituents with the legislative behavior."[70]

A crucial problem, therefore, for a comprehensive analysis of politics is the development and transmission of issues. One approach has been to focus on critical periods. Many authors have argued that during such times political parties become ideologically polarized and offer distinct alternatives to voters.[71] This pattern has been confirmed by many studies of specific periods and places. Recently, a series of national-level studies covering a long time period have built on each other and attempted to integrate the different political elements. The initial article sought to measure national party conflict. Analyzing party platforms from 1844 to 1968, Benjamin Ginsberg concluded that high levels of party cleavage occurred in 1852, 1896, and 1932.[72] Next, considering the transformation of issues into policy, Ginsberg coded all U.S. statutes from 1789 to 1968 and determined that significant policy changes always came shortly after insurgent forces gained control of the government.[73] Adding another component, Michael King and Lester Seligman demonstrated that in critical periods a much higher proportion of incumbent Congressmen were defeated, and that freshman lawmakers represented a new recruitment pattern and supported new legislation.[74] Finally, David Brady argued that turnover of committee members and a higher degree of party voting are related to the major policy changes immediately following critical periods.[75] Thus, it is contended, significant policy choices have been offered once in a generation, and the electorate, in choosing new representatives and disturbing the status quo, has succeeded in implementing its chosen policies.

Although this model has much to commend it, for it provides a plausible means for linking many features of the political system, it is deficient in several respects. First, on empirical grounds, the link between and classification of elections, platforms, and statutes is inadequate. The temporal patterns for each variable do not coincide well enough, with major discrepancies for the periods of 1800 to 1805 and 1852 to 1861, and confusion about 1874 to 1880. Furthermore, the classification of certain elections is dubious, particularly the judgment that 1828 was a defeat for "insurgents." It was, after all, President Adams who lost in that year. Second, the platform analysis ignores the changing roles of platforms themselves, especially in terms of their intended audience, such as party workers, party voters, or the general public. Third, since the platform analysis deals with only two parties, it obscures the conflict in elections with important third (or fourth) parties. Given the significant role of these parties (especially in the 1850s, the 1890s, 1912, 1924, and 1948), this is a damaging omission.

The most serious deficiency, however, is in failing to consider the conclusions of voting studies: that for many places and times religion and ethnicity were the main determinants of voting behavior, that moral and "cultural" issues were often most salient, and that frequently economic issues were only of symbolic importance. The problem with this model, then, is the one raised earlier: the development and transmission of issues.[76] Although moral and cultural issues were more prominent on local and state levels, they were also important nationally, as shown by debates over prohibition, marriage and divorce laws, and sexual purity.[77] Equally significant is the perspective through which issues were viewed. Woman suffrage, for example, was probably considered more often in terms of religious and cultural values than as a secular "democratic" issue.[78] Even economic questions like the monetary standard were perceived in moral terms.[79] As a culminating example, note only a few of the many ways to classify the issue of slavery: moral, legal, or economic.

Attempts to link various political elements have thus far had mixed success. The important possibilities for linking popular voting behavior, institutional change, legislative voting, and legislator characteristics have been adequately demonstrated. The relationship of Congressional recruitment to elections, Congressional voting, and institutional change is clear, though parallel studies are needed on state and local levels. Analysis of issues, however, requires a more thorough, systematic, and complex approach that includes party pronouncements, public debate, and roll-call votes. In addition, this analysis must dispense with a single factor emphasis on economic perspectives and issues. Finally, a more difficult problem is to define the role of leaders in transmitting issues to and from the voters. One concept which might improve the analysis of issues is that of different "publics," as, for example, a "foreign policy public" posited by Ernest R. May.[80] A second and very useful concept is Samuel Hays's community-society continuum, distinguishing different types of relationships "ranging from personal, community, face-to-face contacts on the one hand, to impersonal, mass relationships in the wider society on the other."[81] Taken together, these notions may help to isolate and identify specific voter-leader connections.

The context in which different political elements interact has received considerably more attention since the mid-1960s when Samuel Hays called for a "social analysis of American political life."[82] Political studies now commonly consider social conditions or structure. The concept of modernization, which has recently presented tantalizing possibilities for linking all aspects of American development, has been used frequently by social historians. A rising number of challenges to this theory, however, suggest that it posits an ahistorical dichotomy between traditional and modern. Others have responded that although it may not be predictive or applicable to all societies, the theory does "encompass the parameters of Western change with which the American historian is primarily concerned."[83] The debate is certainly not over, for whether the concept becomes a "catchword whose incantation magically resolves the problem by failing to confront it" or a usable paradigm depends in large measure on work still to be done.[84]

More acceptable for analyzing political life and linking it to society may be the concept of "political culture." As initially defined by Gabriel Almond and Sidney Verba, this term "refers to the specifically political orientations—attitudes toward the political system and its various parts, and attitudes toward the role of the self in the system."[85] This includes ideas about the nature of politics and government, about the proper role of government, about who should participate in government, from voting to officeholding, and about organizations such as political parties. Several different typologies of political culture (or, in cases, subculture) have been developed. Although these typologies agree on the existence of one type—an essentially "traditional" or "premodern" culture—their other categories are unique.[86] American political historians have the data and opportunity to refine these categories. Such an effort would clarify the relationship of politics and society, for though political culture and social culture are distinct, they are also complementary. Also, it could provide a framework for integrating different components of the political system and a better means of comparing different patterns of politics. Moreover, this concept would aid in defining more clearly the areas in need of research.

Another Phase

By introducing new methods, concepts, and approaches, the new political history has thus moved beyond the old. The new political historians have examined in detail popular voting behavior, legislative voting and organization, and the composition of political elites. They have also begun to integrate the findings of these studies into explanations of the political process and more general analyses of American society.

More, however, remains to be done. The most glaring omission in the writing of new political history concerns local politics. This topic has received some attention, but given the importance of the questions, the variety of settings, and the availability of data, far too little. This is true not simply of large cities, but even more of towns and villages, which have been less often considered. In particular, we need to know more about the nature of local political conflict, about the distribution of political power, and about political participation broadly conceived.

We are most familiar with local voting behavior, for in addition to state and regional studies which discuss county or township voting, there are articles on local voting behavior. Less is known in a systematic and general sense about the nature of local conflict over issues, particularly local issues, and their influence on political activity.[87] While manuscript sources may not be available, newspapers often are, and for many areas there exists a wealth of local referenda data on such proposals as taxation for schools and bridges, or the granting of liquor licenses. A similar source is local voting returns on state referenda.[88]

The distribution of political power holds similar significance. What was the social and economic status of local officials; how long did they hold power; what changes occurred over time? Analyzing officeholders is the first, but not the only step in this investigation, for non-officeholders can be equally or more influential.[89] It is necessary, therefore, in a broad examination of the social and economic context, to consider voluntary associations such as social, fraternal, and local improvement organizations, as well as economic interest groups.[90] At this point the similarity to the community studies of social historians is apparent, suggesting the fruitful possibilities of cooperation with them. Furthermore, in learning from these historians, it would be desirable for political historians to initiate parallel studies similar to the Five Cities Project.[91]

The study of local politics is also necessary to illuminate the relationships between politics on different levels: national, state, and local (even ward, township, and county). This approach is essential in order to develop, among other strengths, a complete perspective on recruitment and career patterns. To view these matters from only a state or national level makes it impossible to describe the overall character of these patterns. Did politicians proceed up a ladder of advancement from local to state, and then to federal office? Or was there a circular pattern in which state or national politicians later held local office? Or, to mention one more possibility, were politicians periodically called out of retirement to aid their party's fight for certain offices? Some verification can be found for each of these patterns; the issue, however, is which one predominated, where, and when.

Another aspect of recruitment and career patterns which needs investigation is the role of lawyers. Their political prominence is well known, but the extent of their presence in legislative bodies is worth noting. In every decade since 1810 they have comprised between 50 and 67 percent of all U.S. Representatives, and while their strength in state legislatures was lower (ranging, it seems, between 10 and 50 percent), this too is far out of proportion to their share of the population.[92] Studies of contemporary lawyer-politicians have suggested various reasons: flexible schedules, political and legal skills, political orientation, and monopolization of law enforcement offices.[93] While all of these explanations seem plausible, we know too little about the historical relationship between lawyers and politics to evaluate their significance properly.[94] Here is another instance of a social-political study which would greatly expand our knowledge of the political system.

A final political element that needs special work on the local level is participation.[95] We already know something about voter turnout, although its variation over all the different types of elections is less clear. What still has not been studied systematically is other modes of participation. For example, at a given time, what proportion of a community either had political experience or was holding office? What proportion of the population became involved in political campaigns? This latter question is admittedly difficult to answer at all, let alone with any precision. However, historians have not yet tried to give an answer, and, given their past record of ingenuity, surely some usable methods can be devised. As further encouragement for this effort, one should note its importance, for the nature and extent of campaigns and party activity provide an important indication of political culture.[96] It is necessary, of course, to avoid seeing America through the eyes of one small town, yet without careful analyses on the local level, historians cannot reach their goal of a systematic, comprehensive analysis of American politics.

Notes

1. See, for example, Harry S. Stout, "Culture, Structure, and the 'New' History: A Critique and an Agenda," *Computers and the Humanities* 9 (July 1975): 213–30; Robert P. Swierenga, "Computers and American History: The Impact of the 'New' Generation," *Journal of American History* 60 (March 1974): 1045–70; Swierenga, "Computers and Comparative History," *Journal of Interdisciplinary History* 5 (Autumn 1974): 267–88; Richard Jensen, "Quantitative American Studies: The State of the Art," *American Quarterly* 26 (August 1974): 225–40; Joel H. Silbey, "Clio and Computers: Moving into Phase II, 1970–1972," *Computers and the Humanities* 7 (November 1972): 67–79; and Allan G. Bogue, "United States: The 'New' Political History," *Journal of Contemporary History* 3 (January 1968): 5–27.

2. To cite only two of the responses, see Herbert G. Gutman, *Slavery and the Numbers Game: A Critique of "Time on the Cross"* (Urbana, Ill., 1975); and Paul David et al., *Reckoning with Slavery: A Critical Study in the Quantitative History of American Negro Slavery* (New York, 1976).

3. Richard Jensen ably summarizes the development of election analysis from the nineteenth century to the 1940s in "American Election Analysis: A Case History of Methodological Innovation and Diffusion," in Seymour Martin Lipset, ed., *Politics and the Social Sciences* (New York, 1969), pp. 226–43.

4. See, for example, J. Morgan Kousser, "Post-Reconstruction Suffrage Restriction in Tennessee: A New Look at the V. O. Key Thesis," *Political Science Quarterly* 88 (December 1973): 655–83; Margaret Thompson Echols and Austin Ranney, "The Impact of Interparty Competition Reconsidered: The Case of Florida," *Journal of Politics* 38 (February 1976): 142–52; and Raymond Tatalovich, " 'Friends and Neighbors' Voting: Mississippi," *Journal of Politics* 37 (August 1975): 807–14.

5. "A Theory of Critical Elections," *Journal of Politics* 17 (February 1955): 3–18; "Secular Realignment and the Party System," ibid., 21 (May 1959); 198–210; and Key and Frank Munger, "Social Determinism and Electoral Decision: The Case of Indiana," in Eugene Burdick and Arthur J. Brodbeck, eds., *American Voting Behavior* (Glencoe, Ill., 1959), pp. 281–99.

6. William L. Shade proposes three general types and a total of seven subtypes in *Social Change and the Electoral Process*, University of Florida Social Science Monograph No. 49 (Gainesville, 1973). Essays outlining other typologies are reprinted in Jerome M. Clubb and Howard W. Allen, eds., *Electoral Change and Stability in American Political History* (New York, 1971).

7. Some analyses have simply ignored the conflict, sometimes substituting the word "crucial." See, for example, *Crucial American Elections*, Memoirs of the American Philosophical Society, vol. 99 (Philadelphia, 1973).

8. This point was made initially in a 1960 article by Duncan MacRae, Jr., and James A. Meldrum on "Critical Elections in Illinois, 1888–1958," which, along with other related works, is in Clubb and Allen, eds., *Electoral Change*. For a fuller view see Walter Dean Burnham, *Critical Elections and the Mainsprings of American Politics* (New York, 1970) and James L. Sundquist, *Dynamics of the Party System* (Washington, D.C., 1973).

9. For the latter period consult Bernard Sternsher's fine summary of recent literature: "The Emergence of the New Deal Party System: A Problem in Historical Analysis of Voter Behavior," *Journal of Interdisciplinary History* 6 (Summer 1975): 127–49. Also see Allan J. Lichtman, "Critical Election Theory and the Reality of American Presidential Politics, 1916–1940," *American Historical Review* 81 (April 1975): 79–117. On the earlier period see Burnham, *Critical Elections*, pp. 14–17, 36–38; Sundquist, *Party System*, pp. 63–91; David E. Meerse, "The Northern Democratic Party and the Congressional Elections of 1858," *Civil War History* 19 (June 1973): 119–27; and Gerald M. Pomper, *Elections in America: Control and Influence in Democratic Politics* (New York, 1968), pp. 113–14.

10. *Critical Elections*, p. 24. Sternsher discusses the studies which suggest different timing for the 1928–1936 period in "New Deal Party System." Ray M. Shortridge shows two different state patterns in "The Voter Realignment in the Midwest in the 1850s," *American Politics Quarterly* 4 (April 1976): 193–222.

11. Katherine Brown, a lone dissenter, summarizes in terms of her dissent the consensus on the seventeenth century in "The Controversy over the Franchise in Puritan Massachusetts, 1954 to 1974," *William and Mary Quarterly* 33 (April 1976): 212–41. For later periods see Chilton Williamson, *American Suffrage from Property to Democracy, 1760–1860* (Princeton, N.J., 1960); Richard P. McCormick, *The Second American Party System: Party Formation in the Jacksonian Era* (Chapel Hill, N.C., 1966); and Burnham, *Critical Elections*.

12. Ray Myles Shortridge, "An Assessment of the Frontier's Influence on Voter Turnout," *Agricultural History* 50 (July 1976): 445–59, concludes that turnout was not higher on the frontier between 1840 and 1870. Warren E. Stickle argues that in the 1960s turnout was higher among Indiana ruralites than among urban dwellers: "Ruralite and Farmer in Indiana: Independent, Sporadic Voter and Country Bumpkin?" *Agricultural History* 48 (October 1974): 543–70. C. Richard Hofstadter argues the positive effect of competition on turnout in "Inter-Party Competition and Electoral Turnout: The Case of Indiana," *American Journal of Political Science* 17 (May 1973): 351–66, while Virginia Gray disagrees with that theory in "A Note on Competition and Turnout in the American States," *Journal of Politics* 38 (February 1976): 153–58.

13. *The Shaping of Southern Politics: Suffrage Restrictions and the Establishment of the One-Party South, 1880–1910* (New Haven, Conn., 1974).

14. The most recent statements are Burnham, "Theory and Voting Research: Some Reflections on Converse's 'Change in the American Electorate,' " *American Political Science Review* 68 (September 1974): 1002–23, plus the comments by Rusk and Philip Converse, pp. 1024–49, and Burnham's "Rejoinder," pp. 1050–57. Also consult William H. Flanigan, *Political Behavior of the American Electorate* (2nd ed., Boston, 1972); Walter DeVries and V. Lance Tarrance, *The Ticket-Splitter: A New Force in American Politics* (Grand Rapids, Mich., 1972); Paul R. Abramson, "Generational Change and the Decline of Party Identification in America: 1952–1974," *American Political Science Review* 70 (June 1976): 469–78; and Milton C. Cummings, *Congressmen and the Electorate: Elections for the U.S. House and the President, 1920–1964* (Glencoe, Ill., 1966).

15. In Indiana, for example, literacy and poll tax laws were considered several times, and a poll tax was passed in 1911, only to be voided by the state Supreme Court. Charles Kettleborough, *Constitution Making in Indiana, vol. 2: 1851–1916* (Indianapolis, 1916), pp. 365–370, 387–397.

16. Pleas for greater sophistication have come from Walter Dean Burnham, "Quantitative History: Beyond the Correlation Coefficient: A Review Essay," *Historical Methods Newsletter* 4 (March 1971): 62–66; and J. Morgan Kousser, "The 'New Political History': A Methodological Critique," *Reviews in American History* 4 (March 1976): 1–14.

17. See, for example, Roger L. Hart, *Redeemers, Bourbons & Populists: Tennessee, 1870–1896* (Baton Rouge, La., 1975); and William G. Shade, *Banks and No Banks: The Money Issue in Western Politics, 1832–1865* (Detroit, 1972). Two studies which calculate turnout are Kousser, *Shaping of Southern Politics*, and Kevin Sweeney, "Rum, Romanism, Representation, and Reform: Coalition Politics in Massachusetts, 1847–1853," *Civil War History* 22 (June 1976): 116–37. Also consult the series of articles on the uses of regression analysis appearing in *Journal of Interdisciplinary History* 4 (1973–1974).

18. For an excellent essay on developing a voting behavior model see J. Rogers Hollingsworth, "Problems in the Study of Popular Voting Behavior," in Lee Benson et al., *American Political Behavior: Essays and Readings* (New York, 1974), pp. 1–24.

19. Lee Benson, *The Concept of Jacksonian Democracy: New York as a Test Case* (Princeton, N.J., 1961); Samuel P. Hays, "The Social Analysis of American Political History, 1880–1920," *Political Science Quarterly* 80 (September 1965): 373–94; Paul Kleppner, *The Cross of Culture: A Social Analysis of Midwestern Politics, 1850–1900* (New York, 1970); Richard J. Jensen, *The Winning of the Midwest: Social and Political Conflict, 1888–96* (Chicago, 1971); Ronald P. Formisano, *The Birth of Mass Political Parties: Michigan, 1827–1861* (Princeton, N.J., 1971). Two essays which survey the growth and findings of ethnocultural histories are Robert P. Swierenga, "Ethnocultural Political Analysis: A New Approach to American Ethnic Studies," *Journal of American Studies* 5 (April 1971): 59–79; and Samuel T. McSeveney, "Ethnic Groups, Ethnic Conflicts, and Recent Quantitative Research in American Political History," *International Migration Review* 7 (Spring 1973): 14–33.

20. One study showing special sensitivity to religion is Frederick C. Luebke, *Bonds of Loyalty: German-Americans and World War I* (Dekalb, Ill., 1974). Other works include John L. Shover, "Ethnicity and Religion in Philadelphia Politics, 1924–1940," *American Quarterly* 25 (December 1973): 499–515; Roger E. Wyman, "Middle-Class Voters and Progressive Reform: The Conflict of Class and Culture," *American Political Science Review* 68 (June 1974): 488–504; D. L. A. Hackett, "Slavery, Ethnicity, and Sugar: An Analysis of Voting Behavior in Louisiana, 1828–1844," *Louisiana Studies* 13 (Summer 1974): 73–118; and Michael Holt, *Forging a Majority: The Formation of the Republican Party in Pittsburgh, 1848–1860* (New Haven, Conn., 1969).

21. Hart, *Redeemers*; Kousser, *Shaping of Southern Politics*; Peter H. Argersinger, *Populism and Politics: William Alfred Peffer and the People's Party* (Lexington, Ky., 1974); James Edward Wright, *The Politics of Populism: Dissent in Colorado* (New Haven, Conn., 1974); and Stanley B. Parsons, *The Populist Context: Rural Versus Urban Power on a Great Plains Frontier* (Westport, Conn., 1973).

22. Richard L. McCormick, "Ethno-Cultural Interpretations of Nineteenth-Century American Voting Behavior," *Political Science Quarterly* 89 (June 1974): 351–78; James E. Wright, "The

Ethnocultural Model of Voting," in Allan G. Bogue, ed., *Emerging Theoretical Models in Social and Political History* (Beverly Hills, Calif., 1973), pp. 35–56; and Kousser, "New Political History." Also see Eric Foner's indignant criticism in "The Causes of the Civil War: Recent Interpretations and New Directions," *Civil War History* 20 (September 1974): 197–214.

23. See, for example, Richard Jensen, "Aggregate Versus Survey Data: The Psephologist's Puzzle," paper presented to the Social Science History Association, Philadelphia, 30 October 1976. Paul Kleppner, in "Beyond the 'New Political History': A Review Essay," *Historical Methods Newsletter* 6 (December 1972): 17–26, defends the use of homogeneous units and correlation coefficients, but also presents his own methodological criticisms.

24. The defensive nature of liturgicals is shown for Missouri Synod Lutherans by Heinrich H. Maurer, "Studies in the Sociology of Religion, V: The Fellowship Law of a Fundamentalist Group; The Missouri Synod," *American Journal of Sociology* 31 (July 1925): 39–57. For the Church of Christ see David Edwin Harrell, Jr., *A Social History of the Disciples of Christ*, vol 2: *The Social Sources of Division in the Disciples of Christ, 1865–1900* (Atlanta, 1973), especially p. 226.

25. For a summary, consult the discussion of and data from the *Census of Religious Bodies: 1906* contained in H. K. Carroll, *The Religious Forces of the United States*, rev. ed. (New York, 1912), pp. lvi–lix.

26. One such effort, which also supports the primary importance of religion and ethnicity, is Kevin Clancy and Lee Benson, "America the Fragmented: An Exploration of the Effects of Class, Ethnicity and Religion on Political and Social Attitudes and Behavior," paper presented to the Social Science History Association, Philadelphia, 30 October 1976.

27. My own attempt to deal with some of these problems is "A Social Analysis of Indiana Politics and Politicians, 1896–1920" (Ph.D. dissertation, University of Illinois, 1976).

28. Actually, the broader term for this category is "collegial bodies," which also includes roll-call voting in conventions and courts. Since the number of such studies is relatively small, however, this discussion will not deal specifically with them. For examples, see John D. Sprague, *Voting Patterns of the United States Supreme Court: Cases in Federalism, 1889–1959* (Indianapolis, 1968); and Frank Munger and James Blackhurst, "Factionalism in the National Conventions, 1940–1964: An Analysis of Ideological Consistency in State Delegation Voting," *Journal of Politics* 27 (May 1965): 375–94.

29. This included Joel H. Silbey, *The Shrine of Party: Congressional Voting Behavior, 1840–1852* (Pittsburgh, 1967), David Donald, *The Politics of Reconstruction, 1863–1867* (Baton Rouge, La., 1965); Allan G. Bogue, "Block and Party in the United States Senate: 1861–1863," *Civil War History* 13 (September 1967): 221–41; and Thomas B. Alexander, *Sectional Stress and Party Strength: A Study of Roll-Call Voting Returns in the United States House of Representatives, 1836–1860* (Nashville, Tenn., 1967).

30. Such studies are: Michael Les Benedict, *A Compromise of Principle: Congressional Republicans and Reconstruction, 1863–1869* (New York, 1974); Gerald William Wolff, "A Scalogram Analysis of the Kansas-Nebraska Bill of 1854 and Related Roll Calls," *Computers and the Humanities* 8 (March 1974); 71–83; Rudolph M. Bell, *Party and Faction in American Politics: The House of Representatives, 1789–1801* (Westport, Conn., 1973); Ronald J. Hatzenbuehler, "Party Unity and the Decision for War in the House of Representatives, 1812," *William and Mary Quarterly* 29 (July 1972): 367–90; Allan G. Bogue and Mark Paul Marlaire, "Of Mess and Men: The Boarding House and Congressional Voting, 1821–1842," *American Journal of Political Science* 19 (May 1975): 207–30; William G. Shade et al., "Partisanship in the United States Senate: 1869–1901," *Journal of Interdisciplinary History* 4 (Autumn 1973): 185–206; David W. Brady, *Congressional Voting in a Partisan Era: A Study of the McKinley Houses and a Comparison to the Modern House of Representatives* (Lawrence, Kans., 1973); in addition, Jerome M. Clubb and Santa Traugott, "Partisan Cleavage and Cohesion in the House of Representatives, 1861–1974," *Journal of Interdisciplinary History* 7 (Winter 1977): 375–402.

31. Robert Zemsky, *Merchants, Farmers, and River Gods: An Essay on Eighteenth-Century American Politics* (Boston, 1971); Jackson Turner Main, *Political Parties Before the Constitution* (Chapel Hill, N.C., 1973); Herbert Ershkowitz and William G. Shade, "Consensus or Conflict? Political Behavior in the State Legislature During the Jacksonian Era," *Journal of American History*

58 (December 1971): 591–621; Rodney O. Davis, "Partisanship in Jacksonian State Politics: Party Divisions in the Illinois Legislature, 1834–1841," in Robert P. Swierenga, ed., *Quantification in American History: Theory and Research* (New York, 1970), pp. 149–62; Wright, *Politics of Populism;* Hart, *Redeemers;* and Parsons, *Populist Context.*

32. Glenn M. Linden, " 'Radicals' and Economic Policies: The Senate, 1861–1873," *Journal of Southern History* 32 (May 1966): 189–99; Bogue, "Radical Voting Dimension"; Benedict, *Compromise of Principle;* H. James Henderson, *Party Politics in the Continental Congress* (New York, 1974); Mary P. Ryan, "Party Formation in the United States Congress, 1789 to 1796: A Quantitative Analysis," *William and Mary Quarterly* 28 (October 1971): 523–42; Bell, *Party and Faction;* and Main, *Political Parties.*

33. For example, Ershkowitz and Shade, "Consensus or Conflict?"; and Wright, *Politics of Populism;* Peter Levine, "State Legislative Parties in the Jacksonian Era: New Jersey, 1829–1844," *Journal of American History* 62 (December 1975): 591–608 attempts to show that both arguments were valid.

34. For example, Silbey, *Shrine of Party;* Shade et al., "Partisanship in the Senate"; and Clubb and Traugott, "Partisan Cleavage and Cohesion in the House."

35. See, for example, the general critique and especially the comments on Guttman scaling by Robert Zemsky in "American Legislative Behavior," in Bogue, ed., *Emerging Theoretical Models,* pp. 57–76. Compare this with Allan G. Bogue's defense and use of Guttman scaling in "The Radical Voting Dimension in the U.S. Senate During the Civil War," *Journal of Interdisciplinary History* 3 (Winter 1973): 449–74. A very useful methodological critique of several recent works is Ballard Campbell, "The State Legislature in American History: A Review Essay," *Historical Methods Newsletter* 9 (September 1976): 185–94.

36. David J. Rothman, *Politics and Power: The United States Senate, 1869–1901* (Cambridge, Mass., 1966); and David W. Brady and Phillip Althoff, "Party Voting in the U.S. House of Representatives, 1890–1910: Elements of a Responsible Party System," *Journal of Politics* 36 (August 1974): 753–75.

37. Shade et. al., "Partisanship in the Senate."

38. Clubb and Traugott, "Partisan Cleavage and Cohesion in the House."

39. *Compromise of Principle,* p. 26.

40. See Bogue's "Radical Voting Dimension."

41. See Campbell's suggestion of four criteria for evaluating roll-call analyses in "State Legislature," p. 186.

42. It is also an old technique. One of the first such studies was Charles Beard's *An Economic Interpretation of the Constitution* (New York, 1913). Cf. Richard D. Brown, "The Founding Fathers of 1776 and 1787: A Collective View," *William and Mary Quarterly* 33 (July 1976): 465–80. See also Lewis J. Edinger and Donald D. Searing, "Social Background in Elite Analysis: A Methodological Inquiry," *American Political Science Review* 61 (June 1967): 428–45.

43. See, for example, Allan G. Bogue et al., "Members of the House of Representatives and the Process of Modernization, 1789–1960," *Journal of American History* 63 (September 1976): 275–302; Ballard Crooker Campbell, "Ethnicity and the 1893 Wisconsin Assembly," *Journal of American History* 62 (June 1975): 74–94; Thomas Alexander and Richard E. Beringer, *The Anatomy of the Confederate Congress: A Study of the Influences of Member Characteristics on Legislative Voting Behavior 1861–1865* (Nashville, Tenn., 1972); Main, *Political Parties;* and Rothman, *Politics and Power.*

44. William L. Barney, *The Secessionist Impulse: Alabama and Mississippi in 1860* (Princeton, N.J., 1974); Jean H. Baker, *The Politics of Continuity: Maryland Political Parties from 1858 to 1870* (Baltimore, 1973); Robert Sherman Laforte, *Leaders of Reform: Progressive Republicans in Kansas, 1900–1916* (Lawrence, Kans., 1974); and Bruce M. Stave, *The New Deal and the Last Hurrah: Pittsburgh Machine Politics* (Pittsburgh, 1970).

45. Leonard Tabachnik, "Political Patronage and Ethnic Groups: Foreign-born in the United States Customhouse Service, 1821–1861," *Civil War History* 17 (September 1971): 222–31; Kenneth Prewitt and William McAllister, "Changes in the American Executive Elite—1930–1970," in

Heinz Eulau and Moshe M. Czudnowski, eds., *Elite Recruitment in Democratic Politics: Comparative Studies Across Nations* (New York, 1976); Ralph A. Wooster, *Politicians, Planters and Plain Folk: Courthouse and Statehouse in the Upper South, 1850–1860* (Knoxville, Tenn., 1975); and Kermit L. Hall, "Social Backgrounds and Judicial Recruitment: A Nineteenth Century Perspective on the Lower Federal Judiciary," *Western Political Quarterly* 29 (June 1976): 243-57.

46. Edward M. Cook, Jr., *The Fathers of the Towns: Leadership and Community Structure in Eighteenth-Century New England* (Baltimore, 1976); Gerald W. McFarland, *Mugwumps, Morals, and Politics, 1884–1920* (Amherst, Mass., 1975); and Hart, *Redeemers*.

47. To mention only two: William T. Kerr, Jr., "The Progressives of Washington, 1910–12," *Pacific Northwest Quarterly* 55 (January 1964): 16–27; and E. Daniel Potts, "The Progressive Profile in Iowa," *Mid-America* 47 (October 1965): 257–68.

48. See Malcolm E. Jewell and Samuel C. Patterson, *The Legislative Process in the United States* (New York, 1966), pp. 101–22. Richard G. Miller provides a useful table showing the rise of mean wealth for both Republican and Federalist candidates over a range of office categories. *Philadelphia—The Federalist City: A Study of Urban Politics, 1789–1801* (Port Washington, N.Y., 1976), p. 18.

49. For examples of such an error see Laforte, *Leaders of Reform;* Baker, *Politics of Continuity;* and O. Gene Clanton, *Kansas Populism: Ideas and Men* (Lawrence, Kans., 1969).

50. Barney, *Secessionist Impulse,* p. 70; also pp. 65–76.

51. Heinz Eulau et al., "Career Perspectives of American State Legislators," in Dwaine Marvick, ed., *Political Decision Makers,* International Yearbook of Political Behavior Research, Vol. 2 (New York, 1961), pp. 219–20, 259. Also, see Eulau and Czudnowski, eds., *Elite Recruitment;* and Lester G. Seligman et al., *Patterns of Recruitment: A State Chooses Its Lawmakers* (Chicago, 1974).

52. Parsons, *Populist Context;* and Clanton, *Kansas Populism.*

53. Considerations of this factor would have been very useful for Barney, *Secessionist Impulse,* passim; and Hart, *Redeemers,* pp. 125–31.

54. Bogue et al., "Members of the House," is based on this data collection. See also Rothman, *Politics and Power;* James Sterling Young, *The Washington Community, 1800–1828* (New York, 1966); and Donald R. Matthews, *U.S. Senators and Their World* (Chapel Hill, N.C., 1960).

55. Seligman et al., *Patterns of Recruitment,* p. 5. Also consult Chong Lim Kim, Justin Green, and Samuel C. Patterson, "Partisanship in the Recruitment and Performance of American State Legislators," in Eulau and Czudnowski, eds., *Elite Recruitment,* pp. 79–104, which cites much of the relevant literature.

56. See Jewell and Patterson, *Legislative Process,* pp. 118–21; David Ray, "Voluntary Retirement and Electoral Defeat in Eight State Legislatures," *Journal of Politics* 38 (May 1976): 426–33; David Ray, "Membership Stability in Three State Legislatures: 1893–1969," *American Political Science Review* 68 (March 1974): 106–12; and James B. Kessler, ed., *Empirical Studies of Indiana Politics: Studies of Legislative Behavior* (Bloomington, Ind., 1970). For the U.S. Congress, see the sources in note 54, as well as Nelson W. Polsby, "The Institutionalization of the U.S. House of Representatives," *American Political Science Review* 62 (March 1968): 144–68.

57. For example, George B. Galloway, *History of the House of Representatives* (New York, 1962); and George Haynes, *The Senate of the United States, Its History and Practice,* 2 vols. (Boston, 1928).

58. Polsby, "Institutionalization of the U.S. House"; and Nelson W. Polsby, Miriam Gallaher, and Barry Spencer Rundquit, "The Growth of the Seniority System in the U.S. House of Representatives," *American Political Science Review* 63 (September 1969): 787–807.

59. For example, see Charles O. Jones, *The Minority Party in Congress* (Boston, 1970); and Randall B. Ripley, *Majority Party Leadership in Congress* (Boston, 1969).

60. Some of these factors are considered by David W. Brady, "Congressional Leadership and Party Voting in the McKinley Era: Comparison to the Modern House," *Midwest Journal of Political Science* 16 (August 1972): 439–59; Brady, *Congressional Voting;* and Brady and Althoff, "Party Voting in the U.S. House."

61. One exception is Zemsky, *Merchants, Farmers, and River Gods,* a good study of the colonial Massachusetts legislature. See also Douglas C. Chaffey, "The Institutionalization of State Legislatures: A Comparative Study," *Western Political Quarterly* 23 (March 1970): 180–196.

62. For studies of bureaucracy consult Sidney H. Aronson, *Status and Kinship in the Higher Civil Service; Standards of Selection in the Administrations of John Adams, Thomas Jefferson, and Andrew Jackson* (Cambridge, Mass., 1964); Matthew A. Crenson, *The Federal Machine: Beginnings of Bureaucracy in Jacksonian America* (Baltimore, 1975); and Paul H. Bergeron, "Politics and Patronage in Tennessee During the Adams and Jackson Years," *Prologue* 2 (Spring 1970): 19–24. For courts see Hall, "Social Backgrounds and Judicial Recruitment"; and Larry L. Berg et al., "The Consequences of Judicial Reform: A Comparative Analysis of the California and Iowa Appellate Systems," *Western Political Quarterly* 28 (June 1975): 263–80.

63. See William Nisbet Chambers and Walter Dean Burnham, eds., *The American Party Systems: Stages of Political Development,* 2nd ed. (New York, 1975); Frank J. Sorauf, *Party Politics in America,* 2nd ed. (Boston, 1972); Ronald P. Formisano, "Deferential-Participant Politics: The Early Republic's Political Culture, 1789–1840," *American Political Science Review* 68 (June 1974): 473–87; David Hackett Fischer, *The Revolution of American Conservatism: The Federalist Party in the Era of Jeffersonian Democracy* (New York, 1965); and Robert D. Marcus, *Grand Old Party: Political Structure in the Gilded Age, 1880–1896* (New York, 1971).

64. See Jensen, *Winning of the Midwest;* Kleppner, *Cross of Culture;* and Ronald P. Formisano, "Political Character, Antipartyism and the Second Party System," *American Quarterly* 21 (Winter 1969): 683–709.

65. Chambers and Burnham, eds., *American Party Systems;* Burnham, *Critical Elections;* Sundquist, *Party System;* Formisano, "Deferential-Participant Politics"; Ronald P. Formisano, "Toward a Reorientation of Jacksonian Politics: A Review of Literature, 1959–1975," *Journal of American History* 63 (June 1976): 42–65; and Sternsher, "New Deal Party System."

66. *Critical Elections.*

67. For example, Campbell, "Ethnicity and the 1893 Wisconsin Assembly"; Alexander and Beringer, *Confederate Congress;* Main, *Political Parties;* and Parsons, *Populist Context.*

68. Alexander and Beringer, *Confederate Congress;* Main, *Political Parties;* Sheldon Hackney, *Populism to Progressivism in Alabama* (Princeton, 1969); Barbara Sinclair Deckard, "Electoral Marginality and Party Loyalty in House Roll Call Voting," *American Journal of Political Science* 20 (August 1976): 469–81; and Owen S. Ireland, "Germans Against Abolition: A Minority's View of Slavery in Revolutionary Pennsylvania," *Journal of Interdisciplinary History* 3 (Spring 1973): 685–706.

69. *Congressional Voting;* Brady and Althoff, "Party Voting in the U.S. House."

70. Campbell, "State Legislature," p. 189. As an example of the use of this false assumption see John D. Buenker, *Urban Liberalism and Progressive Reform* (New York, 1974).

71. For example, Burnham, *Critical Elections,* pp. 7–10.

72. "Critical Elections and the Substance of Party Conflict: 1844–1968," *Midwest Journal of Political Science* 16 (November 1972): 603–25.

73. "Elections and Public Policy," *American Political Science Review* 70 (March 1976): 41–49.

74. Michael R. King and Lester G. Seligman, "Critical Elections, Congressional Recruitment and Public Policy," in Eulau and Czudnowski, eds., *Elite Recruitment,* pp. 263–99.

75. David W. Brady, "Congressional Policy Responses to Issue and Elections: A Time Series Analysis," paper presented to the Social Science History Association Convention, Philadelphia, 30 October 1976. Another study which shows the important relationship between committee membership and policy output is John A. Ferejohn, *Pork Barrel Politics: Rivers and Harbours Legislation, 1947–1968* (Stanford, Calif., 1974).

76. Richard McCormick discusses this problem with regard to ethnocultural histories in "Ethnocultural Interpretations," pp. 70–78.

77. See, for example, David J. Pivar, *Purity Crusade: Sexual Morality and Social Control, 1868–1900* (Westport, Conn., 1973); Norman H. Clark, *Deliver Us from Evil: An Interpretation of Amer-*

ican Prohibition (New York, 1976); and William L. O'Neill, *Divorce in the Progressive Era* (New Haven, Conn., 1967).

78. For example, Luebke, *Bonds of Loyalty;* and Alan P. Grimes, *The Puritan Ethic and Woman Suffrage* (New York, 1967).

79. Irwin Unger, *The Greenback Era: A Social and Political History of American Finance, 1865–1879* (Princeton, N.J., 1964); and Frederick C. Luebke, *Immigrants and Politics: The Germans of Nebraska, 1880–1900* (Lincoln, Neb., 1969), pp. 156–68.

80. *American Imperialism: A Speculative Essay* (New York, 1968), pp. 17–43, 226–30. Also see Thomas J. Pressley, "The Systematic Study of Public Opinion Without the Use of Modern Opinion Polls," in Bogue et al., eds., *American Political Behavior*, pp. 335–47.

81. "Political Parties and the Community-Society Continuum," in Chambers and Burnham, eds., *American Party Systems*, pp. 153–54.

82. To cite only one of his discussions, see "The Social Analysis of American Political History, 1880–1920."

83. Stout, "Culture, Structure, and the 'New' History," p. 216.

84. The quotation is from Formisano, "Reorientation of Jacksonian Politics," p. 65. For another critical appraisal see Dean C. Tipps, "Modernization Theory and the Comparative Study of Societies: A Critical Perspective," *Comparative Studies in Society and History* 15 (March 1973): 199–225. A recent and sophisticated use of the theory by an historian is Richard D. Brown, *Modernization: The Transformation of American Life* (New York, 1976).

85. Gabriel A. Almond and Sidney Verba, *The Civic Culture: Political Attitudes and Democracy in Five Nations*, rev. ed. (Boston, 1965), p. 12.

86. For discussions about the factors and categories of political culture see Almond and Verba, *Civic Culture*, passim; Daniel J. Elazar, *Cities of the Prairie: The Metropolitan Frontier and American Politics* (New York, 1970), pp. 256–363; Formisano, "Deferential-Participant Politics," pp. 484–87; and J. Rogers Hollingsworth, "Perspectives on Industrializing Societies," in Bogue, ed., *Emerging Theoretical Models*, pp. 108–119.

87. A useful essay relating to this topic is Robert R. Dykstra, "Stratification and Community Political Systems: Historians' Models," in Bogue, ed., *Emerging Theoretical Models*, pp. 77–96.

88. As examples of the use of referenda see John M. Rozett, "Racism and Republican Emergence in Illinois, 1848–1860: A Re-Evaluation of Republican Negrophobia," *Civil War History* 22 (June 1976): 101–15; Phyllis F. Field, "Republicans and Black Suffrage in New York State: The Grass Roots Response," *Civil War History* 21 (June 1975): 136–47; Larry Englemann, "Dry Renaissance: The Local Option Years, 1889–1917," *Michigan History* 59 (Spring–Summer 1975): 69–90; and John M. Allswang, *A House for All Peoples: Ethnic Politics in Chicago, 1890–1936* (Lexington, Ky., 1971).

89. On officeholders see, for example, Michael E. Frisch, *Town into City: Springfield, Massachusetts, and the Meaning of Community, 1840–1880* (Cambridge, Mass., 1972); and Cook, *Fathers of the Towns*.

90. Richard S. Alcorn, "Leadership and Stability in Mid-Nineteenth Century America: A Case Study of an Illinois Town, *Journal of American History* 61 (December 1974): 685–701; Don Harrison Doyle, "Social Theory and New Communities in Nineteenth Century America," *Western Historical Quarterly* 8 (April 1977): 160–63; and Carl V. Harris, "The Underdeveloped Historical Dimension of the Study of Community Power Structure," *Historical Methods Newsletter* 9 (September 1976): 195–200.

91. See Theodore Hershberg et al., "Occupation and Ethnicity in Five Nineteenth Century Cities: A Collaborative Inquiry," *Historical Methods Newsletter* 7 (June 1974): 174–216.

92. See Bogue et al., "Members of the House," p. 284; VanderMeer, "Social Analysis," pp. 252–54; and the sources listed in note 43.

93. In particular, see Paul L. Hain and James E. Piereson, "Lawyers and Politics Revisited: Structural Advantages of Lawyer-Politicians," *American Journal of Political Science* 19 (February 1975): 41–51; Heinz Eulau and John D. Sprague, *Lawyers in Politics: A Study in Professional*

Convergence (Indianapolis, 1964); and Kan Ori, "The Politicized Nature of the County Prosecutor's Office, Fact or Fancy?—The Case in Indiana," in Kessler, ed., *Indiana Politics,* pp. 157–73.

94. Two recent historical studies of lawyers are Jerold S. Auerback, *Unequal Justice: Lawyers and Social Change in Modern America* (New York, 1976); and Maxwell Bloomfield, *American Lawyers in a Changing Society, 1776–1876* (Cambridge, Mass., 1976).

95. A recent and valuable evaluation of contemporary participation is Sidney Verba and Norman H. Nie, *Participation in America: Political Democracy and Social Equality* (New York, 1972).

96. Richard Jensen provided one classification scheme for campaigns in "Armies, Admen, and Crusaders: Types of Presidential Election Campaigns," *History Teacher* 2 (January 1969): 33–50.

7 LEONARD KRIEGER

The Autonomy of Intellectual History*

Intellectual historians have become cuckoos in the historical nest. To the consternation of their colleagues they like to think and to talk about method—and thereby hangs our tale. For the problem of intellectual history is not that, like political and institutional history, it has a method too long unexamined or that, like social history, it has a method modeled on more methodical disciplines and requiring adaptation. The problem of intellectual history, epitomized in the current disputes about the social relations of ideas, is that it has too many methods, that this plurality reflects the diversity of its objects, and that this diversity has raised serious doubts about its integrity as a distinct and autonomous field of history.

Indeed, the very propensity of intellectual historians for discussions of method is a symptom rather than treatment of their problem. For the discussions are not about more or less valid ways of processing a commonly acknowledged material; they are about the appropriate way of processing more or less valid materials. The respective claims of work, propositions, ideas, styles, attitudes, and mentalities to be the authentic objects of intellectual history furnish the primary issue of controversy, and the dubiety of one or another class of this material has evoked the presentation of one or another plausible method to validate it. The hope, then, is that the means will justify the end. In any case, if the plurality of its current species defines the leading problem of intellectual history to be its generic identity, then method would certainly seem to be a derivative dimension of the problem. It is not in the infinite variety of its specific methods that a genus of intellectual history—if there is such a thing—can be found.

Nor can we deduce the integrity of intellectual history from some principle, whether from the principle of special history, abstracted from the seamless web of the past by analogy with other established special fields of history, or from the general principle of intellectual history itself considered in its universal sense

*This paper was originally delivered in a shortened version at the session on Methodology in the History of Ideas during the December 1971 meeting of the American Historical Association. It was first published in the *Journal of the History of Ideas* 34 (1973): 499–516. It is reprinted here with the consent of that journal and with the addition of one paragraph.

of the history of man thinking as distinct from man doing. Neither principle quite holds because, as it is actually practiced, intellectual history is more general than special histories and more specific than any categorical definition of it.

Unlike the specific fields of literary history, history of philosophy, economic history, or even history of science, intellectual history has had no special complementary discipline outside the general field of history to supply the internal analysis of its objects and thereby to define the special historical field essentially in terms of external and temporal relations. As for the generic principle of intellectual history, men have deduced from it positions as contradictory as the proposition that all history is intellectual history, that is, the history of thought, and that no history is intellectual history, since the very definition of history as *res gestae,* as past acts and events, requires that what men have thought should always be subsumed under one or another special form of what men have done. However influential these principles may have been on the actual varieties of intellectual history they do not explain these varieties, which have in fact tended to define the realm of ideas for historical purposes to consist of something less than everything man has thought, something more than the separate compartments into which the products of thought have been traditionally divided, and something different from—albeit conditioned by and contributory to—the realm of deeds. Since the understanding of such intermediate enterprises is usually more susceptible to the historical than the principled approach, let us look beyond the principles to the history of intellectual history, with the expectation that even if we do not find there a valid ground for the autonomy of intellectual history upon which we can agree, we ought at least to discover why intellectual historians act as if they had one. This history goes back a long way and demonstrates that the current distinction of intellectual history as a historiographical field has grown out of the distinct role which has been attributed to ideas in the historical process.

The terminological discrimination between intellectual history and the history of ideas is recent,[1] but the differentiation to which it refers is ages old and has roots in the separate origin of each genre. The history of ideas refers to a category of literature in which articulate concepts have themselves been the primary historical agents, with their personal bearers and external relations adduced as conditions of them. Until recently the history of ideas in this sense has not been a discrete field; it has been closely associated with the special departments of thought and has its early model in Aristotle's metaphysical history of first principles. Intellectual history refers to an overlapping category of literature that has been more comprehensive than history of ideas in two dimensions: it has included inarticulate beliefs, amorphous opinions, and unspoken assumptions as well as formal ideas; and its primary unit of historical concern has not been the set of these notions as such but rather their external relations with the larger life of the people who have borne them. By its very orientation intellectual history has tended to go beyond the formal contours of the special disciplines and to identify the distinctive role of ideas and attitudes vis-à-vis the other historical activities of men. As such an identifiable and distinctive arena, intellectual history had its earliest model in the accounting for the role of revealed religion in our culture during the early Christian era. The model of the two cities was articulated into the categorically separate processes of sacred and worldly history, the first subsuming men's actions and institutions under the sequential stages in the incarnation of the true doctrine, the second subsuming earthly ideas as well as earthly desires under the category of the flesh and its aimless cycles of mundane events. This scheme initiated the pattern, which would be so long-lived, of vesting the unifying threads of history in the mind, the spirit, the ideas of men. Whether such a distinctive level of intellectual history would be thought to require a distinctive method was to vary from period to period, but certainly in its early phase it did require one. The method appropriate to Christian sacred history was *exegesis*, usually biblical and patristic, and it was a method distinctive enough for Bodin and Vico to exclude sacred history explicitly from consideration when they were experimenting with their new methods of organizing worldly laws and cultures into some kind of loose political order.

The exclusion was symptomatic, for whatever their contributions to general history the secular historians of the early modern period contributed little to the specific enterprise of intellectual history—a judgment, surprisingly enough, as applicable to the historian-intellectuals of the Enlightenment as to their predecessors. What contribution was made continued to be made by historians of religion, whether clerical or anticlerical, Christian or unchristian. For through both their positive and their negative approaches confessional Christians, unorthodox Christians, and anti-Christians all alike perpetuated the traditional version of a segregated sacred intellectual history into the nineteenth century, even honing upon it the advanced techniques of authentication and criticism that were diffused through all kinds of historical research by the end of the eighteenth century, and constituted a benefaction of intellectual history for the discipline at large. But in the secular historiography of the early modern centuries worldly attitudes, motives, and ideas were acknowledged for their historical relevance rather than for their historical autonomy. The political focus of the secular historians was too intense, or their impetus toward extended historical coherence too weak, or their feeling for the legal, cultural, and anthropological interpenetration of ideas and acts within an integral humanity too strong, or their faith in the timeless source of universal historical patterns too classical for the developments in their historiography to have any discriminatory effect upon the historical status of ideas as such. In this early modern period we can see ideas as inseparable ingredients of ecclesiastical, constitutional, legal, and political history; ideas as one of several sets of events comprising the history of culture, of languages, and of the arts; and ideas as suprahistorical abstractions epitomizing the anthropological history of the species. But what we do not see is a distinctly intellectual history, for if early modern historiography accustomed men to think of secular ideas as part of their history, it was only insofar as those ideas were tied to and defined by the rest of men's earthly existence. At the end of the Enlightenment as at its beginning, the only ideas with an independent historical role were the ideas inhabiting a separate spiritual space.

The crucial modulation in the history of intellectual history was from the spatial model prototyped in the spiritual city of the Middle Ages into the functional model authoritative in modern times, and its mechanics are most accessible in the historicized systems of the nineteenth century. Comte and Mill, Marx and Engels integrated the realms of universal and particular history by expelling transcendent absolute principles from universal history and positing a single social world with a single history constituted by general laws of development. These laws, in turn, followed continuously as scientific generalizations from the particular facts of history. The pattern is, of course, familiar to us all, but what may not be so familiar is the role of ideas in it. Historically relevant ideas were now considered to be functions of society rather than a distinct level of history leading from God, the recesses of the individual soul, or the eternal principles of human nature, but their function for society was distinctive, autonomous, and even, by dint of the fashionable tie of society with nature and the linguistic fashion of patterning social on natural science, still spatialized. Comte's and Mill's investment of intellectual history in "social dynamics" and Marx's and Engels' in "superstructure" betray the continuing tendency to think of autonomous function in terms of spatial distinctions. For all these thinkers the distinctive function of ideas, the function in which they were autonomous, was their primacy in providing structural unity to history.

But if all agreed in the formal, unifying function of ideas, there was a fundamental divergence in the kind of unity that ideas were deemed to provide, and this divergence is important not only for the understanding of nineteenth-century attitudes toward intellectual history but for its origination of the division within intellectual history which would last down to the present. In the view pioneered by Comte and given a mantle of respectability in Mill's *System of Logic,* "the order of progression in all respects will mainly depend on the order of progression in the intellectual convictions of mankind, that is, on the law of the successive transformations of human opinions." For ideas, operating through the intellectual elite in which they predominate, constitute "the prime agent of the social movement," the "central chain" to "each successive link of which the corresponding links of all other progressions" are "appended" and which confer "a kind of spontaneous order" upon "the succession of facts."[2] In this view, then, ideas are determining agents in the universal laws of *progress* and they function especially as the laws of the movement *between* static epochs. Spencer characterized Comte's whole purpose as the description of "the necessary, and the actual, filiation of *ideas*" in contrast to his own purpose of describing "the necessary, and the actual, filiation of *things.*" It may count as a negative proof of intellectual history's integrative function, moreover, that this same Spencer, who professed to think in terms of things rather than ideas, was contemptuous not only of most historians but of history as such, because it could not by its very nature be anything other than "heaps of stones and bricks," "material for a Comparative Sociology."[3] Here was a striking, albeit admittedly negative, testimonial to the association of intellectual autonomy with lawful history in the nineteenth-century school of progressive sociology.

In Marx and Engels the one indisputable function of autonomous ideas in history was the provision of a unity of a different kind and along another temporal axis: it was a *regressive* unity for the historical facts of the same period. The role of ideas in the progressive movement of history from stage to stage was ambiguous enough in Marx and Engels to provoke the discussions we have had in twentieth-century Marxism on the role of consciousness in revolution and on the differences between Marx and Engels in this respect. Without entering into this intricate discussion of Marxian consciousness in the *general* process of history, we must stress the undeniable attribution of autonomy to the superstructure, at first operational and then explicit, in consequence of its comparative rigidity and growing unresponsiveness to economic change *within each period* before its revolutionary progression to the next. Marx's growing concern with "fetishism" and other modes of "capitalistic false consciousness" definitely implied such autonomy. Engels' actual engagement with intellectual history—in his works on Feuerbach and Dühring—his later notice of the reciprocal "influence" exerted by the superstructure "on the whole development of society, even its economic development," and his frank admissions of Marx's and his early neglect of the way in which "ideological notions" were formed—these were express formulations of the same point, of the braking action of the superstructure, for they were made at the very time—around 1890—that Engels was also stressing the connection between the dynamic movement of nature and the ineluctable development of society's economic base.[4] The distinctive role of ideology within the regressive superstructure, moreover, was its unifying function: it spread a conservative consensus over the fruitful conflicts of the society. As Ernest Labrousse, a later link between Marxism and social history, has phrased it: "movement is *par excellence . . . economic. . . .* The social retards the economic when the social has the initiative itself. . . . But above the social the mental retards in its turn, and the restraints of the mental are the strongest of all. . . . The resistance of static mentality is one of the great factors of regressive history." It is the factor, moveover, which transcends historical fragmentation: ". . . Our goal remains the restitution of global mentality."[5]

Nor was the modified perpetuation of the distinctive unifying role of ideas in Western history embodied only in the abstract historical systems of the nineteenth century. In the unquestionably historical works of William Lecky, Leslie Stephens, William Draper, Andrew White, and even of Leopold von Ranke himself in his *History of the Popes* (1834–1836), ideas of religion and of scientific or utilitarian reason summarized the historical forces of regression and progression whose conflict made Western history a comprehensible whole.

Thus when, around the beginning of our century, the awareness of historical ideas, in general, the self-conscious attribution of the term "intellectual history" and its foreign cognates to their sphere, and the application of the recently sanctified historical methods to them, initiated the discipline of intellectual history in the forms familiar to us,[6] this foundation was itself a sequel to a long tradition certifying the independent role of ideas in our culture. The five easily identifiable schools of modern intellectual history which dominated the first half of our century and remain the bases of current developments in the field are, indeed, reducible for purposes of analysis to two main directions, and the relevance of the tradition to them will become readily apparent. The five schools are: first, the German-Italian historicist school featuring a mix of historical philosophers and philosophical historians running from Dilthey and Croce to Cassirer, Meinecke, and Carlo Antoni; second, the group of sociointellectual historians centering on Marc Bloch, Lucien Febvre, and the periodical *Annales;* third and fourth, the two schools which can be regarded as American counterparts of these two European tendencies, the *History of Ideas* group of Arthur O. Lovejoy and George Boas, and the New History of Robinson, Becker, and Beard; and fifth, the historians of assorted philosophical, literary, artistic, and politico-scientific theories and theorists—Bury, Barker, Randall, Sabine, Auerbach, Mornet, Hauser, Laski, and their ilk—who accommodated their special subjects to the new standard of historical research. This last group too is divisible for our purpose between the historicists and the sociointellectuals, since its works were written within its respective special disciplines, and its historical dimension was more purely represented by one of the two mainline historical groups—the philosophers and aestheticians by the historicists, the social scientists and social *littérateurs*, like Laski and Mornet, by the historians of the *Annales*.

If we ask, then, just what it was that our immediate ancestors originated and what they carried over from *their* past, we shall look for our answers to the two main directions just indicated. Let us first limit the field of the answer and indicate what the new awareness of intellectual history was not yet, for otherwise we shall not understand what we ourselves are doing in the field. The new intellectual history was not yet a separate field of history, with its own method. Certainly there was a novel concern with method and certainly ideas were identified as distinctive objects in history, but the new methods came from outside of history—from neo-idealism and phenomenology in philosophy and especially from sociology among the newly specialized social sciences—and they were designed for integration in the method of all of history, to import principles of coherence into that method, and the awareness of the intellectual dimension of history was a function of these imported general principles. Thus while the *Annales* group and the New Historians wrote deliberate intellectual history, they did not regard themselves as primarily or distinctively intellectual historians: they stressed the historical relevance of the methods and concepts of the social sciences, and they arrived at an appreciation of ideas in history by virtue of their function in retarding or advancing—but in either way in linking—the centrifugal facts on an increasingly specialized society subject to incessant change. Marc Bloch's subjects were primarily social; those of his friend and associate, Lucien

Febvre, were primarily intellectual; but the essential interest of both was in the mental attitudes most closely engaged in social relations as their preservatives. Robinson, Beard, and Becker were similarly sociointellectual historians in varying proportions, with an interest in ideas as the comprehensible measure of the relations between atavism and reform in society.

The other early schools of modern intellectual history—notably historicism and the History of Ideas—drew their methods from philosophy and used them in intellectual history to circumvent the uniqueness of every individual cultural product and every particular event which had been established for the methods both of humanities and of general history as a humanistic discipline. Both schools revealed their philosophical origins by segregating, albeit in varying degrees, the realm of ideas from the realm of social action which had been the traditional focus of history, and if they ultimately drifted into social schematizing it was, as Antoni has shown, in betrayal of their historicist principles.[7] Further, each of these schools defined the history of ideas by a different principle of selection, according to the dimension wherein the continuity was sought. The historicist school, highlighted by Cassirer and Meinecke, looked to the configuration of ideas and found relevant, therefore, ideas that were configurable, whether they were in the form of Cassirer's attempt at what he called the "phenomenology" of the spirit of an age—that is, the essential pattern distillable from the internal relations among its ideas—or Meinecke's attempt to show the complete reflection of political conflicts in the conceptual relations of a dramatized world of interactive ideas. In Lovejoy's *History of Ideas,* on the contrary, the "unit-ideas" which were the objects of his concern were components analyzed out of the systems and combinations in which they were originally invested and followed for their continuity and development through time and discipline. Although Lovejoy seemed to provide a porosity and extensibility for his unit-ideas by admitting "implicit or incompletely explicit assumptions, or more or less unconscious mental habits" among them, his associate George Boas's recent categorical pronouncement that "ideas, after all, exist on the conscious level and their history has to stay on that level" would seem far more faithful to the logic and to the actual performance of the school.[8] To fulfill their function both within and between periods the ideas in the history of ideas must be articulate and recognizable.

It should be clear by now what was common to the men who earlier in this century identified a kind of history which they labeled variously as intellectual history or history of ideas, which applied to different levels of ideas, and which was worked by methods applying to more or less than the category of all ideas in history—by methods, that is, applying to all of the social past or to only certain kinds of ideas. What was common to them and new for historiography was the loss of faith in the underlying lawfulness either of the principles of human nature or the pattern of social development. What was common to them and old for historiography was their persistent faith in the immanent continuity of history itself, and it was to this continuity that they geared their methods.

The connections which could be formerly assumed *for* history had now to be demonstrated *in* history.

What is distinctive about our own generation's approaches to intellectual history? A caveat is required before attempting an answer. Earlier schools and tendencies continue to be influentially represented, by those like Labrousse and Braudel who look directly to the original social and anthropological inspirations of the *Annales* school,[9] by those like Jean Hyppolite, Raymond Polin, and Ernst Nolte who still prosecute genetic and phenomenological studies of individual systems and collective ideologies in depth; and by those like Isaiah Berlin, Passarin d'Entrèves, and Heinz Gollwitzer who actively pursue the history of unit-ideas across the disciplines. Obviously, current protagonists of vintage approaches need be neither epigones nor anachronisms, and the long-lived historiographical fertility of Marxist "consciousness" together with the recent large-scale enterprise of the *Dictionary of the History of Ideas*[10] offer impersonal confirmation of the truth that in intellectual history anteriority is not equivalent to inferiority.

What is most distinctive, albeit not necessarily most distinguished, then, about the contemporary approaches to intellectual history can best be understood as counterbalancing developments from these earlier forms of it. On the one hand, we have separated intellectual history out as a discrete historical field, not only in the mechanical terms of so classifying the historians who profess it and the courses which they teach, but in the constructive terms of detaching ideas and attitudes in history both from their origins in other kinds of disciplines and from their involvement with other kinds of history and collecting them in their own field, defined by their substantive function in the historical process or by the peculiar methods required to know them or by both. On the other hand, the new autonomy thus granted to intellectual history has brought the various forms and levels of man's mental life within the same universe of discourse, has evoked critical discussions over the definition of the field in terms of the relationships among its various intellectual objects and has eventuated either in an academic struggle for domination or in a permissiveness perilous to the integrity of the field itself. Behind these current developments, helping to explain them and posing new challenges to the longevity of the older schools of intellectual history, have been two contextual developments in our own intellectual and cultural life which have set off the third quarter from the first half of the century and carry a step further the disenchantment with the orderliness of things—a disenchantment which, as we have seen, has ever been the spur in shifting our perspective on the role of ideas in history. The first of these altered cultural conditions, with a constructive effect upon the new intellectual history, has been the dramatic shrinkage in the historical branches of the substantive disciplines traditionally bordering on and overlapping intellectual history—notably of philosophy, of literature, and of the arts—with the consequence that their specific historical effluence has passed into the general pool of intellectual history.[11] The second of the altered cultural circumstances, with caustic effect on intellectual history, has been the eruption of the belief in discontinuity as a necessary condition of all human affairs. Since the earlier schools of modern intellectual history had strenuously substituted a belief in a man-made continuity *within* human affairs for the older belief in the natural continuity *behind* them, our latest cultural innovation would seem to mark an even sharper break with traditional assumptions about the role of ideas in history.

Because the various current tendencies in intellectual history have responded to both of these contemporary cultural conditions, these tendencies evince common features which cut across their original variety. First, they all legitimate the field of intellectual history both by distinguishing the role of ideas from the other functions of society, unlike the older sociointellectual history, and by building a social relevance into the ideas themselves, unlike the older philosophical history. Secondly, they all adapt the traditional function of intellectual history to the present requirements of our culture by describing "continuities in the mode of discontinuity," to generalize François Furet's telling characterization of contemporary "serial history."[12] Because of these common features we can arrange the current approaches to intellectual history in a single spectrum composed by the various combinations of social relevance with distinct ideas, and we can hope to find in the alignment of these combinations, however different the kinds of ideas and methods in them, a relationship among them which may help us to define their common field, or at least, their complementary functions.

We may distinguish three main groupings of current approaches—if we permit ourselves to distinguish for analysis what overlaps in practice—as we move from the more explicitly social to the more explicitly cultural and philosophical ends of the spectrum. The first grouping is composed of new directions in sociointellectual history. It continues to focus on the popular levels of ideation in society and to deny special methods for ideas as such, but now it identifies ideas and attitudes as the products of a distinct function of society and takes their special requirements into account by drawing new distinctions between the method of social history, which necessarily includes intellectual history, and the method of the other social sciences. What is autonomous about intellectual history here, then, is acknowledgment of an autonomous facet in the historical role of ideas and, because of the quality that ideas may contribute to history, its insistence on the autonomy of the specifically historical methods vis-à-vis the generic social scientific ones. The most prominent of these tendencies is represented in the current merger of the *Annales'* type of approach to sociointellectual history with Daniel Mornet's type of the sociology of literature that appears in the work of the Sixth Section of the Ecole Pratique des Hautes Etudes and that has been labeled by Robert Darnton, its most articulate reviewer in this country, "sociocultural history."[13] The aspect of its work most germane to the category we are now discussing is its inquiry into the notions and attitudes of the nonintellectual classes, and the novel feature in its inquiry is its interest in the reception of articulate ideas as an autonomous component of these notions and attitudes. Obviously the most responsive tendency within intellectual history to the general democratic movement for the inclusion of the anonymous and inarticulate masses in the historical suffrage, sociocultural history has especially developed methods of quantification and correlation of gross attitudes which are most appropriate to the measurement of mass mentality, but this obvious feature should not obscure its recognition of the qualitative and autonomous factor in ideas that is entailed in both the diffusion of published ideas and in the variation of ideological level with the social stratification of their recipients. Furet, who works in this field of intellectual diffusion and in other dimensions of social history as well, has reformulated the *Annales'* methodology to meet the new equivalence of his interests. He categorically distinguishes the quantifying methods appropriate to the other social sciences and to homologously quantifiable kinds of history, e.g., econometric history, from the quantifying methods appropriate to "serial history," which takes definite time series as the basic realities of the past, constituted by the measurable relations of comparable homogeneous units in that series. Fed too by the extension of Namierian collective biography to include ideas and principles as independent variables and by the sophisticated Marxist stress of an E. P. Thompson on attitudes and beliefs in constituting the "logic" of the social relations which define a class,[14] the new sociocultural history both registers the distinctive role of ideas in the social past and responds to the current demand for historical discontinuity. Furet's emphasis on the series rather than the fact and Thompson's on class as a relation rather than a thing show that ideas are still involved in a connection, while their stress on persistence and cohesion within a single period serves to define both the outer limits and the inner homogeneity of each of their plural series and relations.

Clustered around the middle of the spectrum which runs from mass attitudes to theoretical systems are those tendencies in intellectual history which have become most characteristic of the field—the tendencies which posit ideas and behavioral circumstances as two autonomous levels of history and apply characteristically hybrid methods to relating them. In the form of mere juxtaposition or simple provision of a social context which *ipso facto* makes ideas historical or which somehow socializes them by an invisible osmosis, the approach is scarcely new. What are new are the acknowledgment of formulated ideas and circumstantial conditions as different kinds of historical realities whose mutual relations must be conceived as a historical problem rather than a historiographical assumption, and the innovations in the methods which have been devised to discover actual relations between them. One such method—the use of psychology—is hardly new itself, recent as Erikson's popularization of the term "psychohistory" may be. We may not go back with Frank Manuel as far as Vico for a precedent psychological history, but we must certainly agree that both Dilthey and Febvre have been our predecessors in focusing upon psychic configurations and structures as the kind of intellectual history which was the matrix of men's past behavior.[15] We can go beyond these particular forebears, moreover, to note that in general the centuries-old association between psychology and philosophy in the common enterprise of investigating the origins and validity of ideas—an association persistent to the present through phenomenological psychology—continues to support the long-standing affinity between psychology and intellectual history. What is new in the current vogue of psychohistory is the prominent role of psychoanalysis, which brings two distinctive qualities to the intellectual history it features. First, because psychoanalysis organizes mental life into a process with clearly delineated temporal dimensions, it has underlined the historicity of men's ideas, the multiform vitality of the mental realm, and hence the centrality of intellectual history. Secondly, the obvious stress on the unconscious which psychoanalysis brings to the understanding of mental life has had the effect, in applications like Marcuse's, Erikson's, and Norman Brown's to intellectual history, of grounding the traditional individual of consciously articulated ideas in the common subterranean impulses of the group or the species.

In addition to the implicit social function of the new historical psychology, there are two other methods which explicitly relate the realms of ideas and social behavior. These methods focus on the specifically intellectual classes—that is, on groups whose precise function, as groups, has been to produce or disseminate ideas. One device, at the social end of this cluster, close to the other work of the Sixth Section but distinct in principle, has been the expansion of inquiry from the intellectual elite to all intellectual producers, whether personally identifiable or not, with the purpose not of explaining the origin of individual ideas, but of establishing typical correlations among the ideas of intellectuals numerous enough to be considered a social group or active enough to be socially linked by an intellectual institution, such as a journal or an academy. A second socioideological device of this kind is the selection, for study, of those intellectual groups which have also been collectively active in those societies which have organized intellectual activities into corporate functions. In these groups there are manifested, as matters of historical fact, connections between ideas and social status, between principles and social action, between the autonomy of ideas and the imperiousness of social circumstances. Patently encouraged by Mannheim's sociological notion of the free-floating intellectual but using it rather as an historical pointer than as a general truth, this device has been especially appropriate to the histories of the German and Russian intelligentsia, a term which connotes precisely the separate social existence and distinct social function of an idea-bearing class and transfers the problem of relating idea and social action from the assumptions of the historian to the process of history.

Because this middle cluster of approaches to intellectual history is geared to register the diachronic development of the individual or group as well as the synchronic relations between ideas and their context within the individual or group, it functions not only as a structural link for the life of a society at any one time but also as a thread through changes in limited time—that is, a thread which lasts as long as the lives of the individual or the group whose personality is the mold for the change.

The final set of contemporary approaches to intellectual history is composed of those which seek within the intellectual sphere itself the larger context—preferably some linkage to society—through which alone ideas become historically knowable and historically respectable. The ideas which have evoked these approaches are still the highly individuated and articulated concepts associated with one or a few definitely identifiable historical personages that have been the stock-in-trade of the older philosophical schools of intellectual history. But new methods have been devised in response to the new emphasis upon historical discontinuity and to the growing historical indifference of the substantive humanistic disciplines, with the consequent devolvement upon intellectual historians of the responsibility to vest their philosophical, aesthetic, and doctrinal ideas with the internal dimension that was formerly supplied by the special histories of the respective disciplines. The consequence of the shift has been to dislocate the older tacit arrangement which assigned to the special historian of philosophy or the arts the internal relations of ideas and to the intellectual historian their external relations. At the same time that the intellectual historian must thus bring a new specialization and a new internality to his perception of his intellectual historical object, thereby attenuating the older connections between externally classified ideas and the respectable historical activities of men, his isolation is intensified by the contemporary cultural movement which underlines the discontinuity, both within history and between history and the historian, above all of those formal ideas, doctrines, and world views whose historical function has traditionally been deemed to inhere precisely in their built-in continuity. The sins of continuity, whether in the form of the belief in universal truths or the belief in transepochal influence, loom large, for example, in the depressing syllabus of errors compiled against the historiography of "classic texts" by the contemporary analyst, Quentin Skinner.[16]

The intramural methods recently put forth for this level of intellectual history, however responsive they may be to these limiting conditions, merely take them as their point of departure, and within their limits construct new continuities and especially new bridges to the social experience of man which remains the central reference point of history as a discipline. The new movement toward the specialized, internal understanding of the art or "ology" laying claim to the idea in historical question has not replaced the old awareness of temporal relations as the essence of the historical discipline. What the new movement has done is simply to displace the old awareness in the direction of stressing simultaneous rather than successive relations and of attenuating the distinction between the internal and the external relations of ideas. Again, historians now do stress the disconnectedness of their intellectual objects both from any long-range developments of ideas and from any community of constant values through or above time; and yet the traditional proclivity of intellectual historians to establish continuity persists, for they treat each disassociated idea or thinker as a microcosm that internalizes the macrocurrents of past and present through its own medium, and the junctures which the historian no longer permits *between* ideas are permissibly relocated in the combinations entering into the structure *of* any particular historical idea. The methodical innovations in the service of adjusting the old role to the new conditions seem infinite in their variety, so powerful is the urge to retain the temporal axis of historical relations and to reconstitute connections. Five such innovations, representing both the diversity of practice and the community of purpose which marks this kind of intellectual history, may be mentioned here.

First, the application of linguistics, with its quantitative, analytical, and structural varieties and its range from language games to sociolinguistics, itself recapitulates the whole spectrum of intellectual history in the large. This variegated linguistic approach serves to reconstruct the socialized modes of communication which link the individual idea or syndrome of ideas, meaningless and unknowable in itself, with the contemporaries who gave it meaning and with the historian who can know it only with such mediation.[17]

Second, and most akin to the traditional methods of the historian, is the selection of social theory and theorists as the objects of intellectual history. Highlighted by H. Stuart Hughes's attention to the consciousness of society, by Frank Manuel's social prophets, and Jacob Talmon's social messiahs, this method of internal intellectual history is automatically socially relevant by virtue of its content and authentically historical when it treats its theorists as historical sources, contemporary witnesses of their society, subject to the same critical processing as any other historical source or witness.

A third method seeks to resolve the problem of the historian's new responsibility for the specialized internal relations of ideas by locating these internal relations in the historical process itself and thus converting their challenge for the historian from a problem of historiography to a question of history. The inquiry here is into the impact of a thinker's social experience upon the formation of his ideas, and the method comes into play when direct evidence fails and the pattern of his ideas affords the only extant traces of the impact.[18] The discontinuities in thought furnish the opportunities of ingress for the thinker's contemporary social experience, which becomes visible in his thought and optimally functions as a kind of bypass connecting the logically discontinuous elements of this thought—that is, precisely as a "continuity in the mode of discontinuity."

A fourth method of this internal intellectual history expands the field of ideas to include the arts in a new way. It goes beyond the older method of treating artistic works as expositions whose discursive ideas are to be abstracted from the whole composition, and it also goes beyond the older treatment of finished artistic products as intellectual events, to be aligned with other such events in the contours of an age's general style or spirit. Predicated on the insight into the implicit connection between the narrower and broader senses of culture, the new method is designed to perceive aesthetic modes of expression as autonomous kinds of thinking—as acts of thought immediate to experience, irreducible to discursive ideas or to the orthodox criticisms of their final products, and more open than either formal ideas or finished works of art are to the social matrix which cradles them all. The arts are here regarded as comprising a distinct medium of social communication, connected with other channels of ideas through the social community that sponsors them all as so many articulations of its joint existence.[19]

The recent development of structuralism constitutes a fifth direction in the internalized genre of contemporary intellectual history; it is accorded a place of finality here, despite its paramount reputation, because it both epitomizes the distinctiveness of the genre and affords a reminder of its connection with the other genres of intellectual history. The native habitats of structuralism lie, of course, either outside of history—e.g., in the permanent human nature of Lévi-Strauss's anthropology—or in the economic and social history of Bloch and Braudel—in the "long-term . . . fairly stable relationships between social realities and masses," and, as we have seen, in the comparatively static "collective mentalities" which are continuous with such social structures. What is novel in structuralism amends the original orientation in two consistent ways: the new versions internalize structure within intellectual history and, pursuant to the tradition of such internalizations, seek to posit intellectual structure as the continuity in change. The prime sources of the recent structural intellectual history have been psychology and the history of science, precisely the fields in which stable lawfulness and incessant development have posed equal but unreconciled claims. Through such contributions as Kuhn's structure of scientific revolutions, Piaget's psychology of self-regulatory transformations, and Foucault's mutant and perishable archeology of the linguistically defined human sciences, structuralists now employ intellectual history as the "mode of being" which diachronizes—albeit with moot success—the hitherto synchronously integral scientific and social structures and replicates their connective functions. Such historiographical neologisms as "paradigm," "genetic epistemology," and "episteme," are the visible marks of the pioneering bidimensionality which shows both the means between and the stitching across the traditional unities of intellectual history.[20]

This set of internalized approaches thus testifies as much as the variable socialization of intellectual history to the current substantive plurality and methodic specialization in the field—but it testifies even more to the unbroken drive of intellectual historians, from the dawn of our culture until the present, to hypostatize ideas as the bridges of our history.

What answers does our survey of past and present approaches to intellectual history yield to our initial questions about the relationship of its varieties and its integrity as an autonomous field of history?

First, if intellectual history is conceived as a field in spatial terms, requiring products more akin to one another than to products outside the field and requiring common methods of appropriate cultivation in some measure independent of methods outside the field, then it must be owned that intellectual history is not now an integral or autonomous field of history. At its social end, it studies mass attitudes with extensive methods common to other social history; at its philosophical and aesthetic end, it studies formalized terms and ideas with intensive methods common to other disciplines that are not historical.

But, secondly, intellectual historians, whatever their variety, share the attribution of a common function to ideas in history, whatever the form and level of the ideas—namely, to serve as connections, both among historical agents and between the historical agents and the historian.

Thirdly, the varieties of intellectual history may be aligned as complementary functions of their common service to continuity. The more social varieties have demonstrated their virtuosity in establishing the literal continuity of persistent attitudes; the more philosophical and aesthetic varieties have been addressed to establishing the gossamer continuity through change.

But finally—and here we pass from summary to conclusion—our survey has itself raised a further question which threatens to undercut these general answers. Sociointellectual history and sociolinguistic history have shown themselves to be especially appropriate to the current conditions affecting the discipline of history at large: they are in tune with the democratization of the scope of history, and they have responded with special sensitivity to the requirement of discontinuity that each temporal series be known and understood in its own terms. Despite the usual fragmentation of their results yielded by the masses of their relevant agents for dimensions of ideas other than persistent attitudes and meanings, in principle the socially oriented varieties of intellectual history are surely on the side of the angels. But how can the more insulated varieties of intellectual history still be justified when to the old charge of social indifference there are now added the charges of elitism and anachronism, since the historical validity of the universal ideas on which they have traditionally depended for the long-range continuity both within history and between history and the historian is now so widely denied?

An answer to this question too can be given if we adduce a second set of functions which overlap the functions of understanding persistence and change in ideas and serve them similarly as complements to the varieties of intellectual history. It is a truism that historical knowledge is a compound of sympathy and criticism, and if we translate sympathy into truth seen from the point of view of the historical agent and criticism into truth seen from the point of view of the historian, it is clear that in principle our standard operating procedure is a combination of opposites, and that in practice there has always been a valid range of varying proportions in which historians have employed them. The diversity of these principles roughly overlaps the diversity between the more social and the more philosophical species of intellectual history—but in an unexpected way. Earlier in the century, under the aegis of continuity, historical sympathy was deemed particularly appropriate to individual change and historical criticism to social stasis. But now, under the aegis of discontinuity, the qualities are reversed: socially oriented intellectual history stresses sympathy with the past in its own terms, and philosophically oriented intellectual history assumes a critical connection between the historian and the past. For those who believe that history is the past restored, society is undoubtedly the only possible framework for its restoration. But for those who believe that history is the answer which the past gives to the questions of its successive futures, the common ground afforded by the rational forms of articulated ideas provides a communication through time that offsets their isolation from their contemporary society. And for those who believe that both reconstruction and restoration are required by the historical enterprise, conversation with the great dead joins the resurrection of the souls of the mute in a common perspective upon the autonomous role of ideas in our history.

Notes

1. Esp. Maurice Mandelbaum, "The History of Ideas, Intellectual History, and the History of Philosophy," *History and Theory* 5 (1965): 33–66; and Franklin L. Baumer, "Intellectual History and Its Problems," *Journal of Modern History* 21 (1949): 191–203.

2. John Stuart Mill, *A System of Logic Ratiocinative and Inductive*, 8th ed. (New York, 1881; reprinted New York, 1952), pp. 604–6.

3. Herbert Spencer, *The Evolution of Society: Selections from Herbert Spencer's Principles of Sociology*, ed. R. L. Carneiro (Chicago, 1967), pp. xxii, xxv. Italics in the original.

4. Karl Marx, *Selected Works* (London, 1942), I, 380–94, 452–62; and Friedrich Engels, *Correspondence, 1846–1895* (New York, 1933), pp. 510–11.

5. *L'Histoire sociale: sources et méthodes* (Paris, 1967), p. 5.

6. Felix Gilbert, "Intellectual History: Its Aims and Methods," *Daedalus* 100 (Winter 1971): 80–82.

7. Carlo Antoni, *Dallo storicismo alla sociologia* (Florence, 1940), trans. Hayden V. White, *From History to Sociology: The Transition in German Historical Thinking* (Detroit, 1959), passim.

8. Mandelbaum, "The History of Ideas," p. 35; George Boas, *The History of Ideas: An Introduction* (New York, 1969), p. 19.

9. Thus for Labrousse "the history of ideas" still is a history of "collective mentality"—that is, "of judgments, sentiments, and attitudes"—and "a concrete study of collective mentality can only be a study of social mentality"—that is, of the mental in its specific reference to the concrete experience of particular social groups or classes (*L'Histoire sociale*, p. 5).

10. Published by Scribner's, 4 vols. (New York, 1973), edited by G. Boas, S. Bochner, F. Gilbert, E. Nagel, R. Wellek, H. Cherniss, W. K. Ferguson, E. H. Gombrich, P. O. Kristeller, P. Medawar, M. Schapiro, H. A. Wolfson, and P. P. Wiener.

11. An obvious illustration is the very topic of a recent symposium of literary scholars—"Is Literary History Obsolete?"—published, ironically, under the auspices of *The New Literary History*. Characteristically, the concluding attempt at synthesizing the fragmented answers was made by the historian, Hayden V. White, essentially through the translation of literary into intellectual history. (*New Literary History* 2 [1970]: esp. 173–85.)

12. François Furet, "Quantitative History," *Daedalus* 100 (Winter 1971): 161.

13. Robert Darnton, "Reading, Writing, and Publishing in Eighteenth-Century France: A Case Study in the Sociology of Literature," ibid., p. 226.

14. E. P. Thompson, *The Making of the English Working Class* (New York, 1964), p. 10.

15. Frank E. Manuel, "The Use and Abuse of Psychology in History," *Daedalus* 100 (Winter 1971): 188–96.

16. Quentin Skinner, "Meaning and Understanding in the History of Ideas," *History and Theory* 8 (1969): 3–53, passim.

17. John Pocock, *Politics, Language, and Time* (New York, 1971), pp. 3–41.

18. Leonard Krieger, "Culture, Cataclysm, and Contingency," *Journal of Modern History* 40 (1968): 447–73.

19. Carl E. Schorske's presentation in a symposium on "New Trends in History," *Daedalus* 98 (Fall 1969): 930–33.

20. Fernand Braudel, "History and the Social Sciences," in *Economy and Society in Early Modern France*, ed. Peter Burks (New York, 1972), p. 17; Thomas S. Kuhn, *The Structure of Scientific Revolutions* (Chicago, 1962); Jean Piaget, *Structuralism*, ed. and trans. Chaninah Maschler (New York, 1971); Michel Foucault, *The Order of Things* (New York, 1970).

Bibliography

Baumer, Franklin L. "Intellectual History and its Problems," *Journal of Modern History* 21 (1949): 191–203.

Boas, George. *The History of Ideas* (New York, 1969).

Cohen, Sande. "Structuralism and the Writing of Intellectual History," *History and Theory* 17 (1978): 175–206.

Conkin, Paul K. "Intellectual History: Past, Present, and Future," in Charles F. Delzell, ed., *The Future of History* (Nashville, Tenn., 1977).

Foucault, Michael. *The Order of Things* (New York, 1970).

Gilbert, Felix. "Intellectual History: Its Aims and Methods," in Felix Gilbert and Stephen R. Graubard, *Historical Studies Today* (New York, 1972).

Haven, Richard. *Patterns of Consciousness: An Essay on Coleridge* (n.p., 1969).

Higham, John. "Intellectual History and Its Neighbors," *Journal of the History of Ideas* 15 (1954): 339–47.

Holborn, Hajo. "The History of Ideas," *American Historical Review* 73 (1968): 683–95.

Iggers, Georg G. *The German Conception of History* (Middletown, Conn., 1968).

Lovejoy, Arthur O. *Essays in the History of Ideas* (Baltimore, 1948).

Mandelbaum, Maurice. "The History of Ideas, Intellectual History, and the History of Philosophy," *History and Theory* 4 (1965), Beiheft 5, "The Historiography of the History of Philosophy," pp. 33–66.

Parker, Harold T. "Romanticism and Neo-Romanticism: Patterns of Consciousness," *The Consortium on Revolutionary Europe 1750–1850: Proceedings, 1977* (Athens, Ga., 1978).

Skinner, Quentin. "Meaning and Understanding in the History of Ideas," *History and Theory* 8 (1969): 3–53.

Skotheim, Robert Allen. *American Intellectual Histories and Historians* (Princeton, N.J., 1966).

Struever, Nancy S. "The Study of Language and the Study of History," *Journal of Interdisciplinary History* 4 (1974): 401–15.

Welter, Rush. "The History of Ideas in America: An Essay in Redefinition," *Journal of American History* 51 (1965): 599–614.

8 NANCY S. STRUEVER

Historiography and Linguistics*

Formalism and Its Discontents[1]

The relation between linguistics and historiography is not altogether simple and straightforward. The clear gain in theoretical and descriptive power of twentieth-century linguistics was a function of the establishment of language as an autonomous field of inquiry; for the American structuralists who followed L. Bloomfield, for F. de Saussure and the continental structuralists, and for Noam Chomsky and the generative grammarians, it is the formality and systematicity of language which enable the "scientification" of language inquiry. The formalism which has dominated linguists is emphatically disjunctive—it primarily makes distinctions. Thus the strong features of Saussure's theory were *coupure* and *différence:* the unity and autonomy of language as an object of inquiry rests on a *coupure,* or cut, between *parole,* the actual corpus of utterances and texts, and *langue,* a purely "mental" or formal system in which each element, acoustical and grammatical, derives its value (note: not "meaning," a suspect term for formalists; it is an intrasystem exchange value) from its place in a system of *différences.* It is a relational value, where definition depends upon distinction, on a play of contrasts, on what the unit is *not* (1966). The most important modification of Saussure's *coupure* is Chomsky's: while *langue* remains the formal structure which makes natural languages work, here the system is not differential but *generative,* in the sense that it is a species-specific linguistic capability, and thus the cut is between linguistic *competence,* an unconscious but highly complex and abstract syntactical processing potential of humans, and *performance,* a derived and secondary domain (observe that for Chomsky "processing" exists in a tacit, or unconscious, psychological, not a historical, or even a maturational, domain) (1972).

The relation between linguistics and historiography is not simple, then, because a major impulse of formalist theory since Saussure has been to distinguish a domain of timeless and universal structures and structuring principles from

---

* In this article the text and the notes illuminate each other and are to be read together.

that of the contingencies of extralinguistic "reality," from context, from meaning in the sense of reference to that reality, from use, from the speaking or
listening subject and his intentions and understanding—in short, from history.
Chomsky grasps the formalist nettle most firmly when he claims that in order
to proceed to "interesting" topics of inquiry, that is, those hopeful for the construction of "deep" theory, we must cut ourselves off from subjects of "intrinsic" worth; the domain of the actions of the will, and thus of politics and ethics
and history, will remain, he fears, the province of "weak science-making," of
mysteries, in the foreseeable future (1975: 25).

Historians, then, seem to be in the invidious position of being able to live
neither with nor without linguistics: if the linguists' postulates of systematicity
and their descriptions are correct, they affect all historians reading all languages;
on the other hand, these premises stipulate problems and factors of communication—meaning, intention, convention, usage—as refractory, as late and derived, as "trivial." But the impulse of the historian cannot be to protect his
method from the messy problems thrown up by events; rather, a counter impulse
rules to protect his account from naive determinisms entailed by naive methodological rigor. The target of choice for those who deplore the premature use
of linguistic models to explain social process is Cl. Lévi-Strauss. Let me point
to just two of his difficulties: (1) he fails to see there is a historical dimension
to formalism, that is, there are *formalisms,* and his selection of the model of
binary oppositions derived from phonology and cybernetics, which aligns phenomena with "nature" or "culture," seems unfruitful, dated now (1970); (2) his
bias of nonreferentiality, his focus on formal structures, which undervalues content, quickly becomes narcissistic self-referentiality; the only history such efforts
contribute to is a history of the readers, the inquirers themselves, and Lévi-
Strauss's savages turn into *Sorbonnistes.* Finally, eclecticism presents another
danger; historians and literary historians may simply "import" formalist descriptions, which remain undigested lumps in their narrative or explanatory matrices, or merely exploit the striking lexicon of linguistics as metaphor:
Chomsky's "deep" and "surface" structures, for example, appear in increasingly unlikely places.

From Language to Communication[2]

The task for both historian and linguist, then, is to research and develop a
strong theory which is inclusive, not disjunctive, one which will deal with the
structures and processes of communication as well as language, with performance as well as competence, with *parole* as well as *langue.* Fortunately, there
are theoretical moments which criticize "establishment" formalism and its antihistorical tendencies; to these developments the historian seriously concerned
with language analysis must turn. Thus, revisionist theory stigmatizes the Saussurean *coupure* as neurotic, fetishist (Chevalier 1973); while it insured the formal

elegance of linguistics' constituent disciplines of morphology, phonology, and syntax, it insured their triviality; the demarcation simply reified a temporary stage of inquiry and ignored empirical facts (Henry et al. 1973). E. Benveniste, while noting that the initial distinction of linguistic systems from communicative phenomena was fruitful, stipulates that speech, communication is prior, the source of system (1971: 110), and that the search for meaning, not simply for formal features, is an indispensable part of linguistic analysis (1971: 101f); L. Apostel insists that we subordinate linguistics to the study of the total speech act (1972: 220). Using Ch. Morris's triadic division of language study, recent work would erase the boundary not only between syntax, the relations of sign to sign, and semantics, the study of the relation of sign to extralinguistic object, but also between semantics and pragmatics, the study of the relation of sign to use (1946).

There are at least four major sources of disciplinary pressure for a more inclusive theory. J. Moravcsik is perfectly correct in pointing out the resistance of problems of the philosophy of language to easy empirical solutions (1967: 209); three contemporary philosophic schools—phenomenology, hermeneutics, and "ordinary language" philosophy—are all engaged in restating and refining problems of meaning and understanding, of the relation of language to mind, and of private intent to social rule; to be sure, at times the implications for historical method are vague and their function seems merely hortatory or suggestive. A much more concrete pressure is exerted by sociology and anthropology; thus W. Labov insists that the proper focus of a student of society is on the empirical facts of language in social context: that is to say, not on linguistic constants, but on sociolinguistic variables, linguistic facts correlated with extralinguistic factors, a correlation which reveals function and form in society (1972: 237). Critical theory, that refuge for literary critics who do not wish to be limited to "literary" questions and for intellectual historians who distrust the rubrics of the history of philosophy, has ingeniously attempted to assimilate linguistics within its project for a general theory of inquiry. And finally, formalism itself is engaged in a critique of naive formalism which insists on *coupure*, whether philosophical, between formal and natural languages, or linguistic, between *langue* and *parole*.

Anglo-American Ordinary Language Philosophy[3]

The paradigmatic shift from a reductive to an inclusive theory was L. Wittgenstein's, who began with the project of the logical formalist G. Frege to discover the "true logical structure" beneath the false and misleading surface of natural languages, and concluded with the meticulous description of the infinite variety of actually functioning "language games" (Apel 1967: 4f). The followers of Wittgenstein focus on the *context* of sentences, and they see "grammar" not as a Chomskian system of formal devices, but as an explanation of *use* (Moravcsik 1967: 228). J. L. Austin's most significant refinement was in developing the notion of "performatives," of the "illocutionary" nature of language, which deals with the instances where to speak is to act (1962: 6f). H. P. Grice and P. F. Strawson expand this insight by emphasizing reception as well as production, and concentrate on defining the minimal community of speaker and hearer. Grice insisted on the bidirectional nature, on the reciprocity of creation of meaning; like Austin, he sees "meaning" as not simply a matter of speaker/writer intent, but also of securing "uptake," or reader/listener response (1957, 1969). Strawson developed the "layered" nature of meaning, the succession of acts of recognition of intent by the participants (1971: 158f); thus "speech is a social phenomenon that can only exist in an institutional framework of mutually coordinated actions" (Apostel 1972: 220). The most radical statement is that of J. Searle, a philosopher whose analytic methods are most ingeniously employed by the literary historians. Like the structuralists, he insists on the systematicity of language; social rules underlie, are embedded in grammatical rules; to study social rules which control usage *is* to study *langue*, not *parole* (1969: 17). Like Strawson, Searle sees intention and convention, motive and rule as interwoven; while there is a fogginess to their conception of "intention," there is an austerity, which should appeal to historians, to their admission as evidence for intention only public expression, not introspective hearsay. Further, they seek the regulative or constitutive rules which create or define new forms of behavior and which constitute the individual as subject, govern both subject and text. Searle's axiom, "a theory of language is a theory of actions," undermines, of course, the naive separation of "actions" from "ideas" by historians. Certainly the language system they attempt to analyze is much closer to the realities of texts and discourse with which the historian must deal than the abstract formal structures of establishment structuralism.

Sociolinguistics[4]

This "institutional" theory of language has obvious and strong parallels in sociolinguistics; we see the same emphasis on language as process, activity, rather than product, the same shift from a linguistics of states to a linguistics of operations (Culioli 1973: 83). Thus V. W. Turner devalues the formalist taxonomies of Lévi-Strauss in favor of a precise rendering of dynamics: binary oppositions are not simply categories but *actions* of affirming or negating within the give-and-take of social discourse (1967: 112f). There is a rich repertoire of modes of variation which they have isolated to study: sociolinguists describe tactics of standardization, hierarchization, stratification of language use, code-switching, bilinguality, multilinguality—all of which enrich our notion of a given society's "language." Then, the ethnomethodologists utilize the phenomenological emphasis on the social structuring of "reality," the notion of personal identity as constructed in social relationships of G. H. Mead, in a method which analyzes strategies of interaction, the construction of roles, the maintaining of "boundaries" by the speakers. Interaction, meaningful exchange, demands a reciprocity of viewpoint; as in Grice's emphasis on "uptake," the action of decoding is as important as encoding, reception as much as production of a text; the fundamental unit is not the sentence but the "turn," an exchange of sentences: signification pertains to discourse units, not isolated phrases or sentences (Cicourel 1970). They assume the basic rules of social interpretation procedures are like deep grammatical rules, which both generate and explicate behavior displays; and they insist on the centrality of language behavior, that socialization revolves around language use, an emphasis which can only strengthen the historian's commitment to language analysis.

Continental Structuralists and Post-Structuralists[5]

It is not surprising, then, to find a peculiar alliance forming between the sociolinguists, the Anglo-American linguists and philosophers, and the continental theorists with strong Marxist-Freudian ties: while they have radically different vocabularies, they share premises and goals. The French theorists in particular concentrate on the two problems of the speaker—the *sujet parlant* and the process of *énonciation*. J. Kristeva pointed out the difficulties, which of course are difficulties for the historian, of the Saussurean notion of the subject of language as a "collective memory," of Lévi-Strauss's notion of the subject as a "collective unconscious," and of Chomsky's subject as the "neutralized self," a "black box" (1971: 110f). She praises Benveniste for insisting on the *sujet parlant,* immersed in specific institutions of a social-historical nature, as the support, the context of the text (1975: 230). Rather than a formal analysis of an autonomous, "subjectless" text, on the *énoncé* as product, there is a strong empirical bias to observe the constant intervention of the speaker in the act of *énonciation*. Also, the focus is on language as *syntagmatic* (on the structure of relations of words within sentences, of contiguity, linear succession) rather than as *paradigmatic* (on the structure of relations outside the sentence, of differences, of characteristics which mark off one term from other candidate, replacement terms). Thus Jean Dubois appeals to Chomsky rather than Saussure: *énonciation* is a succession of speaker's choices, of employments of ordering rules, transformations, modifications (1969: 107f).

Paul Henry's *Le Mauvais outil* exemplifies the French resort to the two great explanatory hypotheses of contextualization, Marxism and Freudianism; for Henry, every speaking subject is the subject both of an ideology and of the unconscious (1977: 162). But since his appeal is specifically to Althusser's Marx, where ideology deals in illusion, not objectivity—it speaks in figure—and to Lacan's Freud, where the structure of the unconscious is the structure of language, inquiry is primarily linguistic inquiry. Further, Henry also typifies the French concern, which has its German and Italian counterparts, to combine linguistic formalism with broad social investigation and commitment. Frege, Henry notes, claimed that grammar generates illusion; the *presuppositional* nature of language—that sentences imply as well as assert extralinguistic and linguistic facts—allows us to speak seriously and logically of illusion; but Henry does not focus on the *evils* of illusion like Frege, but on the interpretation of the illusions of ideology, dream work, motive in texts. Just so, D. Slatka will use Austinian analysis of performatives, or speech acts, or Fillmore's formal case grammar (1968) to describe ideological structures of political texts (1971, 1974); and R. Robin, D. Maldidier, and M. Pecheux will use Z. B. Harris's discourse analysis to describe the functioning of ideological choices in historical situations.

The New Formalism[6]

These uses of Fillmore, Frege, and Harris indicate that the precision and model-building capacity of mathematics and formal languages remain attractive to social historians. But where grammatical and logical formalism had abetted each other's reductionism, the new formal philosophy of language is inclusive and attempts what could be termed a *synthesis* of Frege and Wittgenstein: it is a project of a *formal* pragmatics of natural languages, a formalization of "use." R. Montague (1974), for example, opened initiatives in formalist semantics, which would include pragmatics as well; and P. Seuren's claim that semantics is on the verge of "going out of philosophy into science" is an assertion of scientification as inclusive, not exclusionary, and not an impoverishment, but an enrichment of humanistic and historical research, since formal semantics must respond precisely to the grammatical facts of natural languages (1974). Formalists will stipulate the employment of a *series* of logics—assertion logic, action logic, deontic logics of obligation and duty—to deal with the full range of discursive tactics employed on historical occasions (Apostel 1972). The new formalism may integrate, then, the two major types of language study defined by Strawson—the communication/intention and the formal/semantic approaches (1971: 171); R. L. Martin sees this concern with semantic issues as deepening, the concern with pragmatic issues as broadening, and the concern with non-bivalent aspects of language (for example, performatives are neither true nor false) as contributing to the flexibility of formalist inquiry (1971:144).

The Theoretical Implications for History[7]

It is obvious that while much of language theory is so difficult and so tentative as to be almost inaccessible to the historian-layman, far from undermining historical issues, the newer moments restate them in formalist terms. Thus, theory is pragmatic in two senses: it demands the consideration of texts in the context of use, and it has practical applications to specific problems of historical inquiry.

The most intriguing, and least well-defined, possibility is the reformulation of social-moral problematic in the description of historic event: from Austin's postulate that performatives are not true or false but "felicitous" or "infelicitous" (1962: 16f) could stem a reconstitution of the problem of "good faith," where "good faith" and "trust" are accessible to analysis. The same emphasis on language as symbolic action, for example, that a given statement of fact is a performance which creates social constraints, stipulates behavior (Apostel 1972: 220) and makes us rethink issues of "commitment" and "obligation"; consider that both J. Habermas (1970) and E. Veron (1973*a*) hypothesize the congruence of linguistic and social rules. Where Searle speaks of social rules as embedded in grammar, Veron sees obligations as made by discourse; motives are not private intentions but are the products of public methods, used by a group to decide the social existence or nonexistence of an action. And Habermas draws the further conclusion that linguistic description leads not to prescription, but directly to therapy and cure; linguistic inquiry is not only social but "political" and moral, since it indicates the process by which pseudoconsensus can be replaced by true consensus. Where ideologies and their rituals control, produce the acts of recognition of the subjects, science produces the cognition of the ideologies (Althusser 1970: 30) and of the systematic distortions of *communicative* (not linguistic) competence and thus generates intellectual emancipation: symptoms, diagnosis, therapy—all are linguistic for Habermas.

The epistemological implications are even clearer. The same emphasis on "publicity," the same distrust for the appeal to private experience invests Wittgenstein's rejection of the "priority" of mental processes to linguistic expression (1958, 1967, 1969). Wittgenstein is a much tougher-minded antimentalist than most behaviorists, and his insistence on the inextricability of thought and language is similar to that of Benveniste, who claimed that ideas were "words with a history." This in turn supports a notion of intellectual history, not as lists of subjective or private insights, but as a history of social process; what is crucial is what is not monologic, but dialogic or reciprocal—and historical. Formalist pragmatics, which attempts a strong theory of speaker-hearer, author-reader relations, coheres with the development of the *nouvelle rhétorique* initiated by Ch. Perelman, which continues the classical emphasis on the relation of speaker, message, and audience, and which elaborates a richer model of argument, the new rhetoricians claim, than post-Cartesian logic (Perelman-Tyteca 1958). All rhetoric has a cognitive dimension, according to D. Sperber, and the most inobvious persuasive technique contributes to meaning: rhetorical analysis, therefore, includes within its scope interlocutions, situations, extralinguistic signals, and anterior *énoncés* (1975: 389); the rhetoric of the *Groupe meta* of Liège contains an ecological model: the value of a term is equal to the sum of the linguistic experiences accumulated by the receiver, the audience (Jac. Dubois et al. 1970: 145f). Then, M. Pecheux, as a historian of science, claims that the vital context of the discourse of the new science of the modern era was the constellation of discursive practices with which it debated (1969: 34f). The most far-reaching claim for reciprocity, for the social nature of thought, is the "rhetorical theory of cognition" which Apostel attributes to the historian of philosophy J. Hintikka: since "defensibility" is one of the criteria of truth, cognition is essentially dialogic, not monologic; truth claims are embedded in dialogue—a Socratic insight, to be sure (1971: 19).

Finally, current theory celebrates temporality: consider Austin and Searle's focus on speech acts, rather than timeless formal systems, and the current interest in pragmatics, with its concern with event, contingency, agency. M. Foucault speaks of the "punctuality" of discourse and devises a complex project of description of discursive events (1969: 39; 1971); Sperber insists on the temporal dimension of dialogue: rhetoric is the mobilization, the putting into play and successive modifications of shared knowledge, *savoir partagé* (1975: 392). For R. Celis as well as the sociolinguists, institutions are dynamic, continually reinvented by the locutors in discourse (1977: 233). There is a shift, then, from a "static" formalism of taxonomies, binary oppositions, differential relations, to one of process, reflexivity, reciprocity, transitivity: a formalism which is "dynamic," and thus essentially, not trivially, historical.

Questions of Method

The historian will find much of interest in linguistic formalism, then, but he must choose his formalism carefully. Linguistics is not simply an auxiliary technique, like statistics, which can be simply "plugged in"; the student of social-historical event must be extremely conscious of the premises and entailments of the formal analysis he employs. Further, it must be emphasized that some of the approaches which are potentially of greatest interest to the historian are at this point theoretical exploration, not yet "in practice." Finally, if a criterion of scientific progress is the capacity to take in and explain new data, a great deal of historically applied linguistics is unprogressive and trite, an exercise in circular thinking, where linguistic analysis is used merely to confirm conclusions developed from other modes of inquiry.

It is, of course, the premise of the formality and systematicity of language which has enabled the new methodology. The historian who wishes an authoritative introduction to the terms and techniques of linguistic formalism could not do better than to turn to the work of E. Benveniste and L. Hjelmslev. Thus, the lexicologist A. Rey invokes chapter 10 of Benveniste's *Problems in General Linguistics* as a "charter" for linguistic analysis (1977:184); Benveniste claims that there are only two basic methods: to define each element by its relation of simultaneity (by means of segmentation) or by its relations of substitutability: these reveal the linear (syntagmatic) and differential (paradigmatic) structure of language; the two premises that form and meaning are defined in terms of each other and that the interrelations of the levels of units (for example, phonemes, words, phrases) vitally concern form and meaning provide the themes for the series of variations which constitute his rich methodology (1971: 101f). Rey also appeals to L. Hjelmslev (1977: 6): elaborating Saussure's definition of the sign as the inextricable unity of *signifier*, acoustic or graphic signal, and *signifié*, meaning (again note, not reference), Hjelmslev stipulates the sign as containing an expression plane and a content plane, each with both substantive (for example, phonic material, concepts) and formal (for example, organizations of phonic, conceptual material) aspects. The "pure" formalist object, then, is "in the interplay between the expression form and the content form" (1961: 111), a statement which epitomizes the linguistic and semiotic program. Differences, disjunctions, and similarities, conjunctions, are relations which are established in analysis (most basically, commutation—trying the sentence without the term—and substitution) and which constitute the structure of the text. In brief, form is evidence of the highest quality.

Next, the historian who wishes to develop a mode of language inquiry must consider its relations with at least three major disciplinary domains: first, he must confront the antipathy of *pure linguistics:* Chomsky insists that "formal devices of language should be studied independently of their use" (1972*b*: 198–9), that is, that linguistics must be disassociated from inquiry which applies linguistics (Dougherty 1975: 173). Second, the historian must note the unhistorical tendency of *sociolinguistic* research design, which responds to an imperative to limit variables in order to establish relevance and effect, a tactic which is either reductive or productive of circular reasoning or begged questions in historical research. Finally, he must consider the relation of linguistics to *semiotics;* semiotics, the study of all systems of signification, is simply a version of Saussure's *semiology,* the general science of signs, nonverbal as well as verbal: "the linguist cannot with impunity study language without the wider horizon that ensures his proper orientation towards these analogous structures" (Hjelmslev 1961: 107). The theoretical choice is either to see linguistics as a species of semiology or to see semiotics as an extrapolation from linguistics (Barthes 1967: 9f). Further, one can emphasize semiotics as a system of nonreferential formal relations or as a patterning of communicative acts. But in any case, vital issues of the relations of verbal to nonverbal evidence are raised.

Inside the Sentence

LEXICON[8] Rey distinguishes lexicology, whose object is a comprehensive theory of lexical facts, from lexicography, the activity of writing dictionary texts; unlike syntactical grammar, its object is not purely formal in the Hjelmslevian sense, but is the treatment of form in its relations to the *substance* of content, referents (1977: 165). Like the historian, the lexicologist must elaborate his methods while dealing with empirical, diachronic, inexhaustible material; his methods gain in coherence by recourse to linguistic models, in richness by recourse to empirical descriptive processes (1977: 188). In much lexical study, a *differential* paradigm has dominated: J. Trier's concept of lexical "fields" is rather intuitionist in its approach, but it employs the Saussurean feature of *différence* in specifying that a particular word is valued by what it is not; it has meaning in relation to other words within its particular semantic or notional field (Pettit 1975: 13). Matoré simply equated lexicology with sociology of language (1953); certainly the fact that the lexicographer deals not simply with words, but with idioms and locutions, involves him with social constraints; further, a study such as S. J. Tambiah's of the enormous weight of a society's taxonomies of terms, and their organizational force, illustrates the relevance of lexical for social study (in Douglas 1973: 127f).

The historian must respond to other imperatives as well: Weinrich warns that "a semantic theory is of marginal interest if it is incapable of dealing with poetic uses of language" (1972: 117). Metaphor is a special and difficult case: metaphors can be seen as strategies of innovation, not mistakes (Schlanger 1970); rhetorical taxonomies of metaphor and trope are structural descriptions of primitive cognitive tactics of conjunction, disjunction, permutation—taxonomies useful in a vitally nonreductive intellectual history (Ja. Dubois 1970; see also White 1973). Further, if some words are simply "lexicalized metaphors" (for example, "carpetbaggers"), products of diachrony, then surely this is evidence of a historical dimension to lexical inquiry. Etymology, the one inalienably historical linguistic discipline, may be polemical, "weighted" in Fillmore's terms, but it also gives information on the development of grammatical forms: it demonstrates that shift, changes in usage of *etymon* or root term leave their residue, and process makes its own contribution to synchronous meaning (*pace* Saussure); it also provides a sharper instrument than archeology for the uncovering of lost layers of social functions, structures, and goals of remote societies (Malkiel 1975).

SYNTAX[9] Weinrich calls for the integration of lexical and syntactic studies (1972: 116); Fillmore analyzed the effect of syntagmatic constraints on lexicon (1971). Robin sees lexical choice as immersed in the microcontext of short-range discursive choices, and in the macrocontext of ideological and grammatical constraints (1970). The *generative* paradigm dominates syntactic inquiry and focuses on process and choice. But the usefulness of pure syntactic descriptions of intrasentence structures for historical inquiry seems problematical, since its goal is to develop a model of linguistic competence, and, in Chomsky's case, cognitive capacity—a Kantian and an antihistorical project (Moravscik 1967: 222). Chomsky's syntax was to *explain* capacity, but it is used by literary historians to *describe* variations by reference to syntactic norms: R. Ohmann notes that the formal statement of alternatives indicates the nature of stylistic choice, idiosyncrasy, conscious deployments of the apparatus in tactics of deletion, reordering, combination, addition (1964: 423–9): it is a pursuit of style or "identity" in short. Slatka regards the connection between syntactic analysis and communication event as illuminating; he employs Fillmore's case grammar, where agent and agency are part of "deep" structure (1968), to reveal the latent engagements and directives of communicative action (1971). And there is indeed a historical dimension to syntax as well as lexicon; we can observe remarkable changes in syntactic theory, which are related to intellectual-historically significant changes in epistemology and to changes in syntactic practice as well; still, the issue of the possible historicity of Chomsky's "universal" syntactic structures is a metaphysical one at present (Valesio 1974).

Beyond the Sentence

The unit of inquiry for both the literary historian and the historian is the "text." Where Chomsky stipulates that the linguistic system has the phrase (technical version of "sentence") for a boundary and that "discourse" represents propositions (the province of logic and rhetoric) plus an effort to communicate (a psychosociological object), Barthes' postulate that signification lies in texts, not in sentences, and Benveniste's insistence that discourse is prior, language systems derived, point to the motive of the current interest of "text linguistics," which finds the notion of the sentence as the limit of formal system dysfunctional and would dissolve the frontier between phrase or sentence and discourse (Veron 1973*b*: 97). There are various disciplines which contribute to textual analysis: the traditional ones of rhetoric, logic, and philology; the sophisticated "literary" stylistics; the anthropologically motivated structural analysis of narrative—of tale and folklore; and the new formal initiatives in discourse analysis.

DISCOURSE ANALYSIS[10] The premise that intersentence relations function in the same way as intrasentence ones governs the discourse analysis of Harris; the linear nature of language suggested that segmentation techniques could be applied to large, discursive units as well. Harris's *distributionalism* deals with how one utterance follows another in a rational, rule-governed manner (Labov 1972: 252) and proposes a syntax of texts, not sentences; Harris studies the distribution of features (phrases, clauses) within the discursive flow and discovers which are members of *equivalence classes*, features with similar linguistic functions, which reveals a text structure which cuts across content structure. Pettit would assert that both Harris's discourse analysis and K. Pike's *tagmemic* analysis are examples of the use of the linguistic model as *homeomorph* (1975: 40), since the focus is on the formal plane of expression, on a structure of purely linguistic derivation. But Pike's method is much richer: it employs a more complicated hierarchical model of language, assuming a relation between text and communicative contexts. Thus his significant units are *behavioremes*. Also, Pike develops a means of distinguishing between that which is intrinsically, systematically relevant, "-emic," and the merely factual, "-etic," a distinction which has obvious analytic advantages for the historian (Pike 1967: 37–72).

The French sociolinguists, who delight in historical problems, see discourse analysis as primarily comparative, whether linguistic (rhetorical) or sociolinguistic (the correlation of textual and contextual facts): one studies the differences manifested in texts, and therefore it is necessary to construct a corpus to limit variables, according to criteria which will also insure their representativeness (Marcellesi 1971*a*). But Marcellesi prefers the analysis of the form of expression to analysis of content: thematic analysis may be circular and self-fulfilling, for in stating the issue one often defines the answer; form, as a less self-conscious vehicle, is more responsive to, say, ideological motive on the part of the speaker. The purely structural problems of form have the capacity to defeat our expectations derived from content (1971*b*). For Robin, the conditions of the production of discourse are not simply context, exterior, but are constitutive of discourse and are therefore accessible to analysis (1973); this notion promises the reformulation of the Marxist-Freudian task of definition of context as discursive analysis. And the formal interrelation of linguistic and extralinguistic (semantics and pragmatics) defines the project of Pecheux, who opts for both rigor and inclusionism; Pecheux would base discourse analysis on mathematical models, but the object of inquiry is the process of production of texts, of the ensemble of formal mechanisms which produce a discourse of a given type, under given circumstances; it is always necessary to study a text in the context of the possible choices of discursive modalities (1969). Maldidier lists four conditions of production of text: linguistic (grammatical constraints), ideological (political-economic formations), analytic (the economy of unconscious processes), and textual (the range of modalities of the discursive field) (1972: 139). The holistic notion of text, of the organizing force of mode or genre, requires the generation of a typology of discourse and specifically of political, ideological discourse. Again, note that most of these projects are attempts to integrate contextualist (easily seen as historical) and formalist (often considered ahistorical) approaches.

NARRATIVE GRAMMARS AND TEXTUAL SEMIOTICS[11]   V. Propp's seminal *Morphology of the Russian Folktale* proposed a formal analysis of *content:* he developed a limited list of functions (actors engaged in actions) which, if they occurred, appeared in a certain sequence; Propp suggests a flexible system where the constants are "slots" filled by variables (this is a common strategy in modern language study—consider Pike's tagmemes or B. Russell's propositional functions), unlike the more rigid constraints—Laws of Repetition, Contrast, Unity of Plot and Logic—of the earlier system of A. Olrik (Hendricks 1973: 105). The narrative grammar of the French structuralist A. J. Greimas depicts the interrelations between the constituent actors, agents, roles, scenes, and pivot points; it is a more sophisticated version of K. Burke's analysis of the "dramatistic" nature of language (1966: 44). Pettit would claim that these narrative grammars use the linguistic model as *paramorph* (1975: 42); that is to say, they use linguistic structures such as sentences only as metaphor, and deal rather with their subject matter. While the analysis may become enormously complex (Barthes 1970), the relations are still the basic linguistic ones of contiguity (syntagmatic) and similarity (paradigmatic); the goal remains the formulation of an abstract structure of relationships which depicts the manner in which content signifies, a semiotic (Todorov 1967: 8). Greimas emphasizes the cognitive dimension of narrative: that narrative points of exchange function as cognitive exchanges of knowledge between enunciator and enunciatee (1976*a*: 458). This initiative is of particular interest to the historian, since one of the more promising uses of narrative grammars is for the description of how narrative instructs; it pertains, then, to the task of historical self-analysis, the critique of historiography and the implications of its formal strategies.

STYLISTICS AND RHETORIC[12] M. W. Bloomfield defines stylistics as "the study or interpretation of the linguistic element . . . in a text" (1976: 271). There are several approaches to the linguistic definition of style: one may see style as the expression of sensibility, of the attitude of the locutor to his topic, and thus style as deviation, *écart,* or intensification (Riffaterre 1971). One may, like R. Jacobson, specify "poetic" as self-referential, point to the poetic message's focus on itself, variously referred to in the literature as "foregrounding," autotelism, intransitivity (1961: 236). Or one may define literary as "rhetorical": that is, focus on the interrelations of audience, text, and speaker, particularly, like S. Fish, on the problem of reception, not production, on the analysis of effect (1970: 123f). Again, the formalists invoke relational definitions by means of the very simple segmentation and commutation processes; but the wide and complex range of objects to be defined is illustrated in Bloomfield's taxonomy of aesthetic, theoretical, descriptive, rhetorical, historical, cultural, visual, and psychological stylistics. Further, if we, like Fish, claim that there is not so much a "poetic language" as a poetic or literary *use* of language, we find that stylistics applies to any text which possesses the formal traits and functions specified, and thus is relevant to historical as well as literary historical investigation; there must be a continuum of analysis to correspond to the continuum of effect. Recall Henry's thesis that ideology, the unconscious, and fiction all occupy the same domain of illusion: all require the description of figurative tactics, not a strategy of reduction to a "logical" truth. Thus Culler claims that both literature and culture are institutions composed of semiological systems, and "it is only within a semiological perspective that one can develop a proper historical method"; one must focus on the process of signification, not on what is signified, "on the formal devices for the production of meaning, in order to do a history of the process of signification" (1976: 268–9).

Thus, congruent with ethnomethodology's model of reciprocity and Grice's construct of "uptake," rhetoric studies, on the one hand, the active reaction of the reader to the text (Ja. Dubois et al. 1970: 145–53), and on the other, it regards as relevant the attention paid by the locutor to his audience (Pecheux 1969). But of peculiar interest to the historian is the rhetorical emphasis on the public and "shared," rather than the subjective and inward; further, since literariness is established by consensus, it is a hermeneutically, not a positivistically determined fact (J. Zimmerman 1975: 309); the new German *Rezeptionsgeschichte* focuses on literary forms, genres, styles as socially "deemed," as creating horizons of expectations, demanding both conformity and innovation from the producer of texts (B. Zimmerman 1977: 14). Barthes has underlined the continuity between ancient rhetoric and new stylistics as a predilection for "inclusive" tactics; certainly inclusionism marks the methodology of Foucault, which describes the formation of enunciative modalities, the status and role of speakers, institutional emplacement, interrogative goals, and so forth (1969: 68f), a method which could be characterized as historical stylistics.

INTERDISCIPLINARY MOMENTS IN TEXT ANALYSIS[13] One should recognize, then, the advantages of the "specificity" of literary studies: by choosing to work with the most complex material, one has the best chance of rendering a precise account of complex cultural processes and structures. But further, the hypothesis that language is a complex, "messy" domain demands generosity on the part of the investigator; he must be willing to consider all relevant modes—philosophical, logical analysis as well as linguistic, philological, stylistic ones: recall that linguistics has not escaped the bounds of philosophical problems (Moravscik 1967: 209). The result is "mixed genres" of inquiry: consider Benveniste's seminal "Categories of Thought and Categories of Language" (1971: 55f), where he points out that Aristotelian philosophical categories are linguistic ones; Ch. Kahn's use of Harris's distributional analysis, philology, and formal logic in his monograph on the verb "to be" in Greek (1974); Douglas's use of Wittgensteinian constructs as frame for anthropological, sociological, and literary initiatives (1973); and J.-P. Vernant's appeal to Benveniste's linguistic categories of agent and action to characterize ancient Greek moral-political institutions (1975: 365f).

Verbal and Non-Verbal Evidence[14]

Hjelmslev suggested a two-stage development: (1) the distinction and analysis of a purely linguistic structure, and (2) the application of this analysis to nonverbal systems. Hjelmslev emphasizes that our access to signs is mediated by language; "language is a semiotic into which all other semiotics may be translated" (1961: 105, 109): examples of the fitting of nonlinguistic material to linguistic models would be Lévi-Strauss's myth analysis, or the narrative grammars. However, there is the counterclaim that the linguistic model does not obtain for all sign systems, for example, for architecture. It is instructive to consult Eco's daunting list of sign domains, which includes, besides linguistic and text analytics, zoosemiotics, kinesics and proxemics, medical semiotics, iconography, music, paralinguistics, formalized languages, codes, riddles, puzzles, mass communication, and so on (1976: 9f). Still, Eco predicates the same *moral* capacity behind nonverbal and verbal sign; this may be aligned with Chomsky's insistence on language as species-specific. Eco claims that semiotics "is concerned with everything that can be taken as a sign; a sign is everything which can be taken as significantly substituting for something else. . . . [It is] the descriptive study of everything which can be used in order to lie" (1976: 7). Certainly semiotics as a discipline is prey to ideological temptation and polemical use; note the peculiar reversal of emphasis in Pettit's claim that "structuralism is the movement of thought which presses and formulates the case for semiology'' (1975: 33).

LANGUAGE AS SIGNIFIER; WORDS AS SIGNS[15] It is vital to recognize the materiality of linguistic expression, that texts are concrete historical factors at more than one level. When Hjelmslev defines a secondary or connotative semiotic as one in which a whole sign system functions as the plane of expression in another sign system, he delimits a domain where historians have made a very rich contribution to linguistics. This material domain of sign as substance includes printing, the book, the alphabet, the mechanics of diffusion and reception of books and other texts, the pedagogy of language, the spread or contraction of literacy, and more; thus, where the techniques of lexicology are useful to the historian, the history of dictionaries reveals fundamental shifts in conventions of usage to the student of language. To be sure, the types of inquiry which mine this domain vary considerably in sophistication and explanatory power. There is the merely popular and pragmatic interest in the media as message (McLuhan 1962). And to a certain extent, the theory of the meaningfulness, semantic capability, of the material expression has not made much progress since W. Benjamin's brilliant ''The Work of Art in an Age of Mechanical Reproduction'' (1969); there has been an access of jargon, with no corresponding increase in insight. But there has been a considerable gain in the precision and range of description, which has added an important dimension to both social-intellectual and linguistic history. Here one would include E. Eisenstein's and N. Davis's work on the history of printing and printers, and the French series *Livre et société*, which considers the book as a cultural fact, showing the changes in form as well as the techniques of diffusion as they relate to changes in social and intellectual attitudes and goals. The analysis of the production and reception of texts is a quintessentially historical task; we have already alluded to the rich German literature in *Rezeptionsgeschichte*, which concerns itself with the characterization of the reading public, that is to say, the reconstruction of the community of receivers, the stipulation of the social and economic contributions to the receptive dispositions of the readers, and the definition of forms and styles, genres as constraints on producer as well as receiver (B. Zimmerman 1977: 14).

The Analysis of Historical Discourse; Self-criticism as Duty and Task[16]

D. Hymes has made the obvious and compelling point that a proper object of inquiry is inquiry itself; he has asserted as a sociolinguistic imperative the inquiry into the ideology of the investigator as reflected in his discourse, and the delineation of professional sociolects, the idioms of the disciplinary matrices which direct communities of inquirers. His program corresponds to the Marxist-hermeneutic project of an *Ideologiekritik* which includes and corrects the inquirer's own ideology; both would recognize the historian as not only observer but participant in history. Again, we note in scholars of a linguistic turn a preference for formal analysis of expression or content (stylistics or semiotics) as more revealing, less liable to circularity and question-begging than simple lists of themes or "unit-ideas"; Barthes's "Le discours de l'histoire" (1967*b*) is exemplary in its brief, clear stipulation of a range of formal concerns and procedures. Then, form reveals a range of phenomena: the "style" or idiosyncratic point of view of the historian, historical modes as expressions of particular ideologies and social structures, history as a genre, as opposed to fiction and myth. H. V. White has pursued Burke's suggestion (1969: 503–17), of a cognitive rhetoric of discourse which focuses on the primitive figurative tactics of disjunction and conjunction of the four major tropes as most significant; one of the four tropological strategies, he claims, must dominate the production of a particular historical text (1973). Besides correlations of narrative or logical form with philosophy of history, with class allegiances, with literary commitments, formal analysis can also discover ambiguities, crosscurrents within the text, underminings of author-reader expectations. Formal analysis can also be diagnostic and therapeutic: the inquiry into narrative suggests that, like the novel, the historical account must be structured so as to achieve a rich and fresh perspective on character, motive, and their transformations; the historian must be self-conscious about what his narrative *does*.

Summary

The most powerful *theories* reflect Wittgenstein's rejection of the existence of a realm of concepts prior to language; linguistic expressions are not derived from, but integrated with, conceptual structures. This not only forces the dissolution of the boundary between ideas and action by making us focus on strategies, on process of signification, but also teaches us that there is no substitute for writing well: clear gains in insight relate to discursive control. The apprehension of the "untidiness" of the linguistic domain forces inclusionism as a tactic upon us; the revelation of the systematic sources of meaning forces rigor. Then, the strongest *methodological* impulses have as dominant model reciprocity: they postulate meaning as a process of reception as well as production. This underwrites the reciprocity of historiography and linguistics: the historians need the formal systematic structures of linguists; the linguists need the historical descriptions of process, of symbolic interaction.

Notes

1. The historian confronting linguistic formalism should be warned at once that he must simply bite the bullet and master the essential repertoire of terms which have technical functions within the systems; a brief essay in definition is Pettit's first chapter, "The Linguistic Model." (Items listed here without full citations may be found in the Bibliography.)

On the history of language study see E. F. K. Koerner, "An Annotated Chronological Bibliography of Western Histories of Linguistic Thought," esp. part 3, 1962–72, *Historiographica linguistica (HL)* 1 (1974): 351–84; H. Aarsleff, R. Austerlitz, and D. Hymes, eds., *Historiography of Linguistics,* in T. Sebeok, ed., *Current Trends in Linguistics* 13 (The Hague, 1975); or, a summary, R. H. Robins, *A Short History of Linguistics* (London, 1967). Consult also the *Bibliographie linguistique/Linguistic Bibliography* (Utrecht, 1949–), and the Centre national de la recherche scientifique (CNRS), *Bulletin signalétique, 524: sciences de langage* (this has a very peculiar analytic table). Also useful are O. Ducrot and T. Todorov, *Dictionnaire encyclopédique des sciences du langage* (Paris, 1972); A. Martinet, ed., *Le Langage,* in the *Encyclopédie de la Pléiade* (Paris, 1968).

There is a very large literature on structuralist/formalist moments in linguistics and the human sciences: a brief, suggestive overview is P. Pettit's *Concept of Structuralism* (Berkeley, Calif., 1975), which also has good, short bibliographies; an interesting historical frame is in R. Anttilla, "Ist der Strukturalismus in der Sprachwissenschaft schon *passé?"* *HL* 1 (1974): 278–81. The debate over the usefulness of Chomsky's theory is perhaps even more heated; see G. Harman's collection (1974) and the ongoing argument between Chomsky and Searle in Chomsky's *Reflections on Language* (1975), and Searle, "Chomsky's Revolution in Linguistics," *New York Review of Books,* 29 June 1972, and his review of Chomsky in the *Times Literary Supplement,* 10 September 1976; the debate has been extended to a confrontation of Searle, as a philosopher of ordinary language, and J. Derrida, a post-structuralist, in *Glyph: Johns Hopkins Textual Studies* 1 and 2 (Baltimore, 1977). Two critiques of Lévi-Strauss's formalistic and nonreferential modes are L. Rosen, "Language, History and the Logic of Inquiry in Lévi-Strauss and Sartre," *History and Theory (HT)* 10 (1971): 269–94; and R. Girard, "Violence and Representation in the Mythical Text," *Modern Language Notes* 92 (1977): 922–44.

There are a number of general studies which attempt to integrate structuralist-formalist modes in historical inquiry: see "Histoire et structure," *Annales, économies, sociétés, civilisations (Annales ESC),* 26, nos. 3 and 4 (1971): 26–344; J. Le Goff and P. Nora, *Faire de l'histoire,* part 2: *Nouvelles approches,* esp. J. Starobinski, "La Littérature"; part 3: *Nouvelles Objets,* esp. J.-Cl. Chevalier, "La Langue: linguistique et histoire" (Paris, 1974); in the series *Langue française,* the issue of J.-Cl. Chevalier and P. Kuentz, eds., "Langage et histoire," 15 (1972), which contains both theoretical and "applied" articles; R. Robin, *Histoire et linguistique* (Paris, 1973); and A. J. Greimas, *Sémiotique et sciences sociales* (Paris, 1976).

2. On the contributions of phenomenology and hermeneutics to linguistic inquiry see J. Edie, *Speaking and Meaning: The Phenomenology of Language* (Bloomington, Ind., 1976), with a good bibliography; T. M. Seebohm, "The Problem of Hermeneutics in Recent Anglo-American Literature, Part 1," *Philosophy and Rhetoric* 10 (1977): 180–98; P. Ricoeur, *History and Truth* (Evanston, Ill., 1965); G. Radnicky, *Contemporary Schools of Metascience* (Göteborg, Sweden, 1968); H. G. Gadamer, *Philosophical Hermeneutics* (Berkeley, Calif., 1976); E. D. Hirsch, Jr., *The Aims of Interpretation* (Chicago, 1976).

3. Because Wittgenstein is the most powerful, most difficult theorist, he is also the most promising, underutilized; but see K.-O. Apel's attempt to fit him into a hermeneutic frame (1967) as well as P. Ricoeur's collection of articles which looks at Wittgensteinian philosophy from various continental points of view (1977). There have been attempts to apply Wittgenstein's insights to social-political-historical problems: P. Winch, *The Idea of a Social Science* (New York, 1958); E. Anscombe, *Intention* (Oxford, 1957); H. Pitkin, *Wittgenstein and Justice* (Berkeley, Calif., 1972); S. Cavell, "The Availability of Wittgenstein's Later Philosophy," in *Must We Mean What We Say?* (New York, 1969) is also useful. Quentin Skinner has suggested the importance of Austin's notion of fermatives and illocutionary acts for history in "Meaning and Understanding in the History of Ideas," *HT* 8 (1969): 3–53; " 'Social Meaning' and the Explanation of Social Action," in P. Gardiner, ed., *Philosophy of History* (London, 1974), pp. 106–26; cf. Ch. Tarlton, "Historicity, Meaning, and Revisionism in the Study of Political Thought," *HT* 12 (1973): 307–28. J. G. A. Pocock's *Politics, Language, and Time* (New York, 1973) probably belongs more to the Anglo-American tradition than any other; see the review essay by R. Buel, *HT* 12 (1973): 251–64.

4. An excellent journal which deals with sociolinguistics is *Language in Society;* see, for example, the review article, "The State of Sociolinguistic Research," 3 (1974): 91–123. An excellent, brief collection, designed for the layman, is R. Harre, *Life Sentences: Aspects of the Social Role*

of Language (London, 1976); consult also, besides V. W. Turner (1967), his *Dramas, Fields, and Metaphors: Symbolic Action in Human Society* (Ithaca, N.Y., 1974); the collection of P. Giglioli (1972); S. Moscovici, ed., *The Psychosociology of Language* (Chicago, 1972); B. Bernstein, *Class, Codes, and Control*, 4 vols. (London, 1972 ff); J. B. Marcellesi and B. Gardin, *Introduction à la sociolinguistique: la linguistique sociale* (Paris, 1974). The articles in D. Hymes, ed., *Language in Culture and Society* (New York, 1964), J. Fishman, ed., *Readings in the Sociology of Language* (The Hague, 1970) and *Advances in the Sociology of Language*, 2 vols. (The Hague, 1971) should indicate the range of sociolinguistic interests.

In ethnomethodology, E. Goffman's *The Presentation of the Self in Everyday Life* (New York, 1959) is archetypal; see also H. Garfinkel, ''Remarks on Ethnomethodology,'' in J. Gumperz and D. Hymes, eds., *Directions in Sociolinguistics: The Ethnography of Communication* (New York, 1972), pp. 301–24; R. Harre and P. F. Secord, ''Research Strategy in the Behavioral Sciences,'' in *The Explanation of Social Behavior* (Oxford, 1972), pp. 293–317.

Of particular interest to historians is the tendency to devalue universal structures, to revalue variability, pluralism, change which accompanies the relativist-functionalist mode of inquiry: see G. J. N. Bailey and R. Shuy, eds., *New Ways of Analyzing Variation in English* (Washington, D.C., 1973); W. Bright, *Variation and Change in Language* (Stanford, Calif., 1976); J. A. Fishman, *Language in Sociocultural Change* (Stanford, Calif., 1972); U. Weinrich, *Languages in Contact* (The Hague, 1974); but this emphasis marks a wide range of linguistic or philological as well as sociolinguistic inquiry: see E. Benveniste, *Indo-European Language and Society* (Miami, Ohio, 1973); M. Wandruszka, *Sprachen: vergleichbar und unvergleichlich* (Munich, 1969); and his ''Über die Natur natürlicher Sprachen,'' in B. Schlieben-Lange (1975), pp. 319–42; F. Rossi-Landi, ''Ideologies of Linguistic Relativity,'' in T. Sebeok, ed., *Approaches to Semiotics* (The Hague, 1973).

5. French theory, of course, makes a major contribution to the ''critical theory'' enterprise. The programmatic Marxist text is the article of Althusser on ideology (1970); on J. Lacan's *Ecrits* (Paris, 1966) see A. Wilden, *System and Structure: Essays in Communication and Exchange* (London, 1972); also J. Mehlmann, ed., *French Freud: Structural Studies in Psychoanalysis, Yale French Studies*, 48 (1972); J. LaPlanche and J. B. Pontalis, *Vocabulaire de la psychanalyse* (Paris, 1967); the articles by E. Bär and A. Lavers on Lacan in *Semiotica* 3 (1971): 241–79.

6. The Synthèse Library (D. Reidel, Dordrecht) offers an excellent series on formal logico-linguistic developments: besides the volumes edited by Bar-Hillel (1971) and Hockney (1975) see among others in the Synthèse series D. Davidson and G. Harman, eds., *Semantics of Natural Languages* (1972), K. J. J. Hintikka et al., eds., *Approaches to Natural Languages* (1973). See also D. Davidson and G. Harman, eds., *The Logic of Grammar* (Encino, Calif., 1975); Ch. Fillmore and T. Langendoen, eds., *Studies in Linguistic Semantics* (New York, 1971); M. J. Cresswell, ed., *Logics and Languages* (London, 1973), as well as the volume on Chomsky edited by Harman (1974).

7. On Habermas see F. Cassano, *Autocritica della sociologia contemporanea* (Bari, Italy, 1971) and D. Lacapra, ''Habermas and the Grounding of Critical Theory,'' *HT* 16 (1977): 237–64; cf. F. Rossi-Landi, *Linguaggio come lavoro e come mercato* (Milan, 1968), reviewed by A. Ponzio, *Semiotica* 6 (1972): 378–90. To be sure, Chomsky also sees his research as emancipatory, as providing empirical evidence for a nonsubjective creativity; see D. Sears, ''Language, Languages, and Grammar,'' in Harman (1974); N. Struever, ''The Study of Language and the Study of History,'' *Journal of Interdisciplinary History* 4 (1974): 401–15.

On rhetorical theory and practice see also the collection *Philosophy and Argument* (State College, Penna., 1971) and ''Recherches rhétoriques,'' *Communications* (1970). Particularly important for intellectual historians, since much of their material is in the form of modal propositions, is the work on modalities: see K. J. J. Hintikka, *Models for Modalities* (Dordrecht, Netherlands, 1970), and I. Darrault, ed., ''Modalités: Logique, linguistique, sémiotique,'' *Langages* 43 (1976): 3–124.

8. On lexicology, see J. Trier, *Aufsätze und Vorträge zur Wortfeldtheorie* (The Hague, 1973); R. Hallig, W. von Wartburg, *Begriffssystem als Grundlage für die Lexicographie* (Berlin, 1952); K. Baldinger, ''Sémantique et structures conceptuelles,'' *Cahiers de lexicologie (CL)* 8 (1966): 359

ff.; J. Rey-Debove, ed., "La Lexicographie," *Langages* 19 (1970): 3–119; J. Dubois and Cl. Dubois, *Introduction à la lexicographie: les dictionnaires* (Paris, 1971); J. Dubois, "Lexicologie et analyse d'énoncés," *CL* 15 (1969): 115–26; R. Williams, *Keywords: A Vocabulary of Culture and Society* (Oxford, 1976). Also, besides the works of Rey (1977) and Matore (1953), see Greimas (1966), Wandruszka (1969), and the methodological articles by A. Fontana and F. Furet, *Le Livre et la société dans la France du XVIIIe siècle* (Paris, 1970), vol. 2; J. B. Marcellesi, "Analyse de discours à entrée lexicale," *Langages* 41 (1976): 79–124.

On metaphor see the issue of *New Literary History (NLH)* 6 (1974), and W. Shibles, *Metaphor: An Annotated Bibliography* (Whitewater, Wisc., 1971); H. Blumenberg, "Paradigmen zu einer Metaphorologie," *Archiv für Begriffsgeschichte* 6 (1970): 7–300; M. Le Guern, *Sémantique de la métaphore et la métonymie* (Paris, 1973); C. Brooke-Rose, *A Grammar of Metaphore* (London, 1970); T. Todorov, *Théories du Symbole* (Paris, 1977); S. R. Levin, *Semantics of Metaphor* (Baltimore, 1977); W. Koller, *Semiotik und Metaphor* (Stuttgart, 1975). See also the study by J. Tamine, "Les Métaphores chez Robespierre et Saint-Just," *Langue française* 15 (1972): 47–55; cf. the comment in the same volume by Chevalier on metaphor as diagnostic of social process, p. 13.

On etymology see P. Guiraud, *Structures étymologiques du lexique français* (Paris, 1969); J. Paulhan, *La Preuve par l'étymologie* (Paris, 1953), besides A. Rey (1977), pp. 203 ff.

Translation is a central issue: premature theoretization underlay the failure of early efforts at machine translation, and the formalization of semantic and pragmatic theory is still in an early stage. The seminal essay on indeterminacy in translation is W. V. Quine, "Translation and Meaning," in *Word and Object* (Cambridge, Mass., 1960); but see also G. Steiner, *After Babel: Aspects of Language and Translation* (London, 1975), with bibliography; K. R. Bausch and M. Gauger, *Interlinguistica: Sprachvergleich und Übersetzung; Festschrift für M. Wandruszka* (Tübingen, Germany, 1971), esp. parts 3 and 4; K. R. Bausch, J. Klegraf, and W. Wilss, *The Science of Translation: An Analytical Bibliography*, 2 vols. (Tübingen, Germany, 1970, 1972); E. Nida, *Linguistic Aspects of Translation*, in T. Sebeok, ed., *Current Trends in Linguistics*, vol. 12 (The Hague, 1974); and also *Language Structure and Translation* (Stanford, Calif., 1975); J. R. L'Admiral, ed., "La Traduction," *Langages* 28 (1972): 18–117, points to the work of the École Supérieure d'Interprètes et de Traducteurs.

9. On the integration of lexical and syntactical analysis see besides Weinrich and Fillmore, S. Delesalle and M. N. Gary-Pieur, "Lexique et grammaire," *Langue française* 30 (1976): 4–33; L. Zgusta, "Syntagms, Transformations, and Lexicography," *Semiotica* 12 (1974): 307–14; illustrative are D. Slatka, "L'Acte de 'demander' dans les Cahiers de doléances," in *Langue française* 9 (1971): 58–73; R. Brown and A. Gilman, "Pronouns of Power and Solidarity," in Giglioli (1972), pp. 252–82; A. J. Arnaud, *Essai d'analyse structurale du code français* (Paris, 1973); R. Robin (1970). On communication and syntax see J. Pinchon, ed., "Communication et analyse syntaxique," *Langue française* 21 (1974), esp. the articles of Robin, Maldidier, Dubois; since the boundary between sentence and discourse is uncertain, see also the articles of method and application listed in note 10.

10. Dougherty (1975) insists that the transformationalisms of Harris and Chomsky must be carefully distinguished; on Harris' transformationalism, see Harris, "Discourse Analysis," *Language* 28 (1952): 1–30; "Transformational Theory," *Papers in Structural and Transformational Linguistics* (Dordrecht, Netherlands, 1970); see also D. Leeman, "Distributionalisme et structuralisme," *Langages* 29 (1973): 6–42; Pecheux (1969); W. Dressler, *Einführung in die Textlinguistik* (Tübingen, Germany, 1972); T. A. Van Dijk, *Some Aspects of Text Grammars* (The Hague, 1972); W. Dressler and S. J. Schmidt, *Textlinguistik: Kommentierte Bibliographie* (Munich, 1973); see also Hendricks (1973), ch. 2.

There is a considerable number of issues of both the series *Langages* and *Langue française* on the theory and practice of discursive analysis; besides Marcellesi's "Linguistique et société" cited in the bibliography see L. Dubois and J. Sumpf, "Analyse du discours," *Langages* 13 (1969), 3–122; J. Dubois and F. Dubois-Charlier, "Analyse distributionelle et structurelle," *Langages* 20 (1970): 3–128; L. Guespin et al., "Le discours politique," *Langages* 23 (1971): 3–24; M. Pecheux et al., eds., "Analyse du discours: langue et idéologies," *Langages* 37 (1975): 3–99; L. Guespin, ed., "Typologie du discours politique," *Langages* 41 (1976): 3–124; P. Encrevé, "Linguistique et sociolinguistique," *Langue française* 34 (1977): 3–16; also "Langage et idéologies: le discours comme objet de l'histoire," in *Le Mouvement social* 85 (October–December 1973): 3–12. All of these have, of course, specific examples of analysis, but see also D. Maldidier and R. Robin, "Du spectacle au meurtre de l'événement . . . à propos de Charléty (Mai 1968)," *Annales ESC*, 31, no. 3 (1976): 552–88; M. Pecheux, *Les verités de La Police* (Paris, 1975); Greimas and Landowski, "Analyse sémiotique d'un discours juridique," in Greimas (1976); E. Landowski, "La mise en scéne des sujets de pouvoir," *Langages* 43 (1976): 78–89; as well as the monographs in "Linguistique et Histoire," *Langue française* 15 (1972).

11. Besides V. Propp, *Morphology of the Russian Folktale* (Austin, 1968), see Pike (1967); A. Dundes, *The Study of Folklore* (Englewood Cliffs, N.J., 1965); Greimas, *Du sens* (Paris, 1970), pp. 157 ff; M. Arrive and J. C. Coquets, eds., "Sémiotiques textuelles," *Langages* 31 (1973): 3–126; C. Chabrol and L. Marin, eds., "Sémiotique narrative: récits bibliques," *Langages* 22 (1971): 3–130; C. Chabrol, ed., *Sémiotique narrative et textuelle* (Paris, 1973); C. Bremond, *Logique du récit* (Paris, 1973); G. Genette, *Figures, III* (Paris, 1972); R. Scholes and R. Kellogg, *The Nature of Narrative* (Oxford, 1966); M. W. Bloomfield, ed., *The Interpretation of Narrative: Theory and Practice* (Cambridge, 1970); V. Chklovski, *Théorie de la littérature* (Paris, 1966).

Oral discourse is often narrative; on oral discourse as a special case of discourse see the collections of sociolinguistic studies cited in the note 4; also see R. Bauman and J. Sherzer, eds., *Explorations in the Ethnography of Speaking* (Cambridge, 1974); M. Bloch, ed., *Political Language and Oratory in Traditional Societies* (London, 1975); R. Finnegan, *Oral Poetry and Society* (Cambridge, 1977); H. Aguessy, "Tradition orale et structures de pensée," *Cahiers d'histoire mondiale* 14 (1972): 269–97; H.-J. Martin, "Culture écrite et culture orale," *Journal des savants* (July–December 1975): 225–82; and the issue "Oral Cultures and Oral Performances," *NLH* 8 (1977).

12. The article cited by Bloomfield has an excellent bibliography; I would only add that *New Literary History, Poétique,* and *Poetics* seem to have the most useful articles for the historian interested in the language of literature: see particularly B. Stock, "Literary Discourse and the Social Historian," *NLH* 8 (1977): 183–94; L. Goldstein, "Literary History as History," *NLH* 8 (1976): 319–33; Q. Skinner, "Hermeneutics and the Role of History," *NLH* 7 (1975): 208–32. Note that genre is a "privileged object" of research, as it is the locus of intersecting literary and social moments: see T. Todorov, "The Origin of Genres," *NLH* 8 (1976): 159–70; E. Staiger, *Grundbegriffe der Poetik* (Zurich, 1963); P. Hernadi, *Beyond Genre* (Ithaca, N.Y., 1972); C. Guillén, *Literature as System* (Princeton, N.J., 1971); K.-H. Stierle seems to carry the argument further when he discusses not simply generic, but discursive identity: "Identité du discours et transgression lyrique," *Poétique* 32 (1977): 422–41.

13. Vague and ambitious as these initiatives are, they may be more fruitful than the self-congratulatory precision of quantification moments: Greimas warns against the danger of "premature" quantification (1976, p. 46). W. Sedelow, Jr., "History as Language," *Computer Studies in the Humanities and Verbal Behavior* 1 (1968): 183–90, is a model of what such studies should not be and illustrates that the measurable is not intrinsically interesting. But see A. Culioli, "La Formalisation en linguistique," *Cahiers pour l'analyse* 9 (1968): 106–17; J. David and R. Martin, *Statistique et linguistique* (Paris, 1974); R. A. Wisbey, ed., *The Computer in Literary and Linguistic Research* (Cambridge, 1971); H. Kreuzer and R. Gunzenhäuser, eds., *Mathematik und Dichtung* (Munich, 1965); A. Culioli, C. Fuchs, et al., *Considérations théoriques à propos du traitement formel du langage: documents de linguistique quantitative* (Paris, 1970); L. L. Heller, *Communicational Analysis and Methodology for Historians* (New York, 1971). Many articles in *Cahiers de lexicologie, Calcoli, Computers and the Humanities,* as well as monographs about quantification in general are useful, of course.

14. The work of Le Cercle de Sémiotique de Paris is particularly ingenious; excellent reviews of current studies can be found in *Semiotica* and *Versus*. See J. Kristeva, "La Sémiologie: science critique et/ou critique de la science," in *Théories d'ensemble* (Paris, 1968), pp. 80–93; Kristeva,

ed., *Essays in Semiotics,* in T. Sebeok, ed., *Approaches to Semiotics,* vol. 4 (The Hague, 1971). All of the work of R. Barthes is stimulating: see esp. *Mythologies* (Paris, 1957); *Le Système de la mode* (Paris, 1967); *L'Empire des signes* (Geneva, 1970); see also the review by P. Valesio of Eco, "Toward a Study of the Nature of Signs," *Semiotica* 3 (1971): 155–85. While J. Nattiez, ed., "Problèmes et méthodes de la sémiologie," *Langages* 35 (1974), deals mainly with verbal material, see N. Goodman, *Languages of Art* (New York, 1968); C. Metz, *Essais sur la signification au cinéma* (Paris, 1968 ff); L. Meteja and I. Titunik, *Semiotics of Art: Prague School Contributions* (Cambridge, Mass., 1976); Y. Delahaye, *La Frontière et la texte: pour une sémiotique des relations internationales* (The Hague, 1970). See also A. J. Greimas et al., èds., *Sign, Language, Culture* (The Hague, 1970); J. Lotman, *Semiotica e cultura* (Milan, 1975); F. Rossi-Landi, *Semiotica e ideologia* (Milan, 1972).

15. The issues of *Livre et société dans la France du XVIIIe siècle,* vols. 1 and 2 (Paris, 1965, 1970), contain both methodological and substantive papers; see also H. J. Martin, *Livre, pouvoirs et société à Paris au XVIIIe siècle* (Paris, 1969), as well as *Etudes sur la presse au XVIIIe siècle: les mémoires de Trévoux* (Lyon, France, 1973); all are reviewed in "Des livres par milliers," in *Annales ESC* 32, no. 3 (1977): 532–43. Consult also R. Darnton, "Reading, Writing, and Publishing in 18th Century France," *Daedalus* 100 (Winter 1971): 214–45, and "Le Livre français à la fin de l'Ancien Régime," *Annales ESC* 28, no. 3 (1973): 735–44; R. Chartier and D. Roche, "Le Livre: un changement de perspective," in J. Le Goff and P. Nora, *Faire de l'histoire,* part 3: *Nouveaux objets* (Paris, 1974), pp. 115–36, is an excellent survey. On printing, besides the work of E. Eisenstein, "The Advent of Printing and the Problem of the Renaissance," *Past and Present* 45 (1969): 19–89 (her long-awaited volume is now published by the Cambridge University Press), see N. Davis, "Printing and the People," *Society and Culture in Early Modern France* (Stanford, Calif., 1975), pp. 189–226; bibliographical journals such as the *Revue française d'histoire du livre* and the *Archiv für Geschichte des Buchwesens* are also useful. On metalinguistic issues, consider B. Quemada, *Les Dictionnaires du français moderne (1559–1863)* (Paris, 1968); G. Matore, *Histoire des dictionnaires français* (Paris, 1968); as well as the work of A. Rey (1977); then F. Furet and J. Ozouf, *L'Alphabétisation des français, XVIIe–XIXe siècles* (Paris, 1977). A good example of a study of the influence of the pedagogy of language on conceptual structures and developments is O. Hannaway, *The Chemists and the Word* (Baltimore, 1975); a technical approach to the history of metalinguistic discourse is J.-Cl. Chevalier, *Histoire de la syntaxe (1530–1750)* (Geneva, 1968).

On the history of the production and reception of texts, see the bibliography in B. Zimmerman (1977); M. Paillet, *Le Journalisme* (Paris, 1974); J. Habermas, *Strukturwandel des Öffentlichkeit* (Berlin, 1971); R. Warnung, ed., *Rezeptionsästhetik* (Munich, 1975). On the particular problem of "reading": "Readers and Spectators: Some Views and Reviews," *NLH* 8 (1976); W. Iser, "The Reading Process," in R. Cohen, ed., *New Directions in Literary History* (Baltimore, 1974); and *Der Akt des Lesens* (Munich, 1976). On the special problem of literacy, see J. Goody, ed., *Literacy in Traditional Societies* (Cambridge, 1968); L. Stone, "Literacy and Education in England, 1640–1900," *Past and Present* 42 (1969): 69–139; K. Lockridge, *Literacy in Colonial New England* (New York, 1974).

Communication research is a problematic field: some of it relates to highly technical information theory, much of it is of a "cookbook" nature, purveying recipes for successful communication, or propagandizing: see, however, K.-O. Apel, *Transformation der Philosophie, II: Das Apriori der Kommunikationsgemeinschaft* (Frankfurt, 1973). Eco (1976, p. 13) claims that "the study of mass communication exists as a discipline not when it examines the techniques or effects of a particular genre (detective story or comic strip, song or film) . . . but when it establishes that all these genres, within an industrial society, have a characteristic in common." Consult C. Cherry, *On Human Communication* (Cambridge, Mass., 1966); W. Schramm and D. F. Roberts, eds., *The Process and Effects of Mass Communication* (Urbana, Ill., 1971); P. Emmert and William Brooks, eds., *Methods of Research in Communication* (New York, 1970).

16. Hymes' assertion, *Sociolinguistic Patterns* (Philadelphia, 1974), has been noted in a review by J. Verhaar, *Language in Society* 4 (1975): 352–61; Barthes's article is both brief and provocative:

it seems to have suggested the work of L. Gossman on Michelet and Thierry—see "Augustin Thierry and Liberal Historiography," *HT*, Beiheft 15 (1976). See also R. Koselleck and W. D. Stempel, eds., *Geschichte-Ereignis and Erzählung* (Munich, 1973), particularly the articles of K.-H. Stierle and H. Weinrich: Stierle's paper is translated as "L'Histoire comme exemple, l'exemple comme histoire," *Poétique* 10 (1972): 176–98; consult Weinrich's *Tempus: besprochene und erzählte Zeit* (Stuttgart, 1964). Traditionally, there has been an emphasis on the analysis of discursive strategies in monographs on classical historiography; but see also B. Guenée, "Histoires, annales, chroniques: essais sur les genres historiques au moyen âge," *Annales ESC*, 28, no. 4 (1973): 997–1016; K. Heitmann, "Das Verhältnis von Dichtung und Geschichtsschreibung in älterer Theorie," *Archiv für Kulturgeschichte* 52 (1970): 244–79; N. Struever, *The Language of History in the Renaissance* (Princeton, N.J., 1970); L. Orr, *Jules Michelet: Nature, History, and Language* (Ithaca, N.Y., 1976); D. Levin, "Forms of Uncertainty: Representation of Doubt in American Histories," *NLH* 8 (1976): 59–74; H. V. White, "Historicism, History, and Figurative Imagination," *HT*, Beiheft 14 (1975): 48–67; P. Hernadi, "Clio's Cousins: Historiography as Translation, Fiction and Criticism," *NLH* 7 (1976): 247–57.

Bibliography

Althusser, L. "Idéologie et appareils idéologiques d'Etat," *La Pensée* (June 1970): 3–38.

Apel, K.-O. *Analytic Philosophy of Language and the Geisteswissenschaften* (Dordrecht, Netherlands, 1967).

Apostel, L. "Further Remarks on the Pragmatics of Natural Languages," in Bar-Hillel, ed., *Pragmatics of Natural Languages*, pp. 1–34.

———. "Illocutionary Forces and the Logic of Change," *Mind* 81 (1972): 208–24.

Austin, J. L. *How to Do Things with Words* (New York, 1962).

Bar-Hillel, Y., ed. *Pragmatics of Natural Languages* (Dordrecht, Netherlands, 1971).

Barthes, R. *Elements of Semiology* (London, 1967). (1967*a*)

———. "Le Discours de l'histoire," *Informations sur les sciences sociales* 6, no. 4 (August 1967): 65–75. (1967*b*)

———. *S/Z* (Paris, 1970).

Benjamin, W. *Illuminations* (New York, 1969).

Benveniste, E. *Problems in General Linguistics* (Miami, Ohio, 1971).

Bloomfield, M. W. "Stylistics and the Theory of Literature," *New Literary History* 7 (1976): 271–311.

Burke, K. *Language as Symbolic Action* (Berkeley, Calif., 1966).

———. *Grammar of Motives* (Ithaca, N.Y., 1969).

Celis, R. "Langage de l'action et activité langagière," in Ricoeur, ed., *Sémantique en action,* pp. 223–236.

Chevalier, J. Cl. "Idéologie grammaticale et changement linguistique," *Langages* 32 (1973): 115–21.

Chomsky, N. *Language and Mind* (New York, 1972). (1972*a*)

———. "Some Empirical Issues in the Theory of Transformational Grammar." in *Studies on Semantics in Generative Grammar* (The Hague, 1972), pp. 120–203. (1972 *b*)

———. *Reflections on Language* (New York, 1975).

Cicourel, A. "Basic and Normative Rules," in Dreitzel, ed., *Recent Sociology 2*, pp. 4–45.

Culioli, A. "Sur quelques contradictions en liguistique," *Communications* 20 (1973): 83–87.

Culler, J. "Literary History, Allegory, and Semiology," *New Literary History* 7 (1976): 259–70.

Dougherty, R. "Harris and Chomsky at the Syntax-Semantics Boundary," in Hockney, ed., *Contemporary Research in Philosophical Logic and Linguistic Semantics*, pp. 137–93.

Douglas, M., ed. *Rules and Meanings* (Harmondsworth, England, 1973).

Dreitzel, H.-P., ed. *Recent Sociology, 2: Patterns of Communicative Behavior* (New York, 1970).

Dubois, Jacques, F. Edeline, J. Klinkenberg, et al. (Groupe *meta*). *Rhétorique Générale* (Paris, 1970).

Dubois, Jean. "Enoncé et énonciation," in J. Dubois and J. Sumpf, eds., "Analyse du discours," *Langages* 13 (1969): 100–110.

Eco, U. *A Theory of Semiotics* (Bloomington, Ind., 1976).

Fillmore, Ch. "The Case for Case," in Harms and Bach, *Universals in Linguistic Theory*, pp. 1–90.

―――. "Types of Lexical Information in Semantics," in Steinberg and Jakobovits, *Semantics: An Interdisciplinary Reader*, pp. 370–92.

Fish, S. "Affective Stylistics," *New Literary History* 2 (1970): 123–62.

Foucault, M. *L'Archéologie du savoir* (Paris, 1969).

―――. *L' Ordre du discours* (Paris, 1971).

Giglioli, P. *Language and Social Context* (Harmondsworth, England, 1972).

Greimas, A. J. *Sémantique structurale* (Paris, 1966).

―――. *Du sens* (Paris, 1970).

―――. *Sémiotique et sciences sociales* (Paris, 1976). (1976*a*)

―――, and J. Cortes, "Cognitive Dimensions of Narrative Discourse," *New Literary History* 7 (1976): 433–48. (1976*b*)

Grice, H. P. "Meaning," *Philosophical Review* 67 (1957): 377–88.

―――. "Utterer's Meaning and Intentions," *Philosophical Review* 78 (1969): 147–77.

Habermas, J. "Towards a Theory of Communicative Competence," in Dreitzel, *Sociology 2*, pp. 115–48.

Harman, G. *On Noam Chomsky* (New York, 1974).

Harms, R. T., and E. Bach. *Universals in Linguistic Theory* (New York, 1968).

Hendricks, W. O. *Essays on Semiolinguistics and Verbal Art* (The Hague, 1973).

Henry, P., Cl. Haroche, and M. Pecheux. "La Sémantique et la coupure Saussurienne," *Langages* 24 (1971): 93–106.

―――. *Le Mauvais Outil* (Paris, 1977).

Hintikka, K. J. J. "Descartes' *Cogito, ergo sum:* Inference or Performance?" in *Knowledge and the Known* (Dordrecht, Netherlands, 1974), pp. 98–125.

Hjelmslev, L. *Prolegomena to a Theory of Language* (Madison, Wisc., 1961).

Hockney, D., et al., eds. *Contemporary Research in Philosophical Logic and Linguistic Semantics* (Dordrecht, Netherlands, 1975).

Jacobson, R. "Linguistics and Poetics," in T. Sebeok, ed., *Style in Language* (Cambridge, Mass., 1960), pp. 350–77.

Kahn, Ch. *The Verb 'To Be' in Ancient Greek,* in *Foundations of Language,* S. S. 16 (Dordrecht, Netherlands, 1973).

Kristeva, J. "Du sujet en linguistique," in J. Kristeva, ed., "Epistemologie de la linguistique," in *Langages* 24 (1971): 107–26.

―――. "La Fonction prédicative," in J. Kristeva, ed., *Langue, discours, société: pour E. Benveniste* (Paris, 1975), pp. 229–59.

Labov, W. *Sociolinguistic Patterns* (Philadelphia, 1972).

Lévi-Strauss, Cl. *The Raw and the Cooked* (New York, 1970).

McLuhan, M. *The Gutenberg Galaxy* (Toronto, 1962).

Maldidier, D., C. Normand, and R. Robin. "Discours et idéologie: quelques bases pour un recherche," *Langue française* 15 (1972): 116–42.

Malkiel, Y. "Etymology and Linguistics," *Lingua* 36 (1975): 101–20.

Marcellesi, J., ed. "Linguistique et société," *Langue française* 9 (1971): 3–5.

―――. "Eléments pour un analyse comparative," in *Langages* 23 (1971): 25–56.

Martin, R. L. "Some Thoughts on the Formal Approach to the Philosophy of Language," in Bar-Hillel, ed., *Pragmatics of Natural Languages*, pp. 120–44.

Matoré, G. *La Méthode en lexicologie* (Paris, 1953).

Montague, R. *Formal Philosophy* (New Haven, Conn., 1974).

Moravcşik, J. "Linguistic Theory and the Philosophy of Language," *Foundations of Language* 3 (1967): 209–33.

Morris, Ch. *Signs, Language, and Behavior* (Chicago, 1946).

Ohmann, R. "Generative Grammars and the Concept of Literary Style," *Word* 20 (1964): 423–29.

Pecheux, M. *Analyse automatique du discours* (Paris, 1969).

Perelman, Ch., and L. Olbrechts-Tyteca. *La Nouvelle Rhétorique: traité de l'argumentation*, 2 vols. (Paris, 1958).

Pettit, P. *Concept of Structuralism: A Critical Analysis* (Berkeley, Calif., 1975).

Pike, K. *Language in Relation to a Unified Theory of the Structure of Human Behavior* (The Hague, 1967).

Rey, A. *Le Lexique: image et modèles; du dictionnaire à la lexicologie* (Paris, 1977).

Ricoeur, P., ed. *Sémantique de l'action* (Paris, 1977).

Riffaterre, M. *Essais de stylistique structurale* (Paris, 1971).

Robin, R. *La Société française en 1789: Semur-en-Auxois* (Paris, 1970).

———. *Histoire et Linguistique* (Paris, 1973).

Saussure, F. de. *Course in General Linguistics* (New York, 1966).

Schlanger, J. "Metaphor as Invention," *Diogenes* 69 (1970): 12–27.

Schlieben-Lange, B., ed. *Sprachtheorie* (Hamburg, 1975).

Searle, John. *Speech Acts* (Cambridge, 1969).

Seuren, P. ed. *Semantic Syntax* (Oxford, 1974).

Slatka, D. "Esquisse d'une théorie lexico-sémantique," *Langages* 23 (1971): 87–134.

———. "Essai pour Austin," *Langue française* 21 (1974): 90–105.

Sperber, D. "Rudiments de rhétorique cognitive," *Poétique* 23 (1975): 389–415.

Steinberg, D., and L. Jakobovits. *Semantics: An Interdisciplinary Reader* (Cambridge, 1971).

Strawson, P. F. "Intention and Convention in Speech Acts," and "Meaning and Truth," in *Logico-Linguistic Papers* (London, 1971), pp. 149–69, 170–89.

Todorov, T. *Littérature et Signification* (Paris, 1967).

Turner, V. W. *The Forest of Symbols; Aspects of Ndembo Ritual* (Ithaca, 1967).

Valesio, P. "The Art of Syntax and Its History," *Lingua e stile* 9 (1974): 1–30.

Vernant, J. P. "Catégories de l'agent et de l'action," Kristeva, ed., *Langue, discours, société*, pp. 365–73.

Veron, E. "Linguistique et sociologie," *Communications* 20 (1973): 246–78 (Bibliography, 279–96). (1973*a*)

———. "Pour une sémiologie des opérations translinguistiques," *Versus* 4 (1973): 81–100. (1973*b*).

Weinrich, U. *Explorations in Semantic Theory* (The Hague, 1972).

White, H. V. *Metahistory: The Historical Imagination in the 19th Century* (Baltimore, 1973).

Wittgenstein, L. *Blue and Brown Books* (New York, 1958).

———. *Zettel* (Oxford, 1967).

———. *On Certainty* (Oxford, 1969).

Zimmerman, B. *Literaturrezeption im historischer Prozess* (Munich, 1977).

Zimmerman, J. "Sprachtheorie and Poetik," in Schlieben-Lange, ed., *Sprachtheorie*, pp. 287–315.

The Reorientation of Historical Studies: Regional and National Developments

PART: **II**

As the articles which follow will show, a broad historical discourse exists today that transcends national and ideological lines. In important areas of historical inquiry, such as social and economic history, including historical demography, a worldwide community of scholars has developed. Nevertheless, differences persist in the social and political conditions under which historical research is carried on, and these conditions in turn have a bearing on the basic assumptions guiding the work of historians and defining their function in society. These divergences in the institutional and ideological contexts in which historical studies are pursued have led us to arrange the following essays into three sections. Two of these represent two large subcommunities within the broader international community of scholars, one comprising the highly industrialized countries of Western Europe, the English-speaking world, and Japan; the other, the socialist countries of Eastern Europe, the Soviet Union, and the People's Republic of China. The third and much more heterogeneous group of articles concerns the countries of the "Third World," each attempting in very different ways to combine the heritage of scholarly institutions and patterns of research exported from Europe with older indigenous traditions of historical thought and at the same time to confront the problems of national identity and of social modernization. Such a classification admittedly includes an element of arbitrariness, but since it offers a way of pointing up certain commonalities within each group, it has seemed preferable to the editors to a mere listing of articles in alphabetical order or in terms of geographical contiguity.

The
Western World and Japan

Despite the diversity of national traditions, historical writing in the countries with which we deal in this section has considerable unity. Not only are there similarities in the external economic and political contexts within which scholarship is carried on, but the institutional conditions under which history is researched, written, and taught show many common characteristics. In all these countries, first in Germany, more slowly in Great Britain, history in the course of the nineteenth century became a university-centered discipline. Professionalization was accompanied by the development of a similar code governing what constituted rigorous historical scholarship. A sharp distinction emerged between the older amateur tradition of literary history, as was still represented in the nineteenth century by Jules Michelet and Thomas Babington Macaulay, addressed to a broad educated public, and the new professionalized historiography directed to a limited audience of historical specialists.

Generally these countries lacked and still lack centralized institutions which plan and direct historical research. If we overlook the interludes of authoritarian political control in Italy, Germany, Spain, and Japan, historical studies have developed relatively independent of overt political direction. Within each university, scholars have largely determined the topics of their own research, and institutes devoted primarily to research are still few in history as compared to the natural sciences. France is a partial exception. Here the Sixième Section of the Ecole Pratique des Hautes Etudes, now the Ecole des Hautes Etudes en Sciences Sociales, and the National Council for Scientific Research (CNRS) in the years since World War II have financed and coordinated an important but by no means comprehensive segment of historical research and created the conditions for teamwork. The fact that except in France historical studies have been poorly supported by the national and private foundations which finance much social science research, a situation which has been changing in recent years as historians have increasingly adopted the research techniques of the social sciences, has contributed to the continued tendency for historians to work individually.

Nevertheless, certain changes have made themselves felt in all the countries under examination in this section. We have discussed this development in the Introduction to this volume and it will again be considered in the Conclusion. In all these countries, the Rankean exemplar of "scientific" history became the dominant paradigm of historical studies. Similar institutions, patterned on the

German seminar, emerged in all these countries, most belatedly in Great Britain, where the amateur tradition of literary history remained strong until the beginning of the twentieth century. Emphasis was given to a person-oriented narrative history of political, particularly diplomatic and military, events based on the critical scrutiny of printed, and more important, of unprinted government records and private papers at the expense of more broadly conceived social and cultural history. The latter continued to thrive, but mostly outside history departments proper. Despite the lack of coordination of historical research, a broad consensus, different in every country, embraced a major part of the historical profession, basically affirmative of the constituted social and political order and defining what constituted topics of historical interest and proper methods of inquiry.

This consensus has undergone progressive change since the early twentieth century, more rapidly in the United States, Belgium, Great Britain, and particularly in France, where traditions of social and cultural history remained viable in the nineteenth century, more slowly in Germany and perhaps in Italy. In the latter countries the crisis of traditional historiography in the face of the economic transformation of modern societies with its social and intellectual concomitants gave impetus to attempts to preserve the traditions of the past by giving new emphasis to the dominant role of ideas in historical change (for example, Croce and Meinecke).

A more significant response to this crisis was to attach greater importance to the role of a broad variety of social factors. Early serious attempts at establishing a closer relationship between historical studies and certain of the social sciences, originally primarily economics and sociology, but later also demography, cultural anthropology, and linguistics, were made in France, Belgium, the United States, and Britain. The essays that follow all show certain similarities in this trend, which has accelerated in the decades since World War II. As the scope of historical studies broadened, much greater attention was given to analysis rather than narration, to processes rather than events, to social structures rather than the agency of individuals. If earlier theorists of history—Wilhelm Dilthey, Benedetto Croce, R. G. Collingwood, and Friedrich Meinecke (and more recently William Dray, Arthur Danto, and Raymond Aron)—stressed the fundamental difference between a historical discipline seeking understanding of unique situations and the social and natural sciences seeking causal explanations, the newer historians, while recognizing the need to comprehend the uniqueness of historical phenomena, have questioned the dichotomy between a logic of historical and one of social scientific inquiry. The tendency to conceive of history as a historical social science became pronounced in all the countries discussed here.

At the same time, the scope of historical studies broadened as changed political, social, and intellectual conditions brought more and more aspects of human life under consideration. As the following essays will show, responses differed within the various countries. The search for a new theoretical framework for a social scientific history has led in many cases to a dialogue with, and less frequently an espousal of, Marxism. Marxism has formed an important subcurrent of historical scholarship in France, Italy, Japan, and in recent years even Great Britain, but it continues to occupy a relatively subordinate role in the United States and West Germany, although West German theoretical discussion is difficult to understand without the background of a critique of Marxism. Nevertheless, national nuances persisted. In France historiography remained deeply influenced by the French tradition of sociology, cultural anthropology, and geography; in Germany, by the tradition of the historical thought which found its great expression in Marx and Weber; in the United States, by a long-established empirical orientation in the social sciences; in Italy, by the heritage first of Croce and then of Gramsci.

Although the diversity of these historical approaches should not be underestimated, in increasing areas of historical inquiry, such as historical demography or economic growth, discussion has spread across national and ideological lines, including participants from the socialist countries. A host of new journals has grown up, with contributors from throughout the world. Thus for the first time since the eighteenth century the beginnings of an international community of scholars have emerged, although admittedly of a community much more fragmented by subdisciplines than that of the eighteenth century, which still possessed an integrated vision of man and of civilization.

9 LAURENCE VEYSEY

The United States

Historical writing in America, like armaments and grain production, appears above all to be vast in quantity. According to a current estimate, there are about 25,000 historians in the United States, as compared with only half that number in the entire remainder of the world.[1] Few of them publish with any regularity. But the number of books they do write must seem large by earlier yardsticks. For instance, in 1976 some thirty-five to forty titles alone were published in the rather arcane and unfashionable subfield of American intellectual history, an area that some scholars pronounce to be dying.[2]

The growth of the historical profession in America was spectacular during the 1950s and 1960s. But it was the result of an academic boom, indeed of a general expansiveness in the American economy, birthrate, and psyche, which ended around 1970. As universities ceased to grow and in some cases contracted, the current output is likely to plateau and only barely maintain itself, if that, for a long time to come.[3]

Thus the figure of some 25,000 historians in a nation of over 200 million people may well prove to represent an all-time peak of historians per capita. Quantification is a current emphasis within American historical writing, yet figures (such as these) do not automatically reveal their own meaning. More than one historian for each 10,000 men, women, and children in America might seem lavish. Yet historians still are thinly represented as compared with lawyers or ministers (groups which offer markedly different outlooks). Historians' monographs can pile up seldom read on library shelves or in publishers' warehouses, and the way in which historians actually spend their time remains not all that widely comprehended. Distinct limits exist even in the historical setting most congenial to the democratization of historical scholarship; moreover, it now seems that we have gone as far as we ever will in that direction.[4] The unusually favorable ratio of historians to people in America is probably best seen as the rather chancy by-product of a now-lost mood of limitless abundance.

Overall figures mislead, in any event, if they imply there is a single unified "impact" of historical scholarship. Instead, it scatters in a host of often unrelated directions. American universities, more resourcefully than those of any other country, try to "cover" the known past of the entire world. This results in a less obvious parochialism (though subtler forms of it certainly remain). But the effort to recapitulate, even if only roughly, the history of humankind by supporting experts in each major region and epoch on the faculties of leading American universities produces an effect of truly awesome subdivision. In this respect, the discipline of history, despite its lack of an esoteric vocabulary, has become far more minutely specialized than such neighboring fields as sociology or economics. Historians have genuinely much less to say to each other than, for instance, sociologists, even if this may mean they also less often bother to argue with each other. Historians are subdivided in more complex ways than members of other disciplines—quadruply, by nation or region of the globe, by time period, by thematic category (political, social, intellectual, and so on), and by cognitive predilection, sometimes but not always tied to a political outlook (for example, Marxist, Weberian, Freudian, or—perhaps still commonest of all—a naively antitheoretical empiricism). It is a mildly shocking thought that of these four kinds of division, time period—our supposed reason for being— may actually strike most of us as the least important.

All that unites historians is a concern for the evolution over time of whatever it is they study—no matter if individual human beings, societies, ideas, or institutional structures—and therefore a desire to explain changes or failures of things to change.[5] This is something definite, to be sure; it clearly separates historians from all other academics. But it is far less compelling as an attribute in most contexts than the diversity of outlooks and interests that splinter historians into minute subgroups, each with its own hierarchy of respected authorities.

In a period of diminishing differences among national styles, an American historian may well wonder whether greater internal heterogeneity of interest and approach does not constitute one of the few remaining genuine distinctions between historical scholarship in the United States and that of other countries. He is liable to accuse historians elsewhere of paying less well-rounded attention to the entire world and therefore of remaining too much under the spell either of conventional assumptions within their own cultural elites (whether ostensibly conservative or radical) or of particular fashionable social theorists. But in fact he must admit that such complaints increasingly lose force, as younger scholars in this and many other countries detach themselves from the more obvious forms of parochial elitism and as the major theorists become the common currency of much of the globe. Greater American historical cosmopolitanism, like the extensive use of soft drinks, may simply have been the transient result of affluence achieved a little sooner.

The extreme internal diversity of American historians has led to growing matter-of-factness in the acceptance of differences of outlook among colleagues, perhaps in a fashion paralleling the rough-and-ready growth of religious toleration in eighteenth-century New York.[6] For the same reason, a somewhat blander, politer tone of discourse prevails among historians in the United States than among economists or sociologists, and perhaps than it does among historians of some other countries. Even the radical upthrust of the 1960s did not produce as irrevocable or bitter a degree of polarization as it appears to have done in some nearby fields.

Nonetheless, the split between leftist and nonleftist factions which erupted in the mid-1960s has greatly affected American historians, as it has members of all other humane or social disciplines, and most observers would probably agree that this division remains the sharpest one running through the profession today. Yet it must be qualified, for nonleftists actually feel little cohesive unity among themselves, not agreeing even on whether to regard "Marxists" as all that undesirable. For nonleftists, traditional categories of thematic interest (for instance, in political, social, or intellectual history) and one's national and chronological specialty remain all-important signposts of self-definition. Nonleftists generally remain dominant in the history departments of prestigious American universities. Such historians claim to support a notion of sheer meritocracy, underlain by an ethic of individual intellectual competition among scholars, and they believe in some mixture of history for its own sake and (if they deal with modern events) utilitarianism in behalf of "liberal" or moderate goals. They are the priests (and indeed almost the entire band of followers) of the religion of history-as-such, history for no ulterior end outside itself.

Leftists, of course, tend to be much younger, the product of the brief wave of radicalism during the 1960s, and to form a distinct band marked by shared support and mutual camaraderie, sometimes to the point of disavowing or soft-pedalling individual intellectual aspirations and judgments. Leftists do not like to admit openly that they too are frequently pulled into an excitement over the past for its own sake; verbally they insist on seeing history as a tool in the further changing of the world. Leftists often face disguised discrimination within universities, though a number have successfully risen to prominence. A very frequent pattern, not much openly talked about, is that leftists merge increasingly into the older scholarly ethos as time passes. For this reason, it is likely that— possibly excepting Third World specialists—the line between leftist and nonleftist will become increasingly blurred.

Nonleftists have often honestly believed that leftist scholarship tends to be inadequately documented or lacks rigor. Leftists, for their part, have accused most nonleftist scholarship of being trivial, of distracting attention from the burning issues, or of reflecting a middle-class bias. It is not easy to step into this emotionally charged debate and attempt fair judgments, yet some things can be said, at least in the context of writing in United States history.[7]

Leftist historians have contributed much to the release of American history from its previously too self-congratulatory and provincial mold. They have done this in at least three important ways. Along with spokesmen who more directly represent various ethnic and sexual groups, they have called attention to the persisting gulfs and diversities within American society, vivifying for the first time, in the 1960s, the goal of recounting the history of an *entire* population.[8] Thereby they have helped to counter the naively holistic view of America put forth a decade earlier, which achieved generalization by ignoring all minorities. Secondly, leftists have launched an offensive in diplomatic history, particularly regarding the Cold War, that has forcefully shifted the discussion toward a greater appreciation of common qualities in the motives of leaders of the several Great Powers and called into question claims for a unique American idealism operating in the realm of actual foreign policy decisions. Finally, the strain of leftist scholarship which stems from C. Wright Mills has successfully legitimated inquiry into the topic of political and economic power, grasped from a more objective standpoint outside the mindset of the politicians, corporate heads, and bureaucratic functionaries themselves, to the point that scholarship in such realms as business and political history which evades the issue of the exercise and distribution of power becomes vulnerable to severe criticism.

These achievements have by no means been slight. They have been somewhat mitigated by several failings. Some leftist scholars tended, at least for a time recently, greatly to exaggerate the weakness of the existing social order (for understandable wishful and tactical reasons that nonetheless confused reality with special pleading).[9] Again, leftists have often emphasized economic motives in policy making beyond all proportion, out of loyalty to a version of Marxism that other "Marxists," such as Eugene Genovese, have repudiated. The argument for a primarily economic explanation of American involvement in the major wars of this century, advanced by William Appleman Williams and his students, has not yet proved generally convincing, leading one to suspect that if the older generation of historians remained too deeply under the spell of an unexamined nationalism, leftists for their part gravely underestimate the independent force of the nation-state as creator of passions, loyalties, and actions at both high and low levels of societies such as our own.

Finally, if cosmopolitanism of outlook is a desirable goal, leftists have too often remained tacitly committed to their own version of a highly idealized American moral mission in the world (represented by drastic alternatives in foreign policy). This has contributed little to the measured appraisal of American uniqueness. Leftists may assume too offhandedly that such questions are solved by labeling us the nerve center for world capitalism.[10]

On another level the recent New Left may be thanked for having reopened the whole question of the merits of simplicity as against complexity in historical explanation. It is far too easy to dismiss a leftist push toward simplicity as mere anti-intellectualism. We might do well to remind ourselves that a canon of scientific inquiry is always to prefer the simplest accounting for phenomena consistent with the known evidence—in contrast to the cumbersomely elaborate pre-Copernican orbs, for instance. Simplicity is an element, at least, in the formula for what is often in this context termed elegance.

In the 1950s, its opposite was frequently regarded by historians and sociologists as the hallmark of sophistication. Daniel Bell then noted that the values of "ambiguity, irony, paradox, and complexity" had become the most highly prized attributes of intellectual discourse.[11] Multicausal analysis was proclaimed as a virtue for its own sake, and the increasingly byzantine constructions of the Parsonian functionalists were greeted with tolerance or with outright enthusiasm. Similarly, Freudian models of the mind reached what may have been their high point of acceptance, in large part because they emphasized the ambivalence— the complicated presence of seeming opposites—in all human behavior.

The New Left struck at the core of this entire intellectual style by relentlessly insisting that basic historical processes were obvious. Much of this dogged repetitiveness could only strike an outsider as unpersuasive sloganeering. But in part it was a healthy corrective. The situation in the profession had swung full circle from Frederick Jackson Turner's day, when relevant theoretical abstraction was so utterly missing. It needed to be said that some historical questions do demand treatment through relatively straightforward depictions of motive. American political life produced its share of such examples. Possibly a psychobiographer would one day emerge for Spiro T. Agnew, but arguably such effort would be misplaced. The New Left, especially its wing devoted to exclusively economic explanations, swung the pendulum too far away from ambiguity, but the underlying issue—whether social reality might contain zones susceptible to simple as well as to complicated treatment—deserved to be raised.

In it lay the germ of a debate which, if it were ever to be held, might interestingly crosscut the clichés advanced by participants of the differing political persuasions. Thus the holistic view of America put forward by many academics in the 1950s was certainly a simpler overall conception than the alternative notion that America contains many diverse and conflicting social units, even though it was upheld by scholars who openly declaimed the virtue of complexity as an intellectual format. Meanwhile, for their part, leftists found that adding the extremely simple label "false consciousness" to all widely held ideas they did not approve of scarcely did away with the recalcitrant realities of a multilayered American social order. It is too bad that such a debate, shifting the issues away from politics and toward underlying cognitive assumptions, will probably never occur.[12]

The accusation that leftist scholarship has tended to be less rigorous than that of nonleftists does not pass muster, if one thinks of the variety of prominent scholars recently associated with a leftist perspective in American history. At the very least, one must distinguish between the dogmatic assertiveness of a Gabriel Kolko, which indeed can far outpace the density of his relevant documentation,[13] and the flood of important evidence brought forth by such outstanding leftist historians as Eugene Genovese and Herbert G. Gutman, which only someone demanding continuous quantification of data would consider woefully inadequate.[14]

Politically defined factions among American historians will grow less important the longer the current age of relative political calm continues. Instead, historical scholarship in the United States will again be sorted most importantly according to thematic categories—at the grossest level, the threefold split between political, social, and intellectual.[15] From this standpoint, the single most important line of division among American historians separates those who see all historical particulars in terms of the evolution of social structures from those who do not. Among the latter are political historians of an older outlook and semipopular orientation, who treat political conflict in much the same spirit as team sport,[16] not inquiring deeply into the social origins of the actors or exploring the ways in which their routinized conflicts might be illusory.[17] But one also finds intellectual historians who reject the centrality of the concept of social structure from their own very different insistence upon the independence (from everything else) of widely shared patterns of thought within people's minds. Perhaps the most exciting contest now occurring among historians in the United States involves the adherents of these three persuasions. In this quite open and self-conscious struggle, during the past dozen years social historians have been the aggressors, while both political and intellectual historians have been placed increasingly on the defensive, though wasting little love on each other.

Political history has always dominated the entire discipline, in precisely those quantitative terms which social historians admire as evidence of anything (courses taught, books published). This has changed only somewhat. Even today, the review sections of journals reveal that the great majority of books published by historians still treat conventional political or diplomatic topics.[18] Clearly, then, some other, nonnumerical standard is being invoked in the common judgment that political history is "threatened" or "on the defensive" in comparison with social history. Indeed, this standard lies in the nebulous, unquantified realm of estimates about intellectual excitement.[19]

Political history, it seems fair to predict, will always endure. It is the kind of history with the broadest lay audience. Its deeply entrenched following, whose appetite a large segment of the historical profession continues to serve, surrenders to the fascination of observing the nuances of more or less ritualized conflicts among contending parties or factions, both within and between nations. To make these spectator enjoyments seem not only fully respectable but even quite essential, we need only remind ourselves that the wielders of governmental power have more potential than ever for helping or harming ordinary folk. Traditional narratives, biographies, and psychobiographies of such leaders may be expected to go on rolling forth regardless of the contempt of social or intellectual historians. A very large share of those currently teaching American history in our universities and colleges, for instance, continue to believe that a "proper" understanding of such topics as Jeffersonianism, Jacksonianism, Progressivism, and the New Deal deeply matters. What to outsiders may seem at times an exquisite squabbling over minutiae (Has this or that "strain" within Progressivism been duly appreciated?) remain central items in the vocabulary and imagination of what is still the largest single fraction of historians of the United States.[20] When a comparably picayunish concern is shown for the mutual relations of Roosevelt, Churchill, and Stalin, only the most inhumanly consistent devotee of the history of anonymous millions in preference to the story of elites might be found to insist that Soviet-American cooperation was already so unlikely in historical terms, outside of a threat to mutual survival, as to make the words and deeds of individual statesmen and their advisers relatively inconsequential.[21] Similarly, at least this close to the events, it would seem very difficult to argue that Richard M. Nixon was simply a man in the general mold of American presidents, only a shade distinguishable from John F. Kennedy or Franklin D. Roosevelt.[22] To the degree that such points are acknowledged, social historians remain unable to convince their peers that all history should be reduced to the study of large groups of people.

Some political historians, adopting what is often called the "new" political history, seek in effect to retain their special concern with electoral politics while making it a branch of social history, particularly (in America) the history of ethnic conflict.[23] Voting, as a customarily recorded act comparable in this respect to being born or dying, is of course highly amenable to quantitative treatment (though not to the sampling of individuals). So too are the backgrounds of groups of officeholders.[24] The relatively few yet highly conspicuous practitioners of the "new" political history gained the prestige of social historians while dealing with the most conventional of historical subject matter, thus having it both ways.

The situation of intellectual history is very different. An upstart persuasion, widely launched in American universities only in the 1940s and 1950s, it furnished for a time much the same spirit of fresh excitement that has more recently centered in social history.[25] As an anti-Marxist approach to history, arguing for the power of ideas as the causes of events, it fit appropriately into the climate of the Cold War. American intellectual history then contributed to the ethos of holistic nationalism, while European intellectual history fostered respect for the heritage of "Western civilization" at a time when both Communist and Third World nations, from varying points of view, were challenging those values as aristocratic or ethnocentric.

Intellectual history was also more demanding than the earlier political history; its subject matter was more rarefied; it required the historian to be more like an intellectual himself. For this last reason it was often strongly disliked by political historians, especially in the Midwest. Intellectual history, in sum, could be attacked as a rather precious cult. Yet it was politically very safe, and—what usually mattered most of all for its adherents—it was deliciously complex, taking seriously as historical sources some of the most obscure and difficult writings of literate minorities.

During the drastically altered period of the 1960s, intellectual history came to be attacked as "minority" history of the wrong kind—reflecting the values of elites rather than of downtrodden groups. Leftists commonly so accused it (unless it dealt with the history of admired radical thinkers), while social and political historians in general were ready to join in the effort to put down what had long been regarded as a pretentious interloper within the guild. Some critics saw intellectual history as highly interesting but untenable in its claims for the causative power of ideas, at least those ideas associated with "high" culture. This was a relatively kind position. For others, formal ideas of any sort were as repugnant as Christian dogma as explanatory tools, in an age which had long since learned to view human motivation more realistically and therefore more skeptically.

Intellectual historians thus emerged with few friends. Marx and Freud remained probably the two most powerful influences upon historians who thought in terms broader than "common sense," and neither of them gave scope to the power of "ideas," taken at face value. In another direction, intellectual historians constantly faced the accusation of being mere dilettantes in their rapid forays over literary or metaphysical terrain, as compared with their colleagues in such fields as literature or philosophy. Confronted by these and other pressures, many intellectual historians retreated into the relatively uncontested arena of social thought, making their field into little more than a background for the understanding of political issues and conflicts. In the late 1970s, it was too soon to tell whether intellectual history would shrink away as a result of these numerous kinds of vulnerability.[26] A much discussed tactic of accommodation to newer strictures has been a shift toward studying popular culture and values rather than those of cultivated elites. Yet to do this from literary sources is extremely difficult, and like the "new" political history (except that it is not usually quantified), the result is something close to annexation into an all-compassing social history.[27]

What, then, finally of social history—the aggressor—itself? A curious aspect of it is that it is almost never pursued as such. Instead, what is pursued is demographic history, urban history, the history of the family, the history of women, the history of blacks, Chicanos, or native Americans, the history of radical social movements, the history of social mobility. *The* society, in its overall dimensions as an evolving structure, is hardly ever studied (so that many of the more myopic specialists among social historians must themselves be counted on the side of the earlier mentioned dividing line that pays almost no heed to social structure!).

A reason is clear. Social historians emphatically reject the holism of the older intellectual historians and also the dualistic lines of conflict (such as progressives versus stand-patters) of the older political historians. Instead the inhabitants of a given nation-state are seen to form an extraordinarily complicated mosaic. City-dwellers are very much unlike country-dwellers, men unlike women, rich unlike poor, "permanent" families unlike those of transients or immigrants, immigrants of one background unlike those of another. Each element in the mosaic must therefore have an utterly separate history. And there is little incentive to try to piece these histories together into a whole, aside perhaps from using the nebulous rubric of "modernization,"[28] because the parts are seen as the reality, the whole as an artificial construction which is sustained by politicians and financiers. "The whole" is the discredited realm of the elite; the parts are the genuine, and genuinely distinct, arenas of everyday life, which for nearly all people is life itself.

Quantification has affected the various important subfields of social history most unevenly. It has gone farthest in such areas as the study of social mobility, the study of economic and family history in early New England towns, the study of ethnic and economic patterns in residential housing, and in urban history generally. It has made far less headway in the history of women, blacks, or other ethnic groups as such. It is especially worth noting that the entire field of women's history, which took off so explosively during the early 1970s, has mainly followed traditional research techniques using literary evidence.

The "new" social history has been greatly influenced by the French *Annales* school; yet, it has turned out to be very diverse. As practiced in America, does it have some general characteristics? Sometimes one also hears the challenge— what is truly new about it? How does it differ in its treatment of topics from the social history of earlier decades? Two brief examples may give depth to our discussion here—the first involving descriptions of eighteenth-century Philadelphia, the second dealing with immigration and social mobility in Boston.

In each case, one may fruitfully compare parallel accounts written by older and younger social historians.

Carl Bridenbaugh's chapter-length discussion of Philadelphia in the age of Benjamin Franklin, published in 1942, has no explicit overall theme; it moves quite randomly from one subtopic to another, with little sense of any connected argument. A few elementary statistics are brought in.[29] Bridenbaugh's tone is friendly toward the cosmopolitan values of the merchant elite and toward high culture (apart from religion). His account gravitates toward the "amenities" of life on that level of society; it is concerned, for instance, with the aesthetics of contemporary buildings. Bridenbaugh was clearly happy to see his summary contribute to a comfortably familiar image of civic pride. Casually at the end, with no real evidence, Bridenbaugh says that Philadelphia at that time was an environment marked both by materialism and idealism, by individualism and social "communion and interchange."[30]

Providing a summary of roughly the same length on the same city in the same period, Sam B. Warner, Jr., in 1968 was concerned with Philadelphia only as an instance of "privatism" (his concept for the kind of mentality that fails to lead to socialism).[31] Most of his evidence is tied to this single dominating argument.[32] Indeed, one senses that Warner cares little about any possible uniqueness of Philadelphia—that he might just as readily have chosen to write about New York or Baltimore to make the same points. Warner is interested only in *types* of cities; Philadelphia is merely a good illustration of the preindustrial city. Warner also sees cities primarily in terms of spatial patterns, not physical textures or mental states (beyond the one of "privatism," which dictates all those patterns).[33] Warner's view is often openly retrospective or presentist in standpoint.[34] Yet, with one map, an extensive use of statistics, and some graphic descriptions of building and land-use patterns, Warner gives us a far more vivid feeling of what it must have been like for most people to be alive in eighteenth-century Philadelphia than we can ever receive from Bridenbaugh. Finally, where Bridenbaugh had lauded the public spirit and charitable works of mid-eighteenth-century Philadelphians, Warner accuses the very same people of having had next to no government and, by implication, extremely little public spirit.[35] Warner's view of Philadelphia is far more factually precise, culturally unspecific, and, above all, bleaker and less flattering.[36]

The contrast between two studies of Boston, Oscar Handlin's *Boston's Immigrants* (1941) and Stephan Thernstrom's *The Other Bostonians* (1973), is at least equally striking. Handlin's book is primarily a narrative. Its use of statistics is more than merely decorative, but figures are brought in only to establish facts on an occasional basis. By a later standard, there is a very offhanded attitude about evidence. Handlin tries to strike a note of comprehensiveness and definitiveness by providing tidy rhetorical summaries of motives and social patterns—for example, "Boston [in 1845] was a comfortable and well-to-do city in which the people managed to lead contented and healthy lives."[37] Today one cringes at such language. Handlin unabashedly quotes an elite literary figure, Ralph Waldo Emerson, to show "the fundamental ideas and basic assumptions permeating the social and economic structure of the society."[38] But Handlin was less theoretically naive than Bridenbaugh, embracing, for conceptual underpinnings, the cultural anthropology of Ruth Benedict.[39]

Many people would regard Stephan Thernstrom's book as a purer instance of the "new" social history than Warner's description of Philadelphia, because the text of his book consists entirely of a discussion of statistical tables—how they were calculated and what they appear to mean.[40] One might interpret the shift to such a format as anticipating an entirely new degree of reader skepticism about the adequacy of the evidence and the diversion of nearly all the author's energies to the attempt to overcome it. Thus history has become far less obviously literary.

With Handlin, a reader might well be mainly concerned about revealing word choices—for instance, is it ethnocentric to use such terms as "pest hole," "slothfulness," "a brood of evils," and, in a most unclear context, "malignant growth" when describing Irish slums?[41] With Thernstrom, one is primarily trying to critique his reasoning about the evidence.[42] The book is, from start to finish, an argument. It begins with a self-conscious listing of the particular questions he intends to ask of the past. His aim is to answer these questions, not to be comprehensive. On the other hand, he wants his study to be systematically comparable with those of other cities and this implies an unstated model of an ultimate geographical comprehensiveness, at least. Like Warner, Thernstrom is not much interested in what is special about the city he is studying; he is concerned with the city and is, so to speak, "rooting" for the typicality of Boston. Thernstrom's Boston is meant to be a building block in a mosaic.[43] Unlike Handlin, Thernstrom will bring in cultural explanations for phenomena only reluctantly and apologetically, as a last resort.[44] His view of human motivation in the Boston context appears to assume that the desire to rise in social position was central to the "inner" outlook of most Bostonians during the past century.[45] Perhaps for these reasons, Thernstrom's version of the "new" social history is far less tuned to conflict than narrative social history such as Oscar Handlin's.[46] Though claiming to arise from a concern for the history of nonelite masses, quantitative history like Thernstrom's has little in common with leftist-inspired history, which is conflict-oriented or at the very least tied to questions of power and domination and is usually antiquantitative in its approach to evidence.[47] Even Sam B. Warner writes more like a would-be city planner than a Marxist.

Quantitative social history such as Thernstrom's has won enormous attention in recent years and gained great prestige—not least from deserved recognition of the arduous character of the research it entails. It is now just about universally conceded to offer, in theory, a greatly enhanced degree of likelihood concerning the kinds of factual statements it can try to establish. (But these are limited by the surviving records to a rather small number of questions. In a spectacular recent case, when historians tried to use quantitative techniques in an area that had only scattered surviving wisps of evidence, the history of slavery, they stumbled very badly.)[48]

As social history has shifted more and more toward an argument over the meaning of evidence, fallacies in historical reasoning have come to be more widely and forcefully perceived.[49] Oddly this has meant that quantitative history, despite its high prestige, has become surprisingly vulnerable to countersuggestion in specific instances. Logical objections can very often be raised, not only as to how the evidence was gathered or sampled, but to central aspects of the ultimate interpretation. For instance, Thernstrom's book discerns a surprisingly high rate of upward social mobility in late nineteenth-century Boston. Yet, as he once briefly admits, the figures largely derive from the more settled spectrum of the population where fathers' as well as sons' occupations appear in the records.[50] The other major point of Thernstrom's book was to establish an enormously high rate of sheer geographical movement—the existence of a large, predominantly poor floating population. If transients are left out of the social mobility statistics Thernstrom has put together with such great pains, then a skeptical reader might well argue that those latter statistics are so biased upward as to be meaningless.

Surprisingly often, quantitative history is brittle as well as rigorous; it sits like an enormous skyscraper of enterprise which can all too often be toppled, or at least partly undermined, with a crowbar supplied from the arsenal of its own kind of logic.

If so, the fact may well stem from a genuinely important rise in the critical standards applied to works of history in the United States over the past fifteen years. Intermittently these standards reveal themselves in published reviews. Never has so much attention been paid to such issues as the adequacy of evidence, the need for precision over the exact nature of the social aggregate being discussed (such as "Americans," "black Americans," "middle-class women," and so on), and the strength or weakness, in logical terms, of particular expla-

nations. Our capacity to criticize works of history as they come forth has outrun
our capacity to write them in terms that will withstand such criticism. Historical
criticism, in the more demanding circles, is in much better shape in the contemporary United States than substantive historical writing.[51]

Yet with all this greater sophistication about historical argument, it remains
true that the very highest amount of prestige is still awarded to an historian who
uncovers (no matter how he does it) some incontestable yet previously unknown
fact of undeniably major importance. Discovery is what still counts the very
most—for instance, Stephan Thernstrom's disclosure of the previously unsuspected huge numbers of transient laborers in nineteenth-century American cities,
Tamara K. Hareven's revelation of kinship patterns affecting work assignments
among New Hampshire textile workers, or Herbert G. Gutman's discovery of
naming practices among some slaves which reveal their continuing autonomy
from white culture in certain crucial respects.[52] On this most fundamental level,
standards of historical excellence have not changed all that much in the last
hundred years.

In another important respect, American historical writing has altered less from
the 1950s to the 1970s than it had in the preceding twenty-year span. I refer to
the general abandonment of a belief in progress. This change occurred in the
immediate wake of Adolf Hitler and the American use of atomic bombs. Despite
a resurgence of some kinds of Marxism among younger historians in the 1960s,
few serious historical writers of any political persuasion in the United States
since about 1950 have assumed that some inbuilt force—whether socioeconomic, cultural, or religious—is propelling the course of history in the direction
they personally favor.[53] Even those who have celebrated American national
"greatness" have, with the probable exception of Daniel J. Boorstin, felt compelled to try to explain its occurrence on some basis other than destiny or providence—that is, with some degree of awareness that it might have happened
otherwise.[54] This watershed in fundamental attitudes toward history, which lies
far back in the 1940s or 1950s and which such a highly respected historian of
that period as David Potter appears somehow to straddle,[55] may well some day
strike us as more profoundly decisive in setting the tone of American historical
writing than the admittedly beguiling shift toward quantitative and mass-oriented
social history in the 1960s and 1970s.

Tied to this, and again broader than the trend toward quantitative social history, or even the rather limited vogue of comparative history as such, is the shift
in just about every phase of American historical writing toward the introduction
of outside points of reference, that is, to analogous phenomena lying beyond the
isolated case being discussed. Thus historians of slavery routinely bring in slavery in Brazil or the ancient world as an element in the appraisal of conditions
in the United States. And historians of the New England town show familiarity
with equivalent communities in England, France, and Sweden. Diplomatic historians increasingly are ashamed to be found using only the archives of one
country.

All this amounts to a trend toward placing any single nation-state, such as the United States, in context, both geographically and intellectually. Our minds recede farther and farther from it (as if looking at it from another planet), while on a different level we retain our intimate familiarity with it. This extreme duality of perception is what gives the best contemporary American historical writing its strength.

A consequence must be the questioning of previously unexamined assumptions about American uniqueness. The internationalism of basic recent historical processes in the modern world, in political as well as economic and social realms of life, will hopefully be agreed upon as the primary historical theme of the near future, drawing United States historians still farther out of their isolation and their sometimes nearsighted preoccupation with local trends and events that were not all that different from those going on in some other continents of the globe at slightly later dates.

Notes

1. Edward Pessen in *The New York Times*, 17 April 1977.

2. This approximate figure results from an attempt on my part to canvass the areas for a prize award, employing the middlingly broad definition of what intellectual history is. The figure was only slightly smaller for 1975.

3. A small number of young historians, trained but unable to obtain academic positions, are publishing, but they are not likely to affect the broad picture.

4. The spread of historical awareness through dramatization, as in the case of Alex Haley's largely fictional *Roots* (Garden City, N.Y., 1976), is of course far more impressive, but the present essay restricts itself to professional historical scholarship in the United States.

5. Leonard Krieger once argued that what characterizes the historian is his concern for change, in his "The Horizons of History," *American Historical Review* 63 (1957): 69–72. This is more sharply pointed than a more recent definition to the effect that "interest in time as a total dated system distinguishes the historian's concern . . . from . . . the social scientist's," in Robert Berkhofer, Jr., *A Behavioral Approach to Historical Analysis* (New York, 1969), p. 267. But it may be ambiguous in the sense that ideally a historian should be equally alert for evidences of continuity or change and must often try to account for failure to achieve change (for instance, of socialism in the United States). Actually historians may well be specialists in trying to explain unevenness in the rates of change (the fact that it is here very fast, there very slow) regardless of subject matter—the evolution of an entire society or of a single individual's career in life.

6. Intellectually diverse, American historians continued to be socially far more homogeneous, because of their relatively advantaged upbringings. See Everett C. Ladd, Jr., and Seymour Martin Lipset, *The Divided Academy* (New York, 1975), p. 173, Table 53.

7. While my opening remarks tried to take into account all historians living in the United States, the rest of the essay mainly of practical necessity confines itself to those who study the United States.

8. Foreshadowings of this aim date back to the "new" history of James Harvey Robinson around 1910. But only in the 1960s was the phrase "the people" truly taken to mean all the people (black, white, male, female) in quite an automatic way.

9. Within the New Left, certain factions accused others of doing precisely this, yet an observer perceives these tendencies across the entire range of the internal debate. See the introduction to James Weinstein and David W. Eakins, eds., *For a New America: Essays in History and Politics from Studies on the Left, 1959–1967* (New York, 1970), pp. 3–33. The problem is exactly parallel

to that of religiously committed historians who want to believe that religion has remained a vital force in American society in recent decades.

10. For example, Joyce and Gabriel Kolko, *The Limits of Power: The World and United States Foreign Policy, 1945–1954* (New York, 1972), pp. 11, 709.

11. Daniel Bell, *The End of Ideology* (New York, 1960), p. 287.

12. One might almost venture the hypothesis that simplicity resides in whatever motive force the historian believes to be central—the national political or cultural unit for historians of the 1950s, the corporate elite and the oppressed for leftists. Yet there is a genuine sense, transcending such a tendency, in which the earlier historians valued complexity in approaching any subject matter whatever. The strength of historical writing in the 1950s at its best had lain in its subtlety; the strength of the best such writing after about 1965 lay in its argumentative forcefulness. The same trend toward such simpler force may be seen operating (albeit in different terms) both in leftist history and in history seeking quantitative definiteness and precision.

13. See, for example, the textual argument in Kolko and Kolko, *The Limits of Power*, pp. 23–28, in relation to notes 22–32.

14. Eugene D. Genovese, *Roll, Jordan, Roll: The World the Slaves Made* (New York, 1974); Herbert G. Gutman, *The Black Family in Slavery and Freedom, 1750–1925* (New York, 1976).

15. Of course various other kinds of history in this sense (diplomatic, economic, psychohistorical) might fairly claim autonomy on a par with these three, so there is more arbitrariness in referring to this threefold division than there was in describing a division between leftists and nonleftists. Yet I believe these three labels do in fact reflect highly recognizable elements or factions within American history departments. Psychohistory, which generally confines itself to studying political or intellectual figures, strikes me more as a curiously intense spin-off from the climate of the 1950s, when Freud was so much in vogue, than as a major new direction in historical writing.

16. Arthur M. Schlesinger, Jr., is no doubt the most distinguished example.

17. The discussion among American historians over the celebrated issue of "consensus" or conflict as the key to American politics and culture has abated, it now being widely recognized that conflicts have been too central and numerous to allow for the kind of argument against their importance put forward by Daniel J. Boorstin, *The Genius of American Politics* (Chicago, 1953), but that, on the other hand, the most important conflicts have been ethnic, regional, or even (in the realm of labor history) class-oriented, rather than involving the election struggles of Republicans and Democrats. American historians of the 1950s who steered relatively clear of the consensus debate (e.g., Richard Hofstadter, David Potter) often emerged in the 1970s with higher reputations than those who had focused their energies on it.

18. Although when the counting is shifted to titles of dissertations in progress, social history (in all its phases) now emerges as the clear winner. From the list of them in the *Journal of American History* 64 (1977): 285–308, I count 121 in political history, 152 in social history, and 64 in intellectual history. However, those that can be called social history are overwhelmingly on rather trivial or conventional topics not inspired by the methods of the "new" social history. The "new" social history is practiced by a tiny elite within the profession.

19. For a recent lament at the loss of prestige of political history within the discipline, see Gordon A. Craig, "Political and Diplomatic History," in Felix Gilbert and Stephen R. Graubard, eds., *Historical Studies Today* (New York, 1972), pp. 356–7.

20. For a recent example of a highly traditional summary narrative of American political history (inspiring one commentator on it to remark, "Those textbooks of the 1940s were not putting us on"), see Robert Kelley, "Ideology and Political Culture from Jefferson to Nixon," *American Historical Review* 82 (1977): 531–62, and comments on it, 563–82. The footnotes to Kelley's article provide a good brief indication of works currently considered important by American political historians.

21. Most American diplomatic history has recently centered on the problem of the origins of the Cold War. For reviews of the literature, see Warren F. Kimball, "The Cold War Warmed Over," ibid., 79 (1974): 1119–36; and Betty Miller Unterberger, "Cold War Revisionism Reinterpreted," *Reviews in American History* 2 (1974): 436–45.

22. Ultimately it may be interesting precisely to try to do this. Yet the same technique clearly would not seem appropriate for Adolf Hitler.

23. Lee Benson, *The Concept of Jacksonian Democracy: New York As a Test Case* (Princeton, N.J., 1961), is widely credited with having moved American political history in this direction.

24. A recent instance of a vast project of this kind is Allan G. Bogue, Jerome M. Clubb, Carroll R. McKibbin, and Santa A. Traugott, "Members of the House of Representatives and the Processes of Modernization, 1789–1860," *Journal of American History* 63 (1976): 275–302; unfortunately the labors seem far more remarkable than the results.

25. For a recent account of the growth of intellectual history as a subfield of historical studies, see Felix Gilbert, "Intellectual History: Its Aims and Methods," in Gilbert and Graubard, *Historical Studies Today*, pp. 141–158.

26. The healthy publishing record of American intellectual historians in 1976 (see above, n. 2) means less in the long run than the question as to whether, in a period of declining resources, intellectual historians will or will not be replaced by their colleagues when they depart. A major effort at self-appraisal by American intellectual historians will appear in a forthcoming volume to be edited by Paul Conkin and John Higham.

27. For their part, social historians usually give lip service, at least, even now to the need to continue working with literary sources alongside the quantitative. The French *Annales* school, which has influenced American social historians as an important symbol of inspiration, legitimizes the effort to study collective mentalities, and is hence one form of intellectual history.

28. The attempt to apply modernization theory to United States history culminates so far in Richard D. Brown, *Modernization: The Transformation of American Life, 1600–1865* (New York, 1977). But the concept of modernization has been attacked as vague, or as unduly deterministic, and its use may have reached its peak. Its great virtue has been the way in which it has worked against nationalistic parochialism, by attempting to see the history of the modern world as a unit and the nations largely as illustrations of universal processes. One must hope that this international perspective can be retained even if historical trends are looked at with less reductionism than the concept of modernization possibly imposes.

29. Carl Bridenbaugh and Jessica Bridenbaugh, *Rebels and Gentlemen: Philadelphia in the Age of Franklin* (New York, 1965; first published 1942), pp. 1–28. In one brief instance, the trend toward irreligion (p. 18), shrewd use of figures is made.

30. Ibid., pp. 26, 27.

31. Sam Bass Warner, Jr., *The Private City: Philadelphia in Three Periods of Its Growth* (Philadelphia, 1968), pp. 3–21.

32. E.g., Bridenbaugh had seen religion as merely fading into irreligion, but Warner (p. 3) sees it as directly overcome by greed.

33. However, Warner has an account of tavern life that parallels Bridenbaugh's.

34. I.e., Warner's aims throughout his account are to identify types and stages in urban history, looking backward from the present, and to indict capitalistic individualism for what it has given us in the twentieth century.

35. Warner's judgment that eighteenth-century Philadelphia was practically ungoverned clearly seems to stem from a planning-oriented perspective in the mid-twentieth century. These conflicting standpoints lead to a highly revealing factual clash. Bridenbaugh (p. 11) had described how "at intervals along [all] these thoroughfares [of Philadelphia in the 1770s] some five hundred public pumps supplied the citizens with their water, and never failed to make an impression on visitors." Warner (p. 10) states: "There were no public schools, no public water, and at best thin charity." For Warner, eighteenth-century Philadelphia was a "community" only in the limited, literal sense of offering a high degree of face-to-face contacts among its inhabitants.

36. The main similarity between Bridenbaugh and Warner, as social historians, lies in their common awareness of the importance of economic conditions and such factors as social class, social mobility, and ethnicity. On topics of this kind the two accounts overlap a good deal, although Bridenbaugh emphasizes trade routes linking Philadelphia with the outside world (their effect in creating a cultural cosmopolitanism is an implicit theme of his chapter), while Warner emphasizes

the work and living patterns of artisans within the city itself, since they formed the bulk of the population.

37. Oscar Handlin, *Boston's Immigrants: A Study in Acculturation* rev. ed. (New York, 1974; first published 1941), p. 20.

38. Ibid., pp. 20–21.

39. Or at least of that generation of anthropologists more generally. The subtitle of his book (above, n. 37) reveals this.

40. Stephan Thernstrom, *The Other Bostonians: Poverty and Progress in the American Metropolis, 1880–1970* (Cambridge, Mass., 1973).

41. Handlin, *Boston's Immigrants*, pp. 107, 113, 117, 206.

42. However, questions of language return in Thernstrom's book at the level of word choices made to describe particular statistical results (e.g., that Bostonians had "good chances" to rise, p. 73), because each such summary statement conveys a given degree of optimism or pessimism in viewing the workings of American society. Any book containing words as well as figures, and not utterly trivial, no doubt will retain this dimension.

43. Thernstrom's image of a city such as Boston also seems more mechanistic than Handlin's, as when he calls Boston "a major importer and a major exporter of human raw material" (p. 29).

44. Ibid., p. 168.

45. In fairness, this is only an inference from Thernstrom's general silence about inner mental states, together with his decision that social mobility is a centrally important theme to explore.

46. Of course this is ironic, since Handlin explicitly dislikes ethnic conflict (e.g., see p. 229).

47. In his treatment of blacks, for one chapter out of his nine (pp. 176–219), Thernstrom uses his statistical sources to emphasize the bleakness of the life-chances of the group, reenforcing a highly critical view of white domination in American society. This is in striking contrast to Handlin's astonishingly rosy view (pp. 179–180, 212–213) of black prospects in a slightly earlier Boston.

48. It is now often implied that Robert W. Fogel and Stanley M. Engerman, *Time on the Cross*, 2 vols. (Boston, 1974) contains so many suspect generalizations on the basis of scanty and unrepresentative (though technically quantitative) evidence that the book ought not to have been published. Among other critiques, see Herbert G. Gutman, *Slavery and the Numbers Game: A Critique of* Time on the Cross (Urbana, Ill., 1975).

49. Symptomatic of this trend is David Hackett Fischer, *Historians' Fallacies* (New York, 1970).

50. Thernstrom, *The Other Bostonians*, p. 80.

51. A suggestion recently made by Henry F. May in conversation with the author.

52. See above, nn. 14, 40; and Tamara K. Hareven, "Family Time and Industrial Time: Family and Work in a Planned Corporation Town, 1900–1924," *Journal of Urban History* 1 (1975): 365–89.

53. Thus leftists have had to confront and explain the failure of socialism in the United States and Western Europe, and indeed in America the decline of milder versions of liberal reformism as well.

54. Boorstin (see above, n. 17) carries his celebratory tone to such a pitch as often to suggest a continuing belief in providence akin to George Bancroft's in the nineteenth century.

55. In his *People of Plenty: Economic Abundance and the American Character* (Chicago, 1954), Potter backs off ironically from celebratory providentialism but avoids the clearcut skepticism about the whole subject of national uniqueness and destiny which has increasingly characterized the thinking of younger American historians more recently. With all its faults, *People of Plenty* may still be the best brief interpretive synthesis of American history in a period when few historians try to write in such terms; it may be compared with Robert H. Wiebe, *The Segmented Society: An Introduction to the Meaning of America* (New York, 1975).

Bibliography

These titles are examples of seminal or otherwise distinguished works in American history, representing a wide variety of fields and approaches, published since 1960. Titles marked with an asterisk (*) illustrate use of quantitative techniques.

Bailyn, Bernard. *The Ideological Origins of the American Revolution* (Cambridge, Mass., 1967).

*Benson, Lee. *The Concept of Jacksonian Democracy* (Princeton, N.J., 1961).

*Bogue, Allan G. *From Prairie to Corn Belt: Farming on the Illinois and Iowa Prairies in the Nineteenth Century* (Chicago, 1963).

Brody, David. *Steelworkers in America: The Nonunion Era* (Cambridge, Mass., 1960).

Davis, David B. *The Problem of Slavery in the Age of the Revolution, 1770–1823* (Ithaca, N.Y., 1975).

Flower, Elizabeth, and Murray G. Murphey, *A History of Philosophy in America*, 2 vols. (New York, 1977).

Genovese, Eugene D. *Roll, Jordan, Roll: The World the Slaves Made* (New York, 1974).

*Greven, Philip J., Jr. *Four Generations: Population, Land, and Family in Colonial Andover, Massachusetts* (Ithaca, N.Y., 1970).

*Gutman, Herbert G. *The Black Family in Slavery and Freedom, 1750-1925* (New York, 1976).

*Katz, Michael B. *The People of Hamilton, Canada West: Family and Class in a Mid-Nineteenth Century City* (Cambridge, 1975).

Kolko, Joyce, and Gabriel Kolko. *The Limits of Power: The World and United States Foreign Policy, 1945–1954* (New York, 1972).

Lasch, Christopher. *The New Radicalism in America, 1889-1963: The Intellectual As a Social Type* (New York, 1965).

May, Henry F. *The Enlightenment in America* (New York, 1976).

Morgan, Edmund S. *American Slavery, American Freedom: The Ordeal of Colonial Virginia* (New York, 1975).

*Pessen, Edward. *Riches, Class, and Power Before the Civil War* (Lexington, Ky., 1973).

Potter, David M. *The Impending Crisis, 1848–1861* (New York, 1976).

Sherwin, Martin J. *A World Destroyed: The Atomic Bomb and the Grand Alliance* (New York, 1975).

*Thernstrom, Stephan. *The Other Bostonians: Poverty and Progress in the American Metropolis, 1880–1970* (Cambridge, Mass., 1973).

Warner, Sam B., Jr. *Streetcar Suburbs: The Process of Growth in Boston, 1870–1900* (Cambridge, Mass., 1962).

Wiebe, Robert H. *The Search for Order, 1877–1920* (New York, 1967).

10 JEAN GLÉNISSON

France*

According to Henri-Irénée Marrou, history as it is practiced today in France is characterized by three main traits: the preeminent position occupied by historians whom it is customary to group together as the *Annales* school, inspired originally by Lucien Febvre, Marc Bloch, and Fernand Braudel; the widespread influence of a Marxism in its sometimes orthodox but more often popularized version—the purveyor, in any event, of specific research topics and a ready-made vocabulary; and finally, the increasing resort to computers and the science of statistics, whether this phenomenon is viewed—according to one's inclinations or one's convictions—as a simple surrender to the dictates of fashion or as a significant victory of "serial" history.[1] At a time when the historiographical landscape is changing with singular rapidity, the above judgment, formulated in 1974, remains exact. It is borne out by the evolution of the ideas, methods, and practices of the two generations of scholars—heirs and successors of the great historians of the 1930s—who have dominated the academic scene since the end of World War II.

The 1930s: The Foundations of a School of History

After half a century, the *Annales* has itself become a historical subject (more often abroad than in France, it is true), and it is possible today to retrace the stages in the formation of this empire of scholarship.[2]

On 15 January 1929, "at a moment when the history of the world suddenly changed direction," two Strasbourg professors, Lucien Febvre (1878–1956) and Marc Bloch (1886–1944), launched their new journal, "no bigger than a toy ship on the broad Atlantic." Today, everyone is conscious of the prophetic timeliness of the occasion, the chosen title *(Annales d'histoire économique et sociale),* and the purpose, as set forth in a very brief note "To Our Readers" which introduced the maiden issue.

It was never a question of creating the official organ of a "school of historiography." The first generation of the *Annales* was above all the "open forum"

*Translated from the French by John Day.

of a historiography that sought to free itself from the constraints of a "positivism" represented, for the sake of polemic, by the coauthors of *Introduction aux études historiques* (1898), Charles-Victor Langlois (1863–1929) and Charles Seignobos (1854–1942). Overtures were made to foreign historiography for the benefit of French academics, immured in a scientific nationalism which was historically the result of Franco-German rivalry and of the humiliating defeat of 1870, and simultaneously to related disciplines previously ignored or abhorred: the geography of Vidal de la Blache, the sociology of Durkheim, the science of economics.

The journal was not without precursors. The *Revue de synthèse historique* of Henri Berr, who died in 1954, had been pursuing similar goals in France since 1900. The new tendencies that it was intended to promote were also perceived in other countries. The *Economic History Review* was founded at about the same time as the *Annales* and was charged with an analogous mission. Lucien Febvre and Marc Bloch were not by any means the only champions of a new departure in history in alliance with the other social sciences. They had a certain number of rivals: Henri Pirenne, who was also their friend and mentor, Johan Huizinga, Mario Praz, and above all Max Weber, none of whom published in the *Annales*. In France other scholars were marching to the same tune: François Simiand, who died in 1935, was busy studying business cycles, both in the present and in the past; Ernest Labrousse, the pioneer, together with Simiand, of serial history, but who never forgot that "the economic man is a pure abstraction"; and Georges Lefebvre (1874–1959), who breathed new life into the social history of the French Revolution.[3] Moreover, Febvre and Bloch preached by example. Their own works nurtured the apostolate of their journal.

But it was the *Annales* itself that over the years undermined the positivist definition of historical fact, destroyed the taboo on unwritten evidence, imposed a dialogue with the sister disciplines, discredited the history of events, rejected the primacy of political history by insisting on its interaction with economic and cultural history, repudiated traditional biography which isolated the individual, and succeeded, finally, in making "sensibility" or modes of feeling the object of serious historical research.

In 1971 the Belgian historian Jan Dhont reminisced:

I left a university at the end of my studies where the students held to the orthodox conception of history as the study of facts in their uniqueness. I discovered, at the end of the war, a university where a mass of students were imbued with the spirit of the *Annales*. I never have discovered how that came about. It certainly had nothing to do with the professors. It must have just been something in the air.[4]

The Second Annales: The Age of Braudel

The professional historians were breathing the same air. The International Congress of Historical Sciences that met in Paris in 1950 was visibly under the spell of the victorious ideas of Marc Bloch and Lucien Febvre. But only Febvre could savor that moment of triumph. Bloch was dead, executed in 1944. And the journal had changed its name. To the word *Annales,* which was already famous, had been added in 1946 three nouns that ring like a slogan from 1789— *Economies, Sociétés, Civilisations*—each clearly in its carefully assigned place, and it is no accident that they are all in the plural. If you were to append "populations," you would have the four cornerstones of one of the most fruitful periods in the history of French historiography, even if Fernand Braudel himself maintains that the golden age of the *Annales* was the decade from 1929 to 1939.

At the end of the war, Braudel was a newcomer to the editorial board of the *Annales,* but he was already a confidant and the chosen successor of Lucien Febvre. In 1946 he defended his thesis, now in print as *La Méditerranée et le Monde méditerranéen à l'époque de Philippe II,* which existed in outline in 1939 and was completed in a German prisoner-of-war camp. At the time of its publication in 1949, the book was greeted by Febvre himself as "a revolutionary new way of looking at history, an upheaval for our old habits of mind, a historical mutation of the first magnitude." And it remains, in the words of its American reviewer, "a prodigiously innovative study of Mediterranean civilizations . . . probably the most significant historical work to appear since World War II."[5]

But one did not have to wait for the revised edition of 1966, nor the English translation of 1972. From the early 1950s a new "model" existed in the world of historians, "a heritage," said R. Chartier, "of the human geography of Vidal de la Blache . . . a geo-history of past societies that promoted land, water, and climate to the front ranks." In Braudel's own words,

Everything converges across time and space to give rise to a history in slow motion, the mirror of permanent values. Geography in the new scheme of things ceases to be an end in itself and becomes the means to an end. It helps us to discover the slowest-moving of structural realities, to create a new long-term perspective.[6]

It was on this interplay of space and time that Fernand Braudel based his conception of history. Time, one might almost say, works out its destiny through the history of mankind, whom it molds unmercifully to its purposes; "time the demiurge" whose power can never be grasped at first hand. At the level of everyday commonsense observation, only the short term (*la courte durée*), the "time of events," exists. The progress in history, its new orientation, its dialogue with the other social sciences, notably the science of economics, suddenly discloses behind the blinding light of events the existence of medium-term economic movements. A special expression soon suggested itself to the economists to designate this still rather breathless respiration of historical time that breaks up into medium-length fragments of ten, fifteen, twenty, or fifty years: *conjoncture.* The long term (*la longue durée*), the conjuncture, and the short term (or event) transformed history into a "dialectic of time-spans."

The vision of the world and of history that Braudel developed and refined over the years in the pages of the *Annales,* during the course of his discussions with Claude Lévi-Strauss, and in his other writings, assumes in retrospect a singular kind of majesty. Would it have carried the day with the same ease if he had not possessed an institutional instrument of extraordinary effectiveness: the Sixth Section (economic and social sciences), established by Lucien Febvre in 1947 as part of the old Ecole Pratique des Hautes Etudes? Traian Stoianovich has recently described the inner workings of that powerful lever of scholarly persuasion.[7] It was there that Braudel's disciples were formed and sometimes employed while waiting for the traditional institutions of higher learning to open their doors to them, however reluctantly. It was from there that their ideas were spread abroad through the pages of the *Annales*. It was there, finally, that their own studies were published in numerous prestigious collections: *Affaires et gens d'affaires, Archéologie et civilisation, Démographie et sociétés, Les Hommes et la terre, Monnaies-prix-conjonctures, Ports-routes-trafics*.

The titles alone of these different series confirm the essentially economic orientation of what had come to be known (especially outside France) as the *Annales* school. At the same time, the goal of a "total" history, from economic history to the history of mental structures, was, within certain chronological and geographical limits, being realized. A truly impressive mass of business and financial records was sifted through. The technical resources of economics and statistics were utilized to study the past. *Annales* historians sailed the Atlantic of the treasure fleets or journeyed deep into the provinces of preindustrial Europe.[8]

The 1970s: History Dismembered

At the start of the 1970s the climate changed. An event occurred that produced a chain reaction in the academic hierarchy: Fernand Braudel reached retirement age. He abandoned his chair at the Collège de France and at the same time, his directorship of the Sixth Section and of the *Annales*. The Braudellian empire disintegrated. The moment of the succession was at hand, and a new generation of scholars seized the reins of power. Braudel retained his immense prestige, but the choice of personnel in the main sectors of teaching and research, the nominations to the scientific committees, and the selection of articles and books for publication in the *Annales* and in the scholarly collections now fell to his different heirs, for the responsibilities were henceforth divided. The unifying role played by the master of the *Annales* disappeared.

The Sixth Section was overhauled in order to conform to the academic system that emerged from the upheaval of May 1968. It gained its independence by seceding from the old Ecole Pratique des Hautes Etudes and was rebaptized Ecole des Hautes Etudes en Sciences Sociales. A new term was coined: "the New History." The expression is no less ambiguous than "*Annales* school."

It sometimes happens, as a matter of fact, that the two are confused to the point of assigning the origins of the New History to the days of Lucien Febvre and Marc Bloch. French scholars, however, cannot claim the invention, nor the monopoly, nor even the trademark. Lawrence Stone understands by the term "New History" a body of related historiographical currents which are dominant today in many Western countries.[9] It is sufficiently vague in any case to guarantee its success. Historians of different generations and varying backgrounds have adapted it to their several purposes and use it indiscriminately in the various forums of scholarly intercourse where it has become the custom to raise questions concerning the methods, the value, and the results of recent historical production.

This epistemological effervescence is in fact one of the most striking characteristics of contemporary French historiography. Methodological inquiry has become a literary fashion: Paul Veyne explains "How History Is Written" (*Comment on écrit l'histoire*, 1971); Emmanuel Le Roy Ladurie republishes several of his articles on methodology in "The Historian's Domain" (*Territoire de l'historien*, 1973); A. Casanova and F. Hincker edit their interviews between 1967 and 1973 with historians of various persuasions in "History Today" (*Aujourd'hui l'histoire*, 1974); Jacques Le Goff and Pierre Nora present three volumes of essays on "Making History" (*Faire de l'histoire*, 1974); Pierre Chaunu meditates on "History and the Social Sciences" (*Histoire, Science Sociale*, 1974); Michel de Certeau analyzes "The Writing of History" (*L'Ecriture de l'histoire*, 1975); Jean Chesneaux asks "Should We Clear the Decks of the Past?" (*Du passé faisons table rase?*, 1976). Only the principal titles have been cited here. The total output is astonishing. The *Cahiers du Forum-Histoire* has counted eighteen such works in four years (1973-1976), not including articles published in journals, which are even more numerous. Truly, we have come a long way since Lucien Febvre found the philosophical laziness of professional historians so disheartening.[10]

Theoretical Positions

Diverse currents run through this prolific literature, and certain representative personalities stand out. Pierre Vilar is the respected spokesman for the classical Marxist position. At the opposite pole, Paul Veyne dares to defend with a literary verve nourished by impeccable erudition the historian's right to construct a "plot" using the "facts" with only "pleasure" as his guide. Between these two tradition-laden extremes, there exists no single body of doctrine. Perhaps, as Jacques Le Goff and Pierre Nora write, the historian is waiting for his Saussure. The self-proclaimed spokesmen for the New History dare not permit themselves the luxury of being openly dogmatic. The times we live in would not tolerate it. From their writings, from their numerous collective works, and from their interviews with the press, a body of concepts and doctrine nevertheless emerges which might be considered, at the risk of oversimplification, a common ideology openly embraced or unconsciously assumed by most French historians of our day.

The renunciation of all claim to objectivity (in the positivist meaning of the term) is one of the basic traits of this general attitude. The historian knows that innocence is denied him. Conditioned by his background, his times, his professional milieu, and caught up in the system of production of historical literature, he tends to agree with Georges Duby that "the results of my inquiry are no doubt predetermined by a programming of which I am not fully conscious."

It is impossible to arrive at the facts. History is nothing more than a contingent reading of the past, related by witnesses who are themselves conditioned by circumstances. The historian moves in a world of relative truths. As Pierre Nora describes it,

Until recently, historians were conscious of a unifying principle in their writings. A royal chronicler wrote for the glory of the king. Bossuet's *Discours sur l'histoire universelle* was imbued with the sense of a historical oneness dominated by God. Voltaire knew that he was writing about human progress. Today's relativism has made historians more modest. Where is their vantage point? The heights of science? Who would dare to make such a claim?

Is it the diffused heritage of psychoanalysis, of German historicism, whose French spokesman is Raymond Aron, of the lessons of the early *Annales* with their censure of the certainties of positivism? Something of all of these and of much else besides which partakes of the spirit of a time that refuses to believe in the virtues of science, and having lost faith in progress, dreams of a happier age which it places in the past. This leads, as Philippe Ariès has remarked, to a sort of rehabilitation of premodern cultures thanks to the opportune mediation of historians. It finds expression in Michel de Certeau's new "time relationship": we have grown conscious of the fact that "tradition which we had consigned to the dead past thinking to exorcise it survives in the practices and ideologies of the present." People hunger for continuity. It is no longer a question of "that unyielding time, irreversible and understandable, which continues to advance in the face of every obstacle," but of a time that repeats itself, that twists and turns and retreats. The linear time of the positivists had been called into question by the "Bergsonian" *Annales* and replaced in the 1950s by Braudel's differential tempos of "what moves rapidly, what moves slowly, and what appears not to move at all."

But it seems that only the third of these, the long-term movement (*la longue durée*), has been retained. For one had to admit that the New History is hardly relevant to periods of rapid change like the present. It is appropriate, paradoxically, to the study of societies which change but little, as E. Le Roy Ladurie, to whom we owe the concept of "motionless history," has observed. Pierre Nora, for his part, has resurrected the significant event, indispensable to the student of recent history.[11] The medium term—the *conjoncture*—so dear to the hearts of historians of the 1950s and 1960s appears to have been consigned to oblivion. The long term is the favorite time of anthropology and ethnology, disciplines that are repeatedly evoked by present-day historians because the organization of relations between history and the other social sciences is at the heart of the philosophical and epistemological "system" embracing the New History as practiced in France.

From the beginning, the *Annales* had advocated a dialogue with the related disciplines, particularly sociology—the primacy of history being taken as self-evident. But by the 1950s it was clear that economics was the new favorite, assigned to play the key role in the system of historical interpretation. That role is denied it today. Jacques Le Goff has protested against the "imperialistic designs of economic history." Georges Duby, who practiced it at the beginning of his career, no longer considers the role of economics decisive.

What bothers me about the idea of determinism which we seem condemned to live with is that it implies a causal relationship. The more my work as an historian progresses, the more suspicious I become of the quest for single causes. We should think rather in terms of a multitude of echoes, of interrelations, of a sort of river where the different currents all run together.

The influence of structuralism? Without a doubt. But who can deny that the antideterminism of today's historians is implicitly a criticism of Marxism? "What is at stake," write M. Grenon and R. Robin (who have not rallied to the colors of the New History) "is the concept of an ordered social hierarchy in social structures, and, beyond that, the place that Marx has assigned to the economy."[12]

The radical antideterminism of the New History is of no small consequence. If you deny any kind of hierarchical organization to history, you reduce it to fragments. In practice it is partitioned into scores of genres and specialties with hardly any connection between them. The impression on reading *Faire de l'histoire*, a manifesto in three volumes of the dominant currents in contemporary French historiography, is one of profusion from which emerges, in fact, a swarm of "New Histories."

Formerly political in orientation, more recently economic and social, historiography today, in seeking to avoid the pitfalls of historical determinism, would dissolve into the common magma of the social sciences had it not discovered a unifying factor—a *specificity*. Thanks in particular to Robert Mandrou, Georges Duby, and Philippe Ariès, history disposes of various concepts—the "mental," the "imaginary," the "ritual"—which make it possible, if not to explain, at least to *illuminate* in a uniform light regardless of time and place the modes of being and behaving of human societies. For, writes Duby,

the sentiments that individuals and social groups feel concerning their different situations, and the conduct dictated by that sentiment, are not directly determined by their economic condition but by their conception of it. This is never completely realistic but always modified by the play of an intricate body of mental images.

Thus was born the history of mentalities, the great specialty of French historians of the 1970s, so much so in fact that Lawrence Stone considers the word untranslatable into English. Judged in the "Rapport de conjoncture" of the Centre National de la Recherche Scientifique in 1969 as "filled with pitfalls and in danger of too hasty realizations," this type of history was not long in defining its field of action by instituting—so reads the report for 1974—a distinction between its own domain, which is that of daily life and long-surviving systems of value, and the history of the culture of the elites, which is creation and change. It presupposes that in principle every society possesses simultaneously diverse cultural milieux which are juxtaposed and interlocking and transmitted by language, myth, and upbringing.

Methodological Consequences

Every dominant ideology leaves its mark on methodology. From this point of view the New History sanctions a particular subject matter, a particular kind of source, and particular techniques.

SUBJECT MATTER Closely allied to anthropology today, but still bearing the deep imprint of sociology, economics, and demography, the New History is concerned almost exclusively with human masses and social groups at the expense of the individual princes, heroes, and leaders who had kept historians occupied for two thousand years.

SOURCES As long as the star performers were kings, statesmen, ministers, prelates, generals, and revolutionary leaders, the rare or unique document relevant to their actions and motivations stood at the top of the documentary hierarchy that every type of history implicitly adopts. But the mass of humanity can be grasped only by studying a mass of sources: financial and judicial archives, property censuses, tithe accounts, parish registers. Written records, moreover, no longer satisfy the historian-ethnologist who has developed a taste for archeological artifacts and oral tradition. The historians of medieval "mentalities" have discovered that practically any kind of source can serve their purposes. Charters and registers are revealing not only for their content but also for their external aspects: narrative sources, neglected for a time; chivalric and courtly literature; works of art; coats of arms; tools and implements—all bear witness to a particular vision of the world.

TECHNIQUES The utilization of these masses of documents is beyond the possibilities of the single historian who once got by on "paper and ink and leisure time." Computer technology is needed to quantify, select, and decompose into comparable elements the "millions of deeds" in Chaunu's hyperbole. The vogue of quantitative history, as opposed to literary or "impressionistic" history, is due to the existence in the past fifteen years of auxiliary electronic brains with infallible memories. "The historian of tomorrow will be a computer programmer or nothing at all," says Le Roy Ladurie.[13]

Historical Production: The Favorite Topics

One of the chief characteristics of French history writing today is the rapidity with which ideological and thematic currents pass into the bloodstream of historical practice and production. This phenomenon is to be attributed first of all to the popular appetite for books and television programs on historical subjects: the professional historian has descended from his ivory tower in order to respond to the growing demand. Spokesmen for the New History have become public figures. They can draw attention to the particular points of view and fields of research. And the influence is reciprocal—historians are sensitive to the popular concerns and "fantasies" of the moment. Ecological history was born, for example, as an instantaneous response to the universal anxiety about the defilement of nature. The history of the human body and the history of sexuality, inconceivable in the age of Queen Victoria and Napoleon III, are clearly the fruit of today's "mentality." Thus the latest achievements of academic historians are transmitted almost without transition to the public by word and picture and through the diffusion of works—unencumbered by scholarly apparatus—which were once reserved for a small circle of specialists. Without question the existence of this new market stimulates and accelerates the production of popular history. The historian no longer addresses himself solely to his peers.[14]

These circumstances help to explain a certain conformity evident among members of the profession who are inevitably borne along on the currents that enjoy the most favor with the public; all the more so, given the present organization of French research, which encourages such standardizing tendencies. The financial largesse of the Centre National de la Recherche Scientifique has made it possible to multiply the number of colloquiums, round tables, and scientific seminars that serve to assure the rapid diffusion of ideas and to introduce new works; the speedy publication of discussions and communications which is now the rule has also contributed to this trend. For innovations to become known and accepted it is no longer necessary to wait for the defense of a *thèse d'Etat*, a handmade masterpiece bulging with footnotes that takes at least a decade to produce. This doctoral dissertation, a key element nonetheless in the system of university appointment and advancement, still constitutes the foundation upon which the French historical school as a whole rests. At worst it represents the accumulation of a veritable treasure trove of information which nourishes or consecrates after a certain lapse of time the new trends in history. At best it creates these new trends themselves. The "Rapport de conjoncture" of the Centre National de la Recherche Scientifique for 1974 noted with regard to mod-

ern and contemporary history that the traditional index of scientific productivity—the number of dissertations defended ("sanctioning a long-term individual
commitment to which the Nation still attaches a certain intellectual and moral
value")—had broken all records.

The Topics

More abundant than ever, historical production at first sight is multiform. It
appears that every practicing historian is trying to stake out his own private
reserve in the diversified domain called the New History. But closer inspection
reveals that traditional categories and periodization have not lost their old vigor
despite the widely declared intention to ignore them. There are still histories of
the economy, of society, and of institutions. There are still histories of the ancient world, of the Middle Ages, and of modern times. It often happens that the
new labels are simply affixed to the old merchandise. It is true, however, that
the introduction of the concept of *mentalité,* combined with the use of quantitative methods, is beginning to stir things up. Cultural, technical, social, and
political elements are interwoven to such a point that the old textbook divisions
tend to disappear. It seems more appropriate to speak of historical topics, viewed
in a different light, than of historical genres.

The primary domain of quantification naturally is economic history, which
continues to flourish despite the loss of its former hegemony and a certain las-
situde observed by Jacques Le Goff. Since 1961 we have witnessed the intrusion
of professional economists into the field once reserved for the historian. Jean
Marczewski and a group of scholars under his direction have launched *L'Histoire
quantitative de l'économie française* and applied to past centuries the "model"
of national income accounting. The historians who had criticized their efforts
(P. Vilar, P. Chaunu, J. Bouvier) now recognize that the long work of retrospective econometrics has renewed the methods and results of economic history
in a very positive way, particularly from the point of view of macroeconomics
(as Denis Richet noted in 1973), but they regret the partial character of the proposed model. The professional historians, for their part, have also sometimes
engaged in collective research, which has the merit of attacking problems of
long-term economic movements without regard for the time periods of traditional
history. But it is chiefly the eighteenth and nineteenth centuries that have been
studied. "In France," writes Jean Bouvier, "economic history has barely entered the twentieth century." He lists the following principal subjects of French
research in this field at the beginning of the 1970s: the history of banking in the
nineteenth and twentieth centuries; industrialization and French economic
growth in the nineteenth century; communications (the railroads, the Renault
automotive industry); and foreign economic relations up to 1914.[15]

In economic history the vogue of quantification naturally favors the age of
statistics. The interest in merchants, trade routes, and commerce in the pre-
statistical period (from the Middle Ages at least to the seventeenth century),

which flourished in the 1950s and 1960s, still survives, however, to some extent in medieval history: Robert Delort's study of the fur trade and Henri Dubois's history of the fairs of Châlons, to mention only these two, have recently enriched our knowledge of international commerce and commercial techniques at the close of the Middle Ages.

But as we well know, one of the main concerns of French historians is to preserve an intimate connection between social and economic history. On this terrain, where they are used to moving with particular assurance, the advance continues, as can be judged from the number of new *thèses d'Etat* and of multivolume historical syntheses, another French specialty. Thus the recently completed *Histoire économique et sociale de la France,* edited by Fernand Braudel and Ernest Labrousse, and the *Histoire de la France rurale,* published in 1975–1976 by Georges Duby and Armand Wallon, present the results of current research by leading specialists along with up-to-date bibliographies.[16] A reading of these works confirms the French taste for the study of sociological categories and their milieux.

A few recent examples representative of historical work in different fields can serve to illustrate this trend. "Sundering the procrustean bed of traditional military history," Philippe Contamine has studied the armies of the kings of France between 1337 and 1494. "Ethnologist of a soldiering fraternity, anthropologist of the entire French society as mirrored in a single profession, he brings to life a heretofore little known institution, the permanent army of 10,000 men forged by the French monarchy, and, at the same time, a new sociological type, the career soldier"—a far cry in status if not in morals from the freebooting soldier of fortune of the mercenary bands. In *La Noblesse bretonne au XVIIIe siècle,* Jean Meyer describes how the nobility of Brittany transformed itself into a closed caste as the unforeseen consequence of an administrative decision: the census of the nobility ordered by Colbert, minister of Louis XIV, for the purpose of unmasking the false nobles trying to avoid paying taxes. For the contemporary period, Antoine Prost has studied the veterans of World War I, figures so familiar in French society over the last half century that one is surprised to discover that they are already historical subjects. They formed a coeval pressure group singularly lacking in social cohesion but subject to collective *élans* and hence a sort of human reservoir for the parties and political movements of the period between the two world wars.[17]

Several recent works of history are devoted to the study of elites. Daniel Roche, for example, has analyzed the composition of the scientific academies in the French provinces in the age of the Enlightenment. And the medievalists have multiplied their monographic studies of noble families (the d'Albret by A. Marquette, the lords of Murol by P. Charbonnier, the Tonnerre by M. T. Caron).

At the other end of the social spectrum, the "active minorities" and their milieux are an object of interest that is particularly revealing of current attitudes as well as a further proof of their direct influence on historical production. Since Robert Mandrou's classic study of witchcraft during a period when the more enlightened members of society (represented by the corps of magistrates) had turned their backs on autos-da-fé, the subject has attracted other scholars.[18] To-gether with Michel Foucault (who shares rather than inspires the curiosity of historians), a host of scholars has suddenly discovered the world of the social outcast, the criminal, and the rebel. Michel Mollat and his students have revealed how diversified was the universe of medieval proverty: underpaid wage workers, the hopeless poor, beggars and wayfarers, and the image of Christ on earth— the adepts of voluntary poverty, the disciples or imitators of Saint Francis of Assisi. Yves-Marie Bercé, like other acolytes of Roland Mousnier, has devoted himself to the study of the popular uprisings of the seventeenth century. He provides us with a typology of the revolts in southwest France from 1590 to 1790, which represented not so much disorderly outbursts as a predictable form of social behavior, and which were directed more against the state and its tax collectors, the billeting of soldiers, and the high price of bread than against the nobility.

The observer who is familiar with the usual categories of historiography brushes up against an uncertain frontier here. Does the history of deviant social groups represent the avant-garde of social and economic history or is it peculiar to the New History of mental structures? For in the process of illuminating cer-tain forms of collective behavior, the authors are also clearly endeavoring to define and delimit social classes. The subject, seen in this light, cuts across the boundaries of recognized historical specialties.

One can say the same for two diversified multiform themes which are the current delight of a host of scholars: festivals and death. Today's historian is fascinated by ritual. He is determined to free it from the constraints of folklore and ethnology which tend to ignore its temporal dimension. It is necessary to distinguish between different levels of culture, for among festivals there were dynastic festivals, court festivals, and official festivals, such as the public re-joicing that greeted the entry of the kings of France into their *bonnes villes* and cost the local bourgeoisie a fortune for wine (which flowed like water from the public fountains) and for stage sets inspired by classical mythology. And there were revolutionary festivals, at once utopian and strictly codified—a permanent psychodrama and theatrical representation of the revolution. But what has most aroused the historians' interest is the popular festival in its relation to violence, religion, and the basic rhythms of the biological world.[19]

The history of death is the subject of a number of lengthy works just recently published. For Philippe Ariès, Jean-Noël Biraben, François Lebrun, Michel Vovelle, and Pierre Chaunu, death occupies a place, as Le Roy Ladurie remarks, at the center of historical interest "like the graveyard in the middle of the vil-lage." It is also located at a methodological crossroads, encroaching simulta-neously on the traditional spheres of cultural, social, and demographic history.[20] Michel Vovelle's work on the attitudes toward death among the population of Provence in the eighteenth century provides a good example of this complex kind of history. It demonstrates the utility of computerization in the history of mental structures. An enormous mass of notarized wills was examined. The different formulas, repeated thousands of times over, were sorted out and classified: provisions for masses for the dead, the choice of a burial place (the church, the convent, the cemetery), bequests to the confraternities and to the poor. The analysis of all of these elements has disclosed how people probably behaved in the face of death: the native of Provence died a good Catholic around 1720 in the Baroque Age; he died a Jansenist around 1750, and a philosophe around 1780. The characteristic attitudes of the different classes also stand revealed: bourgeois detachment, peasant and aristocratic piety.

The originality of serial history *à la française* lies perhaps in this quantitative approach to the great shifts in popular modes of thought and feeling.

Some Final Remarks on Contemporary Historiography

My object in this paper has been to identify and illustrate the current trends in French historiography, not to provide an exhaustive bibliography, which would require many hundreds of pages. I am even less concerned with awarding impossible and embarrassing honors for excellence. Nevertheless, a few last touches should be added to this incomplete and perhaps unwittingly partial sketch of the currents that animate French historical writing today.

Production remains vigorous within the traditional time limits officially assigned to the different historical periods. There was once a time perhaps when the medievalists in the wake of Marc Bloch appeared to have a monopoly in methodological innovation. This is now mainly the prerogative of specialists on the seventeenth and eighteenth centuries (the sixteenth century having been virtually abandoned by professional historians). One of the causes of this shift is doubtless the sociological accident that oriented a number of first-class minds of the same age group toward the same field of specialization and similar careers. Another perhaps is the fact so often pointed out that the general trends in history and the unheard-of development of the tools at its disposal have encouraged the utilization of great masses of documents. Since everything now depends on quantity and numbers, historians of the modern period (ca. 1500-ca. 1789 in France) find themselves at a most strategic crossroads. In that pre-statistical age it is not impossible to lay one's hands on Chaunu's "millions" of documents. Series exist if only one takes the trouble to render the data a little more homogeneous. And yet everything is still on a human scale.

In the days of *l'histoire événementielle* it was permitted to turn the pages of a testament with a certain emotion; to daydream over a parish register. The emotion, fortunately, has not altogether disappeared. It humanizes mathematical calculations and penetrates as far as the "structures" themselves. It is enough to read Pierre Chaunu to be convinced of this. Like everything else in those days, eighteenth-century statistics could not help being likable, a far cry from the lifeless series churned out by modern bureaucracies, which are deliberately designed to be fed into a computer. Seventeenth- and eighteenth-century sources leave room for the imagination and inventiveness of the historian, who despite determined efforts is not yet entirely transformed into a human calculating machine.

History in France—which surely cannot be accused any longer of chauvinism—is concerned essentially with the history of France. This is natural enough in a country whose archives are so rich and so well preserved. Most of the works mentioned in the present essay deal in fact with various aspects of the French past. But there are other countries in which French historians traditionally have shown a special interest, particularly Italy and Spain. Among the recent *thèses d'Etat* in medieval and Renaissance history are those of Pierre Toubert (on Latium), Charles de la Roncière (Florence), Elisabeth Carpentier (Orvieto), Pierre Bonnassie (Catalonia), Claude Carrère (Barcelona), and Bartolomé Bennassar (Valladolid). Certain historians of the modern and contemporary periods, like Claude Fohlen, Maurice Lévy-Leboyer, Frédéric Mauro, and Michel Devèze (these are only examples), have written on North and South America. Finally, the colonial and post-colonial past of the former French possessions in Africa and Southeast Asia is the object of numerous recent studies by specialists in the history of the Third World, notably at the University of Paris VII and the Ecole des Hautes Etudes en Sciences Sociales.

French academic historians were long indifferent to the history of history. But this trend has now been reversed. Charles Olivier Carbonell has studied the historical fraternity in the years that the positivist model, anathema to the *Annales*, dominated the field. Michelet and Mignet are the subject of recent biographies. With Philippe Joutard, the history of history abandons "erudite culture" in favor of the "historical mythology of the ordinary Frenchman." For him, it is a question of analyzing the memories and mental images of "great events," "heroes," and "villains" in history left over from his primary school education.

The vigor of local history (of provinces, towns, or villages) is one of the significant traits of French historiography today. The success of this specialty, described by Pierre Goubert, has varied with time. But it is certainly true that French historiography in the nineteenth and early twentieth centuries put the emphasis on the unifying activities of the state and the growth of the nation and usually only studied French culture and civilization from this point of view, neglecting the infinite diversity of the popular and regional cultures. The feverish activity that now reigns in this sector of history is a reflection of the surprising resurgence of regionalism in a country that once seemed to offer the perfect example of the unified nation-state. Certain well-conceived series, particularly the *Histoire des provinces* under the editorship of Philippe Wolff, have given a new lease on life to a genre which has not enjoyed so much success since the great age of erudition. The change in status manifests itself by an infallible sign: the number of doctoral dissertations on regional subjects is on the rise.

The auxiliary historical sciences and the critical editions of source materials are also experiencing a revival, especially in the field of medieval studies. The history of historiography will take note of the obvious decline of French erudition between 1914 and the 1950s, almost half a century during which the publication of narrative and nonnarrative sources almost came to a halt. At a time when writings on the auxiliary sciences were also increasingly rare, the scientific societies whose editions of texts were so numerous in the nineteenth century managed to survive only with the greatest difficulty. Various factors of a demographic, economic, and social nature doubtless help to explain this phenomenon. But one is also forced to recognize that beginning in the 1930s the victorious progress of the *Annales* school hastened the decline of an erudite tradition that was already faltering. Was it not said to be the purveyor of the very positivist historiography that was under attack? At a time when Marc Bloch was adding new luster to medieval studies, pure erudition, without which these same studies are doomed, seemed to have been irremediably compromised.

The situation has changed since then under the dictates of necessity. The stock of documents patiently accumulated in the course of the nineteenth century was being used up and had to be renewed and enriched. The publication of archival sources has therefore resumed. Auxiliary sciences that had been discredited as old-fashioned are enjoying a revival in the fresh light of the history of mental structures; heraldry, for example, is now infused with a certain nobility and sparkle thanks to the interest in symbolism. The computer has made it possible to constitute enormous banks of documents. The use of sophisticated scientific techniques revives the hope of being able to date and localize objects previously difficult if not impossible to interpret.

Conclusion

I am very conscious of the fact that contemporary French historiography does not have a monopoly on vigor and inventiveness. It is enough to read the works which are increasingly numerous, especially in the United States, on epistemology and the history of history to be convinced that the French current has joined the mainstream of Western historiography. The principal traits that I have endeavored to describe are to be found in America, in England, in Italy, and elsewhere.

Viewed from Paris, the undeniable strength of French historiography is a little surprising. It appears at a time when the teaching of history as a fully independent discipline is in the process of disappearing from the official curriculum of the elementary and secondary schools. History is now considered only one social science among many, and no privileged treatment is reserved for it. There are a number of historical reasons for this decline. It seems, however, a singular phenomenon at a moment when the general public has developed a taste for history that is something more than a collection of anecdotes or biographies of notable persons.

The historians who are struggling for the survival of their discipline in the schools are conscious of the dangers facing historical studies. Jacques Le Goff and Pierre Nora plead the cause of a return to historical synthesis or global history which refuses to let itself be submerged by the social sciences. We have come a long way since French historians proclaimed far and wide that theirs was the queen of sciences. They seem to feel the need nevertheless to preserve an independent status and a distinctive role in the life of the nation.

Finally, certain signs have appeared of a revolt against the hierarchy and ideology that now dominate the field of history. Groups of young historians, most of them from the far Left, have begun to question the concepts and practices, judged conformist and conciliatory, of a historiography in the service of the power structure. Several little journals of historical dissent have appeared on the scene: *Cahiers du Forum-Histoire, Le Peuple français, Revue d'histoire populaire, Espaces-Temps.* The *Annales,* in a different spirit, began life in the same way. But has a new *Annales* seen the light of day?

Notes

1. Henri-Irénée Marrou, "L'Epistémologie dans l'histoire en France aujourd'hui," in F. Engel-Janosi, G. Klingenstein, and H. Lutz, *Denken über Geschichte* (Vienna, 1974), p. 97; P. Goubert, "Sur trois siècles et trois décennies: passage des méthodologies," in *Mélanges en l'honneur de Fernand Braudel,* 2 vols. (Toulouse, 1973), I, 251–58.

2. On the *Annales* in general see Georg G. Iggers, "The *Annales* Tradition: French Historians in Search of a Science of History," chapter 2 of his *New Directions in European Historiography* (Middletown, Conn., 1975); and Marina Cedronio, "Profilo delle 'Annales' attraverso delle pagine delle 'Annales'," in *Atti dell'Accademia di Scienze morali et politiche della Società Nazionale di scienze, lettere e arti in Napoli* 83: 179–260. For the period 1929–1945 see L. Febvre, *Pour une histoire à part entière* (Paris, 1962); M. Bloch, *Apologie pour l'histoire ou métier d'historien* (written in 1941–42; published Paris, 1945); M. Bloch, *Les Caractères originaux de l'histoire rurale française* (Paris, 1956; first published 1931); M. Bloch, *La Société féodale* (Paris, 1939); L. Febvre, *Le Problème de l'incroyance au XVIe siècle: la réligion de Rabelais* (Paris, 1942); and H.-D. Mann, *Lucien Febvre: la pensée vivante d'un historien* (Paris, 1971).

3. See François Simiand, *Les Fluctuations économiques à longue période et la crise mondiale* (Paris, 1932), and *Recherches anciennes et nouvelles sur le mouvement général des prix du XVIe au XIXe siècle* (Paris, 1932); Ernest Labrousse, *Esquisse du mouvement des prix et des revenus en France au XVIIIe siècle* (Paris, 1933); and Georges Lefebvre, *Les Paysans du Nord pendant la Révolution française* (Paris, 1924), and *La Grande Peur de 1789* (Paris, 1932).

4. Jan Dhont, "L'Histoire recurrente," *Diogène,* no. 75 (1971): 26.

5. R. M. Andrews in the *New York Times Book Review,* 18 May 1975. On the *Annales* in the time of Fernand Braudel, see F. Braudel, *La Méditerranée et le monde méditerranéen à l'époque de Philippe II,* 2nd ed. (Paris, 1966; English translation by Sîan Reynolds, New York, 1973); F. Braudel, *Civilisation matérielle et capitalisme (XVe-XVIIIe siècles)* (Paris, 1967); F. Braudel's collection of articles entitled *Ecrits sur l'histoire* (Paris, 1969); F. Braudel, personal testimony, *Journal of Modern History* 44 (1972): 448–67; J. H. Hexter, "Fernand Braudel and the 'Monde Braudellien . . .,' " ibid., 480–539; Robert Forster, "Achievements of the *Annales* School," *Journal of Economic History* 38 (1978): 58–76.

6. Braudel, *La Méditerranée,* I, 21.

7. Traian Stoianovich, *French Historical Method: The Annales Paradigm,* foreword by Fernand Braudel (Ithaca, N.Y., 1976).

8. See P. and H. Chaunu, *Séville et l'Atlantique, 1504–1650* (Paris, 1959–1960), and F. Mauro,

Le Portugal et l'Atlantique au XVIIe siècle, 1570–1670 (Paris, 1960); P. Goubert, *Beauvais et le Beauvaisis, de 1600 à 1730* (Paris, 1960); P. Vilar, *La Catalogne dans l'Espagne moderne* (Paris, 1965), and E. Le Roy Ladurie, *Les Paysans de Languedoc* (Paris, 1966). For a general survey of historical works during these years, see J. Glénisson, "L'Historiographie française contemporaine: tendances et réalisations," in Comité français des sciences historiques, *La recherche historique en France de 1940 à 1965* (Paris, 1965), pp. xiv-lxiv.

9. Lawrence Stone, "History and the Social Sciences in the Twentieth Century," in C. F. Delzell, ed., *The Future of History: Essays in the Vanderbilt University Centennial Symposium* (Nashville, Tenn., 1977).

10. The following account is based on the works cited in this paragraph, all of which were published in Paris. In addition much that is of interest has appeared in interviews with the historians who are considered—and consider themselves—representatives of the "New History." Number 123 (April 1977) of the *Magazine littéraire* was devoted essentially to this subject. Participants in the discussion included Philippe Ariès, Michel de Certeau, Georges Duby, Jacques Le Goff, Emmanuel Le Roy Ladurie, and Paul Veyne. Le Roy Ladurie granted a long interview to *Lire, le magazine des livres*, no. 23-24 (Summer 1977), pp. 31-53. See also the article "Histoire et historiens," *Politique aujourd'hui*, no. 11–12 (1975); the special issue of *Dialectiques*, no. 10–11 (1975) on "Histoire et société"; and the chapter on history in vol. VIII of the *Encyclopaedia universalis* (Paris, 1970), by Paul Veyne, Robert Mandrou, H.-I. Marrou, G. Palmade, C. Higounet, P. Vilar, and C. Mazauric; and *L'Historien entre l'ethnologue et le futurologue* (Paris-The Hague, 1972).

11. A special issue of *Communications*, no. 18 (1972), was devoted to *l'événement*. E. Le Roy Ladurie and P. Nora were among the contributors.

12. Michel Grenon and Régine Robin, "Pour la déconstruction d'une pratique historique," *Dialectiques*, no. 11 (1975): 5–32. We have relied heavily on this excellent article, an intelligent critique of the most recent essays on epistemology, devoted essentially to *Faire de l'histoire*. The attitude of present-day historians towards Marxism is carefully analyzed. In this connection E. Le Roy Ladurie writes: "All these different problems or subjects—social groups, élites, revolution, the poor—skirt Marxism without ever meeting it head on. Up to this point we only dimly perceive that great ideological system. Should we take the bull by the horns then? As a matter of fact every study of social history utilizes ipso facto certain Marxist (and sometimes pre-Marxist!) concepts such as social class, class struggle, and even mode of production. But whatever dogmatism, rigidity, and absurdity there is in the standard version (at least in the Latin countries) of Marxism-Leninism or crypto-Stalinism should be shunned like the plague. One wonders even if a perfectly non-Marxist history might not present a certain interest and certain advantages. I say this naturally with the feeling that I am walking on eggs and profaning the most sacred vases of our times." (*Bulletin de liaison*, no. 3 (April 1978): 12.

13. On quantitative history, see F. Furet, "Le quantitatif en histoire," in *Faire de l'histoire*, I, 42–61; and E. Le Roy Ladurie, *Le Territoire de l'historien*, pp. 11–138.

14. The proof is the extraordinary success of E. Le Roy Ladurie's *Montaillou, village occitan* (Paris, 1976), a serious work of retrospective ethnology which was read by a large public. The magazine *Histoire*, founded in 1978 as "a permanent source of information on the entire field of historical research," has been well received by the public.

15. J. Bouvier, "Tendances actuelles des recherches d'histoire économique et sociale en France," in *Aujourd'hui l'histoire*, pp. 130–42. On the endeavor of J. Marczewski and his team, see Denis Richet, "Histoire quantitative ou économétrie rétrospective?" (communication to the Department of History of the University of Ottawa in November 1975). For an account of the French reactions to the "new economic history" see the introduction ("Le Dossier de la question") written by Jean Heffer for Ralph Andreano, ed., *La Nouvelle Histoire économique: éxposés de méthodologie* (Paris, 1977).

16. G. Duby and A. Wallon, *Histoire de la France rurale*, 4 vols. (Paris, 1975–1976): vol. I, *La Formation des campagnes françaises des origines au XIVe siècle* (G. Bertrand, C. Bertrand, M. Le Glay, G. Fourquin); vol. II, *L'Age classique des paysans, 1340–1789* (H. Neveux, J. Jacquard, E. Le Roy Ladurie); vol. III, *Apogée et crise de la civilisation paysanne, 1789–1914* (M. Agalhon,

G. Desert, R. Specklin); and vol. IV, *La Fin de la France paysanne de 1914 à nos jours* (M. Gervais, M. Jollivet, Y. Tavernier). More specific information on the rural history of the Middle Ages can be found in R. Fossier, ''Sources et problématique de l'histoire des campagnes (France du Nord),'' and Ch. Higounet, ''Sources et problématique de l'histoire des campagnes (France du Midi)'' in *Tendances, perspectives, et méthodes de l'histoire mediévale* (Paris, 1977); Comité des travaux historiques, *Actes du 100e congrès des sociétés savantes* (Paris, 1975). Still, urban studies are not neglected. These efforts also bring to our attention ''local history,'' which will be discussed later. The latest available at the time this essay was written is Robert Favreau, *La Ville de Poitiers à la fin du moyen âge: une capitale régionale* (*Mémoires de la Société des Antiquaires de l'Ouest*, ser. 4, 14 (Poitiers, 1978).

17. Philippe Contamine, *Guerre, état et société à la fin du moyen âge: étude sur les armées des rois de France 1337–1494* (Paris-The Hague, 1972); Jean Meyer, *La Noblesse bretonne au XVIIIe siècle* (Paris, 1966); the dissertation of Antoine Prost is in press.

18. Robert Mandrou, *Magistrats et sorciers en France au XVIIe siècle* (Paris, 1968); Michel de Certeau, *La Possession de Loudun* (Paris, 1970); Michel de Certeau, ''Ce que Freud fait à propos de l'histoire: 'Une Névrose démoniaque au XVIIe siècle','' *Annales, économies, sociétés, civilisations* 25 (1970): 654–67; Jacques Sprenger, *Le Marteau des sorcières*, introduction by Armand Danet (Paris, 1973); M. S. Dupont-Bouchat, W. Frijhof, and R. Muchembled, *Prophètes et sorciers dans les Pays-Bas XVIe-XVIIIe siècle* (Paris, 1978).

19. Within one year four important works appeared dealing with festivals: Yves-Marie Bercé, *Fêtes et révoltes: des mentalités populaires du XVIe au XVIIIe siècles* (Paris, 1976); Michel Vovelle, *Les Métamorphoses de la fête en Provence, de 1750 à 1820* (Paris, 1976); Mona Ozouf, *La Fête révolutionnaire 1789–1799* (Paris, 1976); and Rosamonde Sanson, *Les 14 juillet (1789–1975): fête et conscience nationale* (Paris, 1976). On the festivals during the monarchy and court festivals, see Bernard Guenée and Françoise Lehoux, *Les entrées royales, de 1328 à 1515* (*Sources d'histoire mediévale publiées par l'Institut de Recherche et d'Histoire des Textes*) (Paris, 1968); Jean Jacquot, ed., *Les Fêtes de la Renaissance*: vol. I, *Les Fêtes de la Renaissance* (Paris, 1956), and vol. II, *Fêtes et cérémonies au temps de Charles Quint* (Paris, 1960).

20. F. Lebrun, *Les Hommes et la mort en Anjou aux XVIIe et XVIIIe siècles* (Paris-The Hague, 1971); Ph. Ariès, *Essais sur l'histoire de la mort en occident du moyen âge à nos jours* (Paris, 1976); J. N. Biraben, *Les Hommes et la peste* (Paris-The Hague, 1975); and M. Vovelle, *Mourir autrefois: attitudes collectives devant la mort au XVIIe et XVIIIe siècles* (Paris, 1974); P. Chaunu, *La Mort à Paris: 16e, 17e, 18e siècles* (Paris, 1978).

Bibliographical Orientation

No single work embraces every aspect of the history of French historiography since World War II. For a general orientation see J. Ehrard and G. Palmade, *L'Histoire*, 2nd ed. (Paris, 1965); Pierre Chaunu, *Histoire, science sociale: la durée, l'espace et l'homme à l'époque moderne* (Paris, 1974); Jean Glénisson, ''L'Historiographie française contemporaine, tendances et réalisations,'' in Comité français des sciences historiques, *La recherche historique en France de 1940 à 1965* (Paris, 1965). The current bibliography concerning France, and consequently a very large part of the French production, appears in *Bibliographie annuelle de l'histoire de France*. Obviously, one should also consult the book reviews and bibliographical notices in the principal historical journals: *Revue historique, Bibliothèque de l'Ecole des Chartes, Le Moyen Age, Revue d'histoire moderne et contemporaine*.

11 HAROLD T. PARKER

Great Britain

Nineteen forty-five was not a significant date in British historiography: 1929 has greater claim for significance, as does 1886. The two dates remind us that in the last one hundred years British historiography has passed through two revolutions, the one completed, the other still under way.

Prior to the 1880s British history writing was the province of gifted amateurs, men of letters (Thomas Carlyle, Thomas Babington Macaulay, John Richard Green) who produced literary masterpieces that entered the stream of national literature.[1] Since their time, the study of history in Great Britain has become increasingly the province of the professional expert, university-trained and usually university-connected. This process of professionalization in Great Britain was gradual.[2] Starting, let us say, in the 1880s or thereabouts, it was virtually complete by the 1930s. By then historians were established as a professional group with its own code and rituals that governed how the members related to each other, to outsiders, to reality, and to what it valued most. The group had its own publication, the *English Historical Review*, founded in 1886. In accord with international trends already described in the Introduction to this volume, it had its own canons and style of professional work, its ideal being, usually, an accurate narrative of events of prominent people based on critical examination of the written evidence. Lurking in the minds of quite a few professionals was another noble dream, the dream of constructing a moving, flowing synthesis that approximates what actually happened in all its detailed interrelatedness.[3]

Over the decades there has been a massive continuity of professional British historiography in its concern with political, constitutional, economic, social, and local history, established in narrative form by critical historical method. Yet over the decades there have been innovations and changes in subject-matter, perspective, and methodological approach. Changes in the views professionals had of British history came apparently from three sources. They came, first, from the impact of public events upon the mentality of the working historians. The agricultural depression prior to 1914, the continuing plight of the urban poor, the two world wars, the decline of Great Britain as an imperial power, and the reforms in the university educational system affected British historiography in manifold and subtle ways that will not be discussed in this methodological essay.

Second, change in views of the British past came from the almost inexorable operation of the processes of cooperative-competitive erudition. The steady search by many scholars for new documentary evidence, the prolonged absorption of many scholars of diverse minds in the evidence, the verification of their conclusions by publication and by scholarly debate—all this steadily transformed the scholarly view of British history on many subjects. Sometimes the change of view came gradually and peaceably. At other times it came through battles royal in scholarly controversies that lasted decades and even generations. Thus for years scholars debated and sometimes are still debating[4]

(*a*) the relative importance in medieval English history of Anglo-Saxon institutions and of the innovations of the Norman Conquest, especially with respect to the nature of English feudalism in Anglo-Saxon times and after the conquest (J. H. Round, F. M. Stenton, Carl Stephenson; H. G. Richardson and G. O. Sayles, D. C. Douglas, C. W. Hollister, Eric John, H. R. Loyn),[5]
(*b*) Domesday Book (J. H. Round; F. W. Maitland, V. H. Galbraith; R. W. Finn, Carl Stephenson, P. H. Sawyer, D. C. Douglas, H. C. Darby),[6]
(*c*) The origins and early development of Parliament (William Stubbs; L. Riess, J. H. Round, L. O. Pike, F. W. Maitland, C. H. McIlwain, A. F. Pollard, H. G. Richardson and G. O. Sayles; B. Wilkinson, Maurice Powicke, T. F. T. Plucknett; Helen Cam),[7]
(*d*) The nature of the Tudor monarchy (A. F. Pollard; G. R. Elton; W. C. Richardson, P. H. Williams, G. L. Harriss),[8]
(*e*) The rise of the gentry during the sixteenth and early seventeenth centuries (R. H. Tawney; L. Stone; H. R. Trevor-Roper; P. Zagorin; J. H. Hexter, A. M. Everitt, B. Manning),[9]
(*f*) The Glorious Revolution of 1688 (G. M. Trevelyan; L. Pinkham; S. B. Baxter),[10]
(*g*) The nature and origins of political parties in the seventeenth and eighteenth centuries (Thomas Babington Macaulay, W. Lecky, G. O. Trevelyan, G. M. Trevelyan; L. Namier, J. Brooke, B. Donoughue, I. R. Christie; H. Butterfield, J. Cannon, Paul Langford, Frank O'Gorman, H. T. Dickinson, J. Brewer),[11]
(*h*) The origins of the Industrial Revolution (P. Mantoux; W. Rostow, N. Smelser, P. Deane and W. A. Cole, T. S. Ashton, D. Landes, R. M. Hartwell),[12]
(*i*) The social consequences of the Industrial Revolution (A. Toynbee, J. L. Hammond, G. D. H. Cole, C. Clark, J. Kuczynski; J. H. Clapham, T. S. Ashton, F. A. Hayek, R. M. Hartwell; E. Hobsbawm, A. J. Taylor, E. P. Thompson, J. E. Williams, M. W. Flinn).[13]

Each of these controversies followed, with individual variations, the same pattern: the classic statement of a generally accepted view; challenge by forceful revisors, who may overstate their case; equally vigorous revision of the proposed revised version; gradual settling to a new agreed-upon synthesis; the net result of the vivid, stimulating, sometimes acrimonious dispute being increased knowledge and deeper understanding of the past.

Changes in the views of the British past came, thirdly, through the application of new approaches and perspectives identified with Lewis Namier, with the social sciences and quantification, and with the Marxists.[14] The Namier controversy followed the classic pattern of thesis (old view), antithesis (Namier), protest against antithesis (Butterfield), and then new synthesis, with the special feature that the entire dispute generated significant methodological consequences. The debate concerned the nature of English politics during the first two decades of the reign of George III. The old view, represented by George Otto Trevelyan's *Early History of Charles James Fox* (1880) and *The American Revolution* (1898), thought of eighteenth-century politics in terms of a contest between Whig and Tory parties, each party united by devotion to principles. It told in narrative form a story of how an ambitious, scheming George III had tried unconstitutionally to establish a personal tyrannical monarchy, only to be frustrated overseas by the American rebels and at home by the Whigs, the Liberals of the eighteenth century, who heroically made a stand against the threat of royal despotism.[15] Intending to write a political history of England during the American Revolution, Namier published in 1929 a two-volume cross-sectional analysis entitled *The Structure of Politics at the Accession of George III*.[16] Where Whig historians had seen well-organized parties, Namier perceived only political connections based on family relationship, personal friendship, and self-interest. Where the Whig interpretation saw general elections as tremendous debates fought out on great national issues, Namier perceived within each borough or county constituency only rather sordid local contests among great lords and country gentlemen for place and gain. The circumstances varied from constituency to constituency (so each one must be analyzed) and from candidate to candidate (so each one must be studied). George III was to be viewed less as a tyrant than as a monarch who entered the political game to exercise his legitimate royal authority.

Against the implications of Namier's first two volumes, Herbert Butterfield and others protested.[17] History is not simply an analysis of structure; it is also a narrative of events. Men, even politicians, are not simply manipulative creatures and repositories of self-interest; they sometimes have rational intentions and ideas which affect their conduct. History within Parliament is not to be explained entirely by factional power games within the two houses: history was affected by extra-parliamentary events as well and by public opinion. Nor should one overlook the growth of political parties with the advent of the American war. In Namier's essays and in his ultimate narrative of the elections of 1754 to 1784, written by his collaborator John Brooke, Namier either answered these criticisms or absorbed into his account the truth that seemed to be in them. Narrative, he agreed, was the paramount form for the historian: "As history deals with concrete events fixed in time and space, narrative is its basic medium"— but analysis of structure has its place.[18] For the period he was describing, the 1760s, the power game among factions was all-important and would remain important, but (he agreed) with the American war, issues, public opinion, and political parties that were centered to a degree on issues began to affect parliamentary history.[19]

What then was the lasting significance of the "Namier" controversy? As Butterfield correctly pointed out, on the nature of eighteenth-century British politics Namier had been anticipated, by John Adolphus (1802) and W. T. Laprade

(1916).[20] Why then was Namier important? First, he was listened to. His massive researches commanded attention. The eighteenth century became "Namier's century." For several decades the essential structure and functioning of eighteenth-century parliamentary politics were viewed through his spectacles, and researches into constituencies, connections, and political biographies were conducted along the lines of his paradigm.[21] Today, even if a historian disagrees with Namier, he still has to come to terms with his method and conclusions.[22] Second, Namier influenced the way the collaborative history of Parliament, projected in 1929, is being written. In its densely packed volumes appear, century by century, detailed descriptions of each constituency and minute biographies of each and every member of the House of Commons, as Namier desired.[23] Third, he offered an approach, that of collective biography (prosopography), that could be applied to other fields besides parliamentary history.[24] Fourth, and most important, he was the first British historian to look influentially beneath the flowing story of events to underlying structures. Most people, unless they are geniuses (like the elder Pitt), rebels, or madmen, dance according to the patterns of social structure. In a sense people are self-willed, but they are self-willed within a pattern. Namier asked historians to notice these patterns. They have arisen in the narrative of events, and they are profoundly affecting it. Today, to be sure, the scholarly study of political ideas and of extra-parliamentary influences has been revived,[25] but now factional and personal interests, ideas, and extra-parliamentary influences are being fused into a new synthetic political narrative that is different because of Namier's forceful intervention. Out of the clash of scholarly wills that Namier's book had precipitated a synthesis is arising that no single scholar had willed.

A second source of new approaches to professional history was the social sciences, both native to Britain and foreign. Hitherto, the development of British historiography had been largely indigenous to the country and to the historical discipline. Explanations, concepts, and generalizations grew out of the historian's association with the evidence. History was used to explain history. The one philosophical theorist of the profession, R. G. Collingwood, was himself a historian, and he essentially defended what most working historians were then doing anyway—empathically, imaginatively reenacting when they could the thinking of historical actors.[26] But starting in the 1920s and continuing ever since, an increasing number of British historians borrowed subjects to investigate, questions to ask, concepts, approaches, techniques, and methods to apply, and theories from the social sciences. Social historians borrowed from sociology and anthropology, economic historians from post-Keynesian economic theory, historical demographers from analytical demography, and historical geographers from geography. In time British historians entered the stream of international methodological learning and discussion. The British urban historians learned from the Chicago school of urban sociology,[27] the historical demographers from their French counterparts, and economic historians from the New Economic History (USA). The thinking of British historians who followed the social science route was to a degree now governed by developments in other disciplines that were responses to the needs, opportunities, and perspectives of these disciplines. Almost inadvertently, these British historians entered a new historical reality as the operations of their own minds altered.

It is difficult to specify a single date when this shift began. Perhaps 1926 will do as well as any. In that year Richard H. Tawney published his *Religion and the Rise of Capitalism*. Tawney took his subject—the interrelation of religion and other social institutions—from Max Weber's sociology and then developed it brilliantly. However, 1933 is another significant year in the development of British historical methodology. On 18 January 1933 Eileen Power, hitherto a descriptive social historian of the Middle Ages, delivered her inaugural lecture as a professor of economic history at the University of London. In it she came out for the close integration of the labors of "anthropologists, sociologists, economists, and historians." Social history must become the structural analysis of society; social historians must investigate "the general problems with which sociology is concerned"; they must do this by an inductive-deductive scientific method that uses comparison and abstraction. In her address the telltale term "variable" slipped in. "What are the variables in the [historical] situation?"[28] An intellectual revolution lay within the word "variables." Power was putting on a new thinking cap, as Butterfield would say. On 7 February 1946 her successor in the chair of economic history at the University of London, Thomas S. Ashton, in *his* inaugural lecture, "The Relation of Economic History to Economic Theory," anticipated the consequences of the social science approach. Historians will become concerned "with large groups: with the general, rather than the particular; with processes, rather than with events; with the typical, representative or statistical fact, rather than with the unique, individual fact." Increasingly the historian will be "feeling for the structure that underlies the surface of events." He will be guided by the theorists to see how social and economic phenomena are related to each other in ways he did not suspect. But Ashton warned that all generalizations, however useful, are "but causal factors at one remove." We must not forget that "it is the wills and choices and acts of men and women that are the ultimate data" for theorists and historians alike.[29]

As in any age of intellectual transition, there were books (and articles) on old subjects applying old-time descriptive methods, often superbly; books on old subjects using the new analytical methods; books on new subjects using old methods; and books on new subjects using new methods. T. F. T. Plucknett's *Edward I and Criminal Law* (1960),[30] an excellent essay on a traditional subject of English political and constitutional history, applies critical, intuitive erudition of the traditional sort to define time, place, personal movitation and action, and consequences. Nearly all the articles of the *English Historical Review* and, one is tempted to remark, a clear majority of the historical monographs published in Great Britain are still of this variety. George Homans's *English Villagers of the Thirteenth Century* (1942)[31] treats an old subject, the English village, with scholarly thoroughness but from a sociological perspective. The title suggests the differences between the old and the new approaches: the subject is not the village but the villagers and how they interrelated to each other in social processes of functional interdependence that are set forth in the concluding chapter. Keith Thomas's *Religion and the Decline of Magic* (1971),[32] which covers sixteenth- and seventeenth-century England, likewise treats an old subject with massive descriptive erudition but does it from a new ethnographic and anthropological perspective. Reading anthropology apparently helped Thomas to view magic and religion as a cultural phenomenon to be observed dispassionately; it offered a store of explanatory theories, chiefly functionalist, on which he could draw and then use cautiously and with qualifications; and it gave him descriptions of African tribal practices that by comparison suggested or confirmed interpretations of English magical usage. Anthropology added to erudition yielded a richer, deeper, surer account.

New subjects included social structure, a social class, a professional group, the family, and so on. New subjects might be treated by old descriptive methods, often quite appropriately, or by new methods. Over the decades the new methods became increasingly sophisticated. Increasing sophistication appeared in successive articles and monographs on salient issues: for example, in those on the rise of the gentry, from the rather amateurish counting of manors by Tawney (even a genius can make mistakes) to the matured, monumental work of Lawrence Stone (*Crisis of the Aristocracy, 1558–1641*);[33] or in the controversy over the standard of living of the British working class (1780–1850), from the impressionistic descriptions of the Hammonds through the relatively simple indices of prices and wages of Ashton and Eric Hobsbawm to the more intricate calculations of recent articles.[34]

The most powerful sophistication emerged in the interrelated fields of historical demography, economic history, and local history.* Here real breakthroughs occurred in the use of new methods of analysis to discover new phenomena in the historical data, and new interrelationships. The breakthroughs can be dated from 1956, the year when in France Louis Henry announced the method of family reconstitution and in the United States Alfred Conrad and John Meyer issued the first manifesto of the New Economic History.[35] In Great Britain the significant years might be 1964, when the Cambridge Group for the History of Population and Social Structure was set up, 1966, when articles about the New Economic History, using its methods, began to appear in significant numbers in the *Economic History Review,* and some indeterminate year in the late 1960s when computer technology began to be important in historical research. We might also mention the opening application in the mid-1970s of network analysis to the history of local communities, an approach that seems of great promise.

---

*The next four paragraphs of this chapter presume a prior reading of two preceding essays in this book, "The New Demographic History" by Richard T. Vann and "Some Recent Tendencies in Social History" by Geoff Eley, which substantially present aspects of British historiography in their respective fields. These two articles and this essay on Great Britain complement each other.

The goal of the Cambridge Group was ambitious: the numerical study of society over time; the recovery of facts about the numbers of persons, their propensity to be born, to marry, and to die, "their arrangement in families, villages, towns, regions, classes, and so on, as accurately as we can and from as far back as we can go."[36] In their work simple counting and simple statistical manipulation of aggregate figures yielded crude birth rates, marriage rates, and death rates. But the specialized techniques of family reconstitution and computerized record linkage proved unexpectedly useful in refining the conclusions with respect to age of marriage, "age-specific fertility rates for married women, age-specific mortality rates for younger people, expectations of life, infantile mortality," and even "the presence or absence of (voluntary) family limitation."[37] Using chiefly family reconstitution, E. A. Wrigley thus reconstructed from inferior data the demographic history of the parish of Colyton in Devonshire after 1538. Employing among other techniques that of record linkage, Michael Anderson studied "the impact of urban-industrial life on the kinship system of the working classes of nineteenth-century Lancashire." His methods enabled him to penetrate in both rural and urban environments to the residence and coresidence patterns and even to relationships between father, mother, and children within the nuclear family.[38] The first effect of seeking statistical variables is often to lose the individual within a general statistic. The second effect, with the Cambridge Group at least, was to revive the individual: to identify the ordinary individual person and family, to place them firmly in context, and to learn more about them than the traditional intuitive and pictorial social historian ever could; and to do all this more surely. The Cambridge Group related their discoveries to vital economic questions (for example, Were demographic changes connected with the Industrial Revolution?) and to significant social issues (as, for instance, What was the effect of industrialization on the social structure?).

British historiography has had a long and distinguished tradition in economic history. Merely to mention the names of Thorold Rogers, William Cunningham, George Unwin, John Clapham, Ashton, and Michael Postan is to communicate a sense of its excellent quality. What then was new about the New Economic History?[39] It was not measurement and quantification: as early as the 1880s Rogers was publishing his long and famous series on prices and wages, and in the 1930s Clapham quantified whenever he could.[40] Nor was the application of economic theory novel: when in 1948 Ashton suggested that the low rate of interest in the mid-eighteenth century may have facilitated the founding of business enterprises during those years, he was self-consciously applying classical Marshallian economics to the problem of the origins of the Industrial Revolution.[41] What was new was that the economic historians now had a focus—the study of economic growth and the factors entering into it. They now had more abundant theory, post-Keynesian economics as well as the concepts of the equilibrium models of classical economics. And they now had the instruments of counterfactual analysis, intricate econometric models, and eventually computer technology to deploy in a powerful inductive-deductive method that was used to deduce from known data the unknown.[42] In Great Britain the method was applied to such controversial subjects as the per capita cost of the British Navigation Acts to the American colonials[43] and the alleged rise and fall of the manorial system in the twelfth and thirteenth centuries.[44] More synthetically, post-Keynesian economics and the great wealth of new information supplied by economic historians, old and new, have been merged in new economic histories of Great Britain, notably in *A History of the British Economy 1086–1970* (1973) by Brian Murphy.[45] In it he interrelated birthrates, age of marriage, fertility, disease, inoculation, death rates, population totals, food supply, technological inventions, business firms, interest rates, market demand at home, market demand abroad, innovative spirit, prices, wage rates, profits, savings, capital export, foreign competition, governmental policy, taxation, national income total, national income per capita, growth rates, and one person who made a difference (Richard Arkwright) in an ongoing analytical narrative of variables interrelating in time. Murphy's book and others like it suggest that British historiography was moving toward a new paradigm of historical thinking and presentation.

For British historians local history is a rich vein that has been exploited for over four centuries.[46] Its prosecution has passed through the same phases as British historiography in general. At first it was the province of the amateur, in this case enthusiastic local antiquarians, often the country squire or the parson, whose writings ranged from detailed essays on bells, fonts, and family lineages to the uncritical reproduction of cartularies.[47] Toward the close of the nineteenth century professional historians moved in with their disciplined methods of historical criticism. In 1884 F. W. Maitland published the thirteenth-century *Pleas of the Crown for the County of Gloucester,* for the social and legal history they contained.[48] His student, Mary Bateson, followed in 1899 with a critical edition of the cartularies of the borough of Leicester.[49] Meanwhile in 1898 the *Victoria History of the English Counties* had been started—on each county a series of huge, double-columned, folio volumes. Although a disproportionate amount of space was still allotted to the leading families and their lineages, within separate sections on geology, topography, archaeology, political history, social and economic history, ecclesiastical history, and parishes, professionally trained scholars presented a carefully substantiated mass of historical data.[50] The publication of new volumes in the series still continues today. Then, in the 1930s a new breed of local historians arrived, signaled by the appearance in 1932 of *Nottinghamshire in the Eighteenth Century* by J. D. Chambers[51] and in 1935 of *Industry, Trade, and People in Exeter 1688–1800* by W. G. Hoskins.[52] The two authors placed people, agriculture, industry, and trade in their geographic and cultural setting, and did this in such a way that local history could serve general history. For over fifty years, Hoskins and his associates and students have continued along the same route. In writing local history they merge topography, geography, population, agriculture, industry, trade, and above all people in descriptive accounts critically documented and richly evocative of the atmosphere and doings of the past.[53] Local history in the 1950s expanded into the history of cities,[54] an example being the two-volume history of Birmingham by C. Gill and Asa Briggs, and of their suburbs, for example, *A Victorian Suburb* by H. J. Dyos.[55] The history of cities brought British historians within the orbit of international social science theory. The motto of Hoskins, drawn from William Blake and oft repeated, was "To Generalize is to be an Idiot. To Particularize is the Alone Distinction of Merit." But British urban historians began to compare, to contrast, and to generalize, to test against British experience the models of Gideon Sjoberg for the preindustrial town and of Ernest Burgess for the modern metropolis, and to build models of their own.[56] Still more recently in the 1970s they have been rigorously applying network analysis and exchange theory to the history of local communities.[57] Retaining all that was good of past historiography—its rich accumulation of documents and descriptive histories, its dedication to critical method, its sense of the multiple interrelations of local and national history, and its concern for people—the younger British local historians have joined this heritage to newer computer technologies and social science theory in research that is as exciting and as valuable as any in the world.

A third source of new approaches to professional history was Karl Marx and Marxism. British historians became aware of Marx and Marxism only gradually. In 1888 Thorold Rogers could still publish an economic history of England entitled *The Economic Interpretation of History* without a single reference to Marx. George Unwin's essay entitled "The Philosophy of Value" (1900) and Michael Postan's "Karl Marx: A Democrat?" (1934) reveal serious reading and mature understanding of Marx's philosophy, but the two authors described his views only in the end to reject them.[58] Only after World War II, roughly a century after the publication of the *Communist Manifesto,* did British history written by recognized British Marxist historians and exhibiting a "Marxist approach" appear in the flow of British history-writing.

The Marxist approach to history is difficult to define and circumscribe, for Marxist historiography was not monolithic. Marxist historians came in a number of varieties, and over the years the views of each one evolved. Nevertheless, if we take five leading British Marxist historians and in chronological order read all their books and their articles published in *Past and Present,* the *New Left Review,* and the *Socialist Register,* perhaps we can define Marxism in terms of what they did. We can at least inquire: Do they have anything in common? If so, what is it? We note, first, that the five historians chosen were born within twelve years of each other: Christopher Hill (1912), Rodney Hilton (1916), Eric Hobsbawm (1917), Raymond Williams (1921), and Edward Thompson (1924).[59] The first two were educated at Oxford University, the last three at the University of Cambridge, and they all entered the academic world of teaching, of publication, of professional reviewing of other books and of being reviewed. Very early, then, they were educated to see history as a sequence of connected events and factors over time; they were reared in the practice of reading historical reality through intense, critical scrutiny of documents, and they were associating with mentors, colleagues, and reviewers who were insisting that they get their concrete facts straight, that they bring each noun, verb, adjective, adverb, and preposition to the empirical test of correspondence to what had occurred. Briefly, they were working in the idiom of English empiricism and in that special orbit of English empiricism known as academic history. In their writings they never lose the continuing reference to concrete historical experience.

However, they came of age during the 1930s and the war years in the atmosphere of intense discussion of socialism at Oxford, at Cambridge, and at London.[60] At some point, they were each converted to Marxism as a structure of feeling, a theory of understanding, and a guide to public policy. Although in later years they lived through different moods of commitment and semidetachment toward the Marxist doctrine, the conversion experience indelibly affected their histories. Where traditional academic historians focused in their political and constitutional histories on the maneuvers of those who were making it in the established order, Marxist writers often directed their sympathy and attention to the dispossessed and the exploited, to those in society who were being hurt, often badly hurt. Hill wrote of the Levellers, Hilton of the peasant rising of 1381, Hobsbawm of the primitive rebels and Captain Swing, Thompson of the English working class, and Williams of the long revolution toward a democratic society. Where traditional academics distrusted speculative views, theoretical structures, even generalizations, these five Marxist writers gave theory, specifically Marxian theory, an important role in their thinking about the past. The Marxian approach reaffirmed their empirical drive for documentary evidence and concrete fact (they, too, like Marx, were driving researchers), but it encouraged them to interplay theory and concrete reality, past and present. Specifically, Marxist theory taught them to notice, when appropriate, classes and class interaction as well as the importance of economic and social conditions as basal influential elements. It disposed them to look for structures within the flow of events and to seek in a given society the interrelations of economics, social organization, politics, philosophy, religion, and art. Theory and the example of Marx himself encouraged them to undertake the large enterprise audaciously: to capture the ethos of an epoch in an essay, to take the long view of economic-social-intellectual transformations, and to attempt the bold synthesis of individuals, events, factors, structures, moving together in British history over time. Marxian theory also gave most Marxist histories a conscious present reference. Traditional academics extolled neutrality, objectivity, and the exclusion from a historical account of a distorting involvement in present concerns, while yet inadvertently composing histories, such as studies of economic growth, that were hegemonic with the existing capitalistic order. Marxist historians, it seems, nearly always wrote with the present in mind, in histories that were congruent with a desired democratic socialist society.

In a lifetime of research and writing these five historians moved toward an ever more complex, nonreductionist description and explanation of historical happenings. Studying history was for them a learning process, as it was for many historians of their generation. We could illustrate this movement of thought in all five authors but limitations of space compel us to consider only Thompson and Williams. As Thompson in his research interplayed theory with concrete historical and contemporary reality, his view of theory, of reality, and of the process of interplay itself deepened. What he gained from Marxian theory, he tells us, was a sense of process, specifically of the process of the interaction of social being and social consciousness.[61] As he tried fluently and sensitively to discover this process in historical situations, he came across particular men and women doing, feeling, thinking, talking, relating to themselves and to each other. Certain Marxian concepts, designed to handle reality for the purposes of understanding and action, may actually screen the historian, Thompson concluded, from the process of what was occurring. Occasionally useful for swift comprehension of a historical pattern, the term "class" easily becomes a structure, a category, a counter to be moved analytically across the checkerboard of historical discourse. Because the historian can verbally maneuver classes, he thinks he understands history. But actually, Thompson said, he may have lost it: history is people acting and interacting; a class is a kernel of people relating to each other in certain ways over time and becoming conscious of their relations; class is a happening, and the formation of the English working class can be described and understood only in a concrete pictorial narrative.[62] The Marxian concept "base/superstructure" is another mechanical metaphor that in advance of any research destroys the possibility of ever apprehending the delicate processes of people interrelating in various kinds of social activity.[63] Similarly, when Thompson came to the early eighteenth century he found the Marxist phrases such as "class dictatorship" or "law as the instrument of the *de facto* ruling class" to be too crude for the complex reality he saw. Other concepts, "hegemony," borrowed from Gramsci, and "role," "norms," and "expectations," taken from role theory, were closer to the reality he perceived and revealed more about it.[64] "The historical discipline," Thompson observed, "is not a fairground in which different interpreters set up their stalls and solicit the preference of their customers. Historical argument concerns always the exposure of concept to evidence, or the organizing of evidence by concept."[65]

The intellectual life of Williams, like that of many thinkers and artists, was a journey outward in thought and a return, enriched. As a literary critic in the Marxist tradition, about 1950 he left behind the Marxian concept of base/superstructure, which implied interrelationships between the social mode of production and its literature, and the crass application of the concept by Marxist literary critics, who interpreted great literature as the simple representation of class values. Disassociating himself from the mechanical implications of the Marxian concept and the reductionist crudities of its application, he journeyed outward in search of a theory of culture. Along the way he discovered the structure of feeling of a long line of British writers, from Burke and Cobbett through Ruskin and Morris to Orwell, who expressed a qualitative disapproval of the life that was emerging from the Industrial Revolution. He invented a theory of culture as a whole way of life, composed of the four systems of maintenance (economy), decision (politics), communication, and reproduction (family).[66] Then, returning enriched to Marxian theory, he discovered that Lukács, with his concept of totality of a culture, and Gramsci, with his complex concept of hegemony of a dominant class permeating all the cultural elements of the totality, confirmed, illuminated, and enriched his own perceptions, independently reached.[67] He could now travel with a more subtle Marxian theory.

It is tempting to speculate why these five Marxist historians moved toward a more complex interpretation of British history. We can point to several influences that played upon them. One was their experiences as Britons and as British Socialists. It was often an experience of defeat: the loss of empire, the decline of Great Britain in world importance, the bureaucratization of Russian Communism, Russia's brutal suppression of the Hungarian rising, the failure of the Labor Party reforms of 1945–1951 to shake the British capitalist order or to change the acquisitive capitalist ethos into one of socialist cooperation. Defeat bred reflection: why so? And as these events were occurring, new editions of the *Grundrisse* of Marx and translations of Lukács and Gramsci surfaced, expressions of thinkers who had also known defeat of their immediate hopes and who offered complex interpretations of historical reality. These writings became a second influence.[68] A third was the steady contact of the five research historians with the concrete, multifarious historical reality in the documentary evidence, a contact that would tend to dissolve any reductionist view. A fourth was conversation with their university colleagues, in common rooms, in offices, and through book reviews, articles, and books. Conversation with empirical narrators would reinforce the necessity to be true to concrete "facts," while listening to social scientists would offer alternative concepts and theories. A fifth influence, finally, was their own intense thinking life as authors. The most important point, of course, is not that these separate influences were playing on the minds of these Marxist historians but that they were interplaying, within their mentalities. It was this interplay of theory and concrete particulars, of past and present references, and of personal temperament and intellectual powers that made Marxist historiography the densest in texture and intellectually the most exciting in the British sector of world history-writing.

From the acculturation process going on among traditional narrators of unique events, Namierites, social science historians, and Marxists, what was emerging? What are the characteristics of current British history-writing? First is its strong empirical strain. For most British historians from Thomas Carlyle to the present, the study of history has been a reality-seeking enterprise. And reality for most British historians is people, the experiences of many, many people doing many, many things. Whether we quote the traditionalist Butterfield ("the genesis of historical events lies in human beings")[69] or the social science theorist Ashton ("It is the wills and choices and acts of men and women that are the ultimate data") or the Marxist Thompson, the refrain is the same. It follows, congruently, that men *to a degree* make their own history. It is also congruent that research historians, in seeking concrete human reality in documentary evidence, will get their facts straight, in accord with the exacting critical standards of that special orbit of English empiricism, academic history.

A second characteristic of British history-writing is its strong narrative sense. British historians love to tell a story, and they tell it very well, whether it be of personalities, motivations, and unique events, or of underlying structures and variables, or of even deeper processes. Though they may on occasion write static cross sections, or problem-oriented monographs, or conceptual analyses of a social situation, they are always looking forward to the time when the results of these investigations can find their place in an ongoing narrative flow.

Third, British historians, no matter what their school of thought, seem to be reaching "a tacit consensus" about how an ongoing synthetic history of society should be organized. To quote Hobsbawm:

One starts with the material and historical environment, goes on to the forces and techniques of production (demography, coming somewhere in between), the structure of the consequent economy—divisions of labour, exchange, accumulation, distribution of surplus, and so forth—and the social relations arising from these. These might be followed by the institutions and the image of society and its functioning which underlie them. The shape of the social structure is thus established, the specific characteristics and details of which insofar as they derive from other sources, can then be determined most likely by comparative study. The practice is thus to work outwards and upwards from the process of social production in its specific setting [to the phenomena of politics, philosophy, religion, and art]. Historians will be tempted—in my view rightly—to pick on one particular relation or relational complex as central and specific to the society (or type of society) in question, and to group the rest of the treatment around it—for example, Bloch's "relations of interdependence" in his *Feudal Society,* or those arising out of industrial production, possibly industrial society, certainly in its capitalist form. Once the structure has been established it must be seen in its historical movement . . . The tensions to which the society is exposed in the process of historical change and transformation then allow the historian to expose the general mechanism by which the structures of society simultaneously tend to lose and re-establish their equilibria.[70]

Within this "tacit consensus" there are still important disagreements and unresolved problems. Nevertheless, narrators of unique events, Namierites, social scientists, and Marxists seem increasingly willing to learn from each other.

These positive characteristics of recent British historiography have an obverse side. Sturdy British empiricism is accompanied, usually, by distrust of speculative thought. The strongest suit of British historiography is political, constitutional, social, economic, and local history, in other words the story of practical people doing practical things. Aside from individual intellectual historians such as Isaiah Berlin, Butterfield (*The Origins of Modern Science*), Alfred Cobban, and Williams, intellectual history has not been prominent in the British scene.[71] Distrust of speculation may also appear in the relatively slight interest in psychohistory. Perhaps because of this lack the British historians' view of man, his energies, motives, and interior compulsions, is rather simplistic. It follows that exploration of the intricate, subtle ways in which individual psychologies and group psychologies interrelate is at present probably beyond the range of British capabilities. However, even with these limitations, the net impression that British historiography leaves is one of strength; of a solidly based empirical enterprise and of a powerful social science and Marxist synthetic thought that is gathering momentum.

Notes

1. George Macaulay Trevelyan, "Clio, A Muse," in *Clio, A Muse and Other Essays* (London, 1930), pp. 140–41. In the preparation of this methodological essay, two excellent bibliographical surveys have been useful for their references: G. R. Elton, *Modern Historians on British History 1485–1945: A Critical Bibliography, 1945–1969* (London, 1970); and Elizabeth Chapin Furber, ed., *Changing Views on British History: Essays on Historical Writing Since 1939* (Cambridge, Mass., 1966). A very useful classified bibliography is W. H. Chaloner and R. C. Richardson, *British Economic and Social History: A Bibliographical Guide* (Manchester, 1976). By voluntary self-limitation this essay deals only with British historians who concerned themselves with the history of Great Britain; the contributions of British historians to the history of other areas of the world, including the British Empire, have been excluded.

2. George Peabody Gooch, *Studies in Modern History* (London, 1931), pp. 315–25; W. G. Hoskins, *Local History in England* (London, 1959), pp. 20–21; Denys Hay, "The Historical Periodical: Some Problems," *History* 54 (1969): 166–68; E. F. Jacob, "Local History: The Present Position and Its Possibilities," *History* 34 (1949): 196–97: A. T. Milne, "History at the Universities: Then and Now," *History* 59 (1974): 33–46; E. A. L. Moir, "The Historians of Gloucestershire: Retrospect and Prospect," in H. P. R. Finberg, ed., *Gloucestershire Studies* (Leicester, 1957), pp. 267–90; J. E. Neale, "Albert Frederick Pollard," *English Historical Review* 64 (1949): 198–205; F. M. Powicke, "The Manchester History School" (1951), in *Modern Historians and the Study of History: Essays and Papers* (London, 1955), pp. 19–95; F. M. Stenton, "Presidential Address: Early English History, 1895–1920," *Transactions of the Royal Historical Society*, 4th ser., 28 (1946): 7–19: Margaret F. Stieg, "The Emergence of the *English Historical Review*," *Library Quarterly* 46 (April 1976): 119–36; J. M. Wallace-Hadrill, "Sir Frank Stenton," *History* 56 (1971): 55–59; Carolyn West White, "The Historiography of the Edwardian Era" (Ph.D. dissertation, Duke University, 1975), pp. 15–52; Llewellyn Woodward, "The Rise of the Professorial Historian in England," in K. Bourne and D. C. Watt, eds., *Studies in International History: Essays Presented to W. Norton Medlicott* (Hamden, Conn., 1967), pp. 16–34.

3. J. B. Bury, "The Science of History" (1903), in Harold Temperley, ed., *Selected Essays of J. B. Bury* (Cambridge, 1930), pp. 19–20.

4. The names of some of the leading protagonists are given in parentheses after each subject; several, it will be noted, are non-British scholars who were yet prominent in a given controversy. There are, of course, many other controversies not listed here.

5. Furber, *Changing Views*, pp. 14–16, 55; Chaloner and Richardson, *British Economic and Social History*, pp. 5–6; recent books include: Donald James Alexander Matthew, *The Norman Conquest* (London, 1966); Michael Altschul, *Anglo-Norman England, 1066–1154* (London, 1969); Rex Welldon Finn, *The Norman Conquest and Its Effects on the Economy: 1066–86* (Hamden, Conn., 1971); Jack Lindsay, *The Normans and Their World* (London, 1973); Kenneth Harrison, *The Framework of Anglo-Saxon History to A.D. 900* (London, 1976); David C. Douglas, *The Norman Fate, 1100–1154* (Berkeley, 1976); R. H. C. Davis, *The Normans and Their Myth* (London, 1976); David Howarth, *1066: The Year of the Conquest* (New York, 1978).

6. Furber, *Changing Views*, pp. 12–14, 55; Chaloner and Richardson, *British Economic and*

Social History, pp. 6–7; see also H. C. Darby, *The Domesday Geography of Eastern England* (Cambridge, 1952); H. C. Darby and T. B. Terrett, eds., *The Domesday Geography of Midland England* (Cambridge, 1954); H. C. Darby and Eila M. J. Campbell, eds., *The Domesday Geography of South-East England* (Cambridge, 1962); H. C. Darby and I. S. Maxwell, eds., *The Domesday Geography of Northern England* (Cambridge, 1962); H. C. Darby and R. Welldon Finn, eds., *The Domesday Geography of South-West England* (London, 1967); R. W. Finn, *The Making and Limitations of the Yorkshire Domesday* (York, 1972); R. W. Finn, *Domesday Book: A Guide* (London, 1973); H. C. Darby and G. R. Versey, *Domesday Gazetteer* (Cambridge, 1975); H. C. Darby, *Domesday England* (New York, 1977); V. H. Galbraith, *Domesday Book: Its Place in Administrative History* (Oxford, 1978).

7. Furber, *Changing Views*, pp. 27–28, 55, 61–64, 71; see also G. O. Sayles, *The King's Parliament of England* (New York, 1974); G. L. Harriss, "War and the Emergence of the English Parliament, 1297–1360," *Journal of Medical History* 2 (March 1976); 35–56.

8. Elton, *Modern Historians*, pp. 26–37, 41; Furber, *Changing Views*, pp. 101–09; see also: G. R. Elton, *The Body of the Whole Realm: Parliament and Representation in Medieval and Tudor England* (Charlottesville, Va., 1969); S. E. Lehmberg, *The Reformation Parliament, 1529–1536* (Cambridge, 1970) and *The Later Parliaments of Henry VIII, 1536–1597* (Cambridge, 1977); Conrad Russell, *The Crisis of Parliaments: English History, 1509–1660* (London, 1971); W. R. D. Jones, *The Mid-Tudor Crisis, 1539–1563* (New York, 1973); G. R. Elton, *Reform and Reformation: England, 1509–1558* (Cambridge, Mass., 1977).

9. On the rise of the gentry and the English revolution in general, see Elton, *Modern Historians*, pp. 51–64; Furber, *Changing Views*, pp. 132–33; Chaloner and Richardson, *British Economic and Social History*, pp. 50–52, 54–59; R. C. Richardson, *The Debate on the English Revolution* (New York, 1977); see also: R. Ashton, "The Aristocracy in Transition," *Economic History Review*, 2nd ser. 22 (1969): 308–22; Stuart Woolf, "The Aristocracy in Transition: A Continental Comparison," *Economic History Review* 23 (1970): 520–31; Lawrence Stone, "The Aristocracy in Transition: A Reply to Dr. Woolf," *Economic History Review* 25 (1972): 114–16; Conrad Russell, "English Land Sales, 1540–1640: A Comment on the Evidence," *Economic History Review* 25 (1972): 117–21; Lawrence Stone, "English Land Sales, 1540–1640: A Reply to Mr. Russell," *Economic History Review* 25 (1972): 121–23; Christopher Thompson, "The Counting of Manors Reconsidered," *Economic History Review* 25 (1972): 124–31; Lawrence Stone, "Counting Manors Again: A Reply to Mr. Thompson," *Economic History Review* 25 (1972): 131–36; B. Manning, "The Peasantry and the English Revolution," *Journal of Peasant Studies* 2 (January 1975): 133–58; Paul Christianson, "The Causes of the English Revolution: A Reappraisal," *Journal of British Studies* 15 (1976): 40–75; Conrad Russell, "Parliamentary History in Perspective, 1604–1629," *History* 61 (1976): 1–27; C. H. George, "Hill's Century: Fragments of a Lost Revolution," *Science and Society* 40 (Winter 1976–77): 979–86; "The First English Revolution, 1640–1660," *Journal of Modern History* 49 (December 1977); J. H. Hexter, "Power Struggle, Parliament, and Liberty in Early Stuart England," *Journal of Modern History* 50 (1978): 1–50.

10. Elton, *Modern Historians*, p. 66; Furber, *Changing Views*, p. 166; see also J. R. Jones, *Revolution of 1688 in England* (New York, 1973); D. H. Hosford, *Nottingham, Nobles, and the North: Aspects of the Revolution of 1688* (Hamden, Conn., 1976); H.Horwitz, *Parliament, Policy, and Politics in the Reign of William III* (Manchester, 1977); J. R. Jones, *Country and Court: England, 1658–1714* (Cambridge, Mass., 1978).

11. Elton, *Modern Historians*, pp. 18, 59, 67, 78–86; Furber, *Changing Views*, pp. 123–24, 187–88, 207–10; see also P. Langford, *The First Rockingham Administration 1765–1766* (London, 1973); Frank O'Gorman, *The Rise of Party in England: The Rockingham Whigs 1760–82* (London, 1975), John Brewer, *Party Ideology and Popular Politics at the Accession of George III* (Cambridge, 1976); N. A. Erofeev, "Lewis Namier and His Place in Bourgeois Historiography," *Soviet Studies in History* 15 (Winter 1976–77): 26–50; H. T. Dickinson, "Party, Principle and Public Opinion in Eighteenth Century Politics," *History* 61 (1976); 231–37; John Dinwiddy, "Party Politics and Ideology in the Early Years of George III's Reign," *Historical Journal* 20 (1977): 983–89; M. S. Anderson, *Historians and Eighteenth-Century Europe 1715–1789* (Oxford, 1979), pp. 223–29.

12. Elton, *Modern Historians*, pp. 93–102; Furber, *Changing Views*, p. 219; Chaloner and Richardson, *British Economic and Social History*, pp. 61–62; see also D. E. C. Eversley, "The Home Market and Economic Growth in England, 1750–80," in E. L. Jones and G. E. Mingay, eds., *Land, Labour and Population in the Industrial Revolution* (London, 1967), pp. 206–59; P. E. Razzell, "Population Growth and Economic Change in Eighteenth- and Early Nineteenth-Century England and Ireland," in ibid., pp. 260–81; J. W. Osborne, *The Silent Revolution: The Industrial Revolution in England as a Source of Cultural Change* (New York, 1970); R. M. Hartwell, *The Industrial Revolution and Economic Growth* (London, 1971); E. L. Jones, *Agriculture and the Industrial Revolution* (New York, 1974); N. F. R. Crofts, "Industrial Revolution in England and France: Some Thoughts on the Question 'Why Was England First?' " *Economic History Review* 30 (1977): 429–41; P. Lane, *The Industrial Revolution: The Birth of a Modern Age* (London, 1978); Anderson, *Historians and Eighteenth-Century Europe*, pp. 191–211.

13. Elton, *Modern Historians*, pp. 95–96; Furber, *Changing Views*, pp. 219–21; see also Institute of Economic Affairs, *The Long Debate on Poverty: Eight Essays on Industrialization and the Condition of England* (London, 1972); Duncan Bythell, "The History of the Poor," *English Historical Review* 89 (1974): 365–77; Chaloner and Richardson, *British Economic and Social History*, pp. 81–82, 86–87; M. W. Flinn, "Trends in Real Wages, 1750–1850," *Economic History Review*, 2nd ser., 27 (1974): 395–413; T. R. Gourvish, "Flinn and Real Wage Trends in Britain, 1750–1850: A Comment," *Economic History Review*, 2nd ser., 29 (1976): 136–42; M. W. Flinn, "Real Wage Trends in Britain, 1750–1850: A Reply," *Economic History Review*, 2nd ser., 29 (1976): 143–45; G. N. von Tunzelmann, "Trends in Real Wages, 1750–1850, Revisited," *Economic History Review*, 2nd ser., 32 (1979): 33–49.

14. Book reviews and review articles indicate that some British historians were aware of Marc Bloch, Lucien Febvre, Fernand Braudel, Emmanuel Le Roy Ladurie, and of other members of the *Annales* circle, but their influence on British historiography has been thus far rather slight. See on this point Geoffrey Parker, "Braudel's *Mediterranean:* The Making and Marketing of a Masterpiece," *History* 59 (1974): 238–43; Peter Burke, "Writing History from the Bottom Upwards," *The Times Higher Education Supplement*, 27 May 1977, p. 17.

15. Herbert Butterfield, *George III and the Historians*, rev. ed. (New York, 1959), pp. 166–68.

16. (London, 1929).

17. Butterfield, *George III and the Historians*, pp. 202–10.

18. L. B. Namier, *Avenues of History* (London, 1952), p. 8.

19. See the Preface and Introductory Survey by John Brooke in Lewis Namier and John Brooke, *The House of Commons 1754–1790* (New York, 1964), especially I, pp. ix, 198–204.

20. Butterfield, *George III and the Historians*, pp. 61–65, 196–98.

21. See, for example, John Brooke, *The Chatham Administration, 1766–1768* (London, 1956); Ian R. Christie, *The End of North's Ministry, 1780–1782* (London, 1958); Bernard Donoughue, *British Politics and the American Revolution* (London, 1964); and John B. Owen, *The Rise of the Pelhams* (London, 1957). For comment see Richard Pares, *King George III and the Politicians* (Oxford, 1953), p. 2. For continued disagreement see John Cannon, *The Fox-North Coalition: Crisis of the Constitution, 1782–4* (Cambridge, 1969), pp. vii, 238–43, and John Brewer, *Party Ideology and Popular Politics* (Cambridge, 1976).

22. Succinct summaries of the "Namier" controversy are found in G. R. Elton, *Modern Historians*, pp. 83–86, and H. T. Dickinson, "Party, Principle and Public Opinion in Eighteenth Century Politics," *History* 61 (1976): 231–37.

23. Lawrence Stone, "Prosopography," in Felix Gilbert and Stephen R. Graubard, eds., *Historical Studies Today* (New York, 1971), pp. 131–32.

24. Ibid., pp. 111–113; J. E. Neale, "The Biographical Approach to History," *History* 36 (1951): 193–203.

25. Dickinson, "Party, Principle and Public Opinion in Eighteenth Century Politics," pp. 231–37; Dinwiddy, "Party Politics and Ideology in the Early Years of George III's Reign," pp. 983–89.

26. Douglas Dakin, "Collingwood's *Idea of History*," *History* 37 (1952): 4, 6.

27. H. J. Dyos, ed., *The Study of Urban History* (London, 1968), pp. ix, 4, 17.

28. Eileen Power, "On Medieval History as a Social Study," *Economica*, n.s. 1 (1934): 13–29, especially pp. 14, 16, 17, 26, 28–29. In 1932 Power had formed a small group in London to discuss the sociological and historical implications of economic problems; this "sociological group" continued to meet for several years. M. M. Postan, "Hugh Gaitskell: Political and Intellectual Progress" (1964), in *Facts and Relevance: Essays on Historical Method* (Cambridge, 1971), pp. 171, 175.

29. T. S. Ashton, "The Relation of Economic History to Economic Theory," *Economica*, n.s. 13 (1946): 81–96, especially pp. 82, 87–88, 92, 94, 96.

30. (Cambridge).

31. (Cambridge, Mass.); see also two books by W. M. Williams, *Gosforth: the Sociology of an English Village* (Glencoe, Ill., 1956) and *A West Country Village: Ashworthy: Family, Kinship, Land* (London, 1963).

32. (London).

33. (Oxford, 1965); see references under footnote 9.

34. See footnote 13.

35. Peter Laslett, "The History of Population and Social Structure," *International Science Journal* 17 (1965): 584.

36. Ibid., p. 583.

37. Ibid., p. 584; see also E. A. Wrigley, ed., *Identifying People in the Past* (London, 1973), pp. 1–40.

38. Michael Anderson, *Family Structure in Nineteenth Century Lancashire* (Cambridge, 1971).

39. For changing styles of doing economic history, see Chaloner and Richardson, *British Economic and Social History*, pp. 1–4; N. B. Harte ed., *The Study of Economic History: Collected Inaugural Lectures 1893–1970* (London, 1971).

40. N. S. Gras, "The Rise and Development of Economic History," *Economic History Review* 1 (1927): 19–20.

41. There are other examples of the early application of economic theory to historical data: for example, the controversy about the effects of the influx of bullion from Spanish America on the European economy (Pierre Vilar, "Problems of the Formation of Capitalism," *Past and Present* 10 [November 1956]: 15–38).

42. Robert W. Fogel, "The New Economic History: Its Findings and Methods," *Economic History Review*, 2nd ser. 19 (1966): 642–56; John Habakkuk, "Economic History and Economic Theory," in Gilbert and Graubard, eds., *Historical Studies Today*, pp. 30–32; E. H. Hunt, "The New Economic History: Professor Fogel's Study of American Railways," *History* 53 (1968): 3–18; G. R. Hawke, "Mr. Hunt's Study of the Fogel Thesis: A Comment," ibid., pp. 18–23; Lance Davis, "Professor Fogel and the New Economic History," *Economic History Review*, 2nd ser. 19 (1966): 657–63; Meghnad Desai, "Some Issues in Econometric History," ibid., 21 (1968): 1–16.

43. Peter D. McClelland, "The Cost to America of British Imperial Policy," *American Economic Review, Papers and Proceedings* 59 (1969): 370–81; Gary M. Walton, "The New Economic History and the Burdens of the Navigation Acts," *Economic History Review*, 2nd ser. 24 (1971): 533–42; Frank J. A. Broeze, "The New Economic History, the Navigation Acts, and the Continental Tobacco Market, 1770–90," ibid., 26 (1973): 668–78; Peter D. McClelland, "The New Economic History and the Burdens of the Navigation Acts: A Comment," ibid., 678–86; Gary M. Walton, "The Burdens of the Navigation Acts: A Reply," ibid., 687–88; David J. Loschky, "Studies of the Navigation Acts: New Economic Non-History?" ibid., 689–90.

44. D. C. North and R. P. Thomas, "The Rise and Fall of the Manorial System: A Theoretical Model," *Journal of Economic History* 31 (1971): 777–803; Edward Miller, "England in the Twelfth and Thirteenth Centuries: An Economic Contrast?" *Economic History Review*, 2nd Ser. 24 (1971): 1–14; Clyde G. Reed and Terry L. Anderson, "An Economic Explanation of English Agricultural Organization in the Twelfth and Thirteenth Centuries," ibid., 26 (1973): 134–37; Edward Miller, "Farming of Manors and Direct Management," ibid., 137–40.

45. (London).

46. For a select list of local, regional, and urban histories, see Chaloner and Richardson, *British*

Economic and Social History, pp. 6, 12–13, 18, 20, 25, 30, 34, 40–41, 56–57, 62, 65, 67–68, 95–97; for comment see A. R. Mitchell, "Regional History or Local History? The Contribution of *Midland History* and *Northern History* to the Writing of English Economic History at a Local Level," *Journal of European Economic History* 2 (1973): 481–93.

47. E. A. L. Moir, "The Historians of Gloucestershire: Retrospect and Prospect," pp. 285, 287.

48. Ibid., p. 289.

49. *Records of the Borough of Leicester, Being a Series of Extracts from the Archives of the Corporation of Leicester, 1103–1603.* 3 vols. (London, 1899–1905).

50. W. G. Hoskins, *Local History in England* (London, 1959), p. 3.

51. (London); also by Chambers, *The Vale of Trent: A Regional Study of Economic Change* (*Economic History Review*, Supplement no. 3 [1957]).

52. (Manchester). To the books by Chambers and Hoskins we should add two books published in 1940 by H. C. Darby: *Medieval Fenland* (Cambridge) and *The Draining of the Fens* (Cambridge).

53. On Hoskins see C. W. Chalkin and M. A. Havinden, *Rural Change and Urban Growth 1500–1800: Essays in English Regional History in Honour of W. G. Hoskins* (London, 1974); H. P. R. Finberg, *The Local Historian and His Theme* (Leicester, 1952), p. 17. Of his many books we might cite: *The Making of the English Landscape* (London, 1954); *The Midland Peasant: An Economic and Social History of a Leicestershire Village* (London, 1957); *Local History in England* (1959); *Two Thousand Years in Exeter* (London and Chichester, 1960); *Provincial England: Essays in Social and Economic History* (London, 1963); *Old Devon* (London, 1966). Illustrative local histories include: Alan Everitt, *The Community of Kent and the Great Rebellion 1640–1660* (Leicester, 1966); Malcolm I. Thomis, *Old Nottingham* (London, 1968); Brian Simon, ed., *Education in Leicestershire 1540–1940: A Regional Study* (Leicester, 1968); Frank Barlow, ed., *Exeter and Its Region* (Exeter, 1969); Joan Thirsk, ed., *History of Lincolnshire* (Lincoln, 1970–   ): vol. 1, Jeffrey May, *Prehistoric Lincolnshire* (1976), vol. 2, J. B. Whitwell, *Roman Lincolnshire* (1970), vol 5, Dorothy M. Owen, *Church and Society in Medieval Lincolnshire* (1971), vol. 6, Gerald A. J. Hodgett, *Tudor Lincolnshire* (1975); Peter Clark and Paul Slack, eds., *Crisis and Order in English Towns, 1500–1700* (n.p., 1972); C. M. Fraser and K. Emsley, *Tyneside* (Newton Abbot, 1973); Margaret Spufford, *Contrasting Communities: English Villagers in the Sixteenth and Seventeenth Centuries* (Cambridge, 1974); David A. Hinton, *Alfred's Kingdom: Wessex and the South 800–1500* (London, 1977). To these should be added the excellent articles and monographs in local and regional history produced by the British school of historical geographers from H. C. Darby to Alan Everitt and Alan Baker. For an anthology of their articles, see Alan R. H. Baker, John D. Hamshere, and John Langton, *Geographical Interpretations of Historical Sources: Readings in Historical Geography* (Newton Abbot, 1970). For other samples see Alan R. H. Baker and Robin A. Butlin, *Studies of Field Systems in the British Isles* (Cambridge, 1973) and articles in the *Journal of Historical Geography* (1975–   ). Two works of synthesis have been edited by H. C. Darby: *An Historical Geography of England before A.D. 1800* (Cambridge, 1936) and *A New Historical Geography of England* (Cambridge, 1973).

54. For general surveys and bibliography of urban history, see Dyos, *The Study of Urban History*, pp. 19–43; Peter Clark and Paul Slack, "Introduction" in Clark and Slack, eds., *Crisis and Order in English Towns 1500–1700: Essays in Urban History* (n.p., 1972); C. S. L. Davies, "Pre-Industrial England," *History* 62 (1977): 433–38; Chaloner and Richardson, *British Economic and Social History*, pp. 12–13, 25, 40–41, 95–97.

55. C. Gill and Asa Briggs, *History of Birmingham*, 2 vols. (London, 1952); H. J. Dyos, *Victorian Suburb: A Study of the Growth of Camberwell* (Leicester, 1961). For other illustrative urban histories, see A. Temple Patterson, *Radical Leicester: A History of Leicester 1780–1850* (Leicester, 1954); Asa Briggs, *Victorian Cities* (London, 1963); Robert Newton, *Victorian Exeter 1837–1914* (Leicester, 1968); Malcolm I. Thomis, *Politics and Society in Nottingham 1785–1835* (London, 1969); Alan D. Dyer, *The City of Worcester in the Sixteenth Century* (Leicester, 1973); Alan Everitt, *Perspectives in English Urban History* (London, 1973); H. J. Dyos and Michael Wolff, *The Victorian City: Images and Realities*, 2 vols. (London, 1973); Jack Simmons, *Leicester, Past and Present*, 2 vols. (Leicester, 1974); C. B. Jewson, *The Jacobin City: A Portrait of Norwich in its*

Reaction to the French Revolution 1788–1802 (Glasgow and London, 1975); Peter Clark and Paul Slack, *English Towns in Transition 1500–1700* (London, 1976); Anthony S. Wohl, *The Eternal Slum: Housing and Social Policy in Victorian London* (London, 1977).

56. David Ward, "Victorian Cities: How Modern?" *Journal of Historical Geography* 1 (1975): 135–51; David Cannadine, "Victorian Cities: How Different?" *Social History* no. 4 (1977): 457–82.

57. Alan Macfarlane, "History, Anthropology and the Study of Communities," *Social History* no. 5 (1977): 631–52; Alan Macfarlane with Sarah Harrison and Charles Jardine, *Reconstructing Historical Communities* (Cambridge, 1977); R. M. Smith, "Conference Report: Communities and Social Contacts in the Past," *Journal of Historical Geography* 2 (1976): 289–91.

58. George Unwin, *Studies in Economic History: The Collected Papers of George Unwin,* ed. R. H. Tawney (London, 1927), pp. xxiii, 437–38; M. M. Postan, "Karl Marx: A Democrat?" in A. B. Brown, ed., *The Great Democrats* (London, 1934).

59. The selection of these five for consideration should not be construed as a reflection on other Marxist historians, such as Perry Anderson, Maurice Dobb, John Foster, Marion Gibbs, and Gareth Stedman Jones. Nor should one overlook the articles, chiefly on social history, in *History Workshop: A Journal of Socialist Historians* (Vol. 1 [1976]–   ). The five historians were selected because they seemed to be leading and representative, they belong (roughly) to the same generation and hence could be compared, and they published over several decades and hence movement (or non-movement) of thought could be observed. For works of other Marxists see, for example, Perry Anderson, *Lineages of the Absolutist State* (London, 1974) and *Passages from Antiquity to Feudalism* (London, 1977); Maurice Dobb, *Studies in the Development of Capitalism* (London, 1946); John Foster, *Class Struggle and the Industrial Revolution: Early Industrial Capitalism in Three English Towns* (London, 1974); Marion Gibbs, *Feudal Order: A Study of the Origins and Development of English Feudal Society* (New York, 1953); and Gareth Stedman Jones, *Outcast London: A Study in the Relationship between the Classes in Victorian Society* (Oxford, 1971). On the evolution of British socialist historians see: Richard Johnson, "Thompson, Genovese, and Socialist-Humanist History," *History Workshop* 6 (1978): 79–100.

The ensuing paragraphs are based on the publications of the five men available to me in the library of my university. The books and several of the key articles included for Hilton: *The Economic Development of Some Leicestershire Estates in the 14th and 15th Centuries* (London, 1947); Hilton and H. Fagan, *The English Rising of 1381* (London, 1950); Hilton, *Communism and Liberty* (London, 1950); Hilton, ed., *Ministers' Accounts of the Warwickshire Estates of the Duke of Clarence, 1479–80* (Oxford, 1952); "Capitalism—What's in a Name?" *Past and Present* 1 (February 1952): 32–43; ed., *Studies in the Agrarian History of England in the Thirteenth Century* by E. A. Kosminskii (Oxford, 1956); ed., *The Stoneleigh Leger Book* (Oxford, 1960); "Annales: Inquiry into Nutrition," *Past and Present* 23 (November, 1962): 86–88; *A Medieval Society: The West Midlands at the End of the Thirteenth Century* (London, 1966); *Bond Men Made Free: Medieval Peasant Movements and the English Rising of 1381* (New York, 1973); "Warriors and Peasants," *New Left Review,* no. 83 (January-February, 1974): 83–94; *The English Peasantry in the Later Middle Ages: The Ford Lectures for 1973 and Related Studies* (Oxford, 1975); ed., *Peasants, Knights and Heretics: Studies in Medieval English Social History* (Cambridge and New York, 1976); "Agrarian Class Structure and Economic Development in Pre-Industrial Europe: A Crisis of Feudalism," *Past and Present* 80 (August, 1978): 3–19.

For Hill: *The Good Old Cause: The English Revolution of 1640–60, Its Causes, Course and Consequences; Extracts from Contemporary Sources,* ed. Christopher Hill and Edmund Dell (London, 1949); *Lenin and the Russian Revolution* (New York, 1950); *Economic Problems of the Church, from Archbishop Whitgift to the Long Parliament* (Oxford, 1956); *Puritanism and Revolution: Studies in Interpretation of the English Revolution of the 17th Century* (London, 1959); "Republicanism After the Restoration," *New Left Review,* No. 3 (May–June, 1960): 46-51; *The Century of Revolution, 1603–1714* (Edinburgh, 1961); "Puritans and 'the dark corners of the land,' " *Transactions of the Royal Historical Society,* 5th ser. 13 (1963): 77-102; *Society and Puritanism in Pre-Revolutionary England* (New York, 1964); "William Harvey and the Idea of Monarchy," *Past and*

Present 27 (April, 1964): 54-72; "Puritanism, Capitalism, and the Scientific Revolution," ibid., 29 (December, 1964): 88-97; *Intellectual Origins of the English Revolution* (Oxford, 1965); "William Harvey (No Parliamentarian, No Heretic) and the Idea of Monarchy," *Past and Present* 31 (July, 1965): 97-103; "Science, Religion and Society in the Sixteenth and Seventeenth Centuries," ibid., 32 (December, 1965): 110–12; *Reformation to Industrial Revolution: The Making of Modern English Society, 1530–1780* (New York, 1967); *God's Englishman: Oliver Cromwell and the English Revolution* (New York, 1970); *Antichrist in Seventeenth-Century England: The Riddell Memorial Lectures* (London and New York, 1971); *The World Turned Upside Down: Radical Ideas During the English Revolution* (London, 1972); *Change and Continuity in Seventeenth-Century England* (London, 1974).

For Hobsbawm: "The Machine Breakers," *Past and Present* 1 (February 1952): 57–70; "The Crisis of the 17th Century," ibid., 5 (May 1954): 33–53, and 6 (November 1954): 44–65; *Primitive Rebels: Studies in Archaic Forms of Social Movement in the 19th and 20th Centuries* (New York, 1959); "Trevor-Roper's 'General Crisis'—Contribution to Symposium," *Past and Present* 18 (November 1960): 12–14; *The Age of Revolution, 1789–1848* (Cleveland, Ohio, 1962); ed., *Precapitalist Economic Formations* by Karl Marx (London, 1964); *Labouring Men: Studies in the History of Labour* (London, 1964); with George Rudé, *Captain Swing* (New York, 1968); *Bandits* (New York, 1969); *Industry and Empire: An Economic History of Britain Since 1750* (London, 1968); "Problems of Communist History," *New Left Review*, no. 54 (March-April 1969): 85–91; "Confronting Defeat: The German Communist Party," ibid., no. 61 (May-June 1970): 83–92; "From Social History to the History of Society," *Daedalus* 100 (Winter 1971): 20–45; "The Social Function of the Past: Some Questions," *Past and Present* 55 (May 1972): 3–17; *Revolutionaries: Contemporary Essays* (New York, 1973); "Peasant Land Occupations," *Past and Present* 62 (February 1974): 120–52; *The Age of Capital, 1848–1875* (New York, 1975); "Some Reflections on 'The Break-up of Britain,' " *New Left Review*, no. 105 (September-October 1977): 3–23.

For Thompson: *William Morris, Romantic to Revolutionary* (London, 1955); ed., *Out of Apathy* (London, 1960); "Revolution," *New Left Review*, no. 3 (May-June 1960): 3–9; "The Long Revolution," ibid., no. 9 (May-June, 1961): 24–33 and no. 10 (July-August 1961): 34–39; "The Freeborn Englishman," ibid., no. 15 (May-June 1962): 43–57; *The Making of the English Working Class* (New York, 1963); "The Peculiarities of the English," *Socialist Register 1965* (London, 1965), pp. 311–62; "Time, Work-Discipline, and Industrial Capitalism," *Past and Present* 38 (December 1967): 59–97; ed., *Warwick University Ltd.: Industry, Management and the Universities* (Harmondsworth, 1970); "The Moral Economy of the English Crowd in the Eighteenth Century," *Past and Present* 50 (February 1971): 76–136; "Anthropology and the Discipline of Historical Context," *Midland History* 1 (1972); "An Open Letter to Leszek Kolakowski," *Socialist Register 1973* (London, 1974), pp. 1–100; *Whigs and Hunters: The Origin of the Black Act* (New York, 1975); "The Crime of Anonymity," in *Albion's Fatal Tree: Crime and Society in Eighteenth-Century England* by Douglas Hay, Peter Linebaugh, John G. Rule, E. P. Thompson, and Cal Winslow (New York, 1975); "On History, Sociology, and Historical Relevance," *British Journal of Sociology* 27 (1976): 387–402; "The Grid of Inheritance," in Jack Goody, Joan Thirsk, and E. P. Thompson, eds., *Family and Inheritance: Rural Society in Western Europe, 1200–1800* (Cambridge and New York, 1976); "Caudwell," *Socialist Register 1977* (London, 1977), pp. 228–76; "Romanticism, Moralism and Utopianism: The Case of William Morris," *New Left Review*, no. 99 (September-October 1976): 83–111.

And for Williams: *Drama, From Ibsen to Eliot* (London, 1952); *Culture and Society, 1780–1950* (New York, 1958); *Border Country, A Novel* (London, 1960); "Working Class Attitudes," *New Left Review*, no. 1 (January-February 1960): 26–30; "The Magic System," ibid., no. 4 (July-August 1960): 27–32; "Freedom and Ownership in the Arts," ibid., no. 5 (September-October 1960): 53–57; *The Long Revolution* (New York, 1961); *The Existing Alternatives in Communications* (London, 1962); *Britain in the Sixties: Communications* (Baltimore, 1962); "A Prologue on Tragedy," *New Left Review*, nos. 13–14 (January-April 1962): 22–35; "Auto-da-Fe (Elias Canetti)," ibid., no 15 (May-June 1962): 103–6; "From Hero to Victim: Notes on the Development of Liberal Tragedy," ibid., no. 20 (Summer 1963): 54–68; "The British Left," ibid., no. 30 (March-April 1965): 18–26;

Modern Tragedy (Stanford, Calif., 1966); *Drama from Ibsen to Brecht* (London, 1968); *Drama in Performance,* new ed. (London, 1968); *The English Novel: From Dickens to Lawrence* (London, 1971); "Literature and Sociology: In Memory of Lucien Goldmann," *New Left Review,* no. 67 (May-June 1971): 3–18; *The Country and the City* (New York, 1973); "Base and Superstructure in Marxist Cultural Theory," *New Left Review,* no. 82 (November-December 1973): 3–16; ed., *George Orwell; A Collection of Essays* (Englewood Cliffs, N.J., 1974); *Television Technology and Cultural Form* (New York, 1975); *Keywords: A Vocabulary of Culture and Society* (New York, 1976); *Marxism and Literature* (London, 1977); "Social Environment and Theatrical Environment," in Marie Axton and Raymond Williams, eds., *English Drama: Forms and Development; Essays in Honour of Muriel Clara Bradbrook* (Cambridge and New York, 1977); "Timpanaro's Materialist Challenge," *New Left Review,* no. 109 (May-June 1978): 3–17.

60. Postan, "Hugh Gaitskell: Political and Intellectual Progress," pp. 169, 173–76, conveys some sense of the atmosphere of discussion.

61. Thompson, "An Open Letter to Leszek Kolakowski," pp. 27, 28; "The Peculiarities of the English," p. 351.

62. Thompson, *The Making of the English Working Class,* pp. 8–11; "The Peculiarities of the English," pp. 342, 346, 356–68.

63. Thompson, "The Peculiarities of the English," pp. 351–52; "An Open Letter to Leszek Kolakowski," pp. 27–28.

64. Thompson, *Whigs and Hunters,* pp. 189, 259, 260, 261, 262, 263, 269; also, "The Peculiarities of the English," pp. 345–46.

65. Thompson, "An Open Letter to Leszek Kolakowski," pp. 48–49.

66. Williams, *The Long Revolution,* p. 114.

67. Williams, "Literature and Sociology: In Memory of Lucien Goldmann," pp. 4, 9, 12, and "Base and Superstructure in Marxist Cultural Theory," pp. 5–10, 12–14.

68. With Thompson, and perhaps with the others, the perceptions of William Morris also lingered and were a factor: E. P. Thompson, "Romanticism, Moralism, Moralism and Utopianism: The Case of William Morris," p. 109.

69. *History and Human Relations* (New York, 1952), p. 66.

70. "From Social History to the History of Society," *Daedalus* 100 (Winter 1971): 31–32. Recent attempts at general or partial synthesis include Asa Briggs, *The Age of Improvement* (London, 1959); S. G. Checkland, *The Rise of Industrial Society in England 1815–1885* (London, 1964); E. J. Hobsbawm, *The Age of Capital, 1848–1875* (New York, 1975); Harold Perkin, *The Origins of Modern English Society 1780–1880* (London, 1969); and Conrad Russell, *The Crisis of Parliaments: English History 1509–1660* (London, 1971).

71. Among British historians distrust of ideas and lack of interest in intellectual history may have been simply a post-World War I phenomenon. So thought Alfred Cobban, who wrote: "It would hardly be an exaggeration to say that the general climate of opinion among British historians since the First World War has been so cold to anything even smelling of an idea that any exotic plants of this kind that happened to be produced were rapidly killed off and those who would rashly have cultivated them taught the error of their ways" ("Editorial Notes," *History* 43 [1958]: 40–42).

Bibliography

Anderson, Michael. *Family Structure in Nineteenth Century Lancashire* (Cambridge, 1971).

Baker, Alan R. H., John D. Hamshere, and John Langton. *Geographical Interpretations of Historical Sources: Readings in Historical Geography* (Newton Abbot, Devon, England, 1970).

Brewer, John. *Party Ideology and Popular Politics at the Accession of George III* (Cambridge, 1976).

Briggs, Asa. *The Age of Improvement* (London, 1959).

Butterfield, Herbert. *George III and the Historians,* rev. ed. (New York, 1959).

————. *The Origins of Modern Science, 1300–1800* (London, 1949).

Chambers, J. D. *Nottinghamshire in the Eighteenth Century* (London, 1932).

————. *The Vale of Trent: A Regional Study of Economic Change (Economic History Review,* Supplement No. 3 [1957]).

Checkland, S. G. *The Rise of Industrial Society in England 1815–1885* (London, 1964).

Clark, Peter, and Paul Slack, eds. *Crisis and Order in English Towns 1500–1700: Essays in Urban History* (n.p., 1972).

Darby, H. C. *A New Historical Geography of England* (Cambridge, 1973).

Dyos, H. J., ed. *The Study of Urban History* (London, 1968).

Elton, G. R. *Modern Historians on British History 1485–1945: A Critical Bibliography, 1945–1969* (London, 1970).

————. *The Practice of History* (New York, 1967).

————. *Reform and Reformation: England, 1509–1558* (Cambridge, Mass., 1977).

Everitt, Alan. *The Community of Kent and the Great Rebellion 1640–1660* (Leicester, 1966).

Finberg, H. P. R., general ed. *The Agrarian History of England and Wales,* vol. IV, *1500–1640,* ed. Joan Thirsk (Cambridge, 1967).

————, and V. H. T. Skipp. *Local History: Objective and Pursuit* (Newton Abbot, Devon, England, 1967).

Foster, John. *Class Struggle and the Industrial Revolution: Early Industrial Capitalism in Three English Towns* (London, 1974).

Furber, Elizabeth Chapin, ed. *Changing Views on British History: Essays on Historical Writing Since 1939* (Cambridge, Mass., 1966).

Hill, John Christopher. *Change and Continuity in Seventeenth-Century England* (London, 1974).

————. *Intellectual Origins of the English Revolution* (Oxford, 1965).

————. *Reformation to Industrial Revolution: The Making of Modern English Society, 1530–1780* (New York, 1967).

————. *The World Turned Upside Down: Radical Ideas During the English Revolution* (London, 1972).

Hilton, Rodney H. *Bond Men Made Free: Medieval Peasant Movements and the English Rising of 1381* (New York, 1973).

————. *The English Peasantry in the Later Middle Ages: The Ford Lectures for 1973 and Related Studies* (Oxford, 1975).

Hobsbawm, Eric J. *The Age of Capital, 1848–1875* (New York, 1975).

————. *The Age of Revolution, 1789–1848* (Cleveland, 1962).

————. "From Social History to the History of Society," *Daedalus* 100 (Winter 1971): 20–45.

————. *Industry and Empire: An Economic History of Britain Since 1750* (London, 1968).

————. *Primitive Rebels: Studies in Archaic Forms of Social Movement in the 19th and 20th Centuries* (New York, 1959).

————, and George Rudé. *Captain Swing* (New York, 1968).

Hoskins, W. G. *Local History in England* (London, 1959).

————. *The Making of the English Landscape* (London, 1954).

————. *The Midland Peasant: An Economic and Social History of a Leicestershire Village* (London, 1957).

————. *Provincial England: Essays in Social and Economic History* (London, 1963).

————. *Two Thousand Years in Exeter* (London and Chichester, 1960).

Jones, Gareth Stedman. *Outcast London: A Study in the Relationship between the Classes in Victorian Society* (Oxford, 1971).

Lane, Peter. *The Industrial Revolution: The Birth of a Modern Age* (London, 1978).

Laslett, Peter. *The World We Have Lost: England before the Industrial Age* (New York, 1965).

————, ed. *Household and Family in Past Time* (Cambridge, 1972).

Macfarlane, Alan. "History, Anthropology and the Study of Communities," *Social History,* no. 5 (1977): 631–52.

————. *Witchcraft in Tudor and Stuart England* (New York, 1970).

————, with Sarah Harrison and Charles Jardine, *Reconstructing Historical Communities* (Cambridge, 1977).

Murphy, Brian. *A History of the British Economy 1086–1970* (London, 1973).

Namier, Lewis B. *Avenues of History* (London, 1952).

————. *The Structure of Politics at the Accession of George III*, 2 vols. (London, 1929).

Perkin, Harold. *The Origins of Modern English Society 1780–1880* (London, 1969).

Postan, Michael M. *Essays on Medieval Agriculture and General Problems of the Medieval Economy* (Cambridge, 1973).

————. *Fact and Relevance: Essays on Historical Method* (Cambridge, 1971).

————. *The Medieval Economy and Society: An Economic History of Britain 1100–1500* (Berkeley, Cal., 1972).

————. *Medieval Trade and Finance* (Cambridge, 1973).

Richardson, R. C. *The Debate on the English Revolution* (New York, 1977).

Russell, Conrad. *The Crisis of Parliaments: English History 1509–1660* (London, 1971).

Sayles, G. O. *The King's Parliament of England* (New York, 1974).

Stone, Lawrence. *Crisis of the Aristocracy, 1558–1641* (Oxford, 1965).

Tawney, Richard H. *Religion and the Rise of Capitalism* (New York, 1926).

Taylor, A. J. P. *English History, 1914–1945* (New York, 1965).

Thirsk, Joan. *English Peasant Farming: The Agrarian History of Lincolnshire from Tudor to Recent Times* (London, 1957).

————, ed. *History of Lincolnshire* (London, 1970–   ).

Thomas, Keith. *Religion and the Decline of Magic* (London, 1971).

Thompson, Edward P. "Anthropology and the Discipline of Historical Context," *Midland History* 1, no. 3 (Spring, 1972): 41–55.

————. *The Making of the English Working Class* (New York, 1963).

————. "The Peculiarities of the English," *Socialist Register 1965* (London, 1965), pp. 311–62.

————. *Whigs and Hunters: The Origin of the Black Act* (New York, 1975).

Williams, Raymond. "Base and Superstructure in Marxist Cultural Theory," *New Left Review*, no. 82 (November-December 1973): 3–16.

————. *Culture and Society, 1780–1950* (New York, 1958).

————. *Drama from Ibsen to Brecht* (London, 1968).

————. *Drama in Performance*, new ed. (London, 1968).

————. *The English Novel: From Dickens to Lawrence* (London, 1971).

————. *The Long Revolution* (New York, 1961).

————. *Marxism and Literature* (London, 1977).

Wrigley, E. A. "Family Limitation in Pre-Industrial England," *Economic History*, 2nd ser., 19 (1966): 81–109.

————. *Identifying People in the Past* (London, 1973).

————, ed. *An Introduction to English Historical Demography* (London, 1966).

12 GEORG G. IGGERS

Federal Republic of Germany

The past fifteen years have seen a remarkable reorientation in German historical scholarship, in methodology, in conceptions of the historical process, and in the interpretation of the national past. Yet this reorientation has only in part followed the major trend of historical studies elsewhere, especially in France, England, and the United States, to a greater reliance on the methods and theories derived from the systematic social sciences. Recent German historical studies have in many cases gone in new directions toward an integration of contemporary empiricism with conceptions of method and social process indebted to a German heritage of social thought influenced by Karl Marx and Max Weber.

German historical studies resisted the influence of the modern social sciences much longer than did historical studies in other countries such as France, the United States, or Poland. Well into the mid-twentieth century, German historians followed the model set by Leopold von Ranke of a narrative, event-oriented history which concentrated on politics narrowly conceived as the actions of government in pursuit of national interest (*raison d'état*) relatively unaffected by social and economic considerations. Moreover, since the mid-nineteenth century, German university-based historians have been committed to an interpretation of the national past that saw the culmination of German history in Bismarck's establishment of a German Empire under Prussian dominance, a state that maintained the privileged political position of the propertied classes and left considerable authority in a monarchy surrounded by an aristocratic aura. The methodological and political conservatism that characterized the German historical profession reflected the "anachronistic" character of German political conditions, the failure of parliamentary and democratic reform in a country that had rapidly undergone economic modernization and contained an industrial working class increasing in size and political awareness. The attempts by Karl Lamprecht and Kurt Breysig at the turn of this century to move from a state-oriented political to a more broadly based social and cultural history were viewed by the profession not only as a threat to the idealistic heritage of German historical thought but to the political status quo as well. In response to Lamprecht,

German historians (Georg von Below and Friedrich Meinecke) and philosophers (Wilhelm Windelband, Heinrich Rickert) asserted the "idiographic" character of historical method concerned with "understanding" (*Verstehen*) unique human intentions and actions and the inapplicability of methods seeking "to explain" historical behavior "nomologically" by means of abstractions or generalizations.

Neither 1918, 1933, nor 1945 initiated a profound reorientation in historiographical outlook. The reaction to defeat in 1918 and the Treaty of Versailles further strengthened the nationalistic, conservative political consensus among German historians, which was accompanied by a continued hostility to a sociologically oriented history.[1] Within the profession a division existed, with roots in the Wilhelminian period, between a politically conservative orientation, opposed to the Weimar Republic and committed to *revanche,* and a more moderate although also strongly nationally oriented group around Friedrich Meinecke, who accepted the republic as an expedient and sought revision of the Versailles Treaty by peaceful means. While Meinecke assigned a greater role to the history of ideas, both orientations shared basic historiographic notions. Historical studies remained remarkably isolated from the social sciences, which in the Wilhelminian and Weimar periods were moving in the theoretically and methodologically innovative directions of a historically oriented sociology (Max Weber, Ferdinand Tönnies, Karl Mannheim). The Nazi seizure of power resulted in the exile of the small number of liberal dissidents, none of whom returned to Germany after 1945.[2] There was considerable discussion after 1945—as there had been after 1918—of a crisis of "historicism." This consciousness of crisis centered around the threat to traditional cultural and political values posed by historical relativism, yet had little bearing on the scholarly practices of the historian.

The 1950s saw an occasional turning to a history that took political and social structures more into account (*Strukturgeschichte*) than the traditional idiographic history had done. Yet the stress continued on legal and administrative institutions and on political and social attitudes. Because they did not have to contend with the modern state as a part of their subject, scholars in medieval studies had never been able to ignore social and economic factors to the extent that studies of modern German history had. Otto Hintze's attempts in the 1920s to introduce typologies into historical studies received new attention.[3] Otto Brunner in *Land und Herrschaft* (1939) provided examples for a structural study of late medieval political relations. The Max Planck Institute for History under the direction of Dietrich Gerhard and Rudolf Vierhaus embarked in the 1960s on a broad comparative study of corporative (*ständisch*) institutions in the Europe of the Old Regime. Werner Conze's Working Circle for Modern Social History examined the conditions of German industrialization within the framework of the legal and administrative structure of the nineteenth-century German states.

But it was Fritz Fischer's *Germany's Aims in the First World War,*[4] published in 1961, that gave impetus to a profound reexamination of historiographical traditions. This reorientation was perhaps bound to come with the profound change

in social structure that affected Western Europe, and West Germany in particular, in the aftermath of World War II. Fischer's book was less innovative in
its methods than in the questions it raised. Most important, Fischer challenged
the thesis held by the majority of moderate conservative historians after 1945
that the Nazi experience of 1933–1945 marked a discontinuity with German traditions and that the roots of Nazism were to be found not in the German or the
Prussian past but as Friedrich Meinecke, Gerhard Ritter, and Hans Rothfels had
maintained, in a radical democratic and socialist tradition that went back to V.I.
Lenin, Karl Marx, and the French Revolution.[5] In contrast to conservative historians such as Ritter, who had maintained that the German civilian government
and its chancellor Theobald von Bethmann-Hollweg pursued moderate war aim
policies distinct from those of the Pan-Germans,[6] Fischer sought to demonstrate
that a broad consensus of German public opinion, from the Majority Social
Democrats to the right, had championed policies of annexation in Europe and
overseas that in their extent resembled those of the Nazis in World War II. These
policies did not emerge in the course of World War I but were formulated well
before and had their origins in the social and economic structure of Imperial
Germany. Fischer's continuity thesis thus differed from that of Ludwig Dehio,[7]
who in 1955 had recognized a continuity in foreign policy from 1871 to 1945
but had seen it as a tragic result of the hegemonic position of Germany in world
politics, relatively independent from domestic political considerations.

Fischer and his students, for example, Imanuel Geiss, however, reversed the
traditional emphasis of German historians on the "primacy of foreign policy"
and raised a host of questions regarding the interrelation of economic interests,
social class relations, and politics; their change in emphasis made necessary new
methodological and conceptual approaches that would deal with the dynamics
of social structures. Fischer's work engendered a controversy that in its emotional intensity and bitterness resembled that which had been occasioned by Karl
Lamprecht's *German History*. In the wake of the Fischer controversy a younger
generation of historians, many not students of Fischer, turned increasingly to a
critical examination of the recent German past. If the few critical studies prior
to 1961, particularly Karl D. Bracher's *Auflösung der Weimarer Republik* (1955)
and later those of Hans Mommsen and Gerhard A. Ritter, had sought to analyze
the phenomenon of Nazism with political science concepts, newer studies began
to look increasingly to the Wilhelminian and Bismarckian periods for an understanding of later German developments. Beginning in 1966 a large number
of studies began to appear that examined the role of economic pressure groups:
Hans-Jürgen Puhle's study of the Agrarian League (*Bund der Landwirte*),[8] Hart-
mut Kaelble's investigation of the Association of German Industrialists,[9] Dirk
Stegmann's study of the role of parties and pressure groups in the formation of
an anti-Socialist coalition (*Sammlungspolitik*),[10] Volker Berghahn's examination
of the function of the construction of the battle fleet for domestic politics[11] (in
a sense a continuation past 1901 of Eckart Kehr's analysis, of which we shall
still speak), and Peter Witt's work on the financial policies of the German Reich

from 1903 to 1913.[12] An important collection of essays from this new critical viewpoint was contained in the volume *Das Kaiserliche Deutschland* (1970), edited by Michael Stürmer.[13] Going back to the Bismarckian period, Helmut Böhme in *Deutschlands Weg zur Grossmacht* (1966) interpreted the struggle between Austria and Prussia for predominance in Germany less as a function of foreign affairs than of trade interests. We shall speak later in greater detail of H. U. Wehler's *Bismarck und der Imperialismus* (1969), which should also be mentioned here in this context as well as Wehler's great synthesis, *Das Deutsche Kaiserreich* (1973).

These studies were less concerned with the direct influence of economic interests, as George W. F. Hallgarten's earlier study on pre-1914 imperialism had been,[14] than with problems of social and political domination. In many ways they returned to themes explored by Eckart Kehr in the last years of the Weimar Republic. Deeply influenced by Marxian concepts of class struggle and Weberian conceptions of bureaucracy and modernization—and by Weber's analysis of the German Junker class—Kehr in a major book, *Battleship Building and Party Politics in Germany 1894–1901* (1930),[15] and in a series of essays on the function of the bureaucracy in early nineteenth-century Prussia[16] had sought to explain the specific setting of the social conflicts that determined the disastrous course of German politics. As did Hans Rosenberg (who had emigrated in 1933) in his *Bureaucracy, Aristocracy, and Autocracy: The Prussian Experience 1660–1815*,[17] Kehr saw the roots of political conflicts in the failure of the German bourgeoisie to obtain a dominant voice in German politics in the nineteenth century. Instead, the peculiar circumstances of German economic modernization favored the dominance of a capitalistic agrarian class of East-Elbian Junkers. Military pressures in the eighteenth century had accelerated the process of bureaucratization in the Prussian Hohenzollern monarchy but at the same time had been accompanied by an increasing aristocratization of the bureaucracy. The Stein Reforms in the aftermath of the Napoleonic defeat of Prussia in 1806 marked the creation of a *Rechtsstaat* that safeguarded officialdom against the arbitrary interventions of the king and confirmed bureaucratic absolutism. Increasing influence of the bureaucracy was intimately interwoven in Kehr's thinking with the development of capitalism. An enlightened bureaucracy fulfilled the economic interests of the bourgeoisie by creating the conditions for capitalist growth; yet at the same time it maintained the political dominance of the agrarian capitalist classes. The industrialization of Germany with the concomitant rise of a politically conscious proletariat consolidated the alliance of a bourgeoisie with the semiautocratic monarchy and effectively prevented the parliamentarization and democratization of Germany. This development led to a dangerous course in international policy. The *Weltpolitik* and navalism of the Wilhelminian period, in Kehr's assessment, were pursued less for the "preservation of national autonomy" than for "economic autonomy and the struggle for economic expansion" but even more so for "stabilizing anew the threatened dominance of industry and agriculture allied against the rise of the proletariat as a political force.''[18] The growing tensions of a capitalistic social order in which a large share of political power was held by an outmoded agrarian aristocracy prevented the social and political modernization of Germany at the very time when the inner contradictions of German society thrust Germany into a militant foreign policy and made such modernization increasingly necessary for Germany's survival on the world scene, ideas which in some ways are reminiscent of Thorstein Veblen's *Imperial Germany and the Industrial Revolution* (1915).

Kehr, who had died in Washington in 1933 at the age of thirty, was rediscovered by a new generation of historians in the 1960s; his essays were collected by Hans-Ulrich Wehler in 1965,[19] and his book on German navalism was republished in 1966. The entire literature on special interest groups, which we mentioned above, with the possible exception of Kaelble's book, shared the basic assumptions of Kehr and Rosenberg that there had been an imbalance between the economic and the sociopolitical modernization of Germany. They saw in this contradiction and in the anti-Socialist coalition (*Sammlungspolitik*) of partners, industry and agriculture, with very different interests, the roots not only of World War I but of a refeudalization of the solid bourgeoisie as well as of the lower middle classes and the artisans (Winkler).[20] The conflicts resulting from this imbalance contributed according to Hans Rosenberg and H. J. Puhle to the emergence of pre-Fascist *völkisch,* anti-Semitic attitudes which, according to Dirk Stegmann, found their fulfillment in National Socialism.

Kehr's generalizations regarding the political activities of economic interest groups are doubtless too sweeping. Since then a good deal of archival research has been done, with the result that these studies have led to a much more differentiated picture of the goals and policies of the various pressure groups. These studies have been interesting for the critical perspective they have introduced into German historical scholarship rather than for their rigorous conceptual structure. They differ in approach and conclusions from the more traditional studies that emerged from Werner Conze's Working Circle for Modern Social History in Heidelberg, which were concerned with the impact of industrialization on politics and society, and which, without overlooking the pseudoconstitutional character of Prussia and the Reich, placed greater stress on the integration of the working class into the German nation in the decades preceding World War I.[21]

The studies of the new critical orientation have not gone unchallenged. The challenges have taken two forms. The concept of "the primacy of domestic politics" has been questioned. Wolfgang J. Mommsen, in a series of studies of German imperialism in the period preceding the First World War, recognized the impact of social and political tensions resulting from the uneven modernization of Germany, yet at the same time assigned a greater degree of autonomy to considerations of foreign policy and military interest.[22] More radically, in an important article the noted diplomatic historian Andreas Hillgruber sought to reassert the autonomy of "political history."[23] He granted that the Treitschkean formula, *"Männer machen Geschichte,"* was inapplicable. The historian could not ignore the structural context in which political developments occur. But there was an element in politics, he argued, that could not be adequately explained by social or structural analysis. "Political history," as Hillgruber maintained, "whether of domestic or foreign policy is 'political' because it emphasizes the role of decisions, against the conception of history as a process." These decisions, particularly in the area of foreign policy, are often determined by factors of power politics that operate relatively independently of "long-term" economic or social forces. The course of general history, Hillgruber affirms in a form reminiscent of the neo-Rankeans, is essentially determined by the conflicting interests of the great powers. Hillgruber is by no means alone. His reassertion of the "primacy of foreign policy" has been supported by other diplomatic historians such as Klaus Hildebrand.[24] On another level, the "Kehrites" have been accused of presentism, as in Thomas Nipperdey's critique of H.-U. Wehler's study of the political and social structure of Imperial Germany,[25] of interpreting Bismarckian and Wilhelminian society in view of the later political catastrophes. Involved in this controversy is the whole question of the role of value judgments in historical studies, which has become increasingly acute for the present generation of German historians.

Yet in fact much of the new history, concerned with the determining role of domestic factors on foreign policy, is not that dissimilar in its methodological approaches from the older scholarship. Except in the work of historians who utilized well-developed concepts of social structure and change—such as Kehr, Rosenberg, Wehler, Jürgen Kocka, or Reinhart Koselleck—theory plays a relatively subordinate role. Much of the literature on pressure groups was written by men who consider themselves in the first place craftsmen and who approach the archival records of economic interest groups, parties, and business enterprise in very much the same manner as an older group of historians examined diplomatic papers, to understand the concrete decisions of men in positions of power, even if these decisions were now seen as guided by different considerations than reasons of state. Generally lacking in much of this literature is an explicit theory of industrialization or of social and political modernization. Lacking also are the empirical, social, and economic investigations that have accompanied studies of industrialization in England and France.

Only in the last several years has serious attention been given to quantitative methods and studies.[26] This has been so despite the wealth of statistics that German officials and scholars, concerned with the scientific study of the social consequences of industrialization, accumulated in the nineteenth and early twentieth centuries and the pioneering work on social structure and social mobility undertaken by sociologists such as Theodor Geiger in the Weimar Republic but little utilized by social historians.[27] In the late 1960s the economic historian Wolfram Fischer called for an "empirical social science" of the past and regretted how German scholarship in this respect lagged behind that of other Western countries.[28] Fischer called upon historians to link quantitative methods of economic history, estimates of gross national product, real income, and price and loan levels with sociological analysis of class. But the demographic studies needed for such an analysis have been few. The careful empirical studies of social mobility based on census materials that have become current in the United States are still largely lacking in Germany. Demographic investigations, such as Wolfgang Köllmann's population studies[29] or Otto Büsch's examinations of industrialization in the Berlin-Brandenburg area, as Büsch frankly concedes, largely lack an interest in a "theoretical discussion regarding the relationship of industrialization, economic growth, and social change." [30] Wilhelm Abel and his Institute for Economic and Social History in Göttingen indeed pursued a highly quantitative approach that sought to investigate on a comparative European basis the interrelations of demographic and economic factors from the beginnings of a market economy in the Middle Ages to the beginnings of industrialization.[31] But the Abel group showed no concern for the relation of these factors to the social or political structure and little interest in the industrial period. The last few years have seen modest beginnings in the utilization of methods of family reconstitution that have been developed in France and Great Britain since the 1950s as part of a broader approach to social history.[32] Probably most significant is the recent attempt by a research team at the Max Planck Institute for History in Göttingen to integrate demography and economic growth theory in an analysis of the process of rural protoindustrialization in the seventeenth, eighteenth, and early nineteenth centuries.[33]

West German historiography has thus with few exceptions moved in directions different from those characterizing the new social history in France, the United States, England, Poland, and elsewhere. A great deal of research has continued to move along the traditional lines of history of politics, defended by Hillgruber and Hildebrand, that is oriented toward events and personalities. Yet even the new "critical" history has gone a different road. The primary concern of German historiography continues to be the history of politics rather than that of long-range social processes. The new school remains much more in the methodological, and in many ways also the conceptual, tradition of the classical tradition than is immediately apparent.

This is not entirely surprising. German historians, more so than historians in other countries, confront their immediate national past. The central question for much of their scholarship remains how the events of 1933 to 1945 were possible. An extensive literature since the 1950s has dealt with all aspects of the Nazi regime as well as with the Nazi seizure of power. The Institute of Contemporary History in Munich, founded in 1950, has been an important center for these studies. Yet the institute has tended to see Nazism as part of a European phenomenon of the twentieth century, has stressed the elements of resistance to the regime, and in its studies of the political and social origins of Nazism has rarely examined the period before 1918 to which the "critical" historians attached such importance. The question of the continuity or discontinuity of German political development has been left open. Yet this question has been central to the newer critical literature, which studied the nineteenth- and early twentieth-century German past less for its own sake than for an understanding of Germany's recent history.

The political concern also explains in part the skepticism of German historians regarding the empirical-analytical approaches of Western historians, for example, the *Annales* school. A vigorous discussion has ensued in recent years, particularly since approximately 1970, on questions of historical theory and methodology that has paralleled similar discussions in other disciplines, especially sociology.[34] The classical tradition of German historicism, with its stress on the uniqueness of historical phenomena, was generally acknowledged as having provided an inadequate theoretical basis for a historiography dealing with the complex realities of a modern technological society.[35] Historians agreed that history must take into account to a greater degree than before the structural context within which historical situations occur and that therefore explicit theories, generalizations, and typologies have a place in historical analysis. Yet the new critical school has generally maintained the sharp distinction of the historicist tradition between natural and historical phenomena. Writers like Wehler would agree with Hillgruber that historical events cannot be reduced to anonymous social processes. Historians, like Dieter Groh, who saw history as a "critical" social science warned against the "objectivism" inherent in the empirical social sciences (and in much of *Annales* historiography), which failed to recognize the extent to which "men made their own history."[36] While a general consensus emerged among historians that history could not be separated from the social sciences—although these sciences were conceived very differently—it was stressed that history, like the social sciences, must utilize generalizations that take into account the elements of intentionality and value orientation characterizing human behavior. This in part explains the persistent influence of a Weberian social science, a *"verstehende Soziologie,"* which utilizes abstractions in the forms of typologies that seek to "understand" and conceptualize the unique purposes and values determining historical change.[37] A point of agreement thus existed between critical historians of the democratic left such as Dieter Groh, indebted to the "critical theory" of Jürgen Habermas, and an older hermeneuticist tradition (H. G. Gadamer).[38]

On the other hand, a fundamental difference existed on the question of the value neutrality of the historian or the social scientist and the possibility of objectivity in historical inquiry.[39] Clearly, historical science was a historical enterprise; all cognition reflected the socially and historically conditioned perspective as well as the value viewpoint of the inquirer. The fact that all inquiry proceeded from value viewpoints was for Max Weber the very condition that made scientific inquiry possible, that enabled the social scientist to identify problems from among the chaos of phenomena. Yet the question remained whether objectivity in method was possible as Weber had maintained, so that "methodologically correct proof in the social sciences" would "be acknowledged as correct even by a Chinese, who, on the other hand, would be deaf to our conception of the ethical imperative." And connected with the problem of objectivity in method was the question of the possibility of value neutrality. Weber's position was that "an empirical science can teach nobody what he ought to do, and—under certain circumstances—what he wants to do."[40] Here a sharp line has developed between the new critical school of historiography of Hans-Ulrich Wehler, Dieter Groh, Wolfgang Mommsen, Jörn Rüsen,[41] and such other historians as Thomas Nipperdey, Karl Georg Faber,[42] Andreas Hillgruber, and Detlef Junker,[43] who still shared a historicist position reminiscent of Ranke, believing that all historical epochs possessed equal dignity and that each must be judged exclusively in its own terms, a position difficult to maintain in view of the Nazi experience. In contrast the critical school, committed to examining the past "in the interest of a rationally organized future society" (Wehler),[44] basically a democratic socialist society in which men would be "emancipated" (Groh) from arbitrary constraints, sees its task in examining the contradictions in the German society of the past that prepared the tragic course of German history in the twentieth century.[45]

A good deal has been said by historians of very different orientations (Koselleck,[46] Rüsen, Faber, Wehler, Kocka, Nipperdey,[47] R. Vierhaus[48]) about the need to formulate explicit theories of explanation, capable of intersubjective validation, which combine hermeneutic (*Verstehen*) and empirical-analytical methods; but as we have indicated, relatively little historical work is guided by explicit historical theories. Rejecting as speculative the kind of comprehensive theories or laws of historical development called for by Marxist historians in the German Democratic Republic,[49] West German historians agree that theories of limited range are required, in part derived from the systematic social sciences. But the test of a historical theory, as H.-U. Wehler has suggested, is not that it fits as many cases as possible but that it explains specific cases. Wehler and Jürgen Kocka have gone farthest not only in exploring explicit theories but in applying these to historical analysis. History, they agree, is to become a social science, but a "historical social science."[50] Wehler, as an editor, has made German historians aware of attempts outside of Germany, particularly in the English-speaking countries and France, to apply social science theories in the empirical tradition to the analysis of historical phenomena.[51] He has called attention to the extensive quantitative work done in the United States, France, and England in demography, economic growth, and political behavior as well as the attempts to utilize anthropological and psychoanalytic concepts in historical explanation. He appreciates the precise formulation and rigorous examination of explicit hypotheses and models by quantitative methods, particularly in modern economic history. But he is also aware of the limitations of these methods in historical studies. He points out that the hypothetical deductive models of the cliometricians in abstracting economics from history ignore the "unavoidable qualitative," political, and other aspects that enter into every historical situation and thus distort both economic and historical reality.[52] Wehler believes that in taking into account the qualitative, historical aspects that affect social, economic, and political development, Marx and Weber thus offer important correctives for a conceptually rigorous "historical social science."

History as a "historical social science," Wehler and Kocka agree, can thus benefit by combining theories derived from Marx, Weber, and the modern empirical social sciences, a combination that Wehler frankly admits contains an element of eclecticism, but one productive for historical explanation. Kocka in particular has sought comprehensive analysis of historical development, integrating Weberian and Marxist with empirical methods. In an early work on the relations of white-collar employees and management in the Siemens firm from 1847 to 1914, he sought to explore Weberian concepts of bureaucratization as applied to private industry and to study the emergence of a white-collar (*Angestellten*) mentality.[53] He has since sought to compare this with the political and social attitudes of American white-collar workers in the period from 1890 to 1940.[54] Theoretically more ambitious, Kocka in his book on class conflict in World War I sought to go beyond the work of Fritz Fischer and his students as well as the literature on economic interest groups, which with the "aid of traditional methods of textual interpretation" had concentrated on the decisions of leading personalities in economic and political life rather than analyzed "social economic structures *per se*." This brief volume is particularly interesting as an attempt to suggest a possible model for the integration of Marxist, Weberian, and empirical social science concepts and methods. Kocka's primary concerns are the political dimensions of the processes of change, an attempt to explain the revolution of 1918 as the "consistent outcome of German social history in the First World War."[55] Kocka seeks to analyze these processes by means of a model derived from Marx's theory of classes, but separated from Marx's philosophy of history, and incorporating more recent theories of conflict. The model constitutes an ideal type in the Weberian sense, a heuristic device that serves to identify and analyze "certain elements and factors of a historical reality." Using extensive quantitative evidence on class structure, union membership, wages, and the material conditions of life, Kocka at the same time takes into account the "subjective" level of political consciousness and the translation of this consciousness into political conflict, which largely defy quantification and call for the methods of a *verstehende Soziologie*. Kocka thus seeks to demonstrate that although there was no direct relation between economic hardship and political protest, class tensions rather than the desire for peace were decisively responsible for the German revolution of 1918. Yet while the state "tendentially" was an instrument of control by the economically dominant classes, the Marxist model, he held, had to be modified to take into account countervailing factors. Such factors included the degree of autonomy enjoyed by the bureaucratic state as well as the alienation of the rank-and-file workers from the bureaucratized organizations of labor and of the Social Democratic Party, which followed their own institutional ends. Hans-Ulrich Wehler in *Bismarck und der Imperialismus* sought to combine Kehr's interpretation of the incongruencies between the political and economic structure of Imperial Germany with a more implicit theory of economic growth, capable of a degree of quantification. Wehler's study was built to an extent on Hans Rosenberg's attempt in his book on the Great Depression of 1873[56] to explore the impact of the depression on the decline of political and economic liberalism and the consolidation of the alliance of agrarian and industrial interests. Wehler sought to relate Bismarck's colonial policy to a broader theory of industrialization which took into account the uneven nature of growth of capitalist economies. Like Rosenberg, he examined the effects of this uneven development on the specific political, social, and ideological setting of Imperial Germany.

Wehler has given leadership to an important orientation in German historiography committed to making history a "critical" social science. Since 1972 an important series entitled *Critical Studies in Historical Science*[57] has focused on the problems Wehler has considered of prime importance to an analysis of political and social developments in the modern industrial world. The series has utilized theories and methods of the systematic social sciences combined with a "critical" perspective that takes into account the dysfunctions in capitalist societies. Since 1975, with Wehler's collaboration, a periodical entitled *Geschichte und Gesellschaft* has been published, conceived as a journal for "historical social science" understood as an interdisciplinary science in "close relationship with neighboring social sciences, especially sociology, political science, and economics."[58] More than any other German historical journal, *Geschichte und Gesellschaft* has attempted to serve as a forum for international discussion and to acquaint German scholars with social-science-oriented research abroad. The first two issues were devoted to areas in which German historical scholarship has been lagging, demography and social stratification and mobility. A special issue in 1977 was dedicated to the role of theory in the work of the historian.[59] In its attempt to integrate the social sciences from a historical perspective, the journal bears certain similarities to the French *Annales*. But the perspective is in many ways very different and reflects a fundamental difference between the dominant trends in social history today in France and West Germany. Unlike the French journal, with its concentration on social processes in preindustrial Europe, *Geschichte und Gesellschaft* is concerned much more centrally with the modern political world in the context of an industrial society. Open to the empirical and analytical methods of the modern social sciences, the editors of *Geschichte und Gesellschaft* nevertheless set much sharper limits to the applicability of these methods than do the contributors to the *Annales* and in the tradition of Marx and Weber emphasize more strongly the qualitative aspects that go into the understanding of history as the product of human actions.

In conclusion, no attempt should be made to reduce the dominant trends in German historical studies to one or two common denominators. There continues to be considerable resistance to the new critical social history of politics practiced by Wehler and Kocka. The demands for a return to a more conventional political history, more sympathetic to national traditions, along the lines defended by Hillgruber, Hildebrand, and Nipperdey,[60] have been given programmatic expression in the pronouncements of the German professional association of history teachers[61] and in the guidelines promulgated by the education ministries in various West German states. Yet it is unlikely that the direction in which the new critical history has gone in recent years will be reversed. At the same time, however, the past several years have seen a broadening of the concept of history as a historical social science and a lessening of the gulf between social-science-oriented historical studies in the Federal Republic, as in France and the English-speaking countries. This development has by no means been resisted by Wehler, Kocka, or other social historians of politics. Indeed it has found a forum in *Geschichte und Gesellschaft* and in the *Critical Studies in Historical Science*. Thus particularly since the mid-1970s there has been an increasing exploration of quantitative studies in diverse areas of investigation—politics, social mobility, economic growth, and demography. In 1976 an association for quantitative studies was formed, with its own series of publications.[62] New demographic studies, such as those of the Göttingen group on protoindustrialization mentioned above,[63] have acknowledged their debt to the *Annales* and the Cambridge Group for the History of Population and Social Structure. At the same time, however, they have taken very seriously the attempts of British Marxist historians, especially E. P. Thompson, to go beyond an analysis of social structures to a critical social history that explores the political aspects of the everyday life and consciousness of broad segments of the population, who are no longer seen as the passive objects of social processes but as themselves active subjects of history. Historical studies in the Federal Republic in the mid- and late 1970s have thus moved closer to the main streams of modern social history without, however, losing contact with distinctive German traditions of social science scholarship.

Notes

1. See Hans Schleier, *Die bürgerliche deutsche Geschichtsschreibung der Weimarer Republik* (Berlin/G.D.R., 1975); also Georg G. Iggers, *The German Conception of History* (Middletown, Conn., 1968), pp. 236–37, and Bernd Faulenbach, "Deutsche Geschichtswissenschaft zwischen Kaiserreich und NS-Diktatur" in Bernd Faulenbach, ed., *Geschichtswissenschaft in Deutschland: Traditionelle Positionen und gegenwärtige Aufgaben* (Munich, 1974), pp. 66–85.

2. See Georg G. Iggers, "Die deutschen Historiker in der Emigration" in B. Faulenbach, ed., *Geschichtswissenschaft in Deutschland*, pp. 97–111.

3. Otto Hintze, *The Historical Essays*, ed. Felix Gilbert (New York, 1975).

4. Fritz Fischer, *Der Griff nach der Weltmacht: Die Kriegszielpolitik des kaiserlichen Deutschlands 1914–1918* (Düsseldorf, 1960); English translation, *Germany's Aims in the First World War* (New York, 1967).

5. Friedrich Meinecke, *Die deutsche Katastrophe* (Wiesbaden, 1956); English translation, *The German Catastrophe* (Cambridge, Mass., 1950); Gerhard Ritter, *Carl Goerdeler und die deutsche Widerstandsbewegung* (Stuttgart, 1955), particularly p. 92; also "The Fault of Mass Democracy" in *The Nazi Revolution: Germany's Guilt or Germany's Fate?*, ed. John L. Snell (New York, 1959), p. 92; Hans Rothfels, *The German Opposition to Hitler*, rev. ed. (Chicago, 1962).

6. Gerhard Ritter, *Staatskunst und Kriegshandwerk*, vol. I (Munich, 1954).

7. Ludwig Dehio, *Gleichgewicht oder Hegemonie* (Krefeld, 1948), translated as *The Precarious Balance: Four Centuries of the European Power Struggle* (New York, 1962); and *Deutschland und die Weltpolitik im 20. Jahrhundert* (Munich, 1955), translated as *Germany and World Politics in the Twentieth Century* (New York, 1960).

8. *Agrarische Interessenpolitik und preussischer Konservatismus im Wilhelminischen Reich 1893–1966* (Hannover, 1966).

9. *Industrielle Interessenpolitik in der Wilhelminischen Gesellschaft: Der Centralverband Deutscher Industrieller 1895–1914* (Berlin, 1967).

10. *Die Erben Bismarcks: Parteien und Verbände in der Spätphase des Wilhelminischen Deutschlands* (Lübeck, 1970).

11. *Der Tirpitz-Plan* (Düsseldorf, 1971). See also his *Germany and the Approach of War in 1914* (New York, 1973).

12. *Die Finanzpolitik des Deutschen Reiches von 1903 bis 1913* (Lübeck, 1970).

13. *Das kaiserliche Deutschland: Politik und Gesellschaft* (Darmstadt, 1970).

14. *Vorkriegs-Imperialismus: Die soziologischen Grundlagen der Aussenpolitik der europäischen Grossmächte vor dem ersten Weltkrieg*, 2 vols. (Munich, 1951).

15. *Schlachtflottenbau und Parteipolitik 1894–1901* (Berlin, 1930), translated as *Battleship Building and Party Politics in Germany, 1894–1901* (Chicago, 1975).

16. See *Der Primat der Innenpolitik*, ed. H. U. Wehler (Berlin, 1966); English version, *Economic Interests, Militarism, and Foreign Policy: Essays on German History*, ed. Gordon A. Craig (Berkeley, Calif., 1977).

17. (Cambridge, 1958).

18. *Schlachtflottenbau*, pp. 447–8.

19. See above, n. 16.

20. Cf. Heinrich-August Winkler, "Der rückversicherte Mittelstand: Die Interessenverbände von Handwerk und Kleinhandel im deutschen Kaiserreich," in Walter Ruegg and Otto Neuloh, eds., *Zur sozialen Theorie und Analyse des 19. Jahrhunderts* (Göttingen, 1971).

21. See Werner Conze and Dieter Groh, *Die Arbeiterbewegung in der nationalen Bewegung: Die deutsche Sozialdemokratie vor, während, und nach der Reichsgründung* (Stuttgart, 1966), but also see Dieter Groh, *Negative Integration und revolutionärer Attentismus: Die deutsche Sozialdemokratie am Vorabend des Ersten Weltkrieges* (Frankfurt, 1973).

22. Wolfgang J. Mommsen, *Das Zeitalter des Imperialismus* (Frankfurt, 1963); "Domestic Factors in German Foreign Policy before 1914," *Central European History* 6 (1973): 3–43; *Imperialismustheorien* (Göttingen, 1977).

23. "Politische Geschichte in moderner Sicht," *Historische Zeitschrift* 216 (1973): 529–52.

24. "Geschichte oder 'Gesellschaftsgeschichte'? Die Notwendigkeit einer politischen Geschichte von den internationalen Beziehungen," *Historische Zeitschrift* 223 (1976): 328–57.

25. "Wehlers 'Kaiserreich': Eine Kritische Auseinandersetzung," *Geschichte und Gesellschaft* 1 (1975): 539–60. See Hans-Ulrich Wehler's reply to his critics, "Kritik und kritische Antikritik," *Historische Zeitschrift* 225 (1977): 347–84, and his earlier reply to Hillgruber, "Moderne Politikgeschichte oder 'Grosse Politik der Kabinette?' " *Geschichte und Gesellschaft* 1 (1975): 344–369.

26. See the new bulletin *Quantum Information*, first published in 1976, and the series begun in 1977, *Historisch-Sozialwissenschaftliche Forschungen*, including vol. 3, *Quantitative Methoden in der historisch-sozialwissenschaftlichen Forschung* (Stuttgart, 1977). See also Konrad Jarausch, ed., *Quantifizierung in der Geschichtswissenschaft* (Düsseldorf, 1976).

27. Cf. James J. Sheehan, "Quantification in the Study of Modern German Social and Political History," in Val R. Lorwin and Jacob M. Price, eds., *The Dimensions of the Past* (New Haven, Conn., 1972).

28. Cf. Wolfram Fischer and Georg Bajor, eds., *Die soziale Frage: Neuere Studien zur Lage der Fabrikarbeiter in den Frühphasen der Industrialisierung* (Stuttgart, 1967), p. 8.

29. For example, his *Bevölkerung in der industriellen Revolution* (Göttingen, 1974).

30. *Industrialisierung und Gewerbe im Raum Berlin Brandenburg 1800–1850: Eine empirische Untersuchung zur gewerblichen Wirtschaft einer hauptstadtgebundenen Wirtschaftsregion in frühindustrieller Zeit* (Berlin, 1971), p. xi.

31. See Wilhelm Abel, *Agrarkrisen und Agrarkonjunkturen in Mitteleuropa vom 13. bis zum 19. Jahrhundert* (Berlin, 1935; 2nd rev. ed., Hamburg, 1966); also *Massenarmut und Hungerkrisen im vorindustriellen Europa* (Hamburg, 1974).

32. See Arthur E. Imhof, *Historische Demographie als Sozialgeschichte*, 2 vols. (Darmstadt and Marburg, 1975); the special issue of *Geschichte und Gesellschaft* vol. 1, Heft 2/3 (1975): "Historische Familienforschung und Demographie"; Arthur E. Imhof, "Bevölkerungsgeschichte und Historische Demographie," in Reinhard Rürup, ed., *Historische Sozialwissenschaft* (Göttingen, 1977), pp. 16–58; and Karin Hausen, "Historische Familienforschung," ibid., pp. 59–95; on the history of the family see also Werner Conze, ed., *Sozialgeschichte der Familie in der Neuzeit Europas* (Stuttgart, 1977).

33. See Peter Kriedte, Hans Medick, and Jürgen Schlumbohm, *Industrialisierung vor der Industrialisierung: Gewerbliche Warenproduktion auf dem Land in der Formationsperiode des Kapitalismus* (Göttingen, 1977).

34. See Th. W. Adorno et al., *Der Positivismusstreit in der deutschen Soziologie* (Neuwied, 1969, with contributions by Th. W. Adorno, Karl R. Popper, Jürgen Habermas, Ralf Dahrendorf, Hans Albert, and Hans Pilot). English translation, *The Positivism Dispute in German Sociology* (New York, 1976).

35. See Wolfgang J. Mommsen, *Geschichtswissenschaft jenseits des Historismus* (Düsseldorf, 1971), and Jörn Rüsen, *Für eine erneuerte Historik* (Stuttgart-Bad Cannstadt, 1976), as two examples of the extensive literature.

36. *Kritische Geschichtswissenschaft in emanzipatorischer Absicht* (Stuttgart, 1973).

37. See Jürgen Kocka's theoretical essays, including *Sozialgeschichte* (Göttingen, 1977).

38. See Hans-Georg Gadamer, *Wahrheit und Methode* (Tübingen, 1960); English translation, *Truth and Method* (New York, 1975).

39. Cf. Detlef Junker, "Über die Legitimität von Werturteilen in den Sozialwissenschaften und der Geschichtswissenschaft," *Historische Zeitschrift* 211 (1970): 1–33; Hermann von der Dunk, "Wertfreiheit und Geschichtswissenschaft," ibid., 214 (1972): 1–25; Jörn Rüsen, "Werturteilsstreit und Erkenntnisfortschritt," in Jörn Rüsen, ed., *Historische Objektivität* (Göttingen, 1975), pp. 68–101.

40. Max Weber, "Die 'Objektivität' sozialwissenschaftlicher und sozialpolitischer Erkenntnis," in *Gesammelte Aufsätze zur Wissenschaftslehre* (Tübingen, 1951), pp. 155 and 151; translated as " 'Objectivity' in Social Science and Social Policy" in *Max Weber on the Methodology of the Social Sciences*, ed. and trans. Edward A. Shils and Henry A. Finch (Glencoe, Ill., 1949).

41. *Für eine erneuerte Historik* (see above, n. 35).

42. *Theorie der Geschichte*, 3rd ed. (Munich, 1974).

43. "Was kann Objektivität in der Geschichtswissenshaft heissen, und wie ist sie möglich?" in *Historische Zeitschrift*, Beiheft N.F. 3, "Methodenprobleme in der Geschichtswissenschaft" (Munich, 1974), and "Über die Legitimität von Werturteilen" (see above, n. 39).

44. *Bismarck und der Imperialismus* (Cologne, 1969), p. 14: see also the Introduction to Wehler, *Das Deutsche Kaiserreich* (Göttingen, 1973).

45. See, for example, the Introduction to Wehler, *Das Deutsche Kaiserreich*.

46. Reinhard Koselleck, "Über die Theoriebedürftigkeit der Geschichtswissenschaft," in Werner Conze, ed., *Theorie der Geschichtswissenschaft und Praxis des Geschichtsunterrichts* (Stuttgart, 1972), pp. 10–28.

47. Thomas Nipperdey, "Kulturgeschichte, Sozialgeschichte, historische Anthropologie," *Vierteljahrschrift für Sozial- und Wirtschaftsgeschichte* 55 (1968): 145–64.

48. Rudolf Vierhaus, "Geschichtswissenschaft und Soziologie," in Gerhard Schulz, ed., *Geschichte heute: Positionen, Tendenzen und Probleme* (Göttingen, 1973), pp. 69–83.

49. See the Marxist critique by Hans Schleier, *Theorie der Geschichte—Theorie der Geschichtswissenschaft: Zu neueren theoretisch-methodologischen Arbeiten der Geschichtsschreibung in der BRD* (Berlin/GDR, 1975).

50. There is as yet little agreement on what a "historical social science" is. For a discussion of the meanings of the term, see the Introduction by Reinhard Rürup to Reinhard Rürup, ed., *Historische Sozialwissenschaft* (Göttingen, 1977). An early use of the term was by Wehler in the title of his collection of essays, *Geschichte als Historische Sozialwissenschaft* (Frankfurt, 1973).

51. See the volumes edited by Wehler, *Geschichte und Psychoanalyse* (Cologne, 1971), *Geschichte und Soziologie* (Cologne, 1972), and *Geschichte und Ökonomie* (Cologne, 1973).

52. Wehler, *Geschichte als Historische Sozialwissenschaft* (see above, n. 50), p. 65.

53. Jürgen Kocka, *Unternehmensverwaltung und Angestelltenschaft am Beispiel Siemens 1847–1914: Zum Verhältnis von Kapitalismus und Bürokratie in der deutschen Industrialisierung* (Stuttgart, 1969).

54. Jürgen Kocka, *Angestellte zwischen Faschismus und Demokratie: Zur politischen Sozialgeschichte der Angestellten: USA 1890–1940 im internationalen Vergleich* (Göttingen, 1977).

55. Jürgen Kocka, *Klassengesellschaft und Krieg, 1914–1918* (Göttingen, 1973), pp. 1, 136.

56. Hans Rosenberg, *Grosse Depression und Bismarckzeit* (Berlin, 1967).

57. *Kritische Studien zur Geschichtswissenschaft*, edited by Helmut Berding, Jürgen Kocka, Hans-Christoph Schröder, and Hans-Ulrich Wehler; published by Vandenhoeck & Ruprecht in Göttingen.

58. "Vorwort der Herausgeber," *Geschichte und Gesellschaft* 1 (1975): 5.

59. Jürgen Kocka, ed., "Theorien in der Praxis des Historikers," *Geschichte und Gesellschaft*, Sonderheft 3 (1977).

60. See Thomas Nipperdey, "Wehlers 'Kaiserreich': Eine Kritische Auseinandersetzung," *Geschichte und Gesellschaft* 1 (1975): 539–60. Nipperdey is, however, much more open to concepts and methods derived from the modern social sciences (see above, n. 47) than Hillgruber or Hildebrand.

61. See "Erklärüng des Verbandes der Historiker Deutschlands zum Studium des Faches Geschichte an den Hochschulen, 14. 10. 1975," *Geschichte in Wissenschaft und Unterricht* 27 (1976): 223–25, 297–304, 566–69. See the critique of this declaration by Jürgen Kocka et al., "Rückzug in den Traditionalismus," *Geschichte und Gesellschaft* 2 (1976): 537–44.

62. (See above, n. 26).

63. (See above, n. 33).

Bibliography

Abel, Wilhelm. *Agrarkrisen und Agrarkonjunkturen in Mitteleuropa vom 13. bis zum 19. Jahrhundert* (Berlin, 1935; 2nd, rev. ed., Hamburg, 1966).

Böhme, Helmut. *Deutschlands Weg zur Grossmacht* (Cologne, 1966).

Bracher, Karl D. *Die Auflösung der Weimarer Republik* (Villingen, 1955).

———. *The German Dictatorship* (New York, 1970).

Brunner, Otto. *Neue Wege der Verfassungs- und Sozialgeschichte*, 2nd ed. (Göttingen, 1968).

Faber, Karl-Georg. *Theorie der Geschichtswissenschaft*, 3rd ed. (Munich, 1974).

Faulenbach, Bernd, ed. *Geschichtswissenschaft in Deutschland* (Munich, 1974).

Iggers, Georg. *The German Conception of History* (Middletown, Conn., 1968).

Kehr, Eckart. *Battleship Building and Party Politics in Germany, 1894–1901* (Chicago, 1975).

———. *Economic Interests, Militarism, and Foreign Policy* (Berkeley, Calif., 1978).

Kocka, Jürgen. *Klassengesellschaft und Krieg, 1914–1918* (Göttingen, 1973).

———. "Recent Historiography of Germany and Austria," *Journal of Modern History* 47 (1975): 101–19.

———. *Sozialgeschichte* (Göttingen, 1977).

Mommsen, Hans. "Historical Scholarship in Transition: The Situation in the Federal Republic of Germany," *Daedalus* 100 (Spring, 1971): 485–508.

Mommsen, Wolfgang J. *Die Geschichtswissenschaft jenseits des Historismus* (Düsseldorf, 1971).

———. "Historical Study in Western Germany," in Boyd C. Shafer, ed., *Historical Study in the West* (New York, 1968).

Rosenberg, Hans. *Bureaucracy, Aristocracy, and Autocracy: The Prussian Experience 1660–1815* (Cambridge, Mass., 1958).
———. *Grosse Depression und Bismarckzeit* (Berlin, 1967).
Rürup, Reinhard, ed. *Historische Sozialwissenschaft* (Göttingen, 1977).
Rüsen, Jörn. *Für eine erneuerte Historik: Studien zur Theorie der Geschichtswissenschaft* (Stuttgart-Bad Cannstadt, 1976).
Schleier, Hans. *Theorie der Geschichte—Theorie der Geschichtswissenschaft: Zu neueren theoretisch-methodologischen Arbeiten der Geschichtswissenschaft: zu neueren theoretisch-methodologischen Arbeiten der Geschichtsschreibung in der BRD* (Berlin/DDR, 1975).
Schulz, Gerhard, ed. *Geschichte heute* (Göttingen, 1973).
Stürmer, Michael, ed. *Das kaiserliche Deutschland: Politik und Gesellschaft* (Düsseldorf, 1970).
Sywottek, Arnold. *Geschichtswissenschaft in der Legitimationskrise* (Bonn, Bad-Godesberg, 1970).
Wehler, Hans-Ulrich. *Bismarck und der Imperialismus* (Düsseldorf, 1969).
———. *Das deutsche Kaiserreich* (Göttingen, 1973).
———. *Geschichte als Historische Sozialwissenschaft* (Frankfurt, 1973).

13 A. WILLIAM SALOMONE

Italy

Since economy dictates a certain brevity, and since this essay cannot be even remotely exhaustive, even were that possible, this study will seek to be suggestive and, again, not without a modicum of rationality, provocative, in the literal as well as in the inspiring and challenging meaning of the word. It seeks this goal if for no other reason than that it cannot always hope to present sufficient "evidence" or satisfactory documentary reference for the adoption of noncomformist—in its best sense of meaning to be fresh and based upon direct exposure to matter and materials treated—points of views and the formulation of possibly unorthodox judgments.

Let me be even more direct at the start. I regard an essay in historiography as an attempt to write a special kind of history of one's own. "To write a critical history of historiography," said Arnaldo Momigliano in 1974, "one must know both the authors one studies and the historical material they have studied." Even more forcefully, back in 1905, our master Gaetano Salvemini had written in a letter to his teacher Pasquale Villari:

. . . There are works of twenty pages that require a year's labor to be done as they should. For ideas are not stones strewn on the road nor like documents on the shelves of archives so that it is sufficient to shuffle one's feet or take down and open a register in order to come upon lots of stones and documents. Indeed, ideas must be sought out, and often they are not there; and even more often, after one has worked like a dog to put them together, he discovers that they were mistaken, and that it is necessary to start all over once again.

For, we take it, historiography deals with facts that, whatever they were originally, become ideas in the works of the historians. As such they may perhaps remain "fixed" forever as works of art worthy of awed admiration and contemplation or, through the active imagination, be themselves converted into new facts, new ideas. Historiography can be mere listing, cataloging, or even critical bibliography, or it can be a form of bio-history. For us, for purposes of this essay, historiography will be an attempt at an introduction to the cultural and intellectual history of contemporary Italy. As we shall see at some length be-

low—exactly because without an understanding of it, little is very clear in contemporary Italian history—World War II, a war of ideologies par excellence for
Italy, was followed by a strenuous, often bitter, political struggle itself inte-
grally, almost organically, related to a new conflict of ideas, Marxist, Christian-
democratic, and secular. It was a philosophical-ideological civil war in which
the liberal "philosophy of the Spirit" of an old but, during the early phases of
the struggle (to 1952), still living contemplative philosopher, Benedetto Croce,
was placed under siege and savagely battered by a partial progeny excogitated
in a fascist prison by the Marxist activist ideologue Antonio Gramsci. For good
or ill, Italian historiography, even that sector of it that continuously, if not always consistently, protested its "virginal" character untouched by ideological
impurities, was somewhere in its products, somehow in its even unconscious
motives, sometimes affected by the atmosphere and the fortunes and misfortunes
of the great political struggle and the conflict of social ideas and cultural values.

Contemporary Italian historiography is a stupendously complicated affair that
must be placed within its immediate matrix of new forms—that is, the conflict
and confluence of politics and culture after the fall of fascism—as well as within
the mainstream of the larger tradition of Italian historical thought and expression.
A consideration of this complex of factors may or may not render completely
inane comparative questions. Those readers without problems—curiosity is not
always enough, since even cats have it but not "real" problems!—who, as one
once did, ask: "Who came after Croce?" can be told that there were Delio
Cantimori and Federico Chabod, that there are Franco Venturi, Leo Valiani,
Rosario Romeo, Giuseppe Galasso, Salvo Mastellone, Rosario Villari, and
Massimo L. Salvadori, to mention only a few from a variety of fields; the answer
can mean little or nothing if he has problems with elementary Italian, historical
more than linguistic. The question, obviously, is not, as it is so often rather
perversely posed: How do these, and other Italian, contemporary historians compare with allegedly more "original," "pioneering," "ground-breaking" American social historians, the French structuralists and *Annalistes,* British empiricists
and Marxists, German culturalists and realist neohistoricists, or even rare unorthodox Russian historical materialists? The wrong methodological question cannot but lead to the wrong or irrelevant historiographical answer. Even before
attempting to learn in the most general way the work of the Italian historians I
have mentioned above, at least for comparative purposes, one would have to
run back, so to speak, through the entire tradition of Italian modern historiography. For those contemporary historians, and others of similar stature to whom
some reference, however brief, will be made some time later in our text or notes,
are also "children," each in his own fashion, of the historiographical epoch of
long duration that runs back from Croce to Machiavelli and Guicciardini with,
in between, the cultural significance and professional contribution and teachings
of masters of history and philosophy. Modern students who have eyes to read
and see for themselves and, even more, the will to understand will certainly find
somewhere within the works of the major modern practitioners of Italian history,

the lessons or the leavening spirit of the giants of the era of the proto-Enlight-
enment, Muratori, Vico, and Giannone; then the genial reformist *Illuministi,*
Beccaria, Genovesi, Galiani, Filangieri; then the vast and keen intelligence of
Carlo Cattaneo, Francesco De Sanctis, and Giuseppe Ferrari, during the Risorgimento, and, in the aftermath, Antonio Labriola and Croce himself dominating
over two generations. Finally, before, during, or after fascism, there was the
first "historical" anti-Croce, Gaetano Salvemini, and, soon from the fascist
shore, Gioacchino Volpe, and, prematurely cut down before the full fruits of his
superb research were gathered, Antonio Anzilotti, followed, through and after
fascism, by a bright company of younger historians and older masters, chief
among them Luigi Salvatorelli, Adolfo Omodeo, Guido De Ruggiero, Arturo
Carlo Jemolo, Nino Valeri, Piero Pieri, Francesco Ruffini, Cesare Spellanzon,
Gino Luzzatto, Ernesto Sestan, the gifted Nello Rosselli, atrociously killed by
the Franco-Italian fascists in 1937, and, in the fields of literary, art, and phil-
osophic-cultural history, Mario Praz, Roberto Longhi, Lionello Venturi, Giulio
Carlo Argan, Massimo Mila, and Eugenio Garin. In itself and in the perspective
of the legacy of these great historical minds, contemporary historiography is as
rich as that of most of its Western counterparts. At any rate, we believe that
there are no spheres of the elect among historiographical traditions and historical
"schools" but only shifting circles of greatness within circles of achievement
in the universal earthly city where historians grapple with understanding and
creative reconstruction of human vicissitudes worthy of remembrance.

Contemporary Italian historiography, understood in a strict sense, now spans
the generation-long cycle from the end of the Fascist War in Italy in April 1945
(which was the unique high or turning point of a period of shorter duration from
the fall of Mussolini in July 1943 to the expulsion of the communists from the
government in 1947 and their drastic defeat in the political elections of April
1948) to the crisis of Italian democracy which, in its acutest moments, encompassed the student revolt of 1968–1969 and, alas! the dark paroxysm of the social
extremist and terrorist movement that culminated with the assassination of Aldo
Moro by the Red Brigades in the spring of 1978. This chrono-substantive character of the period must not be lost sight of even when apparently remote and
unrelated questions of historical research and writing are under consideration.
Though, as I shall point out below, a sort of special tendentious "presentism"
has characterized Italian historiographical production since the days of Machiavelli, Vettori, and Guicciardini—few Italians ever argued too strenuously against
the Crocean dictum that "all history is contemporary history"—that "presentism" was not overevident except in "official" (Marxist, Catholic, liberal) or
subtly disguised but strongly "committed" ideological quarters. The fact was
that the atmosphere of crisis, even when it seemed to oscillate from extremes
of dark pessimism to expectant moments of civil peace, "economic miracles,"
and social conciliation, and, above all, particularly during the promise-filled
pontificate of John XXIII and then again, in the mid-1970s of ideological compromise, the brief Italian idylls were shattered by waves of unrest, uncertainty,

and violence. The stress and strain of society were inescapably felt in the material life and, of course, in the spiritual and moral fibers of the Italian people. In their turn the almost permanent tensions of collective and individual life were reflected, at times openly, often elusively, as if metarationally, in the mind and work of the historians regardless of the period or subject or problem with which they were grappling.

During its first phase, in the late 1940s and 1950s, the mood of tension, despite recurring activist explosions of one kind or another, was peaceably balanced between a collective sense of quiet elation based on a strange subtle concord that the material disaster of Italy had not been in vain since "fascism had to be destroyed" if an organic reconstruction of the country—physical, political, structural—had to be achieved and, on the other hand, at least in large sectors of the popular masses, adherents or sympathizers in most cases of either the Communist or the Socialist party, a sort of chiliastic expectation of a great change, an Italian revolution "at long last" that would fulfill, at one stroke, the Joachimite prophecy of "the Third Kingdom" of the Holy Spirit, the Machiavellian invocation of a redemptive savior of "the people," the Mazzinian vision of messianic fusion of *"Dio e Popolo,"* the ironclad predictions of Marx for the triumph of the proletariat, Lenin's "Red October" in Italy, and, withal, Antonio Gramsci's prison dream of the "New Prince" incarnated in the hegemony of poor peasants and workers sustained and shielded by an unbetraying revolutionary intelligentsia. In the expectations of a great social change and social revolution there was at the same time the stuff of a *gran rifiuto* (great refusal) of not only the immediate but also the long-range Italian past and, even if nowhere clearly formulated, the emotional and vague transconceptual sense of *renovatio* as it had become associated with those four key Italian words: *Rinascita—Riforma—Risorgimento—Rivoluzione.*

It was quite symptomatic of the mood of rebellion against the past that in 1948 an Italian "historian" should have published a work entitled *Antistoria d'Italia.* No less revealing of the paradoxical character of this phase of contemporary Italian history—and, therefore, of the Italian mind's reflections on history—is the extraordinarily celebrated dictum which Prince Tomasi di Lampedusa in his epoch-making novel *Il Gattopardo* (1958) has Prince Salina tell his young protagonist Tancredi, who is utterly stunned by such wise cynicism: ". . . If you wish all to remain the same you must see to it that everything changes! . . ." By 1945 people and their old worlds—political systems, social relations, spiritual values, ideological orientations—seemed to have changed in Italy and Europe. To what extent, in what ways, and for what reasons was the consciousness, vision, and expression of that grand mutation a new function of the long tradition of Italian historiography?

In the light of the substantive points of reference briefly described and the methodological "experimental" approach concisely anticipated in the preceding introductory reflections, the larger, more fundamental, question cannot but arise concerning the general character (insofar as "general" is not equated to universally validated "law" but only observable norm or trend beyond recurring immediacies and particularities) of Italian historiography as a "tradition" and in its "innovative" stage at this juncture of the contemporary era. Obviously, there cannot but be a disparity in the value of judgments on two such different, and of such difference in duration, and yet diachronically related historiographical periods. Grave dangers of misunderstanding can result from lack of awareness or sensitivity to diffractive perspectivism that may lead the historian's "lenses" to be adjusted telescopically for greater visibility but not necessarily for sharper intelligibility.

That there is indeed something elusively "different"—"different," of course, within the Western cultural context—in the general character of Italian historiography can be denied only by the culturally ingenuous. But what is that "difference"? An immediate, almost tautological manner of describing it might be to say that as a whole Italian historiography is uniquely "national," that is— as has been attempted to be elaborately demonstrated again but from a fundamentally nonnationalistic point of view in the latest monumental or at least multivolume history of Italy, the Einaudi *Storia d'Italia*—that both as *res gestae* (history as reality in being) and as *historia rerum gestarum* (history as recounting, recital, reconstruction) the history of Italy possesses some "original characters" that evidently distinguish (but also bind) it from those of other peoples, nations, and cultures. Leaving aside for the moment the problematics of *res gestae*, some of which we have already summarily dealt with in reference to the immediate postwar period and to others to which we will return, it seems beyond question that Italian and, one can safely assume, most sophisticated non-Italian theorists of history accept as the most plausible hypothesis available the dualistic idea that there is indeed an Italian way *to* history as there is an Italian way *of* history. When the problem arises of spelling out the characteristics of that "autonomous" way, almost infinite varieties of interpretations and different emphases of elements inevitably emerge. It would take an almost absurd, certainly impossible, detailed analysis of even the most general "histories of Italy" through the last five centuries, from the collective historical critique contained in Machiavelli's work and Guicciardini's *Storia d'Italia* at least to Croce, Salvemini, and Chabod, to say nothing of the Gramscian-Marxist exegetical interpreters, to trace, perhaps even quantitatively on some sort of statistical scale, the kinds, recurrences, and variations of "qualities" or characteristics ascribed through the ages to the Italian historical mind.

We have already offered more than an intimation of what our tentative judgment on this complex matter may be. In suggesting, as we have done and will do more elaborately below, if from a different direction, that the conflict between "politics" and "culture" tends to resolve itself in their confluence as "history" (*historia rerum gestarum*) we have isolated, for purposes of understanding, a series of "bonds" that may be part or function of the "original characters" of contemporary Italian historiography. Turning our gaze back now across the centuries to what we might analogically call the "original sources" of Italian historiographical endeavor, the era of the Renaissance and its two great masters of political thought and history, Machiavelli and Guicciardini, we can hazard the view that not only in their time but, *mutatis mutandis,* at least in reconstructions of periods of historic tension and crisis and change Italian historians have tended or appeared to be guided by a set of contrasting, almost mutually contradictory, essentially unconscious, motivating "inner" forces. And, for us, insofar as we have succeeded in ferreting out, not from abstract programs or theories but from within actual works of history, through consistently attentive, select but direct inquiry into not only the masterpieces but the generality of worthy products of the Italian historical mind, these "forces" reduce themselves to four general characteristics, together or in various combinations operating within or behind what I have called the Italian way to history: *Historical realism* (or extensions and modifications of models of analysis of political and civil society originally exemplified in the works of Machiavelli and Guicciardini); *tendentious or even organic humanism* (special attention to the centrality, often the predominance, of the human element, as against the abstract, collective, or quantitative factors, in the vicissitudes of nations and peoples); *individuality* (the formation and activity of men and women as bio-spiritual entities contraposed, quite frequently, to the group, the collective body, the corporation, the sect, the church, the state, but sometimes also to the social community and civil society); and, finally, *philosophical pragmatism* (sometimes amounting to a vision of the world that could be interpreted as instrumentalized providentialism or a version of practical pantheism, at other times an apparent inclination to be influenced, guided, or even vitally overwhelmed by ideological passions). Stated or referred to in this schematic manner, without benefit of illustration or documentation, these characteristics may appear to be mere useful (or useless!) fictions of a committed critic's quest for a transcending comprehension of an impossibly huge corpus of historiographical production whose parts would really need to be analyzed if not one by one at least category by category, subject by subject, author by author. This is, of course, more than true, but it would require at least one large volume all its own. Here I cannot but repeat that, as I read the works of the major Italian historians since the Renaissance and, in particular, as I have studied the major products of the contemporary Italian historians I have mentioned in the preceding pages and others to whom I will have occasion to call attention, however briefly, *those* are the four "categorical imperatives" I have found most dominant in Italian historiographical endeavor.

If the premises (they are really "conclusions") are at least tentatively accepted as crystallizing or exemplifying the historiographical counterpart of what in his brilliant book by the same title Leonardo Olschki has called the multifaceted yet often enigmatic "genius of Italy," the inevitable, usually disturbing, question of continuity and rupture in a "tradition" can be confronted. In this case, the question must be faced not only for abstract or theoretical reasons, important as they may be, but by necessity of the very logic of our antecedent emphasis upon the range and depth of the crisis, and change, of Italian politics through the unique quinquennium of the passage from war to peace in 1943–1948. But, as we have pointed out, there was infinitely more than a crisis of politics involved in the war, the fall of fascism, and during the immediate aftermath of necessary reconstruction. There had broken out during those years, finding a first active-collective expression in the organized armed Italian resistance movement against the Nazi-fascist enemy, a desperate open war of ideas that helped to bring about the victory of the antitotalitarian military, political, and ideological forces in Italy. The unity of action against the common enemy during the resistance held in leash the contrast of philosophical views and, more immediately important, the ideological conflicts and programmatic differences. Restrained even through the early phase of the transition to 1947 these subdued tensions all burst loose and continued with virulence for over a decade. The crisis of Italian politics had found its counterpart in a crisis of culture of which one of the major vehicles of formulation and expression was the "new" philosophical-ideological corpus of apparently unsystematized neo-Marxist doctrines, most of them in the guise of "impressionistic" but extremely subtle and brilliant *historical* critiques of liberal thought and bourgeois values, that was published volume-by-edited-volume from 1947 to 1952 as Antonio Gramsci's *Quaderni del Carcere.* Gramsci's *Prison Notebooks* marked a unique event not only in the political and ideological life of the Italian Communist party and its leader and chief sponsor of their publication, Palmiro Togliatti, but also in the intellectual, literary, artistic, philosophical, and historiographical spheres of Italian culture. If a "rupture" must be sought or isolated in the continuum of Italian historical/historiographical "tradition," it seems reasonable or plausible to suppose that it occurred at that point in the postfascist period when not only the politico-philosophical totalitarian actualism of Giovanni Gentile seemed absolutely dead even before he met his tragic end in the spring of 1944 but, more significantly, when the "absolute historicism" of Benedetto Croce, still very much alive during the years of publication of the *Quaderni del Carcere,* was subjected to the violent attack of the exegetical interpreters of the "first" available version of Gramsci's meditations and annotations during the long, atrocious decade of imprisonment (1926–1937).

At the height of its power the fascist regime's vituperation and repudiation of Croce and the "philosophy of the Spirit" had only half, perhaps even less, succeeded, since the old philosopher's "practical" and theoretical historical works—from his history of Italy issued when the Italian dictator was consolidating his power in the mid-1920s to his history of Europe published when the German Fuehrer was on the eve of the seizure of power and then, before the outbreak of the "second" totalitarian Great War, his philosophic testament to the freedom of history in the book *La Storia come pensiero e come azione* (1938)—testified to his resistance and his significance among "free" Italians and "good Europeans." The postwar revolt against Croce conducted under the banner of Marxism and spearheaded by a well-coordinated, quasi-Gramscian intelligentsia was, in reality, only one aspect of a vaster cultural phenomenon,

but it came to have a substantive as well as an emblematic importance dispro-
portionately dramatized for ideological purposes.

The fact is that Croce was swept in a great wave of rejection and reinterpretation whose crest was ridden by neo-Marxist intellectuals and historians whose
span of attack encompassed wider spheres of cultural rebellion. The historiographical iconoclasm, so evident and often so ubiquitous and facile during the
1950s among some of the old and a great number of the younger historians, was
hardly the result of the sudden collective passion for historical truth as against
the "falsehoods and perversions" of the Crocean-liberal, the democratic-Sal-
veminian, the radical-Gobettian, the socialist-Rossellian, the reactionary-fascist,
or the clerical-Christian democratic "schools." Though Croce was the secular
pope—perhaps "antipope" might have been more accurate—of Italian culture,
and therefore a visibly easy target, the attacks were directed against no one in
particular and yet against all who might possibly stand in the way or delay the
consolidation of a new "hegemony" in Italy. All this, perhaps, at its worst. At
its best, what was involved among certain leading sectors of the Italian intelligentsia, even before the publication of Gramsci's *Quaderni*—as Elio Vittorini's
pathetic experience with his periodical *Il Politecnico* (1945–1947) and Cesare
Pavese's suicide (1950) so tragically reveal—was an acute crisis of conscience.
The question among some of the most sensitive young Italians was: What had
really happened, and why, and now—*what is to be done?* Some among the best,
young and old, had long ago perished under the tyranny of fascism—the socialist
Matteotti, the liberal Giovanni Amendola, the child prodigy of the antifascist
intellectual struggle Piero Gobetti, Carlo and Nello Rosselli, and Gramsci himself—or during the war: Duccio Galimberti, Leone Ginzburg, Giaime Pintor,
and thousands of obscure or unknown victims of Nazi-fascist savagery. But
among the survivors the personal and direct experiences, through war and peace,
of a number of Italian intellectuals who had recoiled from the immorality of the
doctrines of fascism and had resisted and fought against the totalitarian corruption of history, impelled them toward a quick and safe restoration not of discredited systems of law and order but of elementary human and historical values.
Thus, from within the most sensitive moral and intellectual quarters in Italy there
came forth during those years excellent examples of a renewed dedication to
"uncommitted" historiographical endeavor, to a quest for newer approaches to
traditional problems, frequently through practical refinements of the theory and
methodology of historical study beyond the beaten paths of the "classic models"
of the nineteenth and twentieth centuries. No invidious comparisons are intended
when one mentions in this connection such names as Federico Chabod, Franco
Venturi, Nino Valeri, A. C. Jemolo, Rosario Romeo, Leo Valiani, Giorgio
Spini, Elio Conti, Furio Diaz, and the superbly intelligent, uniquely productive
mobile band of the select circle of the elect students of Chabod at Croce's newly
founded Neapolitan Historical Institute, or those who worked with Delio Cantimori at the Scuola Normale of Pisa or in Florence, with Eugenio Garin as well,
or others around Walter Maturi at the University of Turin. When, after twenty-

five years in exile after his "expulsion" by the fascists, Gaetano Salvemini returned at the age of seventy-six to his old chair in history at the University of Florence, he began his new course of lectures on 16 October 1949 with an introduction entitled "A Page of Ancient History," by which he meant to celebrate the death of the immediate past—and the dawn of a new day, a *renovatio*, in Italy.

And yet for a long time to come there was no ideological civil peace in Italy. Certain cadres of the Italian intelligentsia, operating upon premises that often seemed obscure in origin but were quite patent in motivation, tended to set the predominant tone and style and kept the atmosphere agitated, often turbulently distractive of constructive cultural labors. Attachment to a partisan cause, political self-interest, personal and professional opportunism, and, if infrequently, plain ingenuousness led to mercurial oscillations in intellectual commitment and ideological temper, depending occasionally on the rise and fall of the political temperature in Italy and Europe as it was affected by the contemporary struggles for power.

In the light of this murky cultural atmosphere which, politically and internationally, corresponded to the erosive glacial years of the Cold War, it would be mistaken, to say the least, to ascribe to the Togliattian use and abuse of his old unfortunate comrade Gramsci's tormented reflections on philosophy and history for mere ideological and partisan purposes. Nor could the neo-Marxist intelligentsia, whatever the momentum of its enthusiasm and inspiration derived from the Gramscian *Prison Notebooks,* be solely credited with the sweep of the quasi-hegemonic impact of the Sardinian revolutionary thinker's sketchy "guidelines" for a total reinterpretation of Italian history. In a sense, the *Quaderni del Carcere* would have had to be invented had they not become available *at that time,* so powerful, so urgent seemed the need, messianic, fideistic, or collective-emotive as it may be judged, for a message of a possible metamorphosis in the nature of things social and historical. Despite the vociferousness of multitudinous evangels, old and new, religious and secular, liberal, democratic, and socialist, an apparent "vacuum" existed in people's spirits emerging from an unparalleled ordeal by the fire of war, civil strife, and the savagery of genocide demanding to be filled by the tenets of a new faith. In Italy, the long and bitter but also decimating communist activism in the antifascist resistance— of which Gramsci was only the most illustrious martyr—combined with the reality of the Soviet Union's fantastically great contribution to the defeat of Nazi Germany to rear the image, symbol and myth at the same time, of an irresistible and invincible "wave of the future" that would revolutionize and change the very foundations of social life. Incredible as it now seems, that Stalin himself should have become in the Italian populist-communist imaginative discourse a sort of "national hero" was testified to by the half-taunting, half-sardonic, slogan of the late 1940s and early 1950s: *"Ha da' vení Baffone!"* ("Wait till Big Whiskers comes!"). One cannot but help wondering how many "light years" away and therefore how far removed from the realm of reality and human sanity even the most tentative, cautious, and bland suggestion of some such idea as an "historical compromise" would have seemed during those days.

The publication of Gramsci's *Quaderni del Carcere* in slow stages, so to speak, and its availability to large numbers of readers in the general public was at best a very intelligent, at worst an astute, cultural operation that succeeded beyond all expectations. Almost without doubt, the cumulative impact of the seven volumes (if one includes the very first to be issued in 1947, containing the often illuminating and beautiful *Letters from Prison,* so revealing of the humanity as well as the intelligence of Antonio Gramsci) was immense. Their appearance constituted an exceptional episode, a truly extraordinary event, in the cultural and intellectual life of modern Italy. Seldom anywhere before had the impact of "mere" books been so immediate, rarely had new ideas exerted their fascination and force upon people's minds, their ways of thinking, and sometimes their very actions. Hardly anyone who read or heard others who interpreted and communicated by word of mouth or mass media, radio, film or newspaper at that time, escaped the spiritual presence of an extraordinary new "hero"—the unique myth whose protagonist had been a revolutionary warrior and a secular saint, a philosopher and an activist, a complete human being and demiurge of socialism, an intellectual and a fighter for the cause of poor peasants and workers, a new Marxist *uomo universale* and a good Italian. No wonder Benedetto Croce himself in one of his last magnificent acts of all-too-human generosity, did homage to the "genius," to the mind and indomitable spirit of Antonio Gramsci. No less important for our purposes here, it must be emphasized that beside and beyond the intrinsic merits, value, and significance of his *Prison Notebooks,* they contributed to the creation in Italy of a pervasive novel *Weltanschauung* that willy-nilly affected Marxist "believers" and Christian "unbelievers," democratic thinkers and socialist ideologues, university professors and journalists, novelists, poets, and artists, members of Communist party cells and members of Parliament or "high society," philosophers and, above all, historians. The corpus of Gramscian notes and other writings together with the exegetical literature that grew over and around it soon hardened into a veritable bloc of new Marxist "sacred scriptures" that, in their frequently vulgarized versions, would have repelled the lonely prisoner of fascism who had jotted down his notes often in quite different fashion, for quite different purposes—as strenuous, tormented, and tormenting efforts at understanding, at *interpreting* the world and human history which he had not been able (contrary to his master Marx's injunction in his theses on Feuerbach) to *change.*

There are still other ironies in the fortune and misfortune, if such they can be called, involved in the "first" version of Gramsci's *Quaderni del Carcere*—made available, and "irony" in this respect is merely another, milder, word for patent contradictions and "defects" and "defections" in the first editions of the *Notebooks* (and some of them had been pointed out by keen critics very early on, even from within the circle of sympathizers or adherents to the Marxist views). Now, in the late 1970s, with the publication, at long last, of a complete, untampered with, "unedited," and truly critical version of Antonio Gramsci's *Quaderni del Carcere*, edited (in this case one should say patiently, carefully assembled by an expert *équipe* for a long time directed) by Valentino Gerratana (in four volumes, Torino: Giulio Einaudi, 1975), the old irony is explicated as a "fact." And the new fact bears the marks of a very important idea. As Gerratana puts it in his sensitive Preface to the "integral" edition, the *Quaderni* have by now become a "classic." Appearing as they do a quarter century after their first version, at a different historic moment in Italy and abroad, we might add, in becoming a "classic" as indeed they were destined to be, Gramsci's *Quaderni del Carcere* have ceased to be instruments of ideological warfare and can now be studied, perhaps as they should have been from the very beginning, as philosophical reflections on people and their worlds, on ideas and theories of revolution, on the art of politics and the meaning of works of literature, on the sources of religious and intellectual hegemonies and the nature of history. One cannot but speculate, in comparing the "first" with the "integral" critical edition, whether had *this* been published in the late 1940s and early 1950s, when, as we have seen, fierce ideological battles were furiously raging in Italy and Europe, Gramsci's thought and "message" would not have been perhaps much less dramatic and wide-ranging but undoubtedly more constructive and profound. For, again, one cannot but warmly agree with Valentino Gerratana that if in their "first form" of 1948–1951 the *Quaderni* served an exceptional purpose—and, for ourselves, we have clearly suggested what *that* was—now, in the new full critical text they serve the truth. We firmly believe that Antonio Gramsci would never have wanted it otherwise.

I have given the elaborate attention I have to Antonio Gramsci's *Quaderni del Carcere* because I believe that, particularly now in the exceptionally trustworthy "second" critical edition by Valentino Gerratana, they constitute, despite their fragmentary character and "dispersive" form, one of the most original contributions to historiographical innovation in Italy. I intend this judgment as both a commentary and a critique. The publication of the "first" version of the *Quaderni*, as I have frequently intimated, inspired a vast-ranging, often bright but not always critical in the best sense of the word, historical corpus. The work of some of the venerable "older men" like Emilio Sereni and Giuseppe Berti, who had for long been militant in the Italian Communist Party, was not above reproach but truly pioneering, particularly vis-à-vis problems of the South, the peasants, and the Italian countryside, and, in many respects, indispensable for an understanding of even the "pre-Gramscian," if we may so describe it, Italian Marxist views of history. Within the "middle generation," naturally affected by the Gramscian "model," Giorgio Candeloro, with his multivolume history of Italy; Franco Della Peruta, with his studies of the "democratic wings" of the Risorgimento currents and, lately, the early Mazzini; Ernest Ragionieri, with the fine "extremes" of his monographic studies of a single town, his own Sesto Fiorentino, and the impact of German social democracy on Italian socialism; Paolo Alatri, with his early, if partly flawed, studies of the origins and structural

"components" of fascism, and D'Annunzio and Nitti, and the documents of
Italian antifascism; Giuliano Procacci, with his work on social classes and absolute monarchy in sixteenth-century France, his monograph on the "fortune"
of Machiavelli, and his essays on figures of the era of the Second International;
Rosario Villari, with his superb book on the Neapolitan anti-Spanish revolt of
the pre-Masaniello generation and his work on the develoment of Italian capitalism; and not least, Paolo Spriano, the quasi-official, if quite independent-
minded, historian of the Italian Communist party, the student of proletarian
Turin before the coming of fascism, the enthusiast of Piero Gobetti—these and
a number of other Italian Marxist historians all have felt, in one way or another,
the deep imprint of the "first" Gramscian *Quaderni*. On the traces of these or
independently, they collectively seemed engaged in a vast, almost organic, critique of apparently "traditional" versions of Italian history—liberal (Crocean),
democratic (Salveminian), socialist (all varieties of noncommunist shades). And,
in their own reconstructions, they tended to put all the epochal phases of modern
Italian history on trial—the Risorgimento (with special anathema against Mazzini—until recently Franco Della Peruta began rescuing him—and his "Party
of Action" for their failure to realize a "Jacobin revolution" in the course of
the national upsurge); the aftermath and the era of Crispian imperialism; the
Giolittian era (at least until Togliatti himself intervened in a "Discourse on Giolitti" in 1950, and in an anti-Salveminian shaft, softened the blows against Giolitti and his regime); and, obviously, the fascist period and all its works. There
are signs that the "new Gramsci" of the Gerratana critical edition, who is not
"softer" but "fuller" than in the "first" version, coincident as it is with the
détente-oriented, expectant day of an Italian Eurocommunist "historical compromise," may perhaps be directed at guiding or inspiring the neo-Marxist historians toward a partial revision of their former absolute historiographical
revision. Perhaps the really supreme substantive or thematic irony lies in the fact
that among other lesser, similar phenomena the year 1975, which brought forth
the "new Gramsci," also saw the publication of a gigantic, 1170-page study by
a former student of Federico Chabod (who himself had written the most brilliant
short essay on "Croce Storico" in the *Rivista Storica Italiana,* in 1952, the year
of the philosopher's death), Gennaro Sasso's *Benedetto Croce: La ricerca della
dialettica* (Naples: A. Morano, 1975). Thus a philosophical-historical (and ideological) cycle of a quarter century's duration seemed to be definitely closed in
Italy.

During those twenty-five years all Italian historiography, practically with
whatever period, problem, aspect, development, and question of politics, society, and culture it was concerned, was affected or influenced in some way,
touched or aroused, stirred or repelled, inspired to enthusiastic adherence and
emulation or spurred to calm countercritique of neo-Marxist methodological,
documentary, and hermeneutic procedure or to passionate iconoclastic fury aim-
ing to bring down the whole structure of the "new history" assertedly raised
upon the sketch drawn from the genial notations of often very profound reflec-

tions contained in the *Prison Notebooks* of a truly original mind, a keen revolutionary thinker, an extraordinary human being—Antonio Gramsci. The temptation and perhaps the necessity to deal in some detail with this fantastically intriguing and complicated "chapter" of the contemporary Italian infra-historiographical "story" are indeed very great (so much so, I might add, that an early attempt to write that "chapter" and then, again, another version of it, was proving literally self-defeating, leading me as it was to an almost infinity of research problems and enticements with the prospective expectation of drafting a whole volume on it!)—but the opportunity, the time, and the lack of space here force us merely to allude, to squeeze, to synthesize and generalize, and to do so with sufficient clarity that may do essential justice to the central question.

At least one point needs to be emphasized again, directly, relating to all that we have said so far concerning the impact of the Gramscian neo-Marxist ethos upon the Italian historiographical "community." Briefly it is this: Whatever the impact and reaction to *it*—positive or negative, sympathetic or critical—that "community" could not at any single moment and in the long run be seen or characterized as having become a mere function of *that* novel and prevailing current of historical thought and practice. The length and depth of the "national" historical tradition with its multiform "original characters" founded upon geography and economics, politics and religion, social structures and visions of life, diversified artistic, literary, and spiritual modes of expression, differences of linguistic, educational, and legal traditions, varieties of personal and collective philosophies—all these and more contributed to the continuing diversification of the well-trodden paths converging into and diverging from what we have described as "the Italian way to history," that is, historical interpretation and historiographical praxis. If, as some believed, philosophy was needed for history, if both theory and praxis were necessary to historiographical creativity, then it was not hard to see, to find, to discover, if one desired, that, for all his encyclopedic and powerful mode of thought, for all his originality of conceptualization and magnificent reinterpretative imagination, for all his inspiring passion at the service of his vision of a new, a socialist, "city of man," Antonio Gramsci had not been alone, not even only in his day, among Italians and Europeans. Heirs to the same tradition which, as we have already pointed out, had been part created, part nourished, part enriched and kept alive, by the "realist" Machiavelli, the "practitioner" Guicciardini, the "scientist" Galileo, the "philosopher" Vico, the "humanistic positivist" Cattaneo, the "messianic visionary" Mazzini, the "literary artist" De Sanctis, the "Marxist" Labriola, the "historian" Salvemini, the "historicist" Croce—there had been also the "socialist martyr" Giacomo Matteotti, the "heroic activist" Carlo Rosselli, and, above all, the legacy of the genius and tragic fate of Piero Gobetti. If other "models" of Italian thought and action were needed in that non-Platonic "academy" of the truly revolutionary elect among whom Gramsci was so specially, deservedly, illustrious, they certainly were not lacking in nearly all varieties of Italian historical and historiographical culture.

It would be an invidious and truly impossible task at this point, for all the reasons we have repeatedly stated and more, to single out the entire body of the most outstanding historians name by name, work by work, even "school" by "school"—and perhaps there was really only one of these, the Marxist, since Catholic, liberal, democratic, socialist, and "independent" belong to a different kind of classification. The sensitive, yet large and influential, voluminous labors of Don Giuseppe De Luca on Italian religiosity, the "history of piety," as he calls it, for the medieval and early modern period is more than well matched by the fine work on church and state in Italy after the Risorgimento by A. C. Jemolo, and that on the ideas of "social" Catholicism by Ettore Passerin d'Entrèves and that of Angelo Gambasin on the activity of the lower clergy in northern Italy—and from these, to the work of the relatively younger generation, such as that of Gabriele De Rosa on Don Sturzo and the rise of political Catholicism and the origins of Christian democracy, of Fausto Fonzi on the conflict of state and church early in the twentieth century, and particularly, the studies of that fine historical intelligence, that of Pietro Scoppola, on the meaning of Italian Catholic modernism. On the other hand, coming from quarters quite diverse from the "Catholic," the works of the liberal, radical, and socialist "secularists" such as Renzo De Felice on Mussolini and fascism; Rosario Romeo on Cavour and the origins of industrialism in Italy; Giuseppe Galasso on Naples in the early modern period and the development of the concept and practice of the modern state in Italy; Leo Valiani on nineteenth- and twentieth-century Italian socialism and the history of the resistance in which he played so crucial a part; Alessandro Galante Garrone with his original works on Buonarroti and, later, Cavallotti; Salvo Mastellone with his studies of Vico's Naples and then of the rise of Mazzini's "Giovane Italia" movement; Ennio Di Nolfo on fascist foreign policy and heroically, in his completion of the last two volumes of Cesare Spellanzon's huge history of the Risorgimento and the Italian national unity movement; the exceptionally committed Carlo Francovich with his monographs on the Tuscan resistance movement and the rare volume on the origins of Italian freemasonry; Roberto Vivarelli on the origins of fascism; Brunello Vigezzi with his incredibly detailed monograph on the Italian time of troubles on the eve of World War I; Mario Isnenghi with his beautiful volume on the myth of World War I as the "metamorphosis of liberation" as envisaged by the proto-fascist intellectuals and literati; Guido Neppi Modona with his unique historical reconstruction of the interrelationship between concepts and practices of "social" law and proletarian activism, particularly the strike, as a weapon of redress in the prefascist period; Massimo L. Salvadori with his works on the "question of the South" and the activity of Salvemini; Elio Conti with his heroic pioneering labors on Quattrocento Florentine economic and social history; and in contrast Guido Quazza, the brilliant historical clinician of the defections of the Italian political classes through wars, "reconstructions," and "revolutions" that "were made to fail." Together with the younger generation of historians formed at the "school" of Chabod during his days of Milanese, Roman, and, particularly, Neapolitan teaching at the Croce Historical Institute (Berengo, Cozzi, Barié, Sasso, Cristiani, Ventura, Marini, Diaz), and those refined transnational scholars like Giorgio Spini, Alberto Tenenti, Ruggiero Romano, Carlo Ginzburg, and Mario Del Treppo, all of these Italian historians and others still younger among them, and their old masters, constitute a formidable company that does honor to the activity, the productiveness and originality, of the contemporary practitioners of Clio's art. I have wanted to single out in this schematic fashion these names—being fully conscious of the "injustices" I may have committed in my neglect or even ignorance of others—to show, at the very least, how rich and free and varied the most constructive labors of contemporary Italian historiography really, and so admirably, are. The student of modern Italian history, I humbly submit, would serve himself and his profession well if he sought for him- or herself to become acquainted with the contours and contents of the works of these historians.

What, in summation, one might ask is the general structure and some of the outstanding features of contemporary Italian historiographical achievement? Within the logic but especially within the economy of the attempt made in this essay, I believe that, synthetically, the following general comments can be safely, or, as all things historical and human, at least tentatively made.

The contemporary Italian community of historical scholarship is absolutely an "open society." In that "society" the "old history," the historiography of the "systems" (be they philosophical, sociological, meta-historical, or ideological) is either waning and dying out or survives merely as a "document" of a historiographical day that is no more. It is rare to find genuine historians referring to or invoking in their support the names of Hegel, Comte, Marx, Dilthey, Max Weber, Meinecke, even Croce and his "executioner" Gramsci. The vogue of Vico survives, quite actively, but more abroad and as a "universal font" of general "human science" than as a guide to historical hermeneutics. Apparently the "old history" no longer responds to the living and historical experience of part of the old and most of the newer generations of Italian historians actually working, as they have been, in the posttotalitarian era—that "old history" no longer seemed to speak an intelligible language and had no relevance or utility in the discourse of historical understanding. Many of the best fruits of the "old history" (whatever its derivation or "school" ties) have been assimilated and transformed by the historical minds of such innovators as Federico Chabod, Delio Cantimori, Franco Venturi, Leo Valiani, Ernesto Sestan, and, for the ancient period as well as the modern, Arnaldo Momigliano, to mention again only some of the most illustrious of the members of the "middle generation." And among quite a few of the "newer," the growing non-ideological inclinations of a Giorgio Candeloro, an Alberto Caracciolo, a Rosario Villari, a Pasquale Villani, a Marino Berengo, a Massimo L. Salvadori, even a Guido Quazza and a Carlo Ginzburg, have become manifest, despite their early or continuing sympathies or adherence to Marxism; the historiographical "praxis" seems infinitely "softer" in their later works insofar as visible ideological tendencies are concerned.

Despite serious oscillations and, occasionally, severe interruptions, the universe of discourse of the Italian historical community has tended to become ecumenical in the secular and spiritual sense of the word, and a spirit of historiographical "compromise" seems to prevail. The Vatican has asserted that it has "opened" its *Archivio Segreto* to all serious and competent scholars, making documents to the end of the pontificate of Pius IX accessible. As a sort of strange parallel gesture, the Marxist intelligentsia in charge of such matters proclaimed over a decade ago that the archives of the Italian Communist party, at the Gramsci Institute, at the Feltrinelli, and possibly at other repositories of official documents, other than those in the Soviet archives (which only Ernesto Ragionieri for a long time before his premature death in 1977, and probably one or two other "official" party historians had had access to), would be open to historians of "all persuasions." In the meantime, at a national congress of Italian historians held at Perugia early in October 1967, an authoritative spokesman of Marxist historiography asserted publicly that unlike, as he put it, stubborn "radical-bourgeois revisionists," "we Marxists recognize and accept the Risorgimento and the Liberal era" as positive historical facts in the making of a "modern people," the Italians as a whole.

The query cannot but arise: Are contemporary Italian historians on their way toward some sort of historiographical consensus—which, of course, could not help raising fears in the hearts of all those among us who passionately believe in the freedom of history that perhaps a subtle, spontaneous, "corporative totalitarian concord" might emerge? If such a "consensus" should mean not merely the end of sterile and divisive ideological history but also of valid dissent and of the variety of contrasting reinterpretations of the past, it would be a dreary prospect indeed. But such a trend does not, fortunately, appear to be the case in Italy, and there will continue to be sufficient struggles of historical reason to make possible a pondered choice of roads to historical truth.

There has, further, come about a general acceptance in Italian historiographical quarters of the view that the fusion of *facts and ideas*—however wide the definition of "fact" may be (and it can range from a political event to a mass of statistical data, from the fall of a dictatorship to a constituent assembly, from a revolution to a world war) and however vast or restricted the meaning of "idea" might be (and it can range from a personal view of public life to a social doctrine, from a theory of art or culture to a philosophic system, a powerful myth, a body of beliefs)—is the best guide to historical understanding. There has naturally been a confluence and transformation of traditional and innovating factors in contemporary historical endeavor, for, as we now know, on the basis of documented facts history deals not merely with the past but with life and on the basis of the ideas behind or beyond those facts history assumes meaning, significance, a sense of the misery and grandeur, the promise and tragedy, of "social" human life, past and present.

As we have emphasized throughout this essay, there is an Italian way to historical reconstruction. This "fact" derives from neither a meaningless chauvinistic fixity of Herderian cultural or "nationalistic" origin nor an atomistic, Leibnitzian "monadology" stemming from the dangerous fable that "national character" is the sole "true reality" of peoples, the *"Ding an sich."* Contrary to such double nonsense, the "Italian way to history," as we have already suggested, is based on the recognition of the strength of a tradition, on the collective experience of a people, on the perceptions of reality, on the realistic intelligence of those who have meditated profoundly upon the distinctive vicissitudes of a people through epochs of both long and short duration. Realistic vision of a unique but not isolated or unrelated historical "character" has not led to philosophical fatalism or historiographical determinism. Indeed, Italians have continued in their quest for historical humanism. How much and in exactly what ways the relatively recent totalitarian-fascist experience in the "corporative" depersonalization of the individual and in domination over mind or the frightening problems created by the nuclear age, on the one hand, or the crisis of philosophical systems and the metamorphoses of ideologies in our time, on the other, have influenced and shaped contemporary Italian consciousness and its "products" can only be guessed at. To me it seems clear that the Italian historical mind of our time has on the whole refused to abandon the search for the concreteness of history as well as for its "humanity." "The pursuit of the human in history": perhaps this could safely be inscribed on the banner of contemporary Italian historiographical endeavor.

Elsewhere, we know, there have been alternative roads to history. Problems of acculturation and, alas!, pseudophilosophies of metahistory, psychoanalysis, psychohistory, depth psychology, sociologism, quantitative analysis, empiricism, neo-positivism, existentialism, even brands of "historical nihilism" have arisen with special force during the post-1945 period, and, obviously, some of them have not been alien to modern and contemporary Italian historical consciousness. But they have not become dominant or principal themes of practical historiographical activity. Despite, or perhaps better, because of the realistic and eclectic character of Italian historical methodology, the search for historical truth has proceeded in contemporary Italy quite freely but not without a sense of direction, this side of the real, the acutest, problems of social life past and present, but not without promising *aperture* (openings) toward the future "city of man." The autonomy of history as a "science" of life and an "art" of the spirit has been firmly maintained in contemporary Italian historical practice, but it has remained the autonomy of a fertile and productive intellectual community working within the larger society of Western and cosmopolitan historiographical practitioners endeavoring to understand and, possibly, to help change the world.

Bibliographical Note

There is no alternative to (and no apology necessary for) this relatively concise Bibliographical Note. The kind of essay on contemporary Italian historiography I have felt obliged to present under constraints of space if not of time has practically forced me to give up any idea or attempt at including the traditional, footnoted reference and documentary apparatus. Had I proceeded with that form, the Notes would have overwhelmed the text not only in terms of length and size but, perhaps worse, in knotty particulars and complexities. I believe the text of the essay speaks clearly for itself, unburdened by unnecessary bibliographic cargo. Here I believe it sufficient to call attention under several special rubrics to the barest bibliographical references which any reader or student of goodwill might want to seek out for him- or herself in order to make palpable acquaintance with ''the real thing''—the products of contemporary Italian historiography.

1. The direct quotations of the passages by Momigliano and Salvemini are to be found as follows: Arnaldo Momigliano, *Essays in Ancient and Modern Historiography* (Middletown, Conn., 1977), p. 373. The whole of Momigliano's book is worth every effort to find and read carefully. Gaetano Salvemini, *Opere,* 9: *Carteggi,* 1 (Milan, 1968), I, 325.

2. For the works in print in 1976 by the historians referred to throughout the essay, see Associazione Italiana Editori, *Bibliografia: Catalogo dei Libri in Commercio 1976,* 3 vols. (Milan, 1976–1977). The three huge, carefully, scientifically prepared volumes render consultation easy under the triple rubric of authors, titles of books, and subjects.

3. The most useful and illuminating series of critical essays on Italian historiography from 1945 to 1970 (despite the title of the volumes) is in Franco Valsecchi and Giuseppe Martini, eds., *La storiografia italiana negli ultimi venti anni,* 2 vols. (Milan, 1970). They contain the revised and, in most cases, elaborated papers presented at the Perugia Congress of Italian Historians in October 1967. For a summary report on the congress, see A. William Salomone, ''A Report . . . to the President of the Society for Italian Historical Studies,'' in *Nuova Rivista Storica* (1968), pp. 423–29.

4. For general historical and bibliographical critiques, see *Itinerari: Rivista Bimestrale di Storia, Letteratura e Società. Prospettive storiche in Italia. Omaggio a Gaetano Salvemini,* nos. 22, 23, 24 (December 1956), particularly the essays by Ugo Azzoni, Piero Pieri, Fausto Fonzi, Enzo Tagliacozzo, and Aldo Garosci. Luigi Bulferetti, *Introduzione alla storiografia* (Milan, 1965), contains excellent bibliographical references on pp. 85–97. On the theories and practice of Italian historiography, see further Arnaldo Momigliano, *Studies in Historiography* (New York and Evanston, Ill., 1966); Albino Babolin, ed., *Le Scienze umane in Italia, oggi* (Bologna, 1971), particularly Paolo Brezzi's essay ''La Storia''; Federico Chabod, *Lezioni del metodo storico* (Bari, 1972); Delio Cantimori, *Studi di storia* (Turin, 1959), and his *Conversando di storia* (Bari, 1967); Pietro Piovani, *Filosofia e storia delle idee* (Bari, 1965); Furio Diaz, *Storicismi e storicità* (Florence, 1956); Eugenio Garin, *La Filosofia come sapere storico* (Bari, 1959); Cesare Vasoli, *Tra cultura e ideologia* (Milan, 1961); Nicola Badaloni, *Marxismo come storicismo* (Milan, 1962); and Aldo Garosci, *Pensiero politico e storiografia moderna* (Pisa, 1954), particularly pp. 193–273, which contain a very famous and polemical series of articles on *totalitarismo* and *storicismo* in the thought of Antonio Gramsci. On Salvemini and his influence, see A. William Salomone, *Italy in the Giolittian Era* (Philadelphia, 1960), pp. 117–69, and ''Salvemini e Giolitti,'' in *Rassegna Storica Toscana* 4, no. 2 (April–June 1958): 121–51; Ernesto Sestan, ed., *Atti del Convegno su Gaetano Salvemini—Firenze 8/10 novembre 1975* (Milan, 1977). On Chabod, see A. William Salomone, ''Federico Chabod: Portrait of a Master Historian,'' in H. A. Schmitt, ed., *Historians of Modern Europe* (Baton Rouge, La., 1971), pp. 255–90. Finally, on Croce, see his self-edited last compendium of his works published the year before his death in 1952 under the title *Filosofia-Poesia-Storia* (Milan and Naples, 1951), and the famous, beautiful, ''commemorative'' essay by Federico Chabod, ''Croce storico,'' in *Rivista Storica Italiana* 64, no. 4 (1952): 473–530; Gianfranco Contini, *L'influenza culturale di Benedetto Croce* (Naples, 1957); and Gennaro Sasso, *Benedetto Croce: La ricerca della dialettica* (Naples, 1875).

5. For brief summary surveys, in English, see Claudio Pavone, "Italy: Trends and Problems," in *Journal of Contemporary History* 2, No. 1 (1967): 49–77; Roberto Vivarelli, "Italy 1919–1921: The Current State of Research," in *Journal of Contemporary History* 2, no. 1 (1968): 103–12; Marino Berengo, "Italian Historical Scholarship Since the Fascist Era," in *Daedalus* (Spring, 1971): 469–84. For a critical biblio-historiographical source on socialism, see Leo Valiani, *Questioni di storia del socialismo* (Turin, 1975). On "Catholic" historiography, Guido Verucci et al., "Storia del cattolicesimo, della Chiesa, e del movimento cattolico italiano nell'età contemporanea," in *Quaderni Storici,* No. 26 (May-August 1974): 569–643. On Marxist historiography and historians, see the famous critique of the Gramscian interpretation of the Risorgimento and the aftermath by Rosario Romeo, *Risorgimento e capitalismo* (Bari, 1959), and the countercritiques it aroused, in Alberto Caracciolo, ed., *La formazione dell'Italia industriale* (Bari, 1963). Furio Diaz, *La Storiografia di indirizzo marxista in Italia negli ultimi quindici anni,* a reprint from *Rivista critica di storia della filosofia* 3 (1961). On Ernesto Ragionieri, Paolo Spriano, and Giuliano Procacci, see Giorgio Napolitano, "I conti con le proprie leggende," in *Rinascita,* No. 43 (3 November 1978): 23–24. For reinterpretations of the Risorgimento, see Walter Maturi, *Interpretazioni del Risorgimento* (Turin, 1962). On Cantimori, see Eugenio Garin, *Intellettuali italiani del XX secolo* (Rome, 1974), pp. 171–213. On Franco Venturi, see, for his contribution to the nineteenth-century Russian revolutionary intelligentsia, Alexander Gerschenkron, "Franco Venturi on Russian Populism," in *The American Historical Review* 78, No. 4 (October 1973): 969–86. The following studies by Venturi are easily accessible and worthy of study: *Settecento riformatore* (Turin, 1962); *Utopia and Reform in the Enlightenment* (Cambridge, 1970); *Italy and the Enlightenment* (New York, 1972); *Roots of Revolution,* trans. by Francis Haskell (New York, 1960).

6. The new, monumental, and problematical Einaudi *Storia d'Italia,* issued as 11 tomes in 6 vols. (Turin, 1972–1976) should be consulted by all students of Italian history who wish to gain a direct sense of what is novel and what is traditional in modern historiography. The work is extremely rich in the parts which, if the paradox does not prove too shocking, do not add to a similarly plausible or recognizable whole. Nevertheless, and despite its persistent and, in certain sections or volumes (those, for instance, on the political and cultural developments of the nineteenth and twentieth centuries assigned to, respectively, Ernesto Ragionieri and Alberto Asor Rosa) pervasive neo-Marxist bias, the Einaudi *Storia d'Italia* constitutes one of the most ambitious innovations in contemporary Italian historical scholarship.

14 YASUSHI YAMANOUCHI

Japan

General Setting

A unique feature of Japan's modern history lies in the fact that it was the only country in Asia that succeeded in establishing a capitalistic economy capable of competing with the economies of the advanced Western countries. Moreover, it has experienced powerful economic growth under this capitalistic system.

The development of modern Japan faced many problems from its start because capitalism, which was originally born in the Western world and developed there as the result of a prolonged historical process, was brought into an Asian country from the outside.[1]

Certainly, at the end of the Tokugawa period (1603–1868) Japan had already developed some of the preliminary conditions which would be necessary for the establishment of a capitalistic economy. However, the establishment of the Meiji government (1868) can best be explained not as the result of the natural growth of these inner potentials but rather as the result of the self-reformation of the old ruling class. The old ruling class, already under pressure from peasant uprisings, grasped the chance of self-reformation when faced with the serious national crisis brought on by Western intrusion from the outside. The interaction between the elements of the capitalist system which was brought into Japan from the outside as a result of decisions made by the old ruling class and the workings of certain preexisting internal social, economic, and cultural tendencies in Japanese society was bound to cause sharp tensions.

The development of historical studies in Japan cannot be viewed in isolation from these characteristics of modern Japanese history. The importance of this interaction can be seen from the following.

1. It has been the central concern of Japanese historians to make clear the relationship between endogenous factors and exogenous ones in modern Japanese history. Among the impacts from outside—economic as well as cultural—those coming from Western Europe and America had the greatest influence. In the methodology of historical studies, too, Western influences have been great. But the Russian Revolution in 1917 and the Chinese Revolution in 1949 also elicited extraordinary responses from intellectuals, and the shock of these events left clear traces on historical studies.

2. After the Meiji Restoration, Japan underwent speedy economic growth and experienced huge social change, even though it continued to keep the traditional base at bottom. As the result of these circumstances, the study of socioeconomic history played a central role. This does not mean, of course, that there were not superb contributions in histories of thought, politics, and culture.[2] What should be noted here is that the lively and pioneering propositions which led to methodological changes in historical studies usually came from socioeconomic history. As will be mentioned later, in recent times this primacy of socioeconomic history is losing its former strength.

3. The primacy of socioeconomic history was firmly related to the primacy of Marxism in methodology. It should be pointed out, however, that a considerable number of historians who were affected by Marx also showed a great interest in Max Weber. For them, the acceptance of the scholarly system of Weber did not necessarily mean they were employing it as a countertheory opposed to Marxism. On the contrary, they studied Weber as a complement to Marx, and vice versa.[3]

Starting Point—Controversies on Japanese Capitalism (1930–1945)

The controversies about Japanese capitalism in the 1930s provided the methodological framework for historical studies of modern Japan (see in the bibliography *Controversies on Japanese Capitalism*). This controversy was created by the extraordinarily unstable social conditions which were manifested internationally by the Russian Revolution and the Great Depression of 1929 and domestically by intensified class antagonism and the rise of the fascist movement (on fascism in Japan, see M. Maruyama, 1957).

The persons who took part in these controversies expected, though vaguely, that there would soon be a social revolution in Japan which would be similar to that in Russia. Concerning the character of this coming revolution, however, the participants were divided fundamentally into two groups. One group, the *Rōnō* (labor and farmer) school, insisted that the character of the coming revolution would be essentially socialistic. According to them, the pivotal task of revolution would be the socialization of financial capital represented by the big *zaibatsus*[4] (H. Yamakawa, 1927; K. Inomata, 1929). The other group, the *Kōza* (lectures) school, asserted that the revolutionary task required the elimination of the remaining feudal strata, especially parasitic landlords who were an important part of the social base of the *Tennō-sei* (emperor system). In short, the *Rōnō* school assumed that the bourgeois revolution had already taken place, whereas the *Kōza* school believed that a bourgeois revolution was still necessary.

This is not the place to judge which of these two groups understood the contemporary historical circumstances better. But it is certain that the ideas of the *Kōza* school were far more sensitive to the interaction of both endogenous and exogenous factors in the history of modern Japan. As the result of this, the analysis of Japanese capitalism by the *Kōza* school was much more influential than that of the *Rōnō* school in the studies of modern Japanese history.

Moritarō Yamada

M. Yamada's *The Analysis of Japanese Capitalsm* (1934) succeeded in representing most systematically the theoretical standpoint of the *Kōza* school (M. Yamada, 1934). He had started with the study of "the theory of reproduction" (M. Yamada, 1931) which was contained in the second volume of Marx's *Das Kapital* (K. Marx, 1885). The aim of this study was essentially to make clear the conditions of equilibrium in the capitalistic system of production and to seek the causes of the breakdown of this equilibrium at a time of economic crisis.

Yamada later compared Marx's theory of reproduction, which fitted the socioeconomic formation of England in mid-nineteenth century, with the theories of F. Quesnay and K. Wittfogel (F. Quesnay, 1758; K. Wittfogel, 1931). Quesnay provided a suggestive model which influenced both Marx and Wittfogel and analyzed the economic formation of French feudal society on the eve of the Revolution. Wittfogel studied the structure of Chinese Mandarin society. Carefully studying their models which represented the economic formation of three different societies, Yamada developed the idea of utilizing the tables of reproduction as a theoretical tool for historical comparison and analysis (M. Yamada, 1935). Japanese capitalism established its structure of reproduction as a result of an industrial revolution which took place between the Sino-Japanese War (1894–1895) and the Russo-Japanese War (1904–1905). Yet, according to Yamada, the structure of reproduction in Japanese capitalism was quite different from the model Marx presented in *Das Kapital*.

First, Marx's model was based on a historical analysis of England, a country which had undergone its bourgeois revolution in the seventeenth century. In addition, Marx's theory of reproduction presumes that the growth of the capitalistic mode of production in agriculture had already taken place. But in Japan, capitalism continued to keep at its base the semifeudal and petty-peasant agriculture. Yamada described the landlord-peasant relationship, which was accompanied by extravagantly high rents in kind and personal subordination, as "debtserfic." Contrary to this, T. Kushida insisted in his definitive statement of the *Rōnō* school's theory on agrarian problems that the landlord-peasant relationship was essentially to be explained by the process of market competition (T. Kushida, 1931).

Second, while opening agriculture to the market economy, the Meiji government exacted a repressive land tax which was similar in impact to the feudal rent in the Tokugawa period. This land tax, which was passed on to the peasant by way of charging exploitative rents, functioned as the financial means for the new government to build up a repressive military-police structure. In this process, a part of the merchant class was appointed to collaborate with the state policy, and this group later grew into the financial-industrial *zaibatsu* concerns.[5] Of course, there was the growth of private industrial capital, especially in the textile industries (cotton and silk), and this caused the reformation of the mode of production into a capitalistic one (reorganization of production). Yet this reorganization of production, according to Yamada, was nothing but a subordinate phenomenon which depended upon the movement of the military-industrial center (pivot of the reorganization of production), which was centralized and controlled by the state. The character of the Japanese industrial revolution, in this sense, was "perversive" compared to that of the precedent cases in Western countries, where the leading part was played by small private capital supplied by the industrial middle class and the conditions for the rise of production-goods industries were created by the earlier development of consumer-goods industries.

Third, the constrictive and militaristic features of Japanese capitalism could not help but bring various kinds of distortions. They restricted, on the one hand, the enlargement of the domestic market, and on the other hand, encouraged Japan's tendencies to expand economically abroad. Japan had to earn foreign currency necessary for industrialization by exporting silk, tea, and other products to the advanced countries. This brought about its commercial and financial dependency on imperialistic Western forces, represented by the United Kingdom and the United States, with which it had originally intended to compete. Thus, it had to find its way hastily into the neighboring Asian countries in order to compensate for foreign currency deficits. This early intrusion in Asian markets was necessary also for securing iron and coal for military industries. Yamada suggested that imperialism in Japan started not as the result of the concentration of production (V. I. Lenin, 1917) or the growth of financial capital (R. Hilferding, 1910), but as the effect of the establishment of nationally centralized military industries.

Fourth, this "perversive" character in the structure of reproduction of Japanese capitalism appeared also in the industrial organization. After the Industrial Revolution, a very large number of small domestic industries with miserable labor conditions existed. Even in the large-scale machine industries, "half-serfic" industrial relations accompanied by personal subordination were still dominant.

As may be seen from these explanations, Yamada considered that Japanese capitalism was cast into a unique "mold" which was quite different from that of Western capitalism. However, he did not consider the "mold" as being fixed without any dynamic possibilities for historical development—although many scholars (for example, I. Sakisaka, 1935; T. Ōuchi, 1962) misunderstood Yamada's writings on this point. Rather, he confirmed that capitalism was necessarily developing even in this strictly conservative "mold," and that within this development, the formation of a stubborn laboring class was advancing inevitably. The growing social tensions after 1929 produced a link between labor movements in urban districts and peasant struggles in rural areas. With the appearance of this political alliance between workers and peasants, Japanese capitalism with its unique "mold" fell into a crisis which would lead to its dissolution. Yamada predicted that "the dissolution of the mold" would necessarily be followed by a socialist revolution.[6]

Shisō Hattori

In his article on the Meiji Restoration published in 1933, Hattori presented a strong implicit critique of the works of M. Yamada, Y. Hirano, and G. Hani (S. Hattori, 1933, 1952). From this time on, controversies among the scholars of the *Kōza* school, in which the rivalry between Hattori and the others was most prominent, became the driving force for the methodological advancement of historical studies in Japan.

Hattori started his career as a Marxist theoretician when he published an influential analysis of the writings of Russian materialism as systemized by Lenin and Deborin (V. I. Lenin, 1909; A. Deborin, 1925). After the appearance of Hattori's essay, the writings of Lenin and Deborin began to have an overwhelming influence among Japanese Marxists. But this was not without its defects. For example, facing the severe criticism of Hattori and the others, Kiyoshi Miki, a philosopher of much originality, who had been endeavoring to introduce into Marxism the recent philosophical current represented by Dilthey and Heidegger (W. Dilthey, 1922; M. Heidegger, 1927; K. Miki, 1928, 1929, 1932), was forced to retreat from the Marxist circle. This incident is thought to have been a cause of the loss of flexibility in the thought of Japanese Marxism afterwards.[7]

Notwithstanding Hattori's impressive initial appearance as an advocate of Russian Marxism, he did not stop there. In his *Treatises on History* in 1935, he strongly criticized the crude notions expressed by some Japanese Marxists, for example H. Aikawa (H. Aikawa, 1935). Unlike Aikawa, who insisted that the logical construction of *Das Kapital* should itself be the methodological standard for historical studies, Hattori stated that even the study of socioeconomic history had its own theme, separated from the logic of economics. Thus he opened new possibilities for Marxist historical studies (S. Hattori, 1935).

Hattori questioned the theories of Yamada and the others because they could not offer a reasonable explanation for Japan's exceptional success in capitalistic development as an Asian country. Was this not in clear contrast with the historical experiences of the other Asian countries such as India and China? (S. Hattori, 1952) He began to believe that there must have been an immanent and transitional "uklad"[8] in Japanese society during the last years of the Tokugawa period and that this uklad later transformed itself into industrial capital, breaking down the feudalistic social order. Selecting "Manufaktur" as this transitional uklad from the historical description of *Das Kapital* (K. Marx, 1867), Hattori asserted that there were "Manufaktur" businesses in the last years of the Tokugawa period. These were, he said, the equivalents to the textile "Manufakturen" which had been the forerunners of the industrial capital in Western societies. Collecting the materials on "Manufaktur" businesses, he later became one of the pioneers of industrial history in modern Japan (S. Hattori, 1934*a*, 1934*b*).

Hattori's new interpretation of economic history entailed a clash with others, even with those in political history. The opposition between them appeared most explicitly in their interpretations of the character of the *Jiyū Minken* (Freedom and People's Rights) movement in the 1880s. Hattori argued that "Manufaktur" businesses were managed mainly by the wealthy peasants who at the same time used to be usurers or parasitic landlords. Paying attention to the latter side of their character, Hirano, who was an eminent Marxist scholar on the history of modern Japanese politics, claimed that the *Jiyū Minken* movement, the leading part of which was carried by *gōnō* (wealthy peasants), was originally limited in its militancy and did not have the intention to break the outer frame of oligarchic *Tennō-sei* absolutism (Y. Hirano, 1933, 1934). Contrary to this, Hattori insisted that *gōnōs* were small capitalist producers with their base in the village industries, and that although they had the inclination to be parasitic landlords, their zeal to achieve democratic reform, at that time, should not be underestimated (S. Hattori, 1933, 1949, 1955).

Opposing Yamada and the others who stressed the dark features of Japanese society, characterizing it as semifeudal or as Asiatic, Hattori depicted the dawn of modern Japan with its intrinsic possibility for economic and political progress.[9] It might not be too much to say that almost all such noteworthy studies which appeared after World War II attempted to harmonize the theoretical contradictions embraced in the *Kōza* school, including not only S. Tōyama and K. Inoue's representative textbooks on modern Japanese history but also G. Fujita, T. Naramoto, and others' specialized works on economic or political history (S. Tōyama, 1955; K. Inoue, 1951; G. Fujita, 1948; T. Naramoto, 1948).

Main Currents After the War

Hisao Ōtsuka and the Marx-Weber Controversy

A distinctive feature of historical studies in postwar Japan was that the scholars of European economic history gathering around H. Ōtsuka provided many important theoretical insights to scholars in all fields of historical investigation and developed an influential set of criteria for comparative historical studies. Among the contributions to the so-called Ōtsuka school, K. Takahashi's study of the French Revolution and T. Matsuda's study of the German March Revolution were pioneering (K. Takahashi, 1950; T. Matsuda, 1948). Ōtsuka's study of European economic history was affected deeply by the prewar controversies on Japanese capitalism, and his theoretical perspective was close to Hattori's. However, Ōtsuka's interpretation of Marx's philosophy was most influenced by K. Miki's works (H. Ōtsuka, 1967). As we have already seen, K. Miki was the scholar who had been criticized by Hattori in his earliest works. Miki tried to reconstruct historical materialism less as economic determinism than as a study of man—as a hermeneutical phenomenology—by connecting Dilthey and Heidegger with Marx. This effort on Miki's part served as a guide for Ōtsuka, who wished to establish, by connecting Marx and Weber, a unique methodology for the study of history.

Accepting the theory of W. Sombart, Ōtsuka at first considered the transformation of commercial capital to industrial capital to be the normal course of the development of capitalism (W. Sombart, 1902; H. Ōtsuka, 1935). Later he revised his thinking as a result of his elaborate study of the history of joint-stock companies, including his comparative work on the East India Companies in the Netherlands and in England (H. Ōtsuka, 1938) and his careful analysis of Weber's *Protestant Ethic* (M. Weber, 1904a). Ōtsuka developed a new thesis which stated that in England, where a genuine modern society appeared autogenously for the first time, the development of capitalism was carried out mainly by the industrial middle class in rural areas, including farmers as well as artificers.

His *Introduction to the Economic History of Modern Europe* (H. Ōtsuka, 1951–1952), in which he demonstrated his new thesis with a wealth of materials (and in brilliant style!), was the most influential book among many noteworthy works in historical studies after the war. Many people believed it necessary for the future of democracy in Japan to remove the traditional elements in the countryside which had been the social base of *Tennō-sei* fascism, and for these people this book had an enormous impact—even though there were many incessant critics of Ōtsuka among orthodox Marxists.

Among the sections in this book, the one entitled "The Country Clothier and the Corporate Town Clothier: Two Antagonistic Types of Clothiers" was the most compelling. The corporate town clothiers had been exploiting the small artificers through a putting-out system (*Verlagssystem*) that controlled the guild organizations, and the country clothiers had been developing free and independent "Manufaktur" businesses in rural areas without troublesome guild regulations. Comparing these two antagonistic types of clothiers, Ōtsuka reached the conclusion that the former had supported Tudor and Stuart absolutism and the latter had been the backbone of the bourgeois revolution.

Later, stimulated by Marx's famous posthumous work (K. Marx, 1857–1858), he published a noteworthy book called *Essentials of the Theories on the Traditional Communities*. In this book, Ōtsuka attempted to complement Marx's theory by incorporating relevant concepts from Max Weber (H. Ōtsuka, 1955, 1964; M. Weber, 1904b). He stated that the formation of modern society in Western Europe was brought about not by the activities of commercial capital which exploited both sides of the communities, utilizing the price differentials between them (*beiderseitige Exploitation;* cf. K. Marx, 1894), but by the internal commercial exchange which evolved among the producers in the community. He categorized the latter type of exchange as the local market area against the former interarea trade between local communities.[10]

It is evident that Ōtsuka's study in European economic history owes much to Marx. However, the ultimate basis of his academic position is, I believe, derived rather from Max Weber. The fact that he learned a great deal from Weber's sociology of religion and, making full use of the knowledge thus acquired, wrote several very intriguing works, testifies to this statement. Ōtsuka's unique reading of Marx may serve as further proof: rather than accepting Marx at face value, he found in Marx some aspects that can have an affinity with Weber, and by extending those aspects to a maximum degree, he succeeded in drawing a very singular picture of Marx. As is evident to a careful reader, even those meth-odological categories which he developed for his study of economic history—commercial capital versus industrial capital; town clothier versus country cloth-ier; industrial middle class; local market area—are inextricably related to a cat-egory in Weber's sociology of religion, namely, the *asketischer Berufsmensch*.

Naturally enough, Ōtsuka's methodology has been subjected to severe criti-cism from self-proclaimed orthodox Marxists (S. Toyoda et al., 1948). How-ever, at the same time, some doubts were also voiced among non-Marxist historians. Shirō Masuda, who is noted for his eminent works on European medieval history, maintained that a deep abyss exists between the Marxist sys-tem, on the one hand, which is built on universal theories of economics, and that of Weber, on the other, who sought to establish a methodology for com-parative culture, based on his understanding of the historical individual who is a unique product of Western Europe (see Correspondence: Ōtsuka and Masuda). Yoshiaki Uchida, renowned not only as a historian of ancient Europe but also for his works on Weber, reveals some very subtle disagreements with Ōtsuka. Uchida stresses a marked difference between Marx and Weber: the former tried to extricate regularity in the basic material and economic processes, whereas the latter strove to construct ideal types of various cultures in terms of historical singularity of spirit and consciousness. He holds that in contrast to Marx's meth-odology, which is influenced by the dynamics of eighteenth- and nineteenth-century natural science, Weber's methodology has as its background the devel-opment of probabilistic natural science in the twentieth century. In this sense, Uchida thinks that Weber's methodology has an advantage over Marx's (Yosh-iaki Uchida, 1972, especially the Introductory Essay).

Masao Maruyama, Shō Ishimoda, and Rekishigaku Kenkyu Kai

Among the several currents in historical studies in postwar Japan, the work of the Rekishigaku Kenkyu Kai (the Historical Science Society)[11] is very im-portant. This society is still the influential center of the dissenting historians.[12] The golden age of this society, however, was the period immediately following the end of the war. The theme of its general meeting of 1949 was "The Essential Contradictions of Each Social Formation." Among the main reports, S. Mat-sumoto's discussion of the primitive and ancient societies, based on the above-mentioned posthumous work of Marx, and K. Takahashi's[13] arguments on the feudal society attracted the audience. The reports of this general meeting were published by the society in a special issue entitled *The Essential Law of World History* (Rekishigaku Kenkyu Kai, 1949).

But the conceptions aired at this meeting were questioned as early as the general meeting of the following year, primarily by scholars of Chinese history (Rekishigaku Kenkyu Kai, 1950). The presentations at the meeting in 1949 had been based on a Marxist interpretation of history, and they described the history of the world as a developmental stage process which is composed of such eras as the ancient Orient, the Mediterranean world, feudal Europe, and modern European capitalism and which finally reaches the stage of socialism. They affirmed that the Marxian theory of history is not confined solely to one of class struggle, but rather that it also considers the community as a network of interrelationships among producers. This affirmation came to have great impact on later studies in history. However, when world history is interpreted as such a developmental process, the history of Asia appears only as one which belongs to the most undeveloped stage, placed at the very beginning of the process. The stage theory of Marx may be effective in accounting for the shaping of modern Europe, but there is serious doubt as to whether it can explain the history of various areas of Asia, especially that of China. (Japan may be considered an exception, since it resembled Europe in its pattern of development.)

In 1949 the Communist party emerged victorious in the Chinese civil war, and this event exerted a great influence on the current historical studies in Japan. The new situation revealed the fact that the former studies of Chinese history, including the spectacular debates over "the Asiatic mode of production," [14] were not without defects. Facing the simultaneous success of both nationalistic liberation from imperialism and socialistic reformation of old society, scholars of Chinese history felt it necessary to search in the history of China for reasons why the Chinese communists were able to carry out a successful revolution.

In order to explain the Chinese Revolution satisfactorily, it was necessary for Japanese historians to reconsider their theoretical concepts and conduct much new empirical research. In studying the historical materials of Japan or China with their knowledge acquired through Western education, it was not necessarily difficult to analyze the difference between Asian and European societies if one depended on the explanations given by Hegel, Marx, Weber and others (G. W. F. Hegel, 1830–1831; K. Marx, 1857–1858; M. Weber, 1916*b*). However, their theoretical framework could not account for the inherent possibility of any independent, uniquely dynamic development in Asian societies.

Mao Tse-tung demanded of intellectuals that they should strictly serve the people, and he established his strategic base not in the advanced cities but in the backward villages. His highly ethical Marxism surprised the Japanese historians, and his strategy seemed itself to be a severe criticism of Japanese intellectuals who were accustomed to consider the Western city culture to be the most advanced. [15] In these circumstances, the impact of the Chinese Revolution on historical studies led to a strong political response in the academic world, even before scholars could search for valid answers to the key questions raised by the new situation. The movement called "The Historical Science for the Nation" strongly reflected this contemporary situation and the Rekishigaku Kenkyu Kai became the center of this movement.

Here let us take up the case of S. Ishimoda, who was the most influential promoter of the movement. His first work, *The Making of the Medieval World* (1944), was a solid study about the growth of the *bushi* (knight) class which made up the new medieval order that broke down the aristocratic hierarchy of the ancient world (S. Ishimoda, 1944). This excellent study, which was prepared during wartime through the discussions in the secret circle of a Marxist study group on history, became the starting point for his followers. Later, Ishimoda explained the main focus of his study in this way: he tried to determine the reasons why, on the one hand, India and China could not get rid of their "Asiatic despotism," eventually becoming victims of Western imperialism, and why, on the other hand, Japan could succeed in building a modern capitalistic society in Asia. He sought the historical origin of this difference in the rise of a medievalistic feudalism in Japan which was comparable to that in Western Europe (S. Ishimoda, 1946).

The theme of Ishimoda's study in socioeconomic history was the same, in essence, as that of Maruyama in his *Studies in the Intellectual History of Tokugawa Japan* (M. Maruyama, 1952). Maruyama detected the birth of the rationalistic way of thinking in the ideas of Sorai Ogyū, the leading Confucian scholar of the Tokugawa period. Like Ishimoda, Maruyama found that this tendency toward modernization of thought was comparable to that in Europe. Maruyama asserted that the thought of S. Ogyū showed the birth of a preliminary potential for the Meiji Restoration. To appreciate the meaning of the studies that Ishimoda or Maruyama produced during the war, the following comment by Maruyama should be considered. The advocates of fascism stressed the necessity of "overcoming" and "negating" the modern thought of Europe or America, and by stirring the antagonistic feeling against Western culture,[16] they repressed people's criticism against the war of aggression. In these circumstances, said Maruyama, stressing "the modern elements in the Meiji Restoration" or "the maturity of modernizing elements in Tokugawa society" meant building up spiritually "the base of resistance" against fascism[17] (M. Maruyama, 1952, postscript to the Japanese edition; author's introduction to the English edition).

It was natural that the orientation of the historians had to change after the defeat of fascism and the success of the Chinese Revolution. Maruyama, turning his concern to the distortions generated in modern Japanese society compared to the Western world, took up the lack of an individualistic ethic of responsibility in Japanese political—and social—phenomena (M. Maruyama, 1957). Outwardly, his postwar judgment about Japanese society might seem to be opposite to that of his wartime viewpoint, but a serious reader will not miss the continuity in his fundamental attitude. This is also manifested in Maruyama's ambivalent attitudes toward Marxism. In defending the democracy which was planted in

Japan after the war, as well as in securing broad channels of intellectual exchange, he has never relinquished his bonds with the Marxists. At the same time, however, he has never stopped criticizing dogmatism—Stalinism or the leftist *Tennō* system—which is contained in the social system of the Soviet Union and the organization of the Japanese Communist party. The idea of the "individualistic ethic of responsibility" served as his criterion of judgment in analyzing fascism and Japanese society as well as the problems of the socialist system.

Compared to the liberalism of Maruyama, the standpoint of Ishimoda, as a Marxist historian, was much more difficult. After developing a brilliant method to analyze ancient national literature in 1948 (S. Ishimoda, 1948), he took up a new problem which was quite different from that of his first work. The essays collected in *Discovery of History and Nation* were proof of the Marxist scholar's struggle to include the problem of nationalism in historical studies (S. Ishimoda, 1952–1953). Previously, following the orthodox method of Marxism, he had taken up the rise of a new class which would play the leading role in a new society. But in the new book he concentrated his attention on the daily life of common people, and quoting Maxim Gorki, the Russian novelist, he insisted on the necessity of discovering the historical meaning of national traditions which had been breathing in folklore through generations. It must be admitted that these ideas were missed in the class conception of history by orthodox Marxism. In these new propositions of Ishimoda, we may recognize not only the influence of Gorki but also the influence of the ideas of K. Yanagida, who was the greatest folklorist in Japan.[18]

However, Ishimoda could not be free from the opportunism of utilizing academic studies for the political mobilization of scholars. After a period of short enthusiasm, "The Historical Science for the Nation Movement" collapsed. In 1956 Ishimoda admitted errors in the idealistic propensity of his thought and acknowledged the necessity of returning to the standpoint of materialism and positivism (S. Ishimoda, 1956). Notwithstanding the prompt bankruptcy of the movement, there were valuable propositions in his arguments. He emphatically stressed the importance to historical study of analyzing the mental structure of common people.

Concurrently with the bankruptcy of the movement, *Shōwa Shi* (The History of the Showa Period), written by three Marxist historians, was published (S. Tōyama, 1955). It was widely read but also faced serious criticism. The focus of this criticism concerned the author's oversimplification of history with "the abstract ideology of the class struggle" and the indifference to "the spiritual agony" of people who were distressed with the cruel disturbance of the age (see "Reviews on Historical Studies," item 3, p. 277). Many of these drawbacks might be evaded if the propositions of Ishimoda were correctly developed.

The Rekishigaku Kenkyu Kai experienced a new swell of popularity at the general meeting of 1961, which publicized the study of "Modern Japan in World History—The Growth of Capitalism and Its International Moments" as its common theme (Rekishigaku Kenkyu Kai, 1961). Energized by this new swell, the society reorganized itself, adopting "The Reformation of the Ideas on World History" as its long-range study program. Yet it is hard to say that this new research plan yielded fruitful results.

New Currents (1960 and After)

Heralds of the Change—Shumpei Ueyama and the Theory of Modernization

Toward the end of the 1950s, the study of history in Japan started to disclose a new trend, not unrelated to the postwar reconstruction of the Japanese economy, and to its entry into the years of rapid growth. The persistent memories of the tragic war were gradually fading, and the reconstructed society encouraged historians to initiate a reassessment of Japanese history.

A series of studies on the Meiji Restoration by Shumpei Ueyama, a philosopher, marked the emergence of the new trend. Ueyama criticized Marxists of the *Kōza* school and Hisao Ōtsuka for their interpretation of the Meiji Restoration as a process led by feudal forces and asserted that it should rather be understood as a bourgeois revolution comparable to instances in the West. His unhesitating adoption of those expressions used by Marxist historians struck the reader as if he had signaled a revival of the Marxism of the *Rōnō* school. Being a non-Marxist, however, his originality lay rather in replacing the Marxian view of history based on a developmental stage scheme by a new one incorporating recent achievements in comparative geography and ecological botany. Instead of the Marxian scheme, which assumes class struggle as the motivating force of history, he insisted upon the explanatory power of a three-stage scheme composed of a natural society, an agricultural society, and an industrial society (S. Ueyama, 1961). Ueyama himself may have been unaware of this, but the presentation of this new scheme indicated a new direction in the interpretation of modern Japanese history: it is understood not so much as a process of contradiction-laden confrontation, but rather as one of remarkable growth aided by the technological development of an industrial society. He also rejected the idea that modern Japanese history is still traditional or distorted when compared to that of Western Europe; on the contrary, he pictured the former as quite comparable to the latter, which was formed through the Puritan and French revolutions. It may be worthwhile to note that this theory emerged during the time when American scholars, represented by E. O. Reischauer, J. W. Hall, M. B. Jansen, and R. N. Bellah, were vigorously asserting, at conferences and in journals, that Japan was indeed an exemplary case of successful modernization in Asia (cf. S. Kimbara, 1968).

But in light of the deep agony that the United States was suffering from the war in Vietnam, as well as of the rapid growth of Japanese economy which not only brought about material affluence but also rapid inflation and serious pollution, many Japanese historians could not but be doubtful as to the rosy future which modernization theories suggested. Thus the new trend in Japanese historical circles, in their effort to break through the stagnation caused by the study of economic history based upon Marxism of the *Kōza* school, addressed a fresh enterprise which attempted to reassess Japanese history by reaching deep down to the mentality of the Japanese people and by appreciating the thought and consciousness, not only of the intellectual elite, but also of the common people.

The Study Group of Tenkō (Recantation)

The excellent group study about *tenkō* by Shisō no Kagaku Kenkyu Kai (Institute for the Science of Thought) was one manifestation of this new current. Although the ideas of this group were mainly supplied by liberals, it should not be overlooked that some Marxists also took part in it and played a leading role. The study undertaken by this group was not concerned with the logical context of political thought such as liberalism or Marxism. What they carefully investigated was the way each intellectual, as an individual, coped with the hardships inflicted by the cruel oppression of fascism or how he failed and was drawn to recant. As a result of this valuable research, the relationship between Western thought, acquired as literary knowledge, and the traditional environment, such as family and nation, was brought to light, and moreover, reflections on the meaning and limitation of Western education in Japanese mental life were presented. With this study, an important gap in the works of orthodox Marxists, such as above-mentioned *Shōwa Shi,* was considerably filled (Shisō no Kagaku Kenkyu Kai, 1959–1962).

Daikichi Irokawa

Some historians who were the members of the Rekishigaku Kenkyu Kai and yet were dissatisfied with the main concerns of the society began to publish new works which explored the consciousness or thought of common people. *A Spiritual History of the Meiji Period* by D. Irokawa is a good example of these new efforts (D. Irokawa, 1964).

According to Irokawa, there were two poles in the mental configuration of modern Japanese society: one pole was "the thought of the base" and the other pole was "the thought of the apex." The making of these two poles, he said, could be explained through a study of the *Jiyū Minken* movement in the 1880s. Irokawa, who was a young friend of Hattori, inherited the ideas of the latter and reevaluated the character of the *Jiyū Minken*'s popular democracy as manifested in the *gōnō* manufacturers' behavior. He concluded that *gōnō* democracy was a counterforce against the governmental line of modernization from above. After the defeat of the *Jiyū Minken* movement in the latter half of the 1880s, however, *gōnōs* left the industrial life and followed the road of parasitic landlords. This caused the members in the movement to split into two groups. On one side, there were persons who became the leaders in the Japanese way of modernization. This type was well exemplified by Sohō Tokutomi, who later became a leading figure among nationalist writers. They responded actively to the call from above and joined in the activities of the new ruling order. Left on the other side were the poor people who had lost their lands during the severe depression caused by the deflation policy of Matsukata (minister of finance, 1881–1891) and who had gathered around the *Konmin Tō* (the Pauper party) at the last stage of the popular democracy movement.

The history of the popular democracy movement in the 1880s was nothing but the history of failure and defeat. Yet, Irokawa insists, this movement was epoch-making in the history of modern Japan, and the impact of the movement did not die but continued to live on in the consciousness of the common people. Thus he undertook in his study to explore "the latent possibilities" in the thought of the common people.

Irokawa's experiment was an attempt to transcend the framework developed by Maruyama, even though he himself used it as the starting point of his study. The two-polar configuration of Japanese modern thought had already been referred to by Maruyama. Yet Maruyama described this characteristic as "the law of structural imbalance" between the apex, which engaged in a ceaseless struggle to reach the pinnacle of world prominence, and the base with its tenacious roots of traditionalism (M. Maruyama, 1968: 144). Irokawa criticized Maruyama's understanding as one-sided because the latter described the consciousness of the common people only as an aspect of traditionalism. According to Irokawa, the initiative of the common people was innovative and even the oligarchic order of *Tennō-sei* could keep its existence only by absorbing it (D. Irokawa, 1970).

Yoshio Yasumaru

Y. Yasumaru is another brilliant figure who represented the new current.[19] He was also influenced by Marxist methodology in the earlier stage of his study. But later, he developed a much wider perspective in studying the religious mentality of the common people. He, like Irokawa, started with the study of the characteristics of peasant thought. At the end of the Tokugawa period, the luxurious customs born in big towns were brought into the country districts and, spreading like a malignant infectious disease, threatened the steadiness of village life. Before the crisis of the dissolution of the village order, a series of preachers appeared. They tried to rebuild the household of the peasantry, insisting on the ethics of thorough frugality and industry and helping the spontaneous endeavor of the peasants to recover. The teachings of these preachers were thoroughly secularized and had nothing like the Calvinist's belief of predestination which posited the existence of an absolute God over all creatures in this world (cf. M.

Weber, 1904*a*). However the influence of these teachings, with their emphasis on strict asceticism and the rejection of magic, was powerful enough to change the mentality of the peasants (Y. Yasumaru, 1974).

Yasumaru did not praise these changes in mentality without reservation. He did not approve of the vulgar utilitarianism of the teachings which urged that industry and filial submission would necessarily bring about materialistic re-munerations. This vulgar utilitarianism provided the preferable foundation for the ruling ideology of the Meiji state, which was expressed from above in the Edict of Education in 1890.

Yet "the primitive accumulation of the capital" (K. Marx, 1867), which pro-ceeded drastically in the 1880s and the 1890s, changed the situation. The intro-duction of machines and the elimination of the old handicrafts created a vast number of ruined paupers who were unable to support themselves, even though they desperately tried to work. Most of these paupers were just the people who endeavored to integrate themselves into the social order of the Meiji state by strictly following the teachings of the preachers. But they were cruelly rejected by the ruling order. From among these paupers, who had not the means to ex-press their thought because of their illiteracy and who were deserted by the in-tellectuals and political parties, not a few of the founders of the new popular religions appeared. Falling into fanaticism and possessed by native and magical gods, they conveyed the prophecies to their fellow people.

Yasumaru recognizes a tough militant figure against the ruling order in one of these prophets. Helped by a native god, Nao Deguchi, who was the founder of the *Ōmoto* (Origin of the World) sect, attacked the cruelty which accompanied the development of capitalism in Japan. With naive words, she preached on behalf of the lowest class of the society, who were deprived of the means to express their ideas (Y. Yasumaru, 1977).

Another conspicuous characteristic of the new current in historical studies is the impact of the folklore studies of K. Yanagida and his successors. For ex-ample, both Irokawa and Yasumaru often utilize not only the ideas of Yanagida himself but also the achievements of the Yanagida school represented by T. Sakurai and N. Miyata (T. Sakurai, 1962; N. Miyata, 1975).

This impact is not limited to the use in historical studies of the empirical findings of the folklorists but also is manifested in changes in the methodologies employed by Japanese historians. The scholars of the cultural sciences, including historians, tended to see history as a series of unique events. According to M. Weber, the epistemology of the cultural sciences is characterized deeply by the "once-ness" (*Einmaligkeit*) of historical events (M. Weber, 1903–1906). On the other hand, Yanagida was concerned mainly with historical phenomena which were repeated over and over again in the daily life of the common people (K. Yanagida, 1944).

Yanagida's unique approach to history may be considered as a reflection of his conservatism. Yet it is certain that in the traditional way of life there are sometimes very precious suggestions for us about the nature of the "perversions'' or ''alienation'' present in modern industrial societies. Using Yanagida's insights as a starting point, some historians are now beginning to reevaluate the meaning of tradition in historical development.

A Provisional Conclusion

Summing up the tendencies of historical studies which appeared after 1960, we may conclude that in contrast to the former focus on socioeconomic history, a new focus was formed which emphasized the history of the thought of common people.[20] The studies in this new field, absorbing insights from religious sociology and folklore, discovered a new historical dimension which was not explored by socioeconomic history based on the method of Marxism.[21] What is the importance of this new current?

First of all, it means that Japanese historical studies began to extricate themselves from the stage of a simple absorption of methodological stimuli imported from abroad and to seek historically relevant elements in Japan itself. The fact that some scholars began to choose the thought of the common people as their object of research, and that they also began to utilize the achievements of Japanese folklore studies, which were established by Kunio Yanagida, are both to be regarded as manifestations of such a trend. This phenomenon is nothing but a reflection of the realization that Western European societies can no longer be taken as a model for Japan now that the latter has already achieved a high degree of development as an industrial state. At the same time, only a small minority thinks that Russian and Chinese varieties of socialism indicate the direction in which Japan should change. Thus Japanese historical studies are directing themselves toward a rediscovery of the individuality which is endogenous to Japan. If, however, rediscovery of this individuality ends up stressing the difference between Japan and other countries, it will lead us nowhere, because individuality becomes relevant only in terms of the role it has played in Japan's historical participation in world history to date and of the meaning it will have in an increasingly important world network. The urgent task of Japanese historical studies is not to reject traditional historical methodologies of universal relevance—those of Marx and Weber and theories of modernization—but to appreciate the possibilities these methodologies may have and to amplify them through research on Japanese individuality. And in Yanagida's folklore studies, too, although they are based on Japanese materials, there are ample suggestions to common understanding of peoples of various nations in the world.

Now, with respect to a reappraisal of universal theories of history, what problems have been indicated by recent trends in Japanese historical studies? Here it should be remembered that in the former studies the common people had been depicted as the passive objects in history. Even in the works of Marxist historians, the common people were not usually the active subject but rather the defensive class who were suffering under the cruelty of the ruling order. In Marxist history, moreover, the common people sometimes appeared only as the means of the iron law of historical development. In the new current, however, the thought or consciousness of the common people has attracted the attention of scholars because they believe that such an approach has much to offer to those historians endeavoring to explain the dynamics of history. This does not necessarily mean that the subjectivity of the common people always functions along the lines of working toward a new reformed society. To the contrary, the subjectivity of the common people often functions as the solid base of the reactionary ruling order.

The discovery of these interesting but complicated facts seems to necessitate a reconsideration of the relationship between intellectuals and common people in history. Or rather, it might be recognized that the crisis in contemporary scholarship is reflected in this new concern of historical studies. It may not be too much to say that historical studies, which have long been developed by elitist intellectuals in the academic establishment and which have lost the lively concern with the actual problems in contemporary society, are deadlocked. Borrowing from Gouldner, who proposed "the sociology of sociology" (A. W. Gouldner, 1970), historians may now find it necessary to explore "the sociology of historical studies." How does Marxism, which has been—and still is—the influential methodology for historical studies in Japan, handle these new situations?

Notes

1. G. Hani skillfully analyzed the complex problems brought about by the intrusion of Western capitalism into Asia and compared the cases of India, China, and Japan. See Goro Hani, *Tōyō ni okeru Shihon Shugi no Keisei* (The Rise of Capitalism in the Orient) (1932).

2. This article deals mainly with the methodology of the study of modern Japanese history. The only exception is H. Ōtsuka's works which grew out of his investigation of European history. As to the general survey of historical studies in Japan, see the beginning of the bibliographical section, "Reviews of Historical Studies," items 1 to 13. For recent developments with regard to statistical studies in socioeconomic history, see the second part of item 9 and the following two special issues: *Atarashii Edo-jidai-shizō o motomete* (Searching for a New Interpretation of the Edo Period) (1977), edited by Shakai Keizai Shigaku Kai; *Explorations on Economic History* 15, no. 1 (1978).

3. Some American studies of Japanese modernization assert that Weber's theory can be employed as a countertheory to Marxism (see John M. Dower, ed., "Japan and the Uses of History," introductory essay to *Origins of the Modern Japanese State: Selected Writings of E. H. Norman* [1974], pp. 62 ff.). However, in Japanese historiography not a few writers have stressed the complementarity of the Marxian and Weberian perspectives. For elaboration of this latter point of view, see the arguments of H.Ōtsuka in this article. The following discussions are also valuable: Yoshihiko Uchida, "Nihon Shisōshi ni okeru Uēbā teki Mondai" (M. Weber in the Historiography of Japanese Thought) (1965), in his *Nihon Shihonshugi no Shisō Zō* (Variations of Thoughts in Japanese Capitalism); Yoshiaki Uchida, *Uēbā to Marukusu* (Weber and Marx) (1972); Takashima Zenya, *Marukus to Uēbā* (Marx and Weber) (1975).

4. *Zaibatsu* was a big financial concern which controlled many enterprises through holding shares. In this, *zaibatsu* was an equivalent to trust or cartel in Western societies. But it has some unique characteristics. (1) *Zaibatsu* was formed not as the result of competition in the free market

but rather through the support of state authority and state capital.(2) At the center of an oligarchic *zaibatsu* concern, there was a ruling clan. The relationship of the members in this clan was paternalistic, and the relationship between the members of this clan and the employees (including eminent directors of big enterprises) was similar to that of a feudalistic master-client nexus.

5. Scholars of the ·*Kōza* school considered that the transformation of commercial capital under the protection of the state should be sharply distinguished from the growth of industrial capital among middle-class producers. It is remarkable that they found the support for this argument not only in Marx and Lenin, but also in Weber; they drew in particular upon the following: Karl Marx, "Geschichtliches über das Kaufmannskapital," *Das Kapital*, Vol. 3 (1894); Vladimir Lenin, *Development of Capitalism in Russia* (1899); Max Weber, "Die protestantische Ethik und der Geist des Kapitalismus," *Archiv für Sozialwissenschaft und Sozialpolitik* 20 (1904); "Konfuzianismus und Taoismus," ibid., 41 (1916); "Hinduismus und Buddhismus," ibid. For example, see G. Hani, *Tōyō ni okeru Shihon Shugi no Keisei* (The Rise of Capitalism in the Orient) (1932). On the other hand, scholars of the *Rōnō* school argued that the transformation of commercial capitalism into industrial capitalism was the common rule for the development of capitalism both in Western societies and in Japan; see Takao Tsuchiya, *Nihon Shihon Shugi Ronshu* (Essays on Japanese Capitalism) (1937). For an interesting dialogue on this problem between Japanese and American scholars, see also "Discussion between Hisao Ōtsuka and Douglas C. North."

6. Yamada's prediction was too optimistic considering the ensuing historical process in which the worker and peasant movements were repressed by and/or absorbed into the militarist regime. Therefore, after the establishment of the militarist regime, scholars found it necessary to reformulate their concepts to explain this new situation. For examples of such attempts see Yasoji Kazahaya, *Nihon Shakai Siesaku Shi* (History of Social Policy in Japan) (1937) and *Rodō no Riron to Seisaku* (Theory and Policy of Work) (1938); Kazuo Ōkōchi, *Shakai Seisaku no Kihon Mondai* (Fundamental Problems of Social Policy) (1940) in *Chosaku Shū* (Collected Works), Vol. 5. and *Senji Shakai Seisaku Ron* (Treatises on Social Policy in Wartime) (1940), in ibid., Vol. 4. Facing the same situation K. Uno reexamined the theory of Marx and built up a unique interpretation of Marx, analytically separating the elements of his theoretical structure and his empirical data. See Thomas C. Sekine, "Uno-Riron: A Japanese Contribution to Marxian Political Economy," *Journal of Economic Literature* 13 (1975): 847–77.

7. See Tōru Miyakawa, *Miki Kiyoshi* (1958) and Ikuo Arakawa, *Miki Kiyoshi* (1968).

8. Uklad, a term which was borrowed from Russian Marxists, means the transitional economic formation which is either the remnant of the old society or the germ of a new one.

9. Japanese Marxist historians are criticized by M. B. Janssen because they provided too "gloomy" views of Japanese modern history (Marius B. Janssen, "On Studying the Modernization of Japan," *Asian Cultural Studies*, no. 3 [1962], pp. 1–11). But if by the use of the word "gloomy" Janssen wants to imply that all such historians underestimated the possibility of economic and political progress, he overlooks the viewpoints of Hattori and many others. What Japanese Marxist historians were saying (at least in case of Hattori) was that the progressive development of history was inevitably accompanied by social contradictions in a class society.

10. For developing the idea of the local market area, the following historical studies were especially suggestive for Ōtsuka; N. S. B. Gras, *The Evolution of the English Corn Market* (1926); E. A. Kosminsky, "Services and Money Rents in the Thirteenth Century," *Economic History Review* 5, no. 2 (1935): 24–45; M. M. Postan, "The Fifteenth Century," ibid., 9, no. 2 (1939): 160–67.

11. As to the historiography of the activities of this society, see at the beginning of the bibliography "Reviews of Historical Studies," item 3.

12. Although the society's core members are historians of the Marxist persuasion, it should also be noted that a number of non-Marxists participate in the society. What may be called a united front is formed between the Marxists and non-Marxists in that they both consider, first, that the factors which caused the imperialistic war of aggression should be sought in the modern history of Japan itself; and second, that historians should be aware of their responsibility to contribute to the maintenance of peace and the development of democracy. With these considerations as a common basis,

the society has consistently taken a very critical position toward the Japanese government's educational policies because the Ministry of Education, reflecting the long-standing monopoly of political power by the Liberal Democratic party, has been seeking to give a certain orientation to the contents of the teaching of history. The ministry has rejected history textbooks that emphasize the tragic side of the war or the oppression of people by the fascist establishment. It has also induced teachers to teach the history of modern Japan as a type of rags-to-riches story. The challenge made by Saburo Ienaga, who is not a Marxist but rather a radical liberal and who presented before the court his claim that the system of textbook authorization by the government is unconstitutional, has now attained a symbolic status in the society.

13. Takahashi is well known as a contributor to the international discussion on "The Transition from Feudalism to Capitalism." He was also the editor of *Seiyō Keizaishi Kōza* (Lectures on European Economic History), 5 vols., with H. Ōtsuka and T. Matsuda.

14. In a series of articles on India written in 1853, Marx had pointed out the following characteristics of Asiatic societies: (1) petty and self-sufficient farming, which also conducts primitive handicraft, is dominant; (2) huge centralized states—Asiatic despotic empires—were formed quite early because of the need for a system of irrigation; (3) feudal lordship and private ownership of land, which were established in Europe, are not evident, and hence what would correspond to rent is quite undeveloped—instead, the tax imposed by the state constitutes the central agent for exploiting surplus products; (4) the caste system developed in India. In what way are these characterizations of Asiatic societies related to the overall schema of world history, in which Marx explained the developmental stages, with modern Europe being the last one to have come into existence? This question concerning Marx's concept of the Asiatic mode of production has generated heated discussions among Japanese historians. See Kimio Shiozawa, "Les historiens japonais et le mode de production asiatique," *La Pensée*, no. 122 (August, 1965).

15. Kōichi Normura's book entitled *Chūgoki Kakumei no Shisō* (Thought in Chinese Revolution) (1971) is representative of the works which analyzed the characteristics of Mao's thought. A recent study by Reiitsu Kojima, *Chūgoku no Keizai to Gijyutsu* (Economy and Technology in China) (1975), on the economy and industrial technology of socialist China, is full of original insights. It is noteworthy that Ōtsuka, who evaluates favorably the changes in Europe during the formation of its modern societies, is now trying to analyze the Chinese experiences—especially the meaning of Mao's ethical Marxism and his strategy of basing revolution in the countryside—in the light of Western experiences during the Protestant Reformation. See: Discussion between Ōtsuka Hisao and Takeuchi Yoshimi, in "Rekishi no naka no Ajia" (Asia in History), *Shisō* (January 1968).

16. This accentuation of antagonism against Western thought was essentially equivalent to the promotion of anti-Semitism by the National Socialists in Germany.

17. The studies of Ishimoda and Maruyama, notwithstanding their indefatigable resistance to fascism, were submitted to severe criticism because of their inability to predict the Chinese Revolution. Few scholars, in fact, wrote about the possibility of a revolution in China. Among the few who did were Karoku Hosokawa, *Shina Kakumei to Sekai no Asu* (The Chinese Revolution and the Tomorrow of the World) (1928); Genichi Suzue, *Chugoku Kakumei no Kaikyu Tairitsu* (Class Antagonism in the Chinese Revolution) (1930); Goro Hani, *Tōyō ni okeru Shihon Shugi no Keisei* (The Rise of Capitalism in the Orient) (1932). This inability to analyze the possibility of revolution in China was a weak point of Japanese historical studies during the interwar period.

18. Afterwards, Ishimoda counted Yanagida as one of the masters by whom he was influenced. See Shō Ishimoda, "San Sensei no Koto" (On My Three Masters) in *Sengo Rekishigaku no Shisō* (A Thought in Postwar Historiography) (1973). As to the essays on Yanagida written by historians, see in the bibliography *Studies on Yanagida Kunio*.

19. American historians might be interested to know that R. N. Bellah's study on Tokugawa religion stimulated Yasumaru and that Yasumaru conceived his work as a critical response to Bellah. See Yoshio Yasumaru, *Nihon no Kindaika to Minshu Shisō* (Japanese Modernization and Thoughts of the Common People) (1974); cf. p. 10 and Postscript.

20. It might not be too bold to call this the equivalent to the English works written by E. P. Thompson and E. J. Hobsbawm. However, the Japanese edition of "modern social history" (see

Georg Iggers and Norman Baker, *New Directions in European Historiography* [1975]) or "new" social history (see Tim Patterson, "Notes on the Historical Application of Marxist Cultural Theory," *Science and Society* 39 [1975]: 257–91) has its particular features because it bears the tradition of Japanese historiography. The New Japanese current was born certainly by breaking through the method of orthodox Marxism. Moreover, it is critical of the method represented by Ōtsuka and Maruyama. Yet, the two polar configurations of "the thought of the apex" and "the thought of the base" by Irokawa show clearly the influence of Marx as well as Maruyama. Yasumaru's approach through religious sociology, too, might not have been produced without the preliminary introduction of Weber by Ōtsuka and the others.

21. As to the discussions on this new focus of historical studies, see in the bibliography "Reviews on Historical Studies," items 12 and 13.

Bibliography

Review of Historical Studies. (1) Japanese National Committee of Historical Science. *Report for International Congress of Historical Science,* 1960, 1965, 1970, 1975. Bibliography and historiography for Japanese editions. Bibliography only for English editions. (2) *Nihon Rekishi* (Japanese History), 23 vols. 1963–4. Historiography at the end of every age. Vol. 22 is a special volume on Japanese historiography. (3) Tōyama Shigeki, *Sengo no Rekishigaku to Rekishi Ishiki* (Postwar Historiography and Historical Consciousness), 1968. (4) *Kōza Nihon Shi* (Lectures on Japanese History), 10 vols. 1970–1971. Vols. 9 and 10 give historiographies. (5) *Gendai Rekishigaku no Kadai* (Themes in Modern History), 1971, Vol. 30 of *Sekai Rekishi* (The World History). (6) *Gendai Rekishigaku no Kadai* (Themes in Modern History), 2 vols., 1971. Supervised by Nagahara Keiju and Yamaguchi Keiji. (7) *Gendai Rekishigaku no Seika to Kadai* (Results and Themes in Modern History), 4 vols., 1974–1975. Edited by Rekishigaku Kenkyu Kai. (8) *Nihonshi o manabu* (Introduction to Studies of Japanese History), 4 vols., 1975. Edited by Ōe Shinobu et al. (9) *Shakai Keizai Shigaku no Kadai to Tenbō* (Themes and Prospects in Socioeconomic History), 1976. Edited by Shakai Keizai Shigaku Kai. (10) *Nihon Rekishi* (Japanese History), 25 vols., 1975–1977. An additional three volumes are on methodology and historiography. (11) Naruse Osamu, *Sekaishi no Ishiki to Riron* (Consciousness and Theories on World History), 1977. (12) "Nihon Minshū Shi Kenkyu no Genjō to Tenbō" (Situations and Outlook of the Studies of the History of the Japanese Common People). Kimbara Samon et al., *Shosai no Mado,* no. 270, 1978. (13) Chizuka Tadami, "Gendai Rekishigaku no Arikata o megutte" (On the Prospects of the Contemporary Study of History), *Rekishigaku Kenku,* no. 455 (April 1978).

Aikawa Haruki. *Rekishi Kagaku no Hōhōron* (Methodology in Historical Science), 1935.

Bellah, Robert N. *Tokugawa Religion: The Values of Pre-Industrial Japan,* 1957.

Controversies on Japanese Capitalism. (1) *Nihon Shihonshugi Ronsō Shi* (History of the Controversies on Japanese Capitalism), 2 vols., ed. by Koyama Hirotake, 1953; (2) Takahashi, H. Kōhachirō, "La place de la Révolution de Meiji dans l'histoire agraire du Japon," *Revue Historique* 210 (1953): 228–70; (3) *Nihon Shihonshugi Ronsō* (Controversies on Japanese Capitalism), by Uchida Jōkichi, rev. ed., 1956; (4) Révolution française et Révolution de Meiji. (*a*) Kawano Kenji, "Aspects économiques et sociaux," (*b*) Toyoda Takashi, "Etude critique dans l'interprétation de Kosa et de Rono," *Annales historiques de la Révolution française* 35 (1963): 1–24; (5) "Fascizumu no moto ni okeru Nihon Shihonshugi Ronsō" (Controversies on Japanese Capitalism under the Fascist Regime), by Mōri Kenzō, 1971, in *Kindai Nihon Keizai Shisō Shi* (History of Economic Thought in Modern Japan), vol. 2; (6) Yasuba Yasukichi, "Anatomy of the Debate of Japanese Capitalism," *Journal of Japanese Studies* 2, no. 1 (Autumn 1975).

Deborin, Abram. "Lenin als revolutionär Dialektiker," *Unter den Banner des Marxismus* 1, no. 2 (1925).

Dilthey, W. *Einleitung in die Geisteswissenschaften*, 1922.

Dower, John W., ed. "Japan and the Uses of History." Introductory essay to *Origins of the Modern Japanese State. Selected Writings of E. H. Norman*, 1974.

Fujita Gorō. *Nihon Kindai Sangyō no Tenkai Katei* (The Rise of Japanese Modern Industry), 1948.

——. *Hōken Shakai no Tenkai Katei* (The Evolution of the Feudal Society), 1952.

Gouldner, Alvin W. *The Coming Crisis of Western Sociology*, 1970.

Gras, N. S. B. *The Evolution of the English Corn Market*, 1926.

Hani Goro. *Tōyō ni okeru Shihon Shugi no Keisei* (The Rise of Capitalism in the Orient), 1932.

Hattori Shisō. Meiji Ishin no Kakumei oyobi Hankakumei (Revolution and Counterrevolution in the Meiji Restoration), 1933, in *Zenshū* (Complete Works), vol. 3.

——. Ishin Shi no Hōhō Ron (Methodology on the History of the Meiji Restoration), 1934*a*, in *Zenshū*, vol. 4.

——. Bakumatsu Akita-Han no Momen Shijō oyobi Momen Kigyō (Cotton Market and Cotton Weaving in Akita-Han at the End of Tokugawa Period), 1934*b*, in *Zenshū*, vol. 6.

——. Rekishi Ron (Treatises on History), 1935, in *Zenshū*, vol. 4.

——. Meiji Ishin no Shidō to Dōmei (Leadership and Alliance in the Meiji Restoration), 1949, in *Zenshū*, vol. 11.

——. Manyufakuchua Ronsō ni tsuite no Shokan (Impressions of the Debates on "Manufaktur"), 1952, in *Zenshū*, vol. 21.

——. Gōnō to Chūnō (The Wealthy Peasant and the Medium Peasant), 1955, in *Zenshū*, vol. 21.

Hegel, G. W. F. *Vorlesungen Über die Philosophie des Geschichte*, 1830–1831.

Heidegger, M. *Sein und Zeit*, 1927.

Hilferding, Rudolf. *Das Finanz Kapital*, 1910.

Hirano Yoshitarō. Jiyu Minken (Freedom and the People's Rights Movement), 1933, in his *Burujyowa Minshushugi Kakumei* (Bourgeois Democratic Revolution).

——. *Nihon Shihonshugi Shakai no Kikō* (Structure of Japanese Capitalistic Society), 1934.

Hosokawa Karoku. *Shina Kakumei to Sekai no Asu* (The Chinese Revolution and the Tomorrow of the World), 1928.

Iggers, Georg G., and Norman Baker. *New Directions in European Historiography*, 1975.

Inomata Tsunao. *Gendai Nihon Kenkyu* (Studies of Modern Japan), 1929.

Inoue Kiyoshi. *Nihon Gendai Shi* (History of Modern Japan), 1951.

International Discussion. *Transition from Feudalism to Capitalism*, 1976; introduction by Rodney Hilton.

Irokawa Daikichi. *Meiji Seishin Shi* (A Spiritual History of the Meiji Period), 1964, rev. ed., 1973.

——. *Meiji no Bunka* (Culture of Meiji), 1970.

Ishimoda Shō. *Chūsei-teki Sekai no Keisei* (The Making of the Medieval World), 1944; extended ed., 1949.

——. "Chūsei Seiritsu Shi no Ni San no Mondai" (A Few Problems in the Growth of Medieval Society), 1946, in his *Chūsei-teki Sekai*, extended ed.

——. "Kodai Kizoku no Eiyū Jidai" (The Heroic Age in Archaic Aristocracy), 1948, in *Ronshū Shigaku*.

——. *Rekishi to Minzoku no Hakken* (Discovery of History and Nation), 2 vols., 1952–1953.

——. "Rekishi Kagaku to Yuibutsu Ron" (Historical Science and Materialism), 1956, in *Kōza Rekishi* (Lectures on History), vol. 1.

——. "San Sensei no Koto" (On My Three Masters), 1973, in his *Sengo Rekishigaku no Shisō* (A Thought in Postwar Historiography).

Janssen, Marius B., "On Studying the Modernization of Japan," *Asian Cultural Studies*, no. 3 (1962): 1–11.

Kazahaya Yasoji. *Nihon Shakai Seisaku Shi* (History of Social Policy in Japan), 1957.

——. *Rodō no Riron to Seisaku* (Theory and Policy of Work), 1938.

Kimbara Samon. *"Nihon Kindaika" Ron no Rekishi Zō* (Historical Concept of the Theories of "Japanese Modernization"), 1968; extended 2nd ed., 1974.

Kojima Reiitsu. *Chūgoku no Keizai to Gijyutsu* (Economy and Technology in China), 1975.

Kosminsky, E. A. "Services and Money Rents in the Thirteenth Century," *Economic History Review* 5, no. 2 (1935): 24–45.

Kushida Tamizō. "Wagakuni Kosaku-Ryō no Tokuhitsu ni tsuite" (On the Characteristics of Peasants' Rent in Our Country), 1931, in *Zenshū* (Complete Works), vol. 3.

Lenin, V. I. *Development of Capitalism in Russia*, 1899.

———. *Materialism and Empiro-Criticism*, 1909.

———. *Imperialism*, 1917.

Maruyama Masao. *Studies in the Intellectual History of Tokugawa Japan*, 1976; Japanese ed., 1952.

———. *Thought and Behaviour in Modern Japanese Politics*, 1968; Japanese 1st. ed., 1957.

Marx, Karl. "The Future Results of British Rule in India," 1853, etc. *Marx and Engels on Colonialism*.

———. Formen, die der kapitalistischen Produktion vorhergehen, *Grundrisse der Kritik der politischen Ökonomie*, 1857–58.

———. Teilung der Arbeit und Manufaktur, *Das Kapital*, vol. 1, 1867.

———. Die sogenannte ursprüngliche Akkumulation, *Das Kapital*, vol. 1, 1867.

———. Die Reproduktion und Cirkulation des gesellschaftlichen Gesamtkapitals, *Das Kapital*, vol. 2, 1885.

———. "Geschichtliches über das Kaufmannskapital," *Das Kapital*, vol. 3, 1894.

Matsuda Tomoo. *Kindai no Shiteki Kōzō Ron* (Theory on Historical Structure of Modern Society), 1948; newly rev. ed., 1968.

Miki Kiyoshi, "Yuibutsu Shikan to Gendai no Ishiki" (The Materialistic Conception of History and the Consciousness of Contemporary World), 1928, in *Zenshū* (Complete Works), vol. 3.

———. "Shakai Kagaku no Yobi Gainen" (Introductory Conception for Social Science), 1929, in *Zenshū*, vol 3.

———. "Rekishi Tetsugaku" (Philosophy of History), 1932, in *Zenshū*, vol. 6.

(On Miki Kiyoshi see: *Miki Kiyoshi*, by Miyakawa Tōru, 1958, and *Miki Kiyoshi*, by Arakawa Ikuo, 1968.)

Miyata Noboru. *Miroku Shinko no Kenkyu—Nihon ni okeru Dentō teki Meshia Kan* (A Study of Miroku Belief—Traditional Messiah Conception in Japan). 1975.

Naramoto Tatsuya. *Kinsei Hōken Shakai Shiron* (Treatises on the History of Later Feudal Society), 1948.

Nomura Kōichi. *Chūgoku Kakumei no Shisō* (Thought in Chinese Revolution), 1971.

Ōkōchi Kazuo. "Shakai Seisaku no Kihon Mondai" (Fundamental Problems of Social Policy), 1940a, in *Chosaku Shū* (Collected Works), vol. 5.

———. "Senji Shakai Seisaku Ron" (Treatises on Social Policy in Wartime), 1940b, in *Chosaku Shū*, vol. 4.

Ōtsuka Hisao. "Iwayuru Zenkiteki Shihon naru Hanchū ni tsuite" (On the Category of So-called Pre-Modern Capital), 1935, in *Chosaku Shū* (Collected Works), vol. 3.

———. "Kabushiki Gaisha Hassei Shiron" (History of the Making of the Joint-Stock Company), 1938, in *Chosaku Shū*, vol. 1.

———. "Kindai Ōshu Keizaishi Jyosetsu" (Introduction to the Economic History of Modern Europe), rev. ed., 1951–1952, in *Chosaku Shū*, vol. 2.

———. "Kyōdōtai no Kison Riron" (Essentials of the Theories on the Traditional Communities). 1955, in *Chosaku Shū*, vol. 3.

———. "The Market Structure of Rural Industry in the Early Stages of the Development of Modern Capitalism," *Second International Conference of Economic History in Aix-en-Provence 1962*, vol. 2, 1964.

———. "The Role of Max Weber's Sociology of Religion in Cultural Exchange Between East and

West—Dealing with Max Weber's 'Confucianism and Purtanism,' " *Asian Cultural Studies* 5 (October 1966).

————. "Shakai Kagaku no Hōhō" (Method of Social Science), 1966, in *Chosaku Shū*, vol. 9.

————. "Miki san to Hattori San" (Mr. Miki and Mr. Hattori), 1967, in *Chosaku Shū*, vol. 10.

————. *Shakai Kagaku ni okeru Ningen* (Man in Social Science), 1977. (See also Correspondence between Ōtsuka Hisao and Masuda Shirō: (*a*) From Masuda to Ōtsuka: "Ōtsuka Shigaku no Gyōseki to Mittsu no Gimon" (Achievements of Ōtsuka's Historical Studies and Three Questions), *Ikkyo Shimbun*, no. 683 (1960). (*b*) From Ōtsuka to Masuda: "Keizai Shigaku no Kadai to Shikaku—Masuda shi no Mittsu no Gimon ni kotae te" (Themes and Viewpoints of Socio-Economic History—Answer to Mr. Masuda's Three Questions), *Ikkyo Shimbun*, no. 691 (1960), in *Chosaku Shū*, vol. 4; in addition see Discussion between Ōtsuka Hisao and Douglas C. North: "Keizai Shi no Kihon Mondai o᠂megutte—Kindai Seiō Shakai no Keisei" (On the Fundamental Problems of Socio-Economic History—Making of Modern European Society), *Shisō* (June 1976); and, finally, see Discussion between Ōtsuka Hisao and Takeuchi Yoshimi, "Rekishi no naka no Ajia" (Asia in History), *Shisō* (January 1968), in *Chosaku Shū*, vol. 7.

Ōuchi Tsutomu. *Nihon Keizai Ron* (Treatises on Japanese Economy), 2 vols., 1962.

Patterson, Tim. "Notes on the Historical Application of Marxist Cultural Theory," *Science and Society* 39 (1975): 257–91.

Postan, M. M. "The Fifteenth Century," *Economic History Review* 9, no. 2 (1939): 160–67.

Quesnay, François. *Tableau économique*, 1758.

Rekishigaku Kenkyu Kai. *Sekaishi no Kihon Hōsoku* (The Essential Law of World History), 1949.

————. *Kokka Kenryoku no Shodankai* (Stages of the State Power), 1950.

————. *Sekaishi to Kindai Nihon* (World History and Modern Japan), 1961.

————. *Gendai Rekishigaku to Kyōkashyo Saiban* (Contemporary Historical Science and Lawsuit on Official Sanction of School Textbook), 1973.

Sakisaka Itsurō. "Shihonshugi ni okeru Kōzōteki Henka no Mondai" (Problem of Structural Change in Capitalism), *Chuō Kōron* (December 1935).

Sakurai Tokutarō. *Kō Shudan Seiritsu Katei no Kenkyu* (A Study of the Rise of Kō Groups), 1962.

Seiyo Keizaishi Kōza (Lectures on European Economic History). 5 vols., 1960–1962.

————. Vol. 1: *Hokensei no Keizai-teki Kiso* (Economic Foundation of Feudalism);

————. Vol. 2: *Shihonshugi no Hattatsu* (Development of Capitalism);

————. Vols. 3 and 4: *Hōkensei Kara Shihonshugi eno Ikō* (Transition from Feudalism to Capitalism);

————. Vol. 5: *Bibliographies*.

Sekine, Thomas C. "Uno-Riron: A Japanese Contribution to Marxian Political Economy," *Journal of Economic Literature* 13 (1975): 847–77.

Shiozawa Kimio. "Les historiens japonais et le mode de production asiatique," *La Pensée*, no. 122 (August 1965): 63–78.

Shisō no Kagaku Kenkyu Kai. *Tenkō* (Recantation), 3 vols. 1959–1962.

Sombart, Werner. *Der moderne Kapitalismus*, 2 vols., 1902.

Suzue Genichi. *Chugoku Kakumei no Kaikyu Tairitsu* (Class Antagonism in the Chinese Revolution), 1930.

Takahashi Kōhachirō. *Shimin Kakumei no Kōzō* (Structure of the Bourgeois Revolution), 1950; extended ed., 1966.

Takashima Zenya. *Marukus to Uēbā* (Marx and Weber), 1975.

Tōyama Shigeki. *Meiji Ishin* (The Meiji Restoration), 1950.

————. *Shōwa Shi* (History of the Shōwa Period), 1955, with Imai Seiichi and Fujiwara Akira.

Toyoda Shiro et al. *Ōtsuka Shigaku Hihan* (Criticism of Ōtsuka's Method of Historical Study), 1948.

Tsuchiya Takao. *Nihon Shihon Shugi Ronshu* (Essays on Japanese Capitalism), 1937.

Uchida Yoshiaki. *Uēbā to Marukusu* (Weber and Marx), 1972.

Uchida Yoshihiko. "Nihon Shisoshi ni okeru Uēbā teki Mondai" (M. Weber in the Historiography of Japanese Thought), 1965, in his *Nihon Shihonshugi no Shisō Zō* (Variations of Thought in Japanese Capitalism).

Ueyama Shumpei. "Meiji Ishin no Bunseki Shiten" (Analysis of Meiji Restoration), *Shisō no Kagaku* (November 1961).

Weber, Max. "Die protestantische Ethik und der Geist des Kapitalismus," *Archiv für Sozialwissenschaft und Sozialpolitik*, Bd. 20 (1904*a*).

———. "Der Streit um den Charakter der altgermanischen Sozialverfassung in der Deutschen Literatur des letzten Jahrzehnts," *Jahrbücher für Nationalökonomie und Statistik* 28 (1904*b*).

———. "Roscher und Knies und die logischen Probleme der historischen Nationalökonomie," *Schmollers Jahrbuch*, 1903–1906.

———. "Konfuzianismus und Taoismus," ibid., Bd. 41 (1916*a*).

———. "Hinduismus und Buddhismus," ibid. (*b*).

Wittfogel, Karl A. *Wirtschaft und Gesellschaft Chinas*, 1931.

Yamada Moritarō. *Sai-Seisan Katei Bunseki Joron* (Introduction to the Analysis of the Process of Reproduction), 1931.

———. *Nihon Shihonshugi Bunseki* (The Analysis of Japanese Capitalism), 1934.

———. "Sai-Seisan Hyoshiki to Chidai Hanchu" (Tables of Reproduction and Categories of Rent), 1935; reproduced in *Jinbun* (March 1947).

Yamakawa Hitoshi. "Seiji-teki Tōitsu Sensen e" (Towards the United Front in Politics), *Rōnō* (December 1927).

Yanagida Kunio. Kokushi to Minzokugaku (National History and Folklore), 1944, in *Yanagida Kunio Shū* (Collected Works of K. Yanagida), vol. 24.

Studies on Yanagida Kunio: (1) "Yanagida Shigaku Ron" (Essays on Yangida's History), by Ienaga Saburo, 1953, in his *Kidai no Nihon Shigaku* (Japanese Historiography of the Modern Age); (2) "Yanagida Kunio no Rekishigaku" (Historical Science of Yanagida Kunio), by Nakai Nobuhiko, 1957, in his *Rekishigaku teki Hōhō no Kijun* (Criteria for the Method of Historical Science); (3) *Yanagida Kunio to Rekishigaku* (Yanagida Kunio and Historical Science), by Wakamori Tarō, 1975; (4) *Yanagida Kunio—Jōmin Bunka Ron* (Yanagida Kunio—Essays on the Culture of Common People), by Irokawa Daikichi, 1978; (5) *Japanese Marxism and Yanagida's Studies of Agricultural Policy*, by Masami Fukutomi, 1978.

Yasumaru Yoshio. *Nihon no Kindaika to Minshu Shisō* (Japan's Modernization and Thoughts of the Common People), 1974.

———. *Deguchi Nao*, 1977.

The
Socialist Countries

The differences in the climate of scholarship between the socialist countries and the nonsocialist societies of the West and of Japan should be neither overstated nor minimized. There exists a broad consensus between both communities on what constitutes critical historical method. Dialogue, therefore, can take place between historians in the two communities, and in recent years it has in fact increased. Nevertheless, there are fundamental differences. In the socialist countries the pluralism of institutions, ideologies, and methodological approaches does not exist in the same form as in the West or in Japan, although this pluralism is by no means replaced by uniformity. As the essays in this section will demonstrate, lively debates abound among socialists on questions of historical interpretation.

All these countries share a common framework in which historical studies take place, though within this framework there is considerable room for diversity. With isolated exceptions, such as Catholic historiography in Poland, historical studies are expected to function within the context of Marxist-Leninist philosophy. Marxism-Leninism not only assumes a theory regarding the manner in which the historical process functions and how it can be understood, but it also defines the function of historical studies. The idea of history as a value-free science, also widely questioned in the West, is repudiated. History is seen as itself an important instrument in the creation of class consciousness. Partisanship (*partinost, Parteilichkeit*) is considered to be in no way incompatible with an objectivity which consists in the correct understanding of the forces and laws of historical development. This stress on lawful development distinguishes the doctrine of Marxism-Leninism as defined in the Soviet Union and the German Democratic Republic from the more eclectic versions of Marxism which inform many historians in Western European countries, for example, in Great Britain.

The relationship between the state and historical scholarship is much more closely established in these countries than in the West. Party resolutions set certain priorities for historical research. The sharp line which often exists in the West between specialized scholarship and political education is lessened. Historical studies are relatively centrally organized and financed: important research is carried on at the universities, but the coordinating function is assigned to the institutes of history of the academies of science, which are the primary centers of research. Generally, nationwide plans are drawn up to distribute foci of research over the universities and research institutes around the country.

Compared with Western European countries we have discussed, although not the United States, the historical profession is numerically large. This as well as the large number of journals and the diverse areas of research make for a degree of diversity. Debate and controversy within the framework of the official ideology are by no means absent, as the articles on the German Democratic Republic and the People's Republic of China demonstrate. Nevertheless, except for the extensive work on nonsocialist and Third World societies done in the Soviet Union and the comparative studies of the Poles, historical endeavor in the socialist countries continues to concentrate heavily on national histories. Political history also continues to occupy an important role. Marxist history always emphasizes the role of political struggle, although this struggle is seen in the context of the social conditions of production. The materialistic assumptions of Marxist-Leninist ideology have raised questions which broaden the perspectives of a political approach, such as the great interest in the material conditions of life, social structure (including class structure), the mentalities of the broad masses of the population—all topics which have also come to be of increasing concern to Western historiographers.

Marxist philosophy is also conducive to a history in which theoretical formulations play a greater role than in traditional idiographic history, and thus opens points of contact and discussion with the recent theory-oriented history in the West. The history of the working class has taken two often very divergent orientations, one which has stressed the organized movements with their leaders, programs, and ideologies, the other more akin to newer Western attempts to write a "history from below."

Despite commonalities among the socialist countries, national divergences exist. In certain countries, the break with older patterns of scholarship was cataclysmic—in the German Democratic Republic in the aftermath of the Nazi interlude, in the People's Republic of China after the conclusion of a bitter civil war and in the wake of the Cultural Revolution, in the Soviet Union with the end of the period of transition in the 1920s. In other countries, as the articles on Poland and Rumania show, personnel and ideas survived the ravages of World War II with much continuity. In Poland in particular a rich tradition of social and economic history existed in the prewar period which made important contributions to the growth of Marxist historiography after 1945. In general, a distinction can be drawn between the history of the recent past, which in all socialist countries requires a much greater attachment to standards of political interpretation, and the history of the more distant past, which is freer of these requirements. Yet even in the case of the former, dialogue has been possible, as can be seen in the efforts of the Polish-West German textbook commission to establish a past which can be taught in the schoolbooks of both countries. But particularly in the interpretation of the less controversial aspects of the past, historians from the socialist countries, again particularly the Poles, have made important contributions to the analysis of social and economic processes. The

Marxist theory of the transition from feudalism to capitalism has here served as an important source of working hypotheses open to discussion. Particularly in the areas of the economic, social, and demographic history of the premodern period, considerable dialogue has taken place between historians in the socialist and the Western countries, for which journals such as *Past and Present* and the *Annales* have provided a forum.

15 SAMUEL H. BARON
and
NANCY W. HEER

The Soviet Union:
Historiography Since Stalin*

The effects of the Bolshevik Revolution on the writing of Russian history in the Soviet Union have been profound. At the outset, the work of the prerevolutionary historians was repudiated and a concerted effort launched to recast Russia's history in a Marxian ideological mold. The works of Marx, Engels, and Lenin were endowed with scriptural authority, and historical writings became heavily seasoned with quotations from these "classics." The sovereignty of economic determinism was proclaimed, and all too often the most complex phenomena were explained by means of a crude reductionism. All history was perceived as a progression through a prescribed sequence of historical stages, and the data of each people's past a priori had to be accommodated to the scheme. Perhaps the most striking result was the classification of far the greatest part of Russian history as a feudal period. Soviet historiography abounded in such endlessly repeated and unchallengeable propositions. Because the "classics" were far from clear on numerous important questions, however, scholastic controversy was also destined to become a feature of Soviet historiography.

From the beginning, sentiment existed for making history directly serve political needs. However, the campaign to subordinate history to politics gained seemingly irresistible momentum only in the Stalin era. To non-Marxist historians in the West the resulting Soviet historiography seemed so supine and so devoid of redeeming qualities that they long tended to ignore it. Yet the tradition of historical scholarship was not extinguished, and efforts by the Communist party (CPSU) to control historical writing fell well short of the goal. To be sure, in the area of party history, where political pressures were most intense, the partisan *History of the CPSU: Short Course* did become the bible. With the

*This article is adapted from *Windows on the Russian Past: Essays on Soviet Historiography Since Stalin,* edited by Samuel H. Baron and Nancy W. Heer. Copyright 1977 by the American Association for the Advancement of Slavic Studies. Reprinted by permission of the AAASS.

waxing of Soviet Russian nationalism, not only were the heroes and achievements of the past celebrated and frequently inflated, but the influence of foreign
cultures upon the development of Russian civilization was systematically dis-
counted. Ideological interpretation proceeded apace on many another theme as
well, but like so much else it was represented as the revelation of the "law-
governed character" (*zakonomernost'*) of the Russian historical process. Nevertheless, the period also produced excellent studies such as those of S. V. Bakhrushin and K. V. Bazilevich on Russia's early history.[1]

In the years immediately following Stalin's death, stirring of new life began
among the historians. In 1955 and early 1956, lively discussions centering in
and around the journal *Voprosy istorii* (Problems of History) eloquently testified
to the developing ferment.[2] Khrushchev's dramatic speech to the Twentieth
Party Congress in 1956, with its call for a new spirit in historical work, legitimized and propelled into full motion changes which had earlier been adum-
brated.[3] Distortions said to have been produced by the "cult of personality"
were condemned. Historians were now admonished to upgrade their methods;
to use documents and data to explain rather than simply proclaim the past victories of the Bolsheviks; and to write a believable story—which would include
setbacks, confusions, and real struggles, along with glorious achievements. Such
pronouncements encouraged criticism and revisionism, and it seemed that an era
of greater freedom for the historian and more accurate historical writing in all
areas of investigation was at hand.

In the next half dozen years, more energy and resources were put into historical study and publication, access to archival sources was eased, the scope
of historical inquiry was expanded, and so were contacts with historians of the
noncommunist world. Such developments inclined some observers to look to the
future with "qualified optimism."[4] Their optimism was qualified because the
progress made had been attended by setbacks such as the "Burdzhalov affair"—
the dismissal of a leader of the critical movement from the editorial board of
Voprosy istorii. Political intervention in historical affairs had become less heavy-
handed, but it had by no means terminated, and there was no way of knowing
how important a part it might play in the future.

The problematic destiny of Soviet historiography at the opening of the 1960s
is intriguingly communicated by a significant editorial in *Voprosy istorii* (no. 8,
1960) entitled "Soviet Historiography at a New Stage of Development." The
piece bristles with endorsements of many shibboleths of the past, but they are
often balanced by pleas for a widening of perspective, greater objectivity, and
more creative work. On the one hand, the editorial ringingly declares, historiography "remains a class, party branch of scholarship." On the other, it cites
this unexceptional precept of historical research from Lenin, which has been
repeatedly quoted in the last fifteen years:

It is necessary to try to establish a foundation of precise and indisputable facts on which
one could rely. . . . If this is to be a real foundation, it is necessary to take not isolated
facts but the *sum total* of facts relating to the question under examination, *without a*

single exception; otherwise a suspicion will arise—and a fully legitimate one—that the facts have been chosen or selected arbitrarily, that a "subjective" concoction perhaps to justify a dirty event is being served up instead of the objective relation and interdependence of historical phenomena in their entirety.

The editorial speaks of the "deepening crisis of bourgeois historiography," but it also advises Soviet historians to "give thoughtful consideration to everything positive which was achieved by their predecessors [as well as to what] is now being produced not only by progressive foreign scholars but by honest researchers who do not subscribe to Marxism-Leninism." On the one hand, it speaks out against those who would construe "the correction of errors engendered by the cult of the individual as [a warrant for] the revision of fundamental theses and conclusions worked out in Soviet historical scholarship in the past"; on the other, it attacks "dogmatism" and calls for "a bold and creative approach." Finally, it attaches the highest importance to work on the history of the CPSU, and hardly less to writings on recent and contemporary history, but it also recognizes that "the development of historiography as a whole is unthinkable without research into the full historical process."

In spite of its apparently conflicting signals, this authoritative document was intended in all likelihood to convey that the Burdzhalov affair did not signify a reversion to the repression of the Stalin era, that although there were limits beyond which historians must not venture, they were encouraged to reach out, to acquire new methods, to seek new contacts, and to strive for a creative and more accurate representation of the past.

Yet the limits were ill defined, and this circumstance invited the conspicuous and restless probing which characterized the era. If all the facts were to be used, if new techniques and concepts were to be employed, if historians were to operate boldly and creatively, then might not their findings necessitate the "revision of fundamental theses and conclusions worked out by Soviet scholarship in the past"? Those who wished to set limits were by no means entirely clear as to which of the many theses and conclusions developed by Soviet scholarship were fundamental. Such ambiguities no doubt worked to the advantage of historians who aspired to produce work of a high professional standard, and the 1960s produced a richer harvest of historical speculation, controversy, and scholarship than any decade since the Revolution.

As Soviet historiography moved toward universally recognized professional standards, it achieved some impressive gains. The historians secured a larger area of autonomy; conversely, until the most recent years—of which more later—political involvement in historical affairs distinctly receded, and when it came into play it often operated more indirectly and discreetly than in the past. Precisely why and how gains were made is often far from clear, and their real extent is not subject to quantification. There are differences of opinion as to whether the observed shifts in the regime's behavior and attitudes toward historians should be viewed as minor and purely instrumental or whether they indeed represent cumulative and significant developments. It is generally agreed, however, that constraints continue to impinge upon historians in varying degrees, depending upon the political sensitivity of their subject matter.[5]

A consideration of the political functions of Soviet historiography suggests that the authorities regard as fundamental the historical perspectives and interpretations which support the legitimacy of the regime and its basic policies. Thus, Soviet historians of late imperial Russia take it as axiomatic that the revolutionary overthrow of the "disintegrating" old order was inevitable, and they studiously refrain from entertaining alternative possibilities. Similarly, they matter-of-factly envisage the October Revolution as the central event in modern history, and their treatments of 1917 make no allowance for any possible outcome other than the Bolshevik victory. In order to foster harmonious relations among the peoples of the Soviet Union, the historians are expected to demonstrate the friendship of Russians and non-Russians in the prerevolutionary era.

Historians concerned with more remote and therefore less politically charged issues enjoy greater freedom to call the shots as they see them. Not surprisingly, perhaps, especially remarkable strides have been made in the study of the Byzantine impact on Russia. To mention another case, recent Soviet historiography on Ivan the Terrible has either parted with or greatly diluted the class-centered interpretation that formerly prevailed. Even on such delicate matters as the last decades of the old regime, Russian imperialism and colonialism, and the leftist rivals of the Bolsheviks, the general formulas which are obligatorily pronounced are often brought into question by the concrete evidence conscientiously presented.[6]

If political interference has diminished, then what of ideological constraints? Soviet publications of course abound in testimonials to Marxism-Leninism's power to fathom not only the present and the future but the past. However, Marxism as a mode of historical analysis has, in fact, always been more indeterminate than its partisans have admitted. In the post-Stalin era, the critics have relied upon Marxism's indeterminacy and ambiguities to support their drive for greater flexibility in research and interpretation. One of their prime targets was the widespread resort to an exclusive or one-sided economic determinism in historical interpretation. Appropriate pronouncements in the Marxian canon were readily recalled, but what may have begun merely as a corrective endeavor developed into something much more far-reaching. In the 1960s historians who honestly strove to order their abundant and complex data into persuasive relationships made use of an ever wider variety of noneconomic causal explanations. The almost infinite range of causalities explicitly or implicitly adduced indicates that economic determinism has been quietly abandoned in favor of a more flexible approach—or, alternatively, that historical materialism is actually so permissive in the matter of causality that it imposes no serious restraints upon the historian.

Diversity and complexity, resort to pluralist explanation, and an increase in overall flexibility are basic features of recent Soviet historiography, at least at its cutting edge. Historians who have assimilated these methodological modes are less and less inclined to think that Russian history—not to mention world history—may be encompassed in simple formulas. The dramatic revival in the 1960s of the long-banned Marxian concept of "the Asiatic mode of production" is instructive in this connection. Its revival was a consequence of a revolt—sparked by non-Soviet Marxists—against the unilinear and allegedly universally operative five-stage scheme of historical development (primitive communism/ slaveholding/feudalism/capitalism/socialism), which was officially upheld in the Stalin era.[7] As opposed to this Eurocentric conception which straitjacketed the historian, the critics advanced a multilinear approach which took account of diversity. The Asiatic mode of production may be favored as a key to Russia's own history by some Soviet historians who find incongruous the prevailing notion of a millennial feudal period. Here, as in the case of economic determinism, Marxism has by no means been repudiated; it has instead been interpreted generously rather than narrowly and thus enabled to deal more convincingly with the historical data.

Another staple of Soviet historical discourse, the law-governed character of the historical process, seems to have undergone a subtle transformation. Of course Soviet historians continue to utilize the term *zakonomernost'*, but it is difficult to escape the impression that many do so ritualistically. Apparently, many have become increasingly aware that the laws of history are less than perfectly clear and that their value to the research worker has been greatly overrated. Less inclined to make grandiose claims, they are more aware of the human limitations to which the historian is subject. When Soviet historians now use the term *zakonomernost'*, more often than not they appear to mean nothing more than "causally related," in much the same way that Western non-Marxists routinely use that term. They can hardly do other than recoil from the extravagant boasts that were once made for their methodology and conceptions when a leading member of the guild can write: "We have not yet learned how properly to examine the phenomenon of the base and superstructure in their actual interaction"; and another can imply that his colleagues do not precisely know "what feudalism and capitalism are."[8]

Not all Soviet historians share these perceptions. Although Western writers often perceive Soviet historical writing as monolithic, abundant evidence of sharp differences of viewpoint on matters small and large is available from the recent period. These differences have come into especially sharp focus in discussion conferences and in the pages of scholarly journals on such issues as the historicity of the Asiatic mode of production, the nature of Russian absolutism, and the transition from feudalism to capitalism in Russia.[9]

Different Soviet historians in fact perceive and employ Marxism-Leninism differently in their work. Not a few who were formed in the Stalin era pay occasional lip service to the new spirit, while they persist in the ways of the past. They are the "citation-mongers," the dogmatic Marxists who write as if the task of the historian is to find supporting data in the sources for the "established truths" of Marxism-Leninism. At the other pole are scholars who may be called "cosmetic Marxists." These writers appear skeptical about the utility and relevance of the official ideology, and the way they handle their material may be almost indistinguishable from that of the non-Marxist. However, they camouflage their skepticism by occasional genuflections to the old gods. Between these types may be found historians who should perhaps be called "pragmatic Marxists." Unlike the cosmetic Marxist, this type freely makes use of Marxist-Leninist concepts in his work, because he is convinced they yield major dimensions of understanding not to be gained from other perspectives. Unlike the dogmatist, he eschews the identification of Marxism-Leninism with pronouncements from the "classics" on particular subjects and instead is concerned with its spirit. He is the sort who is apt to quote approvingly this statement from Lenin: "Marxists take unconditionally from Marx's theory only the precious methods, without which it is impossible to clarify social relations; and, consequently, they see the criteria for their judgment not at all in abstract schemes and other rubbish but in their truth and correspondence with reality." Such a pronouncement affords a large measure of flexibility, and its insistence on reality as the indispensable validation of theory implies that theory itself is subject to change and development. These writers revise Marxism-Leninism or reinterpret it as necessary, and even borrow and incorporate elements of other perspectives to increase its utility. Of course we are speaking of types, and many Soviet writers might have to be placed in some intermediate category. Moreover, depending on circumstances one and the same person may speak with different voices. This is yet another dimension of the pluralism which characterizes the recent Soviet historical scene.

A distinction has been drawn here between political and ideological constraints upon historical work in the Soviet Union, although it is not always easy to separate them. The distinction is useful, nevertheless. Though political intervention has diminished, the political authorities in the final analysis reserve to themselves the right to interpret the ideology, to censor historical publications, and to denounce what they represent as ideological deviation. Without such political intervention, Soviet historiography might remain formally Marxist-Leninist and at the same time sufficiently flexible to generate work no more or less susceptible to objection than that produced under the inspiration of any other perspective.

It is important to add that the peculiarities of Soviet historiography are not to be explained solely by reference to political and ideological constraints. National traditions influence the modes of historical investigation and perception in any setting, and despite a revolutionary upheaval which ostensibly severed all connection with the past, the Soviet Union has not escaped. A whole range of national, cultural, institutional, and subjective factors may explain why the "great reforms" of Czar Alexander II have been rather neglected by Soviet historians and why much of the work they have produced on the subject is undistinguished. Still another factor which helps to explain some features of Soviet historical work is the virtual neglect of the foreign literature on Russian history. In the rare instances where serious consideration of the foreign literature has occurred, as in the case of Byzantine history and the Asiatic mode of production, it has produced signal results.[10]

A high degree of continuity between the Stalin and post-Stalin eras is apparent in the area of historical approaches and methodologies, but there have also been significant changes.[11] Socioeconomic history still predominates, but because it has been defined more broadly and flexibly, we have been given not only more sensitive studies of the prerevolutionary proletariat but also important work on the peasantry and bureaucracy.[12] A growing interest in demographic studies is apparent, as in the work of Kabuzan and Vodarskii.[13] The publication of such books as the symposium *Absolutism in Russia* signals recognition that the state cannot be dismissed as a mere element of the superstructure but demands historical research and analysis.[14] Except for works written for a broader public, Soviet historians still rarely produce biographical, much less psychohistorical, studies. On the other hand, B. F. Porshnev has endorsed the employment of social-psychological approaches by historians. If his apprehension of these is somewhat narrow and rigid, others have conceived them more broadly and used them effectively.[15] Indicative of a commendable openness to some currents of outside thought is the recent translation (1976) of Erich Auerbach's rich, historically relevant book *Mimesis*. Some Soviet historians—I. D. Koval'chenko comes to mind—have joined the international contingent which finds quantitative methods especially useful in solving historical problems. Finally, it should be mentioned that Soviet historians devote an uncommonly large amount of attention to historiographical and source studies.[16]

We are bound to attempt an estimate of the substantive consequences of the change in climate, though we realize how fraught with difficulty the task is. One point is indisputable: Soviet historians have been working with great industry in the archives and have made available a vast amount of new data on a great many themes of Russian history. However, the enormous labor expended has not resulted in major new interpretations of particular themes, nor, it appears, in a recognizably new synthesis. We see modifications of more or less significance and interest, but it turns out when scrutinized that they stem not so much from new insights as from the correction of distortions introduced in the preceding era. For example, the claim for Russia's autochthonous cultural development has been superseded by acknowledgment that it was influenced and shaped in very important ways by Byzantine and, to a lesser extent, Western civilization. The glorification of Ivan the Terrible has given way to a portrayal which allots due emphasis to the irrational and destructive aspects of his reign. Claims that minority nationalities were voluntarily incorporated into the Russian Empire and were treated with unusual consideration have been scotched. And even the leftist rivals of the Bolsheviks are treated not as foul demons but as multidimensional people who presented serious, if mistaken, political alternatives.

It is fair to say that since the Twentieth Party Congress Soviet historiography has succeeded in undoing much, though by no means all, of the mischief perpetrated in the Stalin era. Among other rectifications was the vindication of M. N. Pokrovskii, the key figure in Soviet historiography in the 1920s, from the slanderous charges leveled against him in the 1930s—though there was no disposition to rehabilitate his general interpretation of Russian history. A more important rectification of these years was designed to counteract excesses for which Pokrovskii himself was chiefly responsible: it was publicly acknowledged that prerevolutionary Russian historiography had been too peremptorily dismissed in the 1920s.[17] This acknowledgment corresponds with our perception— and this is a major point—that many insights of prerevolutionary historiography have been found meritorious and have entered into Soviet interpretation both of particular issues and of the general sweep of Russian history.

In the area of Byzantine and Byzantino-Russian studies, it was the colleagues and students of F. I. Uspenskii, the key figure in the field before the Revolution, who prepared the way for the revival of the past fifteen years. Studies of Ivan the Terrible have once again been conducted within the framework established by the conflicting interpretations of prerevolutionary historians V. O. Kliuchevskii and S. F. Platonov. The school of historiography which emphasized the extraordinary role of the state in Russian history was long a principal target of Soviet writers, but in the recent period many of them have candidly admitted their own failure to accord it due weight and have made substantial amends. The revival of the Asiastic mode of production as a distinct Marxian socioeconomic order has occurred concomitantly with a partial resurrection of the views of G. V. Plekhanov, who made that concept central to his interpretation of Russian history.

The continuing deep imprint of the Revolution and Marxist-Leninist ideology on Soviet historiography is of course obvious, but the correction of earlier distortions and the partial readmission of prerevolutionary views plainly make a significant difference. What this all adds up to is difficult to say, and Soviet historians have not been notably helpful in providing answers. Like their colleagues abroad they expend far the greatest part of their energies on specialized studies and leave the problem of synthesis largely unattended to. Perhaps the problem does not exist for the conservatives, in whose eyes the five-stage scheme provides the framework and the chief nodes of the historical process. One or another of the critics has occasionally called the five-stage scheme into question, but for the most part they take another tack. Rather than emphasize the likenesses in the development of all societies, they have stressed the peculiarities of the Russian historical process and so tended to dissolve the grand unity. It is remarkable how often the word *osobennosti* ("peculiarities") appears in the titles of recent articles and books by critically minded Soviet historians.[18] To appreciate the full impact of this development, it should be recalled that in the formative years of Soviet historiography Pokrovskii directed a triumphant campaign *against* the formerly prevalent view that Russia's history was marked by major peculiarities.[19]

Soviet historians engaged in the identification and study of these peculiarities have gradually shaped an alternative interpretation whose central conception is the *mnogoukladnost'* ("multiformity" or "multistructuredness") of the Russian historical process.[20] *Mnogoukladnost'* refers to the coexistence and complex interaction of two or more socioeconomic formations or subformations within a single society. Such factors as diverse geographical-climatic conditions and varied historical experience produced a variety of regional societies with distinct characteristics and markedly contrasting levels of development. Moreover, in the modern period the socioeconomic development of Russia as a whole lagged behind that of the leading countries of Western Europe. To overcome a disadvantage which threatened its security, the state repeatedly introduced political, economic, and technological innovations developed in the West which added significantly to the contrasts and contradictions in Russian society. By the early twentieth century the accumulated contrasts and contradictions had created explosive potentialities. Most significant was the coexistence of a backward agricultural economy manned by a vast population of discontented, land-hungry peasants and an advanced industrial economy whose factory hands were strongly tinged with revolutionary socialist sentiments. The explosive potentialities were fulfilled in 1917, when peasants and workers engaged in mutually supportive activity, notwithstanding the (unrecognized) incompatibility of their basic goals.

The *mnogoukladnost'* approach no doubt appeals to many of the abler historians because it provides the basis for an interpretation of the October Revolution that is better rooted in the peculiarities and complexities of the Russian historical process. Needless to say, the search for these peculiarities has not been confined to the late imperial period. The published proceedings of a conference held in 1965 to discuss the transition from feudalism to capitalism in Russia are a monument to the endeavor. One of the rare works concerned with broad questions of interpretation, it brings together and attempts to synthesize so many unconventional ideas that an opponent castigated the main report presented for its "historiographical nihilism."

The central idea is that the transition—its discussion ranges over a period of four centuries, beginning with the sixteenth—proceeded very differently in Russia than in the West. In the latter, capitalism arose as feudalism declined—the two were reverse sides of a single process. In Russia feudalism was far more solidly entrenched and adaptable, with the result that strong elements of it persisted even into the twentieth century; correspondingly, the development of capitalism was for a long time blocked, and subsequently hindered and distorted. *Mnogoukladnost'* is here connected with Russia's economic backwardness, the powerful compensatory role of the state, the weakness of capitalism and the bourgeoisie, and the relatively short life of both.[21]

The *mnogoukladnost'* interpretation, here greatly simplified, has a familiar ring. Lenin seems to have coined the term, and Soviet advocates of this perception credit him with the inspiration for their interesting studies along this line. But our sense of having met these ideas before is most apt to stem from their likeness to Trotsky's well-known "laws" of uneven and combined development. Although Trotsky's political and historical ideas remain anathema in the Soviet Union, some writers seem to have been impelled to formulate similar concepts as they strove in the freer atmosphere of the post-Stalin era to construct an interpretation that would do justice to the abundant and contradictory historical data at their disposal.

In the late 1960s and early 1970s the critical-revisionist movement was checked as the political climate changed. The events in Czechoslovakia in 1968 and the emergence of articulate political dissidence in the Soviet Union itself strengthened the hand of the conservative and party-minded elements of the historical guild. They were aided and abetted by the political authorities, who, though they must have distinguished between professionals working within the system for change in their field and people who set themselves against the system, instinctively reached for the brakes in times of uncertainty.

Severe attacks upon certain historians and their works have occurred with much greater frequency in the last years than in the 1960s.[22] The dismissal in March 1974 of P. V. Volobuev from the directorship of the Institute of History is a major case in point. Volobuev, a specialist on the Russian Revolution, was actively involved in developments and controversies at the cutting edge of recent Soviet historiography. He was a conspicuous member of the group which mounted a powerful and apparently successful attack on the formerly prevalent view that Russian autocracy was fundamentally like Western European absolutism. He was also associated with the movement which relies on *mnogoukladnost'* as a primary principle of historical explanation.

In the light of our emphasis on this approach, it is significant that a volume condemned in May 1973 bears the subtitle *The Problem of Mnogoukladnost'*. A circumstantial critique of this collection of essays by I. V. Kuznetsov finds objectionable the notion that Russia was a backward country in 1917, the idea that the peasantry was then concerned mainly with the achievement of bourgeois-democratic rather than socialist objectives, and what he considered the undue emphasis his adversaries gave to Russia's peculiarities. His most serious charge was that "the theory of *mnogoukladnost'* . . . breaks with the Marxist-Leninist teaching on the laws of socioeconomic formations."[23]

Kuznetsov's essay was only the most recent contribution to the developing conservative trend in the 1970s. Predictably, the conservatives sought to limit the historian's flexibility, to promote simplistic formulas, and to exhort their colleagues to "rigorous observation of party-mindedness." Uncomfortable with the critical spirit, they balked at the reinterpretation of Marxism-Leninism in the light of new data and instead insisted on the interpretation of new data on social life in the light of an unalterable Marxism-Leninism.[24] Posing as guardians of sanctified precepts against what they depicted as illegitimate and dangerous revisionism, they freely violated the spirit of Lenin's admonitions cited above.

The events of the last several years have clearly altered the atmosphere in Soviet historiography, but how profound and how enduring the change will be no one can foretell. The foes of freer and more supple historical work seem to be in the ascendant. On the other hand, most of the ground gained in the 1960s has been retained, and good work on many themes continues to be written and published. Besides, it is difficult to imagine that the considerable number of able historians who have powered the critical-revisionist movement will renounce their views, but they are likely to proceed more circumspectly. Neither they nor the more sophisticated stratum of the public can believe the simple verities of an earlier age. Though the political authorities want history to serve their purposes, they also have a continuing stake in the production of interesting and credible historical work. On these counts, the progress made since the Twentieth Party Congress seems likely to be irreversible.

Notes

1. John Fennell has called Bazilevich's *Vneshniaia politika russkogo tsentralizovannogo gosudarstva* (The Foreign Policy of the Centralized Russian State) (1952) a "great monograph." See his *Ivan the Great of Moscow* (London, 1961), p.v.

2. Nancy W. Heer, *Politics and History in the Soviet Union* (Cambridge, Mass., 1971), pp. 69–75.

3. Leo Gruliow, ed., *Current Soviet Policies, II* (New York, 1957), p. 188.

4. John Keep and Lilianna Brisby, eds., *Contemporary History in the Soviet Mirror* (New York, 1964), p. 18.

5. The least progress has been made on the history of Soviet Russia itself.

6. On specific interpretations referred to above and below, see the essays in Samuel H. Baron and Nancy W. Heer, eds., *Windows on the Russian Past* (Columbus, Ohio, 1977).

7. In addition to slavery and feudalism, Marx distinguished another precapitalist socioeconomic formation which he called the Asiatic mode of production. It referred to agrarian self-sufficient societies characterized by the absence of private property in land, the prevalence of peasant communes as the basic units of society, and a despotic political authority ("oriental despotism"). He thought that such societies had developed in India, China, and in modified form, in Russia. Marx considered the Asiatic mode an alternative to the sequence from slavery to feudalism, and a static order which could not generate capitalism without a violent shock from the outside. The Asiatic mode of production as a category of thought was suppressed in the Soviet Union in the 1930s but was revived in the 1960s. An account of these developments is given in Samuel H. Baron, "Marx's *Grundrisse* and the Asiatic Mode of Production," *Survey* 21, nos. 1–2 (Winter–Spring 1975): 128–47.

8. V. I. Shunkov et al., eds., *Perekhod ot feodalizma k kapitalizmu v Rossii* (The Transition from Feudalism to Capitalism in Russia) (Moscow, 1969), pp. 108, 365.

9. See Shunkov et al., *Perekhod ot feodalizma*, and S. D. Skazkin et al., eds., *Dokumenty Sovetsko-Ital'ianskoĭ konferentsii istorikov* (Documents from the Conference of Soviet-Italian Historians) (Moscow, 1970). The latter relates to the controversy over absolutism.

10. John Meyendorff, Ihor Ševčenko, and Alexander Paul, "The Cambridge and Soviet Histories of the Byzantine Empire," *Slavic Review* 30 (1971): 634.

11. Some indication of the range of methodologies in vogue may be glimpsed in S. O. Shmidt et al., eds., *Istochnikovedenie: Teoreticheskie i metodicheskie problemy* (The Study of Sources: Theoretical and Methodological Problems) (Moscow, 1969).

12. See L. M. Ivanov et al., eds., *Rossiĭskiĭ proletariat: oblik, bor'ba, gegemoniia* (The Russian Proletariat: Profile, Struggle, Hegemony); I. D. Koval'chenko, *Russkoe krepostnoe krest'ianstvo v pervoĭ polovine XIX veka* (Russian Peasant Serfs in the First Half of the Nineteenth Century) (Moscow, 1967); and S. M. Troitskii, *Russkiĭ absoliutizm i dvorianstvo v XVIII veke* (Moscow, 1974).

13. V. M. Kabuzan, *Narodonaselenie Rossii v XVIII-pervoi polovine XIX v.* (po materialism revizii) (The Population of Russia in the 18th and First Half of the 19th Century [Based on Census Materials]) (Moscow, 1963); Ia. E. Vodarskii, *Naselenie Rossii v kontse XVII-Nachale XVIII veka* (The Population of Russia at the End of the 17th and the Beginning of the 18th Century) (Moscow, 1977).

14. N. M. Druzhinin et al., eds., *Absoliutizm v Rossii* (Absolutism in Russia) (Moscow, 1964).

15. B. F. Porshnev, *Social Psychology and History* (Moscow, 1970); cf. A. Ia. Gurevich, *Problemy genezisa feodalizma v zapadnoĭ Evrope* (Problems in the Genesis of Feudalism in Western Europe) (Moscow, 1970). It should be noted that some of Gurevich's work was censured.

16. Two relevant serials are *Istoriia i istoriki* (History and Historians) and *Problemy Istochnikovedeniia* (Problems of Source Study).

17. L. V. Cherepnin, "50 let sovetskoĭ istoricheskoĭ nauki i nekotorye itogi izucheniia feodal'noĭ epokhi istorii Rossii" (50 Years of Soviet Historiography and Certain Results of the Study of Russia's Feudal Epoch), *Istoriia SSSR*, no. 6 (1967): 78–79.

18. To mention a few: *Osobennosti agrarnogo stroia Rossii v period imperializma* (Peculiarities of Russia's Agrarian System in the Era of Imperialism) (Moscow, 1962); A. L. Sidorov et al., *Ob osobennostiakh imperializma v Rossii* (On the Peculiarities of Imperialism in Russia) (Moscow, 1963); M. P. Pavlova-Sil'vanskaia, "K voprosu ob osobennostiakh absoliutizma" (On the Peculiarities of Absolutism), *Istoriia SSSR* (History of the USSR), no. 4 (1968).

19. See Samuel H. Baron, "Plekhanov, Trotsky, and the Development of Soviet Historiography," *Soviet Studies* 26 (1974): 380–95.

20. A good introduction to the rise and development of the *mnogoukladnost'* conception is K. N. Tarnovskiĭ's "Problema vzaimodeĭstviia sotsial'no-ekonomicheskikh ukladov imperialisticheskoĭ Rossii na sovremennom etape razvitiia sovetskoĭ istoricheskoĭ nauki" (The Problem of the Interaction of Socio-Economic Formations of Imperialistic Russia in the Present Stage of Development of Soviet Historical Science), in V. V. Adamov et al., eds., *Voprosy istorii kapitalisticheskoĭ Rossii: problema mnogoukladnosti* (Problems in the History of Capitalist Russia: The Question of Multiformity) (Sverdlovsk, 1972).

21. Shunkov et al., *Perekhod ot feodalizma*, pp. 5, 41, and passim.

22. See John Keep, "The Current Scene in Soviet Historiography," *Survey* 19, no. 1 (Winter 1973): 3–20; and George M. Enteen, "A Recent Trend on the Soviet Historical Front," *Survey* 20, no. 4 (1974): 122–31.

23. I. V. Kuznetsov, "Ob ukladakh i mnogoukladnosti kapitalisticheskoĭ Rossii" (On Formations and Multiformity in Capitalistic Russia), *Voprosy istorii*, no. 7 (1974): 20–32.

24. I. I. Mints, M. V. Nechkina, and L. V. Cherepnin, "Zadachi sovetskoĭ istoricheskoĭ nauki na sovremennom etape ee razvitiia" (Problems of Russian Historical Science in the Current Stage of Its Development), *Istoriia SSSR*, no. 5 (1973): 5, 17.

Bibliography

Adamov, V. V., et al., eds. *Voprosy istorii kapitalisticheskoĭ Rossii: problema mnogoukladnosti* (Problems in the History of Capitalist Russia: The Question of Multiformity) (Sverdlovsk, 1972).

Baron, Samuel H. "Plekhanov, Trotsky, and the Development of Soviet Historiography," *Soviet Studies* 26 (1974): 380–95.

―――. "The Transition from Feudalism to Capitalism in Russia: A Major Soviet Historical Controversy," *American Historical Review* 73 (1972): 715–29.

Baron, Samuel H., and Nancy W. Heer, eds. *Windows on the Russian Past: Essays on Soviet Historiography Since Stalin* (Columbus, Ohio, 1977). Covers recent treatment of a number of important topics in Russian history.

Black, Cyril E., ed. *Rewriting Russian History* (New York, 1956).

Cherepnin, L. V. "50 let sovetskoĭ istoricheskoĭ nauki i nekotorye itogi izucheniia feodal'noĭ epokhi istorii Rossii" (50 Years of Soviet Historiography and Certain Results of the Study of Russia's Feudal Epoch), *Istoriia SSSR*, no. 6 (1967).

Druzhinin, N. M., et al., eds. *Absoliutizm v Rossii* (Absolutism in Russia) (Moscow, 1964).

Enteen, George M. "A Recent Trend on the Soviet Historical Front," *Survey* 20, no. 4 (1974): 122–31.

Gefter, M. Ia., et al., eds. *Istoricheskaia nauka i nekotorye problemy sovremennosti* (Historical Science and Certain Problems of the Present Time) (Moscow, 1969).

Gerschenkron, Alexander. "Soviet Marxism and Absolutism," *Slavic Review* 30 (1971): 853–69.

Gruliow, Leo, ed. *Current Soviet Policies, II* (New York, 1957).

Gurevich, A. Ia. *Problemy genezisa feodalizma v zapadnoi Evrope* (Problems in the Genesis of Feudalism in Western Europe) (Moscow, 1970).

Heer, Nancy W. *Politics and History in the Soviet Union* (Cambridge, Mass., 1971).

Istoriia i sotsiologiia (History and Sociology) (Moscow, 1964).

Ivanov, L. M., et al., eds. *Rossiĭskiĭ proletariat: oblik, bor'ba, gegemoniia* (The Russian Proletariat: Profile, Struggle, Hegemony) (Moscow, 1970).

Kabuzan, V. M. *Narodonaselenie Rossii v XVIII-pervoĭ polovine XIX v.* (po materialism revizii) (The Population of Russia in the 18th and First Half of the 19th Century [Based on Census Materials]) (Moscow, 1963).

Keep, John. "The Current Scene in Soviet Historiography," *Survey* 19, no. 1 (Winter 1973): 3–20.

Keep, John, and Lilianna Brisby, eds. *Contemporary History in the Soviet Mirror* (New York, 1964).

Koval'chenko, I. D. *Russkoe krepostnoe krest'ianstvo v pervoĭ polovine XIX veka* (Russian Serfs in the First Half of the 19th Century) (Moscow, 1967).

Kritika: A Review of Current Soviet Books on Russian History (Cambridge, Mass., 1964–).

Kuznetsov, I. V. "Ob ukladakh i mnogoukladnosti kapitalisticheskoĭ Rossii" (On Formations and Multiformity in Capitalistic Russia), *Voprosy istorii*, no. 7 (1974): 20–32.

Marko, Kurt. *Sowjethistoriker zwischen Ideologie und Wissenschaft* (Cologne, 1964).

Mendel, Arthur. "Current Soviet Theory of History: New Trends for Old?" *American Historial Review* 72 (1966): 50–73.

Meyendorff, John, Ihor Ševčenko, and Alexander Paul. "The Cambridge and Soviet Histories of the Byzantine Empire," *Slavic Review* 30 (1971): 619–48.

Mints, I. I., M. V. Nechkina, and L. V. Cherepnin. "Zadachi sovetskoĭ istoricheskoĭ nauki na sovremennom etape ee razvitiia" (Problems of Russian Historical Science in the Current Stage of Its Development), *Istoriia SSSR*, no. 5 (1973): 3–16.

Porshnev, B. F. *Social Psychology and History* (Moscow, 1970).

Pundeff, Marin, ed. *History in the USSR: Selected Readings* (San Francisco, 1967).

Rogger, Hans. "Politics, Ideology and History in the USSR: The Search for Coexistence," *Soviet Studies* 16 (1965): 253–75.

Shmidt, S. O., et al., eds. *Istochnikovedenie: Teoreticheskie i metodicheskie problemy* (The Study of Sources: Theoretical and Methodological Problems) (Moscow, 1969).

Shteppa, Konstantin. *Russian Historians and the Soviet State* (New Brunswick, N.J., 1962).

Shunkov, V. I., et al., eds. *Perekhod ot feodalizma k kapitalizmu v Rossii* (The Transition from Feudalism to Capitalism in Russia) (Moscow, 1969).

Skazkin, S. D., et al., eds. *Dokumenty Sovetsko-Ital'ianskoĭ konferentsii istorikov* (Documents from the Conference of Soviet-Italian Historians) (Moscow, 1970).

"Sovetskaia istoriia na novom etape razvitiia" (Soviet Historiography at a New Stage of Development), *Voprosy istorii,* no. 8 (1960): 3–18; trans. in Shteppa, *Russian Historians,* pp. 390–410.

Tillett, Lowell. *The Great Friendship: Soviet Historians on the Non-Russian Nationalities* (Chapel Hill, N.C., 1969).

Troitskiĭ, S. M. *Russkiĭ absoliutizm i dvorianstvo v XVIII veka* (Russian Absolutism and the Nobility in the Eighteenth Century) (Moscow, 1974).

Vodarskiĭ, Ia. E. *Naselonie Rossii v kontse XVII—Nachale XVIII veka* (The Population of Russia at the End of the 17th and the 18th Century) (Moscow, 1977).

16 JERZY TOPOLSKI

Soviet Studies in Social History

Considerable growth of studies in social history is characteristic of Soviet historiography. Two factors may be cited among the causes of this growth: a rich tradition which goes back to the nineteenth century and the inspiring influence of Marxist theory and method. Such outstanding historians as I. V. Lutchitskiĭ (1845–1918), N. I. Kareev (1850–1931), D. M. Petrushevskiĭ (1863–1942), and I. M. Kulisher (1878–1934) left basic studies of Western European social history during the feudal period, mainly with respect to the peasantry, studies which are still valid in their linking of social and economic analysis in a manner which was then very innovative. From this tradition V. I. Lenin's *Development of Capitalism in Russia* (1899) was developed. The latter study pointed to the role of social stratification in the growth of a market, which was in turn indispensable for the growth of capitalism. For Soviet historians, Lenin's study has become one of the principal instances of the application of the Marxist method to the investigation of mutual relations between society and the economy.

Generally speaking, Soviet historical studies have been influenced by Marxism in two important ways. First, it shifted their focus onto research of the social structure with particular stress on the history of the peasants and the working class and on the problems of class struggle and revolution. And secondly, at the same time, Marxism focused attention on the nature of the successive socioeconomic formations of human societies and on the mechanisms of transition from one formation to the other. Studies and discussions on the making of feudalism and capitalism as well as on the Asiatic mode of production proved to be particularly profitable. Of the immense variety of literature and discussion on these subjects, in part published in the journal *Voprosy Istorii* (Problems in History), let us mention some recent titles: *The Transition from Feudalism to Capitalism in Russia* (1969),[1] *The Development of Feudalism* by A. Novoseltsov, V. Pashuto, and L. Cherepnin (1972),[2] and the works of A. Ia. Gurevich (1970, 1972).[3] The first of these three books includes the views of some fifty historians, who generally speaking advocate a greater stress on the peculiarities of capitalist growth in Russia and other areas of the Soviet Union, on the role of such factors as the state, and on various forms of consciousness. The studies on the making of feudalism have also revealed similar postulates. However, while in the case of the genesis of capitalism emphasis was placed on differences between Russia and Western Europe, in the problem of the genesis of feudalism the focus has been on their common elements. Against the judgment of such authors as A. Ts. Merzon, Yu. A. Tikhonov, and N. V. Ustiugov, most historians have preferred to be cautious in discerning the beginnings of capitalism in Russia as early as the fourteenth to seventeenth centuries; they point to dominating reverse tendencies.

The discussions mentioned above and many others, usually very theoretical in nature, have been based on source-field work performed by successive generations of historians, increasingly so in non-European Soviet republics. The most basic studies of landed property, the situation of the peasantry, and the social structure have been written by the following historians among others: I. A. Kossminskiĭ,[4] a pupil of Petrushevskii and founder of a whole school of historical study on the social history of Western Europe and Byzantium which published usually in the series called "Vizantiĭskiĭ Vremennik" and "Srednie Veka"; B. D. Grekov, the author of the basic study *Krest'ianie na Rusi* (The Peasants of Russia; 2 vols., 1946); V. K. Jatsunskiĭ, who has investigated the social problems of industrialization; V. I. Shunkov, an authority on the socioeconomic growth of Siberia; S. V. Bakhrushin, who has studied cities and burghers; and B. F. Porshnev, a historian of class struggle and popular movements. Numerous studies on the social stratification of the peasantry, on their duties, and on the evolution of landed property have been collected in some volumes of an annual publication started in 1958—*Ezhegodnik po agrarnoĭ istorii Vostochnoĭ Evropy* (Annals of the Agrarian History of Eastern Europe). Different volumes refer to different regions of the Soviet Union from the Baltic areas to Moldavia.

Of the varied studies and discussions by the younger generations of social historians, the most creative and at the same time the most typical for the evolution of Soviet historiography after World War II seem to be the ones linked to the following themes:

(1) the history of the peasants in the several regions of the Soviet Union, especially between the fifteenth and nineteenth centuries, and sometimes linked to the studies of cities and markets;

(2) the agrarian reforms of the nineteenth century, especially the reform of 1861;

(3) the class struggle of the peasantry and the peasant wars;

(4) the social background of the history of the Eastern Orthodox Church and of heretical movements;

(5) the history of the class of feudal landowners and the social origins of absolutism;

(6) manufacture-shops and the origins of the growth of the working class and of the labor movement;

(7) changes in the structure of Soviet society.

In the area of peasant history, one should mention the studies of the mechanisms for making feudal fortunes (*votchina*) and of the group that owned them as contrasted with the formation of the class of subjected peasants during the fourteenth to seventeenth centuries in northeastern Russia. For instance, A. I. Kopanov studied the Beloozero country (1951), L. V. Danilova, Novgorod (1955), Yu. A. Alekseev, Pereeslav (1966), and A. D. Gorskiĭ, the situation of peasants throughout the entire area under consideration in the fourteenth and fifteenth centuries (1960). Similar research was carried out with respect to northwestern Russia, mainly by the historians based in Leningrad. I refer primarily to the innovative works of N. E. Nosov, who pointed out the complex nature of the processes of the making of feudal structures; to the studies published under the editorial supervision of A. L. Shapiro (*Agrarian History of Northwestern Russia,* 1971, 1974);[5] and to those by A. M. Sakharov on the growth of the cities during the fourteenth and fifteenth centuries in this same area (1961). If the studies of Russia's northern lands threw a new light upon the making of feudal structure in the regions covered with forests and archaic in social structure, studies of a much more dynamic variety have been conducted on the villages and peasants in Byelorussia and Lithuania (I. Iurginis,[6] P. G. Kozlovskiĭ, V. I. Meleshko, D. L. Pokhilevitch), Latvia (V. V. Doroshenko, H. Strods), Estonia (J. Kahk, Kh. Ligi, E. Tarvel), and the Ukraine (I. D. Boiko, I. M. Grossman, V. A. Markina). They have contributed to our understanding of the making and growth of social structures in the conditions of the manorial-serf economy and the "new" serfdom of the sixteenth through the nineteenth centuries. V. I. Koretškiĭ[7] has made a synthetical investigation of the origins of the new serfdom (*Zakreposhtšchenie*) with respect to the Muscovite state in the sixteenth century, while the seventeenth-century transition of the peasants from the position of hereditary debtors (*kabalnoe kholopstvo*) into that of manorial serfs obliged to work has been studied by V. M. Paneiakh (1967), who decoded this interesting social process.

Another crucial problem which has attracted increasing attention since World War II has been the nineteenth-century agrarian reforms that abolished serfdom. The reforms have been analyzed in the context of broader social change, including the revolutionary situation. The classic study by P. Zajonchkovski has been complemented by numerous works by M. V. Nechkina (and her pupils), N. N Ulashtshik (1965), and J. Kahk (1978). A comparison of their writings with the much simpler analyses which reduce the history of reform to the closed backstage infighting among various groups of higher officials and landowners demonstrates the value of their profound analysis as it relates to the processes of social genesis.[8]

Historical materialist inspiration of research on the peasant class struggle has produced numerous publications on the struggle during the period of the making of the manorial-serf economy, during the peasant uprisings in the sixteenth to eighteenth centuries, in the peasant fight against serfdom, and during their participation in the revolutionary movements of the twentieth century. Here the following studies merit attention: an analysis of the popular uprisings of peasants and city poor in the eleventh to fifteenth centuries by (among others) M. N. Tikhomirov and M. V. Mavrodin; research on antifeudal heretical movements by (among others) Ya. S. Lurie and A. I. Klibanov; and a number of works concerning the increase of class struggle during the sixteenth century. On the basis of the concept of peasant war introduced by M. N. Pokrovskii with respect to Russia the following leaders of uprisings have been investigated: Bolotnikov, 1606–1607 (I. Smirnov, 1947); Razin, 1670–1671 (I. N. Stepanov, 1962, 1972); and especially Pugachev, 1773–1775 (by A. I. Andrushchenko, M. N. Pokrovskiĭ, and M. V. Mavrodin, among others), in this case in connection with the two hundredth anniversary of the uprising. From a scholarly point of view it is interesting to follow the peasant programs and to reconstruct the aims of the struggle.

Looking for deeper reasons, historians have also analyzed the religious aspect of peasant protest. This is linked to the research on the Eastern Orthodox Church, church property, and priestdom as a social stratum, and to studies on the influence of heretical movements (*staroverstvo* and sects) upon social life and culture, by I. U. Budovin and G. A. Nosov, among others. A great variety of sects have been identified; a continuous process of their differentiation because of antagonisms of a social nature has been described, and the diversified links of religious ideology, social customs, social groups, and class movements of peasantry and urban and plebeian masses have been described and analyzed.

The making of the class of feudal landowners and of their ideology has been investigated mainly in the context of the analyses of the peasantry, of the making and the economics of large landed property (see, for example, works by A. N. Anfimov), and of the making and consolidation of absolutism. Absolutism is viewed in Soviet historiography as a political superstructure of late feudalism. Its making is traced to the period of Peter I, but its beginnings are usually placed in the period of Ivan the Terrible, when Russian monarchy still revealed some features of estate representation.[9] In many discussions scholars have debated both a thesis that Russian absolutism is a borrowing from other countries and a thesis that counterposes Russian and Western European absolutisms. Historians have tried to establish the social background of Russia's absolutism, pointing out among other things the complex nature of relationships between feudal landowners and cities. The problem has also been raised as to whether the origin of the absolutist monarchy is to be linked to popular movements which the ruling class wanted to suppress, or to the support of the monarchy expressed by the middle nobility (*dvoramie*) against the aristocracy (*boiars*) (N. I. Pavlenko). Many studies have been inspired by Ivan the Terrible's *oprichnina* (A. A. Zimin, R. G. Skrynnikov, S. O. Shmidt), by estate representation (*sobor, duma*) (M. N. Tikhomirov, L. Cherepnin, S. O. Shmidt, N. E. Nosov), and by the ideology of absolutism (N. M. Druzhinin, N. I. Pavlenko, S. M. Troitskiĭ).

Another topic of heated discussion in the Soviet historical milieu has been the question of the role of the manufacturing shops as a possible origin of modern industry and as a factor in the making of the working class, the latter raising the complex issue of the nature of a labor force for manufacturing shops in the epoch of serfdom. Studies by E. I. Zaozerskaia of textile manufactures (1960) and the salt industry (1970) merit attention for their treatment of this problem. One can safely assert that in the course of discussion the participants have given up linking eighteenth-century manufacturing shops with the transformations of society leading toward the capitalist economy. However, emphasis has been placed upon the studies of the evolution of the working class and of its situation during the nineteenth century (among others, by Z. M. Ivanov) and on the evolution of the peasant class (I. D. Koval'chenko, J. Kahk). The social (class) genesis of the revolutions of 1905–1907 and 1917 has come to be viewed as separate scholarly issues. Lenin's direct and multiaspectual evaluations and analyses have provided universally accepted frames of Soviet conceptualizations of these phenomena.

One should also mention the research on the transformations of the structure of Soviet society which have accompanied the growth of Soviet sociology and demographic studies and the application of computerized data processing. The processes of collectivization in various republics have been investigated (by S. P. Trapeznikov, P. N. Lomashvili, A. T. Tchmyga, and N. A. Ivnitskiĭ, among others) as well as the conditions of life of Kholkhoz peasants (Yu. V. Arutunian). In 1976 P. I. Simush published a separate book entitled *The Social Portrait of the Soviet Peasantry*.[10] S. L. Senavskiĭ's research on the changes of structure of Soviet society in the past twenty years also merits attention.[11]

These analyses are increasingly linked to computerized data processing, now often employed by Soviet historians for social study. The works of I. D. Koval'chenko, L. V. Milov, and the active team from the Institute of History of the Estonian Academy of Sciences (J. Kahk, E. Tarvel, A. Ruusman, H. Palli, R. N. Pullat, L. A. Loone) are among the best of their kind. Their focus is mainly on the peasants and their economy. One should also mention an interesting program for a reconstruction of the family of the seventeenth to eighteenth centuries in Estonia, elaborated by H. Palli. An American scholar, G. F. Eastbrook, provided one of the blueprints for the classification of peasant households.

Generally speaking, social history belongs among the most dynamic fields in Soviet historiography. As far as the development of its methods and the liveliness of its discussions are concerned, it is the central, most advanced domain of history in the Soviet Union. Its characteristic feature is a continuous link with economic and political history and—to a growing extent—with the history of social consciousness.

Notes

1. V. I. Shunkov et al., eds., *Perekhod ot feodalizma k kapitalizmu w Rossii* (The Transition from Feudalism to Capitalism in Russia) (Moscow, 1969).

2. A. Novoselfšov, V. Pashuto, and L. Cherepnin, *Puti razvitiia feodalizma* (The Development of Feudalism) (Moscow, 1972).

3. A. Y. Gurevich, *Problemy genezisa feodalizma v zapadnoĭ Evrope* (Problems of the Genesis of Feudalism in Western Europe) (Moscow, 1970): *Kategorii srednevekovoĭ kultury* (Categories of Culture in the Middle Ages) (Moscow, 1972).

4. I. A. Kossminskiĭ, *Issledovaniia po agrarnoĭ istorii Anglii XIII veka* (Studies in Agrarian History of England in the Eighteenth Century) (Moscow, 1947).

5. A. L. Shapiro, ed., *Agrarnaia istoriia severo-zapada Rossii: Vtoraia polovina XV-nachalo XVI v.* (Agrarian History of Northwestern Russia: Second Half of the Fifteenth to the Beginning of the Sixteenth Century) (Leningrad, 1971): *Agrarnaia istoriia severo-zapada Russii XVI veka* (. . . of the Sixteenth Century) (Leningrad, 1974).

6. The author prepared a synthetical study of the history of the peasants in Lithuania from the oldest periods to 1861: I. I. Iurginis, *Lietuvos valstieciu istorie* (Vilnius, 1978).

7. V. I. Koretski, *Zakreposhchenie krest'ian i klassovaia borba ve vtoroi polovine XVI veka* ("New" Serfdom of Peasantry and a Class Struggle in the Second Half of the Sixteenth Century) (Moscow, 1970).

8. As demonstrated by D. Field, *The End of Serfdom: Nobility and Bureaucracy in Russia 1855–1861* (Cambridge, Mass., 1976).

9. In the years from 1968 to 1971 there was a discussion on Russian absolutism in *Voprosy Istorii* (Problems in History).

10. P. I. Simush, *Sotsiialnyi portret sovetskovo krest'ianstwa* (Social Portrait of the Soviet Peasantry) (Moscow, 1976).

11. S. L. Senavskiĭ, *Izmeneniia v sotsiialnoĭ strukture sovetskovo obshchestva* (Changes in Social Structure of Soviet Society) (Moscow, 1973); S. L. Senavskiĭ and V. B. Telpukhovskii, *Rabochiĭ klass SSSR 1938–1965* (The Working Class of the USSR, 1938–1965) (Moscow, 1971).

17 ANDRZEJ F. GRABSKI

Poland

As in many other European countries, the methodological basis of academic historiography in Poland prior to World War II was the model of individualistic and "objective" historical science, as codified in the well-known works of Ernst Bernheim and Charles Langlois-Charles Seignobos (the latter was translated into Polish at the beginning of the century).[1] To be sure, at the turn of the century the new currents in European historiography had found supporters among the young university students of historical science. Karl Lamprecht, Gustav Schmoller, and Karl Marx all gained adherents among young Polish historians. Later in independent Poland during the 1920s and 1930s, these young disciples, now mature, contributed significantly to the history of culture and to the interlocking fields of economic and social history. In the history of culture they included Stanisław Kot, Stanisław Łempicki, Aleksander Brückner, and others, and in the modernization of the historical profession Marceli Handelsman and his school. The growing interest in economic and social history was represented by the medievalists Kasimierz Tymieniecki, Roman Grodecki, Stanisław Arnold, Henryk Łowmiański and by researchers such as Natalia Gąsiorowska. It was during the period between the two world wars that the Polish school of economic history was founded by Franciszek Bujak of the University of Leopol and Jan Rutkowski of the University of Poznań. During these years economic and social history in Poland had its own university chairs and its own journal and was winning worldwide scholarly esteem. However, at the same time, in Poland as elsewhere, before World War II traditional political history still dominated historical research.[2]

World War II and the German occupation of Poland brought a brutal halt to the development of Polish historical science. Historiography suffered considerable losses: 53 percent of the historians active before 1939 were dead, the universities and institutes were closed, archives and libraries were pillaged and destroyed during the Nazi occupation, and conducting research became impossible.[3] Thus, the essential problem after the liberation of Poland was the reconstruction of Polish historical science. The combined efforts of the state and society and the considerable contribution of scientific circles to this reconstruction soon produced results: new centers for research in the science of history were created, and the material organization of historical studies in Poland began to develop. Reconstruction was linked to transformation: at the very moment of the liberation of the country, certain historians proclaimed the necessity of transforming Polish historical science because of the new social and political situation.

Most of the professors at both the universities and the other institutions of higher learning had been scholars before the war. The circle of Marxist historians—already rather numerous—initiated different discussions to convince their colleagues of the necessity of finding new concepts of the science of history. During the time of political struggle for consolidation of the new system, oversimplifications were not always easy to avoid. As it pertains to the methodological transformation of historiography, the theory of historical materialism was more than once understood in a dogmatic and simplified manner.[4] Despite all this, even during this time, the scientific content of Polish historical writing was not without importance. In our opinion, its most profitable new direction was the polemic, with its idealist theory of history, its struggle against idiographism, and its practical consequences for historical research.

In the debates on the regularity of historical processes, the new nomological position of Polish historical science was elaborated—not, however, without difficulty—and the development in general of methodological thought was stimulated. The nomological position laid the base for considerable development in research in the field of economic and social history, which was directed—especially in the 1940s and the beginning of the 1950s—toward problems in production, the productive forces, and class struggle. The phenomenon of the "superstructure" was often interpreted as the direct result of the economic and social "base"; this point of view was stipulated by the broad interpretation of the theory of historical materialism that was common at the time. The simplistic trends, which could be seen not only in the field of historiography, were soon criticized by historians, philosophers, and other scholars, and gradually they were overcome.

The new structure of the organization of historical science, and especially the creation in 1952 of the Polish Academy of Sciences (which led to the establishment of a series of scientific centers for historical research, including the Institute of History and the Institute of History of Cultural Materialism), and the founding of other centers (which are still not formally tied to the academy), the creation of a coordinating body (the Committee of Historical Sciences of the Academy of Sciences), the planning of research on a national scale—all this stimulated the growing development of historical research in Poland. One can gain some idea of the dimensions of the increase in contemporary Polish historiography by consulting the annual bibliography of historical writings published by Jan Baumgart and his co-workers.[5] In the years just following the war approximately 1500 books, articles, and other publications devoted to the history of Poland were published per year in Poland. Annual output surpassed 2000 titles in 1954, 3500 in 1969, and 4000 in 1974. These figures refer only to publications which have as a subject Polish history; total historical production is much more extensive (5869 titles in 1974). Between 1955 and 1974, according to the bibliography, the number of published works increased approximately 60 percent per year, but in reality this increase was much greater—almost 100 percent—because the selection criteria for inclusion in the bibliography became much stricter as the years went by.[6] The number of historical periodicals published in Poland is at present sixty, of which only eleven appeared before the war. This considerable wealth of historical publications was a function of the modernization of Polish historiography, which influenced both research methods and the subjects of historical studies. The rise in quantity went hand in hand with a rise in quality, and this, in our opinion, has determined the present position of Polish historical science.

Methodological Consciousness

The characteristic and essential trait of historical science in contemporary Poland is doubtless its well-developed methodological consciousness. In the first years after the war, the discussion of methodological problems in history was the domain of philosophers. But professional historians treated philosophical interpretations with reservation because the often extreme generality of the concepts was only loosely connected to the reality of the historical process. Beginning in the mid-1950s, as conditions grew more favorable for the development of historical thought, numerous historians themselves became engaged in methodological research. Intensively discussed by historians, the work of the philosopher Adam Schaff on the objectivity of the laws of the historical process (in which he presents a severe criticism of numerous concepts and theories of history)[7] has opened the way for a series of works, the majority of which were written by historians, devoted to methodological problems. Taught at the universities, the methodology of history has become a well-developed field, and it is tied to the method of research in contemporary Polish historiography. The results of methodological studies are often presented in books or in the pages of scientific periodicals, two of which make a specialty of methodological issues.

As methodological thought developed, different centers for research in the field were established. The most powerful and influential at present is undoubtedly at the University of Poznań, where an internationally famous school of philosophy that specializes in methodological issues has been established. The cooperation between specialists in philosophy, logic, and history has profited from the numerous works devoted to the whole of ontological and epistemological problems of the science of history. The real results of their research were presented in a book of collected essays by various authors, edited by Jerzy

Kmita, which was devoted to the elements of Marxist methodology in the human sciences, and which deals for the most part with questions on the methodology of history.[8]

Jerzy Topolski, who has written several well-known books on methodology and who is an inspiration to his colleagues in research in this field, is attached to this center. As early as 1960, Topolski published—in collaboration with the philosopher and sociologist Andrzej Malewski—a small volume in which he proposes the idea of research "on the empirical methodology of history" (which opposes the a priori methodology), studies which can be considered competent both in the field of methodology of science as a philosophical discipline and in the practice of historical science.[9] Pursuing his research, the author published in 1968 his fundamental work, *The Methodology of History* (recently translated into Italian and English); in Poland the second, revised, enlarged edition was published in 1973.[10] Topolski presented his methodological ideas to the public at large in the popular small volume *The World Without History* (1972; second edition 1976), in which he opposes contemporary antihistorical trends and presents a defense of consciousness and knowledge of history as being necessary for the progress of society.[11] Recently he has published two new books. In one, entitled *Marxism and History* (1977), he collects his studies devoted to Marxist historicism; and in the other, *Understanding History* (1978), he presents an analysis of the problem of explanations in historical science from the viewpoint of the historian.[12]

In his methodological work, Topolski often uses the specialized language of contemporary methodological science. He understands methodology within a very broad framework: as a theory of the historical process (which he calls objective methodology) and also as historical epistemology. In his ontological reflections, the author, inspired by the theory of historical materialism, has developed in his own terminology—the activitist theory of the historical process—by opposing any fatalistic interpretation of history as well as voluntarist ideas. In this context, Topolski entered into a controversy with several theories and trends of contemporary thought (such as structuralism and economic and psychoanalytical history), opposing their automatic interpretation of the historical process as an autodynamic function of a certain sphere of reality. In his epistemological thinking, by opposing concepts which simplify the character of historical recognition and by instead emphasizing its activity, he has presented— among other things—a theory of knowledge that does not derive from sources and that precedes the position of the researcher, as well as a new classification of historical sources, not according to form but according to their informative character. Topolski's methodological ideas have interested many historians, and he has formed a group of researchers who undertake the study of various problems in the methodology of history.

However, the center of Poznań is not the only one where research of this kind is being conducted in contemporary Poland. In Warsaw the methodological problems of historical science were the subject of the work of Wanda Moszczeńska (who died in 1974), professor at the university and author of *A Critical Précis of the Methodology of History* (1968; the second edition in 1977 was complemented by several of her other works).[13] Also interested in methodological problems was the eminent specialist in economic history, Witold Kula, author of the brilliant essay *Reflections on History* (1958)—a short, critical survey of the reductionist simplifications of the historiography of the 1940s and 1950s[14]—and of other works with a methodological character. Another historian who treated methodological questions in his historiographical research was Marian H. Serejski, professor at the University of Łódź and at the Institute of History of the Polish Academy of Sciences, who died in 1975. He wrote a series of articles dealing with these problems, as well as an anthology of texts written by Polish historians from the eighteenth to the twentieth centuries, entitled *Historians on History* (2 vols., 1963–1965).[15]

At present, Stanisław Piekarczyk of the University of Warsaw has employed contemporary mathematics in his research in methodology. His findings are presented in his important book, *History—Culture—Knowledge* (1972).[16] Methodology of history is also the subject of some philosophical works, among which are those of A. Schaff, who has published a book much discussed by historians, *History and Truth* (1970); and those of Jakub Litwin, a researcher interested in the problems of philosophy of history, and his group.[17] There are many other scholars active in this field. In Krakow, the methodology of history is represented by the work of Celina Bobińska, a specialist in economic and social history and professor at the Jagellonian University, who wrote *Historians—Fact—Method* (1964) and who is editor-in-chief of a specialized review of methodological studies.[18] Zbigniew Kuderowicz, a professor at the same university, researches the philosophy of history. He has published numerous works devoted to the historiosophic ideas of various thinkers of the nineteenth and twentieth centuries—particularly the Germans—and a small, popular book on the fundamental problems of the philosophy of history in its development throughout the centuries.[19]

At almost every university or school of higher learning in Poland where history is taught, one can now find people interested in the methodological problems of historical science. We have listed here only the most important centers of research and the best-known scholars, and have only summarized their activities. Works dealing with the questions of methodology appear frequently, not only in specialized periodicals, but also in other historical reviews. The Polish reader is also familiar with the foreign texts indispensable for a better understanding of current questions on contemporary methodology in history, because translations have been prepared of various works by foreign authors such as Marc Bloch, Fernand Braudel, Michel Foucault, Erich Fromm, Philip Bagby, Igor S. Kon, and others. Thus, there is no doubt that the methodology of history is becoming an area of activity for numerous historians, who are concurrently conducting research and that methodological studies are presently closely connected with the historiographic practice of many researchers.

Historiographical Studies

The interest of historians in historical methodology is also manifested in contemporary Polish historiographical works, which constitute a specialized direction in historical research in Poland. Begun shortly after the war[20] and directed specifically toward problems in Polish historiography, historiographic research in Poland displays a variety of modern interests—among them the problems of historical thought, of erudition and the organization of the science, analyzed within the framework of social and economic conditions. The scholar who should be regarded as the true founder of research in this field is M. H. Serejski (mentioned above), who established the center of historiographic research in the Polish Academy of Sciences and developed a following of students who continued his work. Serejski studied all the problems of Polish historiography from the eighteenth to the twentieth centuries. He dealt with historical science in the periods of the Enlightenment and Romanticism, devoting several works to the great Polish historian of the nineteenth century, Joachim Lelewel, and studying the historiography of bourgeois liberalism and the great historical schools of the nineteenth century. He was also interested in the transformations of historical thought and historiography at the dawn of the present century and in the problem of contemporaneity.

Among the most important of his works are his studies of Lelewel, especially one that deals with Lelewel's idea of universal history (1958). In this and other studies, a collection of historiographical and methodological articles, *The Past and the Present* (1965), an important book, *The Nation and the State in Polish Historical Thought* (1973; second edition 1977), and several others,[21] the author shows the great Polish historian at work amid the grand currents of European historiography in his era. Serejski's main contribution was doubtless his fundamental work, *Europe and the Partition of Poland: A Historiographical Study* (1970), which presents a detailed analysis of the opinions of European historiographers in the eighteenth and twentieth centuries on the fall of ancient Poland in relation to the political and social changes in Europe—a work of formidable erudition and astonishingly broad scope.[22]

A remarkable researcher, Serejski did not limit his studies to Polish historiography only: he published articles on methodological questions of history, on the historical ideas of Voltaire, Leopold von Ranke, François Guizot, and Friedrich Meinecke; he even wrote an article on the historical ideas of Charles Darwin. As an editor, he published numerous works of Polish and foreign historians with critical commentaries (for example, von Ranke's *History of the Popes*) and was editor-in-chief of the collection *Classics of Polish Historiography* (now continued under the editorship of Andrzej F. Grabski).

At the University of Łódź, the history of historiography was also the subject of research of other scholars:[23] the legal historian Jan Adamus (who died in 1962) dealt with the great currents and theories of modern Polish historiography; Józef Dutkiewicz, a historian of the nineteenth and twentieth centuries, published a book on the eminent Polish historian Szymon Askenazy and his school, as well as other historiographical works; the historian and bibliographer Helena Więckowska published the correspondence of Joachim Lelewel from his emigration period, as well as other works devoted to this great historian.[24] Krystyna Śreniowska, a student of M. H. Serejski, is the author of two historiographical works, one on the medievalist Stanisław Zakrzewski and the other on the legend of Tadeusz Kościuszko in Polish historical thought. Another student of the same master, Franciszek Bronowski, specializes in the historiography of the Enlightenment and Romanticism.[25] Still other researchers inspired by Serejski (among whom are Jerzy Włodarczyk and Jerzy Danielewicz) have treated historiographical problems.

Besides Serejski—who was very active in Łódź and Warsaw—other inspirational scholars for modern historiographic research were Wanda Moszczeńska (mentioned above), who treated the problems of Polish historiography at the beginning of the twentieth century, and the sociologist and historian Nina Assorodobraj, who studied the historical ideas of Lelewel and Polish historiography of the nineteenth century.[26] At the University of Warsaw at present, historiographical studies are the subject of works by the legal historian Juliusz Bardach, who published a very valuable book on Wacław Aleksander Maciejowski (a well-known historian of the nineteenth century and a pioneer in the comparative research of Slavic law),[27] as well as Jerzy Maternicki, a student of Moszczeńska and author of works on the Warsaw historians of the nineteenth century (1970), historical education in Poland in modern times (1974), and an interesting volume on historical science and Polish historians during the time of World War I (1975).[28] The eminent specialist on modern history, Andrzej Zahorski, devoted two of his books to the history of the Napoleonic legend in Poland and France.[29] Maria Wierzbicka, another of Moszczeńska's students, has published articles on Polish historians who were part of leftist circles at the beginning of the twentieth century, as well as a valuable book devoted to the development and changes in the methodological concepts of the historical synthesis of Polish national history from the eighteenth to the twentieth centuries.[30]

At the Institute for History of the Polish Academy of Sciences, historiographical research is the subject of the work of Andrzej F. Grabski, a student of M. H. Serejski and author of *Directions in Polish Historiography in Modern Times* (1972), *Historical Thought in the Polish Enlightenment* (1976), and the study *Historiography and Politics* (1978), devoted to the historical research in Poland in the nineteenth and twentieth centuries, and other works.[31] Several other authors have collaborated with Grabski in historiographical research. The historian and political scientist Franciszek Ryszka has written a great deal about the historiography of Nazism. Among other researchers in Warsaw interested in historiographical problems, Janina Żurawicka has published a book on the Polish historian and specialist in the history of religions, Ignacy Radliński.[32]

In Krakow, Henryk Barycz, author of numerous studies dealing with the eminent Krakow historians of the past, is engaged in historiographical studies;[33] Danuta Rederowa is interested in similar problems. Helena Madurowicz-Urbańska has chosen to research economic and social Polish historiography, and she has produced studies devoted to the works of Feliks Łoyko, the forerunner of research in the area of economic history in eighteenth-century Poland,[34] along with other works (among them, studies on F. Bujak). Many other authors have analyzed various questions in historiography, among them Helena Rzadkowska, and let us mention again Celina Bobińska. The history of education in Poland was the topic of interest to Tadeusz Słowikowski, who became a specialist in the field.

Historiographical research conducted in Poland has dealt specifically with Polish-German problems, as is evident from the first volume of the collective work (still incomplete) on Polish-German relations in the science of history (1974).[35] The history of German historiography, as well as the methodology of history, have been subjects of research by Gerard Labuda, Jerzy Krasuski, and other historians in Poznań; some of them have also investigated the ancient historiography of the region of Greater Poland and Poznań. A group under J. Topolski initiated research on the development of Polish historical consciousness. We can also mention the fruitful activity of scholars at other centers of research such as Lech Mokrzecki (Gdańsk), author of several works on the early modern historiography of the northern provinces of Poland (sixteenth to eighteenth centuries) and on the history of the instruction of history,[36] Jerzy Serczky (Toruń), and others. We have not yet mentioned the specialized studies by medievalists—Gerard Labuda, Brygida Kürbis, Aleksander Gieysztor, Zofia Kozłowska-Budkowa, Jan Dąbrowski, and others—devoted to the problems of medieval historiography; or research into the Renaissance and Baroque centuries, conducted by specialists in those eras (H. Barycz, Bronisław Nadolski, and others).

Polish historiographical research, which presently constitutes a very well-developed field of historical science, is directed toward Polish problems in particular. Its evident lack is its relatively limited interest in the broader questions of European and world historiography. However, the history of historiography has become the subject of standard university courses.

Developments in Agrarian History

We have already emphasized that the methodological transformation of the Polish science of history influenced research in the area of economic and social history.[37] One result has been that the problem of agrarian history has taken a leading position in the work of historians; as Jerzy Topolski has said, "The growth in agrarian research following the Second World War is linked to a very powerful movement which can be observed in other countries as well."[38] Between 1945 and 1953 the number of works devoted to agrarian problems published in Poland increased by 12 percent, and in 1958 they constituted 34 percent of the total of Polish historical works. In addition to source publications—such as the important series on the general lands of the royal domains—Polish historiography has developed research on all the great problems of agrarian history.

Thus, considerable progress has been made in our knowledge of agricultural and forestry techniques, tools, vegetable and animal production techniques, mechanization of production, and so on from the most ancient times to the modern era. This progress was made possible through the collaboration of various specialists: historians, archeologists, ethnographers, and even technicians. Historians have successfully conducted research on the productivity of rural economy throughout the centuries by analyzing the ties between the field and the marketplace, and the role of the craftsmen and rural industry. The complicated questions of rural colonization and the problems of arable land have also received attention. Numerous specialists have dealt with the development of agricultural knowledge in relation to the question of productivity.

The technical evolution of the rural economy thus has not been the sole field of interest in the area of agrarian history. The most extensively discussed problems have undoubtedly been those of the transformations in the economic and social structure of rural areas. A particularly important topic has been the agricultural system of the countries of Central Europe, especially the origins and development of seignorial reserves and the system of statute labor. This subject had received a great deal of attention from Jan Rutowski, an outstanding scholar of agrarian history, in the years before World War II; he had analyzed the causes for the pattern of the statute labor system and concluded that "the coexistence of the ease of product flow in the rural economy and of increased serfdom was the required condition, which was at the same time indispensable, for the development of the system of statute labor reserves."[39] Later historians have improved their understanding of this phenomenon by examining seignorial reserves in different regions of the country.

Specialists of agrarian history have also generally discussed the causes of economic regression in Poland since the end of the sixteenth century and its consequences for the whole of economic and social life, as well as the problem of the origins of capitalism in rural areas and its development in the different regions of the country. Within this framework, the period preceding the appropriation from the peasants has been studied. Research devoted to later times is rather scarce, as are studies on Polish agricultural history of the twentieth century. An important new aspect of research in the history of the Polish rural community has been the keen interest that has arisen about problems related to social conflicts. These have been analyzed in terms of the social conditions and the position of the rural population from the Middle Ages to modern times.

Other Areas of Economic History

Research in other areas of economic history has been less prolific, but during the 1950s studies were undertaken on the importance of crafts, prices, wages, and other economic questions. These have developed extensively in subsequent years. The problem of production in the artisan and cottage industries in the towns from the Middle Ages to modern times has been discussed, especially the history of manufacturing in the eighteenth century and modern industry in the main industrial centers of Poland—mining, metallurgy, cloth manufacturing, textiles, and so on. Trade problems, very little studied in the 1950s, have been analyzed much more intensely since the 1960s. The trade of the great cities—Gdańsk, Szczecin, Poznań, and so on, and the Vistula—has attracted the most interest; very little attention has been given to the history of transportation and communications. Compared to other areas of research in economic history, relatively little work has been done pertaining to problems of prices, money and credit, or wages. But a most successful area of study in contemporary Polish historiography has been undoubtedly the history of towns. There are dozens of local monographs and studies pertaining to the history of the various Polish towns. Whole series of works, as well as synthesized works written by several authors, are devoted to the history of great centers such as Warsaw, Krakow, Poznań, Gdańsk, Szczecin, and Lublin, among others. These studies have looked beyond purely economic history and analyzed all aspects of historical problems.

Since the 1960s, in connection with the increase in research on the period between the two world wars, studies have been begun on economic policies of the Polish state following World War I. Of central concern to several specialists have been the economic and social conditions in Poland during the Nazi occupation, as well as the economic policies of the German occupiers. Researchers of earlier economic history have been less interested in the economic policies of the ancient Polish state than in the policy on the co-partitioning of the states of ancient Poland, especially the economic policies of Prussia in regard to Polish territory which was annexed by the Hohenzollern monarchy.

In the study of other areas of economic life, as in their research on agrarian society, contemporary Polish historiographers have paid special attention to socioeconomic problems. Research has been developed on social structure, devoted to the processes of the formation, constitution, interior structure, and living conditions of classes and large social groups. This form of historical study, which was inspired by sociology, began immediately after the war—we should here mention the pioneering work by Nina Assorodobraj on the labor force in manufacturing in the eighteenth century (1946)[40]—but it has really become fully developed since the mid-1950s. Most of the works in this genre are devoted to the history of the working class, but a considerable number focus on other social groups: the bourgeoisie, the nobility, the intellectuals, and so forth.

The Integration of Economic and Social History

Thus two trends can be discerned in contemporary Polish economic and social historiography. On the one hand, several scholars, having renounced the simple descriptive style and gone in search of new paths of interpreting the phenomena they study, are engaged in research on materialistic culture, closely linked to the history of techniques.[41] Since the 1950s, this history of materialistic culture has become a special and independent field of historical research in Poland. Its main center of research is the Institute of History of Materialistic Culture of the Polish Academy of Sciences; some specialists also work at the universities and at other centers. This group publishes reviews and special collections as well as synthesized works. Research in this field has a strong interdisciplinary character; the historians work in collaboration with specialists in various disciplines.

On the other hand, a different trend can be observed, a widening of the area of research by including the great problems of social history, which is strictly tied to the development of methodological thought, inquiry into new problems, and to new interpretations and methods. Thus, economic history in contemporary Poland is becoming more and more social history. In the 1960s, in his treatise on problems and methods in economic history and also in a small volume on economic theory of feudal society, Witold Kula spoke out against the increase in monographic and analytical research as well as descriptive trends in research of economic history.[42] These two works, methodological in character, were influenced by new currents in contemporary historical science, especially the ideas of French historiography and the theoretical thought in the economic sciences, and they provoked animated discussion among specialists; they have thus considerably contributed to an acceleration in the modernization processes of economic and social history in Poland.

The trend toward historical research with a global perspective, inspired by the theory of historic materialism and stimulated by the very close relations of the Polish historians with the French *Annales* school, is manifested in the 1960s by an increase in research on economic and social models. In their discussions with foreign scholars, the Polish historians, interested in the problems of the generalization of the view of contemporary historiography, have opposed the tendency to consider models exclusively as instruments of historical epistemology designed by the researcher. They rather tend to study the complexity of historical reality and its actual structure by using the methods of models.[43] Interest in economic structures has resulted in monographs and other works proposing a comparative perspective for analysis of the complexity of historic processes. This trend is manifested in the works of various authors; typical examples are the book by Jerzy Topolski on the origin of capitalism in Europe from the fourteenth to the seventeenth centuries (1965),[44] and the numerous studies by Andrzej Wyczański, Andrzej Mączak, Władysław Rusiński, and several other historians. The economist Stefan Kurowski, inspired by the theories of long-range economic cycles which abound in foreign literature, attempted to analyze "secular trends" according to the development of iron and steel production (1963); the result of this study is very debatable.[45]

The historian-economists who are engaged in the study of new problems have become more and more interested in new methods of research, especially quantitative methods and techniques. These questions were discussed during the international colloquium "History and Modernity, Problems of the Modernization of the Methodology and Profession of the Historian," organized in Warsaw at the Institute of History of the Polish Academy of Sciences in November 1973, with the participation of specialists from several countries—France, the Soviet Union, the Netherlands, Italy, Hungary, and others.[46] The colloquium provided the occasion for a discussion of questions about methods and also for a presentation of results from already completed studies that had been conducted by using quantitative methods and techniques.

Since the 1960s research into economic and social structures has been developed in Polish historical science. On the initiative of Witold Kula, a whole series devoted to the history of social structures in Polish society during the eighteenth and nineteenth centuries has been published, which analyzes the various social groups.[47] Several historians have prepared and published monographs or other specialized studies that use sociological and statistical methods to examine large groups and social classes and their structure in given places and times, especially during the nineteenth and twentieth centuries. Let us mention here the research of Marian M. Drozdowski and other authors on the working class; the studies of Janina Leskiewiczowa, Janusz Zarnowski, Ryszarda Czepulis-Rastenis, and others on the intellectuals (Polish intelligentsia); of Jerzy Jedlicki on the nobility; of other authors on the bourgeoisie (Ryszard Kołodziejczyk), the Jews (Artur Eisenbach), and others. This direction of historical research, which now occupies the specialists of several branches of historical science, has become in recent years one of the principal currents in contemporary Polish historiography.

The History of Political and Social Movements

The history of political and social movements is a new area of historical research, which has drawn the attention of several historians and has taken a prominent position in the total works of contemporary Polish historiography. Before the war, these subjects had received only marginal attention in academic historical science, even though historical reviews were published on the parties which were devoted to the history of the Polish socialist movement. Immediately after the war, small study and documentation centers for the history of the workers' movement were created throughout Poland. These were soon transformed and united into the Institute of the History of the Party and eventually into the Advanced School of Social Sciences, which is tied to the Central Committee of the United Polish Workers' Party (PZPR).[48] In the beginning, activity at this center was mainly concerned with the propagation of the socialist tradition of the Polish workers' movement, but soon studies were begun on the history of the socialist and workers' movement in Poland from the end of the nineteenth century to the present time. The history of the workers' movement has found a secure place in the universities and other centers of historical research; presently it is a very well-developed area of specialized studies. Since the mid-1950s these researches, directed specifically toward the history of movements of the revolutionary left, have expanded to include the history of the parties and organizations of various political and ideological beliefs. During this research, primarily focused on questions of the central organizations of the workers' movement, their program and activities, other problems were also investigated: regional organizations and their members, questions of daily activity, knowledge and culture of the workers, and so on.

The history of the workers' movement is thus becoming more and more a social history, the subject of which at present is not exclusively the history of institutions, their leaders and political actions, but of all the problems of the working class, analyzed on the political and social level. This research is therefore becoming more and more integrated with other directions in the study of economic and social history in Poland. Following the example of studies on the workers' movement in the second half of the 1950s, research was also developed on the peasant movement.[49] Since 1959, the *Annals* of these studies have been published—a specialized review, devoted to the movement's history—and the Institute of History of the Peasant Movement has continued in its productive work since 1960. This area of research is presently represented by an important number of scholars who work at various centers: in Warsaw (Krzysztof Dunin-Wąsowicz, Jan Molenda, Jan Borkowski, Witold Stankiewicz, Józef R. Szaflik, Andrzej Zakrzewski, and others), in Łódź (Helena Brodwoska), in Krakow, in Poznań, and elsewhere.

Until the 1960s, the history of other Polish economic and social movements was not a field of great interest in historical research; the works which attempted to deal with these problems were rare and not very satisfactory. In the last few years, however, interesting results can be observed in this area, especially in research on the nationalist movement (Marian Orzechowski, Jerzy Marczewski, Roman Wapiński, Jerzy J. Terej, and others), Christian democracy (Bożena Krzywobłocka), and other trends.

Cultural History

The increase in new trends in Polish historical science is not limited to the areas mentioned above. We should still mention definite transformations which have occurred in the area of cultural history, where Polish historiography has traditionally displayed valuable historical research. We have already seen that studies on materialistic civilization developed into a specialized branch of historical studies linked to economic and social history; this should not be considered as a general detachment of such interests from the history of culture. To the contrary, works on the questions of materialistic civilization seem to become more and more integrated with research on the totality of culture. In Polish historiography after the war, the simplistic categories for interpreting cultural phenomena as direct results of economic and social conditions were soon abandoned, but this does not mean that efforts to improve understanding of the social dimensions of culture were curtailed. Through their criticism of the more narrow categories of traditional research (which border on studies of sections from cultural activity and are nothing more than a barely coherent collection of results of works in various specialized disciplines—art history, history of literature, etc.) Polish historians, in collaboration with sociologists, historians of literature, and others, have made differentiated attempts to find new categories of research in cultural history.

We emphasize the differentiation of these propositions, because, as is the case with historical science in other countries, no one single concept of research in the history of culture exists in Polish historiography, and several propositions rival one another, each based on a different theoretical idea. Thus, studies have been developed of everyday life in Poland from the most ancient times to the present, as is evidenced by the collection of books devoted to this genre, comparable to the well-known Hachette collection in France.[50] Several researchers have been inspired by the history of mentalities which presently is so well developed in French historical science, and they have proposed works on the history of culture in the categories of the history of mentalities. This is exemplified by the brilliant essay of Andrzej Wyczański on the culture of the Renaissance in Poland, in which he has grasped and analyzed the characteristic features of Renaissance man in his materialistic and social context.[51] Elsewhere in the research dealing with problems of culture, one can see the increasing influence of sociological ideas and cultural anthropology, which is determined by the development of these scientific specializations in Poland. Recently, a lively interest has also been shown by several researchers in semiotic ideas, under the influence of which culture is studied as a system of signs. None of these new propositions has become prevalent in present research on the problems of culture in Polish historiography.

It should be observed that numerous cultural historians—as for example the eminent specialist in problems of Polish cultural history of the sixteenth and seventeenth centuries, Janusz Tazbir,[52] among others—profit in their own works from various theoretical inspirations, and attempt to find general research categories which are practical rather than theoretical by analyzing spheres and ties of culture within its total structure and development. This does not, however, mean that all Polish historians interested in the problems of cultural history have a similar attitude: there are still representatives of traditional *Sittengeschichte*— we can cite here the work of Zbigniew Kuchowicz on the customs of Polish society of the sixteenth through the eighteenth centuries[53]—as well as scholars interested in questions of intellectual culture. These topics are often the subject of studies by historians of the sciences and philosophical thought, which are well-developed and fully independent disciplines in contemporary Polish historical science.

Finally, in the last few years an increasing interest in the forms of culture, such as political culture, social culture, and so forth, can be observed in Polish historiography. This work, the first results of which have already been published, is undoubtedly influenced by sociology and has been directed toward research on the attitudes of social groups, with respect to the different spheres of historical reality.[54]

One can observe a growing process of integration of studies in the history of culture and civilization with the rest of social history. This trend can also be observed in research on the history of classes and large social groups. As studies in the economic, social, and political history of various groups have grown, historians have been obliged to analyze their cultural histories as well. At present, the most thriving seem to be researches on the culture of the working class, largely as a result of the studies by Władysław L. Karwacki.[55] The problems in the culture of the peasants, previously studied only by ethnographers, have now also drawn the attention of historians, as has the culture of the nobility and the bourgeoisie.

A further example of the integration of the history of culture with the whole of research on great historical problems is provided by works on the German occupation of Poland during World War II. Czesław Madajczyk, in his fundamental work on the system of the Nazi occupation of Poland, also dealt with questions of culture;[56] the culture at the time of Nazism has likewise been the subject of the social research of Bogusław Drewniak. Similar problems have been investigated by other researchers, of whom we can here mention Franciszek Ryszka. In 1977, the Polish Commission of History of the Second World War organized an international colloquium in Warsaw, "Inter arma non silent Musae," devoted to problems that arose with the influence of the war and Nazism on the culture of the time.[57]

In present-day Polish historiography, a certain sense of competition may be observed between work on the history of culture and research on collective consciousness. The function of the category of consciousness in the theory of Marxism and its interpretation in the various currents of Marxist thought is recognized. In numerous philosophical works, the importance of analyzing the area of human consciousness as an active factor in historical processes has been repeatedly emphasized; this has even influenced historical research. Current Polish historiography has produced several interesting works on national consciousness, such as the studies of Józef Chlebowczyk.[58] Research has also begun on other similar problems: class consciousness, political consciousness, historical consciousness (which is also of special interest to sociologists), and so on—we are awaiting the results.

At the end of 1977, two colloquia were organized at the Institute of History of the Polish Academy of Sciences which were devoted to problems of research in the field of the history of collective consciousness—social and national—in Poland in modern times.[59] The exchange of ideas during debates such as these has undoubtedly contributed to the growth of research in this field and allows a better specification of its categories.

Political History

We should emphasize once more the already repeatedly observed fact that the especially preferred area of traditional historiography has been political history, in the form of *Haupt-und Staatsaktionen*. Compared to historical science in other European countries, Polish historiography finds itself in a very peculiar situation. During the period of the nonexistent Polish state, it was not easy for political reasons to pursue work on Polish political history, especially on the political history of the modern period. Hence, numerous fundamental problems have not been studied, or have been analyzed only from the point of view of the countries who were the co-partitioners of Poland, in their own historiography. This situation has undoubtedly stimulated interest in the political history of Poland before the war—to a certain degree—and also in the present time. The distinctly controversial nature of the subject of these studies has prevented the research of Polish political history of the twentieth century from developing better until the last twenty years, and numerous questions still remain which have not yet been approached by historians.

Even though political history often was judged (in our opinion, too severely) as a refuge for historiographical traditionalism, even though researchers less inclined to follow each innovation in their science often produce work of a very traditionalist nature in this area, political history is currently a field where new trends are on the increase. The subject of research is thus not only political activities of the great figures in history, but also—not to say specifically—the power elites, political groups and parties, and so on, analyzed within the economic and social context that is presented to us; for example, there are numerous works on the problems of political history of Poland in the nineteenth century. In a general way we may cite the work of Stefan Kieniewicz, author of several works devoted to the history of Poland in the nineteenth century and a fundamental work on the insurrection of 1863,[60] and Henryk Wereszycki, Jerzy Skowronek, Jerzy Zdrada, and the numerous historians who are occupied with Polish political history of the twentieth century, such as Tadeusz Jędruszczak, author of the important volume on the power elite in Poland before the war,[61] as well as other authors of works on the various questions of political history in our century. In this field, too, new research methods are being employed, notably quantitative methods in works dealing with the political attitudes of social groups. Numerous Polish historians interested in political history undoubtedly agree with Jerzy Topolski, who in his essay on its role in historical synthesis has emphasized the importance of research in this field, which simultaneously treats "the subjective and objective side of the historical process," that is, the problems of the activities of man and his motivations as well as political and other factors.[62]

The process of modernization involves both the very traditional form of historiography as well as biographical works. At the time of the transformation of Polish historical science after the war, these forms were considered outdated, and for several years publication of the national biographical dictionary was even halted. Contemporary biographical works are seeking new forms in the presentation of so-called ecological portraits of persons within the context or milieu of their activity. Among the most interesting attempts we may cite the biographical research of groups, especially of generations, such as the work of the literary historian Alina Witkowska on the generation of literary figures contemporary with Adam Mickiewicz, or of the historian Tomasz Kisielewski on the first three generations of activists in the Polish peasant movement, in which he presents their "collective portrait."[63]

Social History

The various areas of research in the Polish science of history are thus becoming more and more a social history. This trend can be observed in the works devoted to medieval history, as well as in modern and contemporary history. It is the eminent medievalist Henryk Łowmiański who in his monumental work on the birth of Poland has presented a truly global analysis of the long-range processes of the formation of Polish society and the Polish state.[64] The trend toward global history from a perspective of social history has intensified from the 1960s to the present.

In this time, collective research on the Polish working class has developed at the Institute of History of the Polish Academy of Sciences, under the leadership of Stanisław Kalabiński, who engaged a number of important specialists and studied all problems of the structure and development of the working class and its place in Polish society. The results of this work are published in the collection *The Polish Working Class*,[65] which in turn has resulted in the preparation—also under the editorship of Kalabiński—of a work of collective synthesis, the first part of which was published in 1974. In this research, the importance of work on "the role of social factors in Polish historical processes" has been emphasized, as has the need to analyze "the anatomy of our society in the past, to explain the mechanisms which determine the social life of our country and the total complex of historical stipulations of the developmental and dynamic directions of social and political changes, the currents of ideas and cultural trends."[66] Work on the history of the great social classes, which is also conducted in other centers of research and has gradually come to include classes other than the working class, has provided the basis for the recent proposition of an ambitious program of research on the whole history of Polish society and its consciousness.

As a result of this program, established in the national plan of scientific research, several works have been initiated in various fields of Polish contemporary historical science, and researchers have been encouraged to intensify their studies and to modernize their profession. A new series of studies has been started dealing with the problems of the history of society in ancient Poland,[67] and work devoted to the history of societies in other eras continues, or is being developed; an example is Janusz Żarnowski's book on Polish society during the period between the world wars.[68] The very wide range of problems requires an increasing integration of work in the different fields of research, as well as the use of new methods. All this actualizes the question of quantitative methods in the science of Polish contemporary history.

The problem is not completely new, because the question of quantitative methods has been posed for some time, even though researchers have only rarely used the computer.[69] In the second half of the 1960s, research in which the authors used quantitative methods was published on the stratification of the Polish peasants at the beginning of the twentieth century and on the agrarian structure of the kingdom of Poland in the second half of the nineteenth century (Juliusz Łukasiewicz, Regina Chomać). In 1966 the center of statistical research devoted to the study of the history of industry was established. Several historians have been interested for some years in the possibility of using quantitative methods in various fields of research. This was discussed at the Tenth Congress of Polish Historians in Lublin in 1969 and during the already-mentioned colloquium in Warsaw in 1973. Despite all difficulties—the most serious of which are source problems—Polish historical science has already produced valuable works that represent research performed with the computer. Andrzej Wyczański conducted research in 1974 at the Center for Historical Research of the School for Advanced Studies in the Social Sciences (Paris) on Polish social structure in the sixteenth century, the results of which were presented in book form in 1977.[70] His work, composed of three studies devoted to questions of social stratification, proposes to "pave the way for this type of study" and especially to present the possibilities of obtaining through new methods much more precise and detailed results than those obtained according to traditional methods of study. In his analysis of the quantitative material, the author has made use of certain statistical methods (the Lorenz curve and the decile method), with significant results.

Other researchers who conduct historical research on society have produced interesting work in the last few years through the use of quantitative analytical methods.[71] Stanisław Kalabiński and Feliks Tych have undertaken research on the structure of members of the workers' parties between 1878 and 1945. They designed a questionnaire with 60 questions and 360 variations in response to analyze a group of 28,000 active participants in the workers' movement. The work is still in progress, but the authors have released the first results. Kalabiński has already published other quantitative studies: on the members of the first Polish socialist organization, on the differences in wages of workers in the kingdom of Poland at the beginning of the twentieth century, and also on the labor strike movement in the kingdom of Poland in the period 1870–1914. Stefania Kowalska-Glikman has conducted a quantitative study of the social and professional mobility of the population of Warsaw in the first half of the nineteenth century by analyzing 10,000 marriage certificates. Irena Rychlikowa is utilizing statistical methods in dealing with the stratification of landowners between the collapse of ancient Poland and the appropriation of peasant lands in the 1860s. Zbigniew Pustuła already has conducted quantitative research on the structure of the working class and its changes according to data on factory workers from the end of the nineteenth century and the beginning of the twentieth. Joanna Hensel has conducted quantitative research on the bourgeoisie of Warsaw in the second half of the nineteenth century by drawing data from legal documents (3879 documents pertaining to 2600 persons). Ludwik Hass has proposed the use of quantitative methods in research on the attitudes and political behavior of the classes and other social groups in Poland between the two wars.

Contemporary Polish historiography has also produced other works in economic and social history in which the authors have used quantitative methods—which is not completely identical to the use of the computer. Recently, interesting studies on prices in Wrocław between 1506 and 1618 have been prepared by Marian Wolański, who used the computer with the help of specialists of the Oskar Lange Economic Academy at Wrocław.[72]

Summary and Conclusion

Contemporary Polish historiography shows very differentiated and intensive new trends in various fields. It undoubtedly attempts to integrate the picture of the historical reality studied, while aspiring to analyze simultaneously both its structure and its dynamics in their dialectic interdependence, its subjective as well as its objective aspects. This it attempts to achieve on the one hand through specialization, and on the other hand through increasing collaboration of the various specializations, in its search for the synthesized perspective of research. We have already stressed the essential importance of the modernization process in Polish historical science, of the new methodological inspirations, of the valued traditions of Polish historiography of the past, as well as the well-developed relations with the modern research centers for history in foreign countries. Contemporary Polish historiography seems to have established its own character; in our opinion it is not a mere compliment when the Polish School of Historical Research is mentioned more frequently today than in the past.[73]

Notes

1. On Polish historiography prior to World War II in general: the special number of the review *Kwartalnik Historyczny* (Quarterly Review of History), 1937, pp. 205 ff; Bronisław Dembiński, Oskar Halecki, Marceli Handelsman, *L'Historiographie polonaise du XIXe et du XXe siècle* (Warsaw, 1933); Kazimierz Tymieniecki, *Zarys dziejów historiografii polskiej* (Summary of the History of Polish Historiography) (Krakow, 1948); Marian H. Serejski, *Zarys historii historiografii polskiej* (Summary of the History of Polish Historiography), 2 vols. (Łódź, 1954–1956) and the third volume by Józef Dutkiewicz and Krystyna Śreniowska (Łódź, 1969); introduction and commentaries of

M. H. Serejski in: M. H. Serejski, ed., *Historyey o historii* (Historians on History), 2 vols. (Warsaw, 1963–1966). On Polish historiography after the war: B. Leśnodorski, "Les Sciences historiques en Pologne 1945–1955" in: *La Pologne au Xe Congrès International des Sciences Historiques à Rome* (Warsaw, 1955); Jerzy Topolski, "Développement des études historiques en Pologne 1945–1968" in: *La Pologne au XIIIe Congrès International des Sciences Historiques à Moscou*, vol. 1 (Warsaw, 1970); Jerzy Topolski and Andrzej Wyczański, "History Research in Poland 1945–1970," *The Western Affairs Review*, no. 3 (1971) (the same text in Polish in: *Nauka Polska* (Polish Science), 1971, no. 2); Tadeusz Manteuffel, *Historyk wobec historii* (Historians vis-à-vis History) (Warsaw, 1976). See also the bibliography in: *La Pologne au XIIIe Congrès des Sciences historiques*, vol. 2 (Warsaw, 1970), pp. 26–31.

2. Helena Madurowicz-Urbańska, "L'histoire économique en tant que discipline universitaire en Pologne: Période d'organisation 1905/6–1921/2, *Studia Historiae Oeconomicae* (1974): 3–20; idem, "Franciszek Bujak—o nowy kształt historii" (Franciszek Bujak—the new form of history) in F. Bujak, *Wybór pism* (Selected Works), vol. 1 (Warsaw, 1976), pp. 7 ff.; Andrzej Wyczański, "The Annals of Polish Social and Economic History," *The Journal of European Economic History*, no. 1 (1977): 215–226; J. Topolski, "Le développement des recherches d'histoire économique en Pologne," *Studia Historiae Oeconomicae* (1966), pp. 3 ff.

3. J. Topolski, "Développement des études," pp. 8–9; Halina Winnicka, "Środowisko historyków w latach wojny i okupacji" (The Environment of Historians During the Years of the War and the Occupation), *Przegląd Humanistyczny* (Humanistic Review), no. 8 (1975): 75–89.

4. See: Andrzej Malewski (and Jerzy Topolski), "Metoda materializmu historycznego w pracach historyków polskich" (Method of Historical Materialism in the Works of Polish Historians) in: A. Malewski, *O nowy kształt nauk społecznych* (On the New Form of the Social Sciences) (Warsaw, 1975), pp. 166–89.

5. *Bibliografia Historii Polskiej* (Bibliography of the History of Poland) is published as a current bibliography by Jan Baumgart et al.; consult: *La Pologne au XIIIe Congrès International*, vol. 2, pp. 13–14, for detailed information.

6. Stefan Kieniewicz, "Perspektywy dziejopisarstwa" (Perspectives of Historiography), *Polityka* (Politics, A Weekly Review), no. 39 (24 September 1977): 1, 15.

7. Adam Schaff, *Obiektywny charakter praw historii* (Objective Character of the Laws of History) (Warsaw, 1955).

8. Jerzy Kmita, ed., *Elementy marksistowskie metodologii humanistyki* (Elements of Marxist Methodology in the Social Sciences) (Poznań, 1973); see also, J. Kmita, ed., *Założenia teoretyczne badań nad rozwojem historycznym* (Theoretical Principles of Research in Historical Development) (Warsaw, 1977).

9. A. Malewski and J. Topolski. *Studia z metodologii historii* (Studies on the Methodology of History) (Warsaw, 1960).

10. J. Topolski, *Metodologia historii* (Methodology of History) (Warsaw, 1968; 2nd ed. 1973).

11. J. Topolski, *Świat bez historii* (The World Without History) (Warsaw, 1972; 2nd ed. 1976).

12. J. Topolski, *Marksizm i historia* (Marxism and History) (Warsaw, 1977); idem, *Rozumienie historii* (Understanding History) (Warsaw, 1978).

13. Wanda Moszczeńska, *Metodologii historii zarys krytyczny* (Critical Outline of the Methodology of History) (Warsaw, 1968: 2nd ed. 1977).

14. Witold Kula, *Rozważania o historii* (Reflections on History) (Warsaw, 1958).

15. Marian H. Serejski, *Przeszłość a teraźniejszość* (The Past and the Present) (Wrocław and Warsaw, 1965); idem, ed., *Historycy*.

16. Stanisław Piekarczyk, *Historia—Kultura—Poznanie* (History—Culture—Knowledge) (Warsaw, 1972).

17. A. Schaff, *Historia i prawda* (History and Truth) (Warsaw, 1970); Jakub Litwin, ed., *Problemy filozofii historii* (Problems of the Philosophy of History) (Wrocław and Warsaw, 1974); idem. ed., *Zagadnienia historiozoficzne* (Historiosophical Questions) (Wrocław and Warsaw, 1977).

18. Celina Bobińska, *Historyk—fakt—metoda* (Historians—Fact—Method) (Warsaw, 1964). The Review "Historyka, Studia metodologiczne" (History, Methodological Studies) has appeared since 1967.

19. Zbigniew Kuderowicz, *Światopogląd a życie u Diltheya* (World Vision and Life in Dilthey) (Warsaw, 1966); idem. *Biografia kultury. O poglądach Jakuba Burckhardta* (A Biography of Culture. On the Ideas of Jacob Burckhardt) (Warsaw, 1973); idem, *Filozofia dziejów* (Philosophy of History) (Warsaw, 1973).

20. See: Jerzy Maternicki, "Narodziny polskiej historii historiografii 1945–1956" (The Birth of the History of Polish Historiography 1945–1956), *Przegląd Humanistyczny* (Humanistic Review), no. 1 (1978): 1–18.

21. Marian H. Serejski, *Koncepcja historii powszechnej Joachima Lelewela* (The Notion of Universal History According to Joachim Lelewel) (Warsaw, 1958); idem, *Przeszłość*, idem, *Naród a państwo w polskiej myśli historyzcznej* (The Nation and the State in Polish Historical Thought). See also by the same author: "The Concepts of 'Nation' and 'State' in the Polish Historical Thought of the Nineteenth Century," *Dialectics and Humanism*, no. 1 (1975): 89–101; "Naród czy państwo?" (Nation or State?), *Kwartalnik Historyczny*, 1973, pp. 324 ff.

22. M. H. Serejski, *Europa a rozbiory Polski. Studium historiograficzne* (Europe and the Partition of Poland: A Historiographical Study) (Warsaw, 1970); see also by the same author: "L'aspect Européen de la question Polonaise. Les réflexions des historiens étrangers sur les partages de la Pologne," in: *Poland at the Fourteenth International Congress of Historical Sciences in San Francisco* (Wrocław and Warsaw, 1975), pp. 135–47.

23. See: J. Maternicki, "Narodziny," pp. 9 ff (see note 20 for full title).

24. Jan Adamus, *Monarchizm i republikanizm w syntezie dziejów Polski* (Monarchism and Republicanism in the Synthesis of History in Poland) (Łódź, 1961); idem, *Polska teoria rodowa* (The Polish Theory of the Clans) (Łódź, 1958); idem, *O kierunkach polskiej myśli historycznej* (On the Currents of Polish Historical Thought) (Łódź, 1964); Józef Dutkiewicz, *Szymon Askenazy i jego szkoła* (Szymon Askenazy and His School) (Warsaw, 1958); Helena Więckowska, ed., *Listy emigracyjne Joachima Lelewela* (Letters from Emigration by Joachim Lelewel), 5 vols. (Krakow and Wrocław, 1948–1956).

25. Krystyna Śreniowska, *Stanislaw Zakrzewski. Przyczynek do charakterystyki prądów ideologicznych w historiografii polskiej 1893–1936* (Stanisław Zakrzewski. Contribution to the Characteristics of Ideological Trends in Polish Historiography 1893–1936) (Łódź, 1956); idem, *Kościuszko—bohater narodowy. Opinie współczesnych i potomnych 1794–1946* (Kościuszko—National Hero. The Opinions of Contemporaries and Posterity 1794–1946) (Warsaw, 1973); Franciszek Bronowski, *Idea gminowładztwa w polskiej historiografii* (The Idea of Democracy in Polish Historiography) (Łódź, 1969).

26. See: J. Maternicki, "Narodziny," pp. 1–18.

27. Juliusz Bardach, *Wacław Aleksander Maciejowski i jego współcześni* (Wacław Aleksander Maciejowski and His Contemporaries) (Wrocław and Warsaw, 1971).

28. J. Maternicki, *Warszawskie środowisko historyczne 1832–1869* (The Warsaw Circle of Historians 1832–1869) (Warsaw, 1970); idem, *Dydaktyka historii w Polsce 1773–1918* (Didactics of History in Poland 1773–1918) (Warsaw, 1974); idem, *Idee i postawy. Historia i historycy polscy 1914–1918. Studium historiograficzne* (Ideas and Attitudes. History and Polish Historians 1914–1918. A Historiographical Study) (Warsaw, 1975).

29. Andrzej Zahorski, *Z dziejów legendy napoleońskiej w Polsce* (On the History of the Napoleonic Legend in Poland) (Warsaw, 1971); idem, *Spór o Napoleona we Francji i w Polsce* (The Controversy about Napoleon in France and Poland) (Warsaw, 1974).

30. Maria Wierzbicka, *Dawne syntezy dziejów Polski. Rozwój i przemiany koncepcji metodologicznych* (Ancient Syntheses of the History of Poland. The Development and the Changes in Methodological Concepts) (Wrocław and Warsaw, 1974).

31. A. F. Grabski, *Orientacje polskiej myśli historycznej* (Directions in Polish Historical Thought) (Warsaw, 1972); idem, *Myśl historyczna polskiego Oświecenia* (Historical Thought in Polish Enlightenment) (Warsaw, 1976); idem, *Historiografia i polityka* (Historiography and Politics) (Warsaw, 1978).

32. Janina Żurawicka, *Twórczość naukowa Ignacego Radlińskiego 1843–1920* (The Scientific Work of Ignacy Radliński 1843–1920) (Wrocław and Warsaw, 1975).

33. Henryk Barycz, *Wśród gawędziarzy, pamiętnikarzy i uczonych galicyjskich* (Amongst the

Conversationalists, Memorialists and Scholars of Galicia), 2 vols. (Krakow, 1963); idem, *Stanisław Smolka w życiu, w nauce* (Stanisław Smolka, His Life and His Science) (Krakow, 1975); idem, *Na przełomie dwóch stuleci* (At the Turn of Two Centuries) (Wrocław and Warsaw, 1977); idem, *Historyk gniewny*.

34. Helena Madurowicz-Urbańska, *Prace Feliksa Łoyki nad historia gospodarczą i ekonomiką Polski* (The Work of Feliks Łoyko on Economic History and the Economy of Poland), vol. 1, (Wrocław and Warsaw, 1976).

35. *Stosunki polsko-niemieckie w historiografii*. (Polish-German Relations in Historiography), vol. 1 (Poznań, 1974).

36. Lech Mokrzecki. *Studium z dziejów nauczania historii* (Studies on the History of the Teaching of History) (Gdańsk, 1973); idem. *W kragu prac historyków gdańskich XVII wieku* (On the Work of the Historians in Gdańsk in the 17th Century) (Gdańsk, 1974).

37. More detailed information may be found in: J. Topolski, "Le développement des recherches," pp. 3–42; J. Topolski and A. Wyczański, "History Research," pp. 46–64; J. Topolski, "Badania nad dziejami miast w Polsce" (Research into the History of the Cities in Poland), *Studia i Materiały do dziejów Wielkopolski i Pomorza* (Studies and Materials for the History of Greater Poland and Pomerania), no. 2 (1960): 5–43; idem, "Développement des études," pp. 7–75.

38. J. Topolski, "Le développement des recherches," p. 31.

39. Ibid., p. 27.

40. Nina Assorodobraj, *Początki klasy robotniczej. Problem rąk roboczych w przemysle polskim epoki stanisławowskiej* (The Origins of the Working Class. Problems of Man-Power in Polish Industry during the Reign of Stanislaus-Augustus), 2nd ed. (Warsaw, 1966).

41. See Julian Bartyś, "Stan i potrzeby badań nad historią techniki rolnictwa w Polsce" (State and Needs of Research of History of Agricultural Technique in Poland), *Kwartalnik Historii Nauki i Techniki* (Quarterly Review of the History of the Sciences and Technology), no. 3 (1977): 577 ff; idem, "Stan i potrzeby badań nad historią techniki przemysłu społywczego w Polsce" (State and Needs of the Research into the History of the Technology of the Food Industry in Poland), *Kwartalnik Historii Nauki i Techniki*, no. 1 (1978): 135 ff.

42. Witold Kula, *Problemy i metody historii gospodarczej* (Problems and Methods of Economic History) (Warsaw, 1963); idem, *Teoria ekonomiczna ustroju feudalnego. Próba modelu* (Economic Theory of Feudalism. An Attempt at a Model) (Warsaw, 1962). Compare the critical observations in: J. Topolski, "Problemy i metody historii gospodarczej. Na marginesie książki Witolda Kuli" (Problems and Methods of Economic History. A Footnote to the Book of Witold Kula), *Ekonomista* (Economist), no. 4 (1964): 824–35: idem, "O potrzebie teorii społeczeństwa feudalnego" (On the Need for a Theory of Feudal Society), in A. Wyczański, ed.. *Społeczeństwo staropolskie* (Society in Ancient Poland), vol. 1 (Warsaw, 1976), pp. 11–26.

43. See J. Topolski, "The Model Method in Economic History," *The Journal of European Economic History*, no. 1 (1972): idem, *Marksizm*, pp. 133 ff: W. Kula, "Analiza modelowa w historii gospodarczej" (An Analysis According to the Models of Economic History), *Historyka*, vol. 1, 1967, pp. 41 ff. See also the analyses of several economic models in the following book: J. Topolski, *Gospodarka polska a europejska w XVI-XVIII weiku* (The Polish and European Economy in the 16th-18th Century) (Poznań, 1977). See also the summary observations in G. G. Iggers, *New Directions in European Historiography* (Middletown, Conn., 1975).

44. J. Topolski, *Narodziny kapitalizmu w Europie XIV-XVII wieku* (The Origin of Capitalism in Europe in the 14th-17th Centuries) (Warsaw, 1965).

45. Stefan Kurowski, *Historyczny proces wzrostu gospodarczego* (The Historical Process of Economic Growth) (Warsaw, 1963).

46. Janina Leskiewiczowa, Stefania Kowalska-Glikman, eds., *Historia i nowoczeność. Problemy unowocześnienia metodologii i warsztatu badawczego historyka* (History and Modernity. Problems of Modernization of the Methodology and the Profession of the Historian) (Warsaw and Wrocław, 1974).

47. *Społeczeństwo polskie XVIII i XIX wieku* (Polish Society of the 18th and 19th Centuries), a series of works published since 1965.

48. Information on this area of research may be found in Tadeusz Daniszewski, "Stan badań nad dziejami ruchu robotniczego i ludowego w Polsce" (State of the Research on the History of the Workers' and Peasant Movement in Poland), *Z Pola walki* (The Battlefield), no. 1 (1965): 7–20, and the records of the colloquium organized on the occasion of the ninetieth anniversary of the creation of the first Polish socialist party: *Wielki Proletariat i jego dziedzictwo* (The Great Proletariat and Its Patrimony) (Warsaw, 1974), pp. 265 ff.

49. Detailed information on this research may be found in Wiesław Piątkowski, *Przegląd badań nad historią ruchu ludowego w latach 1864–1918* (Review of Research on the History of the Peasants' Movement During the Years 1864–1918), *Roczniki Dziejów Ruchu Ludowego* (Annals of the History of the Peasant Movement), 1959, no. 1; Stanisław Kowalczyk, "Przegląd stanu badań nad historią ruchulludowego w latach 1918 do 1939" (Review of the Research on the History of the Peasant Movement in the Years 1918–1939), *Roczniki Dziejów Ruchu Ludowego* 1959, no. 1; Alicja Więzikowa, "Historiografia ruchu ludowego dotycząca jego dziejów do 1944 r." (Historiography of the Peasant Movement Dealing with Its History up to 1944), *Roczniki Dziejów Ruchu Ludowego*, 1975, no. 17; Józef R. Szaflik, "Stan i potrzeby badawcze w zakresie dziejów polskiego ruchu ludowego" (State of the Research and Needs in the Area of the History of the Polish Peasant Movement), *Kwartalnik Historyczny*, no. 3 (1970): 734 ff.

50. This collection was published by Państwowy Instytut Wydaniczy (State Publishing Institute) in Warsaw.

51. Andrzej Wyczański, "Kultura polskiego Odrodzenia. Próba określenia historycznego mentalności" (The Culture of the Renaissance in Poland. Essay of Historical Definition of the Mentality), *Odrodzenie i Reformacja w Polsce* (Renaissance and Reformation in Poland), 10 (1965): 11–51.

52. Janusz Tazbir, *Rzeczpospolita i świat. Studia z dziejów kultury XVII wieku* (The Republic and the World. Studies on the History of Culture in the 17th Century) (Wrocław and Warsaw, 1971); idem, *Kultura szlachecka w Polsce. Rozkwit-upadek-relikty* (Noble Culture in Poland. Bloom-Decline-Remnants) (Warsaw, 1978). See also the collective work: Józef Wójtowicz, ed., *Narodziny i rozwój nowożvtnej kultury polskiej* (Birth and Development of Modern Polish Culture) (Warsaw, 1974).

53. Zbigniew Kuchowicz, *Obyczaje staropolskie XVII–XVIII wieku* (Customs in Ancient Poland from the 17th–18th Centuries), 2nd ed. (Łódź, 1975).

54. See the collective work: Józef A. Gierwoski, ed., *Dzieje kultury politycznej w Polsce* (The History of Political Culture in Poland) (Warsaw, 1977).

55. See: Władysław L. Karwacki, "Piosenka w środowisku robotniczym. Z dziejów kultury i obyczajów klasy robotnitczej" (Song in Working Class Culture. On the History of the Culture and the Customs of the Working Class), *Polska Klasa Robotnicza* (The Polish Working Class), vol. 5 (1973), pp. 98–179: vol. 6 (1974), pp. 84–118, and other works.

56. Czesław Madajczyk, ed., *Polityka III Rzeszy w okupowanej Polsce* (The Politics of the Third Reich in Occupied Poland), 2 vols. (Warsaw, 1970).

57. Czesław Madajczyk, ed., *Inter arma non silent Musae. The War and the Culture 1939–1945* (Warsaw, 1977).

58. Józef Chlebowczyk, *Procesy narodotwórcze we wschodniej Europie środkowej w dobie kapitalizmu* (The Processes of the Formation of Nationalities in Central Western Europe at the Time of Capitalism) (Warsaw and Krakow, 1975).

59. See the materials published in *Kwartalnik Historyczny*, no. 2 (1978): 299 ff.

60. Stefan Kieniewicz, *Powstanie styczniowe* (The January Insurrection) (Warsaw, 1972).

61. Tadeusz Jędruszcak, *Piłsudczycy bez Piłsudskiego* (The Piłsudski Party without Its Leader) (Warsaw, 1963).

62. J. Topolski, "Historia polityczna w syntezie historycznej" (Political History in the Historical Synthesis) in the collective work: *Polska i świat* (Poland and the World) (Poznań, 1978), pp. 449–558.

63. Alina Witkowska, *Rówieśnicy Mickiewicza Życiorys jednego pokolenia*. (The Contemporaries of Mickiewicz. A Biography of a Generation) (Warsaw, 1962); Tadeusz Kisielewski, *Heroizm i Kompromis. Portret zbiorowy działaczy ludówych* (Heroism and Compromise. A Collective Portrait

of the Activists of the Peasant Movement), vol. 1 (Warsaw, 1977). See also: Emanuel Rostwo-rowski, "Biografia, biogram, historia grupy i pokoleń" (Biography, Biogram, History of Groups and Generations), *Kwartalnik Historyczny*, no. 2 (1973): 352 ff; Tadeusz Łepkowski, "Biografis-tyka: żywotność, tradycjonalizm, nowoczesność" (Biographistics: Its Everlasting Character, Its Traditionalism, and Its Modernity), *Kwartalnik Historyczny*, no. 1 (1975): 100 ff.

64. Henryk Łowmiański, *Początki Polski* (The Birth of Poland), 5 vols. (Warsaw, 1964–1973).

65. Polska Klasa Robotnicza—series published since 1970, Stanisław Kalabiński, ed.

66. Stanisław Kalabiński, ed., *Polska klasa robotnicza. Zarys dziejów* (The Polish Working Class. An Historical Summary), vol. 1, part 1 (Warsaw, 1974), pp. 5–7.

67. Andrzej Wyczański, ed., *Społeczeństwo*.

68. Janusz Żarnowski, *Społeczeństwo Drujiej Rzeczypospolitej* (Society in the Second Republic) (Warsaw, 1973).

69. Detailed information on this research may be found in: Marian Wolański, "Zastosowanie komputerów w badanicah historycznych" (The Use of Computers in Historical Research), *Acta Universitatis Wratislaviensis*, no. 279, *Historia XXVII* (1976), pp. 315–54.

70. Andrzej Wyczański, *Uwarstwienie społeczne w Polsce XVI wieku. Studia* (Social Stratifi-cation in Poland in the 16th Century. A Study) (Wrocław and Warsaw, 1977); see also the same author: "Współpraca historyka z komputerem" (The Collaboration between the Historian and the Computer), *Kwartalnik Historyczny*, no. 1 (1976): 65–73.

71. The results of the quantitative works on Polish society in modern times have been analyzed by Stanisław Kalabiński in his "Metody gromadzenia i analizy danych do dziejów społeczeństwa polskiego XIX i XX w." (Methods of Gathering and Analyzing Information on the History of Polish Society in the 19th and 20th Centuries), presented during the international colloquium "Quantum" in Cologne. The text of the presentation, which was kindly provided by the author, will be published in the proceedings of this colloquium. The results of quantitative research mentioned below are presented in *Polska Klasa Robotnicza* and other publications; the most essential information will soon be published in a collective volume under the editorship of Stanisław Kalabiński in collabo-ration with Joanna Hensel and Irena Rychlikowa, entitled: *Metody i wyniki, Z warsztatu historyka dziejów społeczeństwa polskiego* (Methods and Results, The Work of the Historian in Polish So-ciety), which will be issued by the Institute of History of the Polish Academy of Sciences. I have had the opportunity to consult the volume prior to its publication.

72. M. Wolański, op. cit., pp. 335 ff.

73. See Jerzy Topolski, "Les tendances et l'état actuel des recherches historiques en Pologne" (Trends and Actual State of Historical Research in Poland), a paper read in Paris in 1977, the text of which has been graciously made available to me by the author.

18 HANS SCHLEIER

German Democratic Republic

Marxist-Leninist history in the German Democratic Republic (DDR) is still young; its academic institutions have existed for only the last thirty years. Yet it derives from a long tradition, dating back to the works of the brilliant German thinkers Karl Marx and Friedrich Engels. Marx and Engels, in their multifaceted creativity, revolutionized historical thinking and provided it with a new foundation in the form of historical materialism, as expressed in their historical and contemporary writings and conclusions. Since that time leading figures of the revolutionary German workers' movement have intensively investigated historical problems, drawn historical conclusions, and published historical works (A. Bebel, W. and K. Liebknecht to date). The German working class found an outstanding historian in Franz Mehring. The historical thinking and ideas of the German Communist Party (KPD) formed the immediate prehistory of the science of history in the DDR. The KPD adopted the ideas of Leninism and thus had already worked out before 1945 an antifascist, democratic historical perspective.[1] However, only after 1945, following the total defeat of the terror and war policies of German fascism and imperialism, was it possible to win an institutional place for Marxist historical thinking over the hitherto insurmountable barriers of bourgeois scientific monopoly within the territory of the present DDR.

Professional historical research in the DDR has gone through several developmental phases since 1945.[2] In the first phase, from 1945 to 1950–1951, the antifascist German historians were confronted with complicated tasks. The first was to expose and conquer the Nazistic, militaristic, and chauvinistic historical ideology of German fascism and imperialism, and to remove the heavily tainted and incorrigible fascist historians from the academic institutions. Secondly, the roots of the antipeople, imperialistic politics and its reactionary traditions in German history had to be revealed. This necessitated the refutation of bourgeois historical ideology and theory, which was closely linked to the reactionary politics through its theory of the state as power and its ideology of war. Thirdly, progressive German and international historical thinking had to be brought back from oblivion. The true picture of reality had to be placed opposite the reactionary historical legends regarding the revolutionary workers' movement and the first socialist state in the world, the Soviet Union.

The difficulty of these tasks was compounded by the fact that Marxist historians, who were released from fascist prisons or who returned from emigration (among others, W. Bartel, K. Bittel, H. Duncker, E. Engelberg, E. Hoffmann, J. Kuczynski, R. Lindau, W. Markov, A. Meusel, K. Obermann, E. Paterna, A. Schreiner, O. Th. Schulz, L. Stern, H. Wolf) were few in number and had to secure a place at the universities, which were not reopened until 1945/46. Furthermore, their scholarly studies were partially impeded because of the Cold War against socialism, which strengthened reactionary bourgeois historical ideology and became institutionalized within the territory of the later Federal Republic of Germany (BRD, 1949).

Bourgeois historians made laudable efforts in the reconstruction of scientific institutions and in the establishment of antifascist, democratic concepts for teaching in the universities, in historical education for the schools, and in historical research. They were willing—although with different goals—to assist with the democratic restructuring and, following the founding of the DDR (1949), to cooperate with Marxist historians.

At this stage, the few Marxist historians had to limit themselves to the publication of work which had been written during their years in emigration or to the reinterpretation of old research, as well as to the education of a new generation of Marxist historians. The works of the classical authors of Marxism-Leninism (Marx, Engels, Lenin) were published in multivolume editions and placed at the disposition of scholars. The historical writings of the leading representatives of the German labor movement and historical works of bourgeois-democratic authors were newly published. The translations of the works of Soviet historians were a great help in this situation.[3]

The second phase of historical investigation in the DDR, which determined its further development, took form during the 1950s. At the third Party Congress of the Socialist Unity Party of Germany (SED) in 1950, and the seventh meeting of its central committee in 1951, the historians in the DDR were given directional tasks, which were oriented towards the assertion of Marxism at the historical institutions and the formation of a socialist historical self-consciousness.[4] On the agenda now stood the unfolding of revolutionary and progressive German traditions, on which the DDR was based, as well as extensive research and discussions which were meant to lead to a complete picture of German history and the history of the German labor movement from a Marxist point of view.

Simultaneously, the SED took certain governmental actions, which created the institutional and cadre preconditions for the accomplishment of these tasks. From 1 September 1951 a compulsory study and instruction plan with Marxist orientation was established for the study of history at universities. Institutes for German history were created at the universities of Berlin, Leipzig, and Halle in 1951; the Museum for German History was created one year later. In the meantime, a new generation of Marxist historians appeared, who during the 1950s began to teach at the universities and were appointed to professorships in history, or determined the profile of other scientific institutions.[5] Historical research and education started to produce a broad spectrum of writings. Numerous historical source materials, documents, monographs, and articles were published.[6] Lively historical-theoretical discussions were conducted in the *Zeitschrift für Geschichtswissenschaft,* dealing with such questions as the concept of German history and the roots and driving forces of the historical processes.

By 1958–1959 the Marxist interpretation of history had firmly established itself at the historical institutions and had achieved a new scientific quality in its activities. Historical studies on the occasion of the fortieth anniversary of the October Revolution now concentrated on the previously neglected twentieth century. A systematic discussion of bourgeois historiography began, especially concerning the Federal German Republic (BRD). The international contacts of the DDR broadened and gained firm organizational foundations.[7]

The third phase in the development of historical investigation in the DDR began at the end of the 1950s. Historians attained new heights of creativity, as reflected in their broadened tasks, for instance, the all-encompassing socialist rebuilding in the DDR, the close cooperation of the socialist states, and the international ideological class struggles. The institutions for history now had a group of well-educated staff members available. The number and thematic expanse of the source publications and historical studies increased rapidly. Their content improved as scholars learned the creative techniques of applying to historical-theoretical problems concepts that they had developed in debate. The creation of permanent research groups and collaboration with other Marxist social scientists (philosophers, economists, sociologists, archeologists, linguists, etc.) allowed considerable expansion of the subject and the horizon of historical works, and the results of many individual research projects were generalized. Contemporary history since 1945 and the history of the DDR were now included in research projects. For the first time, comprehensive works on German history (high-school textbooks) and the history of the German workers' movement could be presented. A whole arsenal of historical handbooks, reference books, and lexica were produced, largely according to new methods. In accordance with personnel possibilities, the historians in the DDR collaborated in history commissions and also participated in international congresses and meetings.

A fourth phase in historical research in the DDR began in 1971. The eighth Party Congress of the SED (1971) had beneficial effects on the new tasks to be undertaken. Important historical-theoretical problems were discussed and argued, including evolution and revolution in world history and German history, the development and sequence of the successive formations of society, historical epochs, and other broad historical problems; representatives of the different disciplines often met for beneficial discussions. The historical-theoretical quality of historical research generally improved. Specific historical-methodological research was begun. The discussion and testing of new historical research methods and the application of methods of other social sciences increased. Considerable progress was made in incorporating the history of the German people into the process of international development as well as expanding research into non-German history. In addition, internationally recognized collaborative works and handbooks were produced. More complex research, which examined and interpreted the interactions of various areas of societal development, had far-reaching results. Establishment of bilateral commissions led to closer and systematic cooperation of historians in other socialist countries;[8] joint publications increased.

After 1945, the science of Marxist history in the DDR gained a slow entrance into institutions through history seminars and institutes (presently departments) at the universities of Berlin, Leipzig, Halle, Jena, Greifswald, and Rostock, as well as the pedagogic academies. The science of Marxist history was also established at the previously existing scientific institutions of the SED in Berlin: the Party Academy "Karl Marx" (1946), the Institute for Marxism-Leninism (1949), the Center of the Marx-Engels Edition and Research on the History of the Workers' Movement, the Academy (until 1976, Institute) for Social Sciences (1951). A central museum for German history was founded in 1952,[9] and in 1956 historical research institutions were established with a permanent staff at the Academy of Sciences of the DDR (also in Berlin) which are presently known as the Central Institute for History,[10] the Central Institute for Classical History and Archeology, and the Institute for Economic History.

After the prolonged efforts of the association of historians of the BRD to prevent the development of an independent Marxist German science of history and to undermine its international effectiveness, the Historians' Association of the DDR was founded in 1958[11] (presidents have been E. Engelberg, G. Schilfert, and since 1968 J. Streisand). The Historians' Association encouraged the scientific life and cooperation of the different occupational groups of historians in the DDR through its congresses (six until 1977), professional commissions, and meetings. In 1970, the National Committee of Historians of the DDR (founded 1959, chairman E. Engelberg) was formally accepted into the Comité International des Sciences Historiques (CISH), although delegates of historians from the DDR had participated in the International Congresses of Historians since 1955. The scientific and ideological tasks of historians of the DDR had been coordinated and planned by the Council for the Science of History (chairman E. Diehl) since 1968.

The science of history in the DDR has established a broad spectrum of periodicals and yearbooks.[12] The *Zeitschrift für Geschichtswissenschaft* (since 1953)[13] and the *Jahrbuch für Geschichte* (1967) are of a general nature. Specific tasks are fulfilled by among others *Beiträge zur Geschichte der [initially: deutschen] Arbeiterbewegung* (1959), *Marx-Engels-Jahrbuch* (1978), the *Jahrbuch für Wirtschaftsgeschichte* (1960), the *Jahrbuch für Geschichte des Feudalismus* (1977), the *Jahrbuch für Geschichte der sozialistischen Länder Europas*[14] (1956, with changing titles), *Militärgeschichte* (1961), the yearbook

Asien, Afrika, Lateinamerika (1964), and the periodical by the same name (1973).

The results of the new scientific research are the prime indicators of the development of the science of history. Despite the brief thirty-year-old history of the science of history in the DDR, they are (as is proven by the bibliographies)[15] so extensive and diverse that only a few main trends and projects can be listed in the following.

An extensive German history from a Marxist point of view initially required extensive preparatory work, individual research, and source publications. Since 1959, the *Hochschullehrbuch der deutschen Geschichte* has appeared in twelve volumes (fourteen parts); it was written collectively by several authors and offers a composite survey over time from early history to 1945.[16] These volumes include the most recent research, which occasionally is deepened by individual inquiry. This university textbook, which is based on historical materialism, differs from bourgeois works in terms of principles, problem-posing, themes, source materials, and historical declarations.

In addition, complex works appeared which examined particular areas of German history, such as, for example, the forty-volume *Geschichte der Lage der Arbeiter unter dem Kapitalismus* by J. Kuczynski (1960–1972), the *Wirtschaftsgeschichte Deutschlands* (3 vols., 1965–1975) by H. Motteck and others, the *Geschichte der deutschen Arbeiterbewegung* (8 vols., 1966) which was written by a large collective, the *Kurze Geschichte der DDR* (1964) by St. Dorenberg, and later *DDR, Wachsen und Werden* (1974) by H. Heitzer and others, and the handbook *Die bürgerlichen Parteien in Deutschland* (2 vols., 1968–1970) by D. Fricke et al.

Expanded problems and deepened theoretical concepts as well as additional research lie at the basis of a *Grundriss* of the history of the German people. This publication, entitled *Klassenkampf, Traditionen und Sozialismus,* was written by an author-collective headed by E. Diehl and also includes both the period after 1945 and the history of the DDR. Compared to the university textbook, this overview of German history from early times to the present was more uniform and concentrated on the basic historical laws and forces, on the dialectics of the class struggle between progress and reaction, and on the levels of historical progress which take place during the formation of a society.

The intensive research is also reflected in certain reference works, whose problems, methods, and results reveal principal differences in comparison to bourgeois handbooks, treading on completely new ground in many respects. To name just a few: *Einführung in das Studium der Geschichte* (1966); the small encyclopedia *Deutsche Geschichte* (1965) and the *Deutsche Geschichte in Daten* (1967); the biographical lexica of German history (1967) and of the history of the workers' movement (3 vols., 1965–1967); the *Sachwörterbuch der Geschichte Deutschlands und der deutschen Arbeiterbewegung* (2 vols., 1969); and a *Taschenbuch* and a *Lexikon Archivwesen der DDR* (1971, 1976). The following are not limited to German history alone: *Atlas zur Geschichte* (2 vols., 1973,

1975), the small encyclopedia *Weltgeschichte* (1964), and the *Weltgeschichte in Daten* (1966). These and other reference works gained international recognition, and better editions have been reissued since then.

In economic history, J. Kuczynski developed, for the first time, a picture of the workers' position in the nineteenth and twentieth centuries, based on extensive statistical information and other data. Marxist historical research has always been a social history because of its theoretical background (sequential formations of society, classes) and has been a pioneer in the research of class and social stratification in German history. Contrary to bourgeois social history, it does not isolate sociohistorical research from class struggle and political history, and hence does not limit itself to sectors that are cut apart from the entire reality. During the last few years, research into the social structure of the working class has intensified, new methods (such as quantitative techniques) have been tested, and research has been extended to the working class of the DDR. Further research was conducted into class structure and position and the political struggle of farm laborers and farmers in the nineteenth and twentieth centuries, as well as into the agricultural policies of the ruling classes and the revolutionary worker movement.

Other important subjects include the development of the forces of production and the Industrial Revolution, and of the forces of production in agriculture. A summarizing work, *Die Produktivkräfte in der Geschichte* (vol. 1 by W. Jonas et al., 1969) is in preparation.

The economic historians deserve praise for their research into the reciprocal relationships between economy and politics in the period of imperialism, beginning at the end of the nineteenth century. The German monopoly bourgeoisie was proven to be responsible for the expansion policies and for the unleashing of World Wars I and II. Although initially the development of monopoly capital was a prominent research topic in which industrial history was increasingly included, attention has recently been focused on research into state-monopoly capitalism in Germany, its historical position,[17] and the influence of monopolies on the state, on its policies, and on the establishment of the fascist dictatorship. The comprehensive work *Wirtschaft und Staat in Deutschland*, which surveys the period from the end of the nineteenth century to 1945, is based on both earlier and more recent research (vol. 1, 1978).

Research on early history and the history of antiquity was limited at first to crucial points because of restricted research capacities, but considerable expansion has occurred since the 1960s, and some synthesis has been possible.[18] The historical-theoretical discussions centered on the origin, character, and consequence of precapitalistic formations of society and their historical laws. Special attention was given to the old-oriental class society and the problem of the "Asiatic mode of production," its character, and its temporal and regional extent. Attempts to summarize the formation of precapitalistic societies under one model have failed. The concept of different types of movement of peoples and their historical role was deepened.[19] In *Weltgeschichte bis zur Herausbildung des Feudalismus* (1977) J. Sellnow and others followed the sequence of the formation of societies from primeval society through old-oriental class society and slaveholding society to feudal society.

An additional focal point was formed by research into late antiquity which centered on the change to feudalism in Europe with the problems of an "epoch of social revolutions."

The theoretical and methodological bases of primeval and early history were deepened, and the archeological research methods as well as interdisciplinary cooperation were expanded. Research centered on the genesis of the peoples and states of Central Europe, their historical relations, and the laws of their development. As a result of their studies on the Germanic peoples, B. Krüger and others published the first volume of a handbook entitled *Die Germanen* (1976). Intensive research on the ethnogenesis of peoples and their complicated interactions was summarized in the handbook *Die Slawen in Deutschland im frühen Mittelalter* (1970) by J. Hermann and others. This handbook also gives an overview of the medieval German eastward expansion.

Research into feudalism in the DDR developed into a fruitful reciprocity between historical-theoretical disputes and empirical investigations.[20] Valuable historical-theoretical discussions have been concerned with the periodization of feudalism and the determination of its position and its essential characteristics in the sequence of formation of societies, and were complemented by evaluation of feudal societies outside Western and Central Europe. The emphasis of the research was primarily on the relations of feudal production during the formation of feudal society; second, on the formation and character of the German feudal state; third, on the city history research whereby special attention was given to a comparison of European city history in the fourteenth and fifteenth centuries, to the popular movement within the city, and to Hansa history. Intense discussion revolved around the role of the city and the burghers in the city as factors in the complete unfolding of feudal society. Fourth, research was conducted into religious and heretical movements.

As part of the heated discussions about the transition period from feudalism to capitalism, the problem of the early bourgeois revolution in Germany from 1517 to 1525 stood in the center of research, source editions, and controversies. Even though differences of opinion remained, it was generally agreed that in the early bourgeois revolution, all revolutionary movements, independent of the degree of maturity of the bourgeoisie, tended toward a bourgeois nature *(Illustrierte Geschichte der Frühbürgerlichen deutsche Revolution, 1974, G. Vogel et al.).* These investigations deepened knowledge of the German Peasant War, of the Reformation, and especially of the image of Thomas Müntzer.

In investigation of the transition period from the sixteenth century to 1789, research on the Prussian way in the development of German agriculture, on the manufacturing (handicraft) period and the manufacturing bourgeoisie, and on the problem of (enlightened) absolutism in Prussia and in comparison with other countries stood in the foreground.

The following were the focal points for the epoch of the prevalence of capitalism in Germany since 1789; first, the activation of the progressive German forces through the French Revolution of 1789, the activity of the German Jacobins, the Prussian Reforms since 1807, and the War of Liberation (1813–1815); and second, the role of the bourgeois-liberal and democratic forces in the "Vormärz" (1830–1848). Third, a highlight was research into the revolution of 1848–1849. In addition to the democratic movement, interest centered on the role of the German bourgeoisie,[21] their political failure, and the break in German history resulting from the defeat of the revolution.[22] Fourth, the time of the founding of the German Empire until 1871 was intensively researched. This included more particularly the petty-bourgeois and liberal movement; the anti-democratic class compromise of the bourgeoisie with the Prussian crown and the Junkers; progress and reaction at the time of the founding of the Reich; and evaluation of the character of the newly formed empire (*Die grosspreussisch-militaristische Reichsgründung,* 2 vols., 1971, H. Bartel, E. Engelberg, et al.).

The problem of Prussian-German militarism was discussed during the 1950s in comparison with the bourgeois historiography prior to and after 1945; recently it has been considered in the periodical *Militärgeschichte.* Numerous works on German military history of the nineteenth and twentieth centuries were written, as well as one *Illustrierte Geschichte des deutschen Militarismus (*vol. 1, 1971).

The historiography of the time of the Prussian-German Empire (1871–1918) dealt intensively with the authoritarian policies of Bismarck and the failure of his Bonapartism.[23] Furthermore, it examined the role of the German bourgeoisie in the economy, economic policies, party movements, and ideology, as well as those changes which led to the strengthening of the bourgeoisie in the balance of power between the bourgeoisie and the Junkers in the class compromise. A critical evaluation was made of the colonial policies of the empire and its expansive foreign policies prior to 1914.

Research in the DDR about imperialism[24] gave a new basis to knowledge of the driving forces, manifestations, and results of the expansive policies of the ruling classes. Initially, strong monopoly formation, repressive internal policies, bourgeois parties, and foreign policies were examined; later interest concentrated more on conceptually specific and relevant problems, such as the relation between monopolies and the state and the concept of *Mitteleuropa.* Research on World War I was published in *Deutschland im ersten Weltkrieg,* 3 vols., 1968, by W. Gutsche, F. Klein, J. Petzold and others; it examines all aspects of the war and its connections.

The November Revolution of 1918 was extensively studied with respect to its local and regional effects. Until the late 1960s the question of the character and periodization of the revolution stood in the center of the debate. There is also extensive historical literature on the history of the Weimar Republic (1918–1933). The continuity of the militarist and expansive policies of the ruling class was proven not only through studies of foreign policy and its revanchist drive, especially toward the East, but also in terms of the role of the monopoly bourgeoisie in this development in rearmament, and in its influence on parties and mass organizations. The new traits of state-monopoly capitalism were presented in its basic outlines as well as the division of the upper bourgeoisie into separate monopoly groups with different political-ideological tactics. It was proven that the majority of the bourgeoisie eventually strove for an openly dictatorial form of power and opened the way to power for Hitler's fascism.

With the aid of numerous documentary publications and studies, it was possible to prove in German history from 1933 to 1945 the responsibility of the monopoly bourgeoisie for the consolidation of the Hitler dictatorship and their active interest in armament and expansion prior to and during World War II.[25] Following extensive research on the fascist domestic and terror policies (anti-Semitism, concentration camps, fascist organizations, and other questions) and new research in the sources, a comprehensive work in several volumes was published, entitled *Deutschland im 2. Weltkrieg* (1974; G. Hass, W. Schumann, et al.).

The history of the German working class and the labor movement was largely ignored by the bourgeois German historiographers until the beginning of the present century and since then has been presented only in sketchy and in distorted form. Tying in with Marx and Engels, Mehring, and other leading figures of the revolutionary German workers' movement, the historians of the DDR faced the task of fulfilling one of the greatest needs of historical research, namely, to assemble a source basis which would meet the demands of modern scholarship. In a few decades they succeeded to a remarkable degree.

In close cooperation with the Soviet historians between 1956 and 1968, a forty-volume edition of the works of Marx and Engels was published,[26] which provided international science with its rich legacy of thought and a full arsenal of theory and methods. This broad research concerning Marx and Engels showed the development and actual aspects of their theoretical creativity in the fields of philosophy, political economy, and scientific socialism/communism as well as the important elements of their political battles and their influence on the revolutionary and especially the German labor movement. Their biographies were expanded (in summary: Marx biography, 1967; Engels biography, 1970) and the bourgeois interpretation of Marx, Engels, and Marxism-Leninism was debated. In the meantime, Marx-Engels research has progressed to such an extent that in cooperation with Soviet scientists, a definitive Marx-Engels Complete Edition is being published in one hundred volumes which should meet all requirements.

The publication of selected or collected writings of the leaders of the revolutionary German workers' movement (among others the collective writings of F. Mehring in sixteen volumes since 1960) is of great importance, along with the publication of numerous biographies. The source and document publications cover all areas of the German labor movement from its inception to the present. The *Geschichte der deutschen Arbeiterbewegung* in eight volumes (1966) contains the discussions and research to the middle of the 1960s.

In the history of the German labor movement, the following problems were intensively examined: the early history of the German labor movement and the struggle of the worker during the revolution of 1848–1849; the origin of the German labor movement under A. Bebel and W. Liebknecht, as well as the role of F. Lassalle and his party; the victorious battle of the German Social Democrats against Bismarck's Socialists' Law (1878–1890), their battle against Prussian-German militarism; the development of social democracy into a revolutionary mass party, and the success of Marxism as well as the history of the German Trade Union Movement until the 1890s. In the last few years, the history of the First and Second International was examined, as were the relations of the German Social Democrats to other socialist parties.

For the epoch of imperialism, conflict with opportunism and social chauvinism and development of the German Left stood in the foreground of research. The effects of the October Revolution on the German labor movement, the battle of the German working class during the November Revolution, and the founding of the KPD were thoroughly examined (*Illustrierte Geschichte der November-revolution in Deutschland,* by G. Hortzschansky et al., 1968). The development of the KPD into a revolutionary mass party and its battles against monopoly-capitalism, counterrevolution, revanchism, antisovietism, and the fascist danger are especially important for the period of the Weimar Republic.[27] The center of research in the period from 1933 to 1945 focused on the battle of the KPD against fascism.[28] It was shown that the popular front policy of the KPD was the only realistic alternative: it expressed the interest of the country against fascism, terror, and war.

Contemporary history since 1945 was examined in broad outlines during the 1960s but since then has been the subject of intensive research. Thorough studies and debates were devoted to the antifascist-democratic transformation from 1945 to 1949, its periodization, international connections, and the forces supporting it. In addition, research focused on related revolutionary changes in all areas of societal life, ranging from the economic basis to ideology and culture. Great attention was given to the founding of the SED, its leading role in the socialist transformation up until the present, and the strategy and political tactics of its policies.[29] The founding and history of the DDR has increasingly become the center of attention for documentation and research.[30] In addition to the all-encompassing scope of empirical research, conceptual and historical-theoretical problems are discussed and worked over with philosophers, economists, and other social scientists. Topics include the increasing role of the subjective factor in history and the laws of a developed socialist society. Recently a new edition of *Geschichte der SED* by an author-collective appeared (1978, G. Rossmann et al.), which analyzes all aspects of party history since 1946 from a uniform point of view.

The main subjects of contemporary historical analyses are the reemergence of imperialism in West Germany, which caused the division of Germany in 1949, as well as the further development of the BRD (in summary: *Der Impe-*

rialismus in der BRD, 1971) and the bourgeois character of the policies of the SPD.

Studies on the October Revolution and the Soviet Union initially focused on the influence of the October Revolution on the German workers' movement.[31] During the 1960s studies have centered increasingly on the history of the October Revolution and German-Soviet relations. When a new phase in the development of the research was begun in 1967, research centered on questions such as the international aspect of the October Revolution and the role of the Soviet state in world politics. In the 1970s, subjects of inquiry have been relations between the Soviet Union and the DDR, the "Great War for the Fatherland" (1941–1945), and historical experiences and laws which the history of the October Revolution and the Soviet Union reveal. In cooperation with Soviet authors, a university textbook was published in 1976, *Geschichte der UdSSR* (G. Rosenfeld et al.).

History-writing about other socialist countries in Europe concerns especially neighboring Poland and Czechoslovakia, which have suffered most from the aggression of German imperialism.[32] Historical-theoretical studies and discussion have dealt with the particular problems of the people's democratic revolution since 1944, its character, the relation between general and specific, its periodization, along with the origin of the socialist world system and the improvement in international cooperation between socialist states.

Reflecting their research potential, historiographers had to limit themselves to the highlights of contemporary history outside of Germany. Apart from research into the bourgeois revolution cycle (see note 38), special attention was given on the international level to the work of W. Markov on the French Revolution of 1789 (together with A. Soboul: *1789,* 1973) and especially its Left (J. Roux, 4 vols., 1965–1969). Main twentieth-century subjects for analysis were the history of the United States and Great Britain, problems of imperialistic foreign policies, ideology, and historiography.

In 1960, institutes established for studies of Africa, the Near East, Latin America, and Asia[33] at several universities in the DDR, in cooperation with linguists, economists, legal scholars, sociologists, and others, enabled the potential of research and its coordination to be expanded. Apart from previously mentioned studies on German colonial and expansion politics based on governmental sources in Germany, special attention was given to the struggles for liberation by the colonial peoples, their present battle against neocolonialism, and the development of national states (among other publications was a survey entitled *Geschichte Afrikas,* 2 vols., 1976). The history of the Near East and the Arabic peoples in the twentieth century was intensively studied, with the result that the comprehensive *Geschichte der Araber* (to date 4 vols., L. Rathmann et al.) has been published since 1971, covering Arabic history from its beginnings to the present. Numerous monographs and articles dealt with individual states of Asia and the national liberation movement in that area. The main subjects for

Latin America were Iberian colonization, the Iberian revolutions since 1789, and the liberation movement until the present day.

Additional subjects which were built into disciplines by DDR historians, with internationally recognized results, can be mentioned only briefly here: the history of science (L. Stern), the very broad category of regional history, military history, industrial history, Byzantine studies, the history of Prussia and German-Slav relations prior to 1917 (E. Winters and his school),[34] folklore,[35] archive science and information science,[36] and the history of a national minority in the territory of the DDR: the Sorbs.[37]

The broad variety of forms in which historical publications have appeared can be only briefly referred to. They range from comprehensive publications to handbooks, source publications, monographs, and popular historical publications (which at times are conceptually very stimulating). Fortunately, the historical biography has found a place in the last year and a half.

Working out historical-theoretical and methodological problems could be undertaken only step by step. Immediately following 1945, the first task for the few existing Marxist historians was to collect the philosophical heritage of the classics of Marxism-Leninism (Marx, Engels, Lenin) and to apply their historical-theoretical ideas, in a creative manner, to German history. Furthermore, they sought to refresh the memory of the historical works of Mehring and other Marxists, and finally, through discussions with the bourgeois historians at the existing academic institutions, to secure admission and recognition for the theory of historical materialism.

During the 1950s an intensive debate, often an immediate conflict with bourgeois historiography, began on historical-theoretical problems: politics and the science of history; partisanship and objectivity; party of the working class and the science of history; nation and the science of history; basis and superstructure; material forces of production and the totality of the relations of production in history; the role of the masses and of individuals in history; the periodization of German history; critique of the reactionary bourgeois historical theories.

These subjects were broadened and examined more thoroughly during the 1960s, which sometimes led to further historical-theoretical debates. Studies on revolution theory and revolution research[38] gained special international recognition. There was an intensive discussion on the theory of the economic formation of society and its course in world history as a process of evolution and revolution. Additional subjects for study were society as a system, the concept of progress, the problem of societal/natural laws, and questions of periodization. The relation between history and sociology and other social sciences was closely examined. Likewise, theories and methods of historical scholarship were considered, especially the content and goal of Marxist-Leninist historical science and the dialectics of logical and historical structural elements in the science of history.

The period since 1971 is characterized by instructive discussions, in which specialists proceeded from their specific fields through international comparisons and generalizing theories: for example, the sequence of the formation of societies in world history, revolution theory, evaluation of the bourgeois revolution cycle, and the socialist and the people's democratic revolutions. During the discussions, there was wide scholarly participation on problems of the periodization of German history, the relations between German history and world history, and the role of the masses in history. During these debates, empirical and special historical-methodological ideas were worked out, though without resolving all important problems and differences of opinion. The 1970s mark the first time that historical-theoretical research was undertaken[39] with respect to the dialectics of event, structure and development, the problem of the historical fact, concept construction and conceptual history (*Begriffsgeschichte*), and problems of historical-scientific knowledge and explanation.[40] The relation between the scientific and artistic aspects of history was also discussed. Proceeding from the thought of Marx, Engels, and Lenin, the most extensive research was conducted concerning the development of the theory of the economic formation of society, and its application in historical research.[41]

The history of the science of history has developed into a special field since the beginning of the 1960s; its contact and mutual benefit with historical-theoretical and -methodological studies is becoming even closer, both as an international trend and as a scientific, theoretical, and scientific-historical necessity. During the 1960s, analyses of historical-political concepts, individual movements of the bourgeois historiography of the nineteenth and twentieth centuries, and the historical picture that developed from it initially predominated, presenting an ongoing conflict with the traditions and prevailing trends of bourgeois historiography in the BRD. In addition to criticism of reactionary directions and tendencies, there was also a rediscovery and recognition of positive trends and of progressive bourgeois historians. A comprehensive critique of the bourgeois historiography of the BRD was written by numerous authors.[42] Since the 1970s began, the historiography of the United States, France, and Great Britain has been investigated as well as contemporary issues of bourgeois history theory and methodology. New questions have been posed within the framework of studies of the history of social sciences (J. Kuczynski, 9 vols., since 1975).

Special attention was, of course, directed to our own Marxist traditions of historical thought and historiography which had grown from close cooperation with the policies and ideology of the revolutionary workers' movement. Besides studies on the historical thinking of Marx, Engels, and Lenin, and monographs on the historian F. Mehring, the historical picture developed by the KPD between 1919 and 1945 is the best researched. These publications show how closely Marxist historians who participated in the establishment of an antifascist academic science of history could tie into this view.[43]

The history of historical investigation in the DDR—apart from research reports, university histories, and "Festschriften"—has been examined in detail only since the middle of the 1970s; it was discussed in dissertation colloquia in 1977, during a session of the Commission of Historians of the Soviet Union and the DDR.[44]

In only a few decades, the German Marxist-Leninist sciences of history grew from a science repressed by bourgeois politics and completely banned by fascism into an institutionalized and internationally effective discipline in the territory of the DDR. In addition to the history of the German people, its scientific spectrum includes important problems of world history, the theory of history, and the methodology of the science of history, as well as virtually all genres of historiography.

Notes

1. Werner Berthold, *Marxistisches Geschichtsbild—Volksfront und antifaschistisch-demokratische Revolution* (Berlin, 1976).

2. Ernst Engelberg and Rolf Rudolph, "Zur Geschichtswissenschaft der Deutschen Demokratischen Republik," *Zeitschrift für Geschichtswissenschaft (ZfG)* 8 (1960), Sonderheft, pp. 7 ff; Horst Bartel, Ernst Diehl, and Ernst Engelberg, "Die Geschichtswissenschaft der DDR 1960–1970," *ZfG* 18 (1970), Sonderband, pp. 19 ff; Ernst Diehl, "25 Jahre DDR—25 Jahre marxistisch-leninistische Geschichtswissenschaft," *Wissenschaftliche Mitteilungen der Historiker-Gesellschaft der DDR (WIMI)* 2 (1974): 7 ff. Here we refer the reader to these extensive evaluations of individual phases and their research problems.

3. Lutz-Dieter Behrendt, "Zur Hilfe der sowjetischen Geschichtswissenschaft bei der Entwicklung des marxistisch-leninistischen Geschichtsbildes in den Jahren 1945 bis 1949 auf dem Territorium der heutigen DDR," *Jahrbuch für Geschichte der sozialistischen Länder Europas (JbGSLE)* 20/1 (1976): 207 ff.

4. Helmut Heinz, "Die Bedeutung der 7. Tagung des Zentralkomitees der SED vom Oktober 1951 für die Entwicklung der marxistisch-leninistischen Geschichtswissenschaft der DDR," in *Die marxistisch-leninistische Geschichtsschreibung über die Grosse Sozialistische Oktoberrevolution und den gegenwärtigen ideologischen Kampf* (hereafter cited as: *Geschichtsschreibung und Oktoberrevolution*) (Berlin, 1978) (*Die Grosse Sozialistische Oktoberrevolution und der revolutionäre Weltprozess*, vol. 5), Research reports and bibliographies of historical publications of that year are in "Historische Forschungen in der DDR," *ZfG* 8 (1960), Sonderheft.

5. Hans-Thomas Krause, "Zur Rolle der sowjetischen Geschichtswissenschaft bei der Herausbildung der marxistisch-leninistischen Geschichtswissenschaft in der DDR von 1949 bis zur Mitte der 50er Jahre," *Geschichtsschreibung und Oktoberrevolution*, pp. 201 ff.

6. See reports and bibliographies in "Historische Forschungen in der DDR 1960–1970," *ZfG* 18 (1970), Sonderband.

7. Walter Schmidt, "Das 40. Oktoberjubiläum in der DDR-Geschichtswissenschaft," *Geschichtsschreibung und Oktoberrevolution*, pp. 168 ff.; see also the extensive study thereof in *Jahrbuch für Geschichte*, vol. 20.

8. Horst Bartel, "Die Zusammenarbeit der Historiker der DDR und der UdSSR bei der Entwicklung der marxistisch-leninistischen Geschichtswissenschaft in der DDR," *Die Grosse Sozialistische Oktoberrevolution und der revolutionäre Weltprozess* (Berlin, 1977), I, 168 ff.

9. Peter Möbius, "25 Jahre Museum für Deutsche Geschichte," in *Geschichtsunterricht und Staatsbürgerkunde*, 1 (1977): 75 ff.; Horst Haun, "Die Studienreise der Delegation des Museums für Deutsche Geschichte in die Sowjetunion im September 1952," *Geschichtsschreibung und Oktoberrevolution*, pp. 245 ff.

10. Ernst Engelberg, "10 Jahre Institut für Geschichte," *Spektrum, Mitteilungsblatt für Mitarbeiter der Deutschen Akademie der Wissenschaften zu Berlin* 12 (1966), H. 6, pp. 193 ff.

11. Rolf Rudolph, "Zwei Jahre Deutsche Historiker-Gesellschaft," *ZfG* 8 (1960), Sonderheft, pp. 610 ff.

12. A complete survey can be found in the references in the "Historischen Forschungen in der DDR," see notes 4 and 6 above.

13. The *ZfG* published ten-year indices in 1964 (special edition) and in 1972 (No. 12).

14. A table of contents appeared in *JbGSLE* 15/1 (1971): 177 ff.

15. The best survey of the total development and of the individual special fields can be found in the essays "Historical Research," published by the *ZfG* and cited in notes 4 and 6 above; an additional volume covering the 1970s will appear in 1980. Titles in German history are given by "Annual Reports for German History" each year since 1949. Of the special bibliographies we mention only "Beiträge zur Geschichte der Arbeiterbewegung" (BzG). Additional bibliographies can be found in Peter Wick, "Nachschlagewerke und Informationsmittel für die Geschichtswissenschaft," in *Historische Forschungen in der DDR 1960–1970*, pp. 799 ff.; and Rolf-Robert Brückner, "Laufende Bibliographien zur deutschen Geschichte und ihre Stellung im einheitlichen System der Information," *Jahrbuch für Geschichte (JbfG)* 2 (1967): 378 ff.

16. The collective authors, who were headed by A. Meusel, are: K. H. Otto; L. Stern; H.-J. Bartmuss; H. Gericke; E. Voigt; M. Steinmetz; G. Schilfert; J. Streisand; K. Obermann; E. Engelberg (2 vols.); F. Klein; W. Ruge; E. Paterna et al.; W. Bleyer; K. Drechsler; G. Förster; G. Hass. The volumes are now available in new (to a degree improved) editions. Shorter editions were published by the authors in a three-volume *Deutsche Geschichte* (1965 ff) and in a *Deutsche Geschichte in einem Band* (1968) written by J. Streisand. Both shorter editions go up to the history of the DDR.

17. Helga Nussbaum, "Zur Diskussion um den historischen Platz des staatsmonopolitischen Kapitalismus in der neueren marxistisch-leninistischen Literatur," *Jahrbuch für Wirtschaftsgeschichte (JbWG)* 1976/1: 69 ff; Willibald Gutsche, "Zur Erforschung des Verhältnisses von Ökonomie und Politik im deutschen Imperialismus vor 1917," *ZfG* 25 (1977), H. 6, pp. 711 ff.

18. Joachim Hermann, "Ergebnisse und aktuelle Probleme der Forschung zur Geschichte der vorkapitalistischen Gesellschaftsformationen," *WIMI* (1974), No. 2: 42 ff.

19. J. Hermann, Irmgard Sellnow, et al., *Die Rolle der Volksmassen in der Geschichte der vorkapitalistischen Gesellschaftsformationen* (Berlin, 1975).

20. "Probleme der Feudalismusforschung in der DDR (1970–1975)," *Jahrbuch für Geschichte des Feudalismus* 1 (1977): 11 ff.

21. Helmut Bleiber, "Bourgeoisie und bürgerliche Umwälzung in Deutschland: Zum Stand und zu Problemen der Forschung," *ZfG* 25 (1977), H. 3, pp. 305 ff.

22. W. Schmidt et al., *Die bürgerlich-demokratische Revolution 1848/49*, 2 vols. (Berlin, 1972–1973) (*JbfG*, Vols. 7 und 8); W. Schmidt et al., *Illustrierte Geschichte der Revolution von 1848/49* (Berlin, 1973).

23. See Gustav Seeber et al., *Bismarcks Sturz* (Berlin, 1977); G. Seeber, "Preussisch-deutscher Bonapartismus und Bourgeoisie: Zu Ausgangspositionen und Problemen der Bonapartismus-Forschung," *JbfG* 16 (1977): 71 ff.

24. Fritz Klein, "Stand und Probleme der Erforschung der Geschichte des deutschen Imperialismus bis 1945," *ZfG* 23 (1975), H. 5, pp. 485 ff.; Lotte Zumpe, "Stand und Probleme der wirtschaftshistorischen Imperialismusforschung," ibid., pp. 494 ff.

25. Kurt Gossweiler, "Stand und Probleme der Faschismusforschung in der DDR," *Bulletin des Arbeitskreises "Zweiter Weltkrieg,"* 1 (1976): No. 1: 4 ff.

26. The German edition of Lenin's works in forty volumes was of great conceptual importance.

27. Kurt Finker, "Zur Erforschung des Kampfes des KPD gegen Militarismus, Faschismus und imperialistische Kriegsvorbereitung (1919–1933)," BzG 19 (1977), H. 6, pp. 947 ff.

28. Heinz Kühnrich, "Zur Erforschung und Darstellung der deutschen antifaschistischen Widerstandsbewegung während des 2. Weltkrieges: Ergebnisse und Aufgaben," BzG 17 (1975), H. 2, pp. 260 ff.

29. Gerhard Rossmann, "Zum Stand und zu einigen Aufgaben der Erforschung und Darstellung der Geschichte der SED," *ZfG* 23 (1975), H. 12, pp. 1373 ff.

30. See Heinz Heitzer, "Stand und Aufgaben der Forschungsarbeit über die Geschichte der DDR," *ZfG* 23 (1975), H. 9, pp. 989 ff.

31. See Günter Rosenfeld, "Zur Historiographie über die Geschichte der Grossen Sozialistischen Oktoberrevolution in der DDR," *Geschichtsschreibung und Oktoberrevolution*, pp. 151 ff.

32. See Eva Seeber, "Die Erforschung und Darstellung der Geschichte Polens in der DDR," *JbGSLE* 15/1 (1971): 81 ff.; Sibylle Schröder, "Die Darstellung der Geschichte der ČSSR in der DDR," ibid., pp. 97 ff.; Eva Seeber, "Die DDR-Geschichtsschreibung zur Geschichte des sozialistischen Weltsystems," ibid., pp. 67 ff.; and additional research reports in this volume.

33. Annual bibliographies since 1963 can be found in the publication: *Asien, Afrika, Latein America, Bilanz, Berichte, Chronik*.

34. Horst Giertz and Wilhelm Zeil, "Die DDR-Geschichtsschreibung zur Geschichte Russlands und der deutsch-russischen Beziehungen bis zur Grossen Sozialistischen Oktoberrevolution," *JbGSLE* 15/1 (1971): 135 ff.; Günther Jarosch, "Forschungen in der DDR zur Geschichte der deutsch-slawischen Wissenschaftsbeziehungen," ibid., pp. 163 ff.

35. Hermann Strohback, Rudolf Weinhold, and Bernhard Weissel, "Volkskundliche Forschungen in der DDR: Bilanz und Ausblick," *Jahrbuch für Volkskunde und Kulturgeschichte* 17 (1974).

36. See, for example: Hans-Stephan Brather and Peter Wick, "Grundsätze einer Klassifizierung der Geschichtswissenschaft: Eine informationswissenschaftliche Untersuchung," *JbfG* 13 (1975): 351 ff.; Peter Wick, "Methodologische Fragen bei der Erarbeitung und Anwendung einer Informationsrecherchensprache in der Geschichtswissenschaft," in *Evolution und Revolution in der Weltgeschichte: E. Engelberg zum 65. Geburtstag* (Berlin, 1976), I, 285 ff.; *Geschichtswissenschaftlicher Thesaurus*, 3 vols. (Berlin, 1976).

37. J. Šolta et al., *Geschichte der Sorben*, 3 vols. (1974).

38. Manfred Kossok and Walter Markov, "Zur Methodologie der vergleichenden Revolutionsgeschichte," *Studien zur vergleichendan Revolutionsgeschichte* edited by M. Kossok (Berlin, 1974), pp. 1 ff.; Manfred Kossok, "Vergleichende Revolutionsgeschichte der Neuzeit; Forschungsprobleme und Kontroversen," *ZfG*, 26 (1978), H. 1, pp. 5 ff.

39. Engelberg established in 1969 a research facility for methodology and history of the science of history at the Central Institute of the Academy of Sciences of the DDR (Berlin).

40. E. Engelberg, ed., *Probleme der Geschichtsmethodologie* (Berlin, 1972); E. Engelberg and W. Küttler, eds., *Probleme der geschichtswissenschaftlichen Erkenntnis* (Berlin, 1977).

41. E. Engelberg and W. Küttler, eds., *Formationstheorie und Geschichte* (Berlin, 1978).

42. Gerhard Lozek et al., eds., *Unbewältigte Vergangenheit. Kritik der bürgerlichen Geschichtsschreibung in der BRD*, 3rd rev. ed. (Berlin, 1977). The first edition appeared in 1970.

43. *Geschichtsmethodologische Aspekte der Kategorie Gesellschaftsformation: Ernst Engelberg zum 65. Geburtstag* (Berlin, 1974); *Nachdenken über Geschichte in unserer Zeit: Anlässlich der Ehrung für Walter Markov und Albert M. Soboul* (Berlin, 1976); *Universalhistorische Aspekte des Jakobinismus: dem Wirken Heinrich Scheels gewidmet* (Berlin, 1976); *Sitzungsberichte der Akademie der Wissenschaften der DDR*, Nr. 4 (1974), Nr. 13 G (1975), Nr. 10 G (1976); Joachim Streisand, "Alfred Meusels Weg von bürgerlich-demokratischen Soziologen zum marxistisch-leninistischen Historiker," *ZfG* 23 (1975), H. 9, pp. 1021 ff.; Leo Stern, *Im Dienst der Wissenschaft und sozialistischen Politik* (Halle, 1976).

44. See *Geschichtsschreibung und Oktoberrevolution* as well as *JbfG*, vol. 20 (in preparation).

Bibliography

General

"Historische Forschungen in der DDR [1950–1960]. Analysen und Berichte," *Zeitschrift für Geschichtswissenschaft* 8 (1960), Sonderheft.

"Historische Forschungen in der DDR 1960–1970. Analysen und Berichte," *Zeitschrift für Geschichtswissenschaft* 18 (1970), Sonderband.
These volumes contain surveys of the historical periodicals and journals published in the DDR.
Jahresberichte für deutsche Geschichte, new series from report-year 1949 (Berlin, 1952 ff.)
Wick, Peter. "Nachschlagewerke und Informationsmittel für die Geschichtswissenschaft," in "Historische Forschungen in der DDR 1960–1970," l.c., pp. 799 ff.

ESPECIALLY: in addition to the research reports mentioned in the footnotes, on the individual branches and research directions of the science of history in the DDR, the following should also be mentioned:

Bartel, Horst, Heinrich Gemkow, and Gerhard Winkler. "Bericht über die Marx-Engels-Forschung in der DDR auf dem Gebiet der Geschichtswissenschaft," *Beiträge zur Geschichte der deutschen Arbeiterbewegung* 4 (1962), Sonderheft, pp. 13 ff.
Köpstein, Horst, "Veröffentlichungen zum VII. Kongress der KI in der DDR," *Beiträge zur Geschichte der deutschen Arbeiterbewegung* 17 (1975), H. 4, pp. 723 ff.
Schumann, Wolfgang, and Klaus Scheel. "Quellen und Literatur in der DDR zum deutschen Faschismus," *Bulletin des Arbeitskreises 2. Weltkrieg* (1972), H. 3/4, pp. 35 ff.
Steinmetz, Max. "Thomas Müntzer in der Forschung der Gegenwart" in *Zeitschrift für Geschichte* 23 (1975), H. 6, pp. 666 ff.

Most Important Works

ON THE EARLY HISTORY OF THE SCIENCE OF HISTORY IN THE DDR:
Berthold, Werner. *Marxistisches Geschichtsbild—Volksfront und antifaschistisch-demokratische Revolution* (Berlin, 1970).
Heitzer, Heinz. "Über das Geschichtsbild von Karl Marx und Friedrich Engels," *Studien über die deutsche Geschichtswissenschaft,* Joachim Streisand, ed., vol. 1 (Berlin, 1963), pp. 339 ff.
Höhle, Thomas. *Franz Mehring. Sein Weg zum Marxismus* (Berlin, 1956).
Jaeck, Hans-Peter. "Die französische bürgerliche Revolution von 1789 im Frühwerk von Karl Marx. Geschichtsmethodologische Studien." Ph.D. Dissertation, University of Berlin, 1976 (in press).
Kinner, Klaus. "Zur Entwicklung des marxistisch-leninistischen Geschichtsbildes in der KPD in den Jahren der Weimarer Republik," Ph.D. Dissertation, Universiy of Leipzig, 1973 (in press).
Kuczynski, Jürgen. *Memoiren* (Berlin and Weimar, 1973).
Küttler, Wolfgang. *Lenins Formationsanalyse der bürgerlichen Gesellschaft in Russland vor 1905. Ein Beitrag zur Theorie und Methode historischer Untersuchungen von Gesellschaftsformationen* (Berlin, 1978).
Schleifstein, Josef. *Franz Mehring. Sein marxistisches Schaffen 1891–1919* (Berlin, 1959).

ON THE DEVELOPMENT OF THE SCIENCE OF HISTORY IN THE DDR:
Bartel, Horst, Ernst Diehl, and Ernst Engelberg, "Die Geschichtswissenschaft der DDR 1960–1970," *Zeitschrift für Geschichtswissenschaft* 18 (1970), Sonderband, pp. 19 ff.
Diehl, Ernst. "25 Jahre DDR—25 Jahre marxistisch-leninistische Geschichtswissenschaft," *Wissenschaftliche Mitteilungen der Historiker-Gesellschaft der DDR* (1974), H. 2. pp. 7 ff.
Engelberg, Ernst, and Rolf Rudolph. "Zur Geschichtswissenschaft der DDR," in *Zeitschrift für Geschichtswissenschaft* 8 (1960), Sonderheft, pp. 7 ff.
Heinz, Helmut. "Zur Entwicklung der marxistisch-leninistischen Geschichtswissenschaft der DDR vom III. Parteitag bis zur II. Parteikonferenz der SED (Juli 1950 bis Juli 1952)." Ph.D. dissertation, University of Berlin.
————. "Die erste zentrale Tagung der Historiker der DDR 1952," *Zeitschrift für Geschichtswissenschaft* 26 (1978), H. 5, pp. 387 ff.

Schmidt, Walter. "Der 40. Jahrestag der Grossen Sozialistischen Oktoberrevolution und die Entwicklung der marxistisch-leninistischen Geschichtswissenschaft der DDR," *Jahrbuch für Geschichte,* vol. 20 (in press).

Steisand, Joachim. "Alfred Meusels Weg vom bürgerlich-demokratischen Soziologen zum marxistisch-leninistischen Historiker," *Zeitschrift für Geschichtswissenschaft* 23 (1975), H. 9, pp. 1021 ff.

ON THE DEVELOPMENT OF THE DISCUSSION OF HISTORICAL THEORY AND HISTORICAL METHODOLOGY:

Bartel, Horst, et al., eds. *Evolution und Revolution in der Weltgeschichte. Ernst Engelberg zum 65. Geburtstag.* 2 vols. (Berlin, 1976).

Bartsch, Gerhard, Herbert Crüger, and Christian Zak. *Geschichte als gesetzmässiger Prozess* (Berlin, 1976).

Bollhagen, Peter. *Soziologie und Geschichte* (Berlin, 1966).

———. *Gesetzmässigkeit und Gesellschaft. Zur Theorie gesellschaftlicher Gesetze* (Berlin, 1976).

Eckermann, Walther, and Hubert Mohr, eds. *Einführung in das Studium der Geschichte* (Berlin, 1966). (A revised edition is in press.)

Engelberg, Ernst, ed. *Probleme der Geschichtsmethodologie* (Berlin, 1972).

Engelberg, Ernst, and Wolfgang Küttler, eds. *Probleme der geschichtswissenschaftlichen Erkenntnis* (Berlin, 1977).

———. *Formationstheorie und Geschichte. Studien zur historischen Untersuchung von Gesellschaftsformationen im Werk von Marx, Engels und Lenin* (Berlin, 1978).

Kuczynski, Jürgen, and Wolfgang Heise. *Bild und Begriff. Studien über die Beziehungen zwischen Kunst und Wissenschaft* (Berlin and Weimar, 1975).

Marxistisch-leninistisches Geschichtsbild und Weltanschauung der Arbeiterklasse (Berlin, 1975).

Müller, Werner. *Gesellschaft und Fortschritt. Eine philosophische Untersuchung* (Berlin, 1966).

Stiehler, Gottfried. *Geschichte und Verantwortung. Zur Frage der Alternativen in der gesellschaftlichen Entwicklung* (Berlin, 1972).

———. *Gesellschaft und Geschichte. Zu den Grundlagen der sozialen Entwicklung* (Berlin, 1974).

19 LUCIAN BOIA

Rumania

Historiography has deep roots in the Rumanian culture. Situated in a most troubled area of Europe, the Rumanians had to fight for centuries to keep their national identity, their unity and their independence. Their interest in history that has stressed their Latin origin (i.e., a specific national spirit), their uninterrupted continuity on the same land, and the essential unity of the whole Rumanian civilization (in spite of its long-time division into three separate states: Wallachia, Moldavia, and Transylvania) represented a fundamental feature of the Rumanian culture, ideology, and political life. Through history, national self-consciousness had been consolidated and the spiritual unity of the Rumanians had been achieved even before a united national state was created.

There were numerous historians that played an important role in the making of modern Rumania. At the same time, according to their permanent interest in history, the Rumanians have given the world a few names of historians well known in the history of historiography. To give only a few examples of these personalities, Dimitrie Cantemir (1673–1723), the author of a famous history of the Ottoman Empire; then Alexandru D. Xenopol (1847–1920), known as a history theoretician and author of an important synthesis of Rumanian history; Nicolae Iorga (1871–1940), perhaps the most complete historian in the world, author of more than 1300 books and booklets covering the entirety of Rumanian history and many aspects of world history; the remarkable archeologist Vasile Pârvan (1881–1927); and the medievalist and byzantinologist Gheorghe Brătianu (1898–1953)—all are names connected with outstanding contributions to the universal culture.

Current Rumanian historiography respects and continues the great achievements of its predecessors. Certainly, the present research is carried out in the new political, social, and cultural climate instituted after 23 August 1944 which marked the beginning of Rumania's socialist evolution. Thus, the Marxist conception of history, which had already produced interesting results even before 1944 (through the works of C. Dobrogeanu-Gherea, L. Pătrășcanu, and others), has been generalized in Rumanian historiography. The materialist-dialectical conception has not only established a new system of interpretation, but also enlarged the areas of investigation by dealing with some fields less studied in the past. Studies of economic and social history (with a special emphasis on social classes and conflicts), of the history of the working class, and of socialist and communist movements have been developed. Meanwhile—a characteristic of recent years—Rumanian historians stress the national, specific features of the Rumanian past, starting from the idea that each nation develops according to its own conditions. Marxism enriched Rumanian historiography without diluting its national and patriotic traditional accent.

Currently, historical research takes place within various institutions, involving different categories of specialists. The main universities in Bucharest, Iassy, and Cluj-Napoca (the latter with a division in Sibiù) include faculties of history and philosophy, representing centers of academic higher education and of scientific research. There are also, in close connection with these faculties, but having a certain degree of autonomy, a few institutes of history. Among these are the Institute of History "Nicolae Iorga," The Institute of Archeology, and the Institute for Southeastern European Studies, all in Bucharest, the Institute of History and Archeology "A. D. Xenopol" in Iassy, and a similar one in Cluj-Napoca. Besides, in Bucharest there is the Institute for Historical and Social-Political Studies of the Central Committee of the Rumanian Communist Party and also the Center for Military History and Theory. The study of history also flourishes in the vast chain of archives spread out in the country, which belong to the Central Historic State Archives in Bucharest, and in the numerous history museums in many cities and towns, starting with the National History Museum in Bucharest.

The results of the research studies are published in specialized reviews, the most important being the following: *Revista de istorie* (a monthly review issued in Bucharest and published by the Academy of Social and Political Sciences), which covers various topics on Rumanian and world history; *Revue roumaine d'histoire* (four yearly issues), with a similar profile but primarily meant for readers abroad; *Anale de istorie* (six yearly issues, edited by the Institute for Historical and Social-Political Studies), covering mainly subjects on modern and contemporary history, and on the democratic, socialist, and communist movement; *Revue des études sud-est européennes* (four yearly issues, edited by the Institute for Southeastern European Studies); *Analele Universității, din București, istorie* (one yearly issue, published by the Faculty of History and Philosophy); and *Revista arhivelor* (four yearly issues, edited by the State Archives). In the field of archeology, the main publications are: *Studii și cercetări de istorie veche și arheologie* (four yearly issues) and *Dacia: Revue d'archéologie et d'histoire ancienne* (one yearly issue), which is designed for readers abroad. All the reviews mentioned above are published in Bucharest. Besides these, there are some other publications edited in the country: *Anuarul Institutului de istorie și arheologie, Studia Universitatis Babeș-Bolyai, Acta Musei Napocensis* (edited by the Transylvanian History Museum and issued in

Cluj-Napoca), *Anuarul Institutului de istorie şi arheologie* and *Analele ştiinţifice ale Universităţii Al. I. Cuza* (both issued in Iassy), and then *Forschungen zur Volks- und Landeskunde* (in Sibiu), plus other reviews edited by the local history museums.

A very popular review is *Magazin istoric,* a monthly publication addressed to a large audience, which discusses topics in Rumanian as well as in universal history. Actually, history is spread through many news-media channels such as newspapers, magazines, and radio and television. A remarkable aspect of popular awareness of history is the fact that a course on the fundamental problems of Rumanian history is taught in all the schools of higher education in the country, independent of their profile. History is considered an indispensable element in any educational process.

Certainly, the main direction of research concerns Rumania's history, with the aim of achieving the most complete investigation into the nation's past, from the oldest times to the present. The *origin problem,* a traditional one in Rumanian historiography, stands as a focus. Historians have focused their research upon the stages of the formation of the Rumanian people and its permanent continuity on the present territory, thus opposing the "immigrationist" theories that claim the Rumanian people formed south of the Danube and subsequently migrated.

Archeology has lately played quite an important role in clarifying matters connected with the earlier history of Rumania. There is an outstanding school of archeology in Rumania which conducts specific researches all over the territory and covers a vast period of time from the paleolithic era through the Middle Ages. While prehistory is well represented (a series of interesting neolithic and bronze age cultures have been unveiled), a special interest has been directed toward the historic ages, starting with the Dacian civilization. Beyond the narrative sources of antiquity, interesting but incomplete, a deep acknowledgment of the material and spiritual life of the Rumanians' ancestors, demonstrating their high degree of civilization before the Roman conquest, has been reached by means of archeological excavations. All over the country, new discoveries have been added to the old ones from southwest Transylvania, at Sarmizegetusa (the old Dacian capital) and the surrounding area. Special attention has recently centered on Dacian civilization and political history during the reign of Buregista (ca. 82–44 B.C.), the creator of a large state lying from north to south between the Slovak Carpathians and the Balkans, and from west to east between the Tisza and the Bug rivers.[1]

At the same time, archeological research has been carried out along the Black Sea coast, on the sites of the former Greek cities of Histria, Tomis (Constantza today), and Callatis (Mangalia today). The diggings in Histria, initiated by Pârvan in 1914, have continued to disclose remarkable results, and the place has already become a symbol of Rumanian archeology. At Tomis, where the search has been conditioned by the presence of a modern city in a permanent development, a Roman mosaic, a few statues, and other numerous objects have been found. Special attention has been paid to trade and other types of relationship between the Greek colonists and the local Geto-Dacian population.[2]

The period of Roman domination (A.D. 106–271), a fundamental epoch when the basis of the Rumanian people was established by the fusion of the Roman and Dacian civilizations, has always represented one of the prime subjects of Rumanian historiography. Continuing an old tradition, present historiography, based mainly on archeological research, also stresses some aspects less discussed in the past, such as the economic development of Roman Dacia, social structure and conflicts, and the history of the "free Dacians" kept outside the limits of the Roman province. The continuous presence of elements of Dacian civilization, even after the Roman conquest, has been proved by archeological means. Thus has been established the essential role played by the autochthonous Dacian population in the social and economic life of the province and in the process of the formation of the Rumanian people.[3]

The thousand years (from the third to the thirteenth century) that followed the withdrawal of the Roman administration from Dacia has long been considered a totally obscure period in the history of Rumania, mainly because of the lack of written documents. For political reasons, some foreign historians (not too many and not among the most competent) have tried to deny Rumanian continuity, the continuous life of the Rumanian people and their culture on the present territory. Such theories have always been opposed by the Rumanian specialists (backed also by many foreign historians). An impressive amount of archeological material has been added in recent decades to the logical supports of this view while the items of information taken from written sources and studies concerning this period have come to represent a priority topic in contemporary Rumanian historiography. The material proof demonstrates the full continuity of the Dacian-Roman population (that later became the Rumanian people) after the Roman withdrawal in A.D. 271. The latest research also allows us a better understanding of the relations between the autochthonous people and the many migrating peoples who passed through the present Rumanian territory. The lack of proper written documentation and the importance attributed to the knowledge of this millennium for establishing the real origin of the Rumanian people resulted in the development of a very active and efficient medieval archeology in Rumania, more so than in the Western European countries. Incomplete knowledge of the political evolution was compensated for by rich information covering the evolution of material culture.[4]

The next epoch, related to the history of the Rumanian states in the Middle Ages (Wallachia and Moldavia were founded as states in the fourteenth century, while Transylvania had been enclosed in the Hungarian kingdom but kept a certain autonomy), has always been extensively studied by Rumanian historians. While earlier historians discussed merely the political history and the continuous struggle for independence, contemporary historiography, without neglecting these aspects, studies the medieval centuries on a broader basis. Economic and social life, including such social class conflicts as the great peasant revolts, is thoroughly researched. A special emphasis in investigating the history of the peasants has recently prevailed; a characteristic feature of the Rumanian medieval period was the existence of a large stratum of free peasants, who played a basic role in economic as well as in military fields. More and more studies are being devoted to historical demography, a promising school that is already becoming established. A series of original research projects has been directed toward the application of sociological methods to the study of the Rumanian Middle Ages. The unitary evolution of the three Rumanian states, in spite of their separate existences, is being stressed economically as well as politically. Political and economic relations with the Ottoman Empire have been carefully investigated, with special attention being paid to the variation of the tribute and of other material obligations; though the Turkish suzerainty over Wallachia and Moldavia (and over Transylvania during the sixteenth and seventeenth centuries) delayed the progress of Rumanian society, contemporary historiography stresses that the Rumanian states succeeded in maintaining an appreciable degree of autonomy, thus ensuring a more independent development (in contrast to the other Southeastern and Central European peoples who were integrated into the Ottoman Empire).[5]

It is stipulated today that the modern history of Rumania begins with Tudor Vladimirescu's Revolution in 1821, an event of profound social, political, and national significance. The period connected with the dissolution of feudal relations, the emergence of a market economy, the formation of the Rumanian nation, and the birth of national consciousness covers a broad chronological period from the second half of the eighteenth century through the first half of the nineteenth. Contemporary historiography has thoroughly studied the great social, economic, political, and ideological upheavals that took place during this period, especially the agrarian history of the eighteenth and nineteenth centuries. Besides problems of general history, special attention has been devoted to the key historical events of the nineteenth century: the 1821 Revolution, the 1848 Revolution (emphasizing its unitarian character in the Rumanian states), the Unification of Moldavia and Wallachia in 1859, Cuza's reign (1859–1866) with its important reforms that founded modern Rumania, and the 1877 War of Independence. The latter was specially celebrated on the occasion of its centenary in 1977, when works dedicated to its history were published. A few specialists have studied political life in Rumania after its independence in a series of volumes that go as far as 1920. Special attention has been given to economic and social evolution, the development of the proletariat, social class conflicts, and the history of the socialist movement, especially that of the Socialist Party (founded in 1893). Many studies have been devoted to the national problem and especially to the national movement of the Transylvanian Rumanians, which culminated in the unification of that province with Rumania in 1918. The celebrations of that event in 1968 and 1978 have intensified research in this particular field.[6]

The contemporary period that began in 1918, when the national unity was accomplished, is also a major field of research. Special stress has been put on the history of the working-class movement, including that of the Rumanian Communist party (established in 1921 from the old Socialist party). The great class conflicts, culminating with those during the world crisis in the years from 1929 to 1933, have been carefully researched. Interest was shown in other political topics, such as other parties or political groups, in order to integrate the working class movement into the political life of the country and create a more complete general idea of the nation's political breadth. The policy of allying the Communist party with other political groups for the establishment of a large antifascist front in the 1930s has been emphasized. Rumania's foreign policy, directed toward European security and illustrated in the 1930s by the strong personality of Nicolae Titulescu (1882–1941), has also constituted an important field of research. Other studies cover Rumania during World War II, the political act of 23 August 1944 and its profound implications, and the important structural reforms from 1944 to 1948.[7]

Besides the traditional topics in social-economic and political history, there has lately appeared a special interest in the history of culture, the arts, science, and technology, with an emphasis on the Rumanian contributions within the world culture. Research in the history of historiography, related to the work of some historians and to stages and directions in Rumanian historiography, has also been developed. The military history of Rumania has likewise been the object of research, and not a few works on that subject have been published by the Specialized Institute for Military History and Theory.

In addition to works dealing with a specific period or topic, too numerous to be mentioned here, a trend toward synthesis is also present in contemporary Rumanian historiography. Generally, such works are the result of collaboration between many specialists, and they are significant for presenting the research and the conclusions of Rumanian historiography at a certain moment. The most extended of these, so far, is the *Istoria României* (History of Rumania), edited by the Academy of the Rumanian Socialist Republic and accomplished by a group of prominent Rumanian historians (C. Daicoviciu, I. Nestor, Em. Condurachi, A. Oțetea, D. Prodan, M. Berza, Șt. Pascu, P. P. Panaitescu, P. Constantinescu-Iași, V. Maciu, and many others). Four volumes of the *Istoria* appeared between 1962 and 1964, going as far as 1878 (when Rumania's independence was recognized). Recently the editors began revising the work according to a new plan that takes into account progress in documentation and historical conceptualization, and they plan to issue a ten-volume work within the next few years. Many Rumanian historians, representing all the research centers, are collaborating in this important scientific enterprise.

Certainly, there have also appeared brief, one-volume syntheses. One of these is *Istoria României* (History of Rumania), edited by Miron Constantinescu, Constantin Daicoviciu, and Ștefan Pascu, published in 1969 (with new editions and a French translation: *Histoire de la Roumanie des origines à nos jours*, Roanne,

1970). Another is *Istoria poporului român* (The History of the Rumanian People), edited by Andrei Oțetea, with the collaboration of M. Berza, V. Maciu, I. Nestor, and I. Popescu-Puțuri, published in 1970 (with new editions and an English translation: *The History of the Rumanian People*, New York, 1974). Constantin C. Giurescu and Dinu Giurescu have written *Istoria românilor* (The History of the Rumanians), with two editions, 1971 and 1975. Starting in 1974, they began publishing a more extended work under the same title, in eight volumes, two of which have already been issued; it is actually a revised edition of the old *Istoria Românilor* published by the well-known historian C. C. Giurescu (1901–1977) between 1935 and 1946.

In order to draw some conclusions, one can say that, especially in the latest decade, Rumanian historians have succeeded in covering a remarkable variety of topics from the first known signs of human civilization to the history of the new socialist Rumania. They have mainly studied social-economic history, though without neglecting the great subjects and events of political history, and one principal topic of research has been the continuous struggle of the Rumanian people for freedom and independence. They have applied the Marxist doctrine without dogmatism and without minimizing the importance of specific national factors in the development of Rumanian history. As in the work of previous historians, the Rumanian school considers the nations, with their own specific features, evolution, and ideals, as the gravity center of history. While they have followed the old historiographic tradition, Rumanian historians have also envisaged the application of modern methods. Thus, to mention only a few examples, the Rumanian school produced some valuable results in fields like archeology (including the medieval period), historical demography, and historical sociology.

Another direction of research has been the study of world history, or the encompassing of Rumanian history in general history. There is a rich tradition in this field, and one must remember, among others, names like N. Iorga and G. Brătianu. The preeminent specialists in ancient Rumanian history are also distinguished researchers of classical Greek and Roman history, which is so much connected with the evolution of the territories of the Danube and the Carpathians.[8] Regarding medieval history, a particular interest has been given to Southeast European history (a specialized institute of research exists in Bucharest). Byzantine studies, inheriting a long tradition in Roman historiography, are well represented. Research covering Ottoman history has also developed, as has the history of other Balkan peoples—the Rumanian territory is regarded as a contact area between the Oriental and Western civilizations. Modern and contemporary world history appears mainly in synthetic works addressed to a large public. Concerning the history of the most recent decades, for instance, large teams of specialists have written works on the history of World War II and the resistance of the European nations at that time. A special place is occupied by the history of the relationship of the Rumanian people with other peoples, and great attention is paid to the inclusion of Rumanian history within world history.

The question of intensifying studies in world history has arisen lately in response to a wish to cover some untreated areas in Rumanian historiography (such as Latin America, Africa, etc.). This enlargement of the historical and geographical horizon is one of the main challenges to be faced by the younger generation of historians. It is a trend connected with the general present-day Rumanian international policy of cooperation with all nations in the world. Currently, together with the above mentioned synthetic presentations of Rumanian history, a six-volume work on world history is under preparation. Prepared by a large team of specialists, the work will demonstrate the level reached in this field by Rumanian research.

Rumanian historians look forward with interest to the 1980 International Congress of Historical Sciences to be held in Bucharest. This coming event, which has already stimulated historical research in Rumania, will undoubtedly contribute to a better knowledge of Rumanian historiography in the world and to its deeper integration in world historiography.

Notes

1. For the ancient history of Rumania, see *Dicţionar de istorie veche a Românie* (Dictionary of the Ancient History of Rumania), ed. D. M. Pippidi (Bucharest, 1976). For Dacian history, see Dumitru Berciu, *Romania before Burebista* (London, 1967); H. Daicoviciu, *Dacia de la Burebista la cucerirea romană* (Dacia from Burebista to the Roman Conquest) (Cluj, 1972), and *Dacii* (The Dacians), latest ed. (Bucharest, 1972); I. Horaţiu Crişan, *Burebista şi epoca sa* (Burebista and His Epoch), 2nd ed. (Bucharest, 1976; an English edition is in preparation).

2. The results of Histria archeological diggings are included in the collective work *Histria*, 3 vols. (1954, 1966, 1973). See also the numerous studies of E. Condurachi, who also edited the second volume of *Histria*, and those of D. M. Pippidi.

3. Interesting contributions to pre-Roman and especially Roman Dacian history have been made by Constantin Daicoviciu (1898–1974), a remarkable school initiator. His work *La Transylvanie dans l'antiquité* (Bucharest, 1945) is a reference text for the field. More of his research is included in *Dacica* (Cluj, 1971). Many contributions were offered by Dumitru Tudor, among which are *Istoria sclavajului în Dacia romană* (History of Slavery in Roman Dacia) (Bucharest, 1957); *Oraşe, tîrquri şi sate în Dacia romană* (Cities, Towns, and Villages in Roman Dacia) (Bucharest, 1968); and *Oltenia romană* (The Roman Oltenia), 3rd ed. (Bucharest, 1968).

4. For a synthetic review of the formation of the Rumanian people, see Constantin C. Giurescu, *The Making of the Romanian People and Language* (Bucharest, 1972). For the same epoch, see also the collective work *Relations between the Autochthonous Population and the Migratory Populations on the Territory of Romania* (Bucharest, 1975).

5. Concerning medieval social history, see a reference work, David Prodan's *Iobăgia in Transilvania în secolul al XVI-lea* (Servitude in Sixteenth-Century Transylvania), 3 vols. (Bucharest, 1967–1968). For economic and trade history, see Radu Manolescu, *Comerţul Ţării Româneşti şi Moldovei cu Braşovul (secolele XIV-XVI)* (Wallachian and Moldavian Trade with Braşov) (Bucharest, 1965). For the history of the Rumanian provinces, see Ştefan Pascu, *Voievodatul Transilvaniei* (The Transylvanian Principate), Vol. I, 2nd ed. (Cluj, 1972); Dinu C. Girescu, *Ţara Românească în secolele XIV şi XV* (Wallachia during the Fourteenth and Fifteenth Centuries) (Bucharest, 1973); and Ştefan Ştefănescu, *Ţara Românească de la Basarab I "Întemeietorul" pînă la Mihai Viteazul* (Wallachia from Basarab I, the "Founder," to Michael the Brave) (Bucharest, 1970). For a demographic history consult Ştefan Ştefănescu, *Demografia, dimensiune a istoriei* (Demography, a

Dimension in History) (Timişoara, 1974). For application of sociological methods, see Henri H. Stahl, *Les Anciennes Communautés villageoises roumaines* (Bucharest and Paris, 1969); and *Studii de sociologie istorica* (Studies in Historical Sociology) (Bucharest, 1972). The variations in the economic obligations toward the Ottoman Empire were investigated by Mihai Berza. Numerous documents concerning medieval Rumania were published in the collections *Documente privind istoria Românie* and *Documenta Romaniae Historica*.

6. The social-economic events during the years between 1750 and 1850 are covered by Sergiu Columbeanu, *Grandes exploitations domaniales en Valachie au XVIIIe siècle* (Bucharest, 1974): and Ilie Corfus, *L'Agriculture en Valachie durant la première moitié du XIXe siècle* (Bucharest, 1969). For the 1821 Revolution, see Andrei Oţetea, *Tudor Vladimirescu şi revoluţia din 1821* (Tudor Vladimirescu and the 1821 Revolution) (Bucharest, 1971); and Dan Berindei, *L'Année révolutionnaire 1821 dans les pays roumains* (Bucharest, 1973). For the subsequent evolution of the agrarian problem, see Apostol Stan, *Le Problème agraire pendant la révolution de 1848 en Valachie* (Bucharest, 1971); and N. Adăniloaie and Dan Berindei, *La Réforme agraire de 1864 en Roumanie et son application* (Bucharest, 1966). For the movement for unification, see Cornelia Bodea, *The Romanian Struggle for Unification, 1834–1849* (Bucharest, 1970). Various national and social issues are discussed by Vasile Maciu in *Mouvements nationaux et sociaux roumains au XIXe siècle* (Bucharest, 1971). For the 1859 Unification and Cuza's reign, the standard reference is C. C. Giurescu, *Viaţa şi opera lui Cuza Vodă* (Life and Work of Prince Cuza), 2nd ed. (Bucharest, 1970). For the 1877 War of Independence, see Ştefan Pascu, ed., *The Independence of Romania* (Bucharest, 1977). For the Transylvanian national movement and the 1918 unification, see M. Constantinescu and Şt. Pascu, eds., *Unification of the Romanian National State. The Union of Transylvania with Old Romania* (Bucharest, 1971). For Transylvanian history, see also C. Daicoviciu and M. Constantinescu, *Brève histoire de la Transylvanie* (Bucharest, 1965); and C. C. Giurescu, *Transylvania in the History of the Romanian People* (Bucharest, 1968).

7. The working-class and communist movement is represented in various works, many edited by the Institute of Historical and Social-Political Studies. A volume by Gh. I. Ioniţă is to be published in English, concerning the place of the Rumanian Communist party in the political life of the country between the two world wars. For foreign policy, see I. M. Oprea, *Nicolae Titulescu's Diplomatic Activity* (Bucharest, 1968); and Eliza Campus, *The Little Entente* (Bucharest, forthcoming). Concerning World War II, see *România in războiul antihitlerist* (Rumania in the Anti-Hitler War) (Bucharest, 1966). About the Act of 23 August 1944, see Miron Constantinescu and others, *Études d'histoire contemporaine de la Roumanie* (Bucharest, 1970).

8. For example, E. Condurachi, D. Tudor, and especially D. M. Pippidi published not a few studies on these subjects. Pippidi, one of the most appreciated specialists of classical antiquity, wrote *Recherches sur le culte impérial* (Paris and Bucharest, 1939); *Autour de Tibère* (Bucharest, 1944); *Studii de istorie a religiilor antice* (Studies in the History of Ancient Religions) (Bucharest, 1969); and *Formarea ideilor literare în antichitate* (The Making of Literary Ideas in Antiquity), 2nd ed. (Bucharest, 1977).

Bibliographical Note

The few works mentioned here are not listed according to a strict criterion of values, but are cited only as illustrations of major trends and directions. We preferred to select, when possible, books written in English or French. For a complete bibliography (up to 1974) one may consult *Bibliografia istorică a României* (The Historical Bibliography of Rumania), Vol. I, 1944–1969 (Bucharest, 1970), and vol. IV, 1969–1974 (Bucharest, 1975). For a synthetic review of contemporary Rumanian historiography, see V. Ciocîltan, Fl. Constantiniu, "1944–1974; Trente Années de recherche historique en Roumanie (quelques résultats et directions de recherches)," in *Revue roumaine d'histoire* 4 (1974): 625–46.

For synthetic works on Rumanian historiography in general, see *An Outline of Romanian Historiography until the Beginning of the 20th Century* (Bucharest, 1964); Pompiliu Teodor, *Evoluţia gîndirii istorice româneşti* (The Evolution of Rumanian Historical Thought) (Cluj, 1970) and German translation *Die Entwicklung des historischen Denkens in der rumänischen Geschichtsschreibung* (Cluj, 1972); Lucian Boia, *Evoluţia istoriografiei române* (The Evolution of Rumanian Historiography) (Bucharest, 1976); and *Encyclopedia istoriografiei româneşti* (The Encyclopedia of Rumanian Historiography), ed. Ştefan Ştefănescu, which is to be published soon.

20 ARIF DIRLIK and LAURENCE SCHNEIDER

The People's Republic of China

In this discussion of Chinese historiography we focus on the 1960s and 1970s and on the issue of the "historicist" versus the "class" approaches to China's past. We have chosen this narrow scope, first, because useful description of the historiography of the 1950s is readily available in Western languages; and second, because we feel that the focal issue includes most other vital issues, or at least acts as a necessary introduction to them.[1]

There are yet other reasons for choosing this issue. The historicist-class dichotomy, we believe, has more explanatory value than others, such as Marxism versus nationalism. We also think that the historicist-class issue reveals and illustrates the continuity of problems in Chinese historiography from 1949 to the present. Since then the central problem for Chinese historians has been the search for an appropriate methodology which will reconcile the demands of Marxist historical theory with Chinese history. Related to that continuing problem has been another: how should class analysis in history be related to the tasks of revolution in the present? Tied in with this problem is yet a third: what should be the role of the professional historian in a society in revolution?

The continuing discussion of these problems reached crisis proportions in the 1960s, in the polarized debate between the historicists and the class analysts in 1963 and 1964. To a degree this was an intellectual debate between two schools of Marxist thought, but the historicist group also included several non-Marxists.

Two quotations epitomize the issues at the heart of the historicist-class controversy and of this essay. In 1959 Wu Han,[2] a non-Marxist professional historian trained in China during the 1920s and 1930s, wrote:

Class background is not the sole factor in evaluating historical figures. People can change; in the past it was so; it is so in the present, and it will be so in the future. . . . You cannot insist on measuring the ancients with modern standards, or not a one will pass. To do so is not historicism. . . . [Does] our history only start from today? Would you break off history?

In contrast to the orientation expressed by Wu Han, there was the second approach, enunciated in 1958 by Fan Wen-lan.

[This] concerns the survival [of our nation]. It is only natural that, when attempting to apply the Marxist view and method to the study of Chinese history, we must first of all link our study with the reality that is closest or comparatively close to us. . . . In the course of this study, especially in studying contemporary history, we may be able not only to discover the very complex laws of social development, to accumulate the fabulously rich experiences of class struggle, to learn about various theories and methods of a creative nature for economic and cultural reconstruction, but also help the broad masses to see more clearly the unlimited splendors in the future of social development. Writing such historical work would be the best [means] to connect theory and reality; it would be a practical contribution to the Chinese people. . . . Although ancient history is also a kind of reality, it is nevertheless a remote reality (the more ancient, the more remote from us) and can be given only secondary priority.

The Crisis of the 1960s

In statements like these, the historiographical crisis of the 1960s began with a debate over the relationship between past and present in historical work, or, as the Chinese historians put it, "The modernization of the past." This referred to the tendency of some historians to evaluate the past by contemporary criteria, as well as the tendency to discover in the past social and ideological characteristics of the present. From the beginning of the People's Republic, historians had complained of the modernization of the past as a basic deficiency of contemporary historiography.[3] But the issue now emerged as a central theoretical and methodological issue as the revolution in history threatened to subsume the past in the present. To be sure, there were other issues of contention in the 1960s, including the problem of whether theory or historical data should determine historical interpretation, the role to be assigned to individuals in history (some revolutionaries attempted to abolish names in historical work), the evaluation of historical personages, the role of the masses in history, and the problem of cultural legacy. These various issues were now incorporated into the debate on historicism and crystallized around the issue of how class analysis should be applied in historical inquiry.

Class viewpoint as employed in the debate described the view that took class division as the most important datum in the interpretation of the past and regarded the struggle of the oppressed against their oppressors as the motive force of history. Its proponents demanded that historical events and personages be evaluated chiefly, if not exclusively, in terms of their attitudes toward and contributions to class struggle. The historicists, without denying the centrality of class analysis, objected to this view which ignored all aspects of history but the allegedly unabated conflict between the exploiters and the exploited. Historicism, in their view, helped reveal the complexity of class structures in history, and the attenuations of relations between classes, by placing historical events in their temporal social context. Historicists believed that the approaches indeed complemented one another in understanding history. As Jian Bo-zan, the central target of the attacks, explained it, both the relations within classes and the relations between classes were more complex than was allowed for by the class viewpoint. History revealed, on the one hand, that conflict was not restricted to the struggle between the exploiters and the exploited; there were also contradictions within each class. On the other hand, relations between classes did not consist of unabated conflict; classes with objectively contradictory interests could nevertheless share common ideological and political premises which affected their behavior and relationship. Furthermore, these relations were subject to change in the progress of each stage in history; the exploiting classes, in particular, played different roles according to whether the mode of production they represented was in the ascendancy or in decline.[4]

These elements of the historicist argument were echoed in the writings of others who were critical of the "modernization" of the past that styled itself either as unqualified vilification of the ruling classes or the unconditional "beautification" of the oppressed. To the critics, such evaluations followed from the employment of the class viewpoint without any regard for historical circumstances. These tendencies, they argued, appeared most clearly in the study of peasant wars and historical personages. According to Cai Mei-biao, a specialist on peasant wars who favored the historicist position, peasant rebels were endowed with revolutionary qualities which were inconsistent with the limitations of their historical environment. These included the attribution to peasants of a social and political consciousness and an ideological sophistication that could not have existed in the material conditions of "feudal" China. Peasant wars, he conceded, were manifestations of class divisions and oppression, but peasant dissatisfaction was expressed "spontaneously" and not "consciously"; the element of consciousness could enter only with the rise of the bourgeoisie or the proletariat, classes whose historical duty was to abolish the feudal mode of production. Even if the peasants had such revolutionary consciousness, Cai continued, peasant wars could not have changed the situation because a genuine social revolution (which he distinguished from revolution in general) had to await changes in the mode of production, or the economic basis of society.[5] Others objected to the condemnation of historical personages for their class affiliation without regard for their contribution to social progress. They argued that historical figures should be evaluated from the perspective of the conditions or norms that existed in their time (that is, the level of political and ideological development) and not in terms of their class background.[6] In the case of both peasant wars and historical personages, in short, the critics argued that the "modernization of the past" distorted history by abolishing the difference in material conditions and, therefore, in consciousness between the present and the past. The antidote to this tendency, they believed, was more conscientious attention to historical data and to the peculiarities of different historical contexts.

From the perspective of Marxism, the central problem addressed by the debate concerned the relationship between the material base, class relations, and the political and ideological superstructure of society. The discussion of this problem articulated some of the basic issues that had arisen in the study of peasant wars, which Cai Mei-biao had pointed out in his essay of 1961, in particular in his distinction between social revolution and revolutions in general. Cai held that social revolution could only follow upon the transformation of the mode of production and therefore upon the rise of a new class and the political and ideological forms expressing its interests. This meant that for peasant wars in the "feudal" society of imperial China, social revolution was an irrelevant concept since peasants did not represent a new mode of production. This distinction was crucial to the proponents of historicism and underlay many of their arguments in favor of the evaluation of history from the perspective of historical context. The context, in this view, was provided by the stage of history corresponding to the mode of production which shaped class structure and relations and placed limitations on *all* classes with respect to political and ideological consciousness; if the ruling class of imperial China could not have been expected to rise above historical circumstances, neither could the peasantry.[7] The view also implied that while each stage in history contained its particular class divisions, it also imposed unity upon them through its dominant political and ideological forms. The universal values of each stage represented the dominant values of the ruling class; the culture of the rulers also permeated and dominated the consciousness of the ruled. The peasantry in China, for example, accepted the ideology of the ruling class; peasant wars represented responses to particular abuses but not revolutions against the ruling class or the system as a whole, since the peasantry did not have the consciousness of the system as an expression of particular interests. Peasants aspired to acquire for themselves the political and economic prerogatives of their exploiters, not to change the system. The peasantry constituted a "class-in-itself" but not a "class-for-itself," an important distinction in the Marxist theory of revolution.[8] Furthermore, the proponents of historicism argued, Marxism took each stage in history to be necessary to the progress of history. They pointed out, correctly, that Marx and Engels had regarded the ruling classes of the past, no matter how exploitative, to be necessary to history, which required that their progressive role in history be recognized, at least until the point in each stage where the relations of production became fetters on the further development of the forces of production. Even beyond that point, some of the historicists argued, internal contradictions within the ruling class could, and did, lead to the emergence of creative individuals who left a mark upon history.[9]

In some ways, advocates of the class viewpoint regarded the determinism implicit in these arguments to be the most reprehensible aspect of the historicist position. The arguments, with their stress on the unifying features of each stage, seemed to abolish the distinctions between the ruling and the ruled, and, therefore, the role of class struggle in history—except in the transition from one stage to another. They themselves played down the limitations that the mode of production placed upon revolutionary consciousness and stressed class conflict as the context of history. They held that the masses were responsible for all progress in history; it was the struggle of the masses against the ruling class that forced the latter to advance production as well as to transform political and ideological forms, and it was the accumulated experience of the masses, summed up by members of the ruling class, that accounted for the existence of creative individuals in all aspects of culture.[10] Furthermore, they rejected the idea that the values of the ruling class shaped the consciousness of the masses, not for lack of effort on the part of the rulers to universalize their values, but because of the resistance of the oppressed to efforts to dupe them. They conceded that in the case of the peasants in China the upper stratum did aspire to join the ranks of the rulers, but they insisted that such opportunism did not apply to the poor peasants, who were revolutionary and tried to transform the system, as was evident in the egalitarian ideals expressed by peasant wars. Guan Feng and Lin Yu-shi, two experts on philosophy, added that social revolution did not have to await change in the mode of production; rather, the acquisition of political power by the oppressed could precede changes in the mode of production and the revolutionization of society. Peasants had acquired power through revolutionary means but had been unable to realize revolutionary change.[11] In short, while the proponents of historicism stressed that change in the material base was essential to revolution, the proponents of class viewpoint tended to separate class consciousness and ideology from the mode of production and to make revolutionary consciousness into an endowment of the oppressed throughout history.

The major and most consistent difference between the two positions is revealed best in their differences of attitude toward the questions of the relationship between the present and the past and of class relations in history. The advocacy of class viewpoint was informed by the belief that the study of history was not to be isolated from the cause of revolution in the present. The historicists held that while the present provided a necessary perspective on the past, contemporary tasks and loyalties should not enter into the consideration of historical problems. This question of the relationship between history and the outlook of the historian presents dilemmas for all historians; it is especially problematic in the case of the Marxist view of history, where the goal of the study of history, as is also the case with philosophy, is not merely to comprehend the past but to transform the present. Engagement in class struggle, according to Marx and Engels, laid bare to the revolutionary the class basis of contemporary society and, therefore, of the basic processes of history.[12] History, moreover, was a field of forces in whose interaction the revolutionary discovered the parameters of change. It does not follow from this intimate relationship Marx set up between revolutionary consciousness and history that he considered the present to offer a model with which to explain the past, or that he legitimized the use of history as revolutionary mythology. In Marx's view, while the revolutionary consciousness engendered by participation in political struggle generated a new vision of the past, this same vision, by revealing the historical processes which produced the present, sharpened critical awareness of contemporary society and furthered the cause of revolution. The Marxist historian differs from the non-Marxist or anti-Marxist historian not in using the present as a model for historical explanation, but in a different evaluation of contemporary society and, consequently, of historical processes in general—both in the determination of the relative significance of historical data and in the interpretation of the relationship between different historical phenomena. Nevertheless, *because* of Marx's insistence on historical processes as the ultimate source of revolution, revolutionaries inspired by Marxism have frequently molded history in an image most consistent with contemporary perceptions and tasks.

The debate over historicism and class viewpoint was not the result of conflict between "bourgeois" and Marxist views of history, as some claimed, but between two interpretations which could both be defended in terms of the Marxist view of history. The historicists stressed the critical perspective upon the past which Marxist class analysis provided but resisted attempts to portray the past as another variant of the present. The proponents of class viewpoint, in spite of their protestations to the contrary, did endow contemporary perceptions of revolution with a determinative significance in the evaluation of historical phenomena.

The historicists' view that class analysis required qualification according to historical context did not in itself constitute a rejection of the existence of class conflict in history or a betrayal of Marxist theory, as their opponents claimed. Marx was indeed critical of the tendency of historians to identify with the past ("to share in each epoch *the illusions of that epoch*"),[13] that is, to judge the past by its own criteria, which reflected but the reigning ideology of the time. The historicists' insistence on the need to treat the past in its own right was, of course, reminiscent of such a tendency. More importantly, their arguments coincided with the views of historians such as Wu Han or Liu Jie who had never been enthusiastic about the Marxist theory of history and were, in the early 1960s, openly critical of Marxist interpretations of China's past. It seems probable that agreement between the views of the historicists and non-Marxist historians such as Wu and Liu on this methodological question compromised the faithfulness of the historicists to Marxism in the eyes of their more radical colleagues.

It is also possible that radical attacks on professionalism in history served to draw together historians of disparate ideological persuasion, blurring their differences even further. But to reject the historicist critique of current scholarship because it was not always distinguishable from the views of non-Marxist historians was to treat the Marxist theory of history as a closed system. To equate that critique with the idealistic historicism which Marx had criticized, even to the point of arguing that the historicists aimed to abolish class analysis, was to distort the historicist position. Historians like Ning or Cai did not reject the use of class analysis in theory or practice, and Jian Bo-zan, who was regarded as the chief culprit since the 1930s, had nevertheless been regarded as one of the foremost defenders of the applicability of class analysis to Chinese history.[14] That their defense of historicism placed them in the role of apologists for the ruling classes of the past was unavoidable, as they were involved in an attempt to counter tendencies in Chinese historiography to portray history as the story of a simple Manichean struggle between exploiters of unrelieved wickedness and exploited of unblemished goodness. Furthermore, their arguments for the complexity of class relations in history and in favor of greater attention to concrete circumstances had considerable justification in terms of Marxist theory. They had good reason, in terms of both the origins of Marxism and its subsequent development, to stress the equal significance of the "history" component in historical materialism and the "materialist" component.[15]

The arguments of advocates of the class viewpoint that Marxist class analysis incorporated historicism were accurate only to the extent that class analysis took history as its context. Otherwise class characteristics acquired a suprahistorical permanence that made no room for change in the nature of the oppressed and the oppressor, or their relationship, but rather let in by the back door a modified form of idealism, which approached class exploitation and the resistance to it in terms of abstract class orientations. The proponents of class viewpoint allowed little room for subtle distinctions concerning interaction between classes and stratification within the same class in a given historical environment. Their views on the peasants and the ruling classes, in contrast to their formal theoretical statements, left the distinct impression that they believed the oppressors and the oppressed to exhibit permanent characteristics appropriate to their respective roles regardless of the different forms classes and class relations assumed in different stages of history. This was especially evident in their treatment of the problem of ideology. The majority adamantly refused to entertain the possibility that different classes could share political and social values, although Marx had recognized that this might happen in pre-proletarian consciousness.[16]

In Marx's view, only with the rise of the awareness of classes and, therefore, the exposition of thought as ideology, had it become possible to cast away the illusion of the universality of the ideas produced in each stage of history; and only the proletariat had been able to attain this "consciousness of falseness." Even in that case, moreover, revolutionary consciousness was the product of the process of struggle whereby the proletariat was transformed from a class-in-itself to a class-for-itself. The advocates of the class viewpoint in China not only regarded such consciousness as an automatic product of proletarian existence, but universalized it into a characteristic of the oppressed throughout the ages. Their approach to the past corresponded to what Karl Mannheim has called "the particular conception of ideology," which "operates primarily with a psychology of interests," as contrasted with the "total conception of ideology," which seeks to illuminate the relationship of thought to its social context, and which represented the historicist position.[17] This attitude led to a consistently negative evaluation of the dominant values of the past; at the same time, it led to the attribution to the oppressed of the past the revolutionary consciousness of the present.

History After the Cultural Revolution

With the suppression of the historical profession, little in the way of serious historical inquiry (aside from reprints of some earlier works) found its way into print during the decade after 1966.[18] Historical writing during this period con-

sisted mainly of discussions of ideological conflicts in Chinese history, especially the conflict between the ancient schools of Confucianism and legalism,
and discussions of attitudes toward authority, as exemplified in the debate on
the behavior of heroes in the venerable medieval romance *All Men Are Brothers*
(Shui hu chuan). Both discussions clearly bore the imprint of contemporary
struggles between the cultural revolutionaries (the Gang of Four of recent no-
toriety) and their opponents in the party. In addition, the 1970s also witnessed
the publication of a series of pamphlets on modern Chinese history and a similar
series on peasant rebellions in Chinese history.

The attitudes expressed by the proponents of class viewpoint inform these
works, though in some ways the latter go even beyond the earlier advocacy of
class analysis. These recent publications are all marked by a highly moralistic
approach to the past which not only portrays the past in simple black and white
but goes so far as to ignore the social dimensions of class analysis, concentrating
instead on attitudes.

In the years before the Cultural Revolution, emphasis in Chinese political
thinking shifted gradually to the ideological manifestations rather than the social
dimensions of class divisions in history. In the debates of the 1970s, this attitude
seemed to lead its supporters to abandon their concern with the socioeconomic
basis of ideology because of their preoccupation with ideology itself. In the case
of the debate over legalism and Confucianism, for example, writers classified
the one as progressive and the other as regressive, devoting their attention mainly
to the problem of the camp in which various historical figures should be placed.[19]
In the debates on *All Men are Brothers,* the major problem addressed was
whether or not a certain rebel character in the novel had capitulated to the authorities, thus betraying the cause of the oppressed.[20] Likewise, the pamphlets
on modern Chinese history emphasized Western immorality in China, going so
far as to incorporate into their analyses nineteenth-century popular beliefs
(largely uncorroborated) about the evil intentions and activities of missionaries.

This normative approach to history precluded any serious structural analysis
as advocated by the "historicists" and by the class analysts as well. One recent
Chinese critic of the Gang of Four's crimes in historiography has argued concerning the debate over legalism and Confucianism that this approach to history
even drew attention away from the study of the masses and of the nature of class
conflict in Chinese society by its exclusive concentration on what were essentially divisions within the ruling classes of the past.[21] These discussions, to be
sure, made some concession to history in drawing differences between past progressives and contemporary revolutionaries armed with the "weapon" of Marxism, but their most striking aspect is the concern with the conflict between good
(antiauthoritarianism) and evil (submission to authority) in history, a choice that
does not leave much room for discussion or elaboration, except to add to the list
of the goods and the evils perpetrated by each group. Even in the case of de-
nunciation of the West, the reduction of the problems of imperialism to simple
moral terms has prevented Chinese Marxist historiography from making a sig-

nificant contribution to the growing radical literature on this subject, even though Chinese Marxists of the 1920s had been among the first Third World intellectuals to identify some of the basic problems created by imperialism.[22] In fact, this highly attenuated version of Marxism has simplified Marxist theory, including the rather complex account of conflict and change in history that Mao had formulated in his analysis of contradictions.

Some historians, out of empathy for Chinese counterparts or simply from professional conservatism, might choose to overlook all but the historiographical nihilism of the "revolution" in history sponsored by the Cultural Revolution. However, even in their nihilism the revolutionary historians were not all wrong in their criticisms of the historical profession in China, which did contain its share of "antiquarianism," with its small concern for broader human or revolutionary issues. Marxist historians themselves often spent a great deal of time with abstract, and fruitless, discussions that portrayed the past in the mechanical terms of vulgar Marxism. Theory was often quite irrelevant to the data being investigated, and it frequently deprived history of any vitality.

The goal of incorporating into history the experiences of the common people and bringing historical writing closer to the population at large, moreover, should not be dismissed out of hand. The demand to place history at the service of revolution has not been devoid of innovative scholarly value. One product was the Four Histories Movement of the early 1960s, which gained in intensity in 1963 and 1964 as part of the Socialist Education Campaign, the "prelude" to the Cultural Revolution.[23] The Four Histories (the name was not always the same) referred to the histories of the family, the village, the commune, and industries as revealed through the recollections and perspectives of workers and peasants who had lived through the revolution. They were, to use the American analogue which also gained currency in the 1960s, oral history on a mass scale, aimed simultaneously at educating the younger generation that had not experienced the revolution directly and at uncovering an aspect of history that had been ignored by professional historians and that could not be documented through the ordinary methods of history. The disdain of the professional historian for this kind of history was no less conspicuous in China than it has often been in American historiography. Nevertheless, in the 1960s the Four Histories Movement resulted in the collection of an enormous amount of data on popular experiences. Without the "revolution" in history, these data might have been lost forever to historians, who may someday make intelligent use of them.

Furthermore, during the Cultural Revolution, and again in the early 1970s, when intellectuals were "rusticated" in large numbers, closer cooperation was encouraged between "the masses" and intellectuals in historical inquiry and education. For example, the major historical journal of the country, *Historical Studies,* which resumed publication in 1975, has serialized a brief history of China, with the separate sections reputedly having been composed by different mass organizations. Whether or not a certain group in a certain factory actually wrote these histories is less significant than the effort exerted to bring intellectuals together with a mass audience as an education for both on how history can be viewed. These efforts were possibly intended both to purge the populace of traditional notions of history and to instill in them a new historical consciousness. On the other hand, it meant for historians that their work should be more suited to achieving this end and less involved with the abstract and hypostatized history which was the legacy to Chinese historiography from the rigidification of Marxist theory after 1949.

Notes

1. On pre-1949 Chinese historiography and its relationship to post-1949, see Joseph R. Levenson, *Confucian China and Its Modern Fate*, 3 vols. (Berkeley, Calif., 1958–1965); Arif Dirlik, *Revolution and History: The Origins of Marxist Historiography in China* (Berkeley, Calif., 1978); and Laurence A. Schneider, *Ku Chieh-Kang and China's New History* (Berkeley, Calif., 1971).

2. On Wu Han, see James R. Pusey, *Wu Han, Attacking the Present through the Past* (Cambridge, Mass., 1969), and also see Clive Ansley, *The Heresy of Wu Han* (Toronto, 1971), and C. C. Huang, trans., *Hai Jui Dismissed from Office by Wu Han* (especially the introduction by D. W. Kwok) (Honolulu, 1972).

3. Liu Ta-nien, "Zhongguo Lishi kexue xian zhuang" (The Current Status of Historical Studies in China), *Guang ming Ribao*, 1 July 1953.

4. Jian Bo-zan, "Dui chuli ruogan lishi wenti di chubu yijian" (Preliminary Views on the Handling of Certain Historical Problems), in *Jian Bo-zan xueshuo lunzhu ji* (Collection of Jian Bo-zan's Theoretical Essays) (Shanghai, 1966; essay first published in 1961), pp. 3–4; and also Jian, "Muqian shixue yanjiu zhong cunzai di jige wenti" (Some Problems of Contemporary Historiography), in ibid., p. 30, first published in 1962.

5. Cai Mei-biao, "Dui Zhungguo nongmin zhanzheng shi taolun zhong jige wenti di shangjue" (Consideration of Several Questions Concerning the Discussion of Peasant Wars in China), *Lishi Yanjiu*, no. 4 (1961): 67–71.

6. Jian Bo-zan, "Dui chuli ruogan . . ." and "Muqian shixue yanjiu . . . ," pp. 33–36. And also see Kuo Mo-jo, "Guanyu muqian lishi yanjiu zhang di jige wenti" (Some Problems of Contemporary Historical Research), *Xin jianshe* (New Construction), no. 127 (April 1959): 5; Wu Han, "On Appraisal of Figures in History," trans. in *Survey of the China Mainland Press (SCMP)* (Hong Kong), no. 2721, from original in *Renmin Ribao*, 23 March 1962.

7. Ning Ke, "Lun Makesi zhuyi di lishi zhuyi" (Discussion of Historicism in Marxism), *Lishi Yanjiu* 3 (1964): 6–7, 22.

8. Peking Historical Society, "Jieji guandian, lishi zhuyi lilun shi jieho wenti" (Class Viewpoint, Historicism, and the Question of Unifying Theory and History), from an account of a symposium in *Guangming Ribao*, 31 July 1963.

9. Ning Ke, "Lun Makesi zhuyi di lishi zhuyi," p. 25.

10. Zhou Nian-chang and Huang Xuang-min, "Ru he kandai boxiao jieji zai lishi shang di jinbu zuoyong" (How to Deal with the Progressive Function of the Exploiting Classes in History), *Xin Jianshe*, no. 10–11 (1964): 43–46.

11. Guan Feng and Lin Yu-shi, "The Use of Historicism and Class Viewpoint in Historical Research," trans. in *Survey from China Mainland Magazines (SCMM)*, no. 409, from original in *Lishi yanjiu*, 6 December 1963, pp. 11–13, 15.

12. K. Marx and F. Engels, *The German Ideology* (New York, 1969), p. 69.

13. Ibid., p. 30.

14. See James Harrison, *The Communists and Chinese Peasant Rebellions* (New York, 1969), p. 245.

15. F. Engels, "Ludwig Feuerbach and the End of Classical German Philosophy," in *Marx and Engels, Selected Works* (Moscow, 1973), III, 362, 356.

16. *The German Ideology*, p. 39.

17. Karl Mannheim, *Ideology and Utopia* (New York, 1969), pp. 57–58.

18. For discussions of historians' relations with the party, see M. Goldman, "The Role of History in Party Struggle," *The China Quarterly* 51 (July-September 1972): 500–519; and also Jin Chunxin, *"Historical Studies* Is a Reactionary Bulwark of Bourgeois Historical Circles," *SCMP*, no. 3813, pp. 1–8 (from original in *Renmin Ribao*, 23 October 1966); and Qi Ben-yu, "Study History for the Sake of Revolution," *SCMM*, no. 506, pp. 19–28 (from original in *Hong Qi*, no. 13, 6 December 1965).

19. See Li Yu-ning, ed., *The First Emperor of China: The Politics of Historiography* (White Plains, N.Y., 1975), and *Shang Yang's Reforms and State Control in China* (White Plains, N.Y., 1977). These are both excellent anthologies of translations from basic Chinese materials of the 1970s and from earlier background data as well. The editor provides a comprehensive and thoughtful interpretive essay to each volume.

20. For an illustration see Chu Fang-ming, "Criticism of *Water Margin*" [an alternative English translation for the title], *Peking Review*, 27 February 1976, pp. 7–10.

21. Peking University Department of Philosophy Group for the Study of Chinese Philosophy, "Lishi weixin zhuyi di biaoben" (A Sampling of Historical Idealism), *Lishi Yanjiu*, 2 (1977).

22. A. Dirlik, "National Development and Social Revolution in Early Chinese Marxist Thought," *The China Quarterly* 58 (April-June 1974): 286–309.

23. See Richard Baum, *Prelude to Revolution* (New York, 1975), pp. 37–38. For an excellent discussion of the meaning of the movement, see "The Four Histories Movement," *China Report* 2, no. 4 (June-July 1966): 22–26.

Bibliography

Dirlik, Arif. "The Problem of Historicism versus Class Viewpoint in Chinese Historiography," *Modern China* 3 (1977): 465–88.

Goldman, Merle. "China's Anti-Confucian Campaign 1973–74," *China Quarterly* 63 (1975): 435–62.

———. "The Chinese Communist Party's 'Cultural Revolution' of 1962–64," in C. Johnson, ed., *Ideology and Politics in Contemporary China* (Seattle, 1973), pp. 219–56.

Levenson, Joseph R. "The Past Made to Measure, History under Chairman Mao," *Soviet Survey* 23 (April/June 1958): 32–37.

———. *Revolution and Cosmopolitanism* (Berkeley, Calif., 1971).

MacFarquhar, R. *The Hundred Flowers Campaign and the Chinese Intellectuals* (New York, 1960).

———. *The Origins of the Cultural Revolution* (New York, 1974).

Moody, Peter. "The New Anti-Confucian Campaign in China: The First Round," *Asian Survey* 14 (1974): 307–24.

Schneider, Laurence. Review of Li Yu-ning, ed., *The First Emperor of China*, in *Journal of Asian Studies* 36 (1977): 345–47.

Schwartz, Benjamin. "A Marxist Controversy on China," *Far Eastern Quarterly* 13 (1953–54): 143–53.

Wakeman, Frederic. *History and Will: Philosophic Perspectives on Mao Tse-tung's Thought* (Berkeley, Calif., 1973).

———. "Rebellion and Revolution: The Study of Popular Movements in Chinese History," *Journal of Asian Studies* 35 (1977): 201–38.

Wang, Kung-wu. "Juxtaposing Past and Present in China Today," *China Quarterly* 61 (March 1975): 1–24.

PART: C
Other Areas

For over two thousand years the study of history in Western culture, since Herodotus in fact, was in the hands of the amateur, often the gifted amateur, historian. The first major revolution in Western historical investigation—the professionalization of historians who became university-trained and usually university-connected and the application of intense critical scrutiny to historical evidence—originated in Germany in the late eighteenth and early nineteenth centuries and then spread to other Western countries. Its arrival in a country was often signalled by the founding of a professional journal. Thus in Germany the *Historische Zeitschrift* was founded in 1859, in France the *Revue Historique* in 1876, in England the *English Historical Review* in 1886, and in the United States the *American Historical Review* in 1895.

As Western cultural influence was carried overseas from Europe and from the United States by adventurers, missionaries, traders, soldiers, and administrators, historians in Western countries began to write about the history of the regions touched by Western influence. At first these historians were amateurs. Thus James Mill and Mountstuart Elphinstone wrote histories of India, William H. Prescott published his *Conquest of Mexico* and *Conquest of Peru,* and Sir Harry Johnston came out with his *A History of the Colonization of Africa by Alien Races.* But in the first three decades of the twentieth century, professional historians in Western countries began to apply critical methods to the history of these regions. They often formed specialized societies and founded journals. Thus in the United States historians dedicated to the study of Latin America came together at a meeting of the American Historical Association in 1916 and founded the *Hispanic American Historical Review* in 1918.

Meanwhile, the peoples who were being affected in the twentieth century by influences coming from Europe and the United States had their own way of remembering their past and writing their history. In Latin America, whose elite culture was an offshoot and variant of the European, history writing was the province of the amateur historian. To a degree the same was true in nineteenth-century India. In Africa memory of past events was kept alive in the oral literature of the tribe or kingdom.

But beginning in the first decades of the twentieth century historians native to these regions became university-trained, university-connected, and practitioners of critical method. They too formed professional societies, attended professional meetings, and founded professional journals. Thus in 1935 "Indian historians started meeting regularly in Annual Conferences to discuss their professional problems."[1] In Latin America, "the professionalization of Mexican historiography, [for example], can be said to have begun with the founding of El Colegio de México in 1940," followed in 1951 by the appearance of *Historia Mexicana,* a professional journal.[2] A year previously (1950) the University of São Paulo had initiated the publication of *Revista de historia,* a quarterly which became the most important historical journal in Brazil.[3] Other Latin American countries were initiating their professional historical journals, signals of the professionalization of their historians. Meanwhile, the 1950s, it is said, was "the first decade of the introduction of African history as an academic discipline"; it saw the publication of professional periodicals, such as the *Journal of the Historical Society of Nigeria,* whose first number appeared in 1956, and "the organization of seminars, symposia, and international conferences at which various scholarly bodies sought to lay down rules and a theoretical framework for the practice of African history."[4]

So by 1955 the first major revolution in historical investigation—the professionalization of historians and the intense critical scrutiny of documents by accepted procedures—had been diffused throughout the world. Professional historians everywhere accepted the same canons for the establishment of historical "fact," discussed the same issues of objectivity versus subjectivity, moral judgment, and narrative versus analysis, and were subject to the same methodological winds of doctrine from the Marxist, *Annales,* and social science schools of thought. In the intellectual competition among the three schools the influence of the *Annales* and of the Marxists was negligible in India, slightly more important in Africa, and of growing significance in Latin American scholarship. The influence of certain social sciences, notably anthropology, economics, and sociology, was increasingly strong throughout the area.

However, after 1945 history writing in "other areas" of the world, specifically in Latin America, Africa, and India, had certain special features that were variations of international professional historiography. First, there were essentially two groups of professional historians coming to the history of each region: one group based in Europe and the United States, and the other native to the region. They approached the history of the region with a different set of interests and biases. The first group tended initially to be interested in events in which Europeans or citizens of the United States had been involved: in deeds of exploration, invasion, and government. Coming to the history from outside with this bias, they might overlook elements of a historical situation that were essential to the explanation of what had occurred. On the other hand, historians native to the region insisted that one should write the history from within the culture, from its standpoint. In other words, the history should be Indocentric, or Afrocentric, or Latin Americanocentric, rather than Eurocentric. This principle of writing from within the culture has been open to two interpretations. It has meant, quite simply, that in studying a culture the historian gives to each cultural element the importance it had in the society at a given moment of time—with that interpretation nearly every Western historian would now concur, in theory at least. Or it has meant to some native professional historians that they should deliberately use history to help their country's citizens gain a sense of national identity and continuity over time. Actually, historical memory in Western culture has performed that function of nourishing group identity since Herodotus and Shakespeare, and has been used deliberately, self-consciously, and intentionally by professional historians for that purpose ever since Herder or the *Monumenta Germaniae Historica*. So in using history, even in using professional history, to create a sense of national identity, sometimes in hostility to the West, the native historians of the other areas are in line with a sturdy Western tradition.

A second feature of the historiography of the "other areas" was the development or elaboration of special approaches and theories to meet the special challenges and opportunities of the history of each area. For example, the absence of written evidence for most of sub-Saharan African history compelled historians of Africa to refine the techniques of oral history, of interpretation of oral tradition, and of dovetailing oral evidence with results secured by linguists and archeologists. In Latin America the fusion of Indian and Spanish cultural elements into an Indo-Spanish culture along the Andean and Central American highlands has compelled historians and historical anthropologists to become innovative students of the acculturation process which occurs when two peoples live side by side for generations. Indeed, throughout the other areas in Latin America, Africa, and India, the challenges of studying traditional tribes, castes, and other social groups have led historians to turn to the cultural anthropologists for help more frequently than in Europe and the United States. Only in very recent years have economics and sociology, traditional leaders in social science history in Europe and the United States, begun to acquire importance.

Then, the existence of so many countries with similar yet dissimilar historical experiences has lent itself to comparative studies. One can compare the history of slavery in Brazil, the Caribbean, and the United States; or the introduction of British crown colony institutions into a variety of situations; or the introduction of French and British educational systems into West Africa, and so on. Comparison has led to the formulation of overarching theories of development. The fact that in recent centuries Western civilization, as represented by Europe and the United States, has been the most powerful, innovative culture, in technology, in economic organization, in the institutions of the nation-state, and in military weaponry placed other cultures in a position of relative inferiority and dependency. Since 1945 this situation of dependency has been approached by social science historians within the framework of two major explicatory theories, those of modernization and of dependency. The conflict between the two theories is considered by Charles Bergquist in this volume. For our purpose here we need only to note that modernization theory, dominant in the 1950s and 1960s, was essentially a theory of United States sociologists and political theorists, in other words, of Western outsiders. Although often termed ahistorical, it was in fact a theory of how history had happened in Western societies since the eighteenth century, how nations had moved from tradition to modernity, and how with industrialization, developing countries would do the same in virtually the same way. But developing countries have not developed as predicted; indeed, they have remained underdeveloped. Partly to explain this failure in prediction, scholars, some Marxists and others not, have formulated the dependency theory, which proposes that the processes of the international economic order keep underdeveloped societies underdeveloped. Though the intellectual foundation of the theory was laid in the 1950s by Paul Baran, a United States scholar, it was Latin American and African economists and historians who first explored its implications. At present it is being used to reinterpret the development of Europe.

As one leafs through the professional historical journals of India, Africa, and Latin America, reads outstanding monographs and syntheses, and peruses methodological treatises from these areas, several impressions rise in the mind.[5] One impression is of a steadily and rapidly rising level of competence in applying the critical method of appraising historical evidence for authenticity and reliability and of dovetailing the evidences to establish what happened. This method seems to be an international technology, which is being used deftly by a multitude of intelligent, trained historical scholars throughout the world to enlarge our already tremendous store of historical knowledge. The second impression is of the many exciting things that are being done here in interdisciplinary, comparative, and regional studies. The work, for example, of the Berkeley Ibero-Americana school on seventeenth-century New Spain, which combines demography, economics, and ecology, the integral studies of a coffee county in Brazil[6] or of a caste in India,[7] and the deft syntheses of the historians of West Africa[8] will challenge comparison with work done anywhere. One can learn from it not simply information but methodological address as well. The third impression is of the growing sophistication of methodological debate, for example, in the modernization/dependency controversy,[9] or in the perennial discussion over how to understand and present the history of a civilization,[10] or in the concern with the specific methods of economic history.[11] A fourth impression is that few concepts generated in Europe and the United States to handle Western experience fit the historical experience of these other regions. The older categories of "ancient," "medieval," and "modern" have obviously broken down; but so have the newer Marxist stages of feudalism, capitalism, and socialism, and the social science dichotomies of traditional/modern and the Parsonite pattern variables. Even the concept of "class," shared by Marxists and social scientists, may have to be abandoned. Marxist theory and Western social science may turn out to be culture-bound and the explication of social change to be far more subtle, complex, and varied than was ever dreamed in their philosophies.

Notes

1. S. P. Sen, ed., *Historians and Historiography in Modern India* (Calcutta, 1973), p. xii.

2. Charles A. Hale and Michael C. Meyer, "Mexico: The National Period," in Roberto Esquenazi-Mayo and Michael C. Meyer, eds., *Latin American Scholarship Since World War II* (Lincoln, Neb., 1971), pp. 119, 125–26.

3. Stuart B. Schwartz, "Brazil: The Colonial Period," in ibid., p. 24.

4. E. J. Alagoa, "The Interdisciplinary Approach to African History in Nigeria," *Présence Africaine*, no. 94 (1975): 171–72.

5. The following journals have been viewed: *Hispanic American Historical Review, Latin American Research Review, Journal of African History, Indian Economic and Social History Review, Indian Historical Review, Journal of Asian Studies,* and *Modern Asian Studies.*

6. Stanley J. Stein, *Vassouras, A Brazilian Coffee County, 1850–1900* (Cambridge, Mass., 1957).

7. Frank F. Conlon, *A Caste in a Changing World: The Chitrapur Saraswat Brahmans, 1700–1935* (Berkeley, Calif., 1977).

8. For example: E. J. Alagoa, *A History of the Niger Delta* (Ibadan, 1972).

9. Ronald H. Chilcote, "Dependency: A Critical Synthesis of the Literature," *Latin American Perspectives* (1974): 4–29; Richard Higgott, "Competing Theoretical Perspectives on Development and Underdevelopment: A Recent Intellectual History," *Politics* 13 (May 1978): 26–41; J. Samuel Valenzuela and Arturo Valenzuela, "Modernization and Dependency: Alternative Perspectives in the Study of Latin American Underdevelopment," *Comparative Politics* 10 (July, 1978): 535–57.

10. See, for example, the very thoughtful papers in *Problems of Historical Writing in India* (Proceedings of the Seminar held at the India International Centre, New Delhi, 21st–25th January 1963) (New Delhi, n.d.) and the excellent methodological essay by S. C. Malik, *Understanding Indian Civilization: A Framework of Enquiry* (Simla, 1975).

11. *La historia económica en América Latina* (XXXIX Congreso International de Americanistas, Comisión de Historia Económica del Consejo Latinoamericano de Ciencias Sociales), 2 vols. (Mexico City, 1972).

21 CHARLES BERGQUIST

Latin America: A Dissenting View of "Latin American History in World Perspective"

In a recent major evaluation of Latin American historiography, "Latin American History in World Perspective," Woodrow Borah concluded that history writing dealing with this important world area had been largely derivative of ideas and methods in European and United States historiography. Looking to the future, this distinguished North American specialist in colonial Latin American history asked himself, "Is all work, then, to be essentially derivative; is there no promise of innovation within the study of this region?" His answer was not optimistic.

In truly longer-range terms, say of centuries or even millennia, the answer is obviously an unequivocal yes. In the shorter-range terms which we are exploring, that is, the next decades, and within the limitations of the study of history in those decades, the answer must be somewhat different.

"Regional innovation," according to Borah, "is likely when special circumstances favor it"; generally, "such circumstances arise through the existence of unusually rich local materials for study." He went on to list examples of such unusual Latin American source materials, noting quantities of fecund and accessible data for peasant and urban studies, and for work in ethnohistory, the subfield to which Borah himself has made outstanding contributions in the study of colonial Mexican demographic trends. With these exceptions, however, Borah concluded that "writing on the history of Latin America is likely to be derivative in ideas and techniques," although he added that these ideas and techniques would be adapted to local conditions and clothed in the local color of a region distinct geographically, racially, and culturally from Europe and the United States.[1]

I have examined Borah's conclusions here in some detail for reasons germane to the scope and thesis of the essay which follows. Contrary to Borah, I will argue that the historiography of the region since World War II, and particularly in the last decade, features remarkable innovation. During these years there has emerged a new paradigm which challenges the conceptual framework, basic assumptions, and methodology of the liberal historiography long dominant in Latin America, and indeed, the West as a whole. I will argue that "special regional circumstances" and "exceptionally rich local materials for study" of a kind different from those noted by Borah have already acted to produce the innovative historiography Borah fails to find in his survey of the field. In my view, the recent historiography of this subfield offers historians from developed, mature fields (just as the culture of the region as a whole offers the tourist from the developed world) much more than a delayed, underdeveloped (albeit colorful) copy of ideas, techniques, and institutions well established in the developed world. It does that, as recent historiographical studies of the field, noted below, have amply demonstrated. But the subfield also presents new and vigorous historiographical departures. If these new ideas and techniques are as yet rude and unrefined in expression, and careless and exaggerated in application, if they challenge the cherished assumptions and refined sensibilities of those working in the tradition of liberal historiography, they should not therefore be dismissed out of hand. Work within this new paradigm, sometimes called "dependency" analysis, has not only stimulated major reinterpretations of central themes in Latin American history and suggested new issues and methods for future historical research, it has also generated or reinforced a similar revisionism in other Third World areas, particularly Africa, and has recently begun to affect European historiography itself.

This essay will not, therefore, repeat the evaluations of the conventional historiography of the region, a terrain made readily accessible to English readers by a number of excellent recent historiographical studies.[2] Rather, it will focus on the origins and characteristics of the new paradigm and survey some of the most important applications of that paradigm to the study of Latin American history. A final section attempts to appraise critically the significance of the paradigm for Latin American and historical studies in general.

Origins of the New Paradigm

The special regional circumstances and exceptionally rich local materials for study which favored the emergence of an innovative approach to the history of the region centered on what Latin American intellectuals and policy makers in the postwar period perceived as the central issue of their time: the economic underdevelopment of the region. Disillusioned with liberal thought, which had been in crisis since the 1930s, and stimulated by the momentous social forces unleashed in the region by the Great Depression and World War II, these groups came to concentrate in the 1950s and 1960s on two fundamental and related questions or anomalies which liberal thought found difficult to explain. The first of these was the issue of the seemingly chronic underdevelopment of the region and the fact of great and growing inequality between developed and underdeveloped nations in the world. The second was the belief that although Latin

American societies were *changing*, they did not seem to be *developing*—at least in the classic sense of that concept as it is applied to the historical development of Western Europe and the United States in the eighteenth and nineteenth centuries.

The major forum for this kind of thinking was the Economic Commission for Latin America (ECLA), a United Nations agency set up after the war at the insistence of Latin American policy makers and charged with monitoring and fomenting the economic development of the region. Under the direction of Argentine economist Raúl Prebisch, ECLA first advanced the thesis, buttressed by historical investigation, that during the twentieth century the terms of international trade had turned against the primary commodity-producing nations of the "periphery" of the world economic system and that consequently the solution to the problem of development of the region lay in activist governmental promotion of what ECLA termed "import-substitutive industrialization."[3]

Implicit in the ECLA position were three important assumptions which later became fundamental to the new paradigm: (1) that the world was divided into central-developed nations and peripheral-underdeveloped nations; (2) that these two categories of nations were linked together through the world economic system so that development and underdevelopment were interrelated phenomena; and (3) that, at least in the recent past, trade relations in the world system had worked to the disadvantage of the peripheral nations. But it would be a mistake to overemphasize the radical nature of the ECLA position. During the 1950s ECLA economists continued to work within the framework of liberal economic analysis, and as it turned out, their policy of promoting import-substitutive industrialization was fully compatible with the major economic trend of the period, the establishment in the region of branch plants of primarily United States-based multinational manufacturing corporations.

By the 1960s, however, the Latin American economists at ECLA had become disillusioned with the efficacy of the policy of import-substitutive industrialization in promoting development. The larger Latin American nations had indeed experienced rapid industrialization, but their economies were still characterized by an inordinate dependence on primary exports, suffered from chronic inflation and balance-of-payment problems, and generated growing inequality of income distribution. Moreover, the internal market for manufactured goods was limited and skewed toward high-priced consumer goods, and ownership of much of the industrial plant had passed from domestic hands to subsidiaries of multinational corporations which exported a large portion of their profits, monopolized major internal sources of credit, and favored a capital and technologically intensive kind of industrialization inappropriate to capital-short, labor-abundant Latin American economies. Finally, some of the broader-minded developmental economists and other social scientists associated with them began to argue that industrialization in Latin America had failed to engender the social transformation associated historically with the industrial revolution in Europe. Middle-class groups, encased in a society where rural landowners in the export sector were still powerful and industrial leadership had passed to the foreign sector, had failed to create and implement an ideology of national development and foster and defend national culture. Industrialization had not transformed rural economic and social structures, but it had stimulated massive urban migration of lower-class groups to the cities. Since foreign-owned industry was labor-extensive, however, industrial labor, really a labor aristocracy, was easily coopted, while the marginalized urban poor remained politically weak and unorganized. In short, import-substitutive industrialization had created new and formidable structural economic and social problems without generating the social and political forces capable of overcoming these problems and fostering vigorous national economic development.[4]

Disillusioned with the results of import-substitutive industrialization, by the early 1960s Latin American economists began to emphasize structural characteristics which made Latin American economies unique and tended to make standard liberal economic theory inapplicable to Latin American conditions. But by focusing on structural issues such as land-tenure patterns, linkage effects of export economies, and the role of foreign capital, these thinkers were led, contrary to their training in liberal economics, into increasingly broader (extraeconomic) and deeper (historical) analyses of the problem of development in the region.

Perhaps the most exciting center of this new thought in the early and mid-1960s was Santiago de Chile. Santiago was the site of the regional headquarters for ECLA and home of several academic and research institutions with vigorous programs devoted to the study of economic development. Chile in the 1960s not only seemed to be especially affected by the economic and social problems ECLA attributed to the dysfunctional policies of import-substitutive industrialization; it was also the theater of the remarkable political process which led at the end of the decade to the election of a Marxist government bent on radical reform of Chilean economic and social institutions. Attracted by this institutional and political environment, bright young social scientists from Latin America and abroad converged on Santiago to do research, exchange ideas, and hotly debate analyses of the region's past underdevelopment and strategies to achieve development in the future.

In this crucible of Latin American, and especially Chilean, intellectual and political life of the mid-1960s a new paradigm of the history of the region took form. More than a set of specific historical interpretations, the new approach involves a cluster of basic assumptions, a conceptual framework, and methodology which radically differentiate it from the way historians working in the liberal historiographical tradition view the world.[5]

Characteristics of the New Paradigm

Of the many studies conceived in Santiago in the mid-1960s, two stand out for the clarity with which they articulate the new paradigm and the influence they would have in Latin America and abroad in subsequent years. These two works also illustrate a basic cleavage between proponents of the new paradigm, a cleavage which often goes unperceived or ignored by both critics and advocates of the new paradigm, but which is important in assessing the ideological and political, as well as the historiographical implications of the new approach. One of these works, *El subdesarrollo y la teoría del desarrollo,* was written mainly by Chilean economist Osvaldo Sunkel and published with the collaboration of a Mexican historian, Pedro Paz, in 1970. The other, *Capitalism and Underdevelopment in Latin America: Historical Studies of Chile and Brazil,* was written by North American economist André Gunder Frank and rushed into print in 1967. Although published later, Sunkel's book is treated first because it reflects the initial pattern of "dependency" (or, as its practitioners prefer, "historico-structuralist") thought evolved in the postwar period by the developmental economists connected with ECLA. Frank's book, on the other hand, represents a synthesis of the ECLA schools' extant analysis with United States neo-Marxist thought associated especially with the pioneering work of Paul Baran.[6]

For Sunkel, the problem of Latin American historical development cannot be understood outside the context of an evolving world economic system of which Latin America forms a peripheral part. Latin American historical development has been reactive, dependent, not self-generating and autonomous like the historical development of the center of the world system. Problems in the historical development of the region are thus "systemic" and "structural"; they are brought about by Latin America's position and changing role in an evolving world system.

These initial assumptions generate a remarkably fresh and illuminating perspective on the economic history of the region. Sunkel's structural analysis of the region's different and evolving colonial economies offers an interpretation rich in insight not only for subsequent economic, social, and political histories of these separate areas, but a schema within which available data on colonial labor and tax systems, trade and finance policies, and changes in administrative units and laws could be comprehended, reinterpreted, and related to economic change. Similarly, his structural analysis of the different types of export economies which developed in the region during the era of free trade after 1850 allows him to begin explaining the differing responses of Latin American countries to the developmental opportunities afforded by the crisis in the liberal world capitalist system beginning in 1914.

Sunkel divides Latin American history into two main periods: (1) the colonial or mercantilist era, 1500–1750; and (2) the liberal era, 1750–1950. The last phase of the liberal era, 1914–1950, is one of crisis in the center of the world system, of breakdown of the international division of labor, and consequently, of major structural economic change in Latin America. This structural economic change, termed import-substitutive industrialization, not only calls forth new social groups and fosters the growth of state power in Latin America, it also generates a new school of economic analysis attuned to the special problems of the periphery and composed of thinkers who experience underdevelopment first-hand and are committed to overcome it. In the postwar period the liberal era comes to an end, and Latin American states, transformed and strengthened during the previous period of crisis in the liberal world system, stand on the threshold of a new era of potential development. The promise of this new era can be realized if the strengthened national state, supported by a nationalist "populist" coalition of emergent industrialists, urban laborers, bureaucrats, and technocrats, moves to effect basic modifications in the nation's external economic ties to the world system and in its internal, especially its rural, economic structures.

The essence of Frank's book is contained in the essay "Capitalist Development of Underdevelopment in Chile." It attempts to reinterpret Chilean, and by extension Latin American, history, from the sixteenth century to the present day, in terms of one overriding concern: that capitalism itself generates and explains underdevelopment. Underdevelopment is a product not of "traditional" or backward structures, but of capitalist penetration and the incorporation of Latin America into the capitalist world system since the sixteenth century. The capitalist world system is characterized schematically by a series of metropolitan-satellite relationships, both international and internal, which structure the process of expropriation/appropriation of surplus and drain it in stages toward the center of the system. Several corollaries follow. Latin America was never "feudal" but capitalist from the sixteenth century on. Latin American societies do not have a "dual" (traditional-modern) internal structure; rather these two sectors are linked through capitalist exploitation and surplus appropriation of the so-called traditional sector by the so-called modern sector. Since underdevelopment results from close ties to the developed metropolis, developmental progress should occur historically when and where those ties are nonexistent or weak. This conceptual framework leads Frank to a theoretical and political critique of the bulk of liberal and orthodox Marxist history and social science dealing with the problem of development in Latin America. Since both of those schools define development as a process of modernizing the "traditional" or "feudal" sector, both deal with historical pseudoproblems and foster reactionary political postures by aligning themselves with the "national" bourgeoisie. Only the destruction of capitalism through socialist revolution can overcome underdevelopment. In terms of methodology Frank directs the brunt of his critique at liberal social science and its tenet of political neutrality in research.[7]

Despite the similarity of the critique of liberal thought developed in these two books, Sunkel and Frank are radically opposed in their modes of analysis, advocate fundamentally different strategies to achieve development, and offer different assessments of the international and historical significance of the new paradigm. These differences are rooted in the conception of the importance of class struggle as the motor for historical change. Unlike the neo-Marxists, Latin American structuralists like Sunkel deny the inevitability of class struggle. They neglect class conflict in their historical analysis and exclude it from their solution to the problem of underdevelopment. Although structuralists speak of the need for internal reform and greater social justice, unlike the neo-Marxists they seek to narrow the distance between hierarchically structured groups, not to eliminate inequality. Structuralists never attack capitalism or its basic institutions per se, rather, they concentrate their criticism on the skewed, weak, inefficient, dependent capitalism of the periphery. As a result theirs is a national problematic and, in contrast to the neo-Marxists, they have been reluctant to apply the paradigm outside the context of the historical development of the region.[8]

Yet despite these philosophical and political differences both of these works share certain fundamental assumptions radically at odds with traditional liberal historical thought. Liberal historiography tends to view the world as divided into "modern" societies (like those of the developed capitalist West and Japan) and "traditional" or "developing" societies undergoing the difficult but natural and inevitable process of recapitulating the historical process first experienced by the nations of Western Europe. (The nations of the socialist bloc are seen as "traditional" societies that choose a different—and possibly corrupting—means to the same end.) In this view, "modern" societies are those with secular, rational value systems; industrialized, self-generating economies; complex and fluid social structures; rational bureaucratic institutions; and democratic, or at least pluralistic, participatory political systems. Conversely, "traditional" societies have religious or superstitious or unscientific value systems; stagnant, largely agrarian economies, with insufficient capacity to generate self-sustained growth; rigid, hierarchical social structures; and authoritarian, personalist, and clientelist bureaucratic and political structures. In the liberal view, if development along this traditional-modern continuum does not occur as predicted, or if it occurs unevenly, the cause of the delay is internal to the society in question, the result of inappropriate cultural values, retrograde institutions, insufficiency of capital, technological backwardness.

In contrast, the new paradigm relies on the distinction between *un*developed and *under*developed societies. Undeveloped is what societies are before contact with and penetration by the world capitalist system. Underdeveloped is what these societies become as the process of capitalist integration proceeds. While not denying that developed and underdeveloped societies may exhibit many of the characteristics labeled as "modern" and "traditional" in the liberal paradigm, the alternative approach is concerned with showing how many of the features so called are actually created or reinforced as a result of the historical process of integration into the evolving world capitalist system and the international division of labor, regional specialization, and transfers of surplus which that process has involved.

The new paradigm denies that progress from underdevelopment to development is natural, homogeneous, and inevitable. Once there is a developed part of the world (or center), tied to the underdeveloped part (or periphery), progress away from underdevelopment is the exception, not the rule. Primary obstacles to development are social, structural, and systemic, not cultural and institutional. These obstacles are caused or reinforced by external ties. As a result, liberal historiography and the alternative paradigm lead to radically different approaches to contemporary problems of the region. Liberal historiography tends to assume that transfers of Western values, institutions, ideas, capital, and technology will continue to have a positive impact on the historical evolution of the region. Conversely, because they assume that obstacles to development are caused or reinforced by contact with the developed world, advocates of the new paradigm favor the radical restructuring or breaking of contemporary international ties.

Perhaps the most emotional issues separating the two schools of historical analysis are methodological. Perception of these differences leads liberal historians such as Borah to relegate work done in the alternative paradigm into the realm of "politics" and "ideology," not history. For those working in the new paradigm, on the other hand, liberal historians squander their time and resources in an exaggerated, pseudoneutral empiricism designed to answer the wrong questions.

Although liberal historians recognize the problem of bias, they seek a history which is as neutral and objective as possible. "Good" historical research is thus done only by historians whose special training is designed to eliminate bias in their research and handling of evidence. Research is empirical and based on hard documentary and, increasingly, measurable data. In order to document and measure fully, it is necessary to break down historical reality into small components. Specialization, not only on geographical, but also along chronological, topical, and methodological lines, is encouraged.

For advocates of the new paradigm there is no such thing as neutral social science. All social science is socially determined; "good" social science is consciously socially committed. What is essential for science is to state fully one's assumptions and conceptual framework. Because the historical obstacles to development are systemic and structural, it is vital to have a theoretical understanding of how the part relates to the whole before empirical data can be usefully collected and measurement of hard data can become meaningful. Thus specialization, not only within academic disciplines, but *by* disciplines, is dysfunctional. Any social scientist can write history, and all social scientists should. Not an interdisciplinary but a single social science—holistic, profoundly historical, and initially at least, interpretive—is the goal of those working within the alternative paradigm.

Seen from class and national perspectives both paradigms make a great deal of sense. The locus and timing of the liberal paradigm, evolved in the developed nations of the capitalist West over the course of the last two centuries, help to explain its ethnocentric and self-serving world view. Its assumptions and basic conceptual framework rationalize the world capitalist system and the interests of the dominant class within it. Its current methodological canons are appropriate to the resources of developed capitalist nations able to afford a large, full-time historical establishment blessed with huge research libraries and expensive mechanical hardware.[9] On the other hand, the new paradigm builds on dissident, nonliberal, nineteenth-century European intellectual traditions, on Comtian positivism and Marxism, but transforms them in the 1960s to speak to the problem of underdevelopment in the periphery. The new paradigm is the ideological expression of powerful social forces which have emerged in Latin America opposed to the workings of the international capitalist system. The new paradigm, it can be argued, is also appropriate to the limited academic resources of the region. History writing in Latin America, except for the work of a few largely foreign-trained scholars, has traditionally been the preserve and vocation of a social and political elite concerned with justifying the status quo. It is in the social sciences of economics and sociology that an institutional infrastructure is most developed and full-time scholarship judged on intellectual excellence is most possible. Finally, given the limited resources available for training and research in history and the underdeveloped state of the historiography of the region, broad interpretive studies in history would seem to make good economic and intellectual sense.

Promise of the New Paradigm

Unfortunately, however, for all its fresh and provocative insight into the historical evolution of the region and its appropriateness to regional needs and resources, most work within the new paradigm does not qualify as very good history judged by any standards. The two works discussed so far illustrate many of the historiographical deficiencies of this literature as a whole. Although both Sunkel and Frank made an effort to familiarize themselves with historical materials and each consulted trained historians, both authors lacked familiarity with primary historical documents, possessed only a modest acquaintance with the corpus of secondary works available on the history of the region, uncritically accepted evidence and tended to use that evidence selectively, or when evidence was lacking, substituted educated guesses derived from abstract contemporary social science models for hard data generated by the close scrutiny of past social reality. Moreover, perhaps as a result of their initial training in liberal economics, both authors evinced a narrow, economistic, and somewhat mechanical view of the past which neglected the ideas, individuals, and social groups that constitute the human dimension of historical change. Small wonder that few historians of any school took history writing within the new paradigm seriously.

Fortunately for the historiography of the region, however, some historians did. In 1970 two works written by trained historians appeared which reinterpreted the history of the region within the new paradigm. One of these, *The Colonial Heritage of Latin America,* written by North Americans Stanley J. and Barbara H. Stein, dealt with the colonial period, and received wide attention and at least in some circles, critical acclaim. The second work attempted what was perhaps a more difficult task: to apply the new paradigm to the relatively undeveloped historiography of the national period. Written by Argentine historian Tulio Halperín Donghi and published in Spanish in 1970, the *Historia contem-*

poránea de América Latina has been undeservedly neglected outside Latin America and will receive the most detailed attention here.[10]

The Steins' book interprets the legacy of the colonial period through the lens of Iberia's own dependence vis-à-vis the more developed societies and economies of Western Europe. It is this anomalous position in the Atlantic economy, of being at one and the same time colony and empire, that explains the anti-developmentalist character of the institutions and values of the Iberian nations and their American possessions.[11] The Steins' short interpretative essays fall short of a systematic reinterpretation of Latin American colonial history within the new paradigm. But their incisive assessment of issues like colonial mercantile and labor systems and political developments like the Bourbon and Pombaline reforms suggested fresh and meaningful ways to interpret old material in terms of contemporary problems. Moreover, in their almost anthropological emphasis on patterns of behavior and world views and their graphic use of quotations from primary historical documents, they were able to evoke the richness and texture of colonial life. Their book demonstrated both the interpretive possibilities and the subtlety and depth possible in the application of the new paradigm. The central weakness of the book lay in the sketchy and unconvincing efforts of the authors to relate the colonial legacy of the region to nineteenth- and twentieth-century developments in Latin America. To that task, however, Halperín had already set himself.

If Halperín's book owes its interpretive power and revisionist insights to the perspective and ideas of the economists concerned with the roots of Latin American underdevelopment, it tempers these insights with a historian's broad view of historical change, a wide familiarity with primary documents, and an unrivaled command over available secondary sources. The book is divided into six long sections, each of which emphasizes structural changes in the world capitalist system and explores the implications of these changes for Latin America's historical development. Thus Halperín's first chapter, "The Colonial Legacy," sketches the structure of the first "colonial pact" binding the American colonies to their mercantilistic Iberian metropoles and stresses Bourbon efforts to revamp the colonial system under the growing pressures of the more dynamic industrializing economies of Western Europe, particularly that of Great Britain, in the late eighteenth century. Chapter Two, "The Crisis of Independence," involves the struggle for a "new colonial pact" which would integrate Latin America into a closer relationship with the new industrial power in the world system. This chapter, as well as the following one, "A Long Wait," which together cover the period 1810–1850, argue that the process of independence engenders a "ruralization" as well as a "militarization" of power. Economic, political, and institutional changes favor some domestic social and regional groups over others and new groups (such as British merchants) enter the scene in force. The whole process is further complicated by the failure of the new metropolis to live up to expectations and help consolidate the new order through investments in the productive apparatus and transportation. These metropolitan deficiencies begin to be overcome after 1850 during the "Rise of the Neo-Colonial Order'' (Chapter Four), a process which is consolidated after 1880, during the "Maturing of the Neo-Colonial Order'' (Chapter Five), and lasts until the crisis in the world system in 1930. During this classic era of liberalism, the maturing of the industrial economy of Latin America's British metropolis and the international division of labor and massive increase in trade and investment which result create a new order and stability in Latin America built on the thriving export economies which develop in the region. But the new order is almost immediately affected by new tensions: (1) the rise of a new metropolis (the United States) which depends less on the importation of primary commodities and seeks ownership of the means of production itself in Latin America; and (2) the rise of new social groups (middle sectors and labor) which agitate for political and social reform. Finally, in his 180-page Chapter Six, Halperín focuses on the "Crisis of the Neo-Colonial Order,'' which begins in 1930. Halperín breaks this period into two parts. The first analyzes the economic, social, and political ramifications of the breakdown of the world order during two decades of depression and world war. The second deals with the period since about 1955 when the vitality of "import-substitutive industrialization'' has run its course in economies still dependent on agricultural and mineral exports, and social and political tensions reach unprecedented proportions. Unlike many of the Latin American dependency thinkers, however, Halperín stresses the importance of socialist Cuba as a viable alternative to the current crisis.

An overview like this conveys the general lines of the argument of this lengthy and detailed book but cannot hope to suggest the richness and subtlety of Halperín's analysis, much of which derives from a relentless comparative approach to subregional and national variations on the major themes outlined for the region as a whole. Although the weaknesses of the book are many—it suffers inevitably from the underdeveloped state of the historiography of a region for which even good narrative political histories have yet to be written for the period 1850–1930, is written in a complex and sometimes convoluted prose style which attempts to fuse descriptive and analytical modes, fails to distinguish solid historical generalizations from preliminary hypotheses, weakens its argument by neglecting ideological and cultural trends, and on rare occasions (as in the treatment of Brazilian slavery) fails to come to terms with recent historical scholarship—the *Historia contemporánea*, taken as a whole, is a most impressive, although tentative, first approximation of what a mature interpretation within the alternative paradigm might look like. As such it is a book replete with hypotheses in need of empirical evaluation and constitutes an indispensable guide to research issues within the new paradigm.

Significance of the New Paradigm

For ideological, political, and intellectual reasons the new paradigm has proved enormously appealing in Latin American intellectual circles and has had a profound effect on Latin American historical studies. If underdevelopment is a structural problem generated by the region's historical relationship to the developed West—not a cultural problem as liberal thought tends to assume—then development can be achieved through political action to change internal structures and modify or break that external tie. But the new paradigm also exercises an appeal for conceptual and methodological reasons more specifically related to historical studies. By placing the history of the region in the context of an evolving world capitalist system and demonstrating how social, political, institutional, and cultural history can be understood in relation to economic trends, it suggests radical reinterpretations of virtually every aspect of the history of the region. It has also brought into focus new areas for research, especially the need to probe the evolving relationship between dominant capitalist and dependent peripheral social formations and to explore the impact of economic change in the center on economic, social, political, and intellectual developments in the periphery. Whatever the precise combination of reasons for the appeal of the new historical paradigm, recent years have witnessed an explosion of historical writing by Latin American social scientists, journalists, and politicians working within the new approach.[12]

But if the quantity of historical writing done within the new paradigm is impressive, the quality of that work as history continues to suffer from defects of insufficient and selective research, easy generalization, arid schematization, and economism.[13] It is ironic that, given the gross inequality of resources for historical research in a world divided into overdeveloped and underdeveloped nations, most of the best historical research influenced by the new paradigm is now being done in the developed world.[14] Nevertheless, as a result of the influence of the new paradigm, history has become more important to Latin American intellectuals, and there are indications that the professional historians of the region are imbued with the new sense of purpose.[15]

To date the new paradigm has influenced primarily the study of Latin American history, but it also contains within it the germs of a radical reinterpretation of the history of the modern world. If trends in the center account for the underdevelopment of the periphery, might not the very development of the center be linked to the underdevelopment of the periphery? To some extent this radical notion is present in all writing within the new paradigm, but it is within the neo-Marxist variant that economists and sociologists have begun to exploit the revisionist potential of the new perspective for the history of other Third World areas and the developed nations themselves.[16]

How one gauges the significance of a historical paradigm involves questions of judgment based on one's assessment of the degree to which that paradigm approximates an accurate explanation and description of social reality, past, present, and future. Questions of the degree of historical "truth" in a paradigm, in turn, revolve around not only issues of fact but problems of theoretical attractiveness, methodological utility, and practical effectiveness which cannot be separated from personal, class, and national interests. I believe a strong case can be made for the superiority of the neo-Marxist variant of the new paradigm. It has more elegantly and convincingly explained the major anomaly on which the liberal paradigm flounders: the history of chronic underdevelopment in the world system and of the growing gap between developed and underdeveloped nations within that system. It has developed a methodology which, because it is total and dialectical, can more convincingly explain historical change in whole societies—and systems—through time. And it is an explanation of underdevelopment and therefore a strategy for development which has proven to be effective historically in those few Third World nations where class-based political action by the most numerous and disadvantaged in the system has succeeded in breaking out of the pattern of underdevelopment in the world capitalist system. Nevertheless, the new paradigm is faced with some glaring anomalies of its own. It finds embarrassingly difficult the task of adequately accounting for the relative development of white settler colonies like Australia and New Zealand, areas that became integrated into the world system in much the same way as, say, Argentina and Uruguay. Another serious threat to the theoretical integrity of the new paradigm is the issue of the quality of contemporary capitalist development in a nation like Brazil.[17] Issues raised by both of these problem areas seem to point back in the direction of liberal assumptions, and around questions like these will concentrate some of the most important future work in Latin American and world history.

These personal assessments aside, the emergence of an alternative paradigm within which to interpret and study the history of the modern world is clearly an important intellectual development in its own right. This is true however one chooses to assess the relationship of ideas to historical change, or whatever position one takes on the degree of historical "truth" or the methodological validity of work done within the paradigm. The new paradigm is the intellectual analogue of the growing dissatisfaction of people in Third World nations who occupy an ever more disadvantaged position in a grossly unequal world system. Most people in the developed world are now uncomfortably aware of the economic and political dimensions of this new Third World militancy. Historians in the developed world who stand aloof from these economic and political trends will be pleased to learn that there is a historiographical dimension, pregnant with promise and significance, of this same historical process.

Notes

1. Woodrow Borah, "Latin American History in World Perspective," in Charles F. Delzell, ed., *The Future of History* (Nashville, Tenn., 1977), pp. 151–72. The quoted material is from pp. 166 and 167.

2. Borah's article is the most recent and most comprehensive of these. It highlights the thematic and the methodological concerns of foreign scholars and Latin American historians trained abroad and the ideological and political preoccupations of traditional historians in Latin America. It is especially notable for its emphasis on the evolving postwar institutional infrastructure for Latin American history writing within the area and abroad. Also very recent, but narrower in focus, is Charles

Gibson's excellent review of work done in that most developed of Latin American history subfields, colonial Mexican history, "Writing on Colonial Mexico," *Hispanic American Historical Review* 55 (1975): 287–323. Unlike Borah, Gibson takes work done within the "dependency" paradigm seriously and warns his traditionally minded colleagues that they ignore this work "at their peril" (p. 322).

Reflecting current trends in European and United States historiography several articles have surveyed the state and promise of quantitative studies in Latin American history. The most recent of these is Peter H. Smith, "History," in Robert S. Byars and Joseph L. Love, eds., *Quantitative Social Science Research on Latin America* (Urbana, Ill., 1973), pp. 14–61, which laments the meager efforts of historians of Latin America to apply quantitative techniques to political history. A more encouraging evaluation of the application of those techniques to the economic history of the region emerges from the chapters by John J. TePaske (for the colonial period) and William P. McGreevey (for the national period) in Val R. Lorwin and Jacob M. Price, eds., *The Dimensions of the Past: Materials, Problems and Opportunities for Quantitative Work in History* (New Haven, Conn., 1972).

For an overview of the field as a whole which seeks to emphasize progress made since World War II, see the Introduction and chapters devoted to history by John J. TePaske, Stuart B. Schwartz, Richard Graham, Frederick M. Nunn, Joseph T. Criscenti, Charles A. Hale and Michael C. Meyer, and Thomas G. Mathews in Roberto Esquenazi-Mayo and Michael C. Meyer, eds., *Latin American Scholarship Since World War II* (Lincoln, Neb., 1971).

3. Prebisch's seminal essay is *The Economic Development of Latin America and Its Principal Problems* (New York, 1950).

4. Convenient English-language sources for studies of this type are two works edited by the Chilean historian Claudio Véliz: *Obstacles to Change in Latin America* (London, 1965) and *The Politics of Conformity in Latin America* (London, 1967).

5. I have been guided in this approach by Thomas Kuhn's seminal analysis of paradigmatic shift in the natural sciences, *The Structure of Scientific Revolutions* (Chicago, 1962) and, especially, by Aidan Foster-Carter's careful application of Kuhn's concept to the field of developmental economics, "From Rostow to Gunder Frank: Conflicting Paradigms in the Analysis of Underdevelopment," *World Development* 4 (1976): 167–80. A work critical of this approach which covers a great deal of the literature on development is Richard Higgott, "Competing Theoretical Perspectives on Development and Underdevelopment: A Recent Intellectual History," *Politics* 13 (1978): 26–41.

6. Other works could have been chosen, particularly the widely read study by the Brazilian sociologist Fernando Henrique Cardoso and the Chilean historian Enzo Falleto, *Dependencia y desarrollo en América Latina* (Mexico City, 1969). That work is an essentially friendly critique, from within the new paradigm, of the excessively economistic and mechanical nature of analyses like that of Sunkel and a plea for greater attention within the paradigm to the sociological dimensions of economic and political change during the historical evolution of the region. Of works conceived outside Santiago probably the most influential is that of the Brazilian economist Celso Furtado, *Economic Development of Latin America: A Survey from Colonial Times to the Cuban Revolution* (Cambridge, 1970).

7. Several of the basic ideas expounded by Frank were anticipated by Paul Baran in his classic study, *On the Political Economy of Growth* (New York, 1957). These include the central concept that the processes of development and underdevelopment are structurally linked within the world capitalist system, the thesis of the perpetual underdevelopment of Third World nations because of the inevitable historical failure of the national bourgeoisie to promote vigorous capitalist development, the critique of cultural and psychological theories of modernization, and most significantly, the outline of the mechanisms of surplus expropriation and appropriation which historically have drained capital out of Third World nations.

8. Both Sunkel and Frank have been criticized for their failure to incorporate internal class analysis in their historical interpretations of the region, but this is a similarity more apparent than real. In the preface to his book Frank stressed the need for such analysis in the future and, as the simplicity

of his approach and the passionate, almost messianic, language of his book reveals, he aimed his analysis at the dispossessed masses in the system whose mobilization was crucial to bringing about social revolution. Sunkel's book, on the other hand, with its dispassionate, technical language, mathematical proofs of economic theory, and surgical dissection of economic structure, was aimed not at popular forces but at political elites, particularly the bureaucrats and technocrats in the state bureaucracies of the region.

9. I believe, however, that the postwar work on Latin America done by liberal historians in the developed world, no doubt because of its inductive approach and emphasis on primary data, suffers much less from distorted conceptualization and ethnocentric bias than comparable work done by liberal Latin Americanists working within the other social sciences. The careful and important studies of all the major liberal colonial historians and historians of the national period like Alan K. Manchester, R. A. Humphries, Myron Burgin, David Bushnell, John Johnson, and many others, constitute a corpus of historical literature as yet unrivaled in quality and importance in the field.

10. Unlike this book, which was never reviewed in the journal of Latin American historians in the United States, *The Hispanic American Historical Review*, Halperín's narrower, and in my view, less successful and important, political history of the La Plata region in the postindependence decade, *Politics, Economics and Society in Argentina in the Revolutionary Period* (Cambridge, 1975), has been published in English and was promptly decorated with a prestigious historical prize.

11. According to the authors, the dependency concepts which inform their book emerged from contact with the historical documents themselves, but, as their bibliography indicates, they had also read Prebisch and Furtado. One work not cited there, but which anticipates the Steins' thoughtful treatment of the peculiar meld in colonial Iberian economic and social institutions of medieval and feudal legacies with capitalist institutions, is Sergio Bagú, *Económia de la sociedad colonial: Ensayo de la historia comparada de América Latina* (Buenos Aires, 1949). Bagú thus also anticipates, and develops with far more subtlety, Frank's main argument concerning the capitalist nature of the Iberian colonies.

12. During the last decade, in addition to publishing scores of books and founding perhaps a dozen new journals, advocates of the new paradigm have set up new social science research centers in the larger Latin American nations. CEBRAP (Centro Brasileiro de Análise e Planejamento), under the direction of Juarez Rubens Brandão Lopes in São Paulo, and CEDES (Centro de Estudios del Estado y de la Sociedad), directed by Guillermo O'Donnell in Buenos Aires, are the most distinguished of these.

13. There are exceptions, however. For example, Carlos Guilherme Mota's impressive monograph, *Nordeste, 1817* (São Paulo, 1973), uses word analysis within the alternative perspective to explore the consciousness of different social groups involved in that "revolutionary" movement which, Mota argues, conditioned the character of the Brazilian independence movement of 1822. See also the work, both theoretical and empirical, of the prolific Venezuelan Marxist historian, Germán Carrera Damas, especially his *Culto a Bolívar* (Caracas, 1970). A sterling example of detailed historical work within the new paradigm which continues to emphasize the cultural assumptions of the old is the eight-volume *Historia rural del Uruguay moderno* (Montevideo, 1967–1978) by José Pedro Barrán and Benjamín Nahúm.

14. Illustrative of this irony is the fine set of essays published in Heraclio Bonilla, ed., *La independencia en el Perú* (Lima, 1972). Of the six contributors three are Europeans, one a North American. Of the two Latin Americans, only the editor is resident in the region; the other teaches at a major university in the United States. An influential early proponent of the new paradigm in the United States was the North American Congress on Latin America (NACLA), a nonacademic activist group whose important publications also illustrate the link between the neo-Marxist variant of the new paradigm and the emergence of New Left historiography in the United States during the Vietnam war years. For United States academic scholarship on Latin American history influenced by the new paradigm even before 1973, see Part IV of Charles W. Bergquist, "Recent United States Studies in Latin American History: Trends Since 1965," *Latin American Research Review* 9: I (Spring 1974): 3–35. Recent examples of the escalating influence of the new paradigm in the de-

veloped world are David Rock, *Politics in Argentina, 1890–1930* (Cambridge, 1975), and Samuel L. Baily, *The United States and the Development of South America, 1945–1975* (New York, 1976).

15. See the two-volume Sep-Setentas publication, *La historia económica en América Latina* (Mexico City, 1972), especially the thoughtful, wide-ranging essay by Enrique Florescano, II, 11–81, and the monumental *Latin America: A Guide to Economic History, 1830–1930* (Berkeley, Calif., 1977) edited by Roberto Cortés Conde and Stanley J. Stein.

16. See the extraordinary book by the Egyptian economist Samir Amin, *Accumulation on a World Scale* (New York, 1975), and the first of four projected volumes by the North American sociologist Immanuel Wallerstein, *The Modern World-System* (New York, 1974). Frank is also at work on a multivolume history of world capitalism.

17. These issues are forcefully raised in Arghiri Emmanuel, *Unequal Exchange* (New York, 1972), and Bill Warren, "Imperialism and Capitalist Industrialization," *New Left Review* 81 (1973): 3–44.

Bibliography

Amin, Samir. *Accumulation on a World Scale*. New York, 1975.

Borah, Woodrow. "Latin American History in World Perspective," in Charles F. Delzell, ed., *The Future of History* (Nashville, Tenn., 1977), pp. 151–72.

Esquenazi-Mayo, Roberto, and Michael C. Meyer, eds. *Latin American Scholarship Since World War II* (Lincoln, Neb., 1971).

Foster-Carter, Aidan. "From Rostow to Gunder Frank: Conflicting Paradigms in the Analysis of Underdevelopment," *World Development* 4 (1976): 167–80.

Frank, André Gunder. *Capitalism and Underdevelopment in Latin America: Historical Studies of Chile and Brazil*. New York, 1967.

Gibson, Charles. "Writing on Colonial Mexico," *Hispanic American Historical Review* 55 (1975): 287–323.

Halperín Dongui, Tulio. *Historia contemporánea de América Latina*. Madrid, 1970.

Higgott, Richard. "Competing Theoretical Perspectives on Development and Underdevelopment: A Recent Intellectual History," *Politics* 13 (1978): 26–41.

Sunkel, Osvaldo, with the collaboration of Pedro Paz. *El subdesarrollo y la teoría del desarrollo*. Mexico City, 1970.

Wallerstein, Immanuel. *The Modern World-System*. New York, 1974.

22 N. GERALD BARRIER

India: Recent Writing on the History of British India

The study of Indian history during the years of British rule from 1857, when the Mutiny led to the crown's assumption of full control, until 1947, when India became independent, has undergone a turbulent and uneven transformation during the last three decades. In spite of the eclectic nature of the literature, and an overall lack of direction and synthesis about what is and is not known, common historiographic and methodological problems are reflected in current attempts to write a history of the subcontinent. After commenting briefly on the state of the discipline prior to the 1950s, this essay will trace recent major developments and then highlight directions in select areas of research.

Until very recently, two factors influenced perspectives on the history of India under British rule.[1] First, limited access to documents narrowed the scope of research. Immense collections of official records, for example, were out of bounds to serious students. Although several depositories outside India collected publications, those collections tended to be isolated and unpublicized; those in India often were storehouses with librarians who attempted to keep out both white ants and scholars. Even if the documentation had been more available, the dominant mood and ideology associated with British rule would have limited its use. The supporters of official action—imperialist historians either trained in Western institutions or affiliated with the bureaucracy—dominated the handful of professionals with interest in South Asia.[2] Sharing a belief in the value of British rule, these men portrayed government in terms of an "iron frame" (the lauded Indian Civil Service) and a cohesive bureaucratic system run by those with common ideals and purpose. Attention to the formal nature of rule permeated studies of British administration.[3]

Opposition to these views arose among Indians and their allies in Great Britain, but most of these historians were amateurs without formal training. Political or cultural crises also colored handling of issues and sources. Some shunned the British entirely and wrote instead on problems central to Indian daily life, producing histories of caste groups, martyrs, or a religious community.[4] Others sallied forth to battle commonly held views about foreign rule. In their hands, the 1857 Mutiny became the "first war of independence" and the revered administrative system an imperialist tool that destroyed the economy and India's cultural heritage. When the emergence of divergent political patterns, especially communal activity based on religion, threatened a coherent freedom movement against the British, the foreigners received the blame in the form of charges of "divide and rule."[5]

Despite their differences, the focus and assumptions of the two groupings of historians bore close similarity. Though emerging with diverse conclusions, both groups relied on a limited circle of documents (parliamentary papers, biographies, stray statistical accounts, and published records). Moreover, for their own reasons, nationalists and imperial historians alike portrayed developments in terms of all-India events, all-India organizations, and important individuals (viceroys, secretaries of state, and Gandhi). While interpretations of the Indian National Congress varied, it remained at the forefront of political history; similarly, most writers accepted the view that British rule was a monolithic structure, a well-oiled machine in which decisions and policies were emitted from the top and then implemented relentlessly in the districts. The *raj* became a symbol of oppression or of the permanence and civilizing nature of imperialist rule, depending on one's perspective.

If the cupboard of Indian historical research appeared bare in 1947, the roots of a fresh examination were already present in educational developments that would help foster a new generation of historians. The trend emerged almost simultaneously around the world. Within South Asia, the expansion of universities after 1947 was accompanied by emphasis on Indian history as a major field. Local historical societies, once barely surviving, now received grants and applause. The government provided money for research through institutes (often specializing in the history of a region or an aspect of history) or through programs linked to the newly formed Indian Council of Historical Research. Subsidies paved the way for monographs and provocative essays in prestigious journals such as the *Indian Economic and Social History Review*.[6] A similar pattern of new centers and funding can be found also in Australia, England, and the United States (and to an extent in Russia and Japan). In the United States, largely because of federal funds for language and area studies, major centers have trained historians of modern India who in turn have developed smaller programs spread across the nation. Likewise, in England active programs can be found at Oxford, Cambridge, and the University of London, with links to centers and scholars in Europe.

The new historians, both in India and in Western countries, share several characteristics. Many are trained in Indic languages and value the use of non-official, indigenous documents. Although their handling of the material varies, their underlying concern has been with the history of the Indians themselves rather than primarily with British rule. Politics remains a focus, although as will be noted, it is seen from new perspectives. A final pattern in the new historical trend is the association of scholars, formally or informally, who share common interests. In America, for example, committees studying one region (such as Punjab, Bengal, and Maharashtra) hold conferences and sponsor publications.[7] Occasionally one or more centers become identified with research on a particular problem: for instance, Cambridge and Oxford historians are much involved in a reexamination of the Indian political system.

The growth of a profession in South Asian history has been accompanied and in part accelerated by widened access to documents. The explosive spread of the publication industry in nineteenth-century India left a legacy of almost innumerable books, tracts, and newspapers. Loosening of copyright restrictions, recent preservation projects, and an overall improvement of information on depositories has now made available a treasure of printed documents. In addition, archives once closed are now open, frequently offering access to items dated up to 1947. Efforts are being made to preserve the private papers of many influential individuals, and oral history projects attempt to maintain personal accounts of historical experiences. Circulation of contemporary studies on Indian history has also improved; many libraries in the West either are associated with permanent acquisition networks (such as that provided by the Library of Congress) or buy directly from the Indian book trade.[8]

This wealth of documents has nevertheless been a mixed blessing to historians. Bibliographic controls have not kept pace with the improved access to materials. With scattered exceptions, there are no major guides to the literature in Indian languages or to thousands of English-language publications for that matter. Although bibliographies of collections in the British Museum and India Office Library exist, even there information is sparse.[9] The infusion of funds for centers was not matched by resources for preparing guides to source materials.

The problems caused by inadequate bibliographic information have been compounded by inattention to issues concerning methodology and use of documents. Every source on India, whether British or indigenous, has problems that affect interpretation. Students sometimes receive rudimentary training in how to handle materials, but on the whole, publications and conferences pay little heed to the value and possible misuse of tracts, journals, British documents, and local records.[10] The appearance of numerous studies on modern Indian history reflects the zeal of energetic scholars breaking fresh ground, but one senses that they are often frustrated by the lack of communication outside particular reference groups or hampered by the need to devise individual approaches to issues encountered in the field. In most areas, information has accumulated, but at the same time one finds a sense of indirection and uncertainty about how specific research fits together. In short, Indian history is in the midst of an exciting phase of monographic, specialized writing. In order to review trends within a quickly changing profession, this essay will direct its attention to research in three areas—administrative history, social and economic change, and politics.

Interpretations of how the British ruled India have been revised substantially. As in the case of administrative and colonial studies in other geographic areas, students of British India now pay attention to the informal nature of control and the strikingly decentralized fashion in which the government operated. Although revisionist trends among specialists in African and British imperial studies account partially for fresh approaches to India, much of the impetus has come from the recently opened records. For the first time, historians can explore the complexities of governance at each level of administration from the once revered apex—the India Office and the Government of India—to the isolated district. Extensive notations in files and the myriad of correspondence connected with decision making have raised questions about the purpose and day-to-day functioning of the bureaucracy.

Despite occasional narratives mirroring an older emphasis on "policy" or monolithic structures, new research points toward a consensus about the dynamics of administration.[11] British survival in India rested ultimately on the ability of administrators to communicate with each other and to secure accurate information, or "feedback," as to what was happening in Indian society. Both formal and informal networks within the bureaucracy facilitated this flow of information. Communication between ruler and ruled also involved apparatus such as commissions of inquiry, public meetings, and legislative arenas, as well as private discussions and secret "tapping" of "native opinion" through intelligence reports and press surveillance. Decision making and policy implementation similarly reflected diverse origins and a concomitant divergence in implementing orders at the local level. Personalities, factions, and ambition played a major role in administrative decisions. Another emphasis in research on administrative functions has been on the alliance between the government and various support groups. The British were never free agents in India. Rather, their decisions had to be made in light of how they perceived both their goals and the limits of public acceptance. This political calculus meant balancing the claims of segments of society, some labeled "friendly" and others "dangerous" or hostile to foreigners. From the outset, the British counted on Indians to help run offices, collect revenue, man the police, and serve in the army. In return, the government had to defend the interests of their native supporters, whether Sikhs and Jats (thought to be vital to the military), Brahmins in certain provinces (influential in maintaining religions and social order), Muslims, or peasants. Much of British imperial history is now being cast in terms of how the government manipulated or worked with specific classes and how its perception of support changed or became implemented in particular policies.[12]

Following the Mutiny of 1857, British officialdom made a slow but decisive change from bureaucratic to imperial politics. Not only did the British import or create new institutions within which Indian politicians functioned, such as councils or legislatures, but the governors themselves had to work within the evolving framework and political milieu. Recent studies of episodes, viceroys, and provincial arenas continually reflect that theme.[13] Power politics involved the perennial Indian value of maintaining face, or prestige, but it also required interacting with Indians in new ways such as lobbying, debating, and developing a constituency. Force was used occasionally, but the overall rhythm and rationale of colonial rule generally rested on a delicate balance between coercion and conciliation.

Scholarly disagreement about British rule centers on three issues—the effects of administration (to be discussed separately), the manner in which philosophical or cultural norms from the West affected India, and the appropriate use of official documents. The painful period of self-examination after the Mutiny of 1857 initiated a century of debate over how Western ideas reached India and what their implications were. At the time, evangelical and utilitarian influences, as well as Christian missions as a whole, received some blame for upsetting Indians and thereby precipitating unrest. Several monographs have traced the role of such influences with regard to land revenue, education, and attitudes toward Indians. Other studies have tried to revise assumptions about the institutionalization of foreign ideology, arguing that practical issues and local circumstance determined what the British did.[14] While wholesale application of Western ideas has been questioned successfully, research does show that groups of men, frequently in provincial schools or cadres, developed distinct philosophies about how to rule.[15] These were perpetuated, changed as necessary, and viewed by the British and nationalists alike as characteristics of particular provincial administrations. A series of studies have also demonstrated the changes in the British image of both the Indians and the British themselves; in essence, the ability of the government to rule depended on adapting to new conditions and altering positions found to be untenable.[16]

Evaluation of British attitudes is related to a methodological issue concerning sources. Records of administrative proceedings unquestionably reflect what at least some Englishmen thought about problems and how they reached decisions. Given the decentralized administration, however, historians have learned that one set of records does not reveal the entire story. A few years ago, "dominance of the India Office" was frequently heard among historians, a reference to how Western historians relied on the select documents sent to London or on the vice-regal papers housed in the India Office. Similarly, administrative research by Indians utilized the New Delhi files but often ignored supplementary documents in London. Recent studies have followed decisions throughout the administrative system, but books continue to be written from incomplete documentation. Studies on controversial events such as the Deccan riots suggest a more pervasive problem with proceedings, namely, the degree to which imperial perception colors the presentation of data in files or in published records such as censuses and settlement reports.[17] British files do tell what the government thought it was doing, and how episodes were interpreted; what remains unclear, and often undiscussed, is the validity of relying on such records for understanding non-British topics. Some historians would argue that Indian history must be written not from files but from evidence produced by Indians themselves; another group suggests that while records must be handled critically like other documents, they should not be discarded as useless. The issue has not been resolved, and it affects much of the current research on modern India.

Study on another dimension of Indian history, social and economic change, has similarly questioned earlier views such as the existence of an all-India middle class dominated by a small professional group or the destruction of the economy by imperialism. Tilting with older orthodoxies, however, has not furnished an integrated version of what did affect Indians and their institutions. Two current historiographic trends are the prevalence of articles on issues and processes and a paucity of monographs that not only deal with specific topics but add to a general understanding of social developments. At least three elements contribute to this diffuse state of research. First, unlike historians in other world regions, scholars of these subjects in Indian history cannot draw upon a secondary literature as a guide or stimulus for research. Serious writing on economic and social issues in India can be traced back at best through two decades, a short period for developing mature ideas or comparative approaches. Secondly, while individuals have borrowed and adapted methodology from other disciplines (most notably anthropology and sociology), no ideology or model has served to focus discussion. Marxist concepts, for example, have had little impact on social analysis. Scholars tend to deal with a small area of expertise; they either are not concerned with broader implications, or more often they present results in such a way that generalizations do not appear easily. Finally, cultural diversity within the Indian subcontinent lends itself to a balkanization of historical perspective. To work on one region—the Punjab, for example—may require research in several languages and years of familiarization with the culture and documents of the area. The effort to find and use newspapers, tracts, and private papers helps foster specialized, narrow study. Conferences and panels do provide channels for examining problems comparatively, but only recently have organizations such as the Indian Council for Social Science Research or the United States Social Science Research Council attempted to set up forums for integrating scholarly findings.

The choice of what to study in Indian social history thus varies considerably. Although few historians focus on individuals, several new biographies contribute notably to an appreciation of human beings and their milieu (for example, Blair Kling's life of a Bengal entrepreneur and cultural leader and N. Mukherjee's biography of a Bengal *zamindar*).[18] Scholarly analyses, buttressed by the appearance of at least a hundred autobiographical accounts in the last decade, have focused on broader social units such as caste or on groups operating within organizational structures.[19] Important contributions include books on the Marwaris (a trading community), social and religious change among Christians in Punjab, a key Muslim college and its students, and upwardly mobile castes.[20] Leadership and social change in urban settings have been examined, while developments in the countryside have been evaluated either at the provincial or district level.[21]

Common themes receive emphasis in many such works. First, the notion of the West having an "impact" on a dormant, unchanging society has been replaced by a more complex view of cultural contact. India prior to British rule had already been undergoing changes whose speed and direction depended on regional and local events. The appearance of foreigners and their domination of the political system only added another variable, though an important one, to the pattern. Some groups took advantage of changed opportunities and prospered; others once ascendant did not respond creatively and lost economic or social status. Since British rule spread across India at different times, and often pursued different approaches to local situations, the quality and rapidity of change varied.[22] Concern with the economic exploitation of the subcontinent has shifted either to particular sectors of the economy or to what the British did and its results (usually at the provincial level).[23] The forthcoming *Cambridge Economic History of India*, a collaborative project by scholars from throughout the world, should serve as a benchmark in understanding economic developments. Cultural interaction between Indians and Westerners also receives prominence; historians have analyzed the transfer of institutions and ideas as well as the type of associations emerging from cultural interaction.[24] Tradition receives greater emphasis than in the past, and several scholars have stressed the role that heritage and indigenous institutions played in determining how individuals and new groups viewed themselves and their goals. Careful thought is paid to what "modernization" meant in terms of concrete situations rather than as an abstract notion.[25]

Discussion of British India was once based on British sources and English-language materials, but current writing reflects either a balance between British and Indian documents or a preference for the latter. The most heavily used official records are the multivolume series of Indian censuses (decennial since 1871), the district gazetteers, and land settlement reports that registered social and economic changes over a ten- to thirty-year period. While no sustained evaluation has been undertaken of the issues involved in relying on these and similar sources, the imperial documents continue to be used. Some of the most provocative research, however, rests firmly upon distinctly Indian material, a pattern illustrated by three recent contributions.

Thomas Kessinger has combined anthropological and historical methods in his book on the history of one Punjab village, Vilyatpur.[26] Although referring to British sources, Kessinger generated a fresh approach by utilizing village records, genealogies, household censuses, and pilgrimage records. These were tested against extensive interviews with families in the village, where he lived for a year. The research questions commonly held notions about Indian society and economics. Many Indians in Vilyatpur, for example, have not followed traditional occupations for generations. Instead of finding an abundance of wasteland, as recorded in earlier accounts, Kessinger demonstrated a high degree of land utilization on an intensive cropping basis. His research suggests that many families were nuclear in the nineteenth century, thus challenging the notion that the Indian joint family has only recently shown signs of change. In addition, Kessinger sheds light on migration patterns, ties between towns and village, and a multitude of other issues. It is doubtful that the success of the book will generate a rash of village-level historical volumes, but the research serves as a milestone in methodology.

Ken Jones's *Arya Dharm* deals with cultural change and modernization among Hindus over almost half a century.[27] His research sets rigorous standards for handling indigenous documents—for Jones, that necessitated a decade of study of organizational files, newspapers, and tracts in several languages. His treatment of one organization, the Arya Samaj in Punjab, explores a little-known process, the development of ideology and group consciousness. The book links social mobilization to new associational patterns and subsequently to increased tension among various communities in urban society. Other features, which must be taken into account by future writers, include meticulous maintenance of statistics on funding and participation patterns, and detailed records on the lives of several hundred individuals.

A Caste in a Changing World, by Frank Conlon, demonstrates a similar interest in social and cultural developments.[28] The first narrative history of a caste, this book traces how the Saraswat Brahmins have changed as a community since the 1700s and yet maintained authority and tradition as values. Tapping an array of tables and charts (based on British and Saraswat census records), he traces patterns of urbanization and occupational shifts. Conlon manages the difficult task of blending biography with an analysis that registers influence from several social sciences. Also a model of documentation, his footnotes are filled with references to official documents, temple and monastery records, a dozen newspapers, family histories, caste material (usually in Kanarese and Marathi), and extensive interviews.

The enthusiasm and certainly many of the problems inherent in current research on administration and society are duplicated in the reexamination of India's political history. Unlike scholars interested in social or economic matters, the student of politics confronts a historiographical tradition that stretches back to the pre-1947 period and perpetuates particular concerns. Earlier biographies and historical works had described political organizations such as the Indian National Congress, the role of great men (most often Gandhi and Nehru), or the evolution of *the* freedom movement. Political history tended to be associated with agitation against the British or with activities within formal structures. The admitted importance of the Congress and Gandhi has perpetuated this view of recent history, especially among historians who served within the nationalist organization or who had close contact with the Mahatma. Anniversary volumes sketching the lives of martyrs or the history of associations appear frequently. The divisive elements in the society in which scholars must function also helps account for the emphasis on the unifying role of an organization or person. For whatever reason, the lack of documentation, and the admitted ideological commitment of many political historians, leaves this area a zone for "instant revision."

Before turning to changing views on politics, two observations seem appropriate. First, historians are acquiring a broadened understanding of the political process. The concept of a complex political system, with analysis of process and relationships, has percolated throughout much of the profession, either in the form of graduate training or by constant exposure to social scientists who also follow individuals and topics back through time.[29] Among historians themselves, the Namierian approach to groupings and self-interest has undoubtedly influenced views of the Indian experience. While influences cannot be attributed solely to one source, a distinctly "modern" view of politics tends to color contemporary research on India. Politics is viewed as a process of organized efforts by individuals and groups to control resources, to create and hold power, or to legitimize claims to leadership, on the basis of their vital interests. Perception of interest and one's immediate body of reference may change, as may the structures and rules for political participation, but the process continues. Rather than viewing Indian politics therefore as British versus Indian, more attention is being paid to who participates and why, and how groups or organizations function and organize for particular purposes. Interaction between *raj* and local politician still receives prominence, but from a variety of perspectives.[30] Historians also have shown interest in groups upon which the British relied, such as Indian princes.[31]

A series of books by scholars associated with John Gallagher and Anil Seal (Oxford and Cambridge) illustrates a number of these altered perspectives.[32] Their studies, usually published by the presses of the two institutions, explore common themes in spite of regional variations. Politicians are viewed in terms of groups acting essentially from self-interest and moved by economic or status concerns rather than by the factors traditionally judged important, such as caste and religion. Careful reconstruction of career and family patterns also characterizes their work, as does reliance on statistics to explore the dynamics of participation. The British are seen as major actors, actively nurturing supporters among Indians (patron-client relationships) and otherwise evolving as politicians. The structure of governance from the village to the central legislature provided stimulus, according to their interpretations, for tying politicians together vertically as well as horizontally (hence the concern with "locality, province, and nation").

In addition to a broader view of politics, the new research taps sources hitherto unused in understanding political patterns. Newspapers, party documents, and private papers provide chronology or information on events. Problems inherent in using newspapers as sources have been overcome in part by evaluating accounts against other material (a journal by an opposing faction, or a British commentary). In terms of official documents, historians have integrated a wider spectrum of British material into their narratives. References to confidential political files, for example, now commonly appear in footnotes.

Serious source problems nevertheless remain. The preoccupation with English-language material in earlier studies continues, particularly in the mono-graphs appearing from Oxford and Cambridge. Ready access to such sources, plus perhaps a tendency for high-ranking politicians to use English as a medium, probably accounts for the pattern. However, given the expanded use of Indic-language materials by other historians, and the fact that the majority of news-papers and books relating to Indian politics tend to be in the vernacular, one might legitimately inquire as to whether the conclusions of the current generation of monographs will stand the test of time.[33] Moreover, as in the case of other aspects of Indian history, political specialists may have wandered into pitfalls because of unquestioning reliance on British documents. Individuals base chap-ters on confidential translations from the vernacular press, for example, without tracing the original or without pursuing adequate data on the editor and trans-lator. Intelligence reports are similarly suspect, especially in light of the limi-tations of the Imperial C.I.D. (with either Indian sources or paid informers). Perhaps scholars critically evaluate the references, but generally files are quoted without qualification. What the British said thus seems to be taken as a fact. Nor are published documents necessarily sacrosanct. Peter Reeves and Bruce Graham have shown, as an illustration, the difficulty of trying to use official reports as a basis for election data.[34]

A more complex understanding of politics and an expanded base of source materials have helped foster a fresh look at most dimensions of Indian politics. Central organizations continue to be studied, but with attention to general issues, internal dynamics, and participation patterns. In a recent book illustrating the new trends, John McLane has analyzed the social composition of Congress lead-ership and at the same time evaluated nationalist efforts to meet challenges posed by communal tension. Also noteworthy is S. R. Mehrotra's investigation of the early nationalist movement, based on an exhaustive study of newspapers and private collections.[35] More prominent have been studies on the Congress and other parties at the local level. Historians now have assessed politics, particularly between 1880 and 1947, in most geographic regions. Their focus varies, but each is concerned with specific associations, identifiable groups, and parochial issues. Counting is pronounced, either to identify patterns or to explore variables underlying group formation.[36] Political mobilization is also examined in studies of idiom, propaganda, and newspaper networks.[37] At least two scholars, Richard Cashman and Kenneth Jones, have highlighted the role of images, myths, and ideology in politics, while others have studied segments of the population long ignored, such as untouchables, the princes, municipal leaders, and peasants.[38] The Congress and Gandhi were ambivalent toward terrorism and so, apparently, are contemporary historians: except for stray surveys and biographies, no con-nected account of revolutionaries has appeared.[39]

Scholarly inattention similarly characterizes writing on politics associated with religious identification. Articles cover particular riots and events, but except for a few critical monographs (and a large number of books with a Hindu or Muslim viewpoint), the crucial evolution of communal patterns remains uncharted.[40]

Available research does throw light on the British contribution, linking the government not to "divide and rule" strategies but rather to a transfer of arenas of conflict (such as councils or elections) that intensified religious revival.[41] Moreover, some of the basic elements in the politics of religion are beginning to receive attention—regional variations in Hindu-Muslim relations, cultural change that strengthened boundaries between communities, new institutions for defense and attack, and conflict within sects over the control of institutions. Details at the regional level remain sketchy, especially in the case of the Muslim experience (the exception is Francis Robinson's study of Muslims in the United Provinces).[42] Reasons for this inactivity include the sensitivity of issues involved and also the lingering tendency to keep files on communal politics "confidential." If Pandora's box were to open, perhaps the ensuing discussion would further inflame the communal situation.

Alongside new subjects and local history, men and events—the traditional pivots of historical writing—remain prominent. Symposia occasionally provide a platform for examining events, exemplified by collections of essays on World War I and India, the disturbances in 1919, and partition.[43] Participants in the "great events" of the past decades now are writing histories or autobiographical accounts. National leaders such as Nehru, M. N. Roy, Tilak, and Gokhale have been the subjects of recent biographies. The best of these works generally deal not just with the personality and ideas of individuals, but also with the milieu in which they lived and the forces at work in society.[44] Documentation again reflects a balance between local records and British files. Literally hundreds of books and articles have been written on Gandhi since 1945, but four deserve mention because they mirror perspectives that will be more evident in coming years. Eric Erikson's psychoanalytic study of Gandhi has evoked a wave of criticism and support. In the balance, the work serves as a guide in understanding how personality and culture affect great men, in this instance, a most unusual Indian.[45] Although outdated at places, Joan Bondurant's *Conquest of Violence* remains the best overall survey of the interaction between Gandhi's philosophy and practical strategy.[46] Two monographs by Judith Brown probably do more than any other research towards approaching in understanding of Gandhi as a politician.[47] Using almost every conceivable source, from the massive documentation in Gandhi's papers and those of the All-India Congress Committee to hundreds of British files, Brown has presented a connected picture of how Gandhi grew as a politician, making mistakes, achieving victories, and evolving within the political arenas of India. She sympathetically handles Gandhi's intimate interaction with officials, and also his sometimes thwarted efforts to work with fellow congressmen and a range of interest groups.

In summary, research and writing on recent Indian history stands at a juncture. On the one hand, the multiplication of publications based on fresh sources and approaches has dramatically increased the information on the last century of British rule in India. Innovative books appear regularly, as for example, two new books by Indian scholars on the urban history of Calcutta.[48] On the other hand, specialization has meant that historians tend to be unfamiliar with the latest literature outside immediate reference groups or published in other countries. Cross-fertilization of ideas and methodology is minimal. Many historiographic issues have not been evaluated seriously within the profession. Stereotypes and older understandings have been challenged, but except for a handful of general interpretative studies, syntheses of material have not been achieved on an extensive scale.[49] Although research on administration, socioeconomic change, and politics points toward a pulling together of many strands, major syncretic works have not been written. Unlike trends suggested by other essays in this volume, no major philosophy or overview of the historical process significantly affects current writing on British India.

New sources, growing funds for research, and expansion of historians with area training nevertheless will alter these patterns, probably in the near future. Historical traditions and dialogue over issues take time to evolve, and one can see in the present dynamic if fragmented phase of writing on India the appearance of a foundation for interpretations that go beyond immediate monographic concerns. Mechanisms that may facilitate integration of research are not clear, although government funding and efforts by institutes or foundations may furnish a catalyst for comparative interpretation. Summer seminars on new topics such as the use of anthropology for teaching and writing about South Asian history (University of Chicago, 1978, supported by the National Endowment for the Humanities) and the concern with methodology that has emerged in conferences of the Association for Asian Studies suggest movement. Until such syntheses appear, the excitement of working on uncharted frontiers of historical research will continue to be tempered by the frustrations implicit in a transitional phase of Indian studies.

Notes

1. Historiographic issues and interpretations on Indian history are examined in Robert I. Crane, *A History of South Asia* (Washington, D.C., 1973).

2. Much of their work has been surveyed in articles on the British and British India in S. P. Sen, *Historians and Historiography in Modern India* (Calcutta, 1973); S. P. Sen, *History in Modern Indian Literature* (Calcutta, 1975); and C. H. Philips, ed., *Historians of India, Pakistan and Ceylon* (Oxford, 1961). Review articles on themes or periods often are found in *Pacific Affairs, Modern Asian Studies* (*MAS*), and *Journal of Asian Studies* (*JAS*).

3. For example, see the descriptions in Curzon of Kedleston, *British Government in India* (London, 1925); C. E. Backland, *Bengal Under the Lieutenant Governors* (Gurgaon, 1975); and the short monographs in the Punjab Record Office series dealing with education, policy, and major decisions (economic and political). A romanticized view is contained in Philip Woodruff (Mason), *The Men Who Ruled India* (New York, 1964).

4. The process for one community is examined in N. G. Barrier, *The Sikhs and Their Literature* (Delhi, 1970); see also Kenneth Jones, *Arya Dharm* (Berkeley, Calif., 1976).

5. Economic nationalism and imperialist charges are surveyed in Bipan Chandra, *The Rise and Growth of Economic Nationalism in India* (Delhi, 1966). On communalism, see Romilla Thapar et

al., *Communalism and the Writing of Indian History* (Delhi, 1977); and *A History of Hindu-Muslim Relations* (Cawnpqr Riot Commission Report), reprinted with a historical introduction in N. G. Barrier, ed., *The Roots of Communal Politics* (Delhi, 1976).

6. The Indian Council of Historical Research has subsidized a wide range of new monographs as well as bringing out its own reports and journals. Also relevant are the proceedings of the Indian Historical Records Commission and conference publications from state or regional history groups. The Institute of Historical Studies in Calcutta has generated a variety of useful symposia and also a major biographical source, *Dictionary of National Biography* (Calcutta, 1972–1974).

7. Issues and approaches are found in Robert I. Crane, ed., *Symposium on Regions and Regionalism in South Asia* (Durham, N.C., 1966); examples of regional collections include Rachel Van M. Baumer, ed., *Aspects of Bengali History and Society* (Delhi, 1976); Burton Stein, ed., *Essays on South India* (Delhi, 1976); and Harbans Singh and N. G. Barrier, eds., *Punjab Past and Present* (Patiala, 1976).

8. The current status of materials in America is surveyed in Maureen Patterson and Martin Yanuck, eds., *South Asian Library Resources in North America* (Yug, 1975); archives are described in D. A. Low, *Government Archives in South Asia* (Cambridge, 1969); an introduction to tracts and vernacular holdings can be found in N. G. Barrier, "South Asia in Vernacular Publications," *JAS* 28 (1969): 803–10.

9. Useful is Margaret Case, *South Asian History, 1750–1950: A Guide to Periodicals, Dissertations and Newspapers* (Princeton, N.J., 1968); notable among regional bibliographies is Eric Gustafson and Kenneth Jones, eds., *Sources on Punjab History* (Delhi, 1975). Among recent guides to the holdings of the India Office and the British Museum is Ganesh Gaur and Eileen Dimes, *Catalogue of Punjabi Printed Books Added to the India Office Library 1902–1964* (London, 1975).

10. Particularly relevant to methodological issues are the following: Edwin Hirschmann, "Using South Asian Newspapers for Historical Research," *JAS* 31 (1971): 143–50; Thomas Kessinger, "Historical Materials on Rural India," *Indian Economic and Social History Review (IESHR)* 7 (1970): 489–510; and N. G. Barrier, "South Asia in Vernacular Publications,"

11. New perspectives on British administration are found in essays presented at the 1978 conference of the Association for Asian Studies, which are to be published in 1979 (ed. Robert I. Crane). Books by B. B. Misra provide an encyclopedic overview of the bureaucracy: *The Administrative History of India* (Delhi, 1970) and *The Bureaucracy in India* (Delhi, 1977). Also useful are biographies by retired Indian Civil Service officers, such as Malcolm Darling's *Apprentice to Power* (London, 1966).

12. A comprehensive analysis of the bureaucracy is Bradford Spangenberg's *British Bureaucracy in India* (Delhi, 1976). Studies on British political perception and action include the following: Bernard S. Cohn, "The Initial British Impact on India," *JAS* 19 (1959): 418–31; R. E. Frykenberg, *Guntur District, 1788–1848* (Oxford, 1965); Thomas R. Metcalf, *The Aftermath of Revolt* (Princeton, N.J., 1964); Anthony Low, ed., *Soundings in Modern South Asian History* (Berkeley, Calif., 1968); and N. G. Barrier, *Banned* (Columbia, Mo., 1975).

13. See S. Gopal, *The Viceroyalty of Lord Irwin* (Oxford, 1957) and *The Viceroyalty of Lord Ripon* (Oxford, 1953); Stephen Koss, *John Morley at the India Office* (New Haven, Conn., 1969); Stanley Wolpert, *Morley and India* (Berkeley, Calif., 1967); Richard P. Cronin, *British Policy in Bengal* (Calcutta, 1977); N. G. Barrier, *The Punjab Alienation of Land Bill* (Durham, N.C., 1966); and Piet Van den Dungen, *The Punjab Tradition* (London, 1972).

14. Among the major new works on influences and application of ideas are these: Elizabeth Whitcombe, *Agrarian Conditions in Northern India*, vol. I (Berkeley, Calif., 1972); Eric Stokes, *The English Utilitarians and India* (Oxford, 1959); R. E. Frykenberg, ed., *Land Control and Social Structure in Indian History* (Madison, Wisc., 1969); Neil Rabitoy, "System versus Expediency," *MAS* 9 (1975): 505–28; and Eric Stokes, "Agrarian Society and the Pax Britannica in Northern India," *MAS* 9 (1975): 529–46. Also important are numerous essays by Ira Klein in *MAS, JAS,* and *IESHR.*

15. Beautifully illustrated in John Beames, *Memoirs of a Bengal Civilian*, rev. ed. (Delhi, 1978). Also discussed in Van den Dungen, *Punjab Tradition,* and Spangenberg, *British Bureaucracy.*

16. On major ideas, see George D. Bearce, *British Attitudes toward India* (Oxford, 1961); Francis G. Hutchins, *The Illusion of Permanence* (Princeton, N.J., 1967); and Allen J. Greenberger, *The British Image of India* (Oxford, 1969).

17. Useful in this regard are two articles by Clive Dewey, "Images of the Village Community," *MAS* 6 (1972): 291–328, and "The Agricultural Statistics of the Punjab," *Bulletin of Quantitative and Computer Methods in South Asian Studies* 2 (1974): 3–14. Also see Ira Klein, "Death in India," *JAS* 32 (1973): 639–60; and Neil Charlesworth, "The Myth of the Deccan Riots," *MAS* 6 (1972): 401–42. A collection of essays on the use of censuses will be published shortly in N. G. Barrier, ed., *The Census of British India: New Perspectives* (Delhi, 1979).

18. Blair Kling, *Partner in Empire* (Berkeley, Calif., 1977); N. Mukherjee, *A Bengal Zamindar* (Calcutta,1975).

19. For example, S. Mazumdar, *A Pattern of Life*, ed. Geraldine Forbes (Delhi, 1977); Bhagat Lakshman Singh, *Autobiography* (Calcutta, 1965); D. D. Karve, ed., *The New Brahmans* (Berkeley, Calif., 1963); and Prakash Tandon, *Punjabi Century* (Berkeley, Calif., 1968) and *Beyond Punjab* (Berkeley, Calif., 1971).

20. Thomas Timberg, *The Marwaris* (Delhi, 1977); John Webster, *Christian Community and Change in 19th Century North India* (Delhi, 1976); David Lelyveld, *Aligarh's First Generation* (Princeton, N.J., 1977); and Satish Saberwal, *Mobile Men* (Delhi, 1976). Also important are Lucy Carroll, "Caste, Social Change, and the Social Scientist," *JAS* 35 (1975): 63–84; and William Rowe, "Mobility in the 19th Century Caste System," with other related essays in Milton Singer and Bernard Cohn, eds., *Structure and Change in Indian Society* (Chicago, 1968).

21. On urban developments, see Susan J. Lewandowski, "Changing Form and Function in the Ceremonial and Colonial Port City in India," *MAS* 11 (1977): 183–212; Christine Dobbin, *Urban Leadership in Western India* (Oxford, 1972); Ellen Gumperz, "City-Hinterland Relations and the Development of a Regional Elite in 19th Century Bombay," *JAS* 33 (1974): 581–601; and Gautam Bhadra, "Social Groups and Relations in the Town of Murshidabad," *Indian Historical Review* 2 (1976): 312–38. In addition to Whitcombe, *Agrarian Conditions in Northern India*, and Frykenberg, *Land Control and Social Structure in Indian History*, rural studies include Ian Catanach, *Rural Credit in Western India* (Berkeley, Calif., 1970); Girish Mishra, *Agrarian Problem of Permanent Settlement* (Delhi, 1978): Ravinder Kumar, *Western India in the 19th Century* (London, 1968); Ira Klein, "Population and Agriculture in Northern India," *MAS* 8 (1974): 191–215; and two essays by C. A. Bayly, "Town Building in North India," *MAS* 9 (1975): 483–504, and "Local Control in Indian Towns," *MAS* 5 (1971): 289–331.

22. The issues and process of change are discussed in John Broomfield, "The Regional Elites: A Theory of Modern Indian History," *IESHR* 3 (1966): 279–91.

23. See Morris David Morris et al., *Indian Economy in the 19th Century* (Delhi, 1969). New essays or monographs on economics include Clive Dewey and A. G. Hopkins, eds., *The Imperial Impact* (London, 1978); Arthur W. Silver, *Manchester Men and Indian Cotton* (Manchester, 1966); Peter Harnetty, *Imperialism and Free Trade* (Vancouver, 1972); and Ira Klein, "English Free Traders," *MAS* 5 (1971): 251–71.

24. See Geraldine Forbes, *Positivism in Bengal* (Calcutta, 1974), and David Kopf, *British Orientalism and the Bengal Renaissance* (Berkeley, Calif., 1969).

25. Collected essays on these topics may be found in Milton Singer, ed., *Entrepreneurship and Modernization of Occupation Culture* (Durham, N.C., 1972); and Suzanne Rudolph and Lloyd Rudolph, *The Modernity of Tradition* (Chicago, 1967). A survey of issues and literature appears in Yogendra Singh, *Modernization of Indian Tradition* (Delhi, 1973).

26. Thomas G. Kessinger, *Vilyatpur* (Berkeley, Calif., 1974); see also interchanges on the volume and related issues by Kessinger and Dewey in *MAS* 10 (1976): 131–60 and 11 (1977): 615–22.

27. Kenneth Jones, *Arya Dharm*.

28. Frank Conlon, *A Caste in a Changing World* (Berkeley, Calif., 1977).

29. For example, Paul Brass, *Language, Religion and Politics in North India* (Cambridge, 1974); and Richard Fox, *Kin, Clan, Raja and Rule* (Berkeley, Calif., 1971).

30. Especially important are P. D. Reeves, "The Politics of Order," *JAS* 25 (1966): 261–74; and essays in Low, *Soundings*, and the essays in D. A. Low, ed., *Congress and the Raj* (London, 1977), especially the editor's detailed overview.

31. See Bawa Satinder Singh, *The Jammu Fox* (Carbondale, Ill., 1974); Barbara Ramusack, "Incident at Nabha," *JAS* 28 (1969): 563–77, and her forthcoming monograph on the princes, to be published by the University of Cincinnati Press; William L. Richter and Barbara Ramusack, "The Chamber and the Consultation," *JAS* 34 (1975): 755–76.

32. Anil Seal and John Gallagher, eds., *Locality, Province, and Nation* (Cambridge, 1973); Anil Seal, *The Emergence of Indian Nationalism* (Cambridge, 1968); C. A. Bayly, *The Local Roots of Indian Politics* (Oxford, 1975); D. A. Washbrook, *The Emergence of Provincial Politics* (Cambridge, 1976); Christopher Baker, *The Politics of South India* (Cambridge, 1976); Francis Robinson, *Separatism Among Indian Muslims* (Cambridge, 1975); and Gordon Johnson, *Provincial Politics and Indian Nationalism* (Cambridge, 1974).

33. On the languages and other background of the Indian press, see *Statement of English, Foreign, Anglo-Vernacular and Vernacular Newspapers Published in India in 1905* (Simla, 1907). Political literature (tracts and journals) is surveyed in Barrier, *Banned*.

34. P. D. Reeves, B. D. Graham, and J. M. Goodman, *A Handbook to Elections in Uttar Pradesh* (Delhi, 1975); Reeves, "Changing Patterns of Political Alignment in the General Elections to the UP Legislative Assembly, 1937–1946," *MAS* 5 (1971): 111–42.

35. John McLane, *Indian Nationalism and the Early Congress* (Princeton, N.J., 1977); S. R. Mehrotra, *The Emergence of the Indian National Congress* (Delhi, 1974). Also relevant is Briton Martin, *New India 1885* (Berkeley, Calif., 1968).

36. Examples of regional studies include J. C. Masselos, *Toward Nationalism* (Bombay, 1974); R. Suntharalingam, *Politics and Nationalist Awakening in South India* (Tucson, Ariz., 1974); Leonard Gordon, *Bengal: The Nationalist Movement* (New York, 1974); J. H. Broomfield, *Elite Conflict in a Plural Society* (Berkeley, Calif., 1968); Richard Tucker, *Ranade and the Roots of Indian Nationalism* (Chicago, 1972); and N. G. Barrier, "The Arya Samaj and Congress Politics in the Punjab," *JAS* 26 (1967): 363–80. An important statistical analysis appears in Ellen Gumperz, *English Education, Nationalist Politics and Elite Groups in Maharashtra* (Berkeley, Calif., 1968).

37. Ashis Nandy, "The Culture of Indian Politics," *JAS* 30 (1970): 57–79; Gyanendra Pandey, "A Rural Base for Congress," in Low, *Congress*, pp. 199–221; Dipesh Chakrabarty, "Sasipada Banerjee," *Indian Historical Review* 2 (1976): 339–64; G. Pandey, "Mobilization in a Mass Movement," *MAS* 9 (1975): 205–226; Uma Das Gupta, "The Indian Press, 1870–1881," *MAS* 11 (1977): 213–36; and Paul Wallace and N. G. Barrier, *The Punjab Press* (East Lansing, Mich., 1970).

38. See Kenneth Jones, *Arya Dharm*, and Richard Cashman, *The Myth of the Lokamanya: Tilak and Mass Politics in Maharashtra* (Berkeley, Calif., 1975). Among studies of social and political groups, see John Leonard, "Urban Government under the Raj," *MAS* 7 (1973): 227–52; W. F. Crawley, "Kisan Sabhas and Agrarian Revolt in the UP," *MAS* 5 (1971): 95–109.

39. For example, see A. C. Bose, *Indian Revolutionaries Abroad* (Patna, 1971). A biography that explores the evolution of a revolutionary is Emily Brown's *Har Dayal* (Tucson, Ariz., 1975). Also just released is a new study of Indian revolutionaries by a participant, Sohan Singh Josh, *Hindustan Ghadar Party* (Delhi, 1977).

40. See Richard Tucker, "Hindu Traditionalism and Nationalist Ideologies in 19th Century Maharashtra," *MAS* 10 (1976): 321–48; Stephen Dale, "The Mapilla Outbreaks," *JAS* 35 (1975): 85–98; R. Suntharalingam, "The Salem Riots," *MAS* 3 (1969): 193–208; and Richard Gordon, "The Hindu Mahasabha and the Indian National Congress," *MAS* 9 (1975): 145–201. Useful material can also be found in Jones, *Arya Dharm*, and McLane, *Congress*. Essays on the subject also appear in C. H. Philips, ed., *The Partition of India* (Cambridge, 1970).

41. A detailed analysis of these patterns may be found in Gene Thursby, *Hindu-Muslim Relations in British India* (Leiden, 1975); see also N. G. Barrier, "The Punjab Government and Communal Politics," *JAS* 27 (1968): 523–39.

42. Francis Robinson, *Separatism*. In addition, Karen Leonard's study of Kayasthas, Muslims,

and communal identity in Hyderabad will be published by the University of California Press in late 1979.

43. Dewitt Ellinwood, *World War One and India* (forthcoming, 1979); Ravindar Kumar, ed., *Essays on Gandhian Politics: The Rowlatt Satyagraha of 1919* (Oxford, 1971); and Philips, *Partition*.

44. See, for example, S. Gopal, *Jawaharlal Nehru: A Biography*, vol. I (Cambridge, Mass., 1976); John P. Haithcox, *Communism and Nationalism in India: M. N. Roy and Comintern Policy* (Princeton, N.J., 1971); Stanley Wolpert, *Tilak and Gokhale* (Berkeley, Calif., 1962); and B. R. Nanda, *Gokhale* (Princeton, N.J., 1977).

45. Literature on Gandhi is surveyed in *Mohandas Karamchand Gandhi: A Bibliography* (Bombay, 1974). Erik Erikson's analysis is entitled *Gandhi's Truth* (New York, 1969).

46. Joan Bondurant, *Conquest of Violence: The Gandhian Philosophy* (Berkeley, Calif., 1958).

47. *Gandhi and Civil Disobedience* (Cambridge, 1977) and *Gandhi's Rise to Power* (Cambridge, 1972).

48. Pradip Sinha, *Calcutta in Urban History* (Calcutta, 1978); S. N. Mukherjee, *Calcutta: Myth and History* (Calcutta, 1977). Also just released is S. P. Sen, ed., *Historical Writings on the Nationalist Movement* (Calcutta, 1978).

49. Important are the following: Ainslie Embree, *India's Search for National Identity* (New York, 1971); Jim Masselos, *Nationalism on the Indian Subcontinent* (Melbourne, 1972); Peter Hardy, *The Muslims of British India* (Cambridge, 1973); and Stanley Wolpert, *A New History of India* (Oxford, 1977). For an attempt to view Indian developments from a comparative perspective in world civilization, see Edward L. Farmer et al., *Comparative History of Civilizations in Asia*, vol. II (Chicago, 1977).

Bibliography

Barrier, Norman Gerald. *Banned: Political Control and Controversial Literature in British India* (Columbia, Mo., 1975).

Crane, Robert I. *A History of South Asia* (Washington, D.C., 1973).

Dewey, Clive, and A. G. Hopkins, eds. *The Imperial Impact: Studies in the Economic History of Africa and India* (London, 1978).

Embree, Ainslie. *India's Search for National Identity* (New York, 1971).

Gokhale Institute of Politics and Economics. *Annotated Bibliography of Economic History of India, 1500–1947* (Poona, 1977).

Gustafson, Eric, and Kenneth Jones, eds. *Sources on Punjab History* (Delhi, 1975).

Hardy, Peter. *The Muslims of British India* (Cambridge, 1973).

Jones, Kenneth. *Arya Dharm* (Berkeley, Calif., 1976).

Kessinger, Thomas G. *Vilyatpur* (Berkeley, Calif., 1974).

Low, D. A., ed. *Congress and the Raj* (London, 1977).

Masselos, Jim. *Nationalism on the Indian Subcontinent* (Melbourne, 1972).

Patterson, Maureen, and Martin Yanuck, eds. *South Asian Library Resources in North America* (Yug, 1975).

Philips, C. H., ed. *Historians of India, Pakistan, and Ceylon* (Oxford, 1961).

Seal, Anil, and John Gallagher, eds. *Locality, Province and Nation* (Cambridge, 1973).

Sen, S. P., ed. *Historians and Historiography in Modern India* (Calcutta, 1973).

Wolpert, Stanley. *A New History of India* (Oxford, 1977).

23 J. F. ADE. AJAYI and E. J. ALAGOA

Sub-Saharan Africa

The pioneers of African historical studies faced a largely skeptical academic world. Most of the opposition derived from pure racial prejudice, ignorance, imperialist propaganda, genuine scholarly doubt, or varying combinations of these. Some writers, influenced by a narrow perspective drawn largely from accounts of the Atlantic slave trade and European colonial conquest and rule in Africa, took up the position that the African past was devoid of the records of civilizations, empires, kingdoms, and significant activities of kings and leading men that make a reign worthy of historical study. According to these pseudoscientific historians, since history is the account of significant achievement, and since in their view Africa achieved nothing significant in its past, there could be no African history. One notorious and often-cited Oxford pundit (Trevor-Roper) summed up such views by saying that history cannot be created out of the darkness discernible in the African past, or from "the unrewarding gyrations of barbarous tribes in picturesque but irrelevant corners of the globe." Of course, this view that Africa lay in an unhistorical part of the world had been expressed much earlier by Hegel, who declared that "the history of the World travels from East to West, for Europe is absolutely the end of History, Asia the beginning"—Africa being "no historical part of the World; it has no movement or development to exhibit."[1]

Thus one major preoccupation of African historiography in the 1950s and 1960s was to demonstrate how obviously mistaken these arguments were, and to show that Africa had a history beyond an account of the actions of colonial governments and of African reactions to them. This produced a historiography focused on the civilizations, empires, and kingdoms of the Nile Valley, Zimbabwe, the West African Sudan (Ghana, Mali, and Songhai), the Guinea Coast and the Congo Basin, the East African lake region, and others.

There remained, however, other apparently more difficult scholarly doubts and objections. There were reservations about the new methodologies that African historians were adopting in tackling the problem of shedding more light on the African past. In particular there were suspicions that evidence from oral tradition and other nonwritten sources was unreliable and that conclusions

reached from them were not worthy of the tradition of historical discipline hitherto practiced in the West. This important objection challenged those concerned
with the new African historiography to define their methodologies and demonstrate the validity of nonwritten sources as evidence for historical study no less
worthy of attention than written sources. This provided an opportunity for historians of Africa to make original contributions to the science of historical methodology: African historians continue to wrestle with the many specific problems
that arise in the collection and interpretation of data from nonwritten sources for
historical reconstruction; yet each new project successfully completed contributes not only to our fund of knowledge but to a sharpening of our research tools
and equipment as well. We have by no means solved all the problems of oral
traditional history, nor have we completed the task of refining our concepts and
methodology of oral traditions; but African historians no longer have any cause
to feel defensive about their use of oral traditions and other nonwritten sources.
This particular aspect of African historiography can now be accepted as one of
the ways in which the introduction of African history into the general body of
academic disciplines has served to enrich world historiography.

There were also reservations about the emerging pattern of African history.
For example, there was the notion (one which pervaded much writing about
African history even in recent times) that the flashes of achievement to be seen
in the African past derived from sources outside Africa and were introduced
essentially by peoples of non-African or nonblack racial types. In addition, there
was the idea that the black African communities were basically organized inadequately in small-scale agricultural units which were conquered and civilized
by various outside groups and that they were passive recipients of historical
change, not active participants in the shaping of their own historical destinies.
This point of view, usually called the Hamitic Hypothesis, and the tendency to
seek an external source and origin for high cultural, technological, or political
achievement, or any major historical movement in the African past, is not yet
completely absent from some recent accounts.[2] However, this tradition too now
represents a minority position very much on the defensive against the tide and
sweep of African historiography.

Methods of African Historical Research

In spite of the legitimate doubts that have been expressed as to whether written
sources yield adequate and reliable material for writing the history of Africa,
they remain a cornerstone for historical research. In Africa there are very few
places indeed for which written sources date back much more than a century or
two before the colonial period. In the Nile Valley, however, the hieroglyphic
script, one of the first writing systems invented in the world, constitutes the
major resource for reconstructing Egyptian history through three to five thousand
years. Hieroglyphic papyri, inscriptions on statues and in the tombs of the phar-

aohs in the pyramids, and other writings recovered from excavations tell us much about the ideas and activities of this center of African civilization throughout antiquity. In North Africa also, the spread of Islamic religion and Arab settlement that began in the seventh century A.D. introduced Arabic writing and a prolific tradition of documentation. In addition, it is possible to learn something about earlier times through the ancient documents of Greek and Roman activities on the Mediterranean littoral and beyond. But in sub-Saharan Africa, the earliest written sources are usually those of Arab geographers, travelers, traders, scholars, and holy men who operated from North African bases to the West African Sudan and from the Indian Ocean to the Swahili coast of East Africa.[3] The Portuguese arrived in Africa in the fifteenth century, and their records have provided another source of African history, giving fleeting impressions of life in the coastal areas of western, southern, and eastern Africa. They were followed later by other Europeans engaged in the coastal trade, and the body of European accounts of Africa began to grow steadily.

For sub-Saharan Africa then, the major problem with archival sources is their mainly external origin, that is, Arabic or European. However, African historians have become increasingly sophisticated and discriminating in their exploitation of these sources as well as in locating new ones both from unsuspected places within Africa and from different foreign depositories of public or private records abroad. In West and East Africa, for example, efforts have been made to collect records and chronicles written by local scholars; these are generally written in Arabic script, either in the Arabic language itself or in local languages to which the script has been adapted. In the more recent colonial period, African governments have established archives, whose documents provide some of the local information necessary to supplement the external viewpoint of the records in the metropolitan archives in Europe. Further, even data in different metropolitan archives are now being used in a comparative manner to fill out details or to correct misrepresentations or biases in particular bodies of records.

One possible source of documentary evidence remains to be explored by African historians. We now tend to see Arabic and European writing as the only sources of documentation for the history of Africa south of the Sahara, but we have not yet fully investigated the potentialities of the admittedly few cases of local forms of writing in various parts of Africa.[4] The Meroitic script has still to be deciphered, and Meroe itself is beginning to appear as a major crossroads of ideas between the flowering of ancient Egyptian civilization and the historical developments of Ethiopia, the Horn, and the whole of the Western Sudan. Similarly, the *nsibidi* system of communication that developed in the valley of the Cross River in Nigeria has not yet been studied. There are also the *Vai* script of Liberia and the system created by Sultan Njoya of Bamum in the Cameroun in the nineteenth century, among others. It would be unwise to dismiss these possible sources of documentation lightly.

Nevertheless, oral traditions constitute the single most abundant source of information for filling out and correcting the inadequacies and gaps in the external documents. In spite of their central place in the study of African history, oral traditions were not accorded proper recognition among historians outside Africa before the authoritative expositions of their potentialities and challenge by Jan Vansina in the 1960s.[5] It is important, however, to stress that the inability to recognize the validity of oral traditions as an essential storehouse of historical data was mainly a problem among non-African historians and African historians trained in the historiography of the West. African nonliterate societies themselves have always used the oral mode for the transmission of general knowledge, history, and customs without any feelings of inadequacy. Many had evolved various devices for the faithful transmission of those ancient traditions essential to maintaining the identity and integrity of their communities.

For this reason, as soon as Arabic and European writing became established in Africa, local scholars began to exploit these new modes of transmission for compiling written records of oral traditions and writing chronicles of current or recent events. Thus we have the Chronicles or *Tarikh* from the Timbuktu school of Islamic scholars. Similarly, local scholars of the Western Sudan and the East African (Swahili) coast produced Chronicles of Kano, Gonja, and Kilwa, among others.

Other parts of Africa which came under European missionary influence also produced local histories or collections of oral tradition. In Nigeria, Samuel Johnson wrote his monumental *History of the Yorubas*, which remains a valuable repository of Yoruba oral tradition for modern academic historians. Similarly outstanding were the testimonies collected for the Benin kingdom by Jacob Egharevba and those for the Tiv of Nigeria collected by Akiga Sai. In East Africa, Sir Apolo Kagwa was moved by a sense of the enduring value of the oral traditions of the Buganda kingdom and compiled them for the edification of later generations.[6]

When African scholars began to make systematic collections of African oral traditions for the purpose of writing African history, they had to face a number of theoretical as well as practical problems. The first basic problem was to overcome the extreme bias against the validity of orally transmitted evidence that prevails among cultures that commit all or most of their important business to writing. In such cultures, what is left to be remembered and transmitted orally tends to be of marginal importance, and scholars from such cultures tend to accord the lowest rating to orally transmitted testimony. On the other hand, nonliterate cultures tend to develop stronger memories and to fashion institutions and techniques for the transmission of the most important traditions through time. Accordingly, African scholars needed to develop methodologies that are appropriate to probing the limitations of human memory and the extent to which the combined memories of the communities they study will enable them to recover the past.

African historians also face other difficulties with oral tradition than those associated with the weaknesses of human memory. One problem has been that some African cultures tend to regard the formal transmission of traditional history as a function and part of the present political system of the community. Accordingly, distortions occur because the traditions become a charter for the current political structures: for instance, a ruling dynasty can use the king list and genealogy of the kingdom as a charter of legitimacy by telescoping earlier dynasties or by lengthening its own genealogy to incorporate founding ancestors.[7] These and other distortions raise problems in historical interpretation of oral data, and African historians are engaged in refining techniques for dealing with them. One approach to the problem is to collect traditions in depth within a single community in such a way that a number of distortions can be detected by their incongruity with the main body of oral traditions. In another approach, the formal testimonies from within one community may be supplemented and interpreted in conjunction with the less obviously historical evidence of that same community's oral literature, ethnography, and material culture. In this area of detailed knowledge and empathy with tradition indigenous scholars who know the local language and who have the proper background and training in appropriate disciplines should have a clear advantage over scholars from alien cultural environments. Indeed, a major task African scholars have had to face has been the necessity of first sweeping away earlier interpretations of oral data derived from the ethnocentric biases of foreign scholars, however well-meaning many of them may have been.

One trend, then, in the scientific and systematic exploitation of African oral traditions has been that growing numbers of Africans who have an intimate knowledge of local languages and customs have become engaged in the reconstruction of the histories of particular states and peoples. This point underscores a further perspective on the search for answers to the problems posed by oral traditions in African historiography, that is, the peculiar problems brought to the surface by each new study of each community. About a decade ago, only groups organized into state patterns similar to those of Europe were considered suitable for study, in part because these groups usually had court histories, king lists, genealogies, praise literature, and other sources. But now it is becoming clearer that even peoples without the formal apparatus of a state political structure can be studied through a detailed recording of their oral traditions of family lineage and of religious, economic, age-grade, and other varieties of association. In such circumstances, it becomes even more important to apply the comparative method; that is, individual traditions should be analyzed and interpreted in the context of both the totality of the community's oral tradition and the traditions of neighboring related communities. Indeed, as more and more regions and peoples of Africa are covered by systematic collection and evaluation of their traditions, it will become more and more feasible to apply the comparative survey method on an increasingly broader scale.[8]

Recently the comparative method has been applied on a very wide scale indeed in a study of the difficult problem of the chronology of oral tradition. In his work on the subject, D. P. Henige has used king lists and genealogies from all over the world to study the common problems in using this type of data for

dating.[9] Drawing his data for comparison from Asia, the ancient American kingdoms, and Europe, he shows that African king lists and genealogies are normal
products of historical processes, fully comparable to similar material from other
societies around the world. Using material extensive in both the space and the
time it covers, Henige has discovered the areas of weakness and the possible
sources of chronological distortion in oral traditional sources. He has also shown
that "reasonable parameters of expectation are possible" in the computation of
chronologies from oral traditional sources in African historiography. Henige's
work simply confirms what students of African oral tradition have known for
a long time: that mathematically exact chronologies and dates cannot be expected
from oral traditional history and that the chronology from such histories can only
approximate reality. Such limitations, when they are recognized explicitly by
the historians who must work with them, do not necessarily invalidate African
historiography as a scientific discipline; in fact recognition of the limitations
strengthens its claim to be scientific while it stimulates the rigorous search for
other means of achieving reliability.

Another way in which African historiography has attempted to achieve reliability in its conclusions has been its adoption of an interdisciplinary or multidisciplinary approach to the solution of historical problems. At various
conferences of historians of Africa, the need for cooperation between scholars
of different disciplines was early accepted as essential to the full reconstruction
of the African past.[10] At international conferences, historians tended initially to
be at a disadvantage because of the obvious limitations involved in using either
written sources or oral traditions in the reconstruction of early African history.
Anthropologists and other social scientists entered the field of African history
with their process models and field methodology. Indeed, in some instances,
historians tended to take second place in the interpretation of the African past
from nonwritten sources. However, they have begun to regain confidence in
their ability to take the major responsibility for African historiography, even
though they must do so by using insights from the models and methodology of
the social sciences.[11] This new orientation demands that historians acquire competence in at least one of the required related disciplines. African historians have
accordingly grown increasingly adept at the techniques of these other disciplines
and likewise have become more confident about utilizing the results of professionals in the related disciplines for the solution of problems in historical fields.

Of the related disciplines, the ones with the greatest promise for African historiography have been linguistics and archeology. Their promise is so great because of their relevance to a chronological perspective independent of the
estimations available in oral tradition. Thus lexico-statistics and glottochronol-
ogy as means of estimating the separation time span between two languages or
two dialects of the same language have appeared to open up new vistas for historians, in spite of the reservations among linguists.

The radiocarbon method for dating archeological horizons promises even more
to the solution of the problems of chronology in African history. The *Journal*

of African History (based in London) began to publish lists of new radiocarbon dates in 1961.[12] Archeological research is expensive, and the time needed to analyze finds and to process the data is long. For these reasons the areas covered by excavations are still small, and the results so far obtained and available to historians have not produced the measure of impact on African historiography that potentially is there. Nor have many African historians always taken the trouble to study in detail the available technical reports of archeologists or to utilize systematically the lists of radiocarbon dates published in their own professional journals, such as the *Journal of the Historical Society of Nigeria.*[13] Few historians subscribe to the professional archeological journals such as the *West African Journal of Archaeology* or *Azania,* the archeological journal of the British Institute of East Africa. There is a new trend, however, for historians and archeologists to work more closely together. Also, some African historians have moved into archeology themselves. Several universities have established joint departments of history and archeology or have encouraged students to take combined degrees in history and archeology. Such cooperation promises gains in the contributions of each of the disciplines to the historiography of Africa. Combined with improved training in the social sciences, these closer relations with linguistics and archeology have made African historians even more willing to listen to colleagues in related fields and to use the results of their studies for historical research.

Among other developments, this increasing confidence among African historians has changed their approach to projects of interdisciplinary research. In the earlier projects initiated by historians, such as the Benin Historical Research Scheme and the Yoruba Scheme, directed by the Nigerian scholars Onwuka Dike and Saburi Biobaku respectively, the major field research roles were played by nonhistorians from outside. Also, in those pioneer projects the specialists of different disciplines apparently worked independently, without effective collaboration in the field, in the laboratory, or even in a symposium or publication of the results; the expected practical collaboration between specialists from different disciplines was not really achieved. Such wide-scale projects are not as popular as they were a decade ago. In the few that are still current, historians take a more central part in the actual field activities, and their collaboration with other specialists has become more intimate.[14]

The Content of African Historical Studies

African historiography has moved a long way from the 1950s, when its major preoccupation was to establish the very existence and viability of the discipline. It is now more concerned with developing substantive issues of scholarship, interpreting evidence, and relating historical studies to the major concerns of the African peoples. With regard to issues of scholarship, it is concerned, for example, with the wide problem of the origin of man. The earlier discoveries of

Australopithecines in southern Africa, best known through the dramatic finds of ancient humanoids by the Leakeys in Olduvai Gorge, and the more recent indications of even more ancient ancestors of man in Ethiopia have made Africa a prime center of interest in the search for the cradle of mankind.[15] While the work of the archeologists and paleontologists has extended the historical perspective in Africa beyond a million years, other work in the archeology and prehistory of Africa has also extended the scope of research. African historians are now interested in developments in different parts of Africa from the times of the earliest humanoids through the Iron Age. They are interested in the origins of the civilizations of Egypt and the Nile Valley, the influence of Egypt on Greek civilization, and the role of North Africans in the civilizations of the Carthaginian, Roman, and Byzantine periods. In this regard, African historians have taken issue with the attempt of some scholars to deny a black presence in ancient Egypt, and they have stressed the extent to which ancient Egypt can be understood and explained only in the African context.

Cheikh Anta Diop, for example, has used the presence of melanin in the skin fragments of Egyptian mummies as an indication of the black identity of the ancient Egyptians. He has discovered that melanin is found in the skin of blacks but not that of whites. He has also used Egyptian iconography extensively for evidence of ancient Egyptian references to themselves as "black" (the word being, apparently, actually written with charcoal). Other scholars have also cited the writings of Greek and Roman authors who described the Egyptians as black. Theophile Obenga of the University of Brazzaville has continued an earlier and rather controversial line of inquiry by trying to establish a genetic linguistic relationship between ancient Egyptian and Coptic and modern black-African languages. Art historians have likewise called attention to the African anatomy depicted in ancient Egyptian representations of themselves in art.[16] When the Meroitic script is finally deciphered, we may expect considerable assistance from the inscriptions in Nubia in tackling the problems of the historical relationship of the Nile Valley with the rest of Africa and of the history of the racial admixtures within the valley itself. Some historians have connected the concentration of early populations in the Nile Valley with the dessication of the Sahara and the consequent migration of peoples outward from the Sahara to different parts of Africa. But the history of the changing patterns of peoples and relationships through time still remains a subject of speculation and hypothesis based on scanty and perhaps misinterpreted evidence.

The International Congress of African Historians held at Dar es Salaam in 1965 suggested a number of new directions in the writing of African history. The congress formally resolved that "it is only the African people who through an interpretation and safeguarding of their own history can say what they were, what they are, and what they want to be." However, the emphasis of the congress was not on the hue or racial origin of the African historian but on perspective. The continental approach to African history was insisted upon as the only one capable of allowing a perspective internal to the continent and one that views the African as an active and not merely a passive agent in history. The colonial period was singled out as requiring fresh study if the distortions in historical perspective created by the colonial factor are to be corrected. In particular, there was an emphasis on the essential strength and resilience of African institutions in the face of the cultural challenge from Europe. The colonial period was seen as a relatively short episode in the long history of the African past.[17]

Expanding upon the continental view of African history that came to be emphasized, scholars have begun to reappraise not only the precolonial pattern of relationships within the continent but also the contribution of Africans to the development of Europe and the New World through their role in the Mediterranean, especially in the export of gold, and through their labor in American mines and plantations.[18] Emphasis early began to shift from the purely political studies intended to show that Africans had large-scale empires and kingdoms in the past to social and economic studies aimed at unraveling problems of internal African history. Economic historians have increasingly attempted to use statistical methods and quantification to present new interpretations and revisions of established interpretations about intra-African socioeconomic relationships. They are beginning, for example, to show that in precolonial Africa there were considerable changes in economic patterns along with evidence of innovation and risk taking. But some Western scholars have used these same methods to attempt to minimize the demographic impact and the devastations caused by the slave trade in Africa.[19] J. E. Inikori, among others, has produced evidence to show that Western scholars have consistently underestimated the number of slaves shipped out of Africa or received in the Americas. He concludes that "in view of the nature of the methods of computation adopted in [Curtin's] *Census* and the nature of the data upon which they are based, the confidence limits stated for the estimates are unwarranted and likely to mislead."[20]

Marxist historians have drawn particular attention to the importance of socioeconomic factors and the "search for the mode of production" in historical analysis. When applied to particular situations, however, such analysis has been frustrated as much by the preoccupation with European models established by Marx and Lenin as by the paucity of historical data in Africa. Attempts to fit African societies into those models and discover African "primitive communities" and African "feudal societies" have not been very illuminating. They have however, raised several questions worth pursuing about the nature and economic significance of the modes of landholding, the role of markets and long-distance trade, the concept of power, and the interrelationship between economics and politics in African history.[21] More recent attempts to apply Marxist socioeconomic analysis to studies of the colonial period have been more successful. Instead of advancing sterile arguments about the patterns of colonial rule, these later efforts have drawn attention to the effects of colonial rule on African societies and economies. Although the emerging concept of underdevelopment still requires further definition, it already permits a clearer understanding of the processes of change in the colonial period.

East African historians have recently taken up the problem of Bantu origins and migrations, which has long been a subject of debate among linguists. Joseph Greenberg had presented the popular hypothesis that the Benue-Cameroon region of West Africa was the home of the Proto-Bantu. Also by linguistic analysis, Malcolm Guthrie had located the Bantu homeland in Zaire.[22] Other experts had tended to fit their work into the framework of these two hypotheses, in spite of the fact that the central African savanna region is separated from the alleged West African center of origin by 1500 miles of forest land difficult to penetrate. The Ugandan historian Samwiri Lwanga-Lunyiigo has come out in opposition to the idea of mass migration suggested by these hypotheses.[23] From the archeological evidence he contends that the region from East Africa to Central and Southern Africa in which the Bantu are to be found appears to be the homeland of the black, not West Africa as was previously thought. The issue here hangs on the lack of rigor with which evidence from different disciplines has been utilized in the search for solutions to the historical problems of the presence of the Bantu. The case has clearly been made for a review of the evidence from diverse sources, including oral traditions, which have tended to be ignored in the recent discussions.

The objectives of African historical research and writing, then, are no longer those of propaganda about the existence of African history and of the evocation of a glorious past. Rather, the view has become continental, specialized, and concerned with the relevance of this history to the present problems and predicaments of the African in the world. African historians need to examine changes in the economy and technology of African societies, religious systems, modes of warfare, ideas of statecraft, ethics, aesthetics, and so on and to discover ways of bringing this knowledge to bear on the solution of present-day problems. Thus the trend in African history relates it to society, to reality, and to change. African historians, therefore, have to deal with the challenges and problems of committed history.

Conclusion

Has African historiography, then, grown to maturity? We may take two specific developments as indices: first, the level to which African historians are organized as a body of professionals; and second, the progress of the UNESCO project for the writing of a general history of Africa.

Historians in individual African countries have been organized into professional associations and have published research journals for some time. The Historical Society of Nigeria and its counterpart in Ghana already have a history covering two decades; they have published the *Journal of the Historical Society of Nigeria* and the *Transactions of the Historical Society of Ghana* for almost as long. The Nigerian society has even added *Tarikh,* a special journal for school teachers and their students. There have been similar developments in East and Central Africa. African historians in Southern Africa are beginning to follow suit.

In the West African region, the French-speaking countries are generally thought to have developed historical studies at a slower pace than Ghana and Nigeria. Possibly because they feel a need to make up lost ground, the Francophone historians have taken the initiative to form what may be termed the nucleus of a continental association of African historians. The Association of African Historians, however, still has a long way to go to deserve its title. For one thing, it has yet to draw into its fold the effective participation of the large body of African historians in Anglophone East and West Africa. Nevertheless, the association has already launched its own journal, *Afrika Zamani, Revue d'Histoire Africaine,* which began publication in 1974. In the light of its present difficulties of organization and finance the Association of African Historians may be considered mainly as one further step in the movement towards the decolonization of African history and the gradual growth to maturity of African historiography.

The UNESCO project, run under the academic control of an international scientific committee of experts, must be considered an appropriate index for measuring the status of African historiography. It cannot but reflect the progress made to date in the study of African history in all its dimensions. It will be both an assessment and a synthesis of work done thus far, a review of progress to provide signposts to future lines of development.

The organization of the projected eight-volume history of Africa reflects the development by which the major writing and research has shifted from centers mainly in Europe and America to centers in Africa staffed by Africans. In accord with this trend, although the International Scientific Committee is composed of both African and non-African scholars and although the individual contributors of chapters will be chosen on an international basis, each of the eight volumes will have an African editor.[24] Since the departments of history in African universities and the research centers in these universities are relatively young, the individual scholars in them are not as well known internationally as are scholars in Europe and America. But since indigenous African scholars of these young African centers of research represent the vanguard of African historiography, it has also been the policy to use their talents and insights.

The increasing complexity and sophistication of African historiography demands that workers in the field, whether African or non-African, should increasingly use bases and centers in Africa. It has also made it nearly impossible for any single scholar to master more than one subject, geographical area, ecological zone, or cultural region. Accordingly, the major works covering any considerable geographical area or time period involve the cooperation of several scholars.[25] Thus each of the prospective volumes of the UNESCO General History of Africa has a number of contributors. Collaboration of two or more scholars in the production of a single chapter is common, although one scholar, especially the volume editor, may also contribute more than one chapter—usually of a general or evaluative nature. Indeed, the contributors reflect the multidisciplinary nature of African historiography, for the prospectus includes experts from several related fields. The earlier volumes in particular draw upon the knowledge of specialists in such fields as archeology and linguistics, among others. On the other hand, volumes on the more recent periods have called upon the assistance of social scientists, and the last volume, on Independent Africa, is being edited by a political scientist.

Above all, the General History aims at placing African history in a global setting. Each contribution places the history of the locality not in isolation, but in an African perspective, and eventually in a world setting. For instance, it relates developments between Egypt and black Africa, and between Africa and the outside world of Mediterranean Europe or Asia. Similarly, the history of Africans of the diaspora in the New World, and of the contribution of the African peoples and the resources of their continent to world economy and civilization, are treated as an integral part of the history of Africa and a wider world. This project should place the new trend of evaluating the contribution of Africa to world history on a secure and valid basis.

The General History, then, in tune with trends in the development of African historiography, should mirror the degree of maturity that historical work has attained and the problems it still has to solve. It should show that African historiography has passed the point of trying merely to prove a point about the possibility of African history or the past achievements of African civilization; it has entered upon the detailed elaboration of internal developments and the solution of substantive issues of methodology, content, and orientation.

Notes

1. G. W. F. Hegel, *The Philosophy of History* (New York, 1956), p. 99.

2. C. G. Seligman, *Races of Africa* (London, 1930; later eds. 1957, 1966); K. Honea, *A Contribution to the History of the Hamitic Peoples of Africa* (Vienna, 1958); E. R. Sanders, "The Hamitic Hypothesis: Its Origin and Functions in Perspective," *Journal of African History (JAH)* 10 (1969): 521–32.

3. See T. Lewicki, *Arabic External Sources for the History of Africa to the South of the Sahara* (London and Lagos, 1974).

4. See David Dalby, ed., *Language and Africa* (London, 1970).

5. Jan Vansina, "Recording the Oral History of the Bakuba," *JAH* 1 (1960): 46–53, and *De la Tradition orale* (Annales du Musée Royal d'Afrique Centrale, no. 36) (Tervuren, Belgium, 1961).

6. S. Johnson, *History of the Yorubas* (London, 1921); J. V. Egharevba, *A Short History of Benin* (Lagos, 1934); Rupert East, ed., *Akiga's Story: The Tiv Tribe as Seen by One of Its Members* (London, 1939, 1965); and Apolo Kagwa, *Ebika Bya Buganda* (London, 1912), and *Bassekabaka Be Buganda* (London, 1927). See also S. A. Kiwanuka, *History of Buganda from the Foundation to 1900* (London, 1971); compare also E. J. Alagoa and A. Fombo, *A Chronicle of Grand Bonny* (Ibadan, 1972).

7. E. J. Alagoa, "King-list: Myth or History?" *Lagos Notes and Records* 5 (1974): 31–35; L. Bohannan, "A Genealogical Charter," *Africa* 22 (1952): 301–15.

8. Such work is on the increase, especially in East and West Africa; see, for example, B. A. Ogot, *A History of the Southern Luo: Migration and Settlement* (Nairobi, 1967); G. Were, *A History of the Abaluyia* (Nairobi, 1967); and E. J. Alagoa, *A History of the Niger Delta: An Historical Interpretation of Ijo Oral Tradition* (Ibadan, 1972).

9. David P. Henige, *The Chronology of Oral Tradition: Quest for a Chimera* (Oxford, 1974). Henige used data from "737 dynasties from throughout historical time and space, except sub-Saharan Africa" (pp. 123, 124). He then used the general conclusions to analyze the chronologies of the Fante and Asante of Ghana.

10. D. H. Jones, ed., *History and Archaeology in Africa: Report of a Conference held in July 1953 at the School of Oriental and African Studies* (London, 1955). See also R. A. Oliver and J. D. Fage, eds., *History and Archaeology in Africa: Second Conference held in July 1957 at the School of Oriental Studies* (London); R. A. Oliver and J. D. Fage, eds., "Third Conference on African History and Archaeology 1961," *JAH* 3 (1962); C. Gabel and N. R. Bennet, eds., *Reconstructing African Cultural History* (Papers presented at a Northwestern University symposium in 1962) (Boston, 1967); Jan Vansina, R. Mauny, and L. V. Thomas, eds., *The Historian in Tropical Africa* (Report of an international symposium at the University of Dakar, Senegal, in 1961) (London, 1964); and T. O. Ranger, ed., *Emerging Themes of African History: Proceedings of the International Congress of African Historians, Dar-es-Salaam, October 1965* (London, 1968).

11. See R. C. C. Law, "Anthropological Models in Yoruba History," *Africa* 43, no. 1 (1973): 18–26; J. F. Ade. Ajayi and E. J. Alagoa, "Black Africa: The Historians' Perspective," in S. W. Mintz, ed., *Slavery, Colonialism and Racism* (New York, 1974), pp. 125–34; and E. J. Alagoa, "The Interdisciplinary Approach to African History in Nigeria," *Présence africaine*, no. 94 (1975): 171–83.

12. Brian M. Fagan, "Radiocarbon Dates for Sub-Saharan Africa (from c. 1000 B.C.)," *JAH* 2 (1961): 137–39; 4 (1963): 127–28; 6 (1965): 107–16; 8 (1967): 513–27; 10 (1969): 149–69; Frank Willett, "A Survey of Recent Results in the Radiocarbon Chronology of Western and Northern Africa," *JAH* 12 (1971): 339–70; J. E. G. Sutton, "New Radiocarbon Dates for Eastern and Southern Africa," *JAH* 13 (1972): 1–24; and M. Posnansky and R. McIntosh, "New Radiocarbon Dates for Northern and Western Africa," *JAH* 17 (1976): 161–95.

13. T. Shaw, "Radiocarbon Dates from Nigeria," *Journal of the Historical Society of Nigeria* (*JHSN*) 3 (1967): 743–51.

14. See Institute of African Studies, University of Ibadan, *Reports of the Northern History Research Scheme* and *Rivers Research Scheme, First Interim Report* (1975); see also S. O. Biobaku, "The Yoruba Historical Research Scheme," *JHSN* 1 (1956): 59–60; and H. F. C. Smith, "The Benin Study," *JHSN* 1 (1956): 60–61.

15. See L. S. B. Leakey, *Adam's Ancestors: The Evolution of Man and His Culture* (New York, 1960); Mary D. Leakey, *Olduvai Gorge: Excavations in Beds I and II, 1960–63* (Cambridge, 1971); see also *Azania* for recent work of Richard Leakey and others.

16. See the Final Report of the UNESCO Symposium on "The People of Ancient Egypt and the Deciphering of the Meroitic Script," which was held at Cairo, 28 January-3 February 1974; see also J. Vercoutter et al., *The Image of the Black in Western Art* (Fribourg, Switzerland, 1976).

17. J. F. Ade. Ajayi, "The Continuity of African Institutions under Colonialism," in T. O. Ranger, ed., *Emerging Themes of African History* (London, 1968), pp. 189–200; and J. F. Ade. Ajayi, "Colonialism: An Episode in African History," in L. H. Gann and P. Duignan, eds., *Colonialism in Africa 1870–1960* (Cambridge, 1974).

18. Eric Williams, *Capitalism and Slavery* (Chapel Hill, N.C., 1944) is still very relevant; see also Walter Rodney, *How Europe Underdeveloped Africa* (London, 1972).

19. P. D. Curtin, *The Atlantic Slave Trade: A Census* (Madison, Wisc., 1969); Roger Anstey, *The Atlantic Slave Trade and British Abolition 1760–1810* (London, 1975); and Stanley L. Engerman and Eugene D. Genovese, eds., *Race and Slavery in the Western Hemisphere: Quantitative Studies* (Princeton, N.J., 1975), which includes R. Anstey, "The Volume and Profitability of the British

Slave Trade, 1560–1807,'' pp. 3–31, and P. D. Curtin, ''Measuring the Atlantic Slave Trade,'' pp. 107–10. See also P. D. Curtin, *Economic Change in Precolonial Africa: Senegambia in the Era of the Slave Trade* (Madison, Wisc., 1975) for an original contribution to African economic history.

20. J. E. Inikori, ''Measuring the Atlantic Slave Trade: An Assessment of Curtin and Anstey,'' *JAH* 18 (1976): 197–223.

21. See C. Coquery-Vidrovitch, ''Research on an African Mode of Production,'' in M. A. Klein and G. W. Johnson, eds., *Perspectives on the African Past* (Boston, 1972).

22. J. H. Greenberg, ''Studies in African Linguistic Classification, III: The Position of Bantu,'' *Southwestern Journal of Anthropology* 5 (1949): 307–17, and ''Linguistic Evidence Regarding Bantu Origins,'' *JAH* 13 (1972): 189–216; M. Guthrie, ''Some Developments in the Prehistory of the Bantu Languages,'' *JAH* 3 (1962): 273–82.

23. Samwiri Lwanga-Lunyiigo, ''The Bantu Problem Reconsidered,'' *Current Anthropology* 17 (1976): 282–86.

24. The volumes and editors are as follows:

Vol. 1: Methodology and Prehistory, ed. J. Ki-Zerbo (Upper Volta);

Vol. 2: The Classical Period (pre-seventh century), ed. G. Mokhta (Egypt);

Vol. 3: Africa in the Seventh to the Twelfth Century, ed. Mohammed Eli Fasi (Morocco) and I. Hrbek (Czechoslovakia);

Vol. 4: Africa from the Twelfth to the Fifteenth Century, ed. C. T. Niane (Guinea);

Vol. 5: Africa from the Fifteenth to the Eighteenth Century, ed. B. Ogot (Kenya);

Vol. 6: Africa 1800 to 1880 (eve of the colonial period), ed. J. F. Ade. Ajayi (Nigeria);

Vol. 7: Africa under Foreign Rule, 1880–1950s, ed. A. A. Boahen (Ghana);

Vol. 8: Independent Africa, ed. A. Mazrui (Kenya).

The International Scientific Committee has the following additional members: Mrs. Mutumba Bull, J. Devisse, Cheikh Anta Diop, John D. Fage, Jose Luciano France, Musa H. I. Galaal, Vinigi L. Grottanelli, Eike Haberland, Aklihu Habte, Abeodu Jones, Abbe Alexis Kagame, A. Letnev, L. D. Ngcongco, Mekki Shiebeika, Mgr. Th. Tshibangu, S. Exc. Hampate Ba, J. Vansina, F. A. Mourao, D. Chanaiwa, and Ph. Curtin.

25. One recent example of a successful collaboration is J. F. Ade. Ajayi and Michael Crowder, eds., *History of West Africa*, 2 vols. (London, 1974, 1976). One recent example of a work of synthesis by a single historian is J. Ki-Zerbo, *Histoire de l'Afrique noire, d'hier à demain* (Paris, 1972).

Bibliography

Books

Ajayi, J. F. A., and M. Crowder, eds. *History of West Africa*, 2 vols. (London, 1976).

Alagoa, E. J. *A History of the Niger Delta* (Ibadan, 1972).

Alagoa, E. J., and A. Fombo. *A Chronicle of Grand Bonny* (Ibadan, 1972).

Anstey, Roger. *The Atlantic Slave Trade and British Abolition 1760–1810* (London, 1975).

Curtin, P. D. *The Atlantic Slave Trade: A Census* (Madison, Wisc., 1969).

———. *Economic Change in Pre-Colonial Africa: Senegambia in the Era of the Slave Trade* (Madison, Wisc., 1975).

Dalby, David, ed. *Language and History in Africa* (London, 1970).

Diop, C. A. *African Origins of Civilisation* (New York, 1974),

East, R., ed. *Akiga's Story: The Tiv Tribe as Seen by One of Its Members* (London, 1939, 1965).

Engerman, Stanley L., and Eugene D. Genovese, eds. *Race and Slavery in the Western Hemisphere: Quantitative Studies* (Princeton, N.J., 1975). Contains R. Anstey, ''The Volume and Profitability of the British Slave Trade, 1761–1807,'' pp. 3–31, and P. D. Curtin, ''Measuring the Atlantic Slave Trade,'' pp. 107–10.

Gabel, C., and N. R. Bennet, eds. *Reconstructing African Cultural History* (Boston, 1967).

Hegel, G. W. F. *The Philosophy of History* (New York, 1956).

Henige, D. P. *The Chronology of Oral Tradition: Quest for a Chimera* (Oxford, 1974).

Honea, K. *A Contribution to the History of the Hamitic Peoples of Africa* (Vienna, 1958).

Institute of African Studies, University of Ibadan. *Rivers Research Scheme: First Interim Report* (Ibadan, 1975).

Johnson, S. *History of the Yorubas* (London, 1921).

Jones, D. H., ed. *History and Archaeology in Africa: Report of a Conference held in July 1953 at the School of Oriental and African Studies* (London, 1955).

Kagwa, A. *Ebika Bya Buganda* (London, 1912).

Kiwanuka, S. A. *History of Buganda from the Foundation to 1900* (London, 1971).

Ki-Zerbo, J. *Histoire de l'Afrique noire* (Paris, 1972).

Leakey, L. S. B. *Adam's Ancestors: The Evolution of Man and His Culture* (Cambridge, 1960).

Leakey, M. D. *Olduvai Gorge: Excavations in Beds I and II, 1960–1963* (Cambridge, 1971).

Lewicki, T. *Arabic External Sources for the History of Africa to the South of the Sahara* (London and Lagos, 1974).

Obenga, T. *L'Afrique dans l'antiquité* (Paris, 1973).

Ogot, B. A. *A History of the Southern Luo: Migration and Settlement* (Nairobi, 1967).

Oliver, R. A., and J. D. Fage, eds. *History and Archeology in Africa* (London).

Ranger, T. O., ed. *Emerging Themes of African History* (London, 1968).

Rodney, W. *How Europe Underdeveloped Africa* (London, 1972).

Seligman, C. G. *Races of Africa* (London, 1930, 1957, 1966).

Vansina, J. *Oral Tradition: A Study in Historical Methodology* (Chicago, 1965; translated from *De la Tradition orale,* Tervuren, Belgium, 1961).

Vansina, J., R. Mauny, and L. V. Thomas, eds. *The Historian in Tropical Africa* (London, 1964).

Vercoutter, J., J. Leclant, F. M. Snowden, Jr., and J. Desanges. *The Image of the Black in Western Art* (Fribourg, Switzerland, 1976).

Wallerstein, Immanuel. *The Modern World-System: Capitalist Agriculture and the Origins of the European World-Economy of the Sixteenth Century* (New York, 1974).

Were, G. *A History of the Abaluyia* (Nairobi, 1967).

Williams, E. *Capitalism and Slavery* (Chapel Hill, N.C., 1944).

Articles

Ajayi, J. F. Ade. "Colonialism: An Episode in Africa History," in L. J. Gann and P. Duignan, eds., *Colonialism in Africa 1870–1960* (Cambridge, 1974).

―――. "The Continuity of African Institutions under Colonialism," in T. O. Ranger, ed., *Emerging Themes of African History* (London, 1968), pp. 189–200.

Ajayi, J. F. Ade., and E. J. Alagoa. "Black Africa: The Historians' Perspective," *Daedalus* 103 (1974): 125–34.

Alagoa, E. J. "The Interdisciplinary Approach to African History in Nigeria," *Présence africaine,* no. 94 (1975): 171–83.

―――. "King-list: Myth or History?" *Lagos Notes and Records* 5 (1974): 31–35.

Biobaku, S. O. "The Yoruba Historical Research Scheme," *Journal of the Historical Society of Nigeria (JHSN)* 1 (1956): 59–60.

Bohannan, L. "A Genealogical Charter," *Africa* 22 (1952): 301–15.

Coquery-Vidrovitch, C. "Research on an African Mode of Production," in M. A. Klein and G. W. Johnson, eds., *Perspectives on the African Past* (Boston, 1972).

Dalby, D. "The Historical Problems of the Indigenous Scripts of West Africa and Surinam," in D. Dalby, ed., *Language and History in Africa* (London, 1970).

Dike, K. O. and J. F. Ade. Ajayi. "African Historiography," *Encyclopaedia of the Social Sciences,* VI, 394–99.

Fagan, B. M. "Radiocarbon Dates for Sub-Saharan Africa (from c. 1000 B.C.)," *Journal of African History (JAH)* 2 (1961): 137–9; 4 (1963): 127–28; 6 (1965): 107–16; 8 (1967): 513–27; 10 (1969); 149–69.

Greenberg, J. H. "Linguistic Evidence Regarding Bantu Origins," *JAH* 13 (1972): 189–216.

———. "Studies in African Linguistic Classification, III: The Position of Bantu," *Southwestern Journal of Anthropology* 5 (1949): 309–17.

Guthrie, M. "Some Developments in the Prehistory of the Bantu Languages," *JAH* 3 (1962): 273–82.

Inikori, J. E. "Measuring the Atlantic Slave Trade: An Assessment of Curtin and Anstey," *JAH* 18 (1976): 197–223.

Law, R. C. C. "Anthropological Models in Yoruba History," *Africa* 43 (1973): 18–26.

Lwanga-Lunyiigo, S. "The Bantu Problem Reconsidered," *Current Anthropology* 17 (1976): 282–86.

Posnansky, M., and R. McIntosh. "New Radiocarbon Dates for Northern and Western Africa," *JAH* 17 (1976): 161–93.

Sanders, E. R. "The Hamitic Hypothesis: Its Origin and Functions in Perspective," *JAH* 10 (1969): 521–32.

Shaw, T. "Radiocarbon Dates from Nigeria," *JHSN* 3 (1967): 743–51.

Smith, H. F. C. "The Benin Study," *JHSN* 1 (1956): 60–61.

Sutton, J. E. G. "New Radiocarbon Dates for Eastern and Southern Africa," *JAH* 13 (1972): 1–24.

Vansina, J. "Recording the Oral History of the Bakuba," *JAH* 1 (1960): 46–53.

Willett, F. "A Survey of Recent Results of the Radiocarbon Chronology of Western and Northern Africa," *JAH* 12 (1971): 339–70.

Some
Concluding Observations

PART: **III**

Harold T. Parker

To read this book straight through in its entirety, as the two editors have done, is a tremendous experience. So many historians throughout the world, doing so many, many things in so many, many ways blows the mind, to use a popular phrase. There are so many new, or renewed, fields of subject matter—historical demography, historical geography, biography, history of the family, medical history, history of technology, economic and business history, labor history, social history, rural history, political history, diplomatic history, military history, administrative history, institutional history, intellectual history, religious history, literary history, art history, cultural history, *und so weiter*. There are so many approaches, new and old—critical evaluation of evidence, empathy, techniques of oral history, content analysis, information theory, communciation theory, linguistics, search for unit ideas, search for patterns of consciousness, psychohistory, learning theory, small group theory, career-line analysis, prosopography, generation approach, cohort analysis, Thomas S. Kuhn's paradigm, comparative methodology, counterfactual analysis, simulation, typology, role theory, quantification applied to linguistics, to demographic data, to economic data, to political behavior, to social structure and mobility, class analysis, network analysis, exchange theory, organization theory, decision-making, systems analysis, use of images for discovery and presentation, and so on. Historical investigation seems to have disintegrated into anarchy.

Yet if we look again at what has been happening to professional historical studies during the twentieth century and especially since World War II, there seems to have been a double movement. One movement appears, indeed, to have been toward disintegration of old modes of understanding and old forms, disintegration of the old narrative political history, disintegration, even, of more recent modes of thought, such as "vulgar" Marxism and the earliest *Annales* presentations. There has in fact been a movement toward disintegration*s*, plural. But at the same time there has been a movement toward creativity of new forms, and in the last decade *toward* reintegration at a more complex level.

Let us try to work this thesis to a deeper understanding, to see what it will yield. Suppose we think in terms of modes of historical understanding. The oldest mode in Western culture, as old as Homer and Herodotus, is the story. Implicit in the story is our belief that we understand a historical happening if we know the detailed narrative of human beings acting, interacting with each other, interacting with other aspects of nature, moved by human motives, in a continuing linear flow in time of events that are considered, usually, in their unique aspects and assumed to be connected. The story is about human beings; human actions and human motives give momentum to the story; and the story explains as it tells.

A second mode of historical understanding, also as old as Herodotus, is the cross section of a single culture at a given moment of time. Celebrated descriptions of a single culture have been offered by Edward Gibbon (the Roman Empire in the age of the Antonines), by Thomas Babington Macaulay (England in 1685), by Jacob Burckhardt (civilization of the Italian Renaissance), and by Henry Adams (the United States in 1800 and 1817). But Herodotus did it first, in his celebrated second chapter on Egypt. In these descriptions events are still unique, but they are rarely placed in narrative succession. At some point, perhaps with Burckhardt, perhaps with Marx, historians became interested in a homogeneous culture as a total configuration of interdependent parts, with a single ethos.

A third mode of historical understanding was introduced by Thucydides, who perceived that one could do something more with narrative than tell a story: one could combine and compare narratives to discover and support generalizations. One could lay side by side the multiple stories of plague sickness in Athens and then generalize concerning the natural course of the disease. One could do the same for social plague, as Thucydides did in his famous chapter on the revolution of Corcyra in *The Peloponnesian War*. Mentally, he placed side by side the narratives of the revolutions in Hellenic cities during the war, indicated the common course which the revolutions seemed to follow, and going ever deeper, drew out generalizations concerning the behavior of people under the stress of war and revolution, "human nature being what it is." Very early then, with Thucydides, we have a third mode of historical understanding, a mode that views comparable narratives of events in their nonunique aspects, sees that they follow a repetitious course which can be formulated in a natural history, and infers common sets of relationships underlying the common events. The mode slips easily into a cyclic view of phenomena: governments (monarchy, tyranny, aristocracy, oligarchy, democracy, mobocracy, monarchy), coalition wars, civilizations, each has its historical pattern.

A fourth mode of understanding, the dialectical, has viewed history as propelled by contradictions—of good and evil, as with Saint Augustine; of Ideas, as with Hegel; of material and social forces, as with Marx. Saint Augustine linked the dialectical mode to the providential interpretation of history: what is being enacted in human history is the conflict between the kingdom of God and the kingdom of the devil; it will culminate in the Last Judgment, in which the world will come to an end. History was thus conceived in terms of the conflict between two spirits, two moralities, two parties, or as Saint Augustine said, two cities. To believers the interpretation endowed every action, every thought, every feeling with cosmic importance and hence with significant meaning. Also, it offered a comprehensive explanation: everything that happens is either God's grace or God's judgment, or sometimes God's grace within His judgment. At a given moment in the history of Western society, Marx linked the dialectical mode of historical understanding with the reality of class struggle, with a theory of social action moving toward revolution, and with a structure of feeling: hatred of the exploiter (the capitalist) and sympathy for the exploited (the industrial proletariat). It was a powerful, dynamic combination.

This list of historical modes of understanding in Western culture is not meant to be exhaustive—we are evoking only those that are needed later in our discussion—but a fifth concept needs to be mentioned. Sometime in the eighteenth and nineteenth centuries, the idea emerged that the historian should move the cross section of social phenomena through time. The idea is implicit in David Hume's *History of England*. It is explicit in the inaugural lecture in 1848 of the Regius Professor of History at Oxford, H. H. Vaughan,[1] in the theoretical reflections of J. B. Bury of Cambridge University, in Charles Seignobos' *Histoire sincère du peuple français,* in Kliuchevskii's *History of Russia,* and in Henry Adams's *History of the Administrations of Jefferson and Madison.* It became associated with theories of evolution, development, progress, and process. It was at the heart of the Marxian vision of a totality of interrelating forces moving through time.

Now in terms of this introductory analysis, what has happened to history writing in the twentieth century? As we have seen in the Introduction to this volume, toward the close of the nineteenth century among professional historians throughout the world the narrative mode was rather narrowly identified with political history—the story of reigns and ministries, the maneuvers of the political and military elite, and more profoundly, the evolution of political institutions. Moreover, this generation of historical scholars had adopted the critical methods of historical scholarship associated with the name of Leopold von Ranke. So assured were they of their method that they would have approved the celebrated remark of the great French medievalist Fustel de Coulanges to his admiring audience: "Do not applaud. 'Tis not I who speaks, but History, which speaks through me.'"

Embedded in their philosophy was a simple correspondence theory of truth (the image in the historian's mind corresponds to what actually occurred); a passive mirror theory about how historical knowledge is acquired; and a fairly profound but rather unnoticed theory of narrative as a fundamental mode of understanding reality. Lurking in their minds was a noble dream, the dream of synthesis: history, so ran their thinking, is a mysterious flowing puzzle, most of whose pieces have been lost. If by patient effort we can reassemble enough pieces and critically establish their validity and relation to each other, we can construct a moving, flowing synthesis that approximates what actually happened in all its detailed interrelatedness.

Against the narrowness and simplicities of this post-Rankean narrative approach, there developed in the 1890s and the first decade of the twentieth century an international movement of protest, coming from both within and without the historical profession. However, even as the protests were beginning to stir, it was already becoming apparent that even on its own terms the narrative sequence of "unique" events could not handle the problem of a moving synthesis of a national society through time. This became evident with the publication of the first great collaborative histories of a single country: the first American Nation series in the United States, the Oxford History of England, and the *Histoire de France* and the *Histoire de France contemporaine* edited by Ernst Lavisse.

Consider, for example, the volume in the Oxford History entitled *The Fourteenth Century 1307–1399*, by May McKisack. The volume is selected not because it was bad, but because it was excellent.[2] It opened with chapters of detailed political narrative of the reigns of Edward II and Edward III. Here the mode of understanding and explanation was a story, a sequential story in time of events regarded in their unique aspects and assumed to be connected, a story of persons and of their motivations and actions which gave energy and momentum to the account, a self-contained story that explained as it told and thus used history to reveal and understand history. Toward the center of the book there intervened chapters entitled "Parliament, Law, and Justice," "War and Chivalry," "The Church, the People, and the King," "Rural Society," and "Trade, Industry, and Towns." Here we had the second mode of historical understanding: the cross section which arrested time and society for a moment's description. The political narrative was resumed in chapters on the closing years of Edward III and the reign of Richard II. A final chapter, "Learning, Lollardy, and Literature," concluded the book. In tone the book was nonpartisan, nonreverential, nondidactic: in brief, objective. In scope it was total history. In scholarship it was a triumph of erudition. For the author to be able to write so many defensible statements about so many events and conditions presumed the many, many researches of many, many scholars turning over sheaves of many, many documents for many, many years. It assumed the whole complex of formal university instruction, of publication, and of book reviewing that exemplified and communicated the normal practices and values of the professional historians of two generations: the allegiance to objective truth, the quest for what had occurred in terms of the particular definition of historical circumstance at a precise time and place, the critical testing of evidence, the critical scrutiny of each noun, adjective, verb, adverb, and preposition in a history for correspondence to what happened, and the arrangement of happenings in the two then dominant modes of narrative and cross section. But by its own ideal the volume was deficient: at no point did it offer a synthetic, integrated view of the totality of English society at a given moment; and since the narrative was of political events, it did not move the society as a totality through time. This was true of all the great collaborative histories. They left the problem of a moving synthesis of a large society hovering, unresolved.

Protest against the narrative school from within the academic profession came from several sources. It came in part from the philosophers about history. As Louis Mink showed, in the 1920s and 1930s these focused their attention on epistemology (the question of relativism), in the 1940s and 1950s on the problem of explanation, in the 1960s on the nature of narrative, and in the 1970s on a proliferation of issues. Protest came also from professional historians who wished to enlarge the dimensions of historical investigation, the scope of subject matter. The *Annales* school was born of this protest and became a leader. As Jean Glénisson indicates, the *Annales* school was born not of an idea but of a complex of attitudes: acceptance, hostility, and intense curiosity—acceptance of the meticulous, critical documentation of the establishment professional historians, hostility to their narrow focus on political history and the "superficial" narrative of unique events, and the intense curiosity of two brilliant men, Marc Bloch and Lucien Febvre. They, their associates, and successors journeyed into history, made new discoveries about underlying structures, created new forms, and became the establishment. From the standpoint of this essay they invented new ways of doing the cross section: of an epoch (Marc Bloch, *La Société féodale*, 1939); of a national society (Robert Mandrou, *Introduction à la France moderne 1500–1640: essai de psychologie historique*, 1961); of a locality (for example, Pierre Goubert, *Beauvais et le Beauvaisis de 1600 á 1730*, 1960); and of moving a social group within a locality through time (Emmanuel Le Roy Ladurie, *Les Paysans de Languedoc*, 1966). Perhaps because of its initial hostility to the narrative, the *Annales* school was less successful in innovating the history of a *large* society through time.

Indeed, though marvelously rich and innovative in what they did, the *Annales* circle as a group betrayed in their shortcomings the circumstances of their origin. Hostile to a narrow focus on political history, they tended to neglect the political factor. Disdaining the superficial narrative of "unique" events, they rarely faced up to the problem of connecting long-term structures and trends with the flow of everyday happenings. Though aggressive individuals themselves, actively pursuing historical truth in nearly all its interrelations, they almost inadvertently portrayed men as passive, encased in long-term structures and moved about by long-term trends—tools, instruments, and victims of history rather than its makers. And now in the 1970s the *Annales* circle is disintegrating into multiple curiosities resembling in their intricacy and variety the flamboyant tracery of a late Gothic spire or window in the fifteenth century.

Protest against the old style of history also came from the Marxists and neo-Marxists, first from without the profession and then from within. In terms of the analysis in this essay, Marx took the proper stance: he dealt with the totality of a society moving through time. Then he took the turbulence of history into himself and resolved it into order. This was important. It has been observed that one measure of the greatness of an intellectual theory or artistic creation is the magnitude of the turbulence it resolves and contains. Great historians, like Thucydides and Marx, *resolve* turbulence into order; lesser historians, such as Gibbon and the professionals who borrow sociological theories from outside, *impose* ready-made order on chaos. Also, Marx was in research a digger; he had a positive sense of fact; and his theory did point to essential elements of historical reality. Often history does move dialectically through contradictions; human motives, actions, and contradictions do give energy and momentum to the story; most men and women are preoccupied with wresting a survival from nature by available technology; material conditions do give rise to social groupings; societies do pass through stages; within the narrative of events there are moving institutional structures; and historians have neglected the economic factor, the oppressed, and the underlying structures. Marx's theory was tremendously influential and internationally valuable in directing the attention of historians to the exploited, to economic and social conditions, and to institutional structures. In the hands of a master such as Eric Hobsbawm or Jerzy Topolski, it shows a way of moving the totality of a society through time, of interrelating individuals, motives and actions, events, identifiable social groups, and institutional social structures in an ongoing synthesis.

Why, then, don't historians all adopt Marxism as a theory of understanding? There are, of course, several reasons, not all of them intellectual. But in all modesty let me suggest that there is a fundamental intellectual reason. Marx's theory was forged in northwestern Europe in the 1840s. It came closest to fitting historical reality at that place and time. What historians still say about the Revolution of 1848 is what Marx said. But when we move from the 1840s in northwestern Europe either backward or forward in time or outward in space the distance between Marx's model and reality widens. Phenomena appear that the theory cannot handle easily. Among the Marxists there have been two responses to this situation. One is to stick with a doctrinaire version of the theory and impose it on historical reality. The other response, beginning with Marx himself and continuing with Lukács and Gramsci and the neo-Marxist historians, is to revise the theory flexibly and to offer ad hoc interpretations to explain and sometimes to explain away a particular difficulty. This movement toward greater flexibility appears in nearly every article in this book in which Marxism is discussed: in the Soviet Union when historians were freed from political constraints, in Poland, in Rumania, in East Germany, in West Germany, in France, in England, and in Japan. Nevertheless, by now, in my opinion, the Marxian theory has all the symptoms of a paradigm in difficulty: anomalies, ad hoc interpretations, and a dissolution of the pristine simplicity of the original statement. As a theory of understanding, it may have passed its point of greatest usefulness to the historical profession. Why, then, don't Marxists abandon the paradigm? There are many reasons, of course, not all of them intellectual. But one, fundamentally intellectual, can be derived from the analysis of Thomas Kuhn. Scientists and scholars do not abandon a paradigm in difficulty unless there is a better one available.

And in fact, there may be no better paradigm around. Marxists, indeed, still say it is the best: as Jerzy Topolski, author of *Methodology of History,* which is the fairest, most comprehensive and thorough treatise on the subject of methodology in existence, remarks, ''When it comes to the social sciences, it is above all the theory of dialectical materialism which, among the theories marked by a very high level of generality, best satisfies the conditions'' for a sound theory.[3]

This brings us to the social scientists, where the same movement of thought and practice may be observed. The story is familiar, told in this volume again and again, in the Introduction and in the several articles. Protest against the ''narrow'' political history of the pseudo-Rankeans had included from about 1890 advocacy of the application of social science techniques and principles to history. By the 1930s concepts from sociology and economics were being used by a few historians; by the 1950s demography and psychology had been drawn in, and by the 1960s anthropology, to offer a very rapid and rough generalization of a very complex development. By the 1960s quantification and computerization had begun to enter historical procedures. Significant progress was made in social science history in the reorientation of history ''toward the systematic analysis of structure and process and the utilization of theory,'' and to the postulation of generalizations of intermediate range. Statistically historians shifted from relatively simple descriptive tables and linear series and correlation coefficients to multivariate regression, factor analysis, and counterfactual procedures. In the 1950s and 1960s there were two or three major attempts at (as it turned out) interim integration, having in common the idea of a society as a cultural whole of interrelating parts and variables, the old dream of a moving synthesis in the new language and methods of anthropology, sociology, economics, and mathematics. Among the social scientists in the Anglo-Saxon world this attempt at integration was associated most notably with Talcott Parsons and his co-workers and with the structural-functionalist school of anthropology. In France it was connected with certain members of the *Annales* circle. But by the 1970s, these attempts were either in disrepute or forgotten, as social science investigation, in appearance at least, continued its rush toward ever more minute monographic specialization and disintegration.

So since about 1930 the dedication of professional historians to the narrative of unique events about the political elite has been shattered into many, many subject-matter fields and many, many approaches. Even the schools, the *Annales,* neo-Marxist, and the social scientific, have experienced theoretical difficulties. There seem to have been many disintegrations.

However, oblivious of general theoretical difficulties and certainly regardless of historiographers and philosophers about history, specialized investigators throughout the world have continued to churn out monographic books and articles at an astounding rate. Almost inadvertently, there have been movements toward integration within subject-matter fields, between subject-matter fields, of approaches, and of ways of moving a totality of a society through time. Sometimes this integration can be seen in a single sector moving through time, as in the historical demography of a given population or the economic history of a given country.[4] Sometimes the integration has been between sectors, as in the merging of the history of climate, population, the economy, and social groups;[5] or of psychohistory and sociology;[6] or of psychohistory, linguistics, and intellectual history. Sometimes the integration shows itself in the attempted solution of a problem—for example, why did the Industrial Revolution happen in Great Britain? Upon the solution of that problem, not yet achieved, the tools of demography, economic history (old and new), and social and political history have all been convergently focused.

Sometimes synthesis may seem to be occurring in the history of a major event, the French Revolution for instance. In the 1960s there appeared three histories of the French Revolution: *The French Revolution* (London, 1965), by M. J. Sydenham, a narrative-oriented, political-minded historian; *La Révolution* (Paris, 1965), by François Furet and Denis Richet, two authors of the *Annales* circle; and *Précis d'histoire de la Révolution française* (Paris, 1962), by Albert Soboul, a representative of the Marxist world outlook. When these narratives are read side by side, the first impression is one of overwhelming agreement about what scholars then believed concerning the history of the French Revolution. To be sure, the authors have differences of opinion on certain issues. Was there a feudal reaction in the 1780s? How serious was the counterrevolutionary threat? Were the social origins of Girondins and Jacobins diverse? Nevertheless, on first view the essential story seemed to be the same: the nature of the groups composing the National Assembly; the Paris uprising of July 1789; the peasant insurrections of August; the enactment of liberal, constitutional reform; the origins of the war; the reluctance of both Girondins and Jacobins to abandon laissez-faire; the Jacobin adoption of regulation to hold the Sans-Culottes to the war; the Sans-Culotte abandonment of Robespierre at Thermidor; and so on. Time and again Claude Mazauric, the Marxist critic of Furet-Richet, wrote: And then the events of 1790, or Sans-Culotte psychology, or the period of post-Thermidor, are described in the *Annales* account in the classic manner of Lefebvre or Soboul, indicating agreement with the Marxist version.[7] There also seems to be a growing consensus about method, about how the story should be understood and presented: as an enriched analytical narrative of underlying factors, structures, groups, and events. Thus we discover Sydenham, the narrative-oriented political historian, dealing with the psychology of social groups; Furet and Richet, the *Annales* team, finding it necessary to tell the story of unique political events and telling it very well; and Soboul rarely invoking Marxian dialectic to make his case. There seems to be even agreement that the French Revolution was a bourgeois revolution and a growing consensus on what that phrase means: it does not mean that the peasants did not carry through their revolution as well; it does not mean that by 1789 industrial capitalists in great numbers had established their mode of production in France and then by revolution brought the social and political institutions into congruence with their needs and that mode; it does not even mean that financial, commercial, or industrial capitalists were prominent in carrying through the Revolution; it means quite simply and significantly that what may be vaguely called the middle class secured certain reforms which "paved the way for capitalism in France and speeded up its evolution."[8] So there does seem to have been an acculturation process at work among the three groups of historians. Meanwhile, the social scientists have participated in a comparative study of revolutions that was deriving concomitant, congruent generalizations of intermediate range which influence the explanations historians are offering.

And yet the narrative, the *Annales,* and the Marxist authors do betray their origins in several significant ways. Within their growing consensus about method we can still see differences, perhaps even unreconcilable incompatibilities, and certainly there are problems.[9] There is the question of bias. Moved by sympathy for the humble and oppressed, the Marxist writers are especially understanding in dealing with the working classes and with situations of dysfunction, where masses of people were being exploited and hurt—although, to be sure, they are less understanding of the bourgeoisie, who incidentally also suffered. In contrast, a "bourgeois" bias appears throughout the *Annales* volume. The narrative account, of course, attempts to be objective and fair. But there are questions more important than bias. Both the narrative and Marxist authors portrayed men as active, actively making choices; the Marxist authors have perceived that by these choices men build structures and then act within these structures. The Marxist account, indeed, is the stronger one in the perception of these structures. In contrast, the *Annales* authors have repeatedly used the word *dérapage* ("skid"), saying, for example, that after the adjournment of the Constituent Assembly the Revolution "skidded" toward the lower popular and egalitarian side. The figure is unfortunate; not only does it imply a "bourgeois" bias, but more seriously it is a symptom of the *Annales* tendency to make humankind the helpless, passive sport of history.

In the terms of this essay, we are here in the presence of two or three modes of historical understanding. The authors of all three schools were thinking in terms of a flow of time, even a narrative flow in time. (There may be "slow" time, or "fast" time; that is not the question at present.) The persistence of the narrative, despite all criticisms, suggests that the symbol may reflect an essential reality: that electrons, stimuli, sensations, ideas, actions, social structures even, *do* flow in time. (The question of continuity or discontinuity is left aside for the moment.) At a detailed level, social change does proceed through human beings, their energies, motivations, and actions, in a story of "unique" events. But then within the narrative of the three schools divergences appear: the narrative historian tends to remain with the story of human actions and events, though he does note variables and contradictions; the *Annales* group, while telling the story, notices variables, structures, and contradictions; the Marxists do all of these things, but thinking dialectically, they focus on contradictions. In theory, and sometimes in practice, the linear and dialectical modes seem poles apart; in the history of the French Revolution, they seem to be merging. All three schools are perceiving a central unresolved problem: the interrelating of the story of human beings, everyday happenings, and events with the movement of ongoing variables and structures.

Sometimes a new integration of methods and approaches has occurred in tracing the history of a locality—a village, a county, a French *département,* a region, a continuing group within a region. Examples of these abound and are mentioned in nearly every regional article in this volume.[10] Nearly all are excellent, and it would seem invidious and unfair to single out one. But simply by way of illustration, let us consider Georges Dupeux's *Aspects de l'histoire sociale et politique du Loir-et-Cher 1848–1914* (Paris and the Hague, 1962). The title is modest and cautious. It suggests that by voluntary self-limitation of scope, the author proposes to consider only a small area in France through a limited period of time, and in that area only its social and political history, and of that history only certain aspects. The author thus greatly simplifies his problem of a moving synthesis in time. Actually, the book is somewhat broader than its title suggests. It opens with a cross section: a geographic, demographic, economic, and social description of Loir-et-Cher in the 1840s, profusely illustrated by demographic and social structural charts. The second third of the book then traces fluctuations in the economy (prices, wages, and production) from 1850 to 1914, the long-term trends and the short-term cycles. Then, having set the stage, in the last third of the volume Dupeux tells the densely interwoven story, demographic, economic, social, and political, of persons, identifiable social groups, variables, events, structures, and mentalities. Had the book been written in the 1970s, there might have been more economic theory, but the narrative is still worth study. Though a narrative, it is a new form of narrative, indeed a new historical reality, of people and "unique" events, to be sure, but also of groups, structures, variables, and mentalities. Yet problems of moving a synthesis remain, and the book illustrates those, too. For example, by its voluntary self-limitation it evades the central problem: how to move the *totality* of society—not simply the institutions and variables used but also the family, the art, the formal philosophy, and the religion as well.

The problems of a moving synthesis magnify almost exponentially when the subject is the history of a national society or of a civilization through decades or centuries. To relate the masses of people to the decision-making elites, events to structures, the demographic, economic, social, and political world to that of art, formal philosophy, and religion—to do that in an ongoing, all-encompassing account of a large society is the stiffest challenge any historian can face. Most historians, absorbed in their special enterprises, shy away from it. But in every decade a few have responded to the challenge, and in the past decade these few have responded with books that contain much of the discussion of the preceding decades and of the preceding milliennia since Herodotus. I am thinking of such works as Eric Hobsbawm, *The Age of Capital* (1975); Georges Dupeux, *La So-*

ciété française 1789–1960 (1964); Pierre Goubert, *L'Ancien Régime*, I: *La Société*, and II: *Les Pouvoirs* (1969, 1973); Albert Soboul, *La Civilisation et la Révolution française* (1970); and Hans-Ulrich Wehler, *Das Deutsche Kaiserreich 1871–1918* (1973). The reader, from his own background, will doubtless think of others. To compare books such as these with Herodotus prompts one to echo George Bernard Shaw's remark about Shakespeare: "Not greater than Herodotus but better." To compare them with the estimable accounts of the Oxford History variety is an indication of how far history writing has come in two generations and is a cause for optimism. The gains—in the areas of human behavior encompassed, in the density and richness of the narrative, in the narrative integration of structure with event and of people with abstract concepts—are remarkable. History is a reality-seeking, reality-presenting enterprise, in which historians throughout the world are co-workers and colleagues. Few historians in the 1920s anticipated how history was to be investigated, integrated, and written in the 1970s, in all its rich variety. Nor can we, in a fast-moving field, anticipate how it will be written fifty years from now. But if the past is any guide to the future (and often it is not), and if we work, think imaginatively and intelligently, in contradiction and cooperation, we shall be coming closer to realizing that dream of a moving synthesis which has animated the greatest historians.

Notes

1. Lawrence Stone, "History and the Social Sciences in the Twentieth Century," *The Future of History*, edited by Charles F. Delzell (Nashville, Tenn., 1977), pp. 4–5.

2. (Oxford, 1959). Even though the book was published as late as 1959, its approach still represents that of most volumes of the Oxford History, whose pattern was set in the 1930's. The volumes by Austin Poole (*Domesday Book to Magna Carta 1087–1216* [1951]) and R. C. K. Ensor (*England 1870–1914* [1936]) represent interesting variations of the pattern of the McKisack book. Poole opens with three chapters on Government and Society, Rural Conditions, and Towns and Trade, so that the reader gains a sense of the social, economic, and political context in which the royal administration is operating and in which political events occur. Then follow chapters of political narrative so interrupted, however, by chapters on the Church, Learning, Literature, and Art, and the Celtic Fringe, that in the end the reader never has a sense of how English society as a totality moved. The same basic comment applies to Ensor's excellent book.

3. (Translated from the Polish by Olgierd Wojtasiewicz; Dordrecht, the Netherlands, and Boston, 1973), p. 416.

4. For example: William Ashworth, *An Economic History of England, 1870–1939* (London, 1960); E. J. Hobsbawm, *Industry and Empire; An Economic History of Britain Since 1750* (London, 1968); Derek H. Aldcroft and Harry W. Richardson, *The British Economy, 1870–1939* (London, 1969); Witold Kula, *Théorie économique du systeme féodal: Pour un modèle de l'économie polanaise, 16e–18e siècles* (Paris, 1970); William Paul McGreevey, *An Economic History of Colombia 1845–1930* (Cambridge, 1971); M. M. Postan, *The Medieval Economy and Society: An Economic History of Britain, 1100–1500* (Berkeley, Calif., 1972); Lance E. Davis et al., *American Economic Growth: An Economist's History of the United States* (New York, 1972); A. G. Hopkins, *An Economic History of West Africa* (1973); Brian Murphy, *A History of the British Economy 1086–1970* (London, 1973); Douglass C. North and Robert Paul Thomas, *The Rise of the Western World: A*

New Economic History (Cambridge, 1973); Immanuel Wallerstein, *The Modern World-System: Capitalist Agriculture and the Origins of the European World Economy in the Sixteenth Century* (New York, 1974); Carlo M. Cipolla, *Before the Industrial Revolution: European Society and Economy, 1000–1700* (New York, 1976); Fernand Braudel and Ernst Labrousse, *Histoire économique et sociale de la France (1450–1880)*, 5 vols. (Paris, 1970, 1976, 1976); Georges Duby and Armand Wallon, *Histoire de la France rurale*, 4 vols. (Paris, 1976); José Pedro Barrán and Benjamín Nahúm, *Historia rural del Uruguay moderno* (Montevideo, 1967–1978).

5. Philippe Pinchemel, *Structures sociales et dépopulation rurale dans les campagnes picardes de 1836 à 1936* (Paris, 1957); E. A. Wrigley, *Industrial Growth and Population Change: A Regional Study of the Coalfield Area of Northwest Europe in the Later Nineteenth Century* (Cambridge, 1962); Georges Duby, *Guerriers et paysans* (Paris, 1973); Emanuel Le Roy Ladurie, "The French Peasantry in the Eighteenth Century, Viewed in the Perspective of the French Revolution," in *The Consortium of Revolutionary Europe 1750–1850: Proceedings 1975* (Athens, Ga., 1976); Charles Wilson and Geoffrey Parker, *An Introduction to the Sources of European Economic History 1500–1800* (Ithaca, N.Y., 1977).

6. Erich Fromm and Michael Maccoby, *Social Character in a Mexican Village* (1970); Stanley S. Gueterman, *The Machiavellians: A Social Psychological Study of Moral Character and Organizational Milieu* (Lincoln, Neb., 1970); Fred Weinstein and Gerald Platt, *The Wish to Be Free. Society, Psyche, and Value Change* (Berkeley, Calif., 1969); idem, *Psychoanalytical Sociology: An Essay on the Interpretation of Historical Data and the Phenomena of Collective Behavior* (Baltimore, 1973).

7. Claude Mazauric, *Sur la Révolution française* (Paris, 1970), pp. 27, 37, 40. The rejoinder to Mazauric's critique of the Furet-Richet book is found in François Furet, "Le Catéchisme révolutionnaire," *Annales, économies, sociétés, civilisations* 26 (1971): 255–89.

8. Albert Soboul, *The French Revolution 1787–1799 from the Storming of the Bastille to Napoleon* (translation of *Précis d'histoire de la Révolution française*) (New York, 1974), p. 551; also p. 9.

9. For a detailed statement of these incompatibilities and antagonisms, see Geoffrey Ellis, "The 'Marxist Interpretation' of the French Revolution," *English Historical Review* 93 (1978): 353–376.

10. For examples, see references listed in notes 53–57 in the chapter on Great Britain; see also Edward Evans-Pritchard, *The Sanusi of Cyrenaica* (Oxford, 1949); Jean Vidalenc, *Le département de l'Eure sous la monarchie constitutionnelle 1814–1848* (Paris, 1952); Georges Duby, *La Société aux XIe et XIIe siècles dans la région Mâconnaise* (Paris, 1953); F. Dumas, *La généralité de Tours au XVIIIe siècle: Administration de l'intendant Du Cluzel (1766–1783)* (Tours, 1894): Philippe Bernard, *Economie et Sociologie de la Seine-et-Marne 1850–1950* (Paris, 1953); Stanley J. Stein, *Vassouras: A Brazilian Coffee County, 1850–1900* (Cambridge, Mass., 1957); Merle Curti, *The Making of an American Community: A Case History of Democracy in a Frontier County* (Stanford, Calif., 1959); Pierre Goubert, *Beauvais et le Beauvaisis de 1600 à 1730, contribution à l'histoire sociale de la France du XVIIe siècle* (Paris, 1960); Paul Bois, *Paysans de l'Ouest: Des structures économiques et sociales aux options politiques depuis l'époque révolutionnaire, dans la Sarthe* (Le Mans, 1960); André Armengaud, *Les populations de l'Est Aquitain au début de l'époque contemporaine: recherches sur une région moins developpé (vers 1845–yers 1871)* (Paris and The Hague, 1961); Pierre Barral, *Le département de l'Isère sous la Troisième République, 1870–1940: histoire sociale et politique* (Paris, 1962); Pierre Vilar, *La Catalogne dans l'Espagne moderne* (Paris, 1962); Charles Tilly, *The Vendée* (Cambridge, Mass., 1964); Abel Pointrineau, *La vie rurale en Basse-Auvergne au XVIIIe siècle (1726–1789)*, 2 vols. (1965); Fernand Ouellet, *Histoire économique et sociale du Québec 1760–1850* (Montréal, 1966); Olwen H. Hufton, *Bayeux in the Late Eighteenth Century* (Oxford, 1967); Pierre Deyon, *Amiens, capitale provinciale: Etude sur la société urbaine au 17e siècle* (Paris and The Hague, 1967); Richard L. Bushman, *From Puritan to Yankee: Character and the Social Order in Connecticut, 1690–1765* (Cambridge, Mass., 1967); Peter G. Goheen, *Victorian Toronto, 1850 to 1900: Pattern and Process of Growth* (Chicago, 1970); Marcel Couturier, *Recherches sur les structures sociales de Châteaudun 1525–1789* (Paris, 1969); Anne Zink, *Azereix:*

la vie d'une communauté rurale à la fin du XVIIIe siècle (Paris, 1969); Mohamed El Kordi, *Bayeux aux XVIIe et XVIIIe siècles* (Paris, 1970); Kenneth A. Lockridge, *A New England Town, The First Hundred Years: Dedham, Massachusetts, 1636–1736* (New York, 1970); John Demos, *A Little Commonwealth: Family Life in Plymouth Colony* (New York, 1970); Philip J. Greven, *Four Generations: Population, Land, and Family in Colonial Andover* (Ithaca, N.Y., 1970); Thomas Sheppard, *Lourmarin in the Eighteenth Century: A Study of a French Village* (Baltimore, 1971); Patrice L.-R. Higonnet, *Pont-de-Montvert: Social Structure and Politics in a French Village, 1700–1914* (Cambridge, Mass., 1971); A. Temple Patterson, *A History of Southampton, 1700–1914.* Volume 2, *The Beginnings of Modern Southampton, 1836–1867* (Southampton, 1971); Alain Croix, *Nantes et le pays nantais au XVIe siècle: étude démographique* (Paris, 1974); Bernard Chevalier, *Tours: ville royale (1356–1520)* (Louvain and Paris, 1975); Emmanuel Le Roy Ladurie, *Montaillou, village occitan de 1294 à 1324* (Paris, 1975); Alan F. J. Artibise, *Winnipeg: a social history of urban growth, 1874–1914* (Montreal and London, 1975); Michael B. Katz, *The People of Hamilton, Canada West: Family and Class in a Mid-Nineteenth Century City* (Cambridge, Mass., 1975); Maurice Garden, *Lyon et les lyonnais au XVIIIe siècles* (Paris, n.d.); George Frêche, *Toulouse et la région Midi-Pyrénées au siècle des lumières (vers 1760–1789)* (n.p., n.d.).

Select Bibliography on Historiography

"The Achievements of Economic History: Three Schools Compared: The Achievements of the Cliometric School [by Donald N. McCloskey]; The Achievements of the Marxist School [by Jon S. Cohen]; Achievements of the *Annales* School [by Robert Forster]; Discussion [by Douglass C. North]," *Journal of Economic History* 38 (1978): 13–80.

Ajayi, J. F. Ade., and E. J. Alagoa. "Black Africa: The Historian's Perspective," *Daedalus* 103 (1974): 125–34.

Alagoa, E. J. "The Interdisciplinary Approach to African History in Nigeria," *Présence Africaine*, no. 94 (1975): 171–83.

Anderson, M. S. *Historians and Eighteenth-Century Europe 1715–1789* (Oxford, 1979).

Aymard, Maurice. "The *Annales* and French Historiography (1929–1971)," *Journal of European Economic History* 1 (1972): 491–511.

Baron, Samuel H. "The Transition from Feudalism to Capitalism in Russia: A Major Soviet Historical Controversy," *American Historical Review* 73 (1972): 715–29.

Baron, Samuel H., and Nancy W. Heer, eds. *Windows on the Russian Past: Essays on Soviet Historiography since Stalin* (Columbus, Ohio, 1977).

Barraclough, Geoffrey. *Atlante della storia, 1945–1975* (Rome, 1975).

Bartel, Horts, Ernst Diehl, and Ernst Engelberg. "Die Geschichtswissenchaft der DDR, 1960–1970," *Zeitschrift für Geschichtswissenschaft* 8 (1960), Sonderband: 19 ff.

Bergquist, Charles. "Recent United States Studies in Latin American History: Trends since 1965," *Latin American Research Review* 9 (1974): 3–35.

Borah, Woodrow. "Latin American History in World Perspective," in Charles Delzell, ed., *The Future of History* (Nashville, Tenn., 1977).

Ciociltan, V., and Fl. Constantiniu. "1944–1974: Trente années de recherche historique en Roumanie (quelques résultats et directions de recherches)," *Revue roumaine d'histoire* 4 (1974): 625–46.

Cohen, Sande. "Structuralism and the Writing of Intellectual History," *History and Theory* 17 (1978): 175–206.

Committee on Historical Sciences and the Institute of History. *La Pologne au XIIIe Congrès International des Sciences Historiques à Moscou*, 2 vols. (Warsaw, 1970).

Crane, Robert I. *A History of South Asia* (Washington, D.C., 1973).

Davis, David Brion. "Some Recent Directions in American Cultural History," *American Historical Review* 73 (1968): 696–707.

Delzell, Charles F., ed. *The Future of History* (Nashville, Tenn., 1977).

Diehl, Ernst. "25 Jahre DDR—25 Jahre Marxistisch-Leninistische Geschichtswissenschaft," *Wissenschaftliche Mitteilungen den Historiker-Gesellschaft der DDR* 2 (1974): 7 ff.

Dike, K. O., and J. F. Ade. Ajayi. "African Historiography," *Encyclopedia of the Social Sciences,*
VI, 394–99.

Dirlik, Arif. *Revolution and History: The Origins of Marxist Historiography in China* (Berkeley,
Calif., 1978).

Djordjevic, Dimitrije. "Contemporary Yugoslav Historiography," *East European Quarterly* 1
(1967): 75–86.

Eckerman, Walther, and Hubert Mohr. *Einführung in das Studium der Geschichte* (Berlin/GDR,
1966).

Ellis, Geoffrey, "The 'Marxist Interpretation' of the French Revolution," *English Historical Review*
93 (1978): 353–76.

Elton, G. R. *Modern Historians on British History 1485–1945: A Critical Bibliography, 1945–1969*
(London, 1970).

Engelberg, Ernst, and Rolf Rudolph. "Zur Geschichtswissenschaft der Deutschen Demokratischen
Republik," *Zeitschrift für Geschichtswissenschaft* 8 (1960), Sonderheft: 7 ff.

Enteen, George M. "A Recent Trend on the Soviet Historical Front," *Survey* 20, no. 4 (1974):
122–31.

Esquenazi-Mayo, Roberto, and Michael C. Meyer, eds. *Latin American Scholarship Since World
War II* (Lincoln, Neb., 1971).

Faulenbach, B., ed. *Geschichtswissenschaft in Deutschland* (Munich, 1964).

Feuerwerker, Albert, ed. *History in Communist China* (Cambridge, Mass., 1968).

Furber, Elizabeth Chapin, ed. *Changing Views on British History: Essays on Historical Writing
since 1939* (Cambridge, Mass., 1966).

Geiss, Imanuel. *Studien über Geschichte und Geschichtswissenschaft* (Frankfurt, 1972).

Gerschenkron, Alexander. "Soviet Marxism and Absolutism," *Slavic Review* 30 (1971): 853–69.

Gibson, Charles. "Writing on Colonial Mexico," *Hispanic American Historical Review* 55 (1975):
287–323.

Gilbert, Felix. "Intellectual History: Its Aims and Methods," *Daedalus* 100 (1971): 80–97.

Gilbert, Felix, and Stephen R. Graubard, eds. *Historical Studies Today* (New York, 1972).

Glénisson, Jean. "L'Historiographie française contemporaine: tendances et réalisations," in *La
Recherche historique en France de 1940 à 1965,* issued by the Comité française des sciences
historiques (Paris, 1965), pp. ix-lxiv.

Goubert, Pierre. "Historical Demography and the Reinterpretation of Early Modern French History," *Journal of Interdisciplinary History* 1 (1970): 37–48.

Heer, Nancy W. *Politics and History in the Soviet Union* (Cambridge, Mass., 1971).

Hexter, J. H. "Fernand Braudel and the Monde Braudellien," *Journal of Modern History* 44 (1972):
480–539.

Hobsbawm, E. J. "From Social History to the History of Society," *Daedalus* 100 (1971): 20–45.

Honegger, Claudia, ed. *M. Bloch, F. Braudel, L. Febvre, u.a. Schrift und Materie der Geschichte:
Vorschläge zur systematischen Aneignung historischer Prozesse* (Frankfurt, 1977).

Iggers, Georg G. *The German Conception of History* (Middletown, Conn., 1968; German translation, *Deutsche Geschichtswissenschaft,* 3rd ed., Munich, 1976).

———. *New Directions in European Historiography* (Middletown, Conn., 1975; German rev. ed.,
Neue Geschichtswissenschaft, Munich, 1978).

Jay, Martin. *The Dialectical Imagination: A History of the Frankfurt School and the Institute of
Social Research, 1923–1950* (Boston, 1973).

Jones, G. Stedman. "From Historical Sociology to Theoretical History," *British Journal of Sociology* 27 (1976): 295–305.

Keep, John. "The Current Scene in Soviet Historiography," *Survey* 19 (1973): 3–20.

Keep, John, and Lilianna Brisby, eds. *Contemporary History in the Soviet Mirror* (New York,
1964).

Kimio, Shiozawa. "Les historiens japonais et le mode de production asiatique," *La Pensée,* no.
122 (August 1965): 63–78.

Kon, I. S. *Geschichtsphilosophie des 20. Jahrhunderts Kritischer Abriss,* translated from the Russian by W. Hoepp; 2 vols. (Berlin/GDR, 1964).

"Kritik der bürgerlischen Geschichtswissenschaft," special issues nos. 70 and 75 of *Das Argument.*

Le Goff, Jacques, and P. Nora. *Faire de l'histoire,* 3 vols. (Paris, 1974).

Lorwin, Val R., and Jacob M. Price, eds. *The Dimensions of the Past: Materials, Problems, and Opportunities for Quantitative Work in History* (New Haven, Conn., 1972).

Lozek, Gerhard, et al. *Unbewältigte Vergangenheit: Kritik der bürgerlicher Geschichtsschreibung in der BRD,* 3rd ed. (Berlin/GDR, 1977).

Macfarlane, Alan. "History, Anthropology and the Study of Communities," *Social History* no. 5 (1977): 631–52.

Macintyre, S. "The Making of the Australian Working Class: An Historiographical Survey," *Historical Studies* (Melbourne) 72 (1978).

Mandelbaum, Maurice. "The History of Ideas, Intellectual History, and the History of Philosophy," *History and Theory* 5 (1965): 33–66.

Mendel, Arthur. "Current Soviet Theory of History: New Trends for Old?" *American Historical Review* 72 (1966): 50–73.

Meyendorf, John, Ihor Ševčenko, and Alexander Paul. "The Cambridge and Soviet Histories of the Byzantine Empire," *Slavic Review* 30 (1971): 619–48.

Outline of Romanian Historiography until the Beginning of the 20th Century (Bucharest, 1964).

Parker, W. N. "Through Growth and Beyond: Three Decades in Economic and Business History," in Louis P. Cain and Paul J. Uselding, eds., *Business Enterprise and Economic Change* (Kent, Ohio, 1973), pp. 15–47.

Philips, C. H., ed. *Historians of India, Pakistan, and Ceylon* (Oxford, 1962).

Porshnev, B. F. *Social Psychology and History* (Moscow, 1970).

Pundeff, Marin, ed. *History in the USSR: Selected Readings* (San Francisco, 1967).

Ritter, Volker. "Ein Versuch systematischer Aneignung von Geschichte, die 'Schule der Annales,' " in I. Geiss and R. Tamchina, eds., *Ansichten einer zukünftigen Geschichte* (Munich, 1974), I, 153–72.

Schneider, Laurence A. *Ku Chieh-Kang and China's New History* (Berkeley, Calif., 1971).

Schoenwald, Richard L. "Using Psychology in History: A Review Essay," *Historical Methods Newsletter* 7 (1973): 9–24.

Schorske, Carl E., et al. "New Trends in Historiography," *Daedalus* 98 (1969): 891–976.

Sen, S. P. *Historians and Historiography in Modern India* (Calcutta, 1973).

———. *Historical Writings on the National Movement* (1978).

———. *History in Modern Indian Literature* (Calcutta, 1975).

Shafer, Boyd C., et al. *Historical Study in the West: France, Great Britain, Western Germany, and the United States* (New York, 1968).

Sheehan, James J. "Quantification in the Study of Modern German Social and Political History," in Val R. Lorwin and Jacob M. Price, eds. *The Dimensions of the Past* (New Haven, Conn., 1972).

Shmidt, S. O., et al., eds. *Istochnikovedenie: Teoreticheski i metodicheskie problemy* (The Study of Sources: Theoretical and Methodological Problems) (Moscow, 1969).

Sibley, J. "Clio and Computers: Moving into Phase II," *Computers and the Humanities* 7 (1972): 67–81.

Skinner, Quentin. "Meaning and Understanding in the History of Ideas," *History and Theory* 9 (1969): 3–53.

Smith, Peter H. "History," in Robert S. Byars and Joseph L. Love, eds., *Quantitative Social Science Research in Latin America* (Urbana, Ill., 1973).

Social Science Research Council, Committee on Historiography. Bulletin 54: *Theory and Practice in Historical Study* (New York, 1946).

———. Bulletin 64: *The Social Sciences in Historical Study* (New York, 1954).

Stoianovich, T. *French Historical Method: The Annales Paradigm* (Ithaca and London, 1976).

Stone, Lawrence. "History and the Social Sciences in the Twentieth Century," in Charles F. Delzell, ed., *The Future of History* (Nashville, Tenn., 1977), pp. 3–42.

Stout, Harry S. "Culture, Structure, and the 'New History': A Critique and an Agenda," *Computers and the Humanities* 9 (1975): 213–30.

Struever, Nancy. "The Study of Language and the Study of History," *Journal of Interdisciplinary History* 4 (1974): 401–15.

Supple, B. E., ed. *Research in Economic and Social History* (London, 1971).

Swierenga, Robert P. "Towards the 'New Rural History': A Review Essay," *Historical Methods Newsletter* 6 (1973): 111–22.

Teodor, Pompiliu. *Evolutia gîndirii istorice românesti* (The Evolution of Romanian Historical Thought) (Cluj, 1970; German translation, *Die Entwicklung des historischen Denkens in der rümanischen Geschichtsschreibung*, Cluj, 1972).

Tillett, Lowell. *The Great Friendship: Soviet Historians on the Non-Russian Nationalities* (Chapel Hill, N.C., 1969).

Times Literary Supplement. "Historical Writings," 6 January 1956, and "New Ways in History," 7 April, 28 July, and 8 September 1966.

Topolski, Jerzy. "Développement des études historiques en Pologne 1945–1968," in *La Pologne au XIIIe Congrès International des Sciences Historiques à Moscou*, 2 vols. (Warsaw, 1970), I, 7–76.

———. "Le Développement des recherches d'histoire économique en Pologne," *Studia Historiae Oeconomicae* 1 (1966): 3–42.

UNESCO (United Nations Educational, Scientific, and Cultural Organizations), *Main Trends of Research in the Social and Human Sciences*. Part II. Vol. I. *History*. Edited by Geoffrey Barraclough (The Hague, 1978).

Van der Wee, H., and P. M. M. Klep. "Quantitative Economic History in Europe since the Second World War: Survey, Evaluations, and Prospects," *Recherches économiques de Louvain* 41 (1975): 195–218.

Veyne, Paul. *Comment on écrit l'histoire* (Paris, 1971).

Wehler, H.-U., ed. *Deutsche Historiker*, 5 vols. (Göttingen, 1971–72).

Woodman, Harold D. "Economic History and Economic Theory: The New Economic History in America," *Journal of Interdisciplinary History* 3 (1972): 322–50.

Wüstemeyer, Manfred. "Die 'Annales.' Grundsätze und Methoden ihrer 'neuen Geschichtswissenschaft,' " *Vierteljahrschrift für Sozial- und Wirtschaftsgeschichte* 54 (1967): 1–45.

Zeitschrift für Geschichtswissenschaft, vols. 8 (1960) and 18 (1970), *Sonderheft* on "Historische Forschungen in der DDR [1950–1960]" and "Historische Forschungen in der DDR [1960–1970]."

Index